ABERRANT

N! HOME

- N!tertainment
- N!terview
- N! the news
- N!sight
- N!tre nous
- N!ternet
- **N!tv**
- fun N! games

- help!
- awards
- legal stuff

search

[_____]

f i n d !

N! contact us

From N! documentary
*Reaching the Stars:
A Decade of Novas,*
first aired March 23, 2008

We had the chance to sit down and talk with Randel Portman, "The Fireman," in an exclusive N! interview. We discussed what it was like being a nova, how the world has changed since novas' arrival and what the future holds.

• **N!:** So, Mr. Portman, what is it like to be the first known nova?

• **Portman:** It is a distinct honor. Actually it's just luck, really. Fate just decided that I would erupt in a rather spectacular way, and I was lucky enough to save lives. In general, though, being a nova is a wonderful thing. Novas are simply people with special abilities. Yeah, those powers can make us seem weird or unapproachable, but really we are just people.

• **N!:** You may be understating the case a bit. Experts postulate that, in fact, novas have the ability to theoretically do just about anything.

• **Portman:** The theory always sounds better than the actual facts. Novas' powers stem from our ability to manipulate the fundamental forces of nature: gravity, electromagnetism, the strong nuclear force and the weak one. Assuming a nova had no limits in manipulating those forces, then he would effectively be God, but we all have our limits. The Project scientists tell me a lot has to do with how an individual nova sees his abilities and how they emerged.

• **N!:** You emerged — erupted, as the saying goes — spectacularly, saving a school bus full of children. How did that shape your abilities?

• **Portman:** I was a fireman, which is how I got the nickname, and had responded to a traffic accident. When we got to the scene, all I could see was the outline of a school bus in the flames. Fire was coming out of every possible opening in the thing. It was awful. I heard all the little kids screaming, and I just sort of froze. I could feel something happening, and putting out the fire was all I could think of. All of a sudden, my head felt like it was being hit by a sledgehammer. The last thing I remember seeing was a huge gout of flame coming right toward me. After that everything is hazy. The next thing I know, I'm kneeling in a puddle of melted

2

keep reading▶

N

HOME

N!tertainment

N!terview

N! the news

N!sight

N!tre nous

N!ternet

N!tv

un N! games

p!

ards

al stuff

search

[   ]

find!

ontact
s

asphalt. At the time, I didn't even think to wonder why I wasn't hurt. I couldn't see any more flames, and the guys were all standing around me shouting. The rest of it was a blur of sirens and people I didn't know asking me bunches of questions I could barely understand. The headache lasted for almost a week.

The Project docs told me, later, that novas typically emerge during a time of great stress, and their powers reflect that initial situation. I can absorb energy. Only recently have I begun to learn how to redirect it. We aren't all-powerful. Hell, I can't even fly. What kind of superguy can't fly?

• **N!:** How have your quantum powers grown, and how did you learn them?

• **Portman:** The fire-eating thing — "radiant energy absorption," the docs call it — just came naturally. I just *knew* how to do it. Within a few weeks of the initial discovery of novas, the Aeon Society contacted a lot of us and asked us if we would like training on how to use our powers. They had recruited some amazingly smart novas who had figured a lot out about our abilities. I agreed. I spent close to two years with them, on and off, after they set up the Project. They teach various meditation techniques, and they constantly test and challenge us to use our powers in new and different ways. A nova's abilities really are in your mind. You have to convince yourself that you can do something new, and you have to make it an expansion of something you can already do. We even got a crash course in quantum physics, so we would better understand what we were really doing.

• **N!:** What's your take on the recent criticism of Project Utopia? Some people are calling it a conspiracy to take over the world, others are claiming that it wants to create a socialist world government. How do you respond to those claims?

• **Portman:** I don't think that's the case at all. Project Utopia has done great things for everyone on this planet, from the global environmental cleanup to the Palestinian peace agreements to the Ethiopian terraforming project to fighting international terrorism… hell, even the Zurich Accord, that made the world accept novas as people. It shocked people when Project Utopia got an advisory position on the UN Security Council, but as closely as they'd been working with the UN, it shouldn't have surprised anyone. I love my country as much as the next guy — or the next nova — but the recent talk of Utopia being a huge conspiracy comes from a few right-wing nutcases with bad attitudes. Nothing more.

Most of us novas would have been lost without Project Utopia. An erupting nova can be dangerous, whether he means to be or not. At any

3

N!tertainment

N!terview

N! the news

N!sight

N!tre nous

N!ternet

N!tv

fun N! games

help!

awards

legal stuff

search

find !

N contact us

rate, the process is severely painful, as the M-R node just kinda grows in your brain. Hurts like hell, let me tell you. Project Utopia intervention teams show up and offer help and training to new novas. They also offer novas a life and a chance to help society and the world. You remember 1998: People went apesh— err, wacko when they found out there were "superpowered mutant freaks" running around. Project Utopia directed our energies toward helping the world. Without it, people would never have accepted us, and you and I wouldn't be talking right now.

• **N!:** The world has certainly changed in the last 10 years. Do you think it has all been for the better?

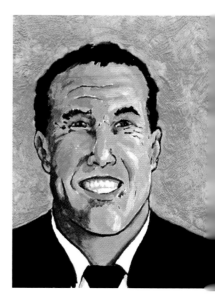

• **Portman:** I don't think anything is that black and white, but the world is definitely a better place. Like I said, the environment is clean, worldwide organized crime is on its way out, Utopia's colleagues at the Triton Foundation have discovered a vaccine for AIDS and cures for many types of cancer and we are even beginning to seriously explore the solar system. Yeah, I think the world is a better place after the arrival of novas. Don't get me wrong, I don't think that this wouldn't have happened without novas. We certainly helped, but anyone with these abilities would. Novas have not just worked toward making the world a better place, but have inspired the rest of humanity to do more. We've changed culture, fashion, politics, even religion in some cases. I mean, isn't this station the highest-rated in the world?

• **N!:** You mentioned the Triton Foundation. Medical and biological science have made prodigious advances in the last decade. What do you think about the recent work on the origins and distinctions of nova biology?

• **Portman:** Everyone knows that novas, or *Homo sapiens novus* as the eggheads like to refer to us, are novas because we have DNA coding allowing us to develop the Mazarin-Rashoud node. Who would have thought that something as small as the M-R node could change us that much? As far as genetics, well, it's not really my field. I know that they are saying that novas have a certain sequence of DNA introns or something, and that is what is responsible for us developing the M-R node. They also say that the DNA can be inherited only from your mother. All I really know is what they tell me; the docs know better than me. I hear that there are over 6000 known novas in the world, now They come from all backgrounds and from around the world.

I do know that we look different. Novas tend to be sleek and buff, with little body fat and great physiques. They say that it comes from our increased metabolism, from forcing the body to channel so much energy. We also eat like pigs. Hell, I had two steaks and three baked

4

keep reading

HOME

N!tertainment

N!terview

N! the news

N!sight

N!tre nous

N!ternet

N!tv

un N! games

p!

ards

al stuff

search

find!

ontact
s

potatoes for dinner last night, but I can also absorb enough energy to turn just about anything into ash. I guess it's the trade-off. Some of us also display what the religious kooks call an "anima." Many novas have a distinct field around them when they use their powers. I guess you've seen the footage — I look like I'm covered in transparent flames when I absorb energy. I've seen weirder displays. I'm just glad that some of the research has helped with older problems like cancer. I haven't had a cold in 10 years, and if a blood sample can keep everyone else from having one, all the better.

• **N!:** Not all novas, especially some who have spoken out recently, have taken such a philanthropic position. How do you respond to Divis Mal's melodramatically dubbed Null Manifesto and organizations like his Teragen?

• **Portman:** I don't know much about this Mal fellow, but I don't like what I've heard. Isn't he the guy who says that we aren't human? Of course I'm human! I can just do things some people can't. He says we're all governments of our own, and that the laws and rules of humans don't apply to us. Personally, if he really believes that, and it's not just a publicity stunt or ratings gimmick, then he's a megalomaniac, and his mom should have spanked him more often. I wish he'd just mouthed off on *Two Minutes Hate*, like the rest of the bored wackos, and left it at that.

As far as the Teragen is concerned, they give all novas a bad name. I can't wait until the Utopians or the UN or someone gets a hold of them. I don't care how popular or "cool" some folks think the Teragen is, Mal's group is nothing but a gang of thugs, the Manson Family with superpowers. They've killed people, destroyed property, intervened in wars — and they say they are acting for the good of all novas? They are no better than Mal. In fact, they're worse. At least Mal just mouthed off. These guys are wreaking havoc. They are the ones who are putting this smear-campaign crap on the Project.

• **N!:** Does the future look bright?

• **Portman:** I think so. We've had problems and bad apples, of course, but all in all, novas have done a lot to make the world a better place. Guys like Mal will always pop up, but they'll get their due. I think the next 10 years will be even better than the last. I really believe that the 21st century will be the dawn of a golden age for mankind.

N HOME

- N!tertainment
- N!terview
- N! the news
- N!sight
- N!tre nous
- N!ternet
- N!tv
- fun N! games

help!

awards

legal stuff

search

find !

N contact us

N the news

The *Galatea* Explosion

From Ultimate Media's "Reliving N-Day" audio collage

"…In the wake of the *Galatea's* explosion, freak accidents and catastrophes are erupting all around the world…"

"…earthquake, at least 4.0 on the Richter scale, rocked Denver…"

"…series of explosions on the streets of New York City, including one threatening a school bus…"

"…United States government has declared a state of Defcon 3…"

"…India is blaming a Pakistani attack for the sudden flood of the Ganges, which has washed away…"

"…teenager was unable to be rushed to the hospital, remaining electrically charged for 20 minutes, despite paramedics' attempts to ground out the electrical charge…"

"…mass suicide of a California religious commune, which detectives are attributing to a millennial death pact…"

> Of all the days to change the world forever, why the hell did God have to pick a fucking Monday?
>
> — Dr. Duke Rollo, post-gonzo journalist

From the final broadcast of the *Galatea*, 03/23/98

• **Galatea:** …Command, we're having some sort of difficulties on board.

• **NASA:** Say again. What kind of difficulties?

• **Galatea:** Lights aren't functioning properly… diagnostic seems to indicate some sort of…

• **NASA:** Come in, *Galatea*. Can you hear us?

• **Galatea:** Yes…the signs are…

• **NASA:** *Galatea*, do you read us?

• **Galatea:** We read you, Command. This isn't… Command, system failure seems to indicate core shielding breach. We…

• **NASA:** Dear God. Hold on, *Galate* Are you sure that—

• **Galatea:** Jesus… Command, we'r gonna… Please, tell our kids…

[Signal ends]

6

keep reading

N!tertainment

N!terview

N! the news

N!sight

N!tre nous

N!ternet

N!tv

fun N! games

elp!

vards

gal stuff

search

[find !]

contact
us

Excerpt from *Reaching the Stars: A Decade of Novas*

• **Chantal D'Aurelion:** "The explosion of the *Galatea*, tragic though it was, was just the first step in that long series of dramatic events that marked the birth of the Nova Age. The first eruptions of novas took the world by surprise, but in America, one particular event stands out. We found an eyewitness to that first dramatic eruption — and what a story it is."

• **Doreen Maxwell [voiceover as "dramatic re-creation" footage rolls]:** "Lord, I'll never forget it. The TVs in the store windows had just started up with the news breaks talking about the *Galatea*. I can remember the *Challenger* explosion, and I was just thinking 'Oh my God, not again — not another crew of astronauts lost,' and that's when I heard this screeching behind me. I turned around, and there was this school bus all smashing across the median and slamming into cars. Fire was coming out of the windows and everything, and the driver actually shot up out of the roof into the air. I don't remember seeing him come down.

"The flames was getting bigger, starting to shoot all over the place, and we could see that the kids couldn't get out. I was screaming for somebody to do something when the fire truck got on the scene. The firemen started moving people back out of the way, trying to get there, and the poor kids was just screaming, and that's when it happened.

"The fire just shot up and out of the windows and twisted up together like a braid, and then it *shot* down at this one fireman and hit him right square in the chest. His helmet blew off and he took a couple of steps back, but he didn't fall over. And that fire just kept on shooting up out of the bus and pouring into him until the bus didn't have any fire in it left at all. And the fireman, he was down on one knee, holding his head, and he looked like he was on fire — but I looked twice, and the fire just soaked on up into his body like he was a sponge, and the asphalt around him was turning all red, and I swear he sank down into the *melted* road!

"Well, things kept on getting crazy after that. The police arrived and started shooing us all back, and I heard about the rest on TV — how this sort of thing was going on all over the place, with earthquakes, explosions, freak thunderstorms and all that, and the government all going to Defcon 'cause they thought it was some kind of attack — but the news finally told us that the fireman was all right, and soon after that, we started finding out about all these people with powers.

"But when people ask me, 'Where were you when the *Galatea* exploded?', I can look them in the eye and say, 'I was on the street where the Fireman erupted.' Ain't too many people can say that."

7

Journal entry, Dr. Phylicia Cassant; February 2, 1999

The public is now fully convinced that the *Galatea* disaster is the link. A payload of radioactive isotopes, detonated in a spectacular explosion and spread via jetstream to every corner of the globe: The image has certainly caught on with the common man. "Radioactivity breeds mutation" — that's all the explanation most people seem to need.

I have to wonder, however, if the isotopes weren't somehow charged with refined "quantum energy" during the process. Nothing in modern science explains how such a thing was possible — but then again, modern science is skating by with the barest excuses for how aberrant powers function, anyway. It seems more plausible to me that the genetic coding for the M-R node would be stimulated by focused quantum than by outright radiation; however, there's no way to test this theory. Quantum is notorious for not remaining in the background long in concentrated quantities; short of having an already-manifested aberrant there at the time, I suppose there's no way we could ever have known for certain. Which is a damn shame, because otherwise, this conundrum may very well haunt me to my grave.

I wonder: Since the most common source of focused quantum appears to be aberrant powers, is it possible that some mutant actually manifested a functioning M-R node *before* the loss of the *Galatea*? Is it possible that one of the men and women aboard was the first aberrant, and that he or she somehow engineered the explosion to create others like himself or herself? If so, then logically this aberrant would still survive; why sacrifice yourself, after all? The question is — where is he?

Must look into this further, preferably by enlisting an aberrant with enhanced reasoning capacities. Are the rumors of psychometric powers true? Whatever the case, I'd better keep this to myself; no need to endanger my current position by earning a reputation as a crank conspiracy theorist. I can collect the Nobel after I've gotten proof.

Timeline

1998

March 23, 12:18 PM GST: *Galatea* research satellite explodes. Its rapidly decaying orbit dumps radioactive material into the jetstream. In a matter of days, increasing radiation levels are reported worldwide.

March 23, 3:31 PM EST: Randel Portman becomes the first publicly known nova. "The Fireman," as the media later dub Portman, emerges during a school-bus fire in New York. His nascent powers absorb the energy from the fire, putting it out and saving dozens of lives.

March-April: Novas emerge worldwide on an almost daily basis. Governments scramble to deal with the phenomenon. International relations become tense, with the US going to Defcon 3. Other nations respond in kind. Emergency sessions of the UN are called. First usage of the term "nova" by the press, in response to scientists' unofficial categorization of the newly erupted as *Homo sapiens novus*.

April 12: The Aeon Society, an international philanthropic organization dating back to the League of Nations, initiates a dialog with the UN, offering to seek out and study novas.

May 1: The Aeon Society publicly announces its UN support and issues an invitation to open dialog with any interested novas. The UN works behind the scenes to calm and reassure the world that Aeon can handle the nova outbreak.

June 30: The UN overwhelmingly passes the Zurich Accord, a document declaring novas to be human beings, with all the rights and responsibilities thereof. A few fundamentalist Islamic nations and dictatorial regimes, all countries with poor human-rights records, protest the resolution.

August 13: Project Utopia, a multipurpose private foundation, is formed under the guidance of both the UN and the Aeon Society. Project Utopia's stated goals are to study the nova phenomenon and utilize novas' abilities to better the quality of life on Earth for all its inhabitants. Membership and training are open to all interested novas, under the direction of Drs. Henri Mazarin and Farah Rashoud.

October: First use of the term "baseline" to refer to humans without an M-R node.

December 4: Dr. Henri Mazarin and Dr. Farah Rashoud release their findings on the discovery of a unique gland found in the brain of novas. The Mazarin-Rashoud, or M-R, node is believed to be the root of a nova's abilities. Novas officially dubbed subspecies *Homo sapiens novus*. An independent pharmaceutical research facility, the Triton Foundation, provides funding for Mazarin and Rashoud's research, and much of the other nova research over the next decade. A nova's powers are theorized to derive from manipulation of the basic forces of the universe, also known as the quantum forces: gravity, electromagnetism, weak nuclear force

and strong nuclear force. The M-R node allows the nova some degree of channeling and control over the quantum forces.

December 31: Aeon Society census reports approximately 600 known novas in the world population.

Inspired by the coming of the novas and fueled by millennialist anxiety, various apocalyptic and transcendentalist religious sects arise throughout 1998. Many of these groups see novas as the chosen of God or the ultimate development of humanity. The most notable of these is The Church of the Immanent Escheaton, founded by a charismatic nova styling himself Chrystian Kalpa. The Vatican does not release an official statement of position on the status of novas. Protestant sects and Judaism release statements of support for novas, with wording in line with that of the Zurich Accord. Fundamentalist Islamic sects decry novas as the Devil's children, but increasingly come into conflict with Sunni philosophy exalting novas as the chosen of Allah.

1999

January 1: In a media spectacle attended by former President Carter and the UN Secretary-General, Project Utopia introduces its "Team Tomorrow," a group of novas from around the world organized to implement Project Utopia's goals of a better future. Team Tomorrow begins to combat global terrorism, organized crime and natural disasters with the cooperation of law-enforcement agencies worldwide. Utopia's fledgling Science and Technology Department begins working on solutions to famine and environmental crises.

January 8: Project Utopia opens the first Rashoud facility in midtown Manhattan. The facility is intended to be a place where nascent novas can go to learn about and explore their powers in a controlled environment. Over the next decade, dozens of other Rashoud facilities open worldwide.

February 18: Boris Yeltsin dies, setting off a breakdown of the Russian government. The chaos leads to Russia's total economic collapse. Russia's financial woes spread through already weakened world markets, and cause the world's worst one-day market losses ever. "The Moscow Crash," as it is later termed, plunges the world into a massive recession.

February 19: The World Bank responds immediately by calling for temporary freezes on all international loan payments. International currency markets close for the week due to pressure from the International Monetary Fund. Wall Street and other world trading centers voluntarily close trading for the rest of the week to allow a thorough assessment of the situation, and to allow the panic to calm. Many governments, including the US and the rest of the G7 nations, implement emergency price controls on consumer goods.

March 1: Project Utopia announces that its nova-employing research department is working on a solution to the economic crisis. It also offers the services of the novas associated with Utopia to the UN, and any government that asks, for relief work. The news leads to a slight upswing in world markets.

April 7: Microsoft becomes the first private company to hire a nova for public relations and research. Mungu Kuwasha is hired for his ability to interface with computer systems.

April 30: World unemployment rates quadruple in only two months. Philan-thropic organizations worldwide follow the Aeon Society's lead in offering relief assistance. Project Utopia novas help with distribution of perishable supplies, creating the most efficient relief effort in history. Governments enlist nova aid in quelling food riots. Some novas use their abilities to keep basic utilities, such as water and electricity, flowing in areas where they would otherwise be inaccessible.

June 2: The International Monetary Fund announces its inability to ameliorate the global financial crisis. The Japanese take the news especially poorly. The Nikkei Index loses 50% of its value overnight. Tokyo newspapers report over 2,000 suicides that night alone.

June 5: Acting on the advice of Project Utopia nova prognosticators, the UN unanimously passes a resolution to freeze exchange rates in the world currency market. The move causes massive inflation in the currency of developing nations, but leads to a gradual strengthening of the industrial powers' economies.

November 21: Japan announces *Saisho*, "The New Beginning," a series of government subsidies designed to employ novas in high-tech industries. The Japanese government agrees to pay for companies to hire novas for research and development purposes, in hopes that new technologies will salvage Japan's economy. The project is a rousing success, and within a decade Japan regains its position as the premier developer of new technologies.

December 2: Project Utopia's Team Tomorrow announces it will be on call around the world to avert any problems that may come from the Y2K millennium bug. Prime-time television specials aired around the world show novas working with computer designers to prevent the problem, and teams of novas performing disaster-control drills.

December 31: Aeon Society census reports approximately 1350 known novas in the world population.

Novas continue to erupt throughout the year, despite falling levels of radiation from the *Galatea* explosion.

2000

January 1: The Year 2000 bug hits many of the world's computer systems, causing moderate problems. Power production, airline traffic control, Internet traffic and financial institution computers are the most affected. Utopia-affiliated novas race around the globe to restore (or, in some cases, generate) emergency power and direct what few planes are in the air. Most people notice only that the airlines and banks are shut down for a couple of days, and that Web pages and e-mail have glitches for a few weeks. Y2K becomes Utopia's biggest public-relations windfall since the coming of the novas.

January 28: The Triton Foundation announces the first successful gene-therapy treatment for breast cancer. By 2006, this treatment, combined with childhood genetic screening, makes breast cancer a thing of the past.

February 1: Project Utopia an-nounces, before the UN General Assembly, its intention to perform a worldwide environmental cleanup. The world press applauds the news, and various countries use the cleanup project as a core to create civil works programs to help alleviate the massive unemploy-ment that has plagued them since 1999.

April 8: Fidel Castro dies. Cuba spends the following weeks in political turmoil. When the dust clears, a democratically elected president and legislative body take control of the government. Cuba's relations with the rest of the world normalize by July.

May 31: The first movie to feature nova actors opens to rave reviews. Steven Spielberg-directed *Nova* is the story of a young man who emerges as a nova, then dedicates his life to righting the wrongs of society. Various famous novas figure prominently in the cast. The movie breaks all previous sales records, staying in the top spot throughout the summer. *Nova* goes on to sweep the Academy Awards, winning a record 18 Oscars.

July 15: Second-quarter financial reports indicate worldwide economic improvement. The upswing marks the beginning of the largest sustained period of economic growth and prosperity in world history. The UN drops its freeze of the currency markets, and most nations of Western and Central Europe agree to the adoption of the euro currency, linking much of Europe into one economic entity. The United Kingdom declines entry into the European Union.

September 6: Project Utopia announces that it has successfully closed the hole in the ozone layer and introduced CFC-eating bacteria into the atmosphere to prevent continued damage. Project Utopia requests that all UN member states begin transporting toxic and radioactive waste to a collection facility in Siberia for future disposal.

November 3: Robert Schroer, a moderate Republican representative from Colorado, is elected President of the United States. Schroer begins the Republican nomination process as a virtual unknown; his platform calls for continued economic reform and a return to so-called "common-sense" values. He wins a narrow victory in the general election over Al Gore, in which the Reform and Libertarian candidates also take sizable proportions of the vote. Following Schroer's win in the primaries, and escalating with his election, many of the Republican Party's far-right elements divorce themselves from the party to found splinter groups more appealing to their agendas.

December 31: With the Y2K problem and millennialist anxiety distant memories, the press realizes that 2001 is the actual beginning of the new millennium. This announcement inspires the largest New Year's celebrations in

memory. Festivities include nova-produced energy releases in orbit that are visible around the world.

Aeon Society census reports approximately 1800 known novas in the world population.

2001

January 24: Project Utopia-mediated negotiations between Israel and the Palestinian Liberation Organization open. The peace talks end with the signing of the London Peace Accord, which establishes a Palestinian state along the border of Israel and Egypt. Project Utopia agrees, as part of the Accord, to monitor the newly created border, although Israel is rumored to have almost a dozen novas under its direct control.

March 18: Project Utopia announces that bioremedial bacteria recently introduced in the world's oceans, along with a large amount of physical cleanup, will restore the water quality of the world's oceans to pre-Industrial Revolution levels by 2006.

March 29: The Russian Confederation rises from the political and economic chaos caused by the Moscow Crash of 1999. Russia's downward spiral reverses, albeit slowly, thanks to nova "economic savant" and Minister of the Treasury, Vladimir Sierka. The reorganized Confederation consists of sovereign member states allied for purposes of economic strength and foreign relations. The Confederation has one currency, the ruble, and representatives of each member-state in the Confederation vote on all foreign trade decisions. The Confederation retains its seat on the UN Security Council, but the member states are represented individually in the General Assembly. In effect, the Confederation functions somewhat like a cross between the European Union and the United States of America. Belarus president Andrei Srebrianski is elected the first Confederation president. Although Srebrianski is officially president, rumors continue in the press that Minister Sierka is the true leader of the Confederation.

May-November: Brushfire wars sweep through sub-Saharan West Africa, as Sierra Leone, Nigeria and Sudan use nova mercenaries, dubbed "elites" by the press, to fight as proxies. While fewer than a dozen elites die in the conflicts, hundreds of civilians are killed as "collateral damage," and the political borders of Africa are redrawn several times throughout the months of conflict. Team Tomorrow takes peacekeeping actions on behalf of the UN and finally negotiates a ceasefire. Press coverage of the conflicts becomes the highest-rated television event of the decade, so far. Various conspiracy theorists claim that the conflicts were instigated by the US and other major powers so they

could see how effective novas were when used as military operatives.

The Equatorial Wars, as the fighting is later dubbed, prompt international negotiations concerning the use of novas in military applications. While the talks are never formalized, the UN and Project Utopia openly support discussion on the issue. International consensus falls short of banning the use of novas in the military, but it is generally agreed that due to the unpredictable nature of novas' powers, they should not be used against civilian or normal military targets unless in all-out war. Strategists and academics quickly devise a new school of military deterrent thought based around novas and formalize the idea of limited-scale conflicts fought by nova proxies. General acceptance of this idea, as an economical alternative to certain types of conventional conflicts, leads to large numbers of elites being contracted by world governments in the following year.

May 21: The Triton Foundation announces a gene-therapy treatment for prostate cancer and a genetic screening process that predicts (with 94% accuracy) whether a person will develop any of the common forms of cancer.

June 10: Representatives of the United States, the Russian Confederation, the UK and Japan meet in Moscow. They agree to form and sponsor a multinational intelligence agency, which they term the Directive. The Directive's primary mission is to monitor the activities of Project Utopia and the world's growing population of novas.

August 7: Aníbal Buendia, a nova with the ability to reconfigure his cellular structure, creates the polymer derivative known as eufiber. This material, which has the ability to bond with nova cell structure and channel and redirect quantum and bioenergies, becomes the most popular fashion accessory for novas and the wealthy. As a side effect, studies of eufiber enable the development of OpNet cable technology.

October: Project Utopia begins coordinating with law-enforcement and intelligence agencies from around the world (Interpol, FBI, Scotland Yard, Mossad) to combat organized crime and terrorism.

December 31: Aeon Society census reports approximately 2100 known novas in the world population.

2002

January 2002-early 2005: Much of the world's copper and fiber-optic cable communications networks are replaced with advanced optic cable derived from studies of Buendia eufiber and wireless networking. The new hardware, coupled with new data-transfer protocols, is dubbed "OpNet." OpNet replaces the Internet, phone systems and cellular networks, allowing for wireless communications from virtually any location. It boasts an initial 700% increase in data speed over conventional telecommunications technology.

March 30: CNN breaks a sex scandal involving US president Schroer. The sordid scandal involves a six-year homosexual affair on the part of the President. Schroer gives a televised address that night and admits to the affair. Even with his immediate response, his approval ratings plummet.

August 12: Project Utopia gives its final report on the state of the environment to the UN General Assembly. Team Tomorrow combines physical cleanup with the introduction of the Zushima macrobe, a genetically engineered self-regulating organism that will regulate further pollution. The environment is in better shape than at any point in the last hundred years, and Project Utopia scientists estimate that a sustainable level of pre-Industrial Revolution air and water quality will be a reality by 2005.

September 15: India, China and Pakistan face off over ownership of the Kashmir region. Quick intervention by Team Tomorrow prevents an all-out war, but several conflicts with government-sponsored novas and mercenary elites occur. Kashmir becomes a demilitarized zone under UN and Project Utopia surveillance.

November 21: The Viacom and Microsoft corporations announce their merger into an enormous corporate entity to be called ViaSoft.

December 4: A subway bombing in Tokyo brings world attention to Kamisama Buddhism, a hybrid of Shinto and Buddhist beliefs that is increasingly popular with Japanese youths. While Kamisama Buddhism professes nonviolence, the media play up the suspects' involvement with the sect. Three young fanatics are charged in the bombing, though the leader of the religion, nova guru Bodhisattva Masato, disavows any knowledge of the attack.

December 31: Aeon Society census reports approximately 2500 known novas in the world population.

2003

January 1: The N! channel debuts on cable and satellite systems in 47 countries. N!, a spinoff of the E! channel, is dedicated solely to covering the lives and exploits of novas. It features biographies of famous novas, quasi-scientific documentaries on nova abilities and physiology, nova sporting competitions, interviews with novas and nova-related news from around the world. Within three months of its initial airing, N! becomes the highest-rated channel ever.

March 9: Team Tomorrow stages a dramatic rescue of the space shuttle *Discovery* after a sizable meteor strikes the shuttle, knocking it off course and igniting an oxygen tank. The entire crew survives the rescue. This event marks the point at which governments begin to consider novas for space operations and exploration.

May 6: Project Utopia announces plans to terraform the Ethiopian Highlands. The project, a cooperative endeavor between Project Utopia, the UN and the Ethiopian government, marks the first attempt at engineering widespread geographical and environmental changes throughout a region.

September 25: A terrorist organization sets off an explosion utilizing primitive fusion technology. Over 30 city blocks are leveled, and hundreds die. Team Tomorrow Americas arrives immediately to supply humanitarian aid and assist in the criminal investigation. Despite repeated reports of nova involvement in the bombing, no one has been charged to date. The Sao Paolo bombing is the most expensive terrorist attack in history, causing an estimated $20 billion in damages.

October 7: The Triton Foundation announces the discovery of an AIDS

vaccine. The World Health Organization declares October 7th "Red Ribbon Day" and, with the help of national and local health organizations, vaccinates 90% of the world population over the next three months.

December 10: Henri Mazarin and Farah Rashoud receive the Nobel Prize in biology for their pioneering research into nova physiology and the discovery of the M-R node.

December 31: Aeon Society census reports approximately 2800 known novas in the world population.

2004

February 19: The Triton Foundation announces an advanced gene-therapy treatment that fights most known forms of cancer.

May 1: The World Health Organization approves a host of new genetic engineering techniques, many of which were developed in conjunction with the Triton Foundation over the past few years. Most national food inspection organizations (such as the Food and Drug Administration in the US) copy this move, marking the first widespread international use of genetic engineering for livestock and crops. World food production increases by 25% over the next two years.

June 1: The hypercombustion engine is released. Designed by nova Tetsuo Yamato, the hypercombustion engine is a super-efficient internal combustion engine, suitable for consumer and industrial applications. It boasts a tenfold decrease in fuel consumption while increasing power by a like amount. Within the decade, all automotive transportation and fossil-fuel-based electric production use hypercombustion engines exclusively.

June 15: In the wake of the Sao Paolo bombing, the UN Secretary-General grants Project Utopia's Science and Technology Department authority to monitor, approve and regulate new technologies, particularly those derived from the "nova boom." Many member nations and corporations vehemently protest this decision.

July 24: The first Summer Olympic games to feature nova-only competitions opens. The nova events include variations on traditional track and field events, and the games become the second-highest-rated sports event of the year.

September 6: Project Utopia opens a special Rashoud facility in Bahrain. This facility is ostensibly designed to assist novas with high levels of quantum buildup, but Utopia is given leeway to confine novas considered in need of therapy by the UN as a whole. The facility's opening is not publicized, nor are the media or public allowed on the facility's grounds, though documentaries of its existence soon flood the OpNet.

September 30: The inaugural match of the Xtreme Warfare Federation, XWF, takes place in Madison Square Garden. The XWF is founded in response to increased demand for nova sporting events, and a corresponding loss of interest in traditional sports over the preceding years. The pay-per-view event garners massive ratings and is carried over OpNet. Licensing revenues top the $1 billion mark in a single year. The initial match is the highest-rated television event of 2004.

November 3: Lauren Pendleton is elected both the first female and first Libertarian president of the United States. The press credits her victory to voters disgruntled with two sex scandals by two consecutive presidents from both major political parties. The Libertarian Party and various independent candidates claim a sizable portion of legislative seats in the election.

December 31: Aeon Society census reports approximately 3000 known novas in the world population.

2005

April 2: Puerto Rico becomes the 51st state of the United States of America.

April 19: Team Tomorrow unseats Macedonian dictator Yaroslav Radocani. Radocani came to power with the aid of military loyalists and high-tech weaponry. Following the revelation that Radocani's weaponry had been produced by Japanese corporations acting in violation of UN norms, Utopia's Science and Technology Department is granted even greater regulatory latitude in monitoring "potentially dangerous technological advancements."

June 15: Pope Benedict XVI issues *Ad Dei Lucem*, a bull declaring that novas, like humans, have immortal souls, are tainted with original sin and can be saved through the grace of Christ.

October 31: A previously unknown nova calling himself Divis Mal issues the Null Manifesto in a broadcast emanating from the Azores. The edict essentially counters the Zurich Accords, and claims that novas are "emancipated" from global citizenship and any responsibilities thereof. The provisions of the Null Manifesto state that novas are not human beings and are therefore not subject to human law, boundaries or moral codes, nor may they claim citizenship in any nation established by human beings. Novas may be granted diplomatic privileges by human governments, but they are essentially "governments" unto themselves.

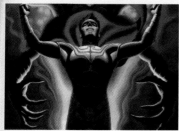

A nova-only dissident group calling itself the Teragen publicly endorses the Null Manifesto and renounces all ties to governmental bodies. Project Utopia comes out in strong public opposition against the Teragen's position, and it promises, in front of a closed UN Security Council meeting, to monitor Teragen activity. Sales of Teragen-specific bootleg merchandise skyrocket, particularly among the First World 18-35 demographic.

Ø

November 7: The first ever surgical trial of a complete spinal cord reconstruction is performed. The trial is a glowing success. Funding for the research comes from the Triton Foundation.

December 31: Aeon Society census reports approximately 3500 known novas in the world population.

2006

May 22: The Ethiopian government announces the completion of the terraforming project. The Ethiopian Highlands, formerly a dry, flat, desert plain, is now a verdant grassland. The grateful Ethiopian government gives Project Utopia a large headquarters in Addis Ababa. Ethiopia soon becomes the breadbasket of Africa.

July 5: A conservative Tehran mullah is openly assassinated by novas declaring themselves "members of the Teragen." Known Teragen sympathizers disavow the assassins, claiming that the Teragen is neither an organized institution nor has any single agenda. Nonetheless, Project Utopia and the UN take greater pains to monitor known or suspected Teragen novas.

August 30: Ongoing tensions in the Kashmir region erupt into a small-scale war. Nova elites representing India, China and Pakistan fight across the region, turning it into a blasted ecological nightmare. Project Utopia steps in to stop the fighting, under UN authority, and arrests several of the novas deemed responsible for the disaster.

November 5: A Quebec separatist group based in Montreal claims responsibility for recent terrorist strikes in Ottawa and Toronto. Given the nature of the strikes, Canadian authorities fear the group may be employing a nova elite.

December 31: Aeon Society census reports approximately 4800 known novas in the world population.

2007

January 1: Nova astronaut Janos Karagian walks across the lunar surface without artificial life support gear. Plans are made to send nova astronauts to Mars.

March 1: The UN promotes a pact banning all nuclear, biological and chemical (NBC) weaponry. The NBC weapons ban is signed by all the member states. Military observers claim that while there is a trend towards disarmament, most of the nuclear powers still have stockpiled weapons.

May-December: Teragen attacks of terror and random violence begin being reported by the media. Although fewer than half a dozen terrorist strikes occur, the media goes into a frenzy.

August 3: Project Utopia receives a permanent "advisory" seat on the UN Security Council. Many political observers credit the unprecedented move as stemming from Project Utopia's agreement to pay off the UN debt, totaling $1.6 billion.

December 31: Aeon Society census reports approximately 6000 known novas in the world population. As of yet, no nova is known to have been impregnated or impregnated others, either baseline or nova. Utopia-affiliated scientists vow to study this phenomenon, at the behest of nova would-be parents.

2008

May 13: Popular Team Tomorrow agent Jennifer "Slider" Landers is killed in Calcutta by parties unknown. The world is shocked at the murder of its "sweetheart."

May 15: Jennifer Landers' closest friend, controversial ex-T2M nova André Corbin, inexplicably flees the site of her funeral.

May 16: UN and Utopia investigations finger Slider's murder as the handiwork of Corbin, who is believed to be linked to the Teragen. This revelation comes as part of a worldwide public broadcast on all major news networks.

May 19: Scandal rocks Project Utopia as unconfirmed reports of mercenary novas, government infiltration and nova black ops leak to the media. Aeon Society and Project Utopia spokespeople immediately counter with evidence of a Teragen frame-up involving the dead Slider. Wary observers and conspiracy theorists see themselves as vindicated and deluge the media with dire predictions.

May 30: Nova Sophia Rousseau contacts fugitive André Corbin. Their underground organization immediately begins contacting friends and acquaintances in the nova community, as well as newly erupting novas. The group's goal is to expose the hidden corruption in Project Utopia, and Corbin dubs its members "Aberrants" in an ironic usage of a popular epithet.

June 2: In a closed UN Security Council meeting, Utopia's Internal Affairs Department reveals findings indicating a frame-up of the organization. The US and British governments are unconvinced, and Directive surveillance of Utopia's operations is stepped up.

June 3: The Teragen meets in council at a hidden retreat. Topics of the meeting include what precisely is going on with the now-weakened Project Utopia, and how to use the group's newfound weakness to dismantle it.

June 4: Project Utopia begins an internal investigation for remaining allies of Corbin within its own ranks.

June 15: There are approximately 40 Aberrants worldwide, all either in deep cover or in hiding. To date, neither Corbin nor Rousseau has been brought to justice, and the identity of Slider's assassin remains a mystery.

Abstract from the Research Project "The Genetic Basis of *Homo sapiens novus*"

Dr. Sarah Lewis, Director of the Brooks L. Miller Center for Biosciences Research, Georgia Institute of Technology

September 13, 2007

Funding provided by the Triton Foundation

In the nine years since the first recorded appearance of novas, many in the scientific community have speculated as to a possible genetic basis for the individuals now classified as *Homo sapiens novus*. The continued emergence of novas, years after the worldwide cleanup of the debris from the *Galatea* explosion, has served only to fuel the controversy.

After five years of research, involving data collected from over 50 novas and the Human Genome Project, I feel confident in saying that *Homo sapiens novus* definitely has a genetic basis. The findings of this project bring into question several long-standing assumptions on human genetics.

Early analysis showed no statistically significant link between *Homo sapiens novus* DNA sequences or chromosomal typing and those of *Homo sapiens*. Without an isolated DNA sequence being responsible for *Homo sapiens novus* development, it led us back to considering environmental causes. A review of the pioneering work of Drs. Mazarin and Rashoud provided the clues to unlocking the mystery of *Homo sapiens novus* genetics.

The M-R node is key to novas' ability to manipulate quantum energies and forces, and provides the most consistent physiological distinction between *Homo sapiens* and *Homo sapiens novus*. The node itself has an internal structure similar to that of a metaphase-stage mitosis division, the second stage of cellular division, in which the DNA has been condensed into sister chromatids, the nuclear membranes have disappeared, and the chromatids are lined up in the middle of the cell on the spindle fibers, preparing to be drawn to the poles of the cell. Interestingly, the M-R node does not contain DNA itself. In a fashion similar to red blood cells, it relies on other cells to create and expand it.

The similarities between the physical structures of metaphase and those of M-R nodes led to an analysis of the genetic material within currently replicating cells of *Homo sapiens novus*. Extensive analysis and mapping of *Homo sapiens novus* dividing DNA showed that particular sections of DNA sequences were common to all the novas tested.

The common sequences were previously thought to be introns. An intron is nontranscribed DNA sequencing. If every individual base pair in all the DNA in an organism were used to make needed proteins, the organism would be highly susceptible to even the slightest genetic mutations. Introns are a kind of blank space in the DNA chain that codes no needed information. In fact, most of the DNA making up a gene are actually introns. As such, their existence means that any particular genetic mutation is statistically much less likely to be fatal to the organism. However, in normal dividing cells, no DNA is being coded, as it is compressed in preparation of division. All novas must have some trigger that codes that DNA immediately preceding duplication of the cellular DNA for replication and mitosis, or that codes introns while the DNA is compressed.

All *Homo sapiens novus* test subjects were found to have the same intron sequences in their DNA. The Human Genome Project did not record sequencing of dividing DNA, so initially, we isolated and tested 30 researchers at our lab. Only one showed the particular sequencing. Her excitement over the find apparently led to the triggering of the latent genetic material, because within days of the discovery, she erupted as a nova.

Subsequently, a double-blind test was run with tissue samples from 5,000,000 different individuals. Six of the samples were from *Homo sapiens novus*. All six of the *Homo sapiens novus* samples showed the DNA sequencing, while none of the *Homo sapiens* samples did. We have not received the funding for more extensive testing, but computer models indicate that our current tests are 99.998% statistically accurate.

M-R Node Development

The latent genetic sequencing in a *Homo sapiens novus* is activated by severely increased cellular division brought about by large-scale adrenaline release. Upon activation, the previously dormant DNA sequences transcribe a series of highly mutagenic hormones. These hormones leave the dividing cell's DNA, and quickly infuse the cell. The hormones are then released from individual cells, and make their way into the bloodstream.

Through an unknown mechanism, the hormones apparently seek out and bind to specific neuron clusters in the frontal lobes. There they cause a rapid mutation of the neurons into the M-R node, much as large doses of highly carcinogenic agents can cause cancerous tumors in a matter of hours. The mechanism by which the M-R node changes or expands after its initial genesis is unknown.

Several of the hormones coded by the DNA sequence were previously unknown, and have resisted all attempts at independent synthesis.

Conclusion

While we have identified the genetic basis for *Homo sapiens novus*, the finding leave more questions and speculations than answers. The specificity of the DNA sequenc-

ing would account for the relative rarity of *Homo sapiens novus*, but it is unknown why novas have continued to appear with greater frequency. The *Galatea* explosion, and its subsequent radioactive fallout, could theoretically have caused the changes in the DNA sequence, but not in the frequency shown by erupting novas.

Given the inheritable genetic basis of *Homo sapiens novus*, it would seem that we can expect further generations. Half of a human being's DNA is from each parent, so it is possible that all or some *Homo sapiens novus* females that have children will produce *Homo sapiens novus* themselves; similarly for *Homo sapiens novus* males. Please note that this assertion is just that; we have been unable to locate any *Homo sapiens novus* who are currently pregnant, or have had children. In light of the physiological changes inherent to *Homo sapiens novus*, it is questionable whether a *Homo sapiens novus* female can bear children at all.

Our testing method would also imply the ability to test people for future M-R node development, possibly even in a prenatal stage. While technically this is now a possibility, the process of harvesting and analyzing DNA is both laborious and very expensive. It requires not just blood samples, but various tissue samples in large quantities. The DNA analysis requires intensive lab work, and even with the best computer analysis, the process is prohibitively time-consuming. Widespread testing for *Homo sapiens novus* is not something that is likely to occur in our lifetime.

From *Encyclopedia Britannica*, 2005 edition

"Mazarin-Rashoud Node"

The Mazarin-Rashoud node, M-R node for short, is a small gland between the frontal lobes of the brain that is found only in novas, *Homo sapiens novus*. The M-R node acts as a catalyst for novas' control and manipulation of quantum energy forces. As the node develops, it increases in size, taking up progressively more space in the cranial cavity. Relatively little is known about how the M-R node functions. The M-R node is named after Dr. Henri Mazarin and Dr. Farah Rashoud, who first documented its existence in 1998 and received a Nobel Prize for their work in 2003. *See NOVA, QUANTUM FORCES*

On a last, purely speculative, note, we found it interesting that the genetic basis for *Homo sapiens novus* came from previously unrecorded introns, and at a time when the cellular DNA is not supposed to be active. The triggering mechanism is still unidentified; it could be a case of spot evolution, or perhaps even outside source influence. Further research on this topic is definitely in order.

Corbin

Birth Name: André Corbin
Date of Birth: March 23, 1985
Place of Origin: Leith, Scotland
Occupation: Ex-soccer player; ex-adult film star; ex-Team Tomorrow agent; co-founder of Aberrant movement

Powers: Corbin was a professional soccer player prior to his eruption, and the transformation from human to nova has enhanced an already exceptional athletic prowess. His strength, speed and reaction time are all well above the human norm, and he possesses uncanny powers of perception, intuition and acuity. Most notable, though, is Corbin's self-titled "Bender" — waves of quantum force that radiate out from his body. Persons bathed in these waves experience exceedingly potent emotional shifts: Would-be lovers hurl themselves at each other (or at Corbin), rivalries flare into violent hatred and mild unease becomes mind-numbing terror.

Background: Born on the date that would become N-Day 13 years later, André Corbin seemed born to stardom. From a working-class family in the industrial town of Leith, Corbin rose to become a professional soccer player in London. One of the most talked-about up-and-coming stars, Corbin seemed destined to save the declining edifice of baseline professional sports — if he didn't destroy it first. His athleticism was almost as notable as the fiery, hell-raising personality that incited riots across the continent and made tabloid headlines across the world.

And that was before his eruption. Corbin manifested as a nova during the World Cup playoffs between the UK and Nigeria, causing a riot in the process. Seeking to bolster its public image, Project Utopia contacted the famous sports celebrity and, amid great fanfare, announced his entry into Team Tomorrow.

This move was, to put it bluntly, a disaster. Corbin's in-your-face, hedonistic personality and lack of respect for authority made him completely unable to get along with his teammates or take his role seriously. Scandal rocked the prodigal's tenure, from the Princess Fazour Affair to the Waldorf-Astoria Incident to the shocking direct-to-OpNet release of *Hardballs*, an "art film" featuring Corbin and several pulchritudinous costars. Suspended from the team, Corbin severed all ties to T2M except for those to his unlikely friend, Jennifer "Slider" Landers.

And so it was to Corbin that Slider turned when she discovered evidence linking Project Utopia to a secret "black operation" called Project Proteus. At first skeptical, Corbin soon became convinced that Slider had uncovered the first layer of a vast global conspiracy. His conviction became concrete when Jennifer was murdered in Calcutta on May 13, 2008. Since that day, Corbin has gone into hiding, allying with mysterious nova Sophia Rousseau. The pair have recruited approximately 40 like-minded novas, some of whom are still officially tied to Utopia. Taking the epithet "Aberrant" as their ironic sobriquet, these novas seek to uncover the truth about Project Utopia and stop the Project's exploitation of novas. Corbin has a lot of growing up to do in a hurry; only time will tell if he succeeds.

Estimated Power Levels:
Strength: 5
Intellect: 3
Speed: 6
Offense: 4
Defense: 7
Versatility: 8

From "The Coming of Novas: Evolution's Next Step" by Dr. Henri Mazarin and Dr. Farah Rashoud, 2003

We are often asked, "What exactly is the M-R node?" Simply put, it is a small gland located between the frontal lobes of the brain. It is significant for two reasons. First, it is the organ with which novas manipulate quantum energies, hence giving them their amazing abilities. Second, it is the most reliable and obvious physiological difference between *Homo sapiens* and *Homo sapiens novus*.

For all of its importance, the M-R node itself is rather unexciting: a rough sphere, approximately 1 cm in diameter, of grayish matter. The node has many blood vessels and nerve fibers extending from it into the rest of the brain, which make it look vaguely like an octopus.

The M-R node's internal structure is much more interesting, and admittedly, more than a bit mystifying. The node consists of a tough outer membrane that surrounds twin poles connected by fibers, with what appear to resemble chromosomes. The outer portion of the chamber, outside the "spindle," contains the blood supply and numerous nerve endings, which relay information back and forth to the rest of the brain. The inner spindle surrounds a matrix of complex proteins. The matrix displays a high level of electrochemical activity, the specifics of which are still a matter of study.

While virtually nothing is known about how the M-R node manipulates quantum forces, it is interesting to note that the node itself highly resembles another biological structure. With the exceptions of the M-R node's connections to the rest of the brain and its size, its structure is very similar to that of metaphase in mitosis.

Even though the M-R node's manipulations of external energies are a mystery, how it affects a *Homo sapiens novus*' individual physiology is much more concretely understood. The M-R node connects to all portions of the brain, both those controlling autonomic functions (such as heartbeat and respiration) and those responsible for creativity, speech, and thought. This allows the node to both influence and draw from all aspects of a nova.

Novas control their abilities with conscious thought, but the specific actions of the M-R node that are responsible for the desired effect are unconscious. Much like walking: The nova decides to walk somewhere, but the actual interplay of his leg muscles is handled outside of his direct conscious awareness. The node seems to respond to subconscious desires and stimuli, in a manner similar to muscular reflexes or other autonomic functions. There also appears to be a psychologically significant influence of the unconscious on the M-R node, as novas tend to display a kind of "signature" when manifesting a power. Examples include

William Thompson, who appears to be surrounded by "serpents" of energy when using his abilities; or Randel "The Fireman" Portman, who appears to be surrounded by flames when absorbing energy from his surroundings. This effect is referred to by scholars as the nova's "anima."

The M-R node's control over autonomic functions within the body is much simpler. The node is able to effect considerable changes in physiology and metabolism within a nova. Indeed, the node seems to adapt a nova's body automatically to compensate for any manipulations that it makes to the external environment. This is not to say that novas are infinitely adaptable. They adapt to environmental changes caused by themselves, but do not necessarily change in response to environmental conditions they did not cause. For example, a nova may need a coat in the snow, but would automatically adapt to his M-R node covering him with cryokinetic frost.

The M-R node is capable of producing great changes within a nova's body. Some general changes include enhancement of physique and improvement of efficiency in all bodily processes. These changes are in response to the increased stress caused by the manipulation of forces and energies that the unaugmented human body is not equipped to channel.

The M-R node itself adapts over time. With increased control of quantum forces, the M-R node of a nova tangibly grows. It appears that the size of the node affects the amount of energy that it can channel, and the level of control it has over those forces. Some novas have displayed M-R nodes as large as an apple. What effect, if any, this has on a nova is unknown at this time.

MEMO

From: Agt. Kyle Landers, DEA
To: Michael Padgett, Northeast Regional Director, D
Date: April 8, 2006
Re: Tri-Cities Operation

The Tri-Cities drug ring has finally been broken up, no conclusive ties to the C-Z were discovered. I just tur evidence over to the District Attorney today. In all, 26 were made, but the group's leader, a suspected nova, elud ture. I guess we need our own nova to get him.

One thing you need to be aware of, though. The Tr ring was peddling a new drug, along with all the old favori dealers call it "soma." They claim it is an extract from a no R node. The lab boys analyzed it, and it is some kind o adrenochrome. This shit is scary. Imagine crack, but about times more powerful. It kills most people that use it, un extremely diluted. Even worse, it's rumored that soma is thing that can give a nova a sustained high. Their metabolis everything else seem like aspirin.

If this shit ever gets out, it could be a real mess. Luc have to kill a nova to get it, and that can't be easy. We sho our eyes open anyway.

From "Quantum Force Manipulations and the Mind" by Dr. Shawn Worth

Scientific American, February 2008

In the decade since their appearance, there has been much speculation about how *Homo sapiens novus*, or novas, manipulate quantum forces. While it is well known that the Mazarin-Rashoud node is the gland that allows these spectacular abilities, little is known about how the node functions. Unfortunately, this mystery is unlikely to be solved in the near future. Novas are understandably reluctant to participate in the direct experimentation needed to validate any theories proposed. This matter remains an issue of much debate in the scientific community.

I wish to offer a theory on the workings of the M-R node. The release of Dr. Lewis' recent study on the genetic basis of novas has opened the doors of speculation on the origin of novas. I feel that the answer to both the origin of novas and their amazing abilities lie in the origins of human consciousness.

Philosophers have long debated the nature of the mind. Human consciousness is a unique phenomenon. In the last decades, computer scientists have begun to claim that consciousness and intelligence are simply a function of a sufficiently complex computational ability. This theory is proposed by those who support what is known as strong AI (artificial intelligence). These thinkers claim that a fast enough and complex enough computer will mimic all the functions of consciousness.

I say "hogwash" to my esteemed colleagues. I say that consciousness is an observable physical phenomenon that happens on the quantum level. The uncertainty inherent to quantum mechanics allows for the self-reflexivity of consciousness, unlike the cold logic of a binary system. Although the proponents of strong AI would deny it, there has been significant research in the last 30 years to point to this conclusion.

The phenomenon of consciousness gives novas their incredible abilities. Novas can manipulate the fundamental forces of nature on a quantum level. Given that our consciousness exists primarily on the quantum level, the abilities of novas are merely manipulations of the primary components of consciousness. Humans manipulate quantum forces every day by merely thinking. Novas, through the M-R node, magnify and externalize those manipulations.

The metaphorical comparison between the M-R node and mitochondria may be more than an interesting coincidence.

From "Introduction to Physics, 12 edition", 2008, entry-level text

Quantum Forces: What are typically referred to as the "quantum forces" are in fact the fundamental forces of the universe. The term "quantum" came to be applied to such forces as physicists began to understand that the forces themselves operate on an absolutely fundamental level and carry aspects of both particles and waves; *see quantum physics* and *quantum theory*. The quantum forces are gravity, electromagnetism, strong nuclear force and weak nuclear force.

Gravity: Simultaneously very well understood and not well understood at all, gravity is a force we're all familiar with, as most of us feel it every day of our lives. Gravity is the attraction of mass to mass. In other words, matter is attracted to other matter, with more attraction being caused by objects with greater mass. Newton was the first to set down concrete laws for gravity, followed by the General Relativity of Einstein. However, gravity has yet to be fit comfortably into the quantum mechanical picture. Many theories have been proposed, but none have been fully satisfactory. The fact that novas can manipulate gravity is perhaps the strongest evidence to date that gravity can be fit into the quantum picture, however.

Electromagnetism: The second-strongest of the four fundamental forces, it also has an infinite range like gravity does. Easily the most fully explored of the quantum forces, electromagnetic fields are fields of photons generated by charged objects. Electromagnetism reflects the tendency of opposite charges to attract. This force is displayed on the atomic level via ionic bonding and on a larger scale with such materials as magnets. Electromagnetism works through the use of electromagnetic fields produced by charged material. These fields are easy to detect: They can be displayed by such pedestrian methods as sprinkling iron filings around the end of a magnet. If the charge is stationary, we call it an electrical field, and if the charge is moving, we also get a magnetic field.

Strong Nuclear Force: This force holds things together on the atomic scale and smaller. It has a range of only a few femtometers (a millionth of a trillionth of a meter), but within that range is the strongest force in the universe. It holds quarks together into hadrons, and holds protons and neutrons together to form nuclei. Only its extremely short range allows other forces to overcome it at all. The particle which carries the strong force is call the gluon.

Weak Nuclear Force: The least understood of all the fundamental forces, it also acts only at the nuclear scale. The weak force is responsible for a number of nuclear decay reactions, but is hard to explain beyond that, as it does not act in any sort of intuitive "push" or "pull" manner like the other three forces. The intermediate boson, W, is responsible for the weak interaction. An early triumph in the search for a Grand Unified Theory (GUT) was the unification of the electromagnetic and weak forces in electroweak theory.

N!tertainment

N!terview

N! the news

N!sight

N!tre nous

N!ternet

N!tv

fun N! games

help!

awards

legal stuff

search

[   ]

find!

N contact us

From N! documentary "Nova Powers!!!"

Novas display a multitude of amazing and incredible powers. Scientists have attributed these powers to a nova's Mazarin-Rashoud node and its ability to manipulate quantum energies and forces. While the mechanics of how the M-R node functions are still a mystery, the effects of the powers themselves are more documented.

Novas tend to "erupt" at points of great stress. The nature of this stress often dictates the kinds of powers the nova possesses. For example, nova Micah Weedman, who emerged during a skydiving accident, gained the ability to fly. Novas often display an outwardly visual effect associated with their powers, called the "anima." As we see, Micah displays a pair of glowing energy "wings" when he flies.

Besides the anima, most novas bear some obvious outward sign of their change. While many novas possess amazing physiques, some novas develop further changes to their appearance, such as bioluminescent auras or silvery skin.

Nova powers can roughly be divided into three categories: internal powers, sensory/ controlling powers and external powers. These categories are merely for purposes of demonstration; few nova abilities are so easily classified.

Internal Powers

Internal powers affect only the nova. Many novas display typical human traits that are heightened to an amazing degree. Some novas are incredibly strong or unbelievably intelligent. A quick look at the evening news sometimes shows novas lifting tractor-trailer trucks or memorizing the complete works of Shakespeare. Many novas seem to display a heightened level of biological attractiveness and natural charisma. The many nova actors and actresses are testament to how seductive and appealing novas can be.

Some novas display useful and amazing body modifications. Novas with claws, wings or the ability to withstand the elements or massive amount of energy are not uncommon. Changing appearance at will or even turning completely invisible are other documented powers. And, of course, so is the ability to fly….

Sensory/Controlling Powers

Potentially even more powerful are novas who can sense things beyond the limits of normal human experience, or control objects through acts of will. At the simplest level, many of these abilities seem nothing more than normal human senses extended and heightened to an impossible degree. Other such powers include seeing in other parts of the electromagnetic spectrum (such as infrared, ultraviolet and x-ray waves) or seeing matter on a microscopic or atomic level.

keep reading

N
HOME

N!tertainment

N!terview

N! the news

N!sight

N!tre nous

N!ternet

N!tv

in N! games

p!

rds

al stuff

search

[   ]

find!

ntact

Novas occasionally display powers that were once considered psychic or extrasensory perception. Acts of clairvoyance or precognition fall into this category. Other so-called psychic powers, such as the spectacular "telekinesis" ability, will be mentioned later. Novas often seem more 'in tune' with the world around them, and some are able to predict future events. No one knows the limits of these abilities, but they seem specialized and relatively rare among the nova population. It probably makes our viewers feel better to know that no nova has displayed the ability to read minds. Yet.

Novas have also displayed even more esoteric abilities. ViaSoft prodigy Mungu Kuwasha, for example, can manipulate and control computers and data seemingly by thought alone. Novas have demonstrated control over purely mechanical devices, too. Most novas with these abilities seem to "interface" with the object in question....

External Powers

By far the most spectacular and impressive of their abilities, the external powers account for the most amazing and unbelievable of nova abilities. These powers allow novas to defy nature — to literally change the world.

Many novas possess the ability to harness ambient energy, then release it in a focused burst. The tabloids have dubbed this ability the "quantum bolt," and it can take many forms. Novas have been observed throwing heat and electrical discharges, even shooting lasers from their eyes. News footage from the Kashmir crisis and African conflicts show the sheer power of these "quantum bolt." They can vaporize tanks, crumple buildings and even simulate atomic discharges. The nova generating a quantum blast seems immune to its effects, sometimes walking unscathed out of a conflagration of his own making.

Just as some novas can create energy from nowhere, other can absorb and destroy energy. Randel Portman, the famous "Fireman," is probably the most widely known energy-absorber. Last year, an unknown nova even walked into the fires of a nuclear power plant during the Calcutta Meltdown, and when she left, there was not a trace of radioactivity left.

External powers displayed by novas take on even more bizarre forms. Sound waves, radioactivity and even biological processes in other creatures can all be controlled by certain novas. Many of the other so-called psychic powers, such as telekinesis, also fall into this category.

From internal Department of Defense memo, EYES ONLY, 6/6/03

Our scientists have completed their studies of known and theorized nova abilities. What they found is shocking. First, some novas do possess the ability to manipulate emotions and even dominate individuals. Mind-reading is not confirmed, but is not out of the question, either. This information should be screened and censored from the media and the scientific community at large. I also recommend that all sensitive operatives be screened for undue influences.

The scientists' conclusion is that novas can potentially do anything, and I mean *anything*. They affect the very fabric of the universe. Our scientists speculate that, given enough time and training, there is literally nothing a nova could not do. Even more frightening are preliminary reports that novas with greater levels of quantum control appear to be less stable. The researchers theorize that the increased growth of the M-R node, necessary for greater power, also impinges the frontal lobe, possibly leading to hallucinations or even personality disorders. The last thing we need is a bunch of psychos with the power of gods....

From a New Nova Orientation Meeting Speech

Greetings, everyone, and welcome to the dawn of your new future. I am Dr. Yuji Go; you will no doubt get to know me and all of the other Project Utopia staff intimately during your training stay here at this Rashoud facility. If you have any questions or concerns during your stay, please contact your personal liaison, who will take the proper procedural steps to have the matter addressed.

As you all undoubtedly know now, you have demonstrated abilities that identify you as novas. Take a quick look around you — most of you are in your 20s, while a few are in your early 30s and a goodly number of you are still in your teens. Obviously, eruption — which is what we call the act of becoming an active nova rather than a latent one — happens to relatively young members of society. By looking around, you've also probably caught on to the fact that novas aren't restricted to any single class, race or ethnicity. Some of you were dirt poor seven days ago, while others of you may have been born with silver spoons in your mouth. That doesn't matter anymore. What is important is that we're here to help you realize your potential and, should you choose to remain among us, become a contributing member of Project Utopia, whose own goal is building a better world for novas and humankind alike.

If you would, think back to the time of your eruption. It may be a bit traumatic for you, but this helps us immensely in directing your potential. Recall the exact circumstances, as they have become psychological catalysts for your burgeoning powers. For example, if you were trapped in a burning building and the stress triggered your eruption, you may find yourself inclined toward the manipulation of fire. If your eruption occurred while falling, you may possess a flight potential. If you erupted while faced by a menacing animal, you may possess control over nature's lesser beasts. Whatever the case, give it a moment of brief consideration. If you'd be so kind, please look over your enrollment dossier and make sure your processing liaison recorded your eruption circumstances correctly. There's nothing to be ashamed of — remember, if you don't help us, we can't help you.

Before we go any further, however, I'd like to offer a bit of preemptory warning. Yes, you are all novas, and you possess tremendous abilities and vast power. But that power comes with a price. I will warn you now about using your powers recklessly: Don't do it. The upcoming months will educate you in the rudiments of why and how your abilities work, as well as the danger inherent in abusing them. For now, simply let us guide and direct you in the use of your nova potentials. Your very health depends on it.

I can see some of you are uncomfortable with this already. We've anticipated that. During your physical examination, you were administered a pill or injection of quantum-retarding moxinoquantamine. Whatever potential you may possess, the drug limits it until you have learned the control and restraint to do it yourself. We cannot control the effects this quantum power has on your bodies, however, and if you insist on rebelling or making a show, you will damage yourself far in excess of the effect you try to create. Please; we do this for a living. Let us work with you.

POWER USE AND TRAINING

M E M O

To: All field operatives, clinic staff and recruitment team captains
From: Michael Hodge, New Personnel Processing Director
Re: Procedural Update

Effective immediately, all recruitment staff are to cease "snatch-and-grab" enrollment methods. While this may be appropriate to "organizations" like the Teragen, it is certainly out of place with the aims of our organization. Project Utopia takes a nurturing stance on nova development. Although I am not a nova myself, I have seen many of you brought into the organization, and encourage you to remember the trauma of your own first eruptions.

All I'm asking is that team leaders show a little sympathy. If we adopt the methods of the other groups, we make ourselves no better than they.

Clinic staff, if you have any reason to suspect that a newly discovered nova has been treated roughly or unfairly by his recruiter, please notify me immediately.

M E M O

To: Michael Hodge, New Personnel Processing Director
From: Bruce McInerny
To: All field operatives, clinic staff and recruitment team captains
Re: Procedural Update

Look, I already told you that McKinney kid refused to calm down once he'd already agreed and his parents had signed the release. Read the report. This job's already hard enough without some pencil-pushing, third-rate bureaucrat trying to tie my hands even more because he's got nothing better to do on Project Utopia time.

The more you complicate this, the more difficult it becomes, and the easier it is for these new novas to fall in with other, potentially dangerous, organizations.

Screw you, Hodge. It's already ridiculous that someone with my capabilities has to file paperwork to keep a tick like you happy, so count your blessings that I haven't had to "ensure complicity" by knocking *you* out with a manhole cover.

From a Progress Report on Nova Development at a Utopia Facility

Date: 10 Jan 2006

Datum/Data: Actualization continues slowly with the newest detachment of recruits. Retarded progress seems to rest in the nature of the recruits: As M-R node eruption can occur in anyone, we have no guarantee of dealing with analytical or even suitably self-aware subjects. Indeed, some among the current roster seem to hail from what could be described as underprivileged, socially inequitable or (for lack of more suitable descriptors) "white-trash" upbringings.

While the development team continues to guide these prospects down their paths of enrichment, it is the opinion of this researcher that some subjects would affect their environment more radically than they possess the conscience or intelligence to understand.

I draw on sociological history to make my point. Star athletes of the latter 20th century made a good deal of money, often with little more than cursory education. This abrupt accumulation of money, combined with poor knowledge bases and insufficient socialization, made for aberrations of society — "hillbillies with money," who could not conceive of the problems they potentially posed.

Taken to the next logical step, novas possess far more environmental influence than money represents in the preceding pro-athlete example. When a subject possesses the ability to distort the minds of those around him or cause a nuclear conflagration in a half-mile radius, yet lacks the ability to distinguish between not only right and wrong but appropriate and inappropriate as well, upon whom does the burden of responsibility fall? As further evidence, I cite case UT-117-UK; Marjorie McCannagh. At 60 IQ, Marjorie was only marginally aware of her surroundings, so her power to sever organic molecular bonds and turn living things into puddles of carbon sludge posed more threat than advantage.

(Granted, these aberrations are isolated occurrences. All evidence suggests that, most frequently, the M-R node acclimates and accelerates the mind and body to peak or even superhuman levels of fitness and performance. This problem, on a larger scale, seems to be more of a sociological phenomenon, though McCannagh is hardly an inappropriate example.)

To that end, this researcher must recommend continued pursuit of the proposed "M-R lobotomy" treatment. In sociopathic, asocial and criminally inclined subjects, the Project must take it upon itself to cauterize the M-R node as early in its eruption as possible. Waiting too long may allow the node to grow back under the healing auspices of its biochemical adjustments.

Welcome to the Nova Site, the only site on the OpNet
devoted to self-made novas by self-made novas.

So you want to be a nova. Join the club. Only one in a million people
becomes a nova, because its really hard to do. First, you have to have the
devotion to do it. Second, you have to have the time to explore your powers.
Third, you have to have an extra bit of meat in your brain, which causes all
your powers to happen.

You can't be a nova without causing that bit of meat (called the node)
to open up. Of course, its not that easy. The node only opens up under
stress. (Mordus says he opened his by drinking an entire case of African
Malt Liquor, but I think he's lying.) That's the hard part. You have to
cause yourself enough stress to open the node, but if whatever you do to
cause the stress might kill you, so be careful.

Also, your nova powers have to do with the thingie that caused your node
to open, so pick something cool. If you open your node by holding up a golf
club in an electric storm you get lightning powers, but if you open your
node by slamming your head in a car door a lot, you probably get some really
crappy powers like only making car doors open.

Learning powers and opening the node usually makes you really sick. Most
people get huge headaches (migraines) when the node opens up, because the
node pushes its way out from the "inactive" part of the brain to the
"active" part physically. Seriously.

Also, the power (we novas call it jolt or juice or magnum) sometimes
causes illness in a body not used to it. Your going to be really tired when
you first become a nova, because all the juice just wears you out because
you don't know how to control it yet. Also, you'll probably get some kind of
disease like a cold or the flu because your so tired your immunity system is
tired with the rest of your body.

The best thing to do is practice your powers, though, so let the headache
and sickness wear off and get to work. Practice makes perfect, but here's a
few easy tips to help you on the way.

1.) Do it (practice) away from people until you get the hang of it. If
you're just learning you might kill someone or hurt them, so stay away from
other people.

2.) Practice at the same time every day. Let your body get used to a
regular series of practice exercises, so you can be at your maximum ability
each day when you "work out."

3.) Go slowly. Only train your powers for a few hours a day — no more
than two until you can learn to control the power flow. Too much will wear
you out and either burn out your node or make you sick again with exhaus-
tion.

4.) Eat a lot. If your really a nova and not a poser, you'll eat a bunch
of food all day long. These munchies are caused by the power in your body,
as you have to keep giving it fuel.

5.) Don't wear a costume. A nova with a costume is either an Elite or a
poser. Do not wear capes especially because when you get in a fight, that's
the first thing people pull. This isn't a comic book, it's real life. Do
pick a cool name for yourself though, but you probably already knew that.
Being a nova is being important. You have to look like somebody worth
noticing for anyone to care.

CLICK HERE to join the OpNet Novas mailing list

CLICK HERE to skip to the next OpNet NovaRing site

CLICK HERE to register with the Renegade Nova League

From a Training Session Video Recording at QuebecFac

[Translated from French]

· **Trainer:** You made some excellent progress yesterday, Jean. How do you feel today?

· **Jean:** A bit tired.

· **Trainer:** Any symptoms to report? Did you need any meds last night?

· **Jean:** I had a nosebleed after dinner last night. And the nurse gave me one adrenocilin, but I only took half the pill. I slept like a baby, but I've got kind of a headache now.

· **Trainer:** I see. What did you do with the rest of the pill? I like your cap, by the way. Are you a Yankees fan?

· **Jean:** Flushed it. Yeah, I like the Yankees. I've got a jersey, too.

· **Trainer:** All right. Are you ready to start for today?

· **Jean:** I guess.

· **Trainer:** Okay. [To technicians] Let's have 400 migs of moxinoquantamine. Okay, Jean, I want you to think about moving this magnet again.

· **Jean:** We did this yesterday.

Trainer: I know, Jean, but I don't want to go forward without making sure you remember how to do what we covered yesterday. [Jean sighs] Ready?

· **Jean:** Yep. [magnet moves visibly, suspended in air. Magnet rotates in air]

· **Trainer:** Fantastic, Jean! Not only do you remember, you're already controlling better than you did yesterday! Great work! Okay, now slow it down...good. Put it down carefully. [magnet clatters to surface of table]

· **Jean:** Dammit.

· **Trainer:** No problem, Jean, we'll just try again. You were doing awesome. This time, though, *feel* the magnet the whole time. I saw you kind of relax your mind before the magnet was on the table. Make sure you give it your full concentration *all the way through*.

PROJECT
UTOPIA

BIOLOGICAL DIFFERENCES

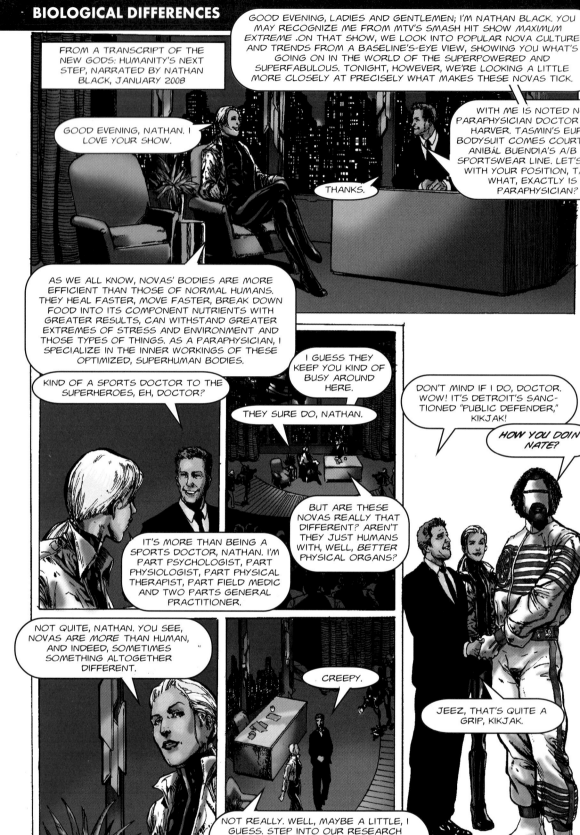

GOOD EVENING, LADIES AND GENTLEMEN; I'M NATHAN BLACK. YOU MAY RECOGNIZE ME FROM MTV'S SMASH HIT SHOW *MAXIMUM EXTREME*. ON THAT SHOW, WE LOOK INTO POPULAR NOVA CULTURE AND TRENDS FROM A BASELINE'S-EYE VIEW, SHOWING YOU WHAT'S GOING ON IN THE WORLD OF THE SUPERPOWERED AND SUPERFABULOUS. TONIGHT, HOWEVER, WE'RE LOOKING A LITTLE MORE CLOSELY AT PRECISELY WHAT MAKES THESE NOVAS TICK.

FROM A TRANSCRIPT OF THE NEW GODS: HUMANITY'S NEXT STEP, NARRATED BY NATHAN BLACK, JANUARY 2008

GOOD EVENING, NATHAN. I LOVE YOUR SHOW.

WITH ME IS NOTED N PARAPHYSICIAN DOCTOR HARVER. TASMIN'S EUR BODYSUIT COMES COURT ANIBÁL BUENDIA'S A/B SPORTSWEAR LINE. LET'S WITH YOUR POSITION, TA WHAT, EXACTLY IS A PARAPHYSICIAN?

THANKS.

AS WE ALL KNOW, NOVAS' BODIES ARE MORE EFFICIENT THAN THOSE OF NORMAL HUMANS. THEY HEAL FASTER, MOVE FASTER, BREAK DOWN FOOD INTO ITS COMPONENT NUTRIENTS WITH GREATER RESULTS, CAN WITHSTAND GREATER EXTREMES OF STRESS AND ENVIRONMENT AND THOSE TYPES OF THINGS. AS A PARAPHYSICIAN, I SPECIALIZE IN THE INNER WORKINGS OF THESE OPTIMIZED, SUPERHUMAN BODIES.

I GUESS THEY KEEP YOU KIND OF BUSY AROUND HERE.

DON'T MIND IF I DO, DOCTOR. WOW! IT'S DETROIT'S SANCTIONED "PUBLIC DEFENDER," KIKJAK!

KIND OF A SPORTS DOCTOR TO THE SUPERHEROES, EH, DOCTOR?

THEY SURE DO, NATHAN.

HOW YOU DOIN NATE?

BUT ARE THESE NOVAS REALLY THAT DIFFERENT? AREN'T THEY JUST HUMANS WITH, WELL, *BETTER* PHYSICAL ORGANS?

IT'S MORE THAN BEING A SPORTS DOCTOR, NATHAN. I'M PART PSYCHOLOGIST, PART PHYSIOLOGIST, PART PHYSICAL THERAPIST, PART FIELD MEDIC AND TWO PARTS GENERAL PRACTITIONER.

NOT QUITE, NATHAN. YOU SEE, NOVAS ARE *MORE* THAN HUMAN, AND INDEED, SOMETIMES SOMETHING ALTOGETHER DIFFERENT.

CREEPY.

JEEZ, THAT'S QUITE A GRIP, KIKJAK.

NOT REALLY. WELL, MAYBE A LITTLE, I GUESS. STEP INTO OUR RESEARCH LABORATORY AND I'LL SHOW YOU A BIT MORE ABOUT HOW THE BODIES OF NOVAS WORK.

MR. KIKJAK IS HERE TO BE A SORT OF GUINEA PIG FOR US IN THE LAB. ISN'T THAT RIGHT, KIKJAK?

HI MOM; HI POP. KIDS, STAY IN SCHOOL AND DON'T DO DRUGS. AND REMEMBER, YOU CAN MEET YOUR POTENTIAL, BASELINE OR NOVA, IN NIKE SPORTSWEAR.

YOU GOT IT, DOC. CAN I SAY HELLO TO SOMEONE REAL QUICK?

NIKE, SEND YOUR ENDORSEMENT CHECK TO...

OKAY, NATHAN, QUIT FOOLING AROUND. COME OVER HERE AND TOUCH THIS GENERATOR TERMINAL.

SURE.

IS IT GOING TO SHOCK ME?

JUST A LITTLE. IT'LL MAKE YOUR HAIR STAND ON END.

OKAY, BUT I'LL WARN YOU: MY INSURANCE RATES ARE THROUGH THE ROOF. I'VE GOT TO CHASE THESE NOVAS ALL OVER THE PLACE TO GET DECENT FOOTAGE—

TOUCH THE TERMINAL, NATHAN.

KRAK, KRAKOKAY, OKAY.

OF COURSE. STEP ASIDE, BUTTERCUP.

AS YOU CAN SEE, LADIES AND GENTLEMEN, NATHAN'S BODY BEGINS TO REACT TO THE ELECTRICAL CURRENT I'M PASSING THROUGH IT AT A GENERATOR SETTING OF 1.

AS A NOVA, KIKJAK CAN WITHSTAND SIGNIFICANTLY GREATER ELECTRICAL CURRENT. I'LL JUST SET THE GENERATOR'S OUTPUT TO 10—

WHICH WOULD KILL A NORMAL MAN, CORRECT, DOCTOR?

NOT IMMEDIATELY, BUT IT WOULD CERTAINLY STIMULATE ALL HIS MUSCLES, PREVENTING HIM FROM MOVING. IN SOME CASES, IT MIGHT STOP THE AVERAGE HUMAN HEART.

WOW, THAT WAS QUITE A JOLT.

BUT KIKJAK DOESN'T FEEL A THING.

NOW, IF YOU'D BE SO KIND, KIKJAK?

NOT A THING. WELL, I FEEL IT, BUT IT DON'T REALLY HAVE MUCH EFFECT. CHECK IT.

AND THIS ALSO APPLIES TO OTHER HOSTILE

STIMULI.

STIMULI, NATE.

25

YES, STIMULI. LIKE HEAT AND COLD?

ABSOLUTELY, BUT YOU'LL HAVE TO TAKE MY WORD FOR IT. I DOUBT MR. KIKJAK WOULD ALLOW US TO SET HIM ON FIRE.

[CENSORED] THAT. IT STILL HURTS, IT JUST HEALS FASTER THAN YOU ALL DO. I'LL LET YOU DO IT IF YOU LET ME SET NATHAN ON FIRE, OKAY?

I DON'T THINK SO. SO, WHAT'S THE DEAL, DOCTOR? WHY DO NOVAS FEEL LESS OF THE PAIN AND HEAL FROM IT MORE QUICKLY?

THEY STILL FEEL IT, ALBEIT DIFFERENTLY. HERE, LOOK AT THIS.

THE NOVA'S CELLS ARE DIFFERENT — DENSER — THAN THOSE OF NORMAL PEOPLE. THE INHERENT ABILITIES NOVAS POSSESS—

POWERS?

NO, IT'S JUICE.

WHATEVER YOUR NAME FOR THEM, THEIR CONTROL STEMS FROM THE FLOW OF "QUANTUM" ENERGY — ENERGY THAT NORMAL HUMAN BODIES AREN'T DESIGNED TO PERCEIVE, LET ALONE MANIPULATE.

ALL OF THESE TINY "PATHWAYS" OR NERVE GROUPS ALLOW THAT ENERGY TO MOVE THROUGH THE NOVA'S BODY. THESE NERVE GROUPS ALSO TRANS-MIT THE FEEDBACK FROM MORE TRADITIONAL STIMULI, LIKE ELECTRIC-ITY, HEAT OR KINETIC FORCE. THAT'S WHY MANY NOVAS CAN WITHSTAND BEATINGS, STABBINGS AND EVEN GUNSHOT WOUNDS.

IT LOOKS LIKE SPAGHETTI. BUT, IF THERE ARE SO MANY MORE NERVES, WHY DON'T NOVAS FEEL MORE PAIN?

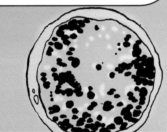

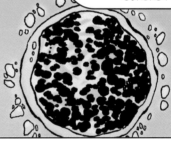

WELL, TO GET TECHNICAL, THEY'RE NOT REALLY NERVES, THEY'RE CALLED M-R COILS, BUT WE'LL GET TO THAT LATER. AS TO WHY IT DOESN'T HURT MORE, THE DELIVERED STIMULUS IS STILL THE SAME, BUT DISPERSED MUCH MORE EXPEDITIOUSLY. LET'S SAY YOU AND KIKJAK GET HIT BY A CAR YOU BOTH FLY THE SAME DISTANCE AWAY, YOU BOTH SUFFER THE SAME AMOUNT OF PHYSICAL KINETIC FORCE ON IMPACT, BUT YOUR BODY DISPERSES THE FORCE THROUGH BILLIONS OF NERVES, WHILE KIKJAK'S BODY DISPERSES IT THROUGH A LOT MORE, GETTING RID OF IT MORE QUICKLY.

AND YOU CRY A LOT MORE, NATHAN.

BUT, DOCTOR, HAVEN'T WE BOTH SUFFERED THE SAME — ER, TRAUMA? I MEAN, WE'LL BOTH STILL HAVE BROKEN BONES, BUT HE'LL JUST FEEL IT LESS, CORRECT?

ALMOST, NATHAN. EACH OF THOSE LITTLE M-R COILS TRANSFERS QUANTUM ENERGY DOWN ITS LENGTH. WITHOUT GETTING INTO LONG-WINDED THEORIES AND METAPHYSICS, QUANTUM ENERGY BASICALLY COMPRISES THE FOUR FUNDAMENTAL FORCES OF THE UNIVERSE: GRAVITY, ELECTROMAGNETISM, STRONG AND WEAK NUCLEAR FORCES. UNDER THE CONTROL OF A NOVA, QUANTUM ENERGY BECOMES...WELL, A SORT OF "COSMIC POWER," IF THAT DOESN'T SOUND TOO CORNY.

HANG ON, THERE, KIKJAK. SO, THIS QUANTUM, IT BLOCKS OUT THE OTHER ENERGY?

ACTUALLY, IT CONVERTS OTHER ENERGIES TO QUANTUM ENERGY. IN FACT, IF YOU WERE FOOLISH ENOUGH TO PUNCH OUR FRIEND KIKJAK—

—YOU MIGHT ACTUALLY BE GIVING HIM MORE POWER, THE CASE OF WHAT ARE CALLED "ABSORBER NOVAS" OR "QUANTUM REPLICATORS."

WAIT, SO NOVAS MAKE THEIR OWN POWER? THEN HOW CAN THEY BE BROUGHT DOWN? I MEAN, JUST LAST WEEK, KIKJAK HERE FOUGHT ONE OF THOSE TERAGEN NOVAS — KNOCKED HIM OUT WITH A FORCE BOLT TO THE HEAD.

KIND OF.

I'LL SHOW YOU SOME COSMIC POWER, SUCKA.

HELL, YEAH. K-JAK OUTTA D-TOWN STRAIGHT TO DOMI-NATE IN OH-EIGHT.

OKAY. SO, ON SOME FUNDAMENTAL LEVEL, THIS HIGH RESISTANCE TO BEING HURT—

THE M-R COILS ONLY TRANSFER QUANTUM. NOVAS HAVE ANOTHER ORGAN — A GLAND, TO BE PRECISE, KNOWN AS THE M-R NODE. M-R STANDS FOR MAZARIN-RASHOUD, THE NAMES OF THE SCIENTISTS WHO DISCOVERED THE NODE A DECADE AGO, BY THE WAY. THE M-R NODE ALLOWS THEM TO CONTROL QUANTUM AND CONVERT THOSE OTHER FORCES INTO PERSONAL QUANTUM RESERVES. WE'VE ALL GOT QUANTUM RUNNING THROUGH US, BUT NOT ALL OF US KNOW HOW TO USE IT CORRECTLY, OR EFFICIENTLY, IF AT ALL.

...IS ACTUALLY HYPERACCELERATED HEALING, AS THE QUANTUM AUGMENTS THE BODY'S NATURAL HEALING PROCESS. KIKJAK MUST HAVE MANAGED TO DOLE OUT MORE TRAUMA THAN HIS ENEMY COULD CONVERT AND HEAL. THE BOTTOM LINE IS THAT EVEN WITH ALL THE QUANTUM IN THE WORLD, IF YOU CAN'T DO ANYTHING WITH IT, IT DOESN'T DO YOU ANY GOOD.

SO FIGHTING MAKES NOVAS STRONGER? AND NOVAS DON'T NEED TO EAT? THEY MAKE THEIR OWN CALORIES OR SOMETHING? BY PUNCHING THEMSELVES?

SNICKER NO, THERE ARE STILL NORMAL, HUMAN BUILDING BLOCKS UNDER THOSE M-R COILS. YOU CAN STILL BREAK BONES AND CAUSE HEMORRHAGES. THEY DON'T ELIMINATE ALL THE NORMAL OBSTACLES. IN MOST CASES, AT LEAST. IN FACT, BECAUSE THEIR BODIES SPEND SO MUCH TIME AND EFFORT DEALING WITH QUANTUM, MOST NOVAS EAT MORE THAN NORMAL HUMANS; SOMETIMES 10 TIMES AS MUCH OR MORE, DAILY.

I LIKE BURGER KING. FIFTY WHOPPERS AND A SMALL DIET COKE, PLEASE. THANK YOU, DRIVE THROUGH.

AS YOU CAN SEE, KIKJAK IS, WELL, GLOWING IN THE DARK. THAT'S HIS EXCESS QUANTUM LEAKING FROM HIS BODY.

NO, NOT PRECISELY. NOVAS BLEED OFF THEIR UNUSED QUANTUM IN DIFFERENT WAYS. SOME MAY HAVE A STRANGE COLOR CAST TO THEIR SKIN; OTHERS MAY "HUM" QUIETLY OR HAVE UNSTABLE CELLULAR BONDS THAT RESULT IN A WATERY CONSISTENCY TO THEIR BODIES. IT ALL DEPENDS ON THE INDIVIDUAL. MOST NOVAS HAVE RELATIVELY MINOR ANOMALIES, BUT THOSE WHO HAVE USED A GREAT DEAL OF QUANTUM IN A SHORT TIME OR HAVE USED IT OVER MANY YEARS, WE SUSPECT, COULD DISPLAY MUCH MORE... PRONOUNCED QUIRKS.

AND QUANTUM IS SORT OF LIQUID. IT "BLEEDS OFF" IN VARIOUS WAYS — HERE, WATCH.

WOW, I NEVER NOTICED THAT BEFORE. ALL NOVAS GLOW IN THE DARK? YOU THINK I'D HAVE SEEN IT IN NIGHTCLUBS—

THIS COMES FROM THE M-R NODE?

NOT DIRECTLY, BUT WE BELIEVE IT TO BE A SIDE EFFECT, SIMILAR TO THE ATTUNEMENT AND "STREAMLINING" OF NOVAS' BODIES. YOU'VE NOTICED HOW MOST NOVAS APPEAR TO HAVE LITTLE BODY FAT?

OF COURSE.

THEY ACTUALLY HOVER BETWEEN ZERO PERCENT AND ONE-HALF PERCENT MORE FAT THAN THE MINIMUM NEEDED FOR BASIC NERVOUS SYSTEM INSULATION, AS THE QUANTUM PROCESSED BY THE M-R NODE MAXIMIZES THEIR BODIES' NATURAL FUNCTIONS AND MINIMIZES THE OBSTACLES THAT IMPEDE THOSE FUNCTIONS. ALONG THE SAME LINES, NOVAS CAN EXIST AT VERY LOW AIR-OXYGEN COUNTS, AND CAN NEUTRALIZE TOXINS ALMOST AS QUICKLY AS THEY ENTER THE BLOODSTREAM.

SO NOVA MEDICINES NEED TO BE CUSTOM-TAILORED?

TRUE, BUT NOVAS RARELY GET SICK — IN ADDITION TO SHUTTING OUT TOXINS, THEIR IMMUNE SYSTEMS WIPE OUT EVERYTHING BUT THE MOST DEBILITATING DISEASES INSTANTLY. NOVA "MEDICINES" LIKE ADRENOCILIN, WHICH ENHANCES QUANTUM CONTROL, ARE VERY PURE RATIOS OF THE COMPONENT CHEMICALS, WHICH WOULD DROP A BIOENGINEERED COW DEAD IN ITS TRACKS. LIKEWISE, IF A NOVA WANTS TO "HAVE A QUICK DRINK" IT HAD BETTER BE VERY NEAR 100 PERCENT ALCOHOL FOR HIM TO EVEN FEEL THE EFFECTS, BUT I CAN'T IMAGINE THAT TASTES VERY GOOD.

IT DOESN'T.

From the journal of Dr. Nimal Dharmasena; November 3, 2001

I wonder if Darwin would feel this way, if he were in my place.

For the last few nights, I haven't even gone home. I've called Imira over and over again, reassuring her that I'm still all right, that I'm just at a critical stage. And I feel like I'm lying when I say that; after all, the last batch of test results has sat on my desk for a long while. But I really am being truthful, after all. I *am* at a critical stage. It's just one of decision, not discovery.

The novas seemed so impossible when they started emerging. I swear, I almost gave up science and ran out to Nevada to preach the gospel of chaos theory by the freeway. But as it turns out, they might just be quantifiable after all — and now that Utopia wants me, I feel like I've been given the keys to the kingdom. No, scratch that — the *blueprints*.

Humanity isn't really evolving anymore, I'm sure of that. And the emergence of the novas tells me that Nature knows this, too; so she jumped a few people ahead, to whatever stage we might normally have reached. The novas are her gift to us, a way of examining what we might become — and evolving *ourselves*. *Us*, not her.

The potential is endless. One nova alone, with the right gifts, could end hunger, rework the world economy or terraform a continent. If we achieve some level of control over nova powers and who we invest them in, we could achieve *Star Trek* several centuries early — my kids could grow up in a world without pollution, without crime, without famine or fear or disease. And the thought that my research might help bring this about....

Who am I kidding? I've wanted to jump aboard Utopia for as long as it's been in existence. I'm sitting here fretting and moaning about what it'll mean to my personal life, what I might have to give up, when all I'm really afraid of is the possibility they'll change their mind.

It's time I made that phone call.

The Genesis

From a Social Sciences lecture, Enka High School, North Carolina

Obviously, nobody knew what to do about the manifesting novas. It turned science, religion and society all on their heads. We didn't even know what an M-R node was. We were baffled.

That's when the Aeon Society entered the picture. This philanthropic organization had an extensive, if not widely publicized, history of assisting and backing various large-scale goodwill programs, such as the Red Cross, the World Health Organization and similar projects. These fellows decided that somebody needed to stick up for the novas, and it might as well be they. Good thing they did, too. So they started talking to the UN, and they eventually worked out a possible solution.

The Zurich Accord of June 1998 — and you had better believe this *will* be on the test — publicly declared novas to be human beings. I know, this kind of sounds like a common-sense thing, but there was a very real case for considering novas an entirely different species, in which case they wouldn't have all the rights and responsibilities that go with being human.

Can anyone name the movement that disagrees totally with the Zurich Accord? Anyone? Good, Emily — the Teragen. But we'll get to them later.

Anyhow, Project Utopia was formed at the same time the Zurich Accord was signed. Its stated goal was "to utilize the vast powers of novas to better the quality of life for all, human and nova alike, on Planet Earth." That's on page 227 — better memorize that. They also wound up having an environmentalist agenda as well, but people have definitely benefited from that as much as animals and plants have.

The next step for Project Utopia was twofold. First, they began their intervention programs, where they'd contact newly erupted novas and invite them to their Rashoud facilities, special clinics designed to help them adjust to their new powers. Then they announced the formation of their special team of all-nova operatives, Team—

Ah, there's the bell. All right, people, finish reading Chapter 24! I want to be able to pick up where we left off tomorrow, and I don't want to have to quiz you — but I will if I don't start hearing some feedback!

Excerpt: "Week in Perspective with Walter Donovan"; show aired January 16, 2008

[00:14:26]

· **DONOVAN:** NEXT TOPIC: THE LATEST POLLS HAVE SHOWN NOTHING BUT AN INCREASE IN POPULAR SUPPORT FOR PROJECT UTOPIA, EVEN THOUGH UN AMBASSADORS FROM SEVERAL NATIONS, INCLUDING THE UNITED STATES, HAVE EXPRESSED GRAVE CONCERN FOR THE AUTONOMY AND AUTHORITY UTOPIA CURRENTLY ENJOYS. GENTLEMEN?

· **CULPEPPER:** WELL, I'LL FRANKLY GO ON RECORD AS DISAGREEING WITH THE MAN ON THE STREET AND AGREEING WITH THE AMERICAN GOVERNMENT ON THIS. PROJECT UTOPIA IS DOING TOO MUCH, TOO SOON, AND I'M HONESTLY VERY WORRIED ABOUT WHAT SORT OF LONG-TERM DAMAGE THEY MIGHT DO IN THE NAME OF A SHORT-TERM FIX.

· **BRYANT:** ARE YOU SERIOUS? LOOK AT THE TERRAFORMING OF THE ETHIOPIAN HIGHLANDS! A VIRTUAL EDEN ON EARTH, BALANCING WILDLIFE PRESERVE WITH HIGH-YIELD CROPLANDS. NEVER MIND THE FACT THAT AT LEAST SIX OF THE MOST PROMINENT ECOLOGISTS IN THE WORLD HAVE PRAISED THE—

· **CULPEPPER:** ECOLOGISTS HIRED BY *UTOPIA*, I MIGHT ADD! ISN'T THAT SOMETHING LIKE THE TOBACCO COMPANIES' HIRED HEALTH EXPERTS OF LAST CENTURY?

· **BRYANT:** OH, PLEASE! IF YOU'D ACTUALLY RESEARCH THE TOPIC, YOU'D FIND THAT THEY ASKED THE 10 FOREMOST ECOLOGISTS IN THE *FIELD* FOR THEIR OPINIONS! IF THEY WANTED YES-MEN, THEY WOULDN'T HAVE GONE TO ALL THAT TROUBLE!

· **CULPEPPER:** WELL, WITH THE AMOUNT OF RESOURCES THEY HAVE AT THEIR DISPOSAL, IT PROBABLY WOULDN'T BE TOO HARD TO PERSUADE—

· **BRYANT:** SO NOW YOU'RE ACCUSING THEM OF *BRIBERY*?

· **CULPEPPER:** NOT AT ALL! I'M SIMPLY HAZARDING AN OPINION!

· **BRYANT:** YOU'RE BEING CONTRARY FOR THE SAKE OF CONTRARINESS! LOOK AT ALL THE OTHER POSITIVE WORKS THAT PROJECT UTOPIA HAS COMPLETED — THE OVERTHROW OF RADOCANI, THE VIRTUAL ELIMINATION OF BANGKOK'S CHILD PROSTITUTION TRADE — *ALL OF WHICH*, I MIGHT ADD, WERE UNDER *COMPLETE* UN SANCTION! AND IF YOU WANT TO TALK SCIENTIFIC ACHIEVEMENTS, WHAT ABOUT THEIR ASSISTANCE IN CURING AIDS AND CANCER, THE HYPERCOMBUSTION ENGINE, THE GLOBAL ENVIRONMENTAL CLEANUP ACTIONS—

· **CULPEPPER:** MAYBE *YOU* LIKE THE IDEA OF THE UN GRANTING VIRTUALLY TOTAL LATITUDE TO A GROUP WITH ALL THE POTENTIAL MILITARY POWER OF ANY TWO EUROPEAN NATIONS, BUT *I* HAPPEN TO THINK—

· **DONOVAN:** GENTLEMEN, PLEASE! IF I MIGHT CHANGE THE SUBJECT....

ACHIEVEMENTS AND GOALS

From an Orientation Speech, Manhattan Rashoud Facility

Believe me, I've seen it before, and I can tell what you're thinking. You're thinking, "What is this 'save the planet' politically correct garbage?" You're thinking, "Why the hell, with all the new opportunities available to me, would I want to throw in with this giant worldwide hippy-dippy love-in?" Well, I'm not going to give you some feel-good, lovey-dovey song and dance about sacrifice and altruism for the greater good. No one — not even the chirpiest Project PR rep — is that naïve. Now, don't get me wrong, Utopia does a lot of good for the world every day, and I'm damn proud to be a part of it. But, first and foremost, Utopia exists for novas. For us — for our protection and, yeah, self-interest, albeit enlightened self-interest. Because underneath all the hype, the cold hard facts are, there are a few thousand of us and billions of them. And those terms — Us and Them, Normal and Aberrant — are exactly what Utopia is committed to avoiding at all costs.

Look, humanity has a long, long history of destroying the Other, the different. We don't want conflict with the baselines. They're our friends, our families. But while my friends aren't a threat to me, they might be a threat to you, for example. Mob mentality and scapegoats are ancient human traditions. What Utopia's doing is aggressively demonstrating what we novas can offer, how we can help. It is and it isn't altruism; you might even call it altruistic self-interest. It's loving your neighbor now so that your neighbors, those billions and billions of anxious, shell-shocked, understandably worried people, will realize that ultimately, we're not so very different after all.

And that's a goal I, for one, can work to support. Your future is your own, but I hope you'll give some thought to staying with the Project. We've got a place for any nova who asks, and the world could use someone like you.

Skew

Birth Name: Andrew Thomas Parker
Date of Birth: September 15, 1989
Place of Origin: Jacksonville, Florida
Occupation: Team Tomorrow agent

Powers: Skew has exceptionally potent control over magnetism, and he is capable of manipulating up to 22 tons of ferrous metal at a distance of 300 meters. He can generate electromagnetic pulses capable of shorting out even shielded electronics and manipulate magnetic fields to create powerful force shields. He has even been noted to exert his power wildly in a 20-meter radius, creating a cyclone loaded with metal weapons. His top flight speed is presently unclocked (or possibly just unavailable to the public), but he is certainly capable of holding his own in a casual dogfight.

Rumors give Skew some ability to affect the iron in a foe's bloodstream, allowing him to tamper with the blood flow to a target's brain and induce vertigo or hallucinations. He is also allegedly able to generate pulses that interfere with the electrical impulses in a human nervous system. However, he has yet to publicly demonstrate anything requiring this level of subtlety and control.

Background: Andrew's eruption wasn't one with a lot of witnesses, but it certainly captured the nation's attention soon enough. After an electromagnetic pulse hit the greater portion of Miami in February of '07, causing widespread blackouts, government and Utopia personnel alike combed the area for months afterward,

Estimated Power Levels:
- **Strength:** 4
- **Intellect:** 3
- **Speed:** 6
- **Offense:** 7
- **Defense:** 7
- **Versatility:** 7

searching for terrorist activity or newly erupted nov[a]
It wasn't until April that they found who they were loo[k]ing for — or rather, he found them. He arrived wit[h] crash at Miami's Utopia offices, dropping an armor[ed] car into the parking lot that was found to contain a sm[all] legion of Spangler Posse repeat offenders. When U[to]pia personnel poured out to investigate, they found t[hat] the self-titled "Skew" wasn't going to take anything fr[om] them but a job application. He got it — delivered in p[er]son by Caestus Pax.

As wildly erratic and creative as the skew-me[tal] music from which he takes his name, Andrew is of[ten] hailed as Team Tomorrow's "loose cannon." He's as li[kely] to wrap a foe up in a midsized sedan as he is to try s[ub]duing him with a barrage of blunt-edged metal pro[jec]tiles (which double as jacket accessories, no less). S[ome] observers wryly note that he has the dubious hono[r of] leader in the "casual property damage" statistics, [but] nobody can accuse Skew of refusing to help out w[ith] cleanup afterwards.

the news

CNN News report, 4/19/2005

N!tertainment

N!terview

N! the news

N!sight

N!tre nous

N!ternet

N!tv

un N! games

p!

ards

al stuff

search

find !

ntact

Daphne Myung; Skopje, Macedonia

• **Myung:** "Suddenly and abruptly, before anyone could blink, it's over. Yaroslav Radocani, the dictator who declared himself the president-for-life of Macedonia, has been removed from power by Team Tomorrow Europe. The operation literally took the world by surprise; not more than 15 minutes after Secretary-General Ghali of the UN announced that Project Utopia had been designated to act as a peacekeeper in this instance, Radocani's personal flag had been toppled from the royal palace.

"Although the exact details of the operation have yet to be fully disclosed, it's apparent that T2M managed to infiltrate the city under cover of nova powers. Radocani and his black-market technology didn't go down lightly — reports of devastation to the royal palace and its bunkers beneath estimate that an earthquake would have been far more gentle. However, T2M has announced that they have suffered no casualties, and that only a few of Radocani's loyalists were killed in the fighting.

"Radocani is, by all reports, scheduled to be entered into Project Utopia's controversial Bahrain rehabilitation center. There he is to, in the words of The Saxon, "receive all the psychiatric assistance and rehabilitation he requires." Many authorities are divided on the issue of whether the intent of this is somehow to cure the "Bitola Butcher" of his sociopathic tendencies and release him back into society, or whether this is simply incarceration by another name. However, at the moment, many of Radocani's former subjects couldn't care less."

From the journal of Dr. Nimal Dharmasena; March 16, 2007

Got to report to Antaeus again today. It gets more unnerving each time. He was very, very deep in Sector 3; I could have sworn that one of the imported leopards was going to take my throat out, safety transmitter or not. I walked around for a whole hour, sweating like a pig, until I finally sat down to rest. And sure enough, there he (she?) was, heaving his body out of the ground, geocarapace and all.

(Is it really a carapace? I'm starting to really wonder. Is it possible that Antaeus' entire cell structure has been replaced with soil and plant matter? Is he really disembodied? Gossip is that he sometimes mentions having "transcended" in some way....)

Anyway, I laid out the month's plan of attack to him. He listened to every word, and then sat there quietly for a few minutes afterward. I was starting to think maybe he wasn't listening after all until that strange, deep, rich voice came welling out of his... well, vicinity.

Turns out that there's some sort of privately owned plant starting up in Madagascar, and Antaeus has just made it our next concern. I double-checked the OpNet for as much info as I could scrounge, and couldn't find a thing about it. But sure enough, there was a dossier waiting on my desk by 5:00.

How the hell Antaeus gets this information is beyond me; we get visits from other directors maybe once every three months, and they don't usually visit the gardens. He makes me redefine my idea of the word "nova," that's for sure. How is it that he can be so impossibly brilliant in the field of ecoscience, so erudite as "Dr. Balmer," and yet, as "Antaeus," practically autistic when dealing with people? I swear, I've learned gigabytes of information since coming to Utopia, but I sometimes feel more confused than ever.

OpNet post, alt.fan.utopia

Subject: Re: LOOK AT THIS!!!!
Date: 9/18/07
Sender: SliderFetish@unca.edu
2Wikkd@im.not.going.to.let.them.trace.me.com wrote:
>i can't believe you people! everyone here is just talks on and on
>about how great project utopia is but none of you see the whole
>picture! what about all the things they don't let us see or have? my
>brother is a scientist, and he was working on something relly important
>that would have made all our live alot easier but they came in and
>took all his files and now he drinks alot and can't get a raise cause
>he just wasted all his time working on something that utopia wont let
>us have! you utopia slaves suck! by the way this story is TRUE but i'm not
going to say who my brother he works for because they (utopia) might
>find out and he'd get fired or arrested or something.
>you all suck!

So? Look, hobgoblin, the UN granted Project Utopia the power of scientific regulation for a reason. Did you hear about the guy who was working on a virtual OpNet interface that would be wired right into the user's pleasure centers? Now, I know that sort of thing sounds pretty good at first, but do you know how damn addictive that'd be? It'd be like unleashing a new drug, something worse than spike! As far as I'm concerned, Project Utopia (something properly spelled with the *shift* key, loser) has every right to their environmental and scientific regulatory powers. Might as well go to somebody with the staff smart enough to use them wisely.

Dev

:::::— If you're reading this, Slider, please marry me. —:::::

**From a guest lecture at Bowling Green University;
featured speaker Damian Lombroso; date 10/02/07**

...I know that when most people think of Project Utopia, they immediately think of Team Tomorrow. But T2M is only part of our organization's overall structure. They're the ones who get a lot of our work done, that's true, but I'd like to focus first on the many thousands of men and women who work just as hard to further the Utopian ideals — the unsung heroes, if you will.

I know that the administrative wing isn't what most people are interested in — after all, when you have Caestus Pax destroying entire chemical weapons plants by his lonesome, the lot of a bunch of paper-pushers doesn't seem all that interesting. But if it weren't for Admin, we wouldn't be here today. Admin keeps our budgets balanced — even though we get a good amount of funding from our parent organization of Aeon and numerous philanthropic organizations, to say nothing of licensing and corporate enterprises, we aren't as filthy rich as you might think. Most of that money gets sunk right back into our various projects. Admin also operates our Rashoud facilities (where we help newly erupted novas come to grips with their new selves) and coordinates our main offices — considering that we've got an office in almost every US state, and almost every country across the globe, that's a lot of coordination!

Oh, and I can't forget our overworked legal department; if it wasn't for their efforts, we'd be so restricted by misguided lawsuits, outmoded strictures and just plain cross-boundary legal confusion that we wouldn't get anything done. The folks in Legal have done a lot for promoting civil rights of nova and baseline alike, as well as helping pass legislation that takes the planet well away from the ecological and societal stagnancy of the late 20th century. Our diplomatic experts, legal eagles, fund-raisers, planners and educators are all part of Admin — as you can see, it's not as boring as you might think. Think of working for a charity organization and a national government at the same time — that's what it's like for us.

I'm sure you've all heard quite a bit about our S&T Department as well. Unless you're in the field yourself, you might not know the names of our top experts — but I'm sure you're familiar with their results. Anybody here been on a cruise lately? Right. Did you notice how much better the ocean looks? If the boys and girls in Science can help it, your children won't believe you when you tell them how polluted and misused the world was when you were their age. There are three major divisions to the scientific wing — Environmental, Medical and Hardtech. Each one has labs scattered around the world, and the staff does a lot of field work. We don't encourage our staff to stay locked in their labs, never seeing much of the world they're trying to better. And the results are pretty dynamic.

The Triton Foundation isn't part of our direct chain of command, but it's the best example of the semi-independent projects that we tend to sponsor. Naturally, it's also one of the divisions that we're most proud of. Not one person in the world — especially you college students — misses AIDS one bit. We can only wait and see what the wizards at Triton cure next.

All right, I can see you're about ready for me to start talking about Team Tomorrow. (*laughter*) As you know, T2M has four main branches, each one with about six to eight nova personnel, plus a rotating pool of floating operatives. Heck, I'm sure you can probably name them all. But T2M is a lot more than just novas. You don't see as much of the pilots, translators, trainers, investigators, support staff and computer wizards who are all as much part of T2M as our nova agents — but they're there. Any one of you could be part of T2M, if you impressed us.

So as you can see, we're keeping ourselves quite busy — and we're doing our best to grow even further all the time. I hope to see some of you in a few years around the offices — trust me, we're always looking for the best.

Now I'd like to open up the floor to questions. Who's first?

'Stasia,

So, you've gotten on the wrong side of the Utopians, have you? Shame on you. You knew they would enjoy nothing better than tweaking our noses, and to actively put yourself on their list before you're ready to cope with the consequences — well, darling, it lacks class. I should leave you to their tender mercies; Mal would like nothing better than such a test, I'm certain. But… well, I've always had a compassionate streak. So at least I can tell you where to hide.

There's no getting around the fact that Project Utopia is quite tight with the United Nations. For Heaven's sake, now they've managed to buy off the UN debts of every single member of the Security Council — and now they're a member, albeit an "advisory" one, of the council itself! This just makes it even more difficult to get an "in" among the right people. Most UN member nations just won't hear it, and the Continent, of course, is right out.

Of course, this heaping helping of goodwill doesn't extend everywhere. The United States, bless its jealous little heart, can't stand Utopia's suc- cess. Of course, the public-opinion polls might not necessarily reflect that — but just try to push some bit of pro-Utopia legislation through Congress and watch what happens. It doesn't seem to bother Utopia much; note that their continental headquarters are situated in the much more recep- tive Mexico City, and nobody seems to be unhappy with that arrangement. But you weren't planning a trip into Mexico, were you?

The United Kingdom's not in love with Utopia, either; that might be a secure place for you to lie low for a while, although you might well be bored to death there. Mumbai might be a better choice, since the Kashmir intervention left a mildly bitter aftertaste in India's mouth. You can mingle with the up-and-coming movie stars while you're there, although for Heaven's sake, don't be *seen* with them!

Ironically enough, Japan seems to be doing its best to create a Project Utopia of its own — or hadn't you noticed the similarities between Nippontai and Team Tomorrow? I suppose Utopia really strikes a chord with the Japa- nese psyche, but it irks them that they've lost a nova or three to Utopia, particularly T2M Asia, rather than to their own patriotic interests. So here they go with their own nationalistic project. What fun. They might ignore you, since they have no personal problems with you — then again, it might tickle them to capture one of Utopia's sworn Teragen enemies.

As a last resort, there's China — but frankly, they're not friendly to anyone. I have a friend or two there, but they're quite busy with their own conversion projects and wouldn't have time to nursemaid a little white girl.

Well, that's about as much as I feel like sharing with you. You really should've thought this thing through a little more before starting your little war with them. I hope this will teach you some subtlety.

Raoul

Nterview

HOME

!tertainment

!terview

!! the news

!sight

!tre nous

'!ternet

!tv

n N! games

p!

rds

al stuff

search

find !

ntact

Is Project Utopia handling its power responsibly?

• **Soon Pak, policeman, Seoul:** "They are a fine example to all of humanity, nova or otherwise. Who else has achieved so much?"

• **Terrence Rather, prosecution lawyer, Chicago:** "I suppose it could be much worse. It's an awful lot of power they've got, but they've done all right by it — so far."

• **Jeanne Griseault, elementary school teacher, Paris:** "What sort of example do they think they are setting if they are willing to resort to violence? Nothing can ever be settled by the fist, no matter how powerful the fist."

• **Cory Evert, student, London:** "Utopia's corkin'! So what if those stateside wankers get all knotted up over 'em? If I had that power, I'd use it too! Screw the polls!"

• **Ketema Alemu, farmer, Inewari:** "What kind of answer could you expect? Ten years ago, I and my children were sick, poor and hopeless. Now I eat three meals a day and my son is second-placed on his university's track team. Utopia and the Team Tomorrow are a blessing, and I cannot believe that you would ask otherwise."

N! HOME

N!tertainment

N!terview

N! the news

N!sight

N!tre nous

N!ternet

N!tv

fun N! games

help!

awards

legal stuff

search

find!

N! contact us

N!tertainment

Excerpt from introductory sequence to N! news show, *Nova Planet*; air date 03/20/0[

Good evening, this is Violet Cameron, and welcome to *Nova Planet*. Tonight, our feature profiles are four of the most prominent figures of Project Utopia — people who daily work harder than we can imagine to make our world a better place. Whether they work on Team Tomorrow or behind the scenes, on-site or in the labs, these four novas are beacons to a brighter future.

Caestus Pax — the center of Team Tomorrow Central, and the heart and soul of the entire Team Tomorrow project. Some say he's the most powerful nova in existence today. But more than that, Caestus Pax is the ideal of dedication — he is the voice of Project Utopia's vision of hope, peace and the betterment of life on Earth. Tonight, we'll follow him around to watch a day in the life of Pax.

Jennifer "Slider" Landers — the spirited young member of T2M whose gifts have saved countless lives from disaster or violence. To many, she is the living counterargument to the Null Manifesto — the girl who proves that no matter what, novas and baselines are not so very different after all. Our cameras go to the locations of her operations, and tonight we'll hear from those who might not be here today if not for her intervention.

Ana Graça Texeira — the Brazilian beauty who's equally at home scouring the ocean bed, taking guns away from terrorist guerrillas or helping in the construction of new housing for the homeless. We trace her career from her eruption to the modern day and collect reports from around the world on her latest activities.

Antaeus — the reclusive ecological mastermind who spearheaded the close of the ozone layer, the revivification of the world's oceans, the terraforming of the Ethiopian highlands, the Amazon restoration project and countless local environmental-recovery programs. Everything he touches turns to green — so what's next on this hypergenius's schedule? We'll find out.

All tonight: on *Nova Planet*.

TEAM TOMORROW (T2M)

Excerpt from a lecture given to prospective Team Tomorrow applicants, 9/14/06

I'll skip introductions. By this point, the five of you should know who I am and why you're here. You'll have plenty of time to get to know one another, too; this training program makes for excellent bonding material. Think of it as a kind of boot camp — if that scares you, you shouldn't even have made it this far. You're powerful, sure, but are you ready to represent all of Project Utopia when the entire world's looking at you?

You've already undergone the Project's training, so we know you're able to control your powers. Here you'll learn how to master them. You need to know everything you're capable of; raw power can cover up for a few mistakes, but one's all it takes to screw you up for good. You'll learn how to apply your potential, and you'll learn self-defense. After all, you're novas — you already have enemies, whether you know who they are or not.

But this isn't the Army. You'll learn much more than self-defense. You'll learn fluency in foreign languages if you didn't have any already. That's right, you have to leave your isolationist ideals at the door here — we're Team Tomorrow, and we represent the world. Not your home country or state or province or county or village — the world. Look around at your fellows here; doesn't seem too representative of any one country, does it? Your cell won't seem that way, either. We take the best, and excellence doesn't recognize political boundaries. It's no accident that Caestus Pax and Slider serve alongside Makara and Ana Graça Texeira, and them alongside André Corbin and Jinshu Shan.

With that in mind, you'll also be taught etiquette. And I damn well recommend you pay attention during your tutoring. You will be taught how to deal with public speaking, how to act responsibly around crowds, how to be an ideal specimen of humanity whenever the cameras are on you. A poor public image won't get you anywhere in this world.

You're probably asking yourselves, "Why should I go to all this trouble when I can get an easier job elsewhere?" You already know the reasons. A generous eight-figure salary. Unmatched health care and insurance benefits. Fame and fortune — a whole world's acclamation, if you think you can handle it. And most importantly, you can go to your beds at night richer, more popular and without a scrap of a guilty conscience — because you are doing the right thing with us. And you cannot get that to such a degree anywhere else.

From Virtual Tours Inc., Package #108

HI! NICE TO SEE YOU! I'M TERRI, AND I'LL BE YOUR VIRTUAL HOSTESS AND TOUR GUIDE. I MUST SAY, YOU'VE CHOSEN A VERY POPULAR PACKAGE. SEEMS LIKE EVERYONE WANTS TO SEE THE INSIDE OF THE FOUR MAIN T2M CELLS' HEADQUARTERS THESE DAYS. WELL, WE'RE HERE TO OBLIGE! NATURALLY, SOME DETAILS HAVE BEEN CHANGED; AFTER ALL, T2M IS HARDLY WITHOUT ITS ENEMIES.

BUT FOR THE MOST PART, THIS TOUR WILL GIVE YOU THE IMPRESSION OF WHAT IT'S LIKE TO LIVE WITH THE BRAVE MEMBERS OF TEAM TOMORROW! THIS TOUR IS PATTERNED, APPROPRIATELY ENOUGH, AFTER THE HEADQUARTERS OF T2M CENTRAL, LOCATED IN THE ADDIS ABABA UTOPIA COMPLEX. AND WHAT A COMPLEX IT IS! ACRES AND ACRES OF LUSH GARDEN PARADISE, FILLED WITH ANIMALS AND PLANTS OF THE MOST PHENOMENAL BEAUTY.

OF COURSE, NO BUGS CAN BITE US HERE — BUT THEY COULDN'T BITE YOU IN THE FLESH, EITHER. VISITORS ARE SUPPLIED WITH SPECIAL PHEROMONALLY TREATED BADGES THAT KEEP THE WORST PESTS AT BAY.
LET'S GET STARTED! FIRST OF ALL, THIS IS THE RECEPTION AREA. I WONDER IF WE'LL SEE ANYONE FROM T2M CENTRAL HERE — OOPS, NO LUCK. I GUESS THEY'RE ALL TOO BUSY TO HANG OUT HERE FOR ANY LENGTH OF TIME.

NOTE THE REPLICA CARPETS — AND YES, THAT RODIN OVER BY THE BAY WINDOWS IS AN ORIGINAL. YOU'LL NOTE THE WONDERFUL LIGHTING EFFECTS. THAT'S BECAUSE THIS COMPLEX, LIKE MOST MAJOR UTOPIA BUILDINGS, WAS DESIGNED BY PIOTR ENRIKSSEN, THE NOVA GENIUS BEHIND MUCH OF PROJECT UTOPIA'S ARCHITECTURAL ENGINEERING PROJECTS. NO, HE DOESN'T JUST BUILD DAMS!

OKAY, NOW LET'S GO TO THE GYM. I HOPE YOU WON'T BE DISAPPOINTED — THERE'S NOT MUCH BY WAY OF COMBAT TRAINING EQUIPMENT THERE. TEAM TOMORROW CON-DUCTS MUCH OF ITS BATTLEFIELD READINESS TRAINING ON HIGHLY SPECIALIZED STAGING AREAS, AND WE'RE NOT TOLD A THING ABOUT THAT. BUT THERE'S STILL PLENTY TO SEE. THERE'S THE OLYMPIC-SIZED POOL — OOH, IT LOOKS REFRESHING.

NOW NOTE THE VARIABLE-LEVEL GYMNASTICS EQUIPMENT; IT'S A LOT MORE IMPRESSIVE THAN YOUR AVERAGE SET OF MONKEY BARS, ISN'T IT? AND WAIT — WHO'S THAT MAN USING THE HYDRAULIC WEIGHTLIFTING PRESS? THAT'S RIGHT, IT'S MAKARA! GEE, HE SURE DOESN'T LOOK LIKE HE NEEDS THE EXERCISE, DOES HE? WHAT A HUNK OF MUSCLE!

NOW WE'LL BE GOING TO THE DINING ROOM. YOU'LL NOTE THE 13TH-CENTURY TAPESTRIES — WE UNDERSTAND THAT THEY—

INTERRUPT
You have chosen to end this virtual tour. Please select alternate headquarters tour:

A T2M Americas
       Mexico City, Mexico
B T2M Europe
       Venice, Italy
C T2M Asia/Pacific
       Talaud Island

From transcript of *Homo Sapiens Novus*, History Channel documentary, original air date February 3, 2008

So what exactly does someone do once his Mazarin-Rashoud node manifests, and he finds himself possessed of the power of a demigod?

Some have joined with Project Utopia, to pit their astounding powers against a challenge just as great — changing the world for the better. Here novas from all countries use earth-shifting telekinesis to dig canals, or superhuman scientific prowess to cure diseases. Some of these even join with Team Tomorrow, the elite cadre ready to fight rogue novas or raise housing, all depending on the needs of the day.

Others follow their patriotism, joining with government agencies such as the armed forces or aerospace programs. Now the human race has walked unaided on the moon, and the possibility of colonizing other planets has leapt centuries toward us. At least one FBI nova has managed to solve baffling cases on an almost daily basis, bringing previously untouchable criminals to justice.

Some have entered the entertainment industry, and they continue to offer us spectacles of sight and sound the likes of which we've never seen.

Some have entered the employment of powerful multinational corporations, serving as spokespersons, special security consultants and even advisors to their employers.

Some have gone freelance, offering their powers to the highest bidder — often in a military capacity. These, the "elites," have been the deciding factor in border conflicts around the globe.

Sadly, a few have decided to use their phenomenal powers for personal gain or advancement. In fact, if not for the efforts of Project Utopia and other novas working for law-enforcement agencies, it's difficult to say if any of these übercriminals would ever have been brought to justice at all. And looming beyond all the independent nova criminals is the terrorist organization known as the Teragen.

The spectre of conflict hangs over all these cliques and organizations. Larger than life in every way, many novas find themselves drawn into conflict with their fellow superpowered beings at least once in their lifetime. Sometimes the deciding factor is egotism run out of hand; sometimes it is a conflict of interest, whether an employer's or one's personal issues. But in a world where the only thing that can reliably stop a nova is another nova, these Promethean giants find themselves thrown against each other by chance or design. And the results are always dramatic.

Tonight we'll be looking at the role of the nova in modern society, from that fateful day in 1998 until...

Alejandra

Birth Name: Alejandra Maria Magdalena Carranza
Date of Birth: February 5, 1984
Place of Origin: Mexico City, Mexico
Occupation: Novox singer
Powers: Alejandra is gifted with the power of enhanced vocal projection, as well as some manner of control over sonic energy. She is capable of producing sounds from 200 dB to subsonic levels. Her ability to control ambient sound is currently unmeasured, but she can lower or increase the volume of background noise in her vicinity, and often does so with precise control as part of her novox concerts. She is also capable of a form of superpowered ventriloquism, mimicking and projecting specific voices or sounds anywhere within earshot.
Background: Alejandra is another of the dramatic rags-to-riches stories that the M-R node has made possible. Her family was eight strong, all stuck in a Mexico City tenement. As she tells it, only their faith kept them going even in the wake of disasters such as the earthquake of 2002.

Alejandra was a member of her church's choir, and it was there that her power first manifested itself, filling the church with a song of celestial beauty. It didn't take long for the news to pick up on this, and almost instantly her family was besieged with offers of employment from music agents, Hollywood and Bombay movie studios, Project Utopia and more. Alejandra and her fa-

ther gracefully shooed the majority of these people away, negotiated a simple contract with New River Records, and proceeded to make novox history.

Estimated Power Levels:
- **Strength:** 2
- **Intellect:** 3
- **Speed:** 3
- **Offense:** 5
- **Defense:** 4
- **Versatility:** 6

I'm waiting on the patio of DuMonde's,

sifting through the publicity photographs her office sent for this interview, and already I don't feel up to writing this article. She's possibly the most beautiful woman I've seen — Elizabeth Taylor and Marilyn Monroe, two of the 20th century's biggest sex symbols, seem almost tawdry when compared to her. As I shift over a shot of her pensively sitting on the balcony of her Cancun home, it occurs to me that words just don't seem to do her justice.

Then she whirls into the room and settles at my table like a summer wind, a zephyr adorned with a white silk button-down blouse and flared collar, perfectly flattering black Rochellaux pants, and the midnight hair and eyes of an Aztlan angel — and I realize that the pictures didn't do her justice, either.

This is, of course, Alejandra — the nova who has redefined Hispanic pop music and is currently shaking the pillars of the entire music industry. She laughs an apology for her tardiness (as if anyone could hold anything against a novox deity-diva like herself) and gently asks the waiter what local fruit is in season right now. I've never seen a DuMonde's waiter so attentive before — he hangs on every one of her murmuring-stream syllables as if she were telling him her phone number, and then he snaps off to the kitchen like St. George after his dragon. Then she turns her attention fully to me, and I feel like Moses having brunch with the burning bush. You would, too.

• **Vox:** I don't know where to begin, except to thank you profusely for agreeing to this interview.

• **Alejandra:** (*laughs*) Oh, it's nothing.

• **Vox:** You've captured the hearts of the world in less than two years. Since your eruption, you've been consistently wooed by music agents, Hollywood and Bombay studios, Project Utopia — the list goes on and on. And yet you signed a contract with the then-obscure New River Records, and went on to make novox history.

• **Alejandra:** And still the offers come. (*smiles*) Thankfully, my family is always there for me; I don't know what I'd do without them politely shooing away some of these people.

• **Vox:** It's common knowledge that you've used a portion of your earnings to move your family to wonderful houses and put your siblings through college. Obviously, there's a strong bond there. Can you tell us something about your childhood?

• **Alejandra:** It wasn't easy. My parents raised us as best they could, but we did not live in one of the better portions of Mexico City. Life was very difficult, and I almost never saw Papa on weekdays or Saturdays unless I had secretly stayed up very late to see him come home. Sunday morning was our special time, when all the family was together and we could go to church together. God was very kind to us in allowing us this time, and I always looked forward to it all week. We had faith — mercifully, enough faith to keep us together during the earthquake of 2002. *(pauses)* We lost almost more than we could bear. But we worked harder, and prayed harder. And then… Well, then I erupted.

• **Vox:** Yes, of course. In your church's choir; we only wish we had a recording of your first song with your new powers. By description, it was positively celestial. But if you'll pardon the question — I know you're probably asked this all the time — what was your eruption like? I mean, can you describe the sensation?

• **Alejandra:** *(laughs)* It's not so easy to describe as you might think!

[She becomes pensive here, and rests one exquisite finger along her chin.]

• **Alejandra:** I think it might be best described as being blind and deaf, and suddenly becoming exposed to light and color and sound all at the same time. It was a tidal wave of new sensation, a wave that drenched me from my skin down to my skeleton. I hear things now that nobody else can, and my voice… *(laughs)* It is something I believe I have to write a song about; perhaps the experience can be properly conveyed only through novox.

• **Vox:** I can hardly wait. Um, now an obvious question is one of musical influences. Apart from your own powers, what other influences have there been on your unique sound?

• **Alejandra:** *(winsome, apologetic smile)* I don't know if I can say for certain. Artists study their art from all angles and choose the elements they prefer. I don't think I can be called an artist — I'm more of a channel for the sound that runs through me. Oh, I've always loved music, everything from older Crystal Method to DJ Faiz to Roy Orbison — but when I am on stage, my voice is not quite my own.

• **Vox:** You make it sound as if it has a mind of its own.

• **Alejandra:** *(silvery laugh)* Oh, I don't think so! A river doesn't have a mind of its own; it just flows where it must and pours through where it was meant to.

• **Vox:** The media has already made a fairly big deal of your open commitment to your religion. With the rise of sects such as Kamisama Buddhism and the Church of the Immanent Escheaton, as well as the media cults to novas in general, it seems almost that traditional religion is falling out of favor.

• **Alejandra:** (*gentle smile*) Religion isn't something that matters only when it's in favor. Christianity was not "in style" in the time of the Roman Empire.

• **Vox:** Good point. Do you like to think of yourself as a role model for Catholicism, then?

• **Alejandra:** Not really, no. I aspire to live a good life. My mother always taught me that pride was the first and worst sin, so I don't want to think of myself as a role model. If other young people look at me and say, "Alejandra is being a good Christian even though it isn't popular — maybe I should give it a second chance," then wonderful. But I cannot let myself believe that this is what *should* be happening.

• **Vox:** So I take it you don't care for Reverend Tuley's accusations that the nova population will naturally set themselves up as, well, gods on earth?

• **Alejandra:** *Madonna*, no! These powers we have are extraordinary, yes — but to place ourselves above God is ridiculous! You might as well have announced Albert Einstein or Kevin Tuleaud as the second coming of Christ! To be sure, these powers are a gift — but how very much different is that from being born rich, or intelligent, or with wonderful parents?

• **Vox:** Beautifully put.

• **Alejandra:** (*laughs*) Why, thank you, sir.

• **Vox:** Does anything else really get under your skin?

• **Alejandra:** Yes. The word "aberrant." What has originally started as a term of misunderstanding is becoming a thing of hate. (*stern tone*) I advise your readers never, ever to use the word around me.

• **Vox:** Oh, of course not! We'll move on. Now, some might say you're bucking all the hottest nova trends. You haven't taken a stage name, and you don't bother with any masks — which, I understand, was a tradition originating in Mexico.

• **Alejandra:** It has something to do with the persona, you see. Many novas, particularly the elites and those who emulate them, believe that the mask is their "battle face" — that their persona and their own, personal self are two different people. I understand that Infierno and Esteban Caraçon are in many ways just that, different people with different goals — but no matter whether I am on stage, in church or here with you, I am always Alejandra. (*scintillating smile*) I am perhaps a minority among novas, but I prefer to think of myself as in the majority of people.

• **Vox:** You're maybe too modest. Do you have any idea how… how easy it is for you to change someone's life, simply speaking a few kind words to them?

• **Alejandra:** (*mischievous smile*) How do you mean? Have I changed yours just now?

• **Vox:** Truthfully?

[A Contract Between a Nova and an Employer]

Contract Between Linda Raphael dba Lotus Infinite and TransEurope Expediting, Inc.

This contract is entered into effect as of 5 October 2007 between the parties hereto, who agree as follows in consideration of the mutual promises contained herein:

1. PARTIES. This is a contract by and between TransEurope Expediting, Inc. (henceforth "Corporation"), whose mailing address is 754 Pharr Rd., Richards Building Suite 1108-D, Atlanta, Georgia 30341; and Linda Raphael dba Lotus Infinite, with offices at the DeVries Agency, 808 7th Avenue, Suite 1301, New York City, New York 10011 (henceforth "Operative").

2. RESPONSIBILITIES OF OPERATIVE. The Operative hereby agrees to locate and retrieve 13 OpNet-capable computer information servers, serial numbered XB4365023WQ, XB4365023WR, XB4365023WS, XB4365023WT, XB4365023WU, XB4365023WV, XB4365023WW, XB4365023WX, XB4365023WY, XB4365023WZ, XB4365024WA, XB4365024WB, and XB4365024WC, tentatively titled "Operation: Upgrade" (henceforth, "the Mission").

This Mission shall be performed according to certain specifications provided by the Corporation, and the Mission shall be undertaken for, and in the name of, the Corporation. The Corporation is the sole owner of copyrights exclusive of the Operative's payment fees; the Mission constitutes "work for hire." The Operative is solely responsible for completion of the Mission.

The Mission shall incur operational expenses of no more than one million (1,000,000) dollars in excess of the Operative's payment fees.

The Mission shall commence upon 11 October 2007.

The Mission shall conclude by 18 October 2007.

3. PAYMENTS TO THE OPERATIVE.

a. The Corporation agrees to pay the Operative a flat fee of four hundred thirty-seven thousand (437,000) dollars in two installments, 10 percent of which shall be paid as management fee to the DeVries Agency.

(i) The first installment, of 1/2 total payment, will be paid upon the Corporation's receipt of the signed contract. The second installment, of 1/2 total payment, will be paid upon receipt of the aforementioned servers.

b. A kill fee equal to 10% of the total payment will be paid to the operative should this contract be terminated by the Corporation.

(i) If the servers or any part of the servers or their required components are delivered to the Corporation after the specified deadline, a penalty of 2% of project's total payment will be imposed for each day that the Mission remains unfinished after the specified date.

c. The Corporation will pay to Operative a royalty of four percent (4%) of the net profit per recovered server sold.

(i) On servers destroyed, given away or sold at or below cost, no royalties shall be paid.

4. RELATIONSHIP. The Operative represents and warrants that, between the Mission Dates specified by the Corporation, the Mission shall be disavowed and denied by the Corporation and representatives thereof, nor shall the Corporate be under any legal liability to avow this Contract or the terms herein. The Operative shall not rely on or reveal the nature of contents of this contract to any individual outside the Corporation or its duly recognized fellows. Should such individuals exist, the Corporation shall provide detailed, written descriptions of them and shall assume all responsibility for the veracity of those descriptions, provided suitable precautions regarding security are taken, in good faith, by the Operative. The Operative shall under no circumstances discuss the Mission with government or law-enforcement agencies, even if the circumstances of the Mission lead the Operative into conflict with said agencies.

5. CIVIL LIMITATIONS. The Operative will endanger no innocent lives, participate in no unwarranted attack upon individuals not associated with the person or entity responsible for theft of the Corporation's property, and kill no individuals directly associated with the person or entity responsible for theft of the Corporation's property. Due to policies upheld by the Corporation, the Operative shall perform neither the Infinite Wind Technique nor the Infinity Justifier while carrying out the terms of this contract. Property damages caused by the Operative are considered to fall under operational expenses outlined in Paragraph 2, and are to be reimbursed by the Corporation to the extent discussed therein.

6. CONFIDENTIALITY. In consideration of the confidential material and business plans supplied by the Corporation to assist in the performance of the Mission, the Operative agrees not to reveal any of said confidential material or business plans to anyone not working for or in behalf of the Corporation without the Corporation's prior written permission.

7. TRADEMARK AND PROPERTY PRODUCTION AND PROTECTION. In consideration of the fee paid under this contract, the Operative agrees that, upon execution of this contract, he will not participate in any Operation: Upgrade-related project except for the Corporation or its licensees, unless the Operative receives direct written permission from the Corporation. "Participation" shall include subsequent "re-recovery" of the specified servers or their contents, destruction of or security relaxation of the specified servers or their contents, tampering

with or other consultation on matters regarding the specified servers or their contents. "Contents" shall include intangible data or information contained as data on the specified servers. This shall in no way limit the Operative's right to write or be interviewed for magazine articles, perform compensated endorsements and the like, subject to Paragraphs 4 and 6.

8. MISCELLANEOUS.

a. Governing Law. This contract, including all matters relating to the validity, construction, performance and enforcement thereof, shall be governed by the laws of the State of Georgia.

b. Severability. The provisions of this agreement are severable, and if any provision shall be held illegal, invalid or unenforceable, such holding shall not affect the legality, validity or enforceability of any other provision. Any such illegal, invalid or unenforceable provision shall be deemed stricken herefrom as if it had never been contained herein, but all other provisions shall continue in full force and effect.

c. Final Agreement. This contract contains the entire agreement between the parties with respect to the subject matter hereof and supersedes any prior agreements between the parties, written or oral, with respect to such subject matter.

d. Notices and Reports. All notices or demands required or permitted under this agreement shall be in writing and shall be deemed served when deposited in the United States Mail, first class postage prepaid, certified or registered mail, return receipt requested, addressed as provided in Paragraph 1 of this contract, or to such other address as either party may from time to time designate in writing. All reports or payments required under this contract shall be served as above, but no certification or registration shall be required.

_____   _____
Corporation Operative

_____
Social Security Number

_____   _____
Date   Date

Estimated Power Levels:
   Strength: 6
   Intellect: 3
   Speed: 6
   Offense: 8
   Defense: 7
   Versatility: 5

Duke "Core" Baron

Birth Name: Louis Martin Freeman
Date of Birth: August 4, 1979
Place of Origin: Brooklyn, NYC
Occupation: Tournament shootfighter; current XWF World Heavyweight Champion

Powers: Core possesses powerful plasma-generation powers, which he can manifest in several ways. Most common is the projection of plasma bolts capable of liquifying solid steel. However, he is also able to manifest a plasma shield that can stop small-arms fire, as well as channel his excess energy through his own form to increase his physical strength and durability.

Background: By his own accounts, Louis Freeman manifested his powers almost immediately after the *Galatea* explosion of 1998. Nobody could approach the whirling mass of plasma that surrounded him — until the effects died down two hours later. Louis fled at that time, evading police and National Guard alike to find his way underground.

He resurfaced in Japan two years later, where the first nova-level shootfight competitions had begun. Having learned to control his innate abilities, as well as keeping his already potent fighting prowess up to date, he rapidly made a name for himself in the independent fighting circuits. When the XWF first formed in 2004, Freeman — now under a new name — became one of its first recruits.

Core is most famous for the radiant yellow-white glow of his energy powers, which emanates from his eyes and mouth when he experiences "power buildup" — an event often accompanying an aggravated emotional state. In other words, the angrier he gets, the more his power builds. This happens now and again in tournaments, and when it does, watch out — because the Core Meltdown™ isn't far behind!

Excerpt: Carson Whitland's orientation interview, Holistics Research, Incorporated, 08/17/05

· **Meade:** Formalities aside, Carson, it's wonderful to have you aboard. We're all very excited about the potential you're bringing to Holistics.

· **Whitland:** Thanks very much, Ms. Meade. I'm looking forward to it.

· **Meade:** Oh, please — call me Sara.

· **Whitland:** Um. Sure thing, Sara.

· **Meade:** Great! Now, let's get started. We're certainly pleased that you've accepted our offer of employment; I can't stress enough how happy we are to have you aboard.

· **Whitland:** Well, to be honest, I *have* heard the stories about nova-run corporations, and it did sound pretty tempting — but I'd rather go ahead and work on research full-time. I don't have much of a head for business, and my... um, powers seem to lend themselves better toward research and analysis than playing the stock market.

· **Meade:** Well, we're certainly glad to hear that. And as I've mentioned before, we're more than willing to make it worth your while to stay on with us.

· **Whitland:** (*laughs*) It's sure hard to say no to a seven-figure startup salary!

· **Meade:** More than that, Carson. Your hyper-enhanced senses are a very valuable asset to us, to say nothing of your ability to handle dangerous chemicals without harm. We've put together one very attractive package of benefits for you — full medical and dental with the Rostrem Clinic—

· **Whitland:** Really! Ahem — sorry.

· **Meade:** Quite all right. Anyway, there's also a multimillion-dollar life insurance policy, expense account, company transport, provisions for retirement, shares in the company stock — I don't think you'll be able to find a better offer out there.

· **Whitland:** Well, uh, probably not. But really, I'd already been kind of keeping track of the various research institutes while I was in college, and this seemed like a great place to come and work. Doing what I want to do, I mean. You know.

· **Meade:** (*laughs*) You've got the job, Carson! There's no need to butter us up — you can save that for your first performance review!

· **Whitland:** (*sheepish laughter*) Yeah, I guess you're right.
· **Meade:** Well, if you'll just sign here, then, I'll give you the full tour of the facilities and start making introductions. All right?

· **Whitland:** Sounds great, so long as we stop somewhere and grab some lunch soon. Nova-sized appetite, you know....

· **Meade:** (*laughter*)

N HOME

N!tertainment

N!terview

N! the news

N!sight

N!tre nous

N!ternet

N!tv

fun N! games

help!

awards

legal stuff

search

[   ]

find!

N contact us

N the news

Excerpt from General Tobias Gahagan's press conference, August 10th, 2000

We are proud to report a unilateral success in the Desert Hawk operation, in the most part owed to the successful deployment of our official US Armed Forces nova operations agents. Over the course of three days — which was the operating window — the United States military suffered only three casualties. Our nova ops completely disabled the enemy's nuclear silos and brought down the two launched missiles without so much as a scratch in the casing.

It is the intention of the United States Armed Forces to continue to recruit novas for just such operations. One nova can prove to have all the firepower of a jet squadron at a fraction of the cost to the taxpayers. That's why I'm pleased to announce the Nova Recruitment Initiative, a program which offers benefits and rewards commensurate to the obviously high value of a nova volunteer. We want any young novas out there to know that they have a place in the United States military, a place where they will be treated with honor and respect.…

It's no surprise that the military potential of novas was put to the test almost immediately. After all, a combat-trained nova is worth a platoon of men, and he doesn't require near the amount of resources to maintain. As costly as retaining a nova (or a force of novas) is for military purposes, doing so relieves a much greater tax burden otherwise spent on conventional armaments, thus freeing up previously unheard-of resources for social programs or otherwise "kinder, gentler" government initiatives.

HOME

N!tertainment

N!terview

N! the news

N!sight

N!tre nous

N!ternet

N!tv

un N! games

p!

rds

al stuff

search

f i n d !

ntact

Script excerpt from documentary program "Cutting Edge" episode #53 (unaired)

The "elites." Nova mercenaries. Superpowered soldiers for hire.

By all accounts, it's a glamorous job. A standard contract can pay an elite over $10 million a year — and that's for a relatively raw and unproven nova. Veterans can demand much, much more. They are among the most notorious and respected men and women in the world — and yet, they are also tied into a world of blood and death, where "minor" wars such as the 2007 Trans-Tanzanian Conflict are fought entirely by elite proxies.

Tonight we delve into the deadly world of the elites, where international boundaries mean little next to nova-level power, tarnished glamour and, of course, the universal law of currency. We look at the practices of these mask-wearing, code-named agents for hire and even travel on a mission with one. All tonight, on the Cutting Edge.

[Opening credits roll]

When discussing the elites, the most obvious place to begin is with the mask. Where so many other novas are proud to let the world look on their features, the elites have evolved a subsociety in which the mask, the persona, is more important than the person beneath. Certainly, some of this stems from the desire to keep one's identity concealed, particularly when jobs take one far from home — or too close to home.

But a mask is hardly anonymity. It's a persona, a character larger than life. Take, for instance, the golden skull mask of Tötentanz. It's a symbol

keep reading

N HOME

N!tertainment

N!terview

N! the news

N!sight

N!tre nous

N!ternet

N!tv

fun N! games

help!

awards

legal stuff

search

find!

N contact us

that has come to represent professionalism and surgical precision — not mercy. When his mask comes into view, his opponents, whoever they may be, give little thought to the man underneath the mask. Instead, it's Tötentanz they fear, a modern-day incarnation of death. The mask is pure intimidation, pure publicity, without giving away anything of the man beneath.

In such a society, it's no wonder that unmasking is a ritual of its own. When two elites develop such a grudge that they're driven to duel with one another, the stakes are rarely to the death. However, sometimes one's whole persona is on the line, as the winner takes the loser's mask as a trophy. In many ways, this is very much like the myth of the Old West, where gunfighters would challenge one another to see whose legend would emerge paramount. The winner of such a duel gains boasting rights, which can lead to more lucrative contracts — after all, he's just proven himself a better fighter than at least one rival. But the loser can never really put on his mask again. The image has been shattered. The immortal is now a little more mortal.

And yet, the power of a nova is such that even an unmasked elite can command great respect. One need look no farther for an example than the self-proclaimed "Stone Badass," Lance Stryker. When unmasked by rival elite Borealis in the spring of 2007, he rallied back with such drive and charisma that his name is now a household word. His licensing arrangements are as profitable as even those of Caestus Pax and André Corbin — not bad for a mercenary.

[Add footage of interview with Lance Stryker, prior to resolution of 5/06/07 Corpus Christi incident]

Stryker: "Yeah, I've heard your fancy-ass press releases about how you think your sorry asses are so superior to normal people and how you think you can lick just about any man on the face of this planet. You bitch and you moan and then you don't get anything done unless you count hiding behind a bunch of women and children. You wanna sit there on top of your "moral superiority"? Well, you're about to get Lance Stryker's boot so far up your ass that your moral superiority's gonna be fired on out your nose, and that's a damn fact!"

[END SCRIPT EXCERPT]

You own the attitude — now own the T-shirt! The meanest, roughest, hardest SOB of an elite ever to draw breath — the Stone Badass, Lance Stryker!

Your ass is living on borrowed time

— and that's a damn fact!

[BEGIN AUDIO CLIP; RECORDED MESSAGE]

Good evening, Dr. Moran. I hope this message reaches you in good health.

My name is Elaine Katzenbaum, and I'll be your contact with the DeVries Agency. First of all, I'd like to thank you for your interest in our operation. We've worked very hard to attain our reputation as the foremost contracting agency for freelance novas, and we hope that we can prove to you that our reputation is justified.

Regulations forbid us from attaching an extended file of our nova operatives, so you'll pardon me for the omission. I'd like to arrange a meeting with you at your earliest convenience; there we can discuss the nature of employment and the available agents that would be best suited for your purposes. Rest assured that should you require a task that runs a high risk of nova-level conflict, we have agents that are fully capable of meeting that challenge. Naturally, our elite agents such as Pursuer are available as well, should you require a very visible presence. Our resources are such that we feel confident we'll have someone available to suit your needs, no matter the place, time or job description.

We've already completed our credit check, so don't let that be a worry. We can discuss exact terms when we meet face-to-face. Again, I look forward to it, and thank you once more for coming to us. Rest assured that your task is as good as completed.

N! the news

...And in Kyoto today, the highly enthusiastic reception for the vacationing Pursuer fell a little flat with the arrival of Caestus Pax. Pursuer was disembarking from his private jet and acknowledging the crowds when Pax dropped out of the skies, landing well clear of Pursuer's entourage but certainly close enough for conversation. Seemingly, no clear words were exchanged, but a staredown of sorts emerged, one that the crowd encouraged with cheers for both sides. It ended inconclusively when Pax pointedly turned his back on Pursuer and lifted off into the skies again.

Although Project Utopia has made no official comment, most experts believe that this was certainly a statement of disapproval regarding Pursuer's part in the latest Argentinian operation. It certainly wouldn't be the first time that the  Utopian agents have clashed with DeVries elites over ideology; the DeVries Agency has constantly and aggressively promoted the belief that their elites are more professional and efficient than the "Tomorrow idealists."

And when these two forces clash, even nonviolently, who benefits? Well, the licensees, for one. Toy sales show an average 10% increase for Utopia and DeVries licensed products just after any threat of hostilities between the two. Apparently if the nation's youth can't see the Highwayman and Skew duke it out on national TV, they'll have to settle for staging their own battles on the playground or in the arcade.

They change the world.

They move mountains.

They define fashion, music, entertainment.

They're the hottest thing on the planet.

They're novas. And we've got them — 24 hours a day, 7 days a week.

N!

Walk among the gods.

(Call your dish network to subscribe today!)

N!tertainment

N!terview

N! the news

N!sight

N!tre nous

N!ternet

N!tv

fun N! games

help!

awards

legal stuff

search

find!

N contact us

N HOME

HOME

N!tertainment

N!terview

N! the news

l!sight

l!tre nous

l!ternet

l!tv

un N! games

p!

ards

al stuff

search

f i n d !

ntact
s

From an N! Broadcast of *Two Minutes Hate* on January 21, 2008

The following television program does not represent the opinions of N! or its employees. *Two Minutes Hate* is intended as a public forum, whereby novas of all creeds and orientations may make their views known. It also serves as an abstract index of nova popularity, as interpreted from independent polls conducted by the N! Network.

Recommended highlights this week on N!:

• **Sunday**, 8 pm: The broadcast premiere of Yoshiro Kumito's controversial film *Hand of God*, starring Michelle Caspar and Tora. Religion and quantum powers are explored in this powerful vision of what it means to have the power to change the world. Viewer discretion is advised.

• **Tuesday**, 9 pm: *Bucking the Odds*, the documentary covering the XWF from its inception to today. See what it's like to work behind the scenes at this multimillion-dollar organization, and find out just how it manages to keep on delivering top-notch battles every week.

• **Wednesday**, 10 pm: The highly controversial interview with Mefistofaleez makes this week's edition of *Constellation* a standout. Parental filters are strongly encouraged.

• **Friday**, 2 pm: Kirsten Dunst returns to *Storms at Sunset* as Violet rises from the dead in the landmark 200th episode. Will anything ever be the same in Storm Bay?

"I hereby swear to become the ravager of humanity, harbinger of misery and the reaper of souls. Everywhere I pass, I will leave despair and wretchedness in my wake. Children will die when I gaze at them and mothers will take ill when I turn in their direction. I will eat only bones and drink only blood. I have become anathema. I have become the absence of hope. My footsteps leave flame and I travel at the velocity of pain. Where I tread, nothing grows; who I touch, never heals. Sickness and famine are my brothers, and I am a companion to owls and a father to bats. The pious curse me as I strike them down; the virtuous shudder as I slay their wives and consume their children. I feel tenfold the pain I inflict, yet it drives me on to greater brutality. Hide your daughters and arm your sons, for I walk among you."

— Count Dragunov, popularity rating 62 percent

"I'm calling you out, Dan Miller and Crystalhawk! You think the Face could give a half a damn about you, Miller, and your pissant problems? Well have no doubt, next week is gonna be the week of the Face. So what the Face wants to know is if you two pansy-ass chuckleheads don't have too much powder in your panties. Yor step up to bat, you face the Face two-on-one, I'll make your chump asses famous, 'cause the Face will be smack dab right in the middle of the intersection of Hollywood and Vine. And what he plans on doing, is the Face will take his right fist, the Face will take his left fist, and then the Face will commence on laying the almighty beatdown on both your punk asses. Now, what the Face will do after that, is he's gonna hulk up the Face Hammer, he's gonna drop the Face Anvil and one of you loudmouth chesters is gonna suffer the Atomic Face Genocide right in the middle of the street. And then the Face will proceed to climb the N! broadcast tower foot by foot *by God-blessed foot*. And when it's all said and done, and when all the world is through chanting the Face's name — and the fireworks are over — you two chuckleheads will have joined the billions and billions of the Face's devoted followers who know damn well that the Face is, and will forever be — and the Face means *forever* be — the most hardcore in the world."

— Rocky "The Face" Elizondo, popularity rating 98 percent

Letter to the Editors

As I had no doubts, Issue 37 sparkled and shone, particularly Will Fraser's fascinating look at the decline of the two-party system in American politics. Not that it's any of our business what the presidents choose to do, but they must accept responsibility for those actions should they come to a public light.

Three years ago, Congress brought up a legislative proposal that would have created a greater role for the government in media, entertainment and cultural development. Proponents of the bill, citing too much emphasis on novas in the media, on the big screen and in other entertainment venues, claimed society sought unattainable role models. Those opposing the bill upheld the independent studios' rights to make whatever their audiences wanted to see, culminating in then-presidential candidate Earvin Waterman remark, "as long as it keeps [novas] out of politics." Well, I've got news for you, Mr. Waterman. From what the public sees of novas, we know their plans and agendas. They don't hide behind petty smokescreens and spin-doctoring campaigns funded by taxpayer money. Perhaps if this country took a *political cue* from its novas, we wouldn't have suffered the collapse of our political engine in the first place.
Anthony Freeman,
Tulsa, OK

Anthony's plea for honesty in politics couldn't come at a better time — to refute his point. See Mim Udovitch's shocking exposé of RusCon's Sierka administration, page 125, for more insight into the nova-political arena. — Ed.

N!tertainment

N!terview

N! the news

N!sight

N!tre nous

N!ternet

N!tv

un N! games

p!

ards

al stuff

N!tertainment

Sports Entertainment

Most team sports simply don't allow nova participants. After all, where's the fun of a basketball game if one man with superhuman reflexes consistently wins every game for his team single-handedly? At least Michael Jordan's opponents had a *chance*....

Nonetheless, the 2004 Olympics saw the first nova-specific track and field events, although naturally, not all countries were able to field a representative, much less a team. Similarly, Project Utopia often sponsors certain all-nova athletic events as charity fund-raisers; even a comparably sedate sport like tennis gets pretty amazing when the participants are Skew and Hammerlock. Conversely, there has been a marked decline in interest for most sports without nova involvement; the glory days of multimillionaire professional athletes are no longer with us.

Of course, there is one arena where novas can test their talents against each other and rake in a fortune in merchandising, pay-per-view proceeds and endorsement deals....

search

find!

ntact
s

- **JERRY "JOJO" DYLAN:** FOLKS, I KNOW I'VE SAID THIS BEFORE, BUT WE REALLY COULD BE LOOKING AT THE GREATEST MATCH IN THE HISTORY OF OUR SPORT! CORE HAS BEEN RIDING HIGH ON TOP OF THE HEAVYWEIGHT DIVISION FOR TWO MONTHS NOW — AND IT'S ONLY NATURAL THAT THESE TWO WOULD NOW COLLIDE!
- **DUSTIN MCSHANE:** ROB "SUPERBEAST" STEELE! THE ONE NOVA WHO'S NOT ONLY MAN ENOUGH TO TAKE CORE DOWN, BUT WHO VERY WELL MIGHT LAND THE INVINCIBLE ONE IN INTENSIVE CARE!

- **DYLAN:** PARTICULARLY WHEN YOU'RE TALKING ABOUT THE VARIABLE-ENVIRONMENT ARENA THAT WE HAVE SET UP HERE TONIGHT! SUPERBEAST EXCELS AT VARIABLE-LEVEL PLATFORMS AND A VARIETY OF SURFACES — AS HIS MATCH LAST MONTH WITH MAXX MAULER PROVED. ALTHOUGH THE EXPIRED TIME LIMIT MADE THE MATCH'S RESULT INCONCLUSIVE—
- **MCSHANE:** MAULER WAS SAVED BY THE BELL! IF THAT MATCH HAD GONE ANY FARTHER, MAULER WOULD BE DOWN DEEPER THAN OUR BOTTOMLESS PIT™!

- **DYLAN:** I DON'T KNOW IF I'D GO THAT FAR, DUSTIN. AND IT LOOKS LIKE OUR ANNOUNCER IS READY TO BRING THE CHALLENGER TO THE RING!

- **ANNOUNCER:** LADIES AND GENTLEMEN, THE FOLLOWING CONTEST IS STIPULATED AS "NO TIME LIMIT," AND IT WILL PROCEED UNTIL ONE OF THE COMBATANTS IS NO LONGER ABLE TO CONTINUE. IT IS FOR THE XWF HEAVYWEIGHT TITLE! HAILING FROM DETROIT, MICHIGAN AND WEIGHING IN AT 613 POUNDS — THE CHALLENGER! HE IS THE NOVA WITH NO HEART — THE LORD OF THE DEAD — THE CORPSEGRINDER! HE IS ROB STEELE — SUUUPERRRBEEEEAST!

- **DYLAN:** GOOD GOD, WHAT A MONSTER!
- **MCSHANE:** LOOK AT HIM LICKING HIS CHOPS! HE CAN'T WAIT TO SINK HIS TEETH INTO CORE!

- **ANNOUNCER:** AND NOW — FROM BROOKLYN, NEW YORK CITY — WEIGHING IN AT 280 POUNDS — HE IS THE REIGNING CHAMPION OF THE SPORT AND THE MASTER OF THE CORE MELTDOWN™. LADIES AND GENTLEMEN, YOUR X! W! F! HEAVYWEIGHT CHAMPION OF THE WOOOOORRRLD — DUKE! CORE! BAROOOONNN!
- **DYLAN:** THE CHAMPION! LOOK AT THAT PLASMA ROLL OFF HIM!

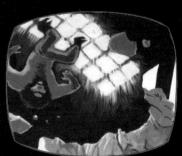

- **MCSHANE:** THESE TWO GUYS ARE GONNA BEAT THE CRAP OUT OF EACH OTHER WITH PUNCHES THAT COULD STOP TANKS! I CAN HARDLY WAIT!

- **DYLAN:** THERE'S THE BELL — AND THERE THEY GO!
- **MCSHANE:** OH YEAH, BABY!

- **DYLAN:** DEAR GOD! LOOK AT THAT! CORE HAS BLASTED SUPERBEAST STRAIGHT UP THROUGH THREE CONCRETE PLATFORMS! NOBODY CAN WALK AWAY FROM THAT!

- **MCSHANE:** DON'T COUNT YOUR CHICKENS, JOJO! LOOK AT THAT!
- **DYLAN:** ALREADY REGAINED CONTROL! SUPERBEAST HAS RICOCHETED OFF A — GOOD LORD!
- **MCSHANE:** I COULD BARELY SEE IT! HE HIT HIM, BUT—

- **DYLAN:** FANS, REMEMBER THAT THE RECORDINGS OF THESE MATCHES — FLURRY OF PUNCHES! NO! CORE'S BLASTED SUPERBEAST FREE! — THE RECORDINGS AVAILABLE FOR SALE THROUGH THE XWF ARE CAREFULLY EDITED FOR THE BEST ANGLE OF EVERY BLOW, AND DOUBLE-TAPED: ONE AT REGULAR SPEED, ONE SLOWED DOWN SO THAT THE HUMAN EYE CAN—

- **MCSHANE:** LOOK OUT! SUPERBEAST HAS A CHUNK OF THAT CONCRETE PLATFORM!
- **DYLAN:** HE'S RUNNING — IS HE GOING TO...? NO! HE'S HURLED IT LIKE A SHOTPUT!

- **MCSHANE:** CORE'S DOWN! CORE'S DOWN!
- **DYLAN:** THAT'S WHAT HAPPENS IN THE XTREME WARFARE FEDERATION — THE UNCHALLENGED LEADER IN NOVA SPORTS ENTERTAINMENT!

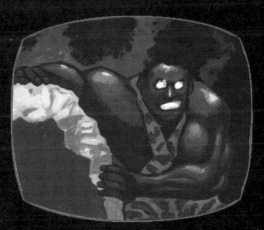

- **MCSHANE:** IS THIS IT? IS IT OVER?
- **DYLAN:** NOT BY A LONG SHOT! CORE'S BACK UP AGAIN — AND SUPERBEAST IS ALL OVER HIM!

From the *Book of Kalpa*

Foreword:

"Response to the coming of the novas and their role in the modern world has been so strong that, as of this printing of the *Book of Kalpa*, membership in the Church of the Immanent Escheaton has eclipsed that of many Christian denominations. Since our inception in 1998, we have converted a vast cross-section of the Western world to our point of view, glory be to the One, through the mysteries with which He has aided our crusade."

— Chrystian Kalpa

Chapter Three: On Holy Living:

"The thetans, which may suffer plague or spiritual decay, may best be kept at peak health through a regimented diet. As the Apostles themselves ate bread and drank wine with the nova Christ at the Last Supper, so should the pure seek to emulate them, succumbing neither to gluttony nor the lusts of indulgence. Bland foods do not excite the body unduly, and so should they support the mind with their foundation of simplicity."

Chapter Four: Ascension to Immanence:

"We may all become Immanent, awakening the blood of the nova within all of us. A proper diet, and observance of the 30 Escheatic Commandments, paves the way. Listen to the higher soul during the daily meditations, for only by denying the lower soul may one reveal the path toward Immanence.

"And those who have earned their transcendence shall bear the Unknown's Eye, though it shall be invisible to all but others who share it. Whether this is known by its temporal name — the Mazarin-Rashoud node — or by its spiritual significance as the mark of the deity's favor, those Immanents who have become so blessed shall know the way to Heaven."

Chapter Six: Meditations:

"Yet the fundaments behind the revelatory Church of the Immanent Escheaton are logical outgrowths of established faith. We do not form a cult, nor are we heretics. Observance of the Immanent Escheaton is a philosophy, a way of life. God is here among us, just as He was among the Catholics of the Middle Ages and the Protestants during the Reformation, and just as He is still among them. God — the One — loves all His children."

Chapter Seven: A Chorus of Voices:

"And so numbered among those practicing the Immanent Escheaton were Gautama Buddha; Jesus Christ; Martin Luther King, Jr.; the Comte St. Germain; Louis XIV of France; and Madame Blavatsky. And so numbered among those practicing the Immanent Escheaton are those who are born into the world, for in the purity of birth lies the introduction to Immanence and the faith that one basks forever in the love of our lord God."

N!tertainment

N!terview

N! the news

N!sight

N!tre nous

N!ternet

N!tv

un N! games

p!

ards

al stuff

search

find!

ontact
s

All eyes in Japan have turned upward to view the grandeur of Bodhisattva Masato, the nova leader of the country's nascent Kamisama Buddhist movement.

According to Kamisama Buddhist belief, novas are reincarnated 'bodhisattvas' and 'asuras,' divine beings placed on Earth as avatars to lead the rest of the world toward enlightenment.

From *Full Nova Extra*, on N!

"Hell, I should go over to Japan. They *worship* novas over there. It's part of that Buddhist thing."

— Starchylde

Such beliefs are not uncommon elsewhere in the world, and this phenomenon sees parallels in the Western doctrine of the Church of the Immanent Escheaton and several smaller, less recognized but no less devout faiths in any number of countries.

The trend has taken a disturbing turn in Japanese culture, however, as the nation's youth, obsessed with the nova as a popular cultural icon, form cults of personality centered on certain members of Japan's nova population. In a society so inundated with a constant flow of media as Japan, these 'new messiahs' come and go as quickly as one can change the channel. For the devoted, however, the nova becomes a way of life as well as a conduit to the heavens.

Seven youths were found in an Osaka school yesterday, naked and cold-bodied, their bloodstreams robbed of oxygen by fatal quantities of adrenocilin, a drug used by fledgling novas to control their quantum powers. Less than an hour after the students' bodies were found, 14-year-old Toshiro Shigematsu turned himself in to Osaka authorities. A documented nova for three months, Shigematsu claimed to have persuaded the other children to take his prescription adrenocilin, telling them it would make them novas. When questioned as to his motive for telling the children this, Shigematsu stated that he was a demon sent back from Hell to reap the souls of the innocent.

Bodhisattva Masato has issued a public censure of the event, but when pressed by Japanese media representatives, he claimed that, quote, 'with good must come evil, and the asuras wickedly follow the paths the bodhisattvas tread.' Other members of the Kamisama Buddhist camp have expressed displeasure at the circumstances surrounding the Osaka child-suicide.

Osaka authorities, with corroboration from other Japanese law-enforcement agencies, claim that incidents like this are not isolated, however. In fact, though the island nation claims as much as a nine percent population of Kamisama Buddhists, several known groups draw constant police scrutiny, as officials grow ever wary of terrorist acts performed under the auspices of religious fervor.

Until further events develop, I'm Lotta Voorhies, CNN Netherlands correspondent in Japan.

57

keep reading

N HOME

N!tertainment

N!terview

N! the news

N!sight

N!tre nous

N!ternet

N!tv

fun N! games

help!

awards

legal stuff

search

find!

N contact us

From the Associated Press

Dime Box, Texas — Houston-sponsored nova Graham "Houston Tornado" Herron was found shot repeatedly with heavy-gauge shotguns and high-powered hunting rifles, then stabbed and beaten Monday night just after nine p.m. Dime Box Sheriff Tom Boddard found the body, which was reported to have been marked with various symbols associated with the Church of Michael Archangel. Powder burns marked the weapons as having been discharged at close range.

"There must have been a lot of the Michaelites to take one of these boys down," stated Sheriff Boddard. "We haven't heard of any of their compounds around here, but maybe they came from Austin or Nacogdoches. We rarely see any of that group around here, let alone novas."

A spokesman for the Church of Michael Archangel's Austin compound, Grand Deacon Micah Piper, had much to say on the subject. "We don't like aberrants. I'm not saying we did what happened to Herron or whoever he was, but he obviously met his match in God's chosen." Other members of the Michaelite church shared the sentiment via OpNet and Internet, issuing letters of support to the Austin branch. According to Disciple Stephen Leeds of Montana, "Aberrants don't belong among normal people"; in the words of Virginia Michaelite Suzanne Haslett, "Why should we weep for the passing of the Devil's own?"

Seven-year-old Lucy Corgan issued perhaps the most telling remark: "My papa has a gun that will drop an aberrant dead in his tracks, and so do all his friends."

The weeks to come may be tense, as Graham Herron's DeVries-represented companions Linda Raphael and Elijah Crane have returned to Houston to "rally some novas interested in justice." Grand Deacon Piper claims not to be scared, boldly responding, "The righteous God is with us, you spawn of Satan. We've got enough guns and faith to lay you out just like what happened to your friend."

Church of Michael Archangel

Take Your Planet Back!

As a HUMAN you are a CHILD OF GOD, and you are DESTINED to INHERIT His garden and everything in it. Stay true to GOD'S ONE WAY and your SALVATION is ASSURED.

But SATAN has sent his DEMONS to plague this earth and to tempt the righteous with their TERRIBLE POWERS. Walk not with the aberrant NOVAS, for in the path follows the DEVIL and his EVIL CURSE.

This is the final dawn, the AGE of APOCALYPSE, and the ANTICHRIST has delivered his MINIONS everywhere across the world.

Take your planet back — reveal these aberrants for what they are: TOOLS of DAMNATION!

Welcome to the **Dark Altar**, the online home of Astaroth and his avatars Beltaine, Belial and Grimskull.

Member Name: |

Password:

"The forth angel poured his bowl on the sun, and it was allowed to scorch people with fire; they were scorched by the fierce heat, but they cursed the name of God, who had authority over these plagues, and they did not repent and give him glory."
— Revelation 16:8

Astaroth has spoken, and his word takes precedence of those of the feeble Christian armies lined up for the slaughter. In the name of our lord Astaroth, the world shall be consumed in a firey cloud, burning those who welcome the Word of God or the Immanent. And lo, the world shall end on the Candelmas of 2017, for that is the number of the great Harbinger Belial.

News of Astaroth:

• Thanks to everyone for the donations for Brother Elias's court appeal legal fees. Send money to Brotther Elias (Stanley Welty), #68291-013, MCFP Springfield, PMB 4000, Springfield, MO 65808-4000. DO NOT TALK ABOUT THE CASE OR THE INFANTS. That will just get your letter torn up. You can also email brother Elias at **Error! Reference source not found.**

• The Burning Man Astaroth Reunion drew over 100 (!) Astaroth servants. Click *here* to see some of the pictures and read the Convocation Litany as spoken by the Astaroth himself!

• Legal procedures have been finished! The Dark Altar, under the name Church of Astaroth, is now a legally-recognised, tax exempt Church!

N HOME

N!tertainment

N!terview

N! the news

N!sight

N!tre nous

N!ternet

N!tv

fun N! games

help!

awards

legal stuff

search

[   ]

find !

N contact us

N sight

From "Masks and Marvels" in *Nova Nouveau* Magazine, April 2007

Novas, often perceived as "superheroes" among the less educated ranks of our society, seem to have adopted a few of the comic-book traditions of their fictionalized predecessors. A Mexican innovation formerly sported only by elites, the mask has become fashionable among other novas recently, and may be well on its way toward becoming the hot accessory for novas and wannabes alike. *Nova Nouveau* looked into this burgeoning trend, hoping to gain a bit of insight into the trend. What we found was… *interesting* to say the least.

Why do you wear a mask?

• **Shannen "Shard" Borland:** Um, I thought all novas were supposed to. You know, part of the tradition and all that.

• **Mefistofaleez:** So when I beat your punk white ass, you can't serve me with a summons. *[Ed. Note: In the case of Hogan v. Mefistofaleez (Dec. 2007), the Supreme Court upheld non-novas' rights to bring charges against the personas of known novas, regardless of whether or not those novas were operating in a public or private capacity.]*

• **Jonas "Kikjak" Kincaid:** A mask commands respect. You know you're dealing with a nova when you see the mask — when I yell at an ogling crowd to get the hell out of the way, they all know that I'm about to throw something big over there.

We asked the same question of baselines: Why have some novas taken to wearing masks?

• **Vernon Gosselaar:** Because they're ashamed of the aberrant freaks they've become. Twenty years ago, it was athletes on steroids; now it's this.

• **Billy Li:** Aren't they like uniforms? A nova with a recognized mask is part of the government or Utopia or something.

keep reading

N!tertainment

N!terview

N! the news

N!sight

N!tre nous

N!ternet

N!tv

un N! games

p!

ards

al stuff

search

find!

ontact
s

• **Nha "Lady Ion" Nguyen:** It lets me adopt a different personality. I've actually got two nova personas, one of which has a contract with ViaSoft and the other with IBM. Of course, they were smart enough to put noncompetition clauses in those contracts, so I just made up another "character" to get around that little obstacle. And my lawyer says it's airtight.

• **Sean "Switch" Connell:** It looks cool, and it hides the fact that my eyebrows grow together. I keep a secret, private identity aside from my public, nova identity, so I don't have to deal with all the public-servant bullshit when I'm not "on."

• **Lance "Stone Badass" Stryker:** Masks are for cowards. I don't do nothin' I'm afraid to own up to, and that's a damn fact!

• **Sabrina Vasquez:** They are so beautiful, it would destroy our minds to look upon them without masks.

• **Joaquin Bialik:** It's all part of the franchise. If Captain Eon or whoever looked like John Q. Public, he couldn't sell T-shirts, Halloween costumes, computer games and posters, you know?

Novas-Only Club Draws Fire From Local Scenesters: When entrepreneusse Travius Diaz designed her latest night-spot for the beautiful people, she had a specific group of beautiful people in mind: novas. A strict novas-only policy at the glamourous Amp Room (with one exception made for hostess Diaz herself) ensures that only the superpowerful get in, and the mundane remain without.

"This isn't bigotry," Diaz claims, despite no intimation of the journalist to that effect. "Novas prefer each other's company. That's what led me to my decision for the novas-only club. Recent research into the sociology of novas indicates that their biochemistries cause sympathetic reactions in other novas. They may fight and feud on N!, but on a basic nova level, they really do share a vibe."

Diaz' theory seems to have more than a grain of truth to it, if her cover charges and refreshment prices are any indicator. The price to pass from the street to the door is £60 and the price of a signature "Amp Well" (a drink consisting of fruit juices, coca extract and dubious other ingredients, rumoured to include adrenaline from human glands and ketamine dosages fatal to baselines). On a special night, the club sees as many as 300 nova guests and mixes as many as 2,000 Amp Wells.

Local nightlife veterans are outraged, however. Ranging from the usual cries of prejudice to the more rare legal actions (which Diaz has already employed a full-time solicitor to handle), local patrons want access.

"It's ridiculous not to let us in. Parties make Ibiza what it is, and the professional partiers should be allowed to enter." So says Nero Krauss, a German transient who washed up on Ibiza's beach with 10 quid in his pocket and half an eight-ball of cocaine in his brain. As part of Ibiza's insolvent population of starstruck, unemployed clubgoers-by-trade, Nero's statement echoes through the ranks of the youth.

Diaz has no sympathy. "These Eurotrash drifters, they want to get in, but all they do is upset the clientele. I vacationed in Ibiza 12 years ago, and all the clubgoers snubbed the visiting middle-class continental men, calling them 'lager louts.' Now that the same thing's happening to them, they're up in arms about it."

Don't expect anything to change, either. Among the jet-setting novas who attend the Amp Room — many of whom travel to Ibiza for one or two nights solely to visit the club — are noted Indian movie producer Deepak Palit, American elite Sarge In-Charge, radical Teragen aristocrat Raoul Orzaiz and even high-society celebs like Amanda Wu. According to all of these and more, novas enjoy the policy. "We're very public figures, and this gives us a place to be private," says supermodel Lydia Divine. (Needless to say, the Amp Room bears a constant wreath of paparazzi.)

"I've got 100-plus enormously famous and fabulous personalities to deal with nightly, all of whom require individual attention," claims Diaz. "My policy is no more restrictive than — and just as appropriate to my patrons as — a dress code."

I VIOLATED RULE #1:

Don't do anything stupid.

As a journalist, I had often found myself in curious places, full of curious foods, looking down the barrels of curious guns and running like all hell with curious people on the lam from even more curious people. All for the sake of the story, I jumped headlong into whatever situation I was supposed to be covering. After a few sessions of balls-out, all-hell, batshit lunacy, I decided that sooner or later this reporting thing was going to get me killed. In an effort to even out some of these rough patches of my investigative techniques, I sat down to make a list of rules that would allow me to get the story and preserve my hide.

I never got past rule one. It seemed to sum up everything I needed to avoid.

The problem with such generalities, however, is that they are, by nature, less than universal in application. While I thought to myself then, "Going with these heroin dealers to seal a buy is just the element I need to lend this story on Russian drug traffic some gravity by way of example," I think to myself now, "What kind of dummy leaves his passport in the hotel and hops into a broken-down Eastern European sedan with a cell phone and expects not to be beaten senseless by the undercover cops who invariably show up for this kind of thing?"

In any event, hindsight is 20/20, and there I stood, handcuffed, legs spread wide and with a mouthful of post-Czarist masonry. No small amount of snow had found its way past the collars of my shoes.

"Barg zerg gudania flovosh harma harma woodle berdla," the cop with his nightstick poking the base of my spine growled at me.

"I'm sorry, I don't speak any Russian. *Habla Englais?*" I replied. My erstwhile companions sneered — they spoke English, but they sure weren't going to translate for me.

"Flermovich grim gram boobla steenick."

"You mean to tell me I'm being arrested? What the hell are you saying? Why don't you hounds speak any English? What the hell is the world coming to? Dammit, I want to see my ambassador!" I quit screaming in time to see the Cyrillic thugs with whom I had foolishly aligned myself pointing at me. The officer above me raised his stick, and about seven marginally interesting seconds of my life passed before my eyes in an instant.

And then my phone rang.

No doubt thinking he was intercepting the cruelest of phone calls, perhaps between dealer and client, the Police Hun grabbed the phone from my belt and answered it with a sneer. Expecting him to offer me a wicked smile and begin dashing my brains out with his stick, I sniffled feebly. Instead, however, he coughed out a few words, turned white, looked around with an air of panic, and placed the phone in my jacket pocket. He then undid my manacles and helped me to my feet.

With my freedom returned, I grabbed my phone and praised the gods.

"Who is this?" I mused.

"It's Lester, you fool, now get out of there and go to the airport. *Flare* wants a video-OpNet documentary on 'the world after the novas came' or something." Bless him; Siegfried Lester, my agent, had pulled my fat from the fire.

"You told them that and they let me go?"

"No, I told them you were a Utopia agent under deep cover and that a field team was surveying them. Now get to the airport!"

I only hope that in the future, when *I* ring up a friend and some foreign brute answers the phone, I have the presence of mind to not only speak the language but come up with an impossibly implausible yet compel-

From Flare's "Normal Lives" column by Dr. Duke Rollo

ling story with which to save my acquaintance's life.

Anyway, without further ado, I headed to the airport, catching the next plane to Amsterdam and billing it to my revolving expense account maintained by N!

● ● ●

I stopped at the hotel in Amsterdam just long enough to shower, shave and pick up my media bag from a rapscallion Hindi named Nazir. A Dutch citizen in only the loosest sense of the word, Nazir had relocated from Saudi about 10 minutes after the Middle Eastern "Midnight Sun" event the rogue nova Asif ibn Karim had caused in late 2004. "It's okay," Nazir told me. "I don't miss it." The little fiend had originally established himself in the global nightlife circuit as part of the late 1990s' world music scene, but that had since gone bottom up and Nazir had reinvented himself as a "shaman" of techno music. That term — techno — has always caused a subconscious shudder in those who don't understand it. Perhaps it's ingrained in us; after centuries of making music with "analog" equipment like sitars, drums and flutes, some people just can't relate to music composed with no instruments. Since its creation in the late 1970s, what may generally be called "techno" has evolved to eclipse the more traditional rock and roll of the late 20th century. Past its primitive (yet compelling) beginnings, techno has become the *lingua franca* of music — the "establishment," as it were. Whereas the American "rebel" would pick up a guitar, his European counterpart would instead learn to make music on a computer. Somewhere after Aerosmith's 75th album, the pop music enthusiasts of the world grew bored with tedious power ballads sung by 60-year-old men pining for the "hot sugar" in teenage girls' panties. They turned to electronic music — dubbed techno for ease of reference — which was created by and for energetic young audiences, and which was performed in the greatest quantity (if not quality) in Europe. Vulgar, raw and at once emotionless and furiously passionate, techno ignites the hearts of the dance floor-regular and partygoer alike. It is not that unrealistic, then, to understand how techno has "taken over the world," to use mediaspeak. Music is an escape, and where better than the synthetic drums and electronic Avalons evoked by techno?

To simply say all that, though, denies the basic attitudes of youth and music. Music is for nightclubs and nightclubs are about excess performed to a backdrop of music. This much always rings true, as Nazir showed me at a nightclub called (roughly translated) the Echo's Lick, no matter where in the world one finds himself. Bodies whirled and pogoed like the pistons in an internal combustion engine. Clubcrawlers threw back drink after drink — beer, liquor, enzyme-boosting vegetable elixirs, you name it — and catapulted themselves back and forth across the dance floor. Every pharmaceutical of man's device and then some could be found in the Echo's Lick, often over the counter. (The club had somehow procured a license to prescribe drugs, which, when coupled with the Netherlands' lax controlled-substance laws, made for one hell of a refreshment bar.) Spikeheads bumped into herb-smokers, who crawled past agitated Mitoids who whirled like dervishes through clusters of hallucinogen trippers and common drunks alike. After taking a pair of red bennies for nostalgia's sake (much to my later chagrin), I cut a rug to an old favorite — Wonder Factory's anthemic "Baby Left Me No Kidney" — and demanded Nazir take me somewhere else.

"These cretins are dancing to the same damn 16-beats I've heard since I was born," I spat at him. "Take me somewhere I can hear some *modern* music, you son of a dingo."

In the cab, my head exploded. My bennies, which I had thought were measured in milligrams of potency, were actually measured in centigrams. The "nickels" I took made up more than a "dollar" worth of dosage. After we found enough pieces of my head to rudely fashion a replacement, we moved on to Groove Yard, a bar specializing in terr'r.

Terr'r music (pronounced "tear") grew, I think, out of the 20th century's nihilistic hyper-affected "gothic" (*sic*) genre. From seeds originally sown by urban industrial and goth music, terr'r takes the experience one step beyond. Using special subsonic frequencies, terr'r music stimulates the fear centers of the human (and nova) brain. These subtle sounds "create" fear in listeners.

Of course, any postgoth worth his salt is going to appreciate the irony of this, and while the vast majority of terr'r bands (like the Crypt Roses and Valhallan Reavers) turn out some truly overwrought spooky tunes, cerebral bands like Lacefisher focus on crafting what would be entertaining, amusing pop and la-la songs if they didn't creep the hell out of you whenever you heard them.

As for the bar's patron's, you've seen them all before: alienated teens, alienated young adults and indulgently alienated Older People. Most of them seemed bored by the scene, but Nazir told me that ennui is part of the culture. "They want to be dead. Or vampires," he told me. I didn't get it. In yr. Corresp.'s opinion, for a group so alienated, these scenesters sure seemed to thrill at sniping at each other. If I had a dollar — excuse me, a euro — for every time one of them called another a poser, I'd be arch-duke of the Low Countries.

It is curious to note that the Dutch have severely limited the venues in which terr'r music may be played. Because of the psychological effects it creates, terr'r is forbidden in moving vehicles and in public houses of less than certain size. It makes a sort of vicious sense; terr'r scares normal people, on the level of mortal fright or amphetamine derangement. Sensible individuals flee from fear, though human society seems to have bred headcases who actually thrive on this sort of thing.

After flogging Nazir, I managed to persuade him to show me a novox bar. Out front, we met a woman who claimed to have a gun "with enough power to stop a nova dead in his tracks." It sounded like a good deal to me, and I looked over her wares. Indeed, the gun looked like it would stop a rampaging nova, primarily by exploding the shooter and everything within a few yards of his vicinity. Thanking her and refusing politely, we entered the bar. On our way out, we noted that her car was a flaming wreck and the woman was no-

where to be seen, but I refuse to render any judgment based on my incomplete observation of the situation.

Novox music (pronounced no-VEAU, sort of like nouveau) is defined not so much by its sound as it is by its creator. Performed by novas, novox may sound like literally anything. Most of it takes the form of enormously accelerated rhythm, but some songs involve a manipulation of soundwaves, distortion of the audience's perceptions and the creation of effects previously impossible without the abilities of the performers.

Aficionados of the movement subscribe to some fairly extreme (though they call it "pure") distinctions. A given novox song, if performed by a non-nova, suddenly ceases to be a novox song. Likewise, a nova may choose to perform an "unplugged" version of a novox song, thus making it no longer novox by removing the "super" elements. Exactly what genre this leaves the song in is not exceedingly clear to me, and Nazir offered little insight on the matter, preoccupied as he was with a cute little Dutch girl with blue hair that had sporadic, visible waves of low-wattage electricity running though it.

"Damn it all," I whispered to the aging Marlene Dietrich clone across the table from me, "what's the word I'm looking for to describe this music?"

"Impossible," came the reply, which was wholly accurate. She punctuated her revelation by standing suddenly and flapping toward the bar amid her wintery leather wrap. With that, I looked around the bar and surmised one of the great, baffling and ultimately stupid truths about novox music: It is for genuine individuals. Because it lacks a genre and a definitive *sound*, novox appeals to those who sub-scribe to the cult of personality surrounding various performers, which may be anyone. Legions of unique conformists, the fans of novox are an unsettling breed, even more disturbing than the most morbid terr'r musician.

By following up with my batlike bar-muse, I learned that she had meant it was "impossible" to define novox, but my first impression seems more poetic and appropriate, so I'll continue to support that.

As the evening waned, Nazir and I left the novox bar. "For God's sake, you shirt-stealing Lowland terrorist, hasn't this city got an aggressive side?" I bellowed, cuffing my guide on the ear and pulling the door off a passing taxi to make my point. "What do you mean?" asked Nazir, wrapping his boxed ear with a bandage he liberated from a drunkard slumbering in the gutter. In tandem, we stomped the hobo and rifled his pockets for loose change, which seemed to come only in the form of French francs.

Violence! Pent-up hostility UNLEASHED!

"Misplaced urban disillusionment diverted into aberrant musical social commentary!" I smashed a passing woman's head through a storefront window for added effect. Nazir kicked a dog that had foolishly wandered over to him. "Why, certainly. You want iso."

Of course; iso. The bastard halfbreed of middle-class malaise and ignorance; the godless child of nihilism and social maladjustment; the sound of poor parenting and barely subjugated deviant whims.

Iso is the music of reaction. Left unemployed by technology and shifts in urban corporate influence, many cities' families have been left destitute, scrambling for whatever jobs unskilled assembly-line ratmen can turn up. It's no wonder, then, that their children are such hollow, monstrous brats. Robbed of a chance to grow up normally, these sons and daughters of the shafted proletariat instead mature into bitter, resentful creatures, blaming the rest of the world (or blaming small parts of it with greater vehemence) for taking away their chances. These kids don't want school — they want to be given a fair shake.

Of course, skipping school leaves them with even fewer chances, but don't tell them that or they'll shiv you and take your wallet. (If you don't believe that kind of thing still happens, go read Punch Nardello's *Detroit to Dresden*.)

Undereducated, mean and angry, they turn to celebrity, which they can attain through catastrophic violence broadcast on local news and OpNet newsfaxes or by making undereducated, mean, angry music. Here, for example, are the lyrics to Blood Simple's underground hit, "Too Big World" (lyrics reprinted by ASCAP permission).

Hate

Hate

Hate

You

Aberrant

Spic

Red-dot

Jew

Charming stuff, to be sure. Upon making it to the iso bar, Nazir and I decided it would be safer to just hang out in the parking lot, where we could still hear the music, and drink malt liquor from the package store. Those clubs are every bit as ugly as the music they play, and they're probably none too receptive to an aging doctor of journalism and his not-white contact.

Here we are again, with a brand new smattering of what's chic and what's plain weak. We editors here at *TechStep* take no small amount of effort to eyeball the current and coming trends, and we pick the most promising of them to relate to you, our loving readers. At the same time, we keep our fingers on the pulse of what's on its way out, because God forbid anyone should see you using outdated apps or last year's floor model. You'll thank us, we promise.

Weak: Internet Diehards   **Chic: OpNet Pioneers**

Okay, call us biased, but as the aging US information network degrades beneath billions of daily Ponzi-scheme e-mails and "I Like Karnage Kombat XIV Gold Turbo" websites, the OpNet looks better and better with each new dawn. Faster data transmit times, hardwired fiberoptic routing, infinite POP subscriber capacity and, most important of all, *registered user licenses* (to filter out the dimwits and plebes) make the OpNet the wave of the digital future — which is here and now.

Weak: Clunky Laptops and Palmtops   **Chic: Cellular Voice-Recognition Interface**

Why carry your computer when you can talk to it from any phone? Typing takes too long and suffers the vagaries of low motor skills and sausage-fingers alike. That, and they always scan your laptop's hard drive at the airport, which is pretty invasive, from a personal privacy standpoint. Instead, adopt any of IBM's, ViaSoft's or Apple's vocal interfaces and telecommute at the speed of thought and speech. As long as your computer's OpNet-capable, processing power is only as far away as your pocket or glove box (or wherever you keep your digital phone).

Weak: Bat-Swinging Vigilantes   **Chic: Nova Activism**

Look, the novas are here to stay. Sure, a few of them are selfish bastards who crash local economies or wipe out city blocks, but most of them are fairly normal people underneath it all. Maybe it's a naïve optimism, but here at *TechStep*, we still believe in the fundamental goodness of all people, novas included. Rather than let a few bad apples spoil the bunch, we'd rather see another Fireman than another Bernard Goetz or Percy Andreesen (the New York fall riots of '03, anyone?).

Weak: Internal Combustion   **Chic: Hypercombustion Engine**

Okay, maybe the hypercombustion engine is still a bit sketchy, but we can hope, can't we? A *twenty-five thousand percent* reduction in global pollution from transportation and maintenance vehicles is a good thing and one that we're willing to risk a few isolated cases of brain cancer for.

Weak: Grass-Roots Ecology Invigoration   **Chic: The Zushima Macrobe**

The editors here at *TechStep* are basically lazy people, but firmly devoted to better life through technology. Now that we have garbage-eating "good" bacteria courtesy of the boys and girls at Utopia, let's use it, dammit! The Zushima macrobe degrades waste material and converts it to carbon dioxide (which, granted, is a simplified statement, but even the post-macrobe undigestibles occupy less than one hundredth of their original mass), which our environment is prepared to handle. Doesn't the grass look particularly green today? Now that we no longer have to bury our trash or shuttle it around the oceans in toxic garbage scows, let's all take a brief moment of reverence to throw a discarded McDonald's cup into the street.

Weak: Proprietary OSs   **Chic: ViaSoft One World**

Yeah, you Mac enthusiasts are going to raise a stink, but *come on*. Enough platform warfare — let's get back to computing. Word is the VS wants to have a remote-compatible version of One World (nicknamed Infra, according to our sources in the R&D labs) by early next year, which should be music to your ears if you're running DeskAway 1.03b. Don't get us wrong, Big Blue; we love using the phone, but that awkward keyword interface needs to go — and to have the Mac's floating-point coprocessor on its side.

Weak: Neural Messaging   Chic: Good Ol' Digital Cellular

Perhaps this seems Luddite of us, but does neural messaging offer anything that pocket or wet phones don't do better? Why read a message when we can talk directly to the person who wants our attention? Global long-distance — when you even need it — is cheaper than neural messaging hubs and backup nerve tapes* anyway. Here's a case of the "breakthrough" not living up to the hype. Sorry, PacBell; nice try.

*Yes, we know they're not tapes, but they may as well be. So sue us.

Weak: Prague and New York City   Chic: Addis Ababa

So long, global telecom. Goodbye, Madison Avenue brand doctors. Hello, entertainment, technology and hospitality. Since Utopia's "terraforming" of Ethiopia, hundreds of thousands have been flocking to A-A to take advantage of the city's boom in growth. Corporate and private citizens have made Addis Ababa a hugely important city, rivaling Tokyo and New York for finance, Bombay for entertainment and any of those crumbling old European cities for culture. Provided you like a warm (er, hot) climate and no humidity, you can live like a caliph in Africa, because it's still burgeoning, so rent can be found on the cheap.

Weak: Endangering Species   Chic: Genetically Engineered Fauna

Hey, we leave the office sometimes. We know that humans aren't the only animals that share the earth. We're happy, though, that new sciences and nova-assisted developments have made it easier for us to exist with those animals. The end of the last century saw over 200 individual species on the endangered list. Through cloning technologies, we've brought that down to a mere 12, and "adaptations" of existing animals (such as the Triton-backed "garbage pigeon") give us a more harmonious environment. Engineered cattle, chickens and fish provide more nutritional output per animal and in less time than Mother Nature's way. Even Utopia's Zushima macrobe is vectored by a specially bred rat. It may not be *Bambi*, but it sure beats eating species like popcorn.

Weak: NBC and Infantry Actions   Chic: Nova Elites

While it pains us to think that we can communicate with our friends nine thousand miles away at the speed of light but we're still fighting with each other over skin color and religion, at least there's a better way to do it. Gas? No thanks. Germ-bombs? Forget it. We'll just hire nova elites to do the necessary ass-kicking and watch it all on the *N! Report*. Why risk countless lives when the novas are willing to pound on each other for a few million bucks plus licensing options?

Weak: Polymer   Chic: Eufiber

Polymers are artificial, expensive, unstable and able to transmit less data per millimeter than the alternative. Eufiber, even the synthetic stuff, is biodegradable, cheap, universal and able to transmit enough data at a one-millimeter thickness to grant everyone in the UK access to every subscription-service OpNet porn site in the world at speeds in excess of a gig a second. And it makes a snazzy running suit. No contest.

Weak: Big Five   Chic: N!

For God's sake, people, how many more sitcoms and gritty UN-agent dramas do we need? The answer is none! Maybe we're just geeks (though the Nielsens suggest otherwise....), but we'd rather watch the Stone Badass duke it out with Electric William any day of the week. And ABC, here's a clue: Urkel is 40 years old. *Retire him!*

Few things frustrate customs officers more than smart-mouthed travelers, and, to their credit, that's probably fair. Spending all day behind a desk while supposedly weeding out international terrorists and the like isn't a very rewarding or fulfilling job, considering that most people who pass through their checkpoints are hopelessly boring. This has the unpleasant result of dulling the officials' senses, making them slothful and irritable. Their vigilance turns to ire, as days pass without a single terrorist or dissident upon whom to swarm and pummel, and their only solace is a half-sleep, which smarminess only serves to agitate.

But then, that's my job — to witness reaction and record it.

Needless to say, customs officials rarely have any degree of tolerance for people who state, "To observe the mating rituals of Mite-dealing ghetto barons in your deca-dent city, you tax-fattened hyenas," when all they really want to hear is "business" or "personal" after asking your reason for leaving your own country. I've had more hands inside me than OpNet interactive porn starlets. My bags have been seized and searched more often than I care to count, and I've had to sit in more national police stations — airport branch — than the most deserving of global felons. Indeed, I'm probably more familiar with evading their long-term scrutiny than the people they're there to protect the good people of the world against.

My wife says I bring it upon myself.

United States

Surely, someone exists somewhere in Los Angeles who doesn't want to kill me, sell me drugs or convert me to some bizarre religion, but I haven't met him.

LA vices begin with the high society and trickle down to the most offensive levels of scum ever seen since the two-party system degraded. Why God hasn't stricken this city from the earth for the modern Gomorrah it has become is beyond me. Like France before its 18th-century revolution, Los Angeles' population consists of a few hyper-rich haves and a hellbroth of have-nots. The haves — crumbling relics from the days of Hollywood's prominence — still lead opulent, drug-addled lives, subsisting on money earned before the entertainment shift to Bombay that they had the sense (then) to invest wisely. The have-nots do what they've always done, killing each other in decrepit housing projects as the tide of cretindom sweeps inexorably over a city that

Excerpts from Dr. Duke Rollo's **Why Customs Officials Hate Me — The Wretched World of Contract Journalism**

Courtesy of ViaSoft Press.

You Tax-fattened Hyenas

was once a pinnacle of American — even Western — civilization.

One modern development, particularly among the crime-ridden warrens of the inner city, seems to be a polarization of gang activity. Once renowned as the United States' breeding ground of low-grade organized crime, Los Angeles appears to have undergone a homogeneity with relation to gangland participation. Signs point to the city's ubiquitous clans of black and Hispanic hooligans rallying under a common anarcho-military banner, though precisely who the leader is remains unknown. Of course, rumors of this sort change little on the surface, as the various warring urban tribes and *vatos locos* continue to gut each other over matters of drug distribution and who be sleepin' wit' who else's bitches, but police and media trends indicate a putting aside of these minor rivalries when something greater looms on the horizon. Of course, LA's police force has one of the greatest reputations for brutality in the free world, but such is the price of eternal vigilance. At least, that's what the nova rent-a-cop tells you when he's ratcheting your arm behind your back....

New York has always been the rotten apple, but those deific novas have certainly done their part in excising the worm from the fruited ovary. By making New York the place to be for novas (as it has been since time immemorial for us baselines), the elite superpeople have breathed new life into what would have certainly festered into another LA. American fashion moves through New York, as does any event of any national or international significance. More culturally diverse than perhaps any other city in the world, New York is a nexus of global civilization. Needless to say, this means you can't park anywhere.

Canada

Yeah, yeah, you know how boring and big and cold Canada is. I've heard those statements of dubious comic value as much as the next person. Go ahead, mock Canada and tell us how Canadians all talk funny.

Dismiss Canada offhand, however, and you leave yourself out of what the United States could have done if they'd wanted to become better people instead of bigger, louder, richer people. Canada enjoys an appallingly *low* crime rate, which works if you like to retain ownership of your belongings but can make things difficult if you find yourself at the tail end of a bender. "May I see your ID, sir?" the officer asked. "Slertainly."

Juss lemme fine It.

"Are you intoxicated, sir?"
"That depenz. Whuss the BAC distincshin? I'm probly toxicainted by my mother's stannerds, but who calls the shots round here?"
"Come with me, sir."

Canada: well-adjusted, civil, respectful, clean and quiet. Probably the scariest place on Earth.

Obviously, none of this applies to Quebec. Once again, the French element has raised its hackles in its long-lived history of being a thorn in the rest of the countryside. Again clamoring for secession, radical elements of Quebecois society have even begun printing their own money, which is worth roughly two quick belly laughs, but little more. Stick with the Canadian dollar, and embargo the hell out of Quebec if it finally does secede.

Mexico

For a destitute nation only marginally above the status of the Third World, Mexico sure knows how to celebrate, though most of the festivities stem from religious events. That's no big deal if you're a heathen like yr. Corresp., but devout individuals of any faith had best acclimate or stay home.

Mexico celebrates the most morbid of affairs, including *Dia de los Muertes*, or the "Day of the Dead," which apparently involves massive amounts of drinking, massive amounts of other ingestions and setting things on fire, but my memory may be a bit fragmented from the festivities. Then again, I speak only enough Spanish to order beer and menace the *caballeros* with a sharpened screwdriver, so I'm not very well versed in the custom's greater meaning.

Other celebrations observed in high style include Cinco de Mayo — the fifth of May — which commemorates Mexican victory over a French invasion at Puebla, and the world-wide N-Day in March. At either of these celebrations (or *any* of the lesser Catholic festivals), Mexican citizens participate with reckless abandon. Beware of partaking of the *cerveza* too liberally, however, as the government has a bit to learn about fairness and honesty, and more than one *gringo* has ended up on the wrong side of a wrought-iron grate forever.

All of these celebrations, of course, involve the ubiquitous *mascaras* for which Mexico is duly famous. No, not the stuff the terr'r kidz put on their eyes, but actual full face masks, which the locals wear to party or hold up liquor stores with little discrimination. Once a localized phenomenon, masks spread to the scurrilous elite caste and, in true consumerist fashion, are now being bought worldwide by skinny white boys who want to play soldier for an evening. Mexico City, home of T2M Americas, has turned itself around miraculously in the past 10 years. Once an overpopulated breeding pit of poverty and violence, Mexico City has benefited greatly from the presence and investment of the novas who dwell there. Now one of the cleanest cities in North America, Mexico City also intends to revive the national economy, starting locally. It is another multicultural hub, and all but the most daft of visitors can find someone who speaks their language. In addition, the young economy-on-the-upswing has drawn a fair share of entrepreneurs who, if you can look past their awful suits and omnipresent cell-phone conversations, may turn Mexico City into a metropolis of global import. Perhaps in spite of themselves....

Central America

I can say little about Central America of timely value, as any given government has shifted hands in three coups in the last 15 minutes. Also, I fear to sit at my desk, as the risk of catching one of the 2,500 stray bullets that have made their way into my room. Racked by popular discontent, poisoned by money from the Medellín drug cartels, and home to what seems like every bushwhacker conflict in the Western Hemisphere, Central America is a dangerous place to live and an ignominious place to die. At night, the fighting dies down in some of the cities, sometimes, and the stalwart or stupid can creep into town for delicious food or to strike up a dalliance with some of the most beautiful Latin people on the continent.

Nova Aníbal Buendia makes his home here, as well, in the relatively calm (meaning that only every *other* citizen carries a firearm openly on the streets) Costa Rica. Costa Rica, (un)fortunately, is one of the places God has created naturally occurring wells of rum, so my experience is limited to sandalwood bars that cool the fevered foreigner's flesh. Also, the "Jesus Christ lizard," which earns its name by running across the surface of still waters, may be seen here, but if one has overin-

dulged, one may take the lizard's name too far. Posting bond in a San José jail costs an arm and a leg, given credit-card conversion rates, and you may not take the lizard with you....

The Caribbean

Once a mainstay of the cruise circuit, the Caribbean has become simultaneously more and less a leisure locale. An influx of wealthy novas who have purchased islands for themselves reduces the amount of public lands available for visit. Of course, the other side of the coin is that many novas have developed their private holdings as commercial resorts, catering to the most lofty and basest whims imaginable. For example, Alain Huur's Heaven resort is a literal garden of earthly delights, at which each visitor receives the services of a slave concubine. Um, or so I've heard. By way of contrast, nova Darryl Kingston's Splash resort sees almost exclusively family traffic, offering scuba tours, fishing charters, coral-gathering expeditions and other fare less suited to the drunken, fornicating hordes of modern Sodom.

Politics have become a pressing issue in the Caribbean recently, and more than one dark rumor has circulated about a secret Teragen stronghold among the region's islands. This is the kind of thing one overhears in dimly lit drinking establishments decorated with posters of Che Guevara and trafficking in knives and boats headed off-island, but those muttered misgivings eventually make it to the press, and certainly have some basis in reality. Again, so I've heard.

Cuba, as anyone with an eye for the decadent knows, has become the Sin Capital of the West. After Castro's death and the island's sudden (read: violent) shift to *laissez-faire* capitalism, money took precedence over morals and the once-poor Cubans established the closest thing to a true "free" market anywhere, at least as far as yr. Corresp. has seen. Like the classic movie *Casablanca*, Havana has become a crossroads of infidels, cretins, archfiends, radicals and other on-the-run sorts, who mix their company with Medellín associates and drug-crazed college students alike....

South America

Colombia (with an "O"; you spell it with a "U," you're talking about the capital of the equally godforsaken South Carolina) is perhaps the only country I have visited in which it is not impossible to order an ounce of cocaine from one's restaurant waiter. Sick with the venom of the resurgent Medellín *trafficantes*, Colombia's government remains weak thanks to drug money and a martial law imposed by the criminals who exist ostensibly on the wrong side of it.

Brazil, on the other hand, has taken a cue from former filth-spawning pit Mexico City and embraced the novas' ameliorating ways. Much of the Amazon deforestation of the past 30 years has been reversed in a scant six, as Utopia-contributed genetic-engineering projects have yielded plants and wildlife that grow to maturity in as little as six months. Project Utopia's Environmental Division maintains a strict quota over what may legally be felled or mined in the area.

Sao Paolo and Rio de Janeiro have risen quickly as well, becoming the third and 12th-largest cities in the world, per capita, respectively. Crossroads of ancient culture and modern technology, these cities have been caught between the rival influences of the ubiquitous Medellín cartels and Utopia crusaders, yet have had the will to remain largely independent for now.

Sooner or later, though, something's got to give, and my money's on basic human greed, which may serve Brazil to the cartels readily.

A few rumors have leaked out of the region concerning a species of super-piranha genetically engineered to combat novas. I hear they're called "Jersey Devils," "chupacabras" and "boogeymen." Is there anything the press *won't* print...?

Europe

The bullheaded, traditional English have largely resisted the efforts of Project Utopia (dragging Ireland and Scotland into the mire with them), and it shows. For a nation that started as a crossbreeding of Roman soldiers who didn't want to go home and Celtic barbarians who drank the blood of their dead, the UK is a needlessly stuffy place.

Such rejection of Utopia's aid is most visible in London, the bacteria-infested armpit of the Sceptered Isle. With London's (and accordingly, the rest of the nation's) refusal to support the euro, accompanied by the degrading value of the pound, the United Kingdom seems doomed in the long term. Largely unaided by the advancements offered by Project Utopia, England slips a little more each day. Violence continues to rise in London, and I'm not talking about the good kind, in which members of the now-extinct House of Lords punched each other and soccer hooligans trampled their own kind beneath their feet. Rather, London has set a tone of ethnic hatred and petty crime that the rest of the nation seems to slowly follow down the trail of general seediness.

On the newly (sort of) united continent, much has shifted within the past 10 years. Antwerp, the diamond capital of Europe, has also become the fashion capital of Europe, usurping that title from Paris and Milan. Perhaps the most unaffectedly and sincerely stylish people of Europe, the Belgians have set a cultural tone that the rest of the Continent would do wise to follow. As genial, hospitable people who value their culture and refuse to take sides in political conflict, Belgium is a model of what an economy should be, if a bit goody-goody for yr. Corresp.'s tastes.

Likewise, Amsterdam has practically mirrored Antwerp's development, with the added bonus of having virtually legalized drug rampages, which goes part and parcel with legalizing almost every pharmaceutical on God's green earth. Removing the "getting away with something" aspect of the drug bender does take part of the mystique away, but I believe that to be part of Amsterdam's intent.

Ibiza, off the coast of Spain, has made similar efforts, but has succeeded largely in only the drug liberalism. You're not going to find any culture in Ibiza, unless it's of the model-who-just-came-off-the-runway-on-the-Groenplatz-seeking-a-meth-binge-so-she-can-dance-all-night-and-not-eat-for-three-days variety. Granted, that's not much cultural significance, but I shall throw no stones from my glass house.

Venice, home to T2M Europe's headquarters, continues to sink into the swamp that seems to want to claim Italy physically as the general chaos of the nation wants to claim it metaphorically. Italy continues the tradition of alternating governmental power between psychotic communists and crazed fascists every other week with the end result of not a damn thing. As it has always been, as it ever shall be, unless nova Giancarlo Vocaccio's eye turns more seriously toward political influence in the boot of the Mediterranean.

War, skirmish, hostility and other bad craziness continue to plague the Balkans, which, true to form, have broken into no fewer than seven million independent nations, some no larger than one street surrounded by other sovereign countries. Likewise, the Balkans continue to be a place where an enterprising journalist — or anyone, really, I suppose — can lose the more dubious threads of his past. The nightclubs have gun checks, the beer contains what passes for antifreeze in civilized nations and low-manufacturer-end technology rules the day in lower Eastern Europe.

Russia, the self-devouring serpent, finally seems to have vomited its own tail and turned its eyes on the rest of the world. Supposedly the seat of the shady "Directive," Russia has once again united after years of Balkanization. Under the charismatic leadership of card-carrying lunatic Vladimir Sierka, the Russian Confederation has made advancements that rival other countries' contributions, including discovering the M-R node at roughly the same time as, well, M and R and engineering the first reliable strain of non-seasonal fruit genomes. Not a bad cop for a nation formerly known mainly for fermented potato juice, but the Confederation's role in both Utopia and global politics remains one of itchy munificence. Of course, Sierka doesn't "officially" lead the Russian Confederation, but yr. Corresp. has experienced enough puppet regimes and banana republics to call them as he sees them....

Africa

Speaking of banana republics, half of Africa's under the open influence of nova elites and the other half remains under the control of maniacal dictators who want to be nova elites. Small-scale wars, either remnants of the Equatorial mess or copycat genocide elsewhere, consume valuable resources from the rest of the world, but anyone who can pull a trigger can pretty much write his own paycheck as a mercenary here. A few notable exceptions, like Addis Ababa and most of Egypt, exist as oases in an otherwise tumultuous continent, but for the most part, Africa is a dumping ground for every experimental explosive, lowest-bidder-produced weaponry and black-market commodity in the world. Any sane person should be at once frightened and titillated by this, but the rational among us should settle somewhere back into fear after the initial response wears off.

The most notorious example of the Africa Syndrome is perhaps the state of affairs in Nigeria. Powermad dictator-thug Alafin Sango, hated by some African factions (particularly Nigeria's neighbors), beloved by many more, put one over on the

Utopians by accepting military and developmental aid and then backing out of the deal. Seems for all their brain trust with the quadruple-digit IQs, the Project couldn't cope with basic baseline no-frills scumbag cheatery. Refreshing, really. Anyhow, Lagos resembles a prewar Berlin of 1935, and bubbles under the surface with weak but fervent internal dissidents and apprehensive neighbors. Unlike some of the region's leaders, Sango is not a nova, and relies on sheer caginess to run his operation. Rumors of Teragen affiliation abound, however, and how exactly Sango has managed to avoid crushing Utopia retaliation is unknown.

Addis Ababa, on the other hand, has become an earthly paradise. As the home of T2M Africa-Mideast, A-A rose from the ashes of the desert like a phoenix as a result of nova terraforming efforts that yielded even more arable land than that surrounding Mexico City. Of course, once you get inside Addis Ababa, all of the glitz, glamour and goodness seems just a bit *too* structured. Is this the result of all Utopia management? Does a "for your own good" ethic pervade the Utopian MO just below the surface? I don't know, but if

Addis Ababa is a model, perhaps I'll settle for a bit of shepherding. It makes you appreciate breaking the rules all the more....

Asia

As fragmented as it has been all throughout history, Asia remains the ultimate place to become lost, both accidentally and electively. The region claims almost as many religions as it does citizens, and any relationship one manages to forge in one country may become null and void in the country 100 yards away.

In the Middle East, for example, religious conservatism yields a grim outlook regarding novas, which reflects in the quality of life established there. As nominal-at-best participants in Project Utopia, the Middle East is split down the middle by a growing faction of moderate Sunnis who regard novas as Allah's chosen. Low-profile military skirmishes involve almost as many nova freebooters as the Central American conflicts, as the strife over matters religious drives neighbors to take up arms. Give peace a chance, though: Long-suffering Palestine has established a national

identity for itself under the guidance of Utopia intervention. Historical archnemesis Israel is, of course, only polite about this for the cameras. Film at 11, undoubtedly, again....

Bombay has become a global entertainment center, taking over the role of schlock- and arthouse film and television producer to the world. Many novas have flocked to the city and taken an active hand in the entertainment industry. Films and television shows featuring nova actors have seen a marked boom in popularity, which has drawn a good deal of advertising and production revenue into the city, making it a new Babylon.

The endless conflict in Kashmir has actually had some positive effect, as ever-swingin' Karachi, Pakistan, has evolved into an industrial power in the region. Enormously populous, Karachi has become the Detroit of the Middle East, but has yet to become as much of a fetid den of violence and decrepitude as its Western cousin. Give it a couple of years.

China, ever the troublemaker, maintains a governmentally mandated distrust of the nova situation, meaning that they abstain from most of Utopia's efforts. Chinese novas either find themselves acquired by the People's Liberation Army (which is, of course, one of the world's largest corporate enterprises), or else they flee to Hong Kong. Hong Kong, of course, has become a super-capitalist den of money-grubbing swine. After it reverted back to Chinese control in the late 1990s, it retained a strong sense of itself, and breaking those old habits engendered by the British Empire was too much for the city to take. Amanda Wu and her nova-employing Novelty consulting firm keeps a steady influx of money into the city, which is truly remarkable: In one of the largest, most business-oriented cities in the world, for a sole company to wield over one percent of the city's private resources is unheard of, and here it has been done. Desire to maintain its affluence also keeps Hong Kong on the fast-and-loose side of trade policy, and literally *anything* can be purchased amid the fabled "midnight markets" or behind closed doors in the highest corporate towers.

For true innovations, however, one must trade in Japan. Following the nation's Saisho revolution, Japan shifted into technological high gear. As they regard Utopia's guidelines on technological development with lip service at best, Japanese manufacturers have rocketed ahead of the industry curve by 20 years or more. In their private lives, however, they still hold a soft spot in their hearts for those little sailor suits the girls wear to school. Bizarre personal penchants notwithstanding, Japanese big business has a curious, shadowy relationship with the nation's Yakuza. Governmental interdict on certain technology — imposed by Utopia pressure, of course — forbids open sale of key items. The criminal organizations, by dint of their lawlessness, elect not to heed these restrictions and move the product for big profit. Part of that profit obviously returns to the manufacturer, who then uses it to pay his taxes and scrub the other money that comes in via various other illicit venues. Obviously, not all Japanese commerce is illegal, but the acceptance of the criminal in the relationship between business and government makes for questionable ethics. Didn't you always suspect as much? The government only differs from the criminals in that they tell you it's okay. At least when you deal with criminals, you *know* you're bad....

Australia/The Pacific

Perpetually part of its self-maintained "Outback," Australia is a national and cultural backwater. It always has been, and it always will be. This isn't necessarily a bad thing (see the efforts of fellow journalist Mim Udovitch in her column for *Forbes*), as sometimes the world just seems too small. Maybe one requires the relative rusticism of eating beetles and drinking beer with no additives to regain a sense of his place in the cosmos.

Nevertheless, the creeping tentacle of technology has not left Talaud Island untouched. Here, Utopia maintains T2M Asia, as well as a facility designed to study the viability of alternative food sources, such as kelp, plankton and lesser fish. All those OpNet rumors about the *enormous* blip on the Talaud facility's sonar have been officially denied by both Japanese and Australian governments, as well as Utopia/Talaud staff. This of course means that either nothing actually happened at all, or something we should fear with all our beings showed its head then promptly vanished. The best way to psyche oneself up to a good, Neptunian dread, of course, is an open-tabbed trip to the nearest pub or tankard.

TOP SECRET

Excerpt from encoded message; dated May 11, 2008

Look, the first thing you need to know is that it's absolutely vital you don't let anyone catch you reading this. I went to a lot of trouble to micronize this print to where it'd be all but invisible to anyone but someone with your powers. Please, if you value my life, don't let on that you got this message. It's that important.

You know how we kept getting that gut feeling that something was going on, something that they wouldn't show us? We were right. I saw it.

It was that espionage mission I took last week; I did a lot better than I thought I would. I wound up tracing back one of the Novelty middlemen through about six miles of false trails, back to the jackpot. He had "orders to cooperate" with at least three elites, including Pursuer. So I started hopping along his contact trails to find out who was paying these three, and why. I almost wish I hadn't.

There isn't space to go into all the details here without making this message look bigger than a pixel. The short of it is — Rourke, Utopia was paying these guys off. Not directly, of course. But I recognized some of the names at the end of the paper trail, and they work in the offices down the hall. These people were authorizing lacing adrenocilin with chemicals that I know are sterility-inducing, in doses that could only be tailored for people like us. There was a coded message concerning the Bahrain facility: something about "detention and treatment" and "Mazarin-Rashoud disorder." There were funds going to pro-Kashmir groups, the groups they send us over there to check. It was like watching a conspiracy-theory movie at three in the morning, only it's all real. Every bit.

Come and talk to me. You wouldn't have gotten this message if I didn't think you would care. But I know you do. We have to figure out what to do.

Jennifer

ND YA THINK THIS IS SOME KIND OF FUCKIN' GLOBAL CONSPIRACY? COME ON, JENNIE, THAT SHITE WENT OUT 10, 15 YEARS AGO.

CORBIN, WON'T YOU LISTEN TO ME? THEY'RE USING US! AEON, UTOPIA, THE WHOLE PROJECT IS RIGGED TO KEEP US IN LINE FOR SOMETHING!

FER CHRIST'S SAKE, JEN, LISTEN TO YERSELF. LISTEN TO WHAT YE JUST SAID. "THEY'RE USING US." "THEY" HAVE SOME SORT OF SUPER-SECRET EVIL AGENDA AND WE'RE JUST PAWNS IN THE GAME; IS THAT IT? YE KNOW WHAT? YE'RE LOSING IT. THEY HAVE NAE LOVE FER ME THERE ANYMORE, BUT EVEN SAE I'M GOING TO CALL THAT OLD BASTARD BLASHILL AND DEMAND HE PUT YE THROUGH PSYCH EVAL. THE STRESS IS GETTING TO YE.

HAT DO YOU MEAN, "SEEN TOO MUCH"? JEN, YE'RE NOT MAKING ANY FUCKIN' SENSE. YE'RENAE GIVIN' ME THE FULL ORY, HERE. I MEAN, YE'RE ASKIN' ME TO WALLOW A PRETTY BIG PILL WITH ALL S, BUT YOU NAE WANT TO GIVE ME THE ETAILS? I CAN'T GO ALONG WITH THIS.

I'M NOT KIDDING, HERE, CORB. AND THIS ISN'T ABOUT SOME KIND OF TV OR OPNET ENTERTAINMENT THING. YOU KNOW ME — I'M NOT SOME WHACKED-OUT CONSPIRACY NUT. I'VE JUST SEEN TOO MUCH TO LET THIS GO BY UNNOTICED.

, YOU'RE NOT, ORB. YOU'RE G TO HEAR ME WHAT'S YOUR ERM COUNT?

BUT IT'S LOW, RIGHT? TELL ME I'M WRONG. TELL ME I'M OUT OF MY MIND ON THIS.

ALL RIGHT, JENNIE. YE'RE CERTIFIABLY OFF THE DEEP END.

FUCK, JENNIE, I DINNAE. MOST MEN DON'T, I'D HASTEN TA POINT OUT.

WHAT'S YOUR SPERM COUNT?

MY LAST PHYSICAL DID HAVE IT BELOW NORMAL, YEAH. NOW, I DON'T KNOW. WHERE'RE YOU HEADED WITH THIS?

AND SHOULDN'T IT HAVE BEEN AT NORMAL, IF NOT ABOVE? I MEAN, DON'T OUR NOVA BODIES OPTIMIZE THAT SORT OF THING?

OKAY, SO WHAT'S YER POINT?

CONTRACEPTION, CORB. THEY'RE PUTTING RACEPTIVES IN OUR FOOD OR ADRENOCILIN OMETHING. JESUS, I COULD TELL YOU THE EXACT HOUR MY PERIOD STARTS.

JH. AND WHY?

SO, BASED ON MY LOW SPERM COUNT — LET ME GET THIS STRAIGHT, JEN — THE PROJECT'S ON SOME KIND OF MIND-CONTROL CAMPAIGN. WAIT — WAIT! ARGH! THEY'RE IN MY HEAD! I'VE BEEN HIT WITH A SHITTIN' ORBITAL BRAIN-WARP LASER! HELP ME, JEN!

MIT, CORB, I DON'T KNOW WHY. IF I ALL THE ANSWERS, I WOULDN'T BE AKING AROUND LIKE THIS. I COULD UST COME FORWARD WITH IT.

SCREW YOU, CORB. NOW YOU'RE JUST BEING A JERK. AND I THOUGHT, DEEP DOWN, I COULD GO TO YOU.

LOOK, HOW LONG HAS THIS KASHMIR THING GONE ON? YEARS, RIGHT? AND THE NOVA BODY COUNT KEEPS GROWING. WHY? JESUS, KASHMIR IS JUST A PISSANT LITTLE STRETCH OF DESERT IN THE MIDDLE EAST. I MEAN, COME ON — IT'S BETWEEN CHINA AND INDIA, FOR GOD'S SAKE — YEAH, THEY'RE A LOT OF PEOPLE THERE, BUT IT'S NOT EXACTLY PRIME TERRITORY. AND UTOPIA KEEPS SENDING US OVER THERE, IN THE INTERESTS OF "MAIN-TAINING PEACE."

M PROJECT UTOPIA CURITY ARCHIVES, ATED MAY 2008

THEY'RE KEEPING THIS THING GOING, CORB. UTOPIA'S MAKING SURE WE KILL EACH OTHER OVER THERE. SAME WITH THAT THING OUTSIDE MEXICO CITY. I COULD'VE HANDLED THAT ALONE, BUT THEY SENT SCHUYLER ALONG WITH ME, AND — LO AND BEHOLD — THOSE ROGUE FEDERALES HAD A NOVA WORKING FOR THEM. EIGHT DAMN DISSATISFIED GOVERNMENT COPS? WHERE'D THEY GET THE MONEY TO HIRE A NOVA?

LOOK, JEN, I'M JUST SAYIN—

NO, YOU LOOK, ANDRE. NOVAS ARE LITERALLY ONE IN A MILLION, MAYBE SIX OR EIGHT THOUSAND WORLDWIDE, EVEN IF THE CURVE IS INCREASING. THEY'RE SYSTEMATICALLY KILLING US OFF, AND THEY'RE GETTING US TO DO IT SO IT DOESN'T LOOK LIKE ANYTHING'S UP. IT'S ALL FOR N! OR FOR PUBLICITY, OR WHATEVER OTHER SCREEN THEY THROW UP AGAINST US.

CHRIST, THE LIST OF EVENTS GOES ON AND ON — MENCKEN DISAPPEARED TWO WEEKS AFTER MIDNIGHT SUN, WEI LOST IN THE SUBMARINE INCIDENT, BHAKRA DEAD IN THE ADDIS ABABA TERRAFORMING UPKEEP.

TERRAFORMING, CORBIN! KILLED WHILE FARMING!

OKAY, THAT'S A LOT O' DEAD IN A SHORT TIME, BUT I'LL NAE GO OFF HALF-COCKED, FOR A CHANGE. ACCIDENTS HAPPEN, JENNIE, PEOPLE GET HURT. IT CAN'T BE A GENOCIDE THING, BECAUSE THEY'VE GOT TOO MUCH MONEY INVESTED IN US. UTOPIA'S OPERATIN' COSTS ARE BLEEDIN' ENORMOUS—

THEY'VE GOT TO BE, JUST TO KEEP US ENGAGED WITH EACH OTHER AND DIVORCE THEM-SELVES FROM ANY IMPLICATIONS—

JEN, SHUT UP A MINUTE, WILL YE? SERIOUSLY, THIS IS SO FAR-FETCHED, THE ONLY THING THAT EVEN MAKES ME BELIEVE IN THE SMALLEST PART OF IT IS THAT IT'S SO BIZARRE THAT THE PIECES SEEM TO FALL INTO PLACE WHEN YE LOOK AT THEM FROM YER DISTORTED ANGLE.

CORB, WHAT MORE DO YOU NEED? LOOK AT IT IN CONTEXT—

SLIDER, THE ONLY REASON I'M GIVING THIS HALF AN EAR IS BECAUSE I TRUST YE AND I KNOW YE'RE NOT AN IDIOT. BEFORE YE GO TO ANYONE ELSE WITH THIS, LET'S TAKE THE TIME TO DO A LITTLE MORE HOMEWORK. I'LL TALK TO EARL ABOUT IT, AND YOU TRY TO GET A FEW OF THE LOOSE THREADS TIED TO SOMETHING.

DID YOU TALK TO PAX OR ANY OF THE OTHER 2MORROW WANKERS ABOUT THIS?

NOT YET.

WELL, DON'T. LET'S LOOK MORE INTO IT BEFORE WE START SOWIN' THE SEEDS OF DISCONTENT. LAST THING I NEED'S MORE FLAK FROM THE MUCKETYMUCKS.

NO, CORB! DON'T TALK TO ANYONE — NOT A SOUL! WE DON'T KNOW IF THEY — DON'T YOU SEE?

WELL, I S SOMETHI SLIDER, BUT KNOW IF IT'S OR JUST S AND BLEE MIRRORS A YET.

55555

5555er55er5

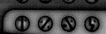

ABERRANT

TOP SECRET

From Project Proteus Audio Files, Delivered to an Operative in Second Week of May, 2008

Clearance Beta.

All field agents' priority.

Concerning nova Jennifer Landers, a.k.a. "Slider."

Nova Slider poses a threat to Utopia and Proteus longevity.

Field observations indicate Slider has made contact with no fewer than 16 novas and no more than 19 novas in a sympathy bid against the objectives of Projects Proteus and Utopia. Known sympathizers include novas Corbin, Meztiszo, Holm, Greer, Yannik, Cherpa and Fong.

Proteus secrecy has not been compromised, but it is of paramount importance to maintain such.

All sympathetic and suspected-sympathetic novas have been assigned to monitored areas for evaluation and damage control. Agents of Proteus are encouraged to assess proximate novas' performance and attitudes, and make necessary adjustments.

Nova Rousseau has not been associated with this group of anti-Utopia novas to date, though records have been incomplete. She's a canny bitch, though, so keep an eye on them and be prepared.

Jennifer Landers, a.k.a. "Slider," presents liability to Projects Utopia and Proteus to such a degree that her continued performance exists more as threat than mere agitation. Act per Code Omega directives, under normal Proteus visibility guidelines.

A Handwritten Note From Slider to Corbin

C—

Forgive me for the Bombay cliché, but they're on to me.

I went to five different people — big mistake — with the story, and they're either part of the cover-up (maybe out of ignorance) or hostile. Obviously, the guy I talked to as my Utopia liaison (Albert Petalan) is part of it, but so are the Calcutta police, the AP reporter and my representative with Amanda Wu's company. I don't know about Rourke anymore.

The bottom line is, we can't go to anyone. Get everyone together and let them know the scale of this thing, but keep it hush-hush. Obviously, if you're not part of Utopia's "solution," you're part of the problem. And Utopia's got almost everyone involved as part of the solution on some level.

Anyway, gotta run. I've left my "resignation" from Utopia here in C. We'll talk later.

Be careful,

S—

P.S. Heard of something called "Proteus"? Let me know.

MEMO

AP Wire Dated Wednesday, May 14, 2008

Calcutta, India — Team Tomorrow nova Jennifer "Slider" Landers, under temporary contract to Novelty Consultation, was reported DOA at UN Franklin Moran field hospital this morning at precisely 4:02 am. Paraphysicians worked tirelessly for eight hours to reinvigorate Slider's failed biological processes, only to declare her dead after unsuccessful attempts.

Slider had been retained by Novelty Consultation to safeguard against Teragen corporate espionage, and agents of that organization are suspected to have some relation to her death.

Details are few and far-between in this event, but the act seems to be one of assassination, possibly linked to Teragen radicalism. Slider's injuries appear to have been caused in conflict with another nova, though no more information is forthcoming at this time.

N! and CNN Televised Live Broadcast from Slider's Funeral and Wake

[BROADCAST JOINED IN MEDIA RES]
...GIVES ME GREAT SADNESS, AS NOVAS AND BASELINES ALIKE HAVE LOST A STRONG HERO NEEDLESSLY.

JENNIFER WAS A CREDIT TO THE CAUSE, BOTH AS A NOVA AND AS AN INDIVIDUAL, AND HER PASSING SHALL LEAVE OUR EARTH A SADDER PLACE FOR A BRIEF TIME, ALTHOUGH I KNOW SHE WOULD WANT US TO MOVE PAST THIS TRAGIC EVENT, HOPEFULLY FINDING IT WITHIN OURSELVES TO—

DAMMIT, SHUKI, WHERE'D HE GO? SARAH, PUT SOMEONE ON IT — THIS IS LIVE, FOR GOD'S SAKE. JESUS CHRIST, SOMEONE GET IN FRONT OF THE CAMERA. SWITCH TO THREE ON THREE, TWO, ONE....

ER, THIS IS N! CORRESPONDENT SANJI RAMANATHAN REPORTING LIVE FROM CALCUTTA, WHEN ONLY MOMENTS AGO, CONTROVERSIAL EX-TEAM TOMORROW MEMBER ANDRÉ CORBIN FLED THE PREMISES, BREAKING OFF HIS EULOGY FOR JENNIFER LANDERS IN MIDSENTENCE.

DETAILS ARE UTTERLY ABSENT AT THIS TIME, AND I'M PROBABLY GOING TO GET FIRED, BUT, UM, THAT'S HOW THIS BUSINESS WORKS. SARAH, I QUIT.

M E M O

5/31/2008

Director Ozaki:

I'm sure I don't have to tell you that we have a problem. However, what you need to know is that you've just been designated a troubleshooter. The information leak on classified material extended beyond Landers and her immediate circle of friends; although our plants on the team were able to minimize the damage control among Team Tomorrow members, she somehow managed to transmit some of her lies to other Utopians, who have subsequently gone rogue. In all likelihood, Park was the one responsible for their evacuation; naturally, he is among the missing. At least 10 have fled [files for each are attached]; although we're waiting for confirmation from all cells, we believe that number could rise to 15 or 20, all told.

The good news in this situation, of course, is that the renegades have very few options at this point. Landers' findings were rather too comprehensive, and we suspect that Landers put a somewhat histrionic, possibly Teragen-inspired, spin on the data, but that may work in our favor. The renegades can be presumed to be aware that Proteus has contacts among global authorities, and they have little reason to trust any particular agency there. Similarly, although our tense relations with the United States government might seem more promising to them, they would have to be fools to try that route openly. The Teragen, though quite possibly behind this whole Landers situation, is hardly an option; these renegades are theoretically smart enough to realize that they can't count on that nest of vipers. And although some media backlash is certainly inevitable, we are already instituting controls to make certain that the damage is minimal. T2M is already being withdrawn, and we won't be making any press conferences until we're certain we know exactly what needs to be said.

Your role in all this is appropriately simple. You are to use whatever resources you can covertly mobilize to track down the rogue novas, silence them however possible, and leave counter-evidence to draw attention away from Utopia. We would of course prefer that you reason with them, convince them of Landers' clearly compromised status, and bring them harmoniously back into the fold; if that option fails, however, you are free to escalate damage control options as you see fit. We cannot afford to be exposed in this; subtlety is of paramount importance here, so don't let any of your agents get too enthusiastic. Especially not Chiraben.

Whatever else, be certain that Mercer doesn't find out about this. He has enough to worry about already, and the world needs him focused on his tasks. It's much better for all of us if he, like the rest of the world, believes these renegades to be just a fringe group of conspiracy theorists.

Director Thetis

F Y I

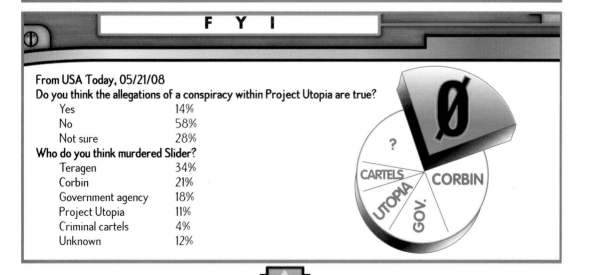

From USA Today, 05/21/08

Do you think the allegations of a conspiracy within Project Utopia are true?

Yes	14%
No	58%
Not sure	28%

Who do you think murdered Slider?

Teragen	34%
Corbin	21%
Government agency	18%
Project Utopia	11%
Criminal cartels	4%
Unknown	12%

T O P   S E C R E T

Excerpt, phone conversation between public terminals, May 30, 2008
Voice 1 [male, estimated age 25]: **Hello?**
Voice 2 [female, indeterminate age]: **Thank you for picking up.**
Voice 1: **Look, who is this?**
Voice 2: **Someone who's well aware of who you are and what you're running from.**
Voice 1: **I dinnae have time for games.**
Voice 2: **Can you guarantee that this phone line is completely secure? Can you guarantee that it'll remain so?**
Voice 1: **...**
Voice 2: **I thought not. Listen to me. I can offer you and your friends shelter. I have resources enough to keep you hidden — but I also have resources enough to back you on a more aggressive course of action, one that stands to help you correct some of your current problems.**
Voice 1: **Can ye prove this isn't a trap?**
Voice 2: **You have a telepath among your number, yes? He will be the proof. Now hang up and start walking south. I'll call you again in five minutes.**
[Transmission ends.]

T O P   S E C R E T

From a Telecom Virus Message Distributed by Sophia Rousseau, Directed Toward Friends and Acquaintances

Greetings, friends. Please listen fully to this message and pass it on via forwarding to someone close to you.

Utopia clearly wants novas under its thumb. Looking at recently discovered evidence (the obtaining of which I relate below), I am forced to conclude that elements within Utopia seek to subjugate or regulate, possibly even systematically eliminate, novas as a whole. How many of us have died in meaningless skirmishes? How many have accepted a corporate-, city- or Utopia-sponsored lifestyle, trading ourselves for money? As we are not the enemies of humankind, nor are we its servants.

The recent death of Jennifer "Slider" Landers is a pivotal point in nova history. Her close associate, André Corbin, has assembled a collection of her notes on the matter, and the aggregate compilation, especially in light of her mysterious death, pleads a very strong case.

However, we need more than a strong case. Utopia has insinuated itself in every aspect of normal life. We have no government to which to turn, nor any police force. At the same time, we cannot become terrorists for fear of losing sympathy for our cause. As well, Utopia has become so entrenched in the geopolitical structure that to overturn public confidence in it could lead to catastrophic panic worldwide. Nor, frankly, do we know a great deal regarding the extent of the conspiracy in Utopia, whether the entire Project has been compromised or only a select cabal within its administration.

Nonetheless, we cannot remain passive against a clear and present threat. Novas interested in defending their rights as individuals are encouraged to gather on June 1 of 2008 at the Amp Room, where a private room has been secured. Matters critical to the future of our role in Earth's history shall be discussed, and your participation is vital to our success.

Thank you for your time.

A Page from Slider's Notes, Presented Before the Assembled Aberrants

Contraceptive compounds mixed into food/adrenocilin (maintains impotency of novas so no more can be born)?
Utopia registration allows constant checkup on status of individual novas (privacy?)?
Nova influence in global governments establishes "watcher" network?
Proteus?
Skirmish — levels of violence to kill off novas/control nova population?
Television ratings peak with internova violence — broadcast "Death of Titan Palmyra" highest rating recorded in history.
Mandatory sterilizations/applications for childhood in high population density cities
Galatea?

N HOME

N!tertainment

N!terview

N! the news

N!sight

N!tre nous

N!ternet

N!tv

un N! games

p!

ards

al stuff

search

find!

ontact
s

the news

HUDDLESTON

From OpNews Live, 11/09/07

…In other news, General Thomas Eddicott was interred today in Arlington National Cemetery with full honors. A long line of Washington's dignitaries turned out to pay their final respects, including Captain Donald R. Baldwin, popularly known as "The Shooter." He is survived by his wife, three children and four grandchildren.

[SCENE: Captain Baldwin's eulogy. On saying Goodbye, Baldwin looks skyward and salutes.]

• **Baldwin:** "No finer soldier ever drew breath than General Thomas Dwayne Eddicott. I had the honor of serving under him for 15 years, and in that I count myself fortunate. I know many of us are gathered here today to mourn the soldier and patriot who always served his country with pride. However, many more of us — including myself — are here to mourn the man who loved his family and his country. He was a good man, first and foremost. And as he looks down from Heaven on us here today, I just want to say: 'Thank you, General…' — and thank you, Thomas. We'll miss you."

83

T O P   S E C R E T

From a Department of Defense memo, classified Deep Black; 08/20/06

Dr. Fielding:

General Endicott is very insistent that Project: Cornucopia be brought up to operating status within schedule. The American military is already over-reliant on nova personnel — we need these exoskeletons up and running, Utopian scientific sanctions be damned. Perfecting the power grids is your only concern — we'll handle the security. General Endicott has told me to reassure you that he is privy to information that will keep the Utopians off our backs, even if they should uncover our research. We can be certain that they won't want to take this to a public arena.

Cpt. Charles Moring

T O P   S E C R E T

Communiqué double-encrypted with Navajo Daedalus 3; dated 6/03/08

I'll presume everything is going well on your end, Director. Nonetheless, my best wishes.

Dr. Enrikssen is showing some signs of restlessness, as I'd projected; all that intellect can hardly be finding sufficient challenge in engineering and architecture. His ability to process and design seems to be speeding up, at least when he's not being currently faced with a direct problem to solve; he's progressed to completing roughly three designs per hour, complete with architectural sketches. He's currently delegating the computer-ized reproductions to assistants — apparently there isn't enough stimulus to finishing a 3-D model of a design that he's already mentally completed.

I'm thinking of testing the new games of chance from Hattori's pet projects on the doctor. With any luck, the advanced probability configurations, when set to cycle through shifting odds in a non-repeating series of patterns, will provide enough stimulation to occupy his mind during non-peak hours. Psych tells me that he has just enough of a gambling bug to take interest, with a minimal chance of overattachment.

In the meantime, all seems to be going quite well with Cocharin. She's continuing to adjust well to life in Engineering, and the department heads worked out a schedule that allows her to use her matter-transmutation abilities on a regular basis without any real quantum-bleeding or signs of stress. I've managed to bond fairly closely to her, and from what she's sharing, she seems to be taking the whole "Slider" incident as she should. There aren't any apparent signs of her having been part of Slider's network, and she's in fact expressed worry as to what the "rogues" might indeed try. I intend to be at confidant-level status within two weeks; she seems glad of the regular non-nova company, as it seems to break down any self-imposed feelings of "being differ-ent."

Advise further as you see fit, of course.
Ruiz

PROJECT PROTEUS

TOP SECRET

Communiqué double-encrypted with Navajo Daedalus 3; dated 6/05/08

Nyeung:

Good job on your recent efforts. Your next bit of business is to prep Ishida and Fashoud and have them ready to support T2MAs in the closing of the Sop Moei plant; they'll be wetworking among the local government and military in order to make certain that the closedown is permanent. A full dossier of their role is enclosed. Business as usual for T2MCe, Eu and Am.

Also, I want an updated full report on the Aeon board — they've taken a few steps I hadn't expected, and I very much dislike surprises. Use a second-tier agent; I want a purer information feed to minimize the chance of discrepancies.

Director Thetis

TOP SECRET

Unmarked communiqué, dated 06/09/08

Chiraben:

I would very politely like to remind you to keep in fucking line. We are not an organization of sadists and bullies. We are not in this for kicks. We have been entrusted with the task of doing what needs to be done in order to better the whole goddamn planet. If that means somebody dies now and again, that's what it means. Our operating principles are here in order to prevent us from paralyzing ourselves with every last ethical question; they were instituted by necessity so that we can achieve actual, regular progress on the betterment of human society as a whole. They do *not* give you *carte blanche* to do whatever the hell you like to somebody that has been designated a liability. We are Project Proteus. We are the oil that keeps the gears turning. We are the screen that keeps the baselines from outright panic. And we are the only thing standing between the status quo and war or genocide, between the rest of the world and lunatics like Mal or those other THINGS. In other words, Chiraben, we do *not* fuck around.

You work alone not because we want you to do whatever the hell you want. You work alone because that is the way we do things. If word comes to me again of you misusing your power to get your own sadistic kicks, then I swear to God that you will be the next designated liability. And don't even fucking think of trying to blow our cover to save your own skin. That didn't save Slider — who was one of the sweetest girls I've ever known — and it by God will not save you. I know where you live, and I know where you sleep. Don't even think of doing a damn thing that might possibly compromise us ever again, or what you did to your last "assignment" will look like a picnic with your grandmother compared to what we will do to you.

Ozaki

THE TERAGEN

From WSSB Eleven o'Clock News, dated 06/08/07

· **MONICA GASPAR:** OUR TOP STORY TONIGHT: TAMPA'S MAYOR FREDERICK RUPERT WAS MURDERED TODAY, IN A BRUTAL RESPONSE TO HIS CONTROVERSIAL ANTI-NOVA SPEECHES AND PROPOSED LEGISLATION. THE TERAGEN MEMBER KNOWN AS "GERYON" APPEARED AT THE MAYOR'S OFFICES AT 2:10 PM, AND FORCED HIS WAY THROUGH THE BUILDING'S SECURITY UNTIL HE REACHED MAYOR RUPERT.

THE ROGUE NOVA SNAPPED RUPERT'S NECK WITH ONE HAND, AND PROMPTLY LEFT THE WAY HE CAME. TWELVE SECURITY GUARDS AND POLICE-MEN WERE SLAIN TRYING TO APPREHEND GERYON, AND 25 MORE — BOTH POLICE AND CIVILIANS — WERE ADMITTED TO ST. JOSEPH'S HOSPITAL WITH VARYING DEGREES OF INJURY.

COUNT RAOUL ORZAIZ, LONG NOTED AS THE MOST PUBLICLY OUTSPOKEN ADVOCATE OF THE TERAGEN'S BELIEFS, OFFERED SYMPATHY FOR THE VICTIMS' FAMILIES, BUT REFUSED TO APOLOGIZE FOR HIS COLLEAGUE'S ACTIONS.

· **ORZAIZ:** REALLY, IT IS UNFORTUNATE THAT THIS INCIDENT HAD TO HAPPEN AT ALL — BUT IN ALL FAIRNESS, WHAT CAN YOU EXPECT? YOU CANNOT LET A RABID DOG RUN LOOSE IN YOUR NEIGHBORHOOD. THIS PERSON WAS NO LESS RABID, AND MIGHT WELL HAVE BITTEN SOMEONE RATHER MORE USEFUL THAN HIMSELF. GERYON'S METHODS ARE BRUTISH, BUT HE DID NOT ACT IN THE WRONG. RUPERT SHOULD HAVE REALIZED THAT HIS SENTIMENTS ARE MOST INAPPROPRIATE FOR THE NEW ERA — TO BE FRANK, THE LOSS OF AN ATAVISM SUCH AS HIMSELF IS NO REAL BLIGHT ON YOUR SPECIES.

· **GASPAR:** HOWEVER, OTHER MEMBERS OF THE NOVA COMMUNITY WERE FAR LESS FORGIVING. PROJECT UTOPIA IN PARTICU-LAR HAS CONDEMNED GERYON'S ACTIONS, AND THAT ORGANIZATION HAS PROMISED TO MAKE THE TERAGEN MEMBER ACCOUNT-ABLE FOR HIS ACTIONS.

· **CAESTUS PAX:** THE NULL MANIFESTO IS NOTHING MORE THAN A TRUMPED-UP EXCUSE FOR TERAGEN MEMBERS TO INDULGE IN WHATEVER CRIMINAL ACTIVITY THEY CHOOSE WITHOUT A PANG OF CONSCIENCE. IT IS FLATLY INTOLER-ABLE. PROJECT UTOPIA IS ASSISTING IN THE AUTHORITIES' MANHUNT FOR GERYON AND WILL BE KEEPING AN ESPE-CIALLY CLOSE EYE ON OTHER KNOWN OR SUSPECTED TERAGEN MEMBERS. SHOULD THEY COMMIT CRIMES SIMILAR TO THIS ACT OF TERRORISM, THEY *WILL* BE CAPTURED AND PROSECUTED UNDER INTERNATIONAL LAW. WE ARE ALL HUMAN TOGETHER — AND THIS DIVIS MAL AND HIS RADICALS NEED TO REALIZE THAT QUICKLY. IF THEY DON'T, THEY WILL FACE THE CONSEQUENCES.

TOP SECRET

[DIRECTIVE FILE]

Director Harris:

Enclosed is my preliminary report on the known personnel and resources of the "Teragen" movement [file PA-2]. Operative "Turncoat" continues with his infiltration, and will update the file as opportunity permits. The evidence supports our theory that this organization seems to be more popular movement and charisma cult than anything else — the key difference being that only aberrants are involved.

Director, the more I learn about this Teragen, the more grave my apprehensions become. I'll leave it to you to pore over the files and piece together the possible extent of this threat, but even a casual scan proves that these people have influence across the continents, possibly even worldwide. I can only presume by the incredibly extensive variety of their contacts and "customers" that they must have a highly cellular setup; there doesn't seem to be much of a regimented central structure at all. Thankfully, we should be able to close in on, say, one of the Zukhov contacts without worrying about the Teragen's contacts in the Vatican.

I highly recommend isolating several of these contact points and moving through them to the Teragen members involved. Of course, we'll need to build up our reserve of reliable aberrant personnel first; of the three aberrants in the Directive I trust, one's in deep cover, the second is a bit unsubtle, and bringing in the third should definitely be a last result if we want to avoid a media fiasco.

I repeat: I'm worried. I think you will be, too, once you go over the file. Although the Teragen has yet to fully blossom into the worst-case scenarios we were projecting back in '98, I have a nagging fear that it's only going to be a matter of time.

Carson

Excerpt: "Null Manifesto"

… The members of *Homo sapiens novus* (also referred to as "novas") are a species separate from *Homo sapiens*. Regulations and laws enacted for the good of *Homo sapiens* are too easily subverted and misinterpreted to abuse the rights of novas, who are required by destiny to attain their full potential — a goal impossible while abiding by strictures set by beings who are not one's peers and who cannot accurately judge what is "ethical" or "moral" for anything other than their own species. As such, the laws and governing bodies established for the purpose of governing *Homo sapiens* must be considered inapplicable to *Homo sapiens novus*.

Until a common governing body, composed entirely of novas qualified to hold authority, is recognized by the majority of the nova population, then it is the duty of every *Homo sapiens novus* to govern himself or herself as he or she sees fit. Just as it is preposterous to ask humans to abide by the strictures of chimpanzee society, any attempt to force a nova to abide by the laws of human society must be seen as an attack on the rights of the individual nova….

Private journal entry: Leland Cornwall; April 23, 2007

Just how I like to begin my days: A telepathic probe just after breakfast. I wish I didn't have to wander into people's minds like this, particularly criminals — and particularly now. I swear to God, walking inside some people's minds is like going into a sewer — it's a hell of a lot different than sexplay with an open partner, that's for sure.

That's how it was with Sluice. To be honest, I was expecting some sort of monstrous asylum dream sequence, like they run on *Telepaths* every now and again. After all, the Teragen are supposed to be brainwashed monsters, full of programmed sadism, right? Not Sluice.

He knew I was coming in, even though we had "Psi-Dancer" in the room as a distraction. He didn't bother with her at all — he was expecting *me*. Don't ask me how; even Pax can't tell her M-R emissions are faked when I don't want him to, so it wasn't a problem with that. He played the gracious host, walking me through the mansion of his cortex and kindly opening doors for me. It was like some drawing-room play.

Worst part is, he kept me out of some of his memories. How the hell?!? He said it had something to do with "meditative exercises" and "funneling potential." Right.

Anyway, I managed to pull out answers to most of the Directors' questions. They weren't happy when he said that the Teragen had no chain of command, no superiors. The only flash of authority-respect that I could glean was when Mal's name came up. The best analogy I could come up with was that the Teragen was like a bunch of graduated college friends who keep in touch and help each other out now and again — and the Directors didn't like that much, either.

Sluice sure seemed to be happy with the arrangement. Even in captivity, facing life in a solitary dark cube, he wasn't bothered by things at all. "You'll come around." That's what he said as he was escorted out. "I can wait, and you'll come around. Then we can talk about this like reasonable novas, without all these monkeys screeching at us."

I didn't like his tone one little bit. Particularly because it seemed so genuine. What does he expect, that I'm going to have some epiphany and spring him, then we can go waltz off to Mal together and make the world a happy place for novas? Where do the people fit in in this arrangement?

I've been stewing over this all day, and I can't think of anything else. I'm going out tonight, no matter what Paxton says. It's going to take a good long evening of sex — sensory sharing and all — to get me to properly unwind. With at *least* three women.

Thank God I'm a nova.

Transcript from a Formative Directive Meeting

Apparently, the meeting from which this transcript originates was held shortly after the St. Petersburg "nova crisis" of 2001. Russian [sic] physiologists made breakthroughs similar to those of Drs. Mazarin and Rashoud, but with far less publicity, prompting government officials to look into the matter. From the spotty records and primary sources we can assemble, the early Directive discussions occurred after some draft of the apocryphal "Sterynch Missive" circulated among carefully selected members of superpower governments (though a few seem to have been selected without regard for their lack of superpower status).

At risk of lending undue editorial to my notes, I find it odd that a loose confederation of EuroSlav states could muster the wherewithal to parallel the M-R discoveries or unite other nations to form one of the most powerful police/ paramilitary organizations in the world when they can't manage to manufacture a decent gas oven. The pre-Sierka problems Russia faced should have been enough to cripple their research, but maybe the triumph of the human spirit is worth more than Hallmark sentiment. Yet, I digress. To get to the point, I suspect guidance or support behind the Russians.

Anyway, I hope you enjoy this. I lost six people to get it. The Ministry of Information is a bit tight-fisted regarding national secrets, even when it comes to public documents. I've taken the liberty of translating, additionally.

— B.F.

· **Ilyanovich (Russian Confederation):** So then, we're agreed? The presence of these "novas" is a concern for all our governments?

· **Stinson (US):** I would imagine so.

· **Nakamura (Japan):** Agreed.

· **I:** Perfect. Now that our semantics coincide, perhaps we should outline exactly how they would best serve us, in the sense that they would be working for their government, of course. If you'll look through my proposal, gentlemen and lady, you'll see we opine that a military structure works best. Although our prior experiment [*I think he's talking about Interpol, but I'm not sure — B.F.*] failed, limiting the structure to fewer participants better able to enforce the Directive code — see the third and fourth attachments — should be far more effective.

· **N:** And the membership is limited to these novas?

· **Lathrop (UK):** No, we've budgeted for a...um, *normal* support team, as well as a joint staff of policy leaders. Leaving the organization solely in the hands of these novas and relying on their sense of patriotism wouldn't work.

· **S:** Pardon me if I'm being a bit slow, but what exactly is the point of this [*sound of papers shuffling*] er, Directive?

I'll tell you right now, my military project expenditures are stretched fairly thin with domestic armed forces spending being cut, 60 "police actions" taking place and UN subsidies on top of it all. I don't know that I can afford another "police force of the world" sort of action, and I'm not sure our people want it.

· **N:** If I may be Devil's Advocate, I'm not sure a nation can afford *not* to be a part of this. We've already seen the power novas possess. Any state without a direct hand in the governance of their, ah, superpowered citizenry is going to have difficulty maintaining its administration without open revolt.

· **S:** And then what are your feelings on China, Miss Nakamura?

· **I:** A vast population, best watched by those sharing our common interests.

· **S:** Well, I didn't ask you, Petr, but I guess that'll do.

[Transcript continues, delving into budget allocations and membership charters.]

From the Sherman Report, presented before Congress in late 2006

Spending to support the Directive must continue, even if additional support from private corporations must be obtained to secure the United States' ongoing membership. Currently, the Directive represents the only viable recourse against placing nearly all faith in nova matters in the hands of Project Utopia.

Directive records show the following countries' contributions and memberships. (All figures shown are in US dollars)

United States	$3.5 billion per annum
30 active members	
Russian Confederacy	$3.2 billion per annum
31 active members	
Japan	$2.85 billion per annum
13 active members	
Germany	$2.1 billion per annum
11 active members	
United Kingdom	$1.2 billion per annum
10 active members	

Directive presence and continued American involvement serves military and intelligence ends, as well as allowing American participation in global policy direction. Withdrawal from the organization places too much power in the collective hands of countries with which the United States has had a history of conflict and enmity.

By maintaining a strong financial and personal presence in Directive affairs, America keeps the strongest weapons in its own hands, or at least under its sway.

From a *CBS Evening News* Broadcast, January 13, 2004

Transmission starts in media res, *owing to storage medium damage.*

...Is why we're here. Federally sponsored nova contractors Karma and Tombstone are with me, describing the presence of these unknown novas as "territorial and cryptofascist."

The cadre of novas, all wearing similar blue-and-white uniforms, appeared on the scene shortly after Karma and Tombstone, and asked the two independents to leave. When Karma and Tombstone refused, the apparent leader of the group displayed an official-looking badge and informed the two interlopers that failure to allow "the Directive" to handle the hostage situation would result in a federal charge of treason.

Onlookers describe the group members as "daunting" and of "a variety of ethnicities."

More on this situation as it develops. Back to you, Dan.

Graffiti from a Subway Train in Japan (Translated)

Super-soldiers or secret police?
The Directive has its eye on you.

From the Transcript of *Klein v. United States*

In 2005, Eugene Klein was arrested by a Russian Directive agent while attempting to burn down a Moscow warehouse stocked with over 4,000 cases of duty-free alcohol, which supposedly belonged to a smuggling ring. The warehouse and attendant property insurance was found to be registered in Klein's name in a Russian court of law. Extradited to America, his land of birth, Klein expected the charges to be dropped, which they were not. After being declared guilty in an American criminal court, Klein sued the American government, claiming financial, physical and emotional damages in excess of three billion dollars.

· **Prosecutor Danvers:** And what precisely is the nature of this Directive, captain?

· **Captain Petrograd:** The Directive maintains global law enforcement. Mr. Klein's actions were criminal, as your own court proved. As a member of the Directive, it was my duty to prevent such illegalities from taking place.

· **PD:** And who, exactly, maintains the Directive?

· **CP:** A joint commission of American, Russian, Japanese and United Kingdom governmental officials. Germany has recently become a member as well.

· **PD:** A global conspiracy, then? No further questions.

· **CP:** No, a check against Utopia's ambitio—

· **PD:** No further questions, witness.

· **CP:** The Directive exists as an alternative to the single-mindedness of Uto—

· **PD:** Your Honor!

With little deliberation, the Supreme Court found in favor of the United States.

From "The Triton Foundation: Curing the World", *Time* Magazine, February 2008

In the decade following the discovery and emergence of *Homo sapiens novus*, the worlds of science and medicine have undergone drastic advancements. Many of the cancers plaguing mankind from the dawn of time now have cures. AIDS, once feared to be the next great plague, is all but eradicated. Doctors even possess cures for spinal injuries that only years ago would have condemned the victim to a life of paralysis.

The Triton Foundation deserves much of the credit for these remarkable advances in medicine. The Triton Foundation is a large medical, pharmaceutical and research conglomerate corporation with ties to the Aeon Society, the philanthropic organization that founded Project Utopia.

"The staff at the Triton Foundation seeks to cure mankind of all the illnesses and injuries that have plagued it throughout history," said Ryan Gill, Triton Foundation CEO. "In that lofty goal, we are no different from any other portion of the medical community." What makes the Triton Foundation different is its unrelenting success rate. In fewer than 10 years, it has found cures that eluded scientists for centuries. Gill claims, "we have simply taken advantage of the vast research that came before us." All this from a company that has been in existence for only 14 years.

In light of the advances made by the Triton Foundation, no one seems too ready to look the proverbial gift horse in the mouth. Of particular note is that the Triton Foundation has funded much of the scientific research into novas. The Nobel Prize-winning Drs. Mazarin and Rashoud have both worked as paid consultants to the Triton Foundation. The company also funded the recent study that discovered a genetic basis for the Mazarin-Rashoud node.

"We have spent a good deal of our research budget on nova physiology because the research has given remarkable insight into the workings of the human body," said Gill. "We have simply followed the cutting edge of scientific research."

The Triton Foundation has no intention of resting on its laurels. Even now the Foundation is striking new ground in various areas of medical science. Current research projects include complete prenatal genetic screening and prenatal gene therapy, which promise to cure, in the womb, many diseases a person could potentially acquire. Serums for viral agents such as anthrax, hepatitis and rhinovirus (the common cold) are also being developed. Possibly the most promising research currently underway involves the cloning of replacement organs and limbs from patients' own DNA. This process promises to make transplantation waiting lists and organ rejection a thing of the past, allowing for virtually any part of the human body to be replaced.

"We see a very bright future for medical research," said Gill. "I can only hope that we can continue to make great strides."

Timeline

1994: Triton Foundation created by the merging of several pharmaceutical and bio-medical research companies under the auspices of the Aeon Society.

2000: Breast cancer cure developed

2001: Prostate cancer cure developed

2003: AIDS vaccine developed

2004: Generic anticancer gene therapy perfected, cures most known forms of cancer; ebola vaccine developed

2006: First prenatal cancer screening for breast cancer; first prenatal gene therapy treatment

2007: Triton-funded research into genetic origins of novas released

Raoul Orzaiz

Birth Name: Raoul Cristóbal Orzaiz
Date of Birth: Unknown
Place of Origin: Valencia, Spain
Occupation: Socialite; Teragen spokesman
Powers: Count Orzaiz refers to himself as "an accomplished athlete of my species." He has distinctively superhuman levels of stamina, speed and strength, although he refrains from publicly demonstrating his prowess. Secondhand rumor (usually attributed to one of his many ladyfriends) cites him as able to lift a dump truck, run as quickly as a cheetah and survive small-arms fire without a scratch.
Background: They don't come any more controversial than the celebrated Count Orzaiz. This European playboy is an unapologetic and public member of the infamous Teragen — and likely the movement's most telegenic spokesman. Although his philosophy is far from popular, the count doesn't lack for popularity of his own.

Count Orzaiz hails from one of the oldest noble families in Europe, a Basque dynasty that stretches back for many centuries. His eruption, which occurred shortly after his graduation from university, was widely publicized throughout Europe. His nova powers didn't seem to affect his jetsetting lifestyle much; if anything, they only encouraged it. Orzaiz is fond of photo safaris, and his work has been featured prominently in *National Geographic Magazine* — his ability to run with the cheetahs and wander with the lions without fear of harm has served his photography talents well.

Orzaiz announced his adherence to the Teragen's creed almost immediately after the release of the Null Manifesto. However, his behavior is a far cry from his more casually sociopathic colleagues such as Geryon — the count is unfailingly polite, and he notably enjoys the company of baselines. Although Project Utopia has stated that they intend to keep a close eye on him, the count has yet to do anything more subversive than lose a few hundred thousand francs in Monaco's casinos.

Estimated Power Levels:

Strength: 6
Intellect: 5
Speed: 6
Offense: 7
Defense: 7
Versatility: 8

Script excerpt from documentary program *Cutting Edge*, episode #41

The state of organized crime at the turn of the century was nothing less than all-out war. The already volatile relations between rival gangs, families and cartels broke down into even more heavy infighting, which was exacerbated when certain organizations (most notably among the Chinese tongs and South American cocaine cartels) began employing nova enforcers. This trend was to get worse when the UN granted Utopia authority to move against international organized crime.

Suddenly the criminal cartels and syndicates of the world found themselves in deep trouble. Not only were they killing each other off at a record rate, but the sudden intervention of Team Tomorrow made the situation much worse for them. By 2004, only a very few cartels were left standing....

Camparelli-Zukhov Megasyndicate

Excerpt from a phone conversation; 03/21/00

· **Voice 1:** I cannot believe you had the audacity to call me. I have nothing to say to you.

· **Voice 2:** If that's so, why are you still on the phone?

· **Voice 1:** Be very careful how you put your words.

· **Voice 2:** I'm not trying to insult you, Zukhov. Get that through your head.

· **Voice 1:** Oh? And what are you trying to do?

· **Voice 2:** Look, this war's been hitting you as bad as me. But you and me, we're both survivors, right? I wanna talk terms.

· **Voice 1:** Of surrender?

· **Voice 2:** Now I should be the one getting insulted. But I'm gonna let that slide. See, I know well as you that we'll be lucky to get out of this alive, much less free and still in business. We've both got contacts in good places, but when it comes down to just the two of us, this Utopia bunch is going to pick off one — then the other. Just like that. We don't have the muscle, and we don't have the freaks to resist them. Not separately. That's why I've got an offer for you.

· **Voice 1:** Is this the same offer you made Serizy and his Frenchmen?

· **Voice 2:** No. No, it isn't. They were wounded a lot

worse than you are; they had no choice but to come under my banner. You... You I respect, Zukhov. You have talents like nobody else in this business; comes of being a damned KGB special talent, huh? I wasn't talking about you working for me. I was talking about us working together.

· **Voice 1:** Hm. And I am to trust your goodwill?

· **Voice 2:** You don't have to. That's the beautiful part. I know you've already been checking up on me and mine. I know you know that we're the last Family standing, and that we've dragged a number of the survivors under our wings. Just like I know you've managed to pick off all your Organizatsiya rivals, and done some recruitment of your own among the Europeans while you were at it. Run your numbers. I'm guessing you'd come out with the same figures I would — that if we tried to do each other dirty, we'd wipe each other out, but if we cooperated...

· **Voice 1:** Yes. That way we stand a chance of survival, and of confounding one another's enemies by pooling resources.

· **Voice 2:** You're quick on the draw, Russkie.

· **Voice 1:** I have done my homework. I will presume that my men will be training yours in proper enforcement techniques, yes? You will abandon your protection operations, of course; there is little need for those when we can make a much greater profit on transporting goods, bookmaking and, of course, "vice." We are both very good at the vice.

· **Voice 2:** Son of a bitch. You were expecting me to call, weren't you?

· **Voice 1:** Is that a problem?

[END PHONE CONVERSATION]

Nakato Gumi

Draft of script from "Gumi Nova Tragic" OAV, aired 07/13/07

· **Ryu:** I don't expect you to understand. You are right to hate me. My hands are soaked in blood — all shed by the order of my *oyabun*. I have killed a hundred men in the name of my gang. I have taken technologies forbidden by Project Utopia and sold them on the black market. I have defied the laws of the world and obeyed only the laws of my family.

· **Ichiko:** But... but you have a choice, Ryu! Everyone has a choice!

· **Ryu:** No, not everyone. I was given no choice to be born, and no choice to live. Now I have no choice how to live.

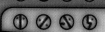

TOP SECRET

From a DeVries briefing letter, dated 03/24/08

Jeffries:

If you've looked over the contract, you've probably already noticed that you're looking at a hell of a lot of money for a simple extraction. Well, don't be fooled — this is no simple extraction. Things are never simple where the Nakato are involved.

I expect you to spend some time doing research on the flight over. You'll need to know everything you can about these people to pull off this mission. I hope your chameleon skills are up to the task; Japan's still fairly xenophobic after all these years.

Of course, it doesn't help that you're up against one of the major organized crime forces in the world, and going after them in their own backyard — where half the *zaibatsu* in Osaka are likely in their pockets. I'm sure you've heard all the stories about the Nakato — amphetamines and spike dealing, vice crimes, money laundering — seems like pretty tame stuff when you compare it to some of the other jobs, right?

Wrong. The Nakato are bad, bad news. I'm serious about doing your research; you won't have a chance in Hell otherwise. For one, you know that smuggling of Utopia-banned technologies they do? Don't think for a minute that there aren't any gimmicks with military applications in their inventory. Some of those might even be capable of dropping Geryon.

For another, you'll have to watch out for the whole neighborhood; in Japan, the Nakato have popularity and approval ratings that are through the roof. The number three comic in Japan is a "true life" rag about a nova who serves his Yakuza masters, helping out the little guy and tweaking the noses of foreign authorities. They've made a damn cartoon out of it, too; and the thing's been exported around to American and European markets, where we can only presume it's stepping up their approval ratings as well.

Finally, you can bet that they've got a nova or two up their sleeves, and we have no idea what sort of powers they're packing. That comic shows somebody with superspeed, but there's no reason to believe it's based on real life; probably just bankrolled by some *kobun*. So be ready to expect anything.

Full dossier's on the chip. Good luck, and watch yourself. If you pull this off, I'll buy you the cognac of your choice, deal?

Khalif

Heaven Thunder Triad

From WXLM-News broadcast, 11/30/06

Police continue to investigate the bizarre murder case of Herbert Wa, who was beheaded in the middle of the Thousand Miracle restaurant last Sunday. Although the restaurant was apparently at peak dining hours when the murder occurred, the police have yet to produce a cooperative eyewitness. As a further outlandish wrinkle, Mr. Wa's head has yet to be recovered; one source at the coroner's office admitted that "it was if his head was bitten off and swallowed."

Excerpt from report filed by Yukiko Takemitsu; 08/09/07

Telepathic scans on the subject are difficult and still not fully conclusive. I have difficulty penetrating the layers of his mental defenses; to do so causes him great pain, and I experience some feedback. As such, I would like to request a prescription of adrenocilin before our next session.

The subject, Ma Yuo, is a lifetime resident of Hong Kong. He was recruited into the triad-sponsored Yellow Silks tong at the age of 13; he killed his first man at the age of 15. This much is easy to discern.

However, it is when I pry behind the door painted with the words "Heaven Thunder" that the defenses become very thick. Either he has been psychologically conditioned to resist telepathic inquiry, or he is holding me out with emotions even stronger than a survival instinct. The threat of something worse than death is very real to him.

The images I receive are fleeting. Ma was apparently only lightly involved in any heroin dealing or use, for it is not a primary motif at all. He does touch on images of fan-tan cards and paigow dominoes, leading me to believe that he is indeed a ranking soldier in the triad's gambling ring, as Investigations reports.

It is as I attempt to go deeper that the other imagery rises up. I catch the repeated chant of oaths of loyalty, many oaths of loyalty. In all, a gruesome fate is promised if he reveals the secrets. The chanting is accompanied by shadowy images — demons with the smiles of sharks, a man on fire, a gout of green smoke with the lips of a woman. At this point, the pain becomes too great, and I am forced to withdraw.

I can only conclude that these final images are how the subject chooses to acknowledge the nova enforcers that we know the Heaven Thunders keep on retainer. There is no evidence to confirm that their chairman is a nova himself. I will attempt to pry further tomorrow, if that is your wish, but I fear that the subject is in very real danger of death if I pry further. His emotional state is such that dying of fright is quite possible. I await your decision.

From a Team Tomorrow Americas trainee briefing; date

MEDELLÍN CARTEL

01/10/07

When it comes to organized crime, we have three real concerns in the Americas. The first is the trouble with various gangs, a few of whom now have nova leaders. You've probably heard enough about the rise of the Crips and the Spangler Posse, and how their leaders have turned them into something much deadlier; however, these are moderately localized threats, and not the subject of this lecture. Secondly, there's the stateside versions of the Nakato, Camparelli-Zukhov and Heaven Thunder — but these are largely United States-local, and small stuff in comparison to their hometown versions. The real lords of organized crime across two-thirds of our protectorate are the Medellín cartel.

The Medellín are virtually unchallenged for their position as kings of the cocaine market. Not long after the *Galatea* explosion, the other Colombian cartels began suffering crippling hits on their farms, processing plants, even households — you name it. To nobody's surprise, this swath of destruction had novas behind it. These novas — two of them at first, although we believe there are more now — turned out to be hired agents of the Medellín drug cartel. The Medellín slaughtered all their rivals and set up their own household as the unquestioned rulers of the South American cocaine and cocaine variants trade. Currently, we suspect that one of these novas is the head of the cartel, and the other serves as his lieutenant; files for both are available on the database.

Ultimately, there's good news and bad news about the Medellín. The good news is that they're pretty localized; they can be found where the cocaine market is, and not much of anywhere else. The bad news is that because they don't really compete with any of the other criminal cartels, there's not much chance of them going to war with, say, the Nakato. They stick to the cocaine business because it's hugely profitable for them, and they're in turn guarded by not only their own nova enforcers, but their layers of contacts. They make more money than they can easily spend; as a result, a lot of their funds are tied up in various Caribbean banks. This "investment" has given them a lot of allies among the appropriate nations, to say nothing of the various Central and South American governments they have in their pockets.

So as you can see, they're a real problem for us. We can't go in after them guns blazing, because they have too many allies that might get us in legal trouble. We can't easily set them against rival syndicates, because they're not in competition. That's why it's one of our primary objectives to continue our goodwill efforts in the Americas; every field we terraform or power plant we set up makes us look a little better to the governmental high-ups. If we can convince the various heads of state that Project Utopia is a better and more valuable friend to have than the Medellín, then maybe we'll get the sanctioning and help we need to remove these parasites once and for all.

Until then, it's going to be very tenuous going. So if you wind up crossing a Medellín in the course of your duties, hold back and play it safe. Let us know. We can still oppose them, but we have to be careful about it.

ABERRANT

RULES

CONTENTS

Printed and bound in Canada

INTRODUCTION

The Basics

Aberrant is a game focusing on the lives and exploits of paranormal humans. Set 10 years after radiation from an exploding satellite triggered bizarre powers in a fragment of Earth's population, Aberrant chronicles the struggles of these "novas," or "new humans," and their quest to fit into — or forever change — human society.

Aberrant is, at its foundation, a game, but a game about telling stories. If you've played other roleplaying games, you should already be familiar with the idea. If not, this section explains what it all means.

Storytelling

Telling stories is a part of our heritage. The oral tradition is the oldest method of communicating information and entertainment. As society progressed and became more diverse and sophisticated, so too did storytelling. Unfortunately, it also became more passive. Where our ancestors took turns telling one another tales, we now watch stories on television.

Yet there are still storytellers among us. The filmmakers who create movies and the writers who create novels and comic books are just a few of those who maintain this ancient art. Aberrant is all about *telling* stories, not just listening to them. It's an opportunity to create new legends — not to merely watch as old legends are recycled on screen.

Roleplaying

Aberrant is a *roleplaying* game; players assume the roles of central characters in an ongoing story. It's much like improvisational acting with a dash of "Cops and Robbers." The make-believe you played as a child — imagining yourself as a knight in shining armor or a brightly clad superhero — was roleplaying. Aberrant is simply a more sophisticated version of those childhood games.

Still, Aberrant needs a few more rules than the playground did; "Got you!" "Did not!" "Did too!" is too simplistic for this sort of game. Aberrant's rules set the story's parameters, allowing the Storyteller to determine each character's abilities and limits. Rules guide the story, eliminating conflict over whether or not a character's actions are plausible — but rules *don't* dictate or restrict the action. The rules provide the basic mechanics for play; beyond that, the game's focus is on the story.

Designed for cinematic storytelling, Aberrant is much like a movie. The game works best when focusing on only a few main characters; thus, a group of only a half-dozen or so players is recommended. Much of the game's intensity and excitement is lost with larger groups, in which players must compete for attention.

The Storyteller

Aberrant has more in common with plays than with card or board games. Most notably, one player, called the *Storyteller*, is a "director" of sorts. In fact, the Storyteller acts as a combination director, narrator and referee, creating the drama through which the players take their characters.

As a Storyteller, you create the environment in which the characters are placed. While players and Storyteller shape events together, you are responsible for tying the story's disparate threads together and making sure that the game runs smoothly. Your most useful tools in balancing story and game are your imagination and the rules systems. Storytelling Aberrant is challenging, but this book makes it a simpler and more enjoyable process. It's a formidable job, but it can be incredibly rewarding — after all, the reward is the story itself.

The Storyteller's role is explored in detail in Chapter Seven: Storytelling.

The Players

Most of the people playing Aberrant assume the roles of the story's protagonists. While the Storyteller sets the stage for the game, it is the *players* who take the stage and create the action there. Being a player demands effort and preparation, but these elements add richness and depth to the story.

As a player of Aberrant, you create a character with incredible powers — a nova. You decide the character's actions over the course of a story as if you were playing a protagonist in a novel or film. Everything you have your character say and do has an impact in the Aberrant universe. Your goal is to help the protagonist overcome the obstacles facing her, thereby achieving her objectives.

After you describe "your" action, the Storyteller will occasionally demand that you roll dice to see if your character succeeds in the attempt. Beyond that, you need only think back to when you played make-believe — it's that simple.

Characters

To play **Aberrant** you create a role and become that person within the context of the game. Just as actors play characters on stage, players are the protagonists in an improvisational story.

While a playwright's characters have a predetermined existence, the **Aberrant** character you create develops according to your desires. The character creation process is relatively simple; it takes only a half-hour or so to work out the Traits and ratings that designate the character's capabilities. Even so, a character is nothing but a collection of numbers on a piece of paper until you breathe life into it.

Character creation is covered in Chapter Two: Character.

The Game

There are no "winners" or "losers" in **Aberrant**. The idea is not to "beat" the other players, as having everyone's characters cooperate is often essential to your own character's survival. Nor is the goal to "beat" the Storyteller, since the Storyteller and players work together to create the best story possible. In the end, the idea is to rise to the challenge, striving to overcome Herculean odds with your powers, wits and courage.

Although this setting's main focus is the struggle for power among the superhuman inhabitants of Earth, **Aberrant** is designed for players to pursue any number of goals. You can explore any concepts that interest you. Your series of stories may deal with matters as epic as saving the entire planet, or as personal as finding true love. It's all up to you and your Storyteller.

Aberrant's "victory conditions" are less tangible than being the only player who isn't bankrupt, or cornering your opponent in checkmate. Success in **Aberrant** may come about for a number of reasons: defeating foes in the course of the story, achieving status within an organization, developing a previously untapped power, uncovering a world-threatening plot or simply enjoying the experience of playing in the game.

There is no official "end" to a storytelling game, merely breaks between game sessions. Each time the players gather, the story picks up again, just like another episode in an ongoing TV series or another chapter in a novel.

The World of Aberrant

Fundamentally, the world of **Aberrant** is much like our own. Though it is set in the near future, the world as a whole is still largely recognizable. People still look and act much as they do now, most of the countries and political divisions remain true to their current parameters, and technology has not advanced beyond what we can presently conceive.

There are two important differences between the

Aberrant world and our own. The first is the presence of superhumans. These beings are referred to as "new humans," or "novas." Novas have a piece of genetic coding enabling them to control the fundamental forces of the universe, thus granting them vast power over their surroundings. Although there are only 6,000 or so novas in the world as of 2008, their coming has had a tremendous impact on culture, politics and scientific theory.

The second important difference is the presence of a powerful global organization, Project Utopia. Founded in 1998 by members of the Aeon Society, Project Utopia's mission is to foster harmonious relations between humans and novas while bettering the world as a whole. In its 10-year history, the Project has had great success, saving countless lives, curing diseases, and ending famine in vast areas of the world. So important has the Project become that Utopia now occupies an advisory seat on the UN Security Council.

The "official" beginning of the Aberrant chronicle is July 2008, a couple of months after a very important event in the **Aberrant** world's history. Recently, the immensely popular nova Jennifer "Slider" Landers was murdered. Evidence currently points to Landers' erstwhile friend, maverick ex-teammate André Corbin. When Corbin fled the site of Landers' funeral and went into hiding, suspicions seemed confirmed beyond all doubt. However, Corbin has apparently founded or joined a renegade group of novas calling themselves Aberrants, and this group has disseminated information suggesting that it was Project Utopia who murdered Slider. The fugitive faction alleges that Slider discovered incriminating information about the Project and was summarily silenced. Utopia publicly scoffs at these accusations, labeling them the desperate defense of a fugitive murderer. Nonetheless, the Slider scandal has shaken novas' confidence in the benevolent Project Utopia, and fallout from the event is polarizing novas worldwide. The balance of power between individual novas and nova factions is shifting, and any nova can make the difference between absolute power and destruction.

As a nova, you are one of the most important beings in the world. Possessed of enough quantum power to change the fate of entire nations, you cannot help but leave an impact on the world around you. Will you join the Aberrants in an attempt to uncover the truth about Utopia, or will you aid the Project against the rogues who would tarnish its good name? Will you ignore the coming struggle, or even exploit it for your own gain? History beckons, and you alone can make the choices that could affect millions.

The Future

Aberrant is a prequel game to White Wolf's **Trinity** science fiction roleplaying game, a far-future setting featuring evolved humans known as psions. As such, events in the **Aberrant** storyline influence and are influenced by the **Trinity** storyline. According to the **Trinity**

timeline, relations between humans and novas will gradually worsen, culminating in the great Aberrant War of 2049-2061. Certain characters introduced in this book will have a greater or lesser impact on the events that lead to — and follow — the Aberrant War.

That having been said, players and Storytellers are free to include as much — or as little — of the "official" **Aberrant-Trinity** metastory as they like. **Aberrant** can easily be played as a stand-alone game without need of **Trinity**, or the characters' actions may forever alter the **Trinity** timeframe to come. It's all up to the players and the Storyteller.

Creating Aberrants in Trinity

Though **Aberrant** is designed as a prequel to **Trinity**, it's relatively simple to use this book to generate the monstrous aberrants of the **Trinity** era. The fundamental difference between the novas of 2008 and the aberrants of 2121 is the amount of Taint accumulated. For **Trinity**-era aberrants, each dot of Quantum translates to one point of initial Taint. **Trinity**-era aberrants cannot save costs on Traits by buying them tainted, but neither are they taken out of play when Taint equals 10.

Moreover, beginning **Trinity**-era aberrants start with a Quantum rating of 3, and may raise starting Quantum scores as high as 7.

Playing Aids

Aberrant is designed for play around a table. You need little besides this book, some 10-sided dice (also called "d10s"), photocopies of the character sheet, pencils and paper for taking notes — and, of course, your imagination.

Still, other props can make the roleplaying experience more vivid. Mood lighting, music, scribbled notes or sketches; all can serve to make the game seem more real. Remember, though, that props are just that; it's the story that matters.

Live-Action

Live-action roleplaying is a natural outgrowth of the "tabletop" storytelling described above. Live-action is even more like improvisational theater; the actors (the players) literally act through the scenes. This can create a very intense and immediate storytelling experience.

In live-action roleplaying, you don't just describe your character's actions; you "are" that character. You actually do what the character does (within reason — obviously, you shouldn't try to simulate flying or lifting a Mack truck). Whether that's simply walking across a room or making a speech before millions, you are physically involved in the action. Imagination is still important, and the Storyteller may still interrupt events to describe objects and special situations.

No dice are used in live-action games; alternate rules (like those in White Wolf's **Mind's Eye Theatre** game products, or simply the result of the Storyteller's judgment), replace dice. The method of adjudicating actions itself isn't important as long as it's consistent, fair and fun for everyone.

Rules of Live-Action

You must follow a few essential rules to ensure that live-action roleplaying is safe and enjoyable for all. These rules must be obeyed in any live-action activity; safety is always the primary concern.

• **Don't Touch:** Players may never actually strike or grapple one another. No combat should ever be performed — that's what the "dice" are for. If anyone gets too rambunctious, the Storyteller should call for a timeout and remind everyone of the rules. Repeat offenders should be asked to leave, or the action should be returned to a tabletop roleplay forum.

• **No Weapons:** No props can be used if they must touch another player to be effective. No real weapons or realistic-looking props (like guns or swords) of any sort are allowed at any time during live-action sessions.

• **Respect People Who Aren't Playing:** Play in a private area where only the players are around (your house, a reserved room on campus or a rented hall). Never perform live roleplay if passersby may be confused or frightened by the event. If nonplayers are around, understand that they probably have no idea what you're doing. Be discrete and considerate; respect their space and don't force them to participate (pausing to explain that you're playing a game is also a good idea).

• **Know When to Stop:** Remember: It's just a game. When anyone calls for a timeout, all action must cease immediately. If the game gets too intense for someone, it's time to stop.

Glossary

The following is a number of terms used in the rules that new players may not be familiar with. Each is described in more detail elsewhere in this book.

Character Terms

• **Aberration:** An odd or detrimental physical or mental quirk gained as a side effect of excessive Taint.

• **Ability:** A Trait describing learning, knowledge or applied experience in a given area. Abilities are added to Attributes to determine your character's skill totals.

• **Allegiance:** The order, government or organization to which your character belongs.

• **Attribute:** A Trait that describes your character's basic characteristics; a reflection of raw, natural capability.

• **Enhancement:** A specialization of a Mega-Attribute that enables you to perform certain superhuman feats.

- **Experience Points:** Points awarded by the Storyteller as "reward" for achieving the story's objective or playing a character well. Experience points can be spent to add new Traits or raise existing ones.
- **Extras:** 1) Special Traits that can be added to quantum powers to enhance their efficiency. 2) The characters (created and played by the Storyteller) with whom the team interacts, from simple passersby and bit characters to trusted allies and dangerous enemies.
- **Group:** The players who adopt the personas of characters involved in the stories told.
- **Mega-Attribute:** A Trait that allows a character's normal Attribute to extend into the superhuman range.
- **Nature:** Your character's core being, her emotional personality.
- **Quality:** A remarkable aspect of one or more of your character's Attributes.
- **Quantum:** A measure of your character's power over the fundamental forces of the universe.
- **Quantum Points:** Points representing residual quantum energy, which a nova expends to activate her powers.
- **Quantum Pool:** The maximum number of quantum points a nova can store under normal circumstances.
- **Quantum Power:** A special manifestation of Quantum your character can generate; for example, flying, generating gravity fields, and projecting force bolts are all considered quantum powers.
- **Skill Total:** The combined rating of an Ability and its base Attribute. Skill total determines the number of dice you roll (called a "dice pool") when your character performs an action.
- **Soak:** Your character's ability to withstand damage and physical trauma.
- **Specialty:** An area of expertise within an Ability.
- **Storyteller:** The person who creates and guides the game by assuming the roles of all characters not taken by the players, and the person who determines all events beyond the players' control.
- **Taint:** A score indicating the degree of change wrought on a nova's mind and body by the channeling of quantum energies.
- **Team:** Specifically refers to the characters *within* the game, not the individuals playing them.
- **Trait:** Any Attribute, Ability, Advantage or other index with a rating.
- **Willpower:** Your character's self-confidence and moral center.

Rules Terms

- **Action,** also **Dice Action:** Performing a task (a consciously willed activity). When you announce that your character is doing something, she's taking an action. This is also called a "dice action" when you must roll dice (known as a "dice pool") to determine whether

or not your character succeeds in an action. Most actions are "standard actions"; see below.

- **Action, Difficult:** A task more challenging than normal. See **Difficulty**.
- **Action, Multiple:** Taking more than one action in a turn. The first action's dice pool is reduced by a number of dice equal to the total number of actions your character will take in the turn. Each following action loses an additional die (cumulative).
- **Action, Resisted:** An action that two or more characters take against one another. Rolls are made for each against Traits designated by the Storyteller, and the character with the most successes wins.
- **Action, Standard:** An action with no difficulty modifiers. You simply roll your Dice Pool and tally any successes. All tasks your character performs are standard actions unless the Storyteller declares otherwise (by applying a difficulty, noting multiple actions or stating that the action is resisted).
- **Botch:** A notable and often dramatic failure when attempting an action.
- **Dice Pool:** The total number of dice available to you for a given action. Your dice pool is equal to the skill total most applicable to the action taken. If your character doesn't have an Ability rating in a task, you default to the base Attribute involved and use its score instead of a Skill Total.
- **Difficulty:** Short for the "difficulty of the roll," a difficulty notes the added challenge involved in accomplishing a task. You must roll the standard base of one success plus the additional difficulty indicated (usually by the Storyteller) to accomplish a difficult action.
- **Dots:** The method used to indicate rating values. Each dot equals a die that may be used to perform actions.
- **Max:** To channel extra raw Quantum into a particular power, thereby increasing the power's potency.
- **Rating:** A numbered Trait value; usually a range from 0 to 5, though sometimes from 0 to 10 (often noted in numbers of "dots").
- **Success:** A die that rolls equal to or higher than the target number of 7. Most actions require only one success; more challenging actions demand more successes.
- **Success, Extra:** Any successes you roll beyond the minimum required to accomplish an action. Extra successes may be used to make a standard success truly inspired.
- **Success, Standard:** Rolling exactly the number of successes required to accomplish an action.
- **System:** A specific set of game mechanics used in a certain situation; rules to help guide dice-rolling resolutions to simulate dramatic actions.
- **Target Number:** The standard rating of 7 over which you must roll for your character to succeed in a dice action.

World Terms

- **Aberrant:** (capitalized) An organization dedicated to uncovering an alleged "conspiracy" in Project Utopia; (lower-cased) a derogatory epithet used to refer to novas.
- **Aeon Society:** A philanthropic organization founded in the early 20th century; founder of Project Utopia.
- **Anima:** A quantum energy field many novas project when using their powers.
- **Amp Room, the:** Private Ibiza nightclub whose membership is open only to novas.
- **Baseline:** "Normal," non-nova human.
- **Blacktech (shadowtech):** Technology that is far ahead of the standard industry curve and is typically developed through studies of novas. Most blacktech is presently banned by Project Utopia's Science and Technology Department.
- **Church of the Immanent Escheaton:** Popular Western religion that upholds novas as highly evolved spiritual beings; similar to the Scientology and theosophist movements of the 20th century.
- **DeVries Agency:** A private firm specializing in the contracting of nova operatives, elites and bounty hunters. A sort of "sports agency" for novas.
- **Directive, the:** A multinational espionage and police agency dedicated to neutralizing threats to world (and particularly First World) security.
- **Dorm down:** To internalize and shut down one's quantum signature, thus appearing as a normal baseline human.
- **Elite:** A nova who uses her powers to act as a mercenary.
- **Equatorial Wars:** A series of resource conflicts fought in Africa in the early 21st century. The Equatorial Wars mark the first use of nova elites in brushfire actions.
- **Eufiber:** A substance secreted by nova fashion designer Anibál Buendia, as well as synthetic derivates of that substance.
- **Franchise:** A nova who accepts an established position of employment with a city, corporation or other body; alternatively, the "identity" of the position itself, independent of the nova filling it. For example, any nova who accepts the Houston Tornado franchise assumes the persona of the Houston Tornado.
- **Inert:** A derogatory term used by certain novas to describe a nonlatent baseline, one without the genetic capability to become nova.
- **Kamisama Buddhism:** A hybrid of Shinto and Buddhist beliefs espousing novas as incarnate spirits.
- **Mascara:** Spanish for "mask"; also, a synonym for "elite," particularly in Latin America.
- **Mazarin-Rashoud (M-R) node:** Gland in a nova's forebrain that allows the nova to channel quantum energies.
- **N!:** A highly rated television channel devoted exclusively to coverage of novas.
- **Nova:** A human with the genetic capability to develop the Mazarin-Rashoud node and channel quantum energies.
- **Novelty Consulting:** A private Hong Kong corporation specializing in consultation and problem-solving.
- **Null Manifesto:** A statement by nova Divis Mal that counters the Zurich Accord, declaring novas to be intrinsically separate from baseline humans.
- **OpNet:** An advanced communications network derived from studies of Buendia eufiber.
- **Project Proteus:** A secret division within Project Utopia whose ostensible goal is to support Utopia's efforts through clandestine actions.
- **Project Utopia:** A private foundation whose goals are to better the quality of life on Earth for all humans, often through use of nova abilities.
- **Quantum energies:** The four fundamental forces of the universe — gravity, electromagnetism, strong and weak nuclear forces — as well as nova-derived and – channeled energies transmuted from those forces.
- **Saisho:** "The New Beginning"; early 21st-century Japanese economic policy.
- **Team Tomorrow (T2M):** The nova-led public relations and defensive arm of Project Utopia.
- **Teragen:** Philosophy/movement founded by nova Divis Mal whose primary precepts are the inherent separateness of baselines and novas and the implicit assumption that novas are more highly evolved beings than baseline humans.
- **ViaSoft:** 21st-century conglomerate created by the merger of 20th-century corporations Viacom and Microsoft.
- **XWF (Xtreme Warfare Federation):** 21st-century sports entertainment enterprise featuring contests of nova-powered shootfighting.
- **Zurich Accord:** UN resolution declaring novas to be human beings.

CHAPTER ONE: SYSTEMS

The systems in this chapter provide a structure by which matters of chance are resolved in the **Aberrant** setting. These rules are quite simple, but even then, you shouldn't feel constrained by them. Be flexible with your adjustments, and be consistent when you make changes.

The Golden Rule

The primary rule of **Aberrant** is simple: *If you don't like it, change it.* The story is more important than any rule. If the systems get in the way, ignore or change them. These rules are merely guidelines; feel free to use, alter or disregard them as you see fit. After all, it's your story. Note that the Storyteller is the final arbiter of any rules question.

Time

Time is a fundamental element of **Aberrant**. There are four distinct ways to describe divisions of time within the game, progressing from the smallest to the largest unit.

• **Turn** — The smallest unit of time in the game, considered long enough to take one *action*. A *turn* is defined as about three seconds in combat situations, although a turn of up to three minutes is acceptable in less dramatic circumstances.

• **Scene** — One compact period of action and roleplaying that takes place in a single location. A *scene* is comparable to a scene in a movie. It takes as few or as many turns to resolve events as are necessary.

• **Episode** — One independent part of a *series*, often played in one game session and made up of scenes connected by *downtime*.

• **Series** — A complete tale, with an introduction, buildup and climax, that often takes several episodes to complete. Your *series* is the continuing narrative that your cast creates. Also called the *story*.

Besides these four active time divisions, **Aberrant** stories sometimes include:

• **Downtime** — Time between scenes or episodes that characters may spend resting, recuperating or possibly learning new talents. Any time that characters are not actively participating in a story is considered *downtime*.

Actions

Characters take lots of *actions* in the course of a story. Players may act out conversations or simply describe actions to the Storyteller. An action can be anything from having a discussion to blasting a building to smithereens.

Some actions, such as talking, walking and other simple physical deeds, are *automatic*, not requiring dice rolls. Other maneuvers, mostly those related to combat, are called *dice actions*, and they demand that you roll dice to determine the outcome.

See "Complications," p. 108, for information regarding specific types of actions.

Dice

Aberrant requires 10-sided dice, which you can find in any game store. Sharing dice between players is perfectly acceptable, but it can slow things down at times. If you prefer your own dice, you'll want around 10. The Storyteller will more than likely want her own dice.

Movement

Your character's actions may depend on how far she can move. These rules keep formulas to a minimum. A *walking* character moves five meters. A *running* character moves her Dexterity rating +12 meters. A *sprinting* character moves (3 x Dexterity) +20 meters. Characters with Traits such as Mega-Dexterity, Flight or Hypermovement can move much faster, though; see Chapters Four and Five for specifics.

Movement is often an automatic action, but a character can take no other action that turn if she moves the entire distance that she's able to. A character may typically move half her running distance and still perform a dice action. Moving under hazardous conditions (combat, rough terrain, buffeting updrafts) may also call for a die roll.

Trait Ratings

A character's *Traits* — innate and learned capabilities, called *Attributes*, *Abilities* and *quantum powers*

— are defined by a number of *dots*. Most Traits are rated from one to five dots; • indicates a poor or beginner level of skill, while ••••• indicates the absolute peak of human capability. Trait ratings are recorded by filling in the appropriate dots on the character sheet.

x	Abysmal/Untrained
•	Poor/Novice
••	Average
•••	Good
••••	Exceptional
•••••	Human maximum

Because of their powers, novas often exceed human capabilities in various Traits.

Rolling Dice and Dice Pools

When your character takes a dice action, you roll one die for each dot you have in the Traits most suited to that task. The Storyteller decides which Traits are appropriate by choosing the *Ability* that best covers the action being attempted.

Attributes (innate capabilities) and *Abilities* (things you know and have learned) have individual ratings, but they are added together to determine a *skill total*. If your character has a 3 Perception and you put two dots in Awareness, your Awareness skill total is 5. Whenever your character performs an Awareness-related action, you roll five dice.

This system holds for novas' *quantum powers*, as well. For example, if a nova has a Dexterity of 4 and a Quantum Bolt rating of 2, and she tries to blast a helicopter out of the sky, the nova's player rolls six dice.

This skill total (also called a *dice pool*) is recorded on the character sheet in the square with each Ability. The dice pool is the total number of dice you roll for a single action. Characters usually perform only one action in a turn, although you may wish to try more than one (see "Multiple Actions"), and some novas can perform many actions in a turn.

Each dice pool derives from a single skill total and *defaults* to the appropriate Attribute if the character has no rating in an Ability. Dice pools figured from Personality Traits are the only exceptions (see p. 144).

Default Traits

On occasion your character may not have a rating in an Ability that the Storyteller designates. If so, you *default* to the Attribute on which the Ability is based. So if the Storyteller calls for an Awareness roll, but you put no points in that Ability, you simply use your character's rating in Perception. This system reflects the idea that someone who improves upon her natural capability through training will generally perform better than someone who tries to get by on raw talent alone.

Option: Cross-Matching Attributes and Abilities

Aberrant's Attribute/Ability combinations match up the most appropriate Attribute to a given Ability, which helps greatly in streamlining game play. Still, the Storyteller may decide that certain unusual circumstances call for a more appropriate Attribute/Ability match.

On these rare occasions, the Storyteller may ask for a cross-matched roll simply by declaring the Attribute and Ability combination he feels is most suitable (this is the only time that the Storyteller need call for the Attribute as well as the Ability to be used). You then take each Attribute rating and Ability rating (*not* skill total) and add them together; this is your dice pool for that roll.

For Example: Kendo Hayashi faces off against a nova enforcer in the service of the Nakato Gumi. Hayashi decides to evaluate his foe's style by observing the opponent's stance and katas. The Storyteller thinks Martial Arts is appropriate, but such a feat really calls for an Intelligence test. Instead of using his normal Martial Arts Skill Total [Dexterity + Martial Arts], Hayashi's player combines the character's 3 Intelligence and 5 Martial Arts for a total of eight dice.

Personality Traits

Three Traits have no Abilities related to them — *Willpower*, *Taint* and *Quantum*. Additionally, Willpower and Taint have both *permanent* and *current* ratings. The permanent rating (designated by dots on the character sheet) usually stays the same. However, the character's current rating (noted by the squares under the permanent rating) can fluctuate during an episode. Dice actions using Willpower are based on the character's permanent score (the dots), not the current rating (the squares).

Personality Traits are discussed in more detail in Chapter Three: Traits, pp. 144-153.

Success and Failure

When you roll your dice pool, you want each die to match or exceed the *target number*. **Unless specifically indicated otherwise, the target number is *always* 7**. So each die that comes up an 7, 8, 9 or 0 (10) is considered a *success* —a favorable resolution. Conversely, if all the dice you roll come up less than 7, your action fails.

All you have to know when you roll is the number of successes you need; if you get at least the minimum quantity, you achieve your goal. The standard number of successes necessary for any task is always one (unless the Storyteller says otherwise). *Extra successes* beyond the minimum can sometimes generate additional effects (at the very least, extra successes mean your character accomplishes the action in a superior and notable fashion). See "Complications" for information regarding easier and more difficult actions.

Total Successes Rolled	Degree of Success
One	Standard
Two	Superior
Three	Remarkable
Four	Astonishing
Five	Phenomenal

For Example: Megan Sensation notices an unknown nova eyeing her at the Amp Room. Not wishing to confront the nova or attract undue attention to herself, Megan tries to slip out unobtrusively during a particularly crowded moment. The Storyteller has Megan's player roll Stealth; Megan's Dexterity is 5 and her Stealth is 2, so the player rolls seven dice. She scores 1, 9, 7, 7, 4, 1 and 10 — four successes. Megan manages to slip easily into a throng of dancers and make her way to the exit.

Complications

It isn't difficult to get at least one success, even with only a couple of dice. If your group is heavily into roleplaying, the simple rolls described above move the game along with a minimum of distraction. The following options serve to accent the game's action and cinematic qualities with an added level of complexity, but they are still designed for smooth gameplay.

Botches

Normally if none of your dice comes up 7 or higher, your character simply fails. If any die on such a failed roll comes up "1," you've *botched*. A botch is an unfortunate result; not only does your character fail the action, but she does so rather significantly. *However, as long as you roll at least one success, you ignore any 1s.*

The specific circumstances of a botch are up to the Storyteller, but they should affect the character adversely and relate to the action being attempted.

For Example: Out of the Amp Room, Megan heads for the beach. The Storyteller asks for an Awareness roll. Megan's player didn't put any points in Awareness, so she defaults to her 5 Perception. Rolling five dice, her player gets 1, 3, 4, 6 and 6: a botch. The Storyteller decides Megan is so pleased with her exit from the Amp Room that she not only fails to see a jacked-up Mitoid in the street, but she runs right into the thug!

Automatic Successes

Your character may be so skilled in a certain task that you need not roll for it. Such is often the case for novas, who perform "impossible" feats with ease. At the Storyteller's discretion, your character has an *automatic success* if her skill total for an action is at least equal to the target number of 7. So if you have eight dice or more, your character succeeds automatically — you don't even need to roll. Still, it's merely a standard success; you might want to roll anyway to achieve extra successes.

You may also spend a Willpower point to earn an automatic success. This "free" success is in addition to any successes gained by rolling dice, but the Willpower point must be spent prior to your roll. You won't want to do so too often. While Willpower points are easy to spend, they're not easy to earn. Only one Willpower point may be spent per turn to gain a free success.

The automatic success rule should never be used in stressful situations, particularly in combat.

Difficulty and Difficult Actions

Most of the time you need only one success to complete an action. However, some tasks, like performing a trick shot or

disabling an encrypted lock, can be more challenging. The Storyteller makes that distinction when appropriate, designating a certain number of successes that you need to roll for your character to complete the task. The *difficulty* to a roll is always listed as a number of additional successes needed beyond the standard one. So a "difficulty penalty of two" (or "+2 to difficulty") means you must get a total of *three* successes. The harder the action being attempted, the more successes are required. Any extra successes you get *beyond* the difficulty indicate that your character does an even more outstanding job than required.

Difficulty Rating	Degree of Difficulty
Zero	Standard
+1	Tough
+2	Challenging
+3	Difficult
+4	Critical

For Example: Megan runs toward the Ibiza beach, the Mitoid hot on her heels. A motorcycle turns the corner casually. Hoping for a fast getaway, Megan jumps for the cycle. The Storyteller decides that landing on a moving bike is tricky and increases the difficulty by two. Megan has an 8 Athletics, so her player needs to get

three successes on eight dice. She rolls: 2, 3, 7, 9, 6, 7, 8 and 9. With five successes, Megan lands squarely on the cycle, grabbing the surprised driver around his waist.

Extended Actions

Some tasks require multiple successes to complete. These *extended actions* often take more than one turn to complete. The additional successes are cumulative, reflecting that sustained effort is needed to accomplish the action. You can keep trying to obtain successes until you gather the required amount or until you botch. If you botch during an extended action, the Storyteller may decide that you lose a "saved" success for each botch, or that you lose them all and must start again from scratch — or even that you messed up so badly that you can't try again.

Extended actions are more complicated than standard actions, and they should seldom be employed in the middle of intense roleplaying. The action in the game should reflect what types of rolls are needed, not the other way around.

For Example: Noticing the commotion Megan is causing, the thug posted outside her flat takes advantage of the distraction and breaks into Megan's apartment. Since he's hired muscle, not a burglar, the thug decides to break down the door. The Storyteller figures the thug must get a total of four successes in an extended action to snap a solid lock. The enforcer has a 10 Might, so his player rolls 10 dice. He gets an abysmal 1, 1, 2, 2, 2, 3, 4, 5, 6 and 9; the door buckles slightly but doesn't give. On his next turn, the player rolls 1, 3, 3, 5, 6, 6, 7, 8, 9 and 10. The four successes this turn plus the one from the previous turn are more than enough to send the door crashing back on its hinges.

Multiple Actions

Your character can also perform *multiple actions* in a turn. The total number of actions the character takes determines how many dice are subtracted from the first task attempted in that turn. Each action after the first loses an additional (cumulative) die beyond that amount. So if your character tries to perform three actions in a turn, you subtract three dice from the first task's dice pool, four from the second and five from the third. If the total actions bring your dice pool for any one task to zero, that action cannot be attempted.

If a nova attempting a multiple action has a relevant Mega-Attribute, dice lost from the multiple action come from the character's normal dice pool first; the Mega-Attribute dice are not lost until the character's normal skill total drops below zero.

For Example: Back on the street, Megan's having trouble getting the irate cycle driver to flee the scene while the Mitoid simultaneously takes aim at them with an SMG. Short on time, Megan performs two actions: shooting a Quantum Bolt at the enforcer and intimidating the driver. With two actions, Megan's player subtracts two from her base 8 Quantum Bolt [Dexterity 5 + Quantum Bolt 3] skill total (rolling six dice for: 2, 2, 5, 5, 6 and 6) and three from her 8 Intimidation (rolling five dice for: 2, 4, 7, 7, 0). Megan's shot misses the thug, but the weapon's scream combined with Megan's shouting startles the driver. He cranks the throttle, and the cycle tears off down a side alley.

Resisted Actions

Sometimes your character's efforts oppose another's, just like in a tug of war. During *resisted actions*, opposing players roll using the appropriate Traits. If you score more successes than your opponent does, your character succeeds at her action before the other character does. Your total successes are then reduced by the amount that your opponent rolled; the successes remaining then apply to the action itself. In this way, even if your opponent can't beat you, she can diminish your efforts.

Examples of Rolls

The following are a few examples of how to use these rules. Remember, each of the Abilities mentioned ties directly to a specific Attribute; unless stated otherwise, you can always default to that Attribute if you don't have the appropriate Ability. The entire list of Attributes and Abilities is detailed in Chapter Three: Traits, p. 134.

• An electrical conduit blows nearby. Roll Athletics or Martial Arts to dodge out of the way.

• Sneaking through the Nakato warehouse, you stumble across a guard. You both roll Initiative to see who reacts first.

• The power is out and the warehouse door is jammed. Roll Might at a difficulty penalty of two to pry the doors open.

• You've been driving across the Midwest for the past 10 hours straight, hoping to reach Chicago by dawn. Roll Endurance to avoid nodding off.

• Two overly curious soldiers question you about your "borrowed" officer's uniform. You could roll either Command to order them away or try Savvy to offer them a bribe.

• No matter what you do, you can't get the young girl to tell you what's wrong. Roll Rapport to get a sense of what's troubling her.

• You need to jump across the service bay to the exit while avoiding Overkilla's Quantum Bolt. Roll Athletics at +2 difficulty.

• Suspicious customs officials don't like the look of your briefcase. Roll Subterfuge, at +1 difficulty, to assure them that everything's cool.

• You speak Mandarin, but your Cantonese is very rusty. Roll Linguistics at +2 to difficulty to figure out what the shopkeeper is yelling about.

• Despite your best efforts, it looks as though this Mitoid won't listen to reason. Roll Brawl or Martial Arts to show him the back of your hand.

• The gangbangers outnumber you five to one and they don't look like they're in the mood to talk. Roll Intimidation at +3 to difficulty to impress upon them that this will hurt them more than it'll hurt you.

• You burst into the cockpit to discover that the pilot is dead and the plane is hurtling directly toward a mountain. Roll Pilot to steer out of harm's way.

• This tech can't have been approved by Utopia S&T. Roll Engineering at +1 to difficulty to determine its origin.

• A pair of jet fighters screams out from behind the cloud bank. Roll Firearms to fire your 50mm cannon right back at them.

• It's your first time at this Utopia branch, and you've forgotten your security code. Make a straight Intelligence roll to recall it.

• You could really use that fellow's platinum card. Roll Streetwise at +1 to difficulty to lift the wallet from his breast pocket.

• What's that chiming noise? Roll Awareness to find out.

For Example: The cyclist's surprise lasts only for a moment, and he tries to bring the bike to a stop. Megan reaches forward and tightens her grip over the driver's, hoping to force the throttle back up. The Storyteller calls for both players to make Might rolls. The characters are evenly matched with no Might Ability and 4 Strength ratings. The Storyteller rolls for the driver, getting 2, 3, 5 and 8. Megan's player rolls 4, 4, 8 and 9. While the driver resists her, Megan has just enough leverage to goose the bike's speed back up.

Some actions are both extended *and* resisted. One opponent must collect a certain number of successes in order to win. All successes rolled above the opponent's total number of successes in a single turn are added together. The first opponent to collect a designated number of successes wins the contest.

For Example: Megan's impromptu chauffeur loses his temper and tries throwing Megan off the bike. The Storyteller states that whoever gets three successes first on resisted Might rolls stays on the hovercycle, while the losing character gets tossed to the ground. In the first turn, the Storyteller rolls for the driver and gets 3, 4, 5 and 9; Megan's player comes up with 1, 2, 4 and 6. In the second turn, the Storyteller's roll is 3, 4, 7 and 8; Megan's player gets 5, 5, 5 and 8. At the start of the third turn, the cycle driver is up by two successes with the Storyteller rolling again for 5, 6, 9 and 0; Megan's player, astounded by the Storyteller's successes, rolls 1, 3, 3 and 7. With a total of three successes, the driver shoves Megan off the back of the careening cycle. Adding injury to insult, the Storyteller imposes two health levels of bashing damage on Megan as she slams into the unforgiving cobblestones. Megan lifts her head in stunned disbelief as the cycle speeds away.

Teamwork

Characters can combine successes, generally during an extended action. At the Storyteller's discretion, two or more players can roll separately and total their successes. While teamwork is effective in repairing devices, collecting information or combat, the tag-team approach can be confusing in social situations.

For Example: Since the enforcer in the street had no chance to catch up to Megan, he goes inside her flat to help his partner. The two thugs ransack the place, trying to find the notes that Megan took of her last conversation with Count Orzaiz. The Storyteller decides that the enforcers will need to get three successes to find Megan's safe since it's hidden behind a false panel. The first enforcer has a 5 Investigation and his player rolls 5, 5, 6, 9 and 0. The second thug must default to his 3 Perception, his player getting 1, 3 and 8. The enforcers discover the small safe; now all they need to do is find a way to open it.

Second Chances

Failure is frustrating. If you're having trouble with your computer and can't figure out why, you're in for an evening of increasing frustration and decreasing productivity. **Aberrant** reflects this "frustration with failure" by allowing the Storyteller to increase the successes needed for any action that you try again after an initial failure. So if a first attempt at picking a simple manual lock fails, a character's frustration with her failure could make her try too hard the second time. To reflect this overcompensation, the Storyteller asks for two successes. Of course if the character fails yet again, things will continue to escalate....

The Storyteller shouldn't invoke this rule in instances such as combat. Missing a target isn't terribly surprising under such circumstances, considering that everyone is dodging about, ducking for cover and generally not being polite enough to stand still.

Power Use

Novas employ many powers. The Traits representing these powers typically rate from 1 to 5. A nova's dice pool for power use typically consists of the sum of an Attribute (listed with the power) and her rating in the power itself.

For Example: Embarrassed by her fall, Megan notices an opportunistic shutterbug racing her way, camera in hand. To preserve her public image (such as it is), she decides to deter the photographer with a Quantum Bolt. Megan's player spends two quantum points and rolls her Dexterity (5) plus her Quantum Bolt rating (3), generating a result of 1, 3, 5, 5, 7, 9, 0 and 0. The uncannily accurate Bolt blows the camera out of the photographer's hand, and the man decides to reconsider his front-page exclusive for now.

CHAPTER TWO: CHARACTER

Before you enter the **Aberrant** universe, you must create a character. However, the character creation process involves more than just saying, "I want to be a..." You need to know who your character is and what she has the potential to do, her likes and dislikes, her background and more. This chapter provides a step-by-step plan for discovering these facets of your character, giving you the chance to create a unique nova you will enjoy playing.

Character creation starts with a basic concept. After deciding on that, you assign the character's normal and nova Traits to determine what she can do, then fill in the details of her personality and life. You should create a character who is interesting for you to play, for your friends' characters to interact with and for your Storyteller to incorporate into the story. Although your nova will indeed be one of the most powerful beings in the world, the goal is not to make the ultimate superbeing, capable of destroying cities with a thought; if you easily trounce everyone you meet, your series is likely to be extremely dull. Indeed, novas with weaknesses are far more interesting; vast power is all the more poignant when contrasted with human foibles.

Role of the Storyteller

The Storyteller should guide the players through character creation. It helps move the process along with a minimum of time and fuss if the Storyteller is on hand to offer assistance.

First, pass out the character sheets and give the players a few minutes to look them over and ask questions. Then go through the character creation process, helping the players create well-balanced characters.

Sometimes character creation can take an entire game session, which is fine. The players shouldn't feel rushed, and they should take the time to create believable characters. If you want to cut down on time spent, encourage your players to have their ideas ready beforehand.

Once you're done with the practical details of creating characters, you can spend the rest of the session running *prologues*. These serve as introductory stories, allowing both you and your players to get to know the characters and the **Aberrant** setting.

Character creation is not a random process; you build your character from the ground up, to your own specifications. You assign Traits and choose everything about your character. That way, you're certain to play a character you find entertaining.

Aberrant's primary theme concerns the ability of the individual to impact her world, and your character should choose and uphold personal goals accordingly. Nonetheless, it is vital to consider how well your character will interact with the rest of the group. The **Aberrant** milieu is a dangerous place; a team has enough to worry about without dealing with internal strife. It also helps to figure out why the members of your team are together. Cultural, ethical or personal ties are just a few reasons why novas might work together. If your character doesn't fit in with the rest of the group, you may find yourself either sitting out of a lot of the action or splintering the group.

Character Creation

All the steps of character creation are detailed here. You'll create a character in less than an hour by following this process. This chapter deals primarily with the mechanics of allocating points for Traits and with filling in the blanks of other areas of your character.

Because novas are born as normal humans who then "erupt" into their full potential at a later point in life (typically between the ages of 16 and 36), character creation actually takes place in two phases. In Phase One, you build your character as a normal person, allocating Attributes, Abilities and quantum potentials. Once the "normal" part of your character is established, you take the character through Phase Two, the origin. Phase Two is where you transform your character from normal human to nova, giving her the awesome quantum powers that forever differentiate her from other mortals.

Chapters Three, Four and Five give expanded and detailed information on each of the following sections.

Phase One: Human

Here you decide what your character was like prior to his eruption. For all intents and purposes, you are creating a normal human being, just like any one of us, with talents, skills and aptitudes appropriate to his background and profession. Don't worry, you'll get to add plenty of powers during Phase Two. For now, though, decide what your nova was like before the change. After all, a featureless menu of powers isn't any fun to play. The best heroes, antiheroes and even villains are people first and "supers" second.

Step One: Concept

You begin by formulating a basic concept for your character. You don't need to know all the details of her life at this point; you just need to have a general feel for who she is. You can add specifics later on in the process; right now you're just interested in the basics.

You need to determine two things at this stage: who you are, and what you're like.

Concept

Novas don't spring fully formed into the **Aberrant** universe. Your character had a life before she erupted. You must decide what she did, how she lived and what was unique about her. This concept may describe her profession, her personality or her interests. The following concepts are merely suggestions; if none of them fits the idea you have in mind for your character, feel free to create your own.

- **Affluent**: Connoisseur of fine things (idle rich, executive, dilettante).
- **Artist**: A creative personality (writer, dancer, actor, painter).
- **Gambler**: Life is a game (thrill-seeker, irreverent, daredevil).
- **Hermit**: Cast adrift in the universe (vagabond, recluse, scarred veteran).
- **Nobody**: Just an average, everyday person (student, working stiff, grunt).
- **Outsider**: Fallen through society's cracks (slummer, dispossessed, neurotic).
- **Philosopher**: Yours is a world of potentials (dreamer, student, idealist).
- **Pioneer**: The universe is a wonderful mystery (researcher, trailblazer, environmentalist).
- **Protector**: One who cares for others (police, doctor, missionary, teacher).
- **Rebel**: Shaking up the status quo (criminal, gang member, politician).
- **Saint**: You follow a higher purpose (priest, visionary, theologian).
- **Scholar**: Learning is its own reward (professor, theorist, scientist).
- **Warrior**: Conflict draws you (vigilante, soldier, crusader).

For Example: Rob decides to create an Aberrant character. Although Rob likes comics and bustin' heads as much as the next guy, he decides that he doesn't want to play another tedious ass-kicker or mercenary. Instead, he wants to play someone whose powers are more subtle, used to further the character's whims and indulgences. He decides that his character is a "playa"-type: smooth, charming in a shallow way and always up to something not quite good. Rob decides to make the character American and male; however, tired of gun-flicks and bad rap videos that present the stereotypical ghetto-dwellin' New Jizack Hustla, Rob decides that his character is of Asian descent; a child of a two-parent nuclear family who simply went shady somewhere along the way. Rob settles on the Gambler concept, and he names the character Philip Long.

Nature

As living icons, novas often shape their quantum gifts into the embodiments of themselves or of concepts dear to them. Accordingly, you should choose your character's *Nature*, a personality archetype that best suits her true personality. This self-perception guides how your character interacts with the universe (see "Nature," in Chapter Three, for detailed information).

For Example: Rob has to pick Philip's Nature. This one's pretty easy: Although the Gallant and Conniver Archetypes might work, Hedonist stands out as the obvious choice. Philip lives for the good times, and he does what he has to do to keep the money coming.

Allegiance

In the world of 2008, novas often act at very high levels of geopolitical power. Accordingly, many novas have an allegiance to one or more important organizations. You may pick your allegiance at this time, though you certainly don't have to have one; should you have no allegiance, simply write "Independent" in the space provided.

For Example: Looking over the possible allegiances, Rob tries to imagine what Philip would think about joining any of them, and he comes up with a resounding "Hell, no!" Philip, like many novas, will be his own person at the beginning of the chronicle, although he could possibly shift toward the side of the Aberrants or even the Teragen as his character develops. For now, Rob writes "Independent" on Philip's sheet. As a side note, Rob decides that Philip entered one of Utopia's Rashoud facilities upon first erupting; the experience was straight out of One Flew over the Cuckoo's Nest, and Philip has had quite enough of Utopia's rather cloying presence in his life, thank you very much.

Step Two: Choosing Attributes

The nine Attributes are innate potentials represented by numerical ratings. All humans have Attributes, though novas often enhance their Attributes to superhuman levels. These Traits are the basis for all of your character's capabilities. Each character's Attributes are rated on a scale of one to five and represented by dots: • is poor, •• is average and ••••• is the peak of human potential (though, for a nova, a ••••• may be quite... mediocre). Novas start with a rating of one dot in each of the nine Attributes, which may then be improved upon by spending Attribute points on a one-for-one basis.

Attributes are divided into three areas: Physical, Mental and Social (see "Attributes," pp. 133-135, for detailed information). You must prioritize these three Attribute categories, determining one area in which your character is particularly adept (primary), one in which she's fairly average (secondary) and one in which she's weak (tertiary). You spend *seven* Attribute points in your primary area, *five* Attribute points in your secondary area and *three* Attribute points in your tertiary area. Allocate the points within each group however you see fit. If an Attribute ends up lower than you'd like, don't worry. You may improve it later with bonus points or experience, and if you supplement your Attribute with a Mega-Attribute (p. 164) during Phase Two, you'll have transcended the human norm anyway.

Any element of your character's concept may suggest the placement of Attribute points. A crusading journalist or scientific prodigy might have strong Mental Attributes, while a scheming con man probably has high Social Attributes.

If any of your character's Attributes are rated at four dots or higher, you need to choose a quality for it. See "Qualities," p. 134, for specifics.

For Example: Rob determines Philip's Attribute categories as follows:

Social is primary. Philip's always had a charming, conniving air about him and can seamlessly insinuate himself into any group or situation. He always knows just the right thing to say, just the right clothes to wear and just the right time to get out of town.

Rob splits the seven points available to the primary Attribute group as follows: three in Appearance, three in Manipulation and one in Charisma. Rob adds these points to the one free point that novas receive for each Attribute, putting Philip at Appearance 4, Manipulation 4 and Charisma 2. Philip is a ladies' man, no question, and he can con an Eskimo into buying an igloo, but he's better at leading a girl into his bedroom than leading a platoon into battle. Since Philip has two Attributes of 4, Rob must choose a quality for each. He picks "Smooth" for Philip's Appearance, and "Hustler" for his Manipu-

lation.

Rob makes Physical Philip's secondary Attribute category. Although his early years were spent at home, Philip had a troubled adolescence and ran away young; as such, he's been in his share of rough situations. Then, too, he's too narcissistic to be out of shape....

Of the five points available to secondary Attributes, Rob allocates two to Dexterity, one to Stamina and the last two to Strength, giving Philip a 3 Strength, 3 Dexterity and 2 Stamina. Philip is naturally graceful, and he works out to keep himself looking fine for the ladies, but he's lazy and prone to beer-and-cigarette breakfasts.

Rob makes Mental Attributes the remaining, tertiary category. Philip is impulsive and prefers to solve problems through negotiation rather than analysis; he's not dumb, but he's no egghead.

With only three points to spend, Rob goes for the average, assigning one dot to all categories. Philip's not stupid or weak in any area, just not particularly sharp, either.

Step Three: Choosing Abilities

As Attributes are your character's innate qualities, Abilities are the skills and talents that she has developed in her life (see "Abilities," p. 136, for specifics). Abilities are rated from • (rudimentary) to ••••• (superior). Abilities begin with ratings of zero, not 1 as Attributes do. You have 23 points to spend on Abilities as you choose. You may distribute Ability points on a one-for-one basis however you see fit, although individual Ability ratings cannot be higher than 3 during this phase of character creation. Bonus points may be spent here, as they can be with Attributes.

Concept is important when deciding where to assign Ability points. A street thug probably won't be very skilled at mingling in high society, while a marine biologist won't likely know much about heavy weaponry. On the other hand, choosing seemingly odd Abilities can enhance your character concept; for example, the street thug might be a runaway from a rich family, or the marine biologist might have served in the Navy for years and know plenty about heavy weapons. You may choose an area of specialization within an Ability; see "Specialties," p. 136, for more information.

Remember that, as a nova, you automatically start with three free dots in Endurance and Resistance; see the Mega-Stamina Mega-Attribute (p. 160) for details.

Skill Totals

As Attributes are raw capabilities and Abilities are learned talents, the two combine to form your character's

skill totals. To calculate a skill total, take the base Attribute, add the relevant Ability and write the total after the Ability rating on your character sheet (in the box after the row of five dots). Whenever you make a roll, your dice pool equals the skill total in that box.

For Example: *Rob has 23 points to spend on what Philip knows, plus his automatic 3 minima in Endurance and Resistance. He spends three points each on Style, Streetwise and Subterfuge; two points on Athletics, Intimidation and Rapport; and one point on Might, Drive, Firearms, Martial Arts, Stealth, Awareness, Linguistics (Cantonese) and Etiquette.*

Step Four: Backgrounds

Backgrounds measure your "place" in the **Aberrant** universe. They represent whom you know, who knows you and what resources you can draw on in times of need. You have *seven* points to allocate among your character's Backgrounds. Your choices should reflect your character concept (see "Backgrounds," p. 139, for details).

For Example: *Rob has seven points to spend on Philip's Backgrounds. Philip's the kind of character for whom Backgrounds will be very important, so Rob gives this section a fair bit of thought.*

Philip has all kinds of casual, shallow acquaintances, so Rob assigns three points to Contacts. Like it or not, Philip's tightly knit family still cares about their wayward son, so Rob puts a dot in Allies. Philip loves the fast life, but he spends money as fast as he gets it, so Rob assigns a single point to Resources (impressive clothes, equally impressive creditors). A little raw power can't hurt, so Rob drops a point in Node, to give Philip a second-instar Mazarin-Rashoud node potential. Finally, Philip's all about the stylin' threads, so Rob spends his last Background point on Eufiber (a Buendia original, cute little tag and all, baby).

Step Five: Finishing Touches

Phase One's about over. All that's left to do is to fill out or develop the last elements of the character. These final details are as important as any other element of bringing your character to life.

Willpower

Willpower measures the power of convictions and self-control. The circles on your character sheet reflect your character's maximum or *permanent* Willpower rating (also called the *score*), which is the theoretical limit of determination. The squares track your character's momentary force of will; this *current* rating (also referred to as *points*) drops as will is exerted (by spending Willpower points) and grows as your character reinforces her belief in herself (by acting true to her Nature) — see "Willpower," p. 144, for further details.

Permanent Willpower begins at a base rating of 3, and bonus points may be spent to raise it to a maximum of 10. Current Willpower starts equal to your character's permanent score.

Quantum

Novas are novas because they can manipulate quantum energies, the fundamental forces of the universe. With sufficient control of these energies, they can do anything from hyperevolving their basic capabilities to creating miniature black holes. The measure of a nova's control over Quantum is the Quantum Trait. This Trait, more than any other statistic, is a measure of a character's "power."

Novas-to-be start with Quantum ratings of 1, though you may use bonus points to increase it in Phase One, as well as nova points to improve the Trait in Phase Two. In any event, no nova may begin the game with a Quantum Trait above 5.

Initiative

Initiative is used whenever there is a question as to which character performs an action before another character. Initiative is the total of your character's Dexterity and Wits. As with other advantages, you may raise this score with bonus points; certain nova powers allow positively obscene Initiative ratings as well.

Movement

Movement indicates the distance your character may travel in one action. Your character may *walk* seven meters, *run* her Dexterity rating +12 meters and *sprint* (Dexterity x 3) +20 meters. As with Initiative, certain nova powers enable a character to travel much, much faster than the human norm.

Quantum Pool

A nova's Quantum Pool is the total amount of "juice" or energy a nova uses to power her abilities. Quantum Pool begins at 20 + (Quantum x 2), and it can be raised with nova points in Phase Two of character creation.

Quantum points are spent from the Quantum Pool when using nova abilities; the character starts the series with a full Quantum Pool.

Bonus Points

Bonus points are used to fill in the blanks left on the character sheet during basic character creation. You have 15 bonus points, and you may spend them on any Attributes, Abilities, Backgrounds, Quantum or Willpower. However, Trait costs vary (see the Character Creation Table). At this time, you may raise Abilities to 4 or above if you wish, though you should have a good reason for doing so (your character is a renowned scientist, champion prizefighter or other prodigy).

For Example: Before spending bonus points, Rob notes that Philip's Quantum rating is 1, his Willpower is 3, his Quantum Pool is 22 and his Initiative is 5.

Now Rob gets to spend his bonus points. He spends seven points to raise Philip's Quantum to 2 (doing so also raises his Quantum Pool to 24). Rob spends five more points to raise Philip's Wits to 3 (he's too smooth to be caught off guard very much). With the last three points, Rob adds a dot in Followers (a rotating posse of equally dissolute sycophants and hangers-on who hang out with Philip now that he's a nova) and raises Philip's Willpower to 4.

Phase Two: Nova

Now you know what your character is like. Or rather, what she *was* like before her Mazarin-Rashoud node changed her from human to nova. In this phase of character creation, you take the man or woman you've created and turn him or her into a demigod.

Step One: Eruption

The defining moment of a nova's existence is her eruption — the moment at which her M-R node "turns itself on" in response to a stimulus. The circumstances surrounding eruption generally dictate the basic parameters of the character's powers. Before continuing, the player should decide on the general events surrounding eruption: what triggered it, why and what powers it prompted.

One thing to keep in mind is that quantum control often manifests itself according to the nova's conscious and subconscious desires, fantasies and needs. As such, players should think about spending at least some of their nova points on their characters' normal Traits and Mega-Attributes. If your character had been a pudgy wallflower up until the time of eruption, it makes more sense to spend nova points on Charisma and Appearance (perhaps even the appropriate Mega-Attributes) than to jack up Quantum Bolt and Force Field to obscene levels. If your character has always wanted to be the greatest musician in creation, raise that Arts Ability before buying the world-wrecking stuff.

Here is a list of possible triggers for a nova eruption:

• **Accident:** The node erupts while the nova is caught in a dangerous accident: a fire, a flood, whatever. Some novas have erupted after taking enough damage to kill them; a clinically dead character suddenly rising Osiris-like from his coma.

• **Deliberate:** Though rare, this eruption happens when a latent nova suspects herself of harboring an M-R node and takes steps to activate it. Most such people, of course, end up injured, crippled or dead, but it's been known to work in a few cases.

• **Emotional Trauma:** The character erupts after a particularly traumatic experience. This trauma could be sudden (intense torture, watching a loved one in peril) or gradual (a runaway teenager who's been starving and cold on the streets for days).

• **Excitement:** The character erupted during a sudden surge of passion — excitement over winning the lottery, a sexual encounter or a sudden discovery.

• **Exposure to Quantum Powers:** It has been documented that exposing latent novas to active novas' quantum energies occasionally causes the latents to erupt. Perhaps your character was an innocent bystander in the midst of a nova-level conflict; the charged quantum energies activated her own M-R node.

• **Revelation:** The nova just realized she could "do things." (This type of eruption is usually accompanied by days of splitting headaches, as the node swells in the forebrain.)

• **Threatening Situation:** Similar in some ways to an accident, a threatening situation involves the nova erupting during a mugging, war, animal attack or similar event.

Of course, no two novas erupt in quite the same ways; feel free to make up any eruption that suits your fancy (subject to the Storyteller's approval).

For Example: Rob wants Philip to be a somewhat sleazy character, so he decides that Philip's M-R node manifested in a somewhat sordid fashion. Philip's eruption, Rob decides, occured in response to an attack from someone whom Philip had crossed earlier: perhaps one of Philip's shady creditors; perhaps a jealous husband or lover whom Philip had cuckolded. In the end, Rob decides that, in fact, Philip seduced the lover of the mob racketeer to whom he owed an overdue loan, giving the crook two reasons to kill him. Philip's powers enabled him to survive the gangster's assault, implying that Philip will have some sort of special defenses, at least enough to survive street-level small-arms fire. Coupled with the superhuman presence and charm that Rob already wants Philip to have, these powers should make for a pretty tough character.

Step Two: Nova Points

Now that you've established the circumstances behind your character's eruption, pick the powers most suited to her. Chapters Four and Five list a wide variety of Mega-Attributes, enhancements and quantum powers to choose from; characters may increase some normal Traits during this stage as well, by means of *nova points.* Beginning characters get 30 nova points, which they can use to increase Quantum or Quantum Pool, buy Attributes, Abilities, Backgrounds, Mega-Attributes, enhancements and quantum powers. As with bonus points, different Traits and powers cost different amounts of nova points (see the Character Creation Table, p. 120).

Note that most Mega-Attributes and quantum powers have a Quantum Trait minimum to purchase; before you buy that power, you must raise your Quantum to the appropriate level, with either bonus or nova points.

When buying nova Traits, you can purchase them more cheaply by designating certain Traits as tainted. A tainted power is purchased at half cost (rounded up); however, for each dot of power so purchased, the nova begins the game with one point of permanent Taint (p. 148).

Remember, as well, that no nova may begin the game with a Quantum Trait above 5. Furthermore, if you raise your character's Quantum Trait to 5, he gains an additional dot of permanent Taint.

For Example: Rob decides that Philip's powers involve a heightening of his own natural charm, as well as a measure of control over the forces of chaos and probability. First of all, he spends five nova points to raise Philip's Quantum rating to 3 (which in turn bumps his Quantum Pool to 26). He now spends 12 points to buy Mega-Manipulation at • • (with the Trickster enhancement), Mega-Appearance at • (with the Seductive Looks enhancement) and Mega-Stamina at • (with the Regeneration enhancement). Philip is extraordinarily resilient, fascinating and persuasive.

With 13 points left, Rob has to select Philip's remaining powers carefully. He decides that Philip's the sort who can stand a little Taint, so he buys a point of tainted Quantum for half cost (three rather than five nova points), raising Philip's total Quantum to 4 (his Quantum

Pool is now 28). A Quantum this high enables him to purchase the Entropy Control quantum power, and Rob again decides to save quantum points by adding Taint. Philip purchases two tainted dots of Entropy Control at half cost (or three nova points per dot rather than five), spending six dots on the power. Since Entropy Control provides a suite of techniques, and since Philip may select one technique per dot in the power, Rob selects Bioentropy Storm (a good all-purpose area attack) and Entropic Shield (a useful defense — Philip's tough by human standards, but nowhere near tough enough to suck up a serious nova attack). Philip can use the other techniques in the Entropy Control suite, but they'll cost six quantum points to activate rather than three, and they activate at +1 difficulty, since he hasn't mastered them yet.

Rob has four remaining nova points to spend. Even with Mega-Stamina and Entropic Shield, he's not entirely comfortable with Philip's defenses, so he spends two points add the Resiliency enhancement to Philip's Mega-Stamina (this allows Philip's Mega-Stamina to soak two levels of bashing and lethal damage rather than one). Rob spends his last two nova points to add six dots to Philip's normal Attributes; he raises Philip's Charisma to 3, Manipulation to 5, Appearance to 5, Dexterity to 4 and Stamina to 4.

Step Three: Finishing Touches

Here's where you have to do a little bookkeeping. Your character begins with one permanent Taint point for each tainted Mega-Attribute dot, quantum power dot, Quantum dot or enhancement purchased. Remember that if your Quantum is 5, you gain an extra Taint dot on top of any other Taint accumulated. If doing so drives your Taint above 3, you gain one aberration (p. 151) per additional Taint point.

You should fill in your speeds for walking, running and sprinting, as well as speeds for any other forms of locomotion (for example, Flight or Hypermovement). The character sheet has space for you to write in extra movement speeds.

Finally, add together all soak gained from Stamina, Mega-Stamina and Armor, then calculate your soak totals for bashing and lethal damage. Extra space on the sheet lets you write in situational soak (for example, from a Force Field, Invulnerability or an Elemental Mastery technique).

For Example: Philip has three Taint points, which Rob dutifully records in the Taint section of the character sheet. A Taint this high does not impose any aberrations — yet — but Philip is nonetheless fairly discernible as a nova.

Philip does not have any special movement powers, so he gets around the same as any baseline. His walk rate is five meters, his run rate is 16 meters (12 + his Dexterity of 4) and his sprint rate is 32 meters (20 + three times his Dexterity of 4).

Now Rob calculates Philip's starting soak scores. Philip's Stamina of 4 gives him four soak versus bashing damage and two soak versus lethal damage; to this base, his Resiliency-enhanced Mega-Stamina adds two soak versus bashing and lethal, for a total of six soak versus bashing damage and four soak versus lethal damage. Philip's incredibly tough by human standards, but he probably should stay out of serious nova-level combat, and his Entropic Shield and Regeneration abilities will doubtless see a fair bit of use.

One more detail needs to be taken care of: Since Philip raised his normal Dexterity and Stamina to 4, he may select qualities for these Traits. He chooses "Run Like Hell" for Dexterity and "Function on Almost No Sleep" for Stamina.

Spark of Life

Now that you have the dots and Traits out of the way, you can personalize your creation and make her uniquely yours. The more details you work out, the more depth your character has. While they have no direct rules impact, these details make it easier for both you and your Storyteller to know who your character is and how she fits into the series.

• **How old are you?** Most novas are relatively young, between 16 and 36 years of age at eruption, though there are exceptions. Also think about what events took place during your character's life. Experiences have as much impact on how old you feel as your physical age does.

• **What do you look like?** While the Appearance Trait indicates how attractive you are, it doesn't say what it is that makes you attractive, nor anything else about your physical identity. Consider your other Traits, including Nature and Backgrounds. Also remember that, unless the Storyteller specifies otherwise, you can be from any culture, of any religion, race or sexual orientation.

While you're thinking about your character's appearance, decide exactly how your quantum powers manifest. Even novas with low or no Taint typically look somewhat different from the human norm. Do your eyes glow when you activate your Force Field; do flames roar from your mouth when you fire your Quantum Bolt?

• **Did you ever notice you were different?** The trauma of eruption merely unlocks a previously latent quantum potential. Many latents experience brief, uncontrolled flashes of power prior to eruption, whether they realize it or not. You may have already been aware of your potential before eruption, or you may have been baffled and confused by the tremendous energies you unleashed. Perhaps you have lived blissfully unaware of your nature.

• **How were you discovered?** Many erupting novas are approached by Project Utopia psychologists and encouraged to enter training at the nearest Rashoud facility. Others find themselves sought out by government agencies, corporations or other groups, though many use their newfound power simply to slip away and avoid detection by potential exploiters.

• **What are your quirks?** Everyone has interesting personal idiosyncrasies; what are yours? They can be anything from always wearing a fedora to having a morbid sense of humor. Good quirks help define your personality and also give the Storyteller more to work with for character interactions and story hooks.

• **Who is important in your life?** How do you feel about your family (or do you even have one)? Are your friends close or merely casual acquaintances? Do you even keep in touch with your loved ones now that you're a nova, or did eruption sever ties between yourself and your baseline compatriots? Just because you've become a nova doesn't mean you lose your previous ties — although it may certainly change how people feel toward you and *vice versa*.

• **What do you own?** This consideration is usually an afterthought, but a little attention to it is useful. Mundane things like an apartment or clothes are considered to be covered by the Resources Background. However, certain weapons, vehicles or unusual items are covered in the Appendix.

• **How do you perceive other people?** Are you tolerant of other cultures and lifestyles? Do you envy other novas? Do you yearn for your old life? Do you consider yourself superior to baselines, perhaps condescending to or even bullying them? Do you remain among baseline society or prefer the company of other novas?

• **How did you meet the rest of your team?** The "team" refers to the other players' characters. While the team itself can take many forms, you still need to figure out how you all came together. Whether it's a willing alliance or a marriage of convenience, be sure that there is some level of trust between yourself and the others.

• **What are your motivations?** No one lives without some sort of motivation. What are your goals? What do you fear? What gives you strength? Also ask yourself "why?" regarding these questions. Motivations can be vague (a desire to improve the world) or very specific (you have sworn vengeance on the Directive agent who murdered your family). You understand who you are in fleshing out your ambitions and priorities.

For Example: Rob wants to establish some more details about Philip's priorities, origin and relationships with others. The Storyteller wants to keep the general details a little vague, but Rob fills in some basic information.

As far as physical appearance goes, Philip is a stunning Asian male of 23, with long black hair in a ponytail, a wiry build and a sharklike smile. He's always dressed to the nines, he favors flashy jewelry and he takes special pride in his Buendia eufiber suit. Although Philip hasn't manifested any aberrations, his Taint is pretty high for a beginning character; Rob decides that harmless but eerie black sparks occasionally crackle from Philip's eyes and across his body, flaring strongest when Philip uses his Entropy Control powers or soaks damage with his Resiliency.

Philip's basic disposition is pretty nailed down, but Rob thinks that some more work could be done in this area. He decides Philip is the youngest son of a family of hard-working Chinese immigrants (which is, of course, where he learned to speak Cantonese). The family was poor and lived in a bad neighborhood; early on, the clashes between the values of Philip's frugal parents and those of his street-rat friends pulled Philip away from his family and onto the streets. Mixing with the wrong crowd, Philip became a gambler, small-time hustler and occasional pimp; these activities combined to get him into some trouble with a local branch of the Camparelli-Zukhov megasyndicate, and his powers activated while defending himself from a pissed-off mob goon.

Early on, Philip entered a Rashoud facility to control his powers; Utopia's nauseating, PC feel-goodism and authority-with-a-smile didn't sit well with him at all, and he left the facility on less than equitable terms. He's sure that the Project is monitoring him as a potential threat, and this suspicion has gnawed at him to the point of paranoia.

Philip currently lives in a small downtown apartment, but he is on the cusp of doing bigger and better (well, bigger) things. He's already attracted a crew of hangers-on and "best buddies"; for now, he's living the high life, impressing (and occasionally freaking out) the ladies and spending money as fast as he makes it. The syndicate arm that had previously been threatening him has "generously" dropped all of his owed gambling debts and is cajoling him into working for them, but Philip has bigger dreams than being a small-time syndicate boss. His family still cares about him and wants him to use his powers responsibly, but Philip has ambiguous feelings about them. More than anything, he wants to avoid Utopia's scrutiny, and this paranoia conflicts with his desires for wealth, fame and attention. Perhaps if he could hook up with others of his kind....

Character Creation Table:

Phase One: Human

This cheat-sheet covers the character-creation process in short form; refer to the appropriate sections for details. Available points are listed where relevant.

- **Step One: Concept**

   Choose Concept, Nature and Allegiance (p. 127)

- **Step Two: Select Attributes (p. 133)**

   Prioritize the three areas: Physical, Mental and Social

   Choose primary Attributes (7 points)

   Choose secondary Attributes (5 points)

   Choose tertiary Attributes (3 points)

- **Step Three: Select Abilities (p. 136)**

   Choose desired Abilities (23 points)

   No Ability higher than 3 at this time.

   Calculate skill totals

- **Step Four: Select Backgrounds**

   Choose Backgrounds (p. 139) (7 points)

- **Step Five: Phase One Finishing Touches**

   Record initial Willpower (3), Quantum (1), Initiative (Dexterity + Wits), Movement (walk 7 m, run Dex +12 m, sprint [Dex x 3] +20 m)

   Spend bonus points (15 points)

Bonus Points

Trait	Cost per dot
Attribute	5
Ability	2
Specialty (max. three per Ability)	1
Background	1
Willpower	2
Quantum	7
Initiative	1

Phase Two: Nova

This section tells how to change your character from normal human to nova.

- **Step One: Origin**

   Choose the circumstances of your character's transformation.

Step Two: Nova Points

   Spend 30 nova points on Mega-Attributes; enhancements; quantum powers; Quantum; Quantum Pool; or extra Attributes, Abilities and Backgrounds.

   Quantum cannot be raised higher than 5; if Quantum is 5, the character gains +1 permanent Taint.

- **Step Three: Phase Two Finishing Touches**

   Record Taint and aberrations (if any), changes to skill totals (if any), changes to Initiative and movement (if any); bashing and lethal soak; decide on any physical changes made by eruption.

Nova Points

Trait Cost	Nova Point
Mega-Attribute	3
Enhancement	3
Quantum	5
Quantum Power (Level 1)	1
Quantum Power (Level 2)	3
Quantum Power (Level 3)	5
Quantum Pool	1/2
3 Attribute dots	1
6 Ability dots	1
5 Background dots	1
Willpower dot	1

Italicized items can be bought as tainted powers; tainted powers cost half the normal cost per dot (round up), but they impose one point of permanent Taint per dot so purchased. A tainted Level 1 power costs one nova point per two dots purchased.

Adding an Extra to a Level 1 or 2 quantum power increases the level of the power by one for purposes of purchasing the power. So, a Level 2 power purchased with an Extra costs five nova points (or three nova points if bought tainted) per dot.

The Team

The majority of novas in 2008 are solitary, focusing on their own lives and goals. Sure, they come together to socialize, and novas' titanic egos often lead to highly publicized (and ratings-drawing) clashes, but by and large, each nova is an island unto herself. Therefore, the team that your characters are to form is a rarity, one sure to turn heads in governments, corporations and international organizations alike.

Because novas are so individualistic, a functional team of them is an entity of great power. It is thus highly desirable that the characters basically trust and support each other. Much like a family, the team may not always get along — individuals could even have distinctly opposing philosophies — but there remains a foundation of respect and reliance on one another that can weather almost any storm.

Creating a Team

The type of team the characters comprise has a tremendous bearing on what the series will be like. If the Storyteller plans to run a series steeped in intrigue and geopolitical machinations, he should make sure the players know this before they create a group of combat-hungry elites. In the end, the story revolves around the team (and, therefore, the characters); understanding what the team is about helps both players and the Storyteller to immerse themselves in the **Aberrant** milieu.

The following are a few questions that should be considered about the team during character creation and (hopefully) answered by the end of the prologue.

• **Where is the team based?** The answer to this question depends on where the Storyteller sets his series. Knowing that the team operates out of T2M Addis Ababa, DeVries corporate offices, a New York penthouse or someone's flat gives a good basis for both Storyteller and players.

• **How do the team members interact?** A team's internal dynamics can give everyone a wealth of roleplaying opportunities and story hooks. Are the members all close friends? Is the team a business or entertainment venture? Are there jealousies or rivalries among members? Are there any secrets kept from certain members? What's the level of trust and camaraderie?

• **What is the team's purpose?** A team's purpose usually ties closely with the type of series the Storyteller runs. The team may have a specific charter given to it by backers (contain and control rogue novas, act as PR reps and special agents for their corporations), or it may have its own agenda (expose Utopia's hidden activities, subjugate the human race). The team's focus may be on combat or intrigue, and the Storyteller should be sure that missions are geared accordingly. However, it always helps to mix things up a bit (having a cadre of masked elites escort a high-ranking diplomat to an international symposium can make for some interesting roleplaying).

• **Is there a team leader?** Decisions must be made somehow. Does your team go by military rank or corporate structure? Is it a democratic group? Are the members well-disciplined and respectful of others' suggestions, or do they tend toward petty squabbling?

• **What is the team's allegiance?** Depending on Backgrounds, your characters may work for (or found/own) Utopia, a powerful corporation or a government agency. A group with the support of an agency or government can draw upon this resource for finances, gear and backup — although usually at the cost of restrictions on the members' freedoms and responsibilities. A team that goes it alone can call its own shots, but it operates without a safety net.

• **Who are the team's enemies?** The team might consciously choose to defy a specific group. What does that group plan to do about the characters' considerable threat? Are there other agencies operating contrary to the team's goals? Is the team aware of these forces? What do these enemies intend?

• **Why does the team exist?** This is perhaps the most important question of all. There's a reason why the characters got together and remain together. Did they have a friend in common? Are they all on the run from Utopia or some other group? Were they drawn together by similar goals or philosophies, or is it simply a marriage of convenience?

Prologue

The prologue is your character's introduction to the world and story. It combines back history, personal details and transformation into a nova. The prologue is usually a short, one-on-one roleplaying session between player and Storyteller that introduces you and your character to the **Aberrant** universe.

Fine Tuning

The prologue lets you test your character, making sure she can do the things you want her to. It's not unusual to discover that an Ability functions differently than you thought, or that a higher (or lower!) Trait makes more sense for your character. After the prologue, you may modify your character (with the Storyteller's supervision), adjusting her to better fit your concept and the series. You don't get any more development points, but you may shift existing points around as appropriate. Once you begin the regular series, any further modifications must be made with experience points.

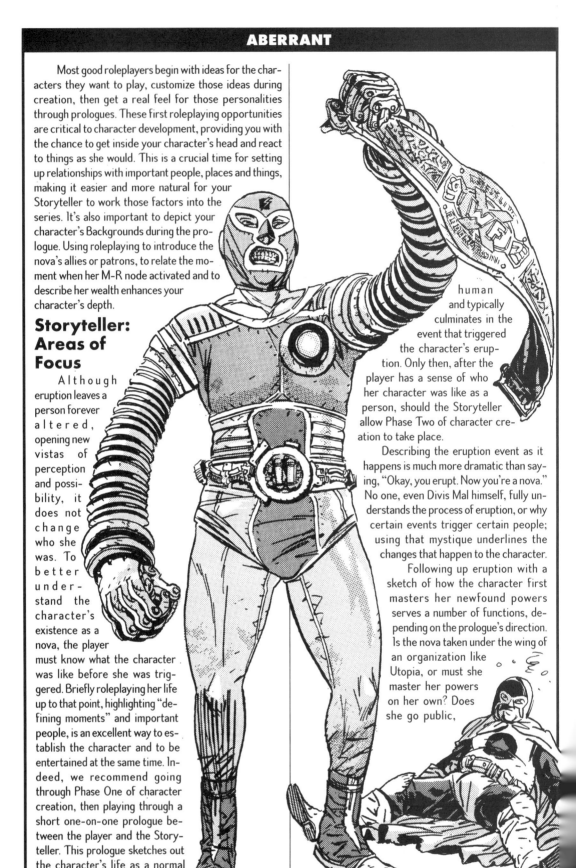

Most good roleplayers begin with ideas for the characters they want to play, customize those ideas during creation, then get a real feel for those personalities through prologues. These first roleplaying opportunities are critical to character development, providing you with the chance to get inside your character's head and react to things as she would. This is a crucial time for setting up relationships with important people, places and things, making it easier and more natural for your Storyteller to work those factors into the series. It's also important to depict your character's Backgrounds during the prologue. Using roleplaying to introduce the nova's allies or patrons, to relate the moment when her M-R node activated and to describe her wealth enhances your character's depth.

Storyteller: Areas of Focus

Although eruption leaves a person forever altered, opening new vistas of perception and possibility, it does not change who she was. To better understand the character's existence as a nova, the player must know what the character was like before she was triggered. Briefly roleplaying her life up to that point, highlighting "defining moments" and important people, is an excellent way to establish the character and to be entertained at the same time. Indeed, we recommend going through Phase One of character creation, then playing through a short one-on-one prologue between the player and the Storyteller. This prologue sketches out the character's life as a normal

human and typically culminates in the event that triggered the character's eruption. Only then, after the player has a sense of who her character was like as a person, should the Storyteller allow Phase Two of character creation to take place.

Describing the eruption event as it happens is much more dramatic than saying, "Okay, you erupt. Now you're a nova." No one, even Divis Mal himself, fully understands the process of eruption, or why certain events trigger certain people; using that mystique underlines the changes that happen to the character.

Following up eruption with a sketch of how the character first masters her newfound powers serves a number of functions, depending on the prologue's direction. Is the nova taken under the wing of an organization like Utopia, or must she master her powers on her own? Does she go public, or does she try to hide from intrusive government agents, Utopia recruiters and media barracudas? Whatever the specific focus of a prologue, the key is to give the players a taste of the universe, thus making each character and the setting all the more real and dynamic in subsequent sessions.

Each character's prologue should ultimately set the scene for the team as a whole. This introduction could culminate in the characters uniting, or could set things in motion to bring them together in the first episode. Whatever the case, the Storyteller should ensure that individual prologues reinforce, however subtly, the goals to which the team will dedicate itself.

Character Development

During a story, your character learns many things about himself, his abilities and his areas for improvement. Success and failure combine to teach you about your character's limitations and potential. Your character will make mistakes, gain insight, practice and hopefully not repeat past errors. All of these things are measured in a game through *experience points*.

Experience

The Storyteller has the responsibility of quantifying each character's experiences. While the knowledge *you* gain concerning plotlines, supporting characters and your team cannot be measured, *your character's* experience can. Experience points are an artificial measure of success or accomplishment that translate into enhanced power and capability. The dramatic situations in which **Aberrant** characters often find themselves promote fast learning as a means of survival.

Awarding Experience Points

The Storyteller should award experience points at the end of every story. All characters typically get the same number, although particularly outstanding accomplishments or roleplaying can earn an individual bonus experience. The amount of experience points given depends on a number of factors.

Keep in mind that a story might continue for more than one game session, although withholding experience points for too long can frustrate players. Generally, if the Storyteller sees a particular story arc continuing for more than three sessions, she should give experience about halfway (or even a third of the way) through the story.

The categories below describe areas in which characters can win experience. Each category is worth one experience point. No character should ever fulfill every single category at one time, although multiple characters may qualify for the same award.

- **Automatic** — Each character receives one point at the end of every story.
- **Discovery** — The character understands something new and significant about himself, his fellow novas or the universe.
- **Exceptional Roleplay** — The player roleplayed his character particularly well. This behavior should be appropriate to the character; points should not be awarded for outlandish, out-of-character antics.
- **Heroism** — The character risked life and limb to save the day. Only the most dramatic situations qualify for this award — stupidity does not count.
- **Wisdom** — The character discovered a way out of a trap or learned the truth behind a mystery. The group often deduces solutions together, in which case everyone should be awarded. However, if one character pieces everything together by himself, only he gets the award.
- **Creativity** — This point is reserved for players who add to the story's enjoyment without detracting from the game. This includes, but is not limited to, well-developed backgrounds, character journals or introducing new story elements. This bonus is highly discretionary and should be awarded infrequently.
- **Cohesion** — The characters worked exceptionally well together, defeating their opponents or strategically investigating all avenues of information.

Roleplaying Development

Skill doesn't develop spontaneously. The dots on your character sheet are easy to fill in, but improving such capabilities in real life takes time, practice and application. **Aberrant** characters, like real people, can improve only Traits that they exercise. There are three key ways to justify increasing your character's capabilities: application, research and training. As such, you can spend experience points on a particular Trait only if your character has used that skill, performed thorough research or received additional training.

It is vital, whatever method of development that you follow, that the growth be roleplayed. Whether that means seeking out your mentor for formalized training or swapping tips of the trade with others, development must be part of the story. Taking an entire game session to roll dice and increase your character's Brawl Ability isn't the point. The Storyteller and player should agree upon the circumstances and time necessary to improve a Trait. Skill improvement need not be the focus of the story, but it should derive logically from the plot.

Experience Costs

Once experience is doled out, players can spend it in any of the following areas. Costs vary depending on the Trait involved. Also, increasing Traits or buying new ones must be roleplayed before spending any points (it's the roleplaying that's important).

Trait Increase	Cost
Attribute	current rating x 4
Ability	current rating x 2
Background	current rating x 2
Mega-Attribute	current rating x 5
Quantum Power (Level 1)	current rating x 3
Quantum Power (Level 2)	current rating x 5
Quantum Power (Level 3)	current rating x 7
Willpower	current rating
Quantum	current rating x 8
Quantum Pool	3 per dot
Initiative	current rating

New Trait	Cost
Ability	3
Specialty (max. three per Ability)	1
Background	2
Enhancement	5
Mega-Attribute	6
Quantum Power (Level 1)	3
Quantum Power (Level 2)	6
Quantum Power (Level 3)	9

Note: A level of Quantum, Mega-Attribute, enhancement or quantum power can be bought tainted for half cost (rounded up); however, the nova immediately acquires a permanent Taint point, along with all the associated negative effects.

Application

Using a Trait repeatedly is the primary way to exercise it. Abilities that you use regularly are perfect to spend experience on. Such "training in the field" is suitable for virtually all Traits.

Even if you fail in a task, related Traits still qualify as practiced or applied. Sometimes we learn more from our mistakes than from our successes. The Storyteller should allow you to spend experience on Traits used ineffectively as well as on those used effectively.

Research

Research is useful for improving knowledge-related Traits. Simple study, however, does not complete the process. Real-world application cements such information, giving your character a solid foundation of knowledge and practical experience.

You can increase knowledge-related Traits at low levels with in-depth research. At higher ratings, however, you must combine study with application.

Research material for raising Traits can be found almost anywhere. Websites, educational programming, printed books or even scientific experimentation can increase your character's knowledge base. New material appropriate to a Trait must be studied each time you wish to increase that Trait.

Training

If your character isn't exposed to situations in which her Abilities improve naturally, she can seek training. Formalized training focuses on improving a certain Trait through rigorous repetition in a controlled environment. Any Trait can be improved through training, although some skills develop better through "real-world" application.

Your character can seek training from numerous sources. Gyms promote physical fitness, schools educate and various programs are designed to improve social skills. Also, the Aeon Society offers its Rashoud facilities, through Project Utopia, for novas who wish to better their quantum powers (so long as the novas in question are on the Project's good side, of course...). Attending most of these training institutions costs money and time. The Storyteller should attach an appropriate price tag and training time, in addition to the experience-point cost.

Finding and indulging in training is more than a way to improve Traits. A resourceful Storyteller can tie training sessions into the series, plumbing new depths in your character's identity and in the story.

Increasing Attributes

Each of the Attribute groups demands a different focus for improvement. Physical Attributes can be improved through rigorous training or exercise. Combat experience, manual labor or athletic pursuits can all improve your character's physical prowess. Mental Attributes develop mostly through discipline and constant exposure to new material. A stagnant mind never improves, while an active one can overcome any limitation. The major component of improving Social Attributes is human interaction. Practice and some training with others can help mold social skills.

Increasing Abilities

Aberrant characters possess a wide range of Abilities, which improve readily with the proper focus. Any Ability can be increased given the proper training. While such improvement is rapid at low levels, the cost increases dramatically as your character's expertise grows. Even among novas, only the most dedicated individuals can master their fields.

An Ability in which your character has a specialty increases just like any other. When the specialized Ability raises to the next dot, your character's specialty automatically goes up as well, remaining one dot higher than the Ability itself. This increase works the same for all of the specialties that your character has in that Ability (remember that your character is limited to a maximum of three Specialties in each Ability).

Say your character currently has two dots in Firearms, and you had previously purchased the Targeting specialty (giving your character an extra die when aiming). Raising the Firearms Ability to 3 costs eight experience points, and you still keep the extra die for targeting (giving your character a 4 Firearms rating when aiming).

Increasing Nova Powers

The means for increasing nova powers are as individual as novas themselves, though a few commonalties have presented themselves. Tapping into quantum powers typically involves some degree of light meditation or disciplinary exercises, though the techniques vary depending on the powers invoked and, of course, the individual nova herself. Project Utopia's Rashoud facilities offer opportunities for training; most countries and many major cities host at least one Rashoud facility. However, the individuality of novas' powers means that one nova's training techniques do not necessarily apply to another; a nova who specializes in Mega-Strength might have little to offer a student seeking to master an Elemental Anima. Furthermore, novas are still exceedingly rare; an "appointment" to be tutored might need to be set up months in advance. Ultimately, many novas must train themselves, through trial and (sometimes dangerous) error. On a more dubious note, the Teragen eagerly assists any novas who ask, but only in exchange for favors or future service.

Developing new powers is typically a touch-and-go process, and accompanied by searing headaches to boot, as the M-R node channels energies in new ways. Accordingly, for the first story or two after developing new powers, all uses of those powers are made at a greater difficulty — typically +1 or +2. This penalty is offset if the nova takes adrenocilin (see the Appendix, p. 281).

Increasing Backgrounds

Backgrounds can be improved only through actual roleplay. New contacts cannot be studied, nor can you practice increasing your number of close allies or your mentor's power and influence. Backgrounds develop strictly over the course of a story. The Storyteller can introduce a new contact, but if you botch the connection, the contact might never call back. Likewise, your character may actively seek to gain more influence by manipulating politicians and local authorities. Backgrounds developed through roleplay then cost experi-

Development and Backgrounds

Certain Backgrounds can reduce the costs of improving a Trait. Most notably, the Mentor Background provides you with direct access to training or research materials. Although the mentor acts as an advisor and confidant, she also can provide your character with the means to improve himself. The Storyteller should decide what Abilities your patron might have (determined by the Background's rating and the mentor's nature). Mentors aren't automatons that simply improve your character's capability with a snap of their fingers. Your character still has to work at the Trait and may even owe his mentor a favor or two.

Contacts, allies and even followers may possess superior skill in certain areas. These people may prove more difficult to tap for education and training than going to a mentor, but they are still excellent resources. Contacts usually charge fees (favors, money, information), and they certainly aren't as helpful as a real teacher. However, your character may have access to a wide range of training through contacts. Allies are often very helpful, and they can present a wide array of abilities. Still, social or family obligations between you and your allies can interfere with training. Followers may feel obligated to teach you, although they may resent the new responsibility, depending on the nature of the bond.

Overall, your character's Backgrounds provide a vast range of potential educational opportunities. The ease of drawing upon these resources depends on the nature of the relationship, the background character's capability and your character's own initiative.

ence points to raise. To make the new rating an intrinsic part of your character, a key element of his ongoing story, you must spend the appropriate experience.

New Backgrounds develop in much the same way. They're introduced into the story by you or the Storyteller. They are then made permanent by spending experience points.

This is not to say that your character can have friends, resources or gear only if she buys them as Backgrounds. If she stumbles across a case full of money or lucks onto an armored jumpsuit, you needn't spend experience to keep it.

Backgrounds represent special relationships that you feel create an important dynamic for your character. Friends, money and connections that aren't purchased as Backgrounds still exist, but they don't have the same strong ties to your character as those bought as Backgrounds do. You need to spend experience only on the

Backgrounds that you want to be a central part of the story, a sort of "supporting cast" of your very own. Backgrounds give your character special benefits and shouldn't be treated frivolously (by either player or Storyteller).

Losing Traits

Generally, Attributes, Abilities and powers can be reduced only due to extreme injury, loss of a limb or a similar condition. If your character suffers an injury sufficient to impair her, the Storyteller must decide what impact the accident has on her Traits. Your character's Traits should be reduced only in the most extreme cases.

Backgrounds, unlike most Traits, can actually lower in rating over time. Contacts, mentors and allies may cease assisting you (whether due to poor treatment by your character, disappearing or even dying), while influence can end with the next election or coup. Backgrounds should be reduced only if you abuse them (assaulting allies, squandering resources) or if the reduction furthers the plot — in which case the Storyteller should restore or replace the Background at a later date.

The Storyteller should make sure any changes to a character's Backgrounds are justified through the character's own actions or that they contribute productively and significantly to the story. Followers don't exist for the Storyteller to snuff; they're just as much a part of the character as her Attributes and Abilities, and they should be given the same consideration.

Personality Development

Your character's personality can change radically over time. Innocent youths can become hardened veterans, while cynics can learn to believe in truly good causes. These changes cannot be mapped on a character sheet. They develop through roleplaying and interaction with other characters. Certain Traits, however, define your character's personality. Nature describes true personality, Allegiance reflects loyalties, Willpower rates strength of will and Quantum assesses ability to interact with the fundamental forces of the universe.

Changing Nature

Nature defines a personality's overriding focus. The forces that shape a child into an adult mold the basic fabric of her personality. These influences (parents, siblings, friends, enemies) cannot be denied. Even if you reject the tenets these influences uphold, they still alter your perception and compel you to accept an alternative.

Changing the course of these personality influences can be impossible as the child reaches maturity.

For the purposes of **Aberrant**, your character's Nature should rarely shift. It might change only after long-term influence from outside forces, in-depth "soul searching" or after a particularly traumatic event.

If you wish to change your character's Nature, discuss it with the Storyteller so the adjustment may be tied into the game. Whatever the specific circumstance, the change should be a dramatic story element.

Changing Allegiance

Allegiance can be changed as the story warrants (an Individualist nova seduced by the Teragen, a Proteus nova betraying the agency to Utopia, etc.). Though switching allegiance can have grave consequences in the story — and betraying a geopolitical power is almost certain to make many enemies for the character — a change of allegiance costs no experience points to implement.

Increasing Willpower

Willpower is a quantified Trait that may be increased with experience points. However, this Trait should not increase without some logical reason. For example, a traumatic event may harden your character's heart, strengthening her resolve. Focus and meditation could lead to an improved understanding of her core being. In short, events during the story have a direct effect on Willpower, much as they do on any other Trait. The main difference between Willpower and other Traits is that Willpower cannot be researched or taught. Increases in Willpower should never be approved casually by the Storyteller.

Increasing Quantum and Quantum Pool

More than any other Trait, Quantum is a measure of a character's potential for power. Accordingly, Quantum can be increased only by continuously practicing one's powers and exploring one's nova nature. Characters who routinely push the limits of their power (for example, spending Willpower to max powers or attempting high-difficulty actions) might be eligible for a rise in Quantum or Quantum Pool. (Note that, after game play begins, an increase in Quantum does not dictate an automatic increase in Quantum Pool; the two Traits must be raised separately.)

As always, the Storyteller has final say as to whether spending experience points in this area has been justified in the game.

CHAPTER THREE: TRAITS

Traits register your character's capabilities, strengths and weaknesses. While little more than marks on paper, Traits enable you to translate a complex personality into the strictures of game reality. This framework gives you the general parameters of what your character can accomplish, but your imagination and roleplaying shape what she actually does. **Aberrant** Traits are designed to be broad; this game is about characters, not statistics.

The previous chapter outlined the character creation and development process; this chapter contains many of the Traits you may choose from to design your character. Mega-Attributes and quantum powers are detailed in Chapters Four and Five, respectively.

Nature

Nature is a basic description of your character's self-perception; no character fits any Nature exactly, but one usually describes his concept well enough. Nature isn't all that a character is about. Rather, it serves as a basic guide to your character's perspective on the **Aberrant** universe and how to act in and react to that universe.

While Nature helps describe who your character really is on the inside, this may not be the facade he presents to the world. However, a person's mood and demeanor can change depending on whom he's with and what situation he's in. Your character's outward personality is handled entirely through roleplaying (although his Nature should accent his general disposition).

In game terms, Nature is important because it enables the character to regain Willpower points. Each Nature archetype lists the criteria necessary to regain Willpower. "See Willpower," p. 144, for specifics on spending and recovering Willpower. Additionally, novas' quantum powers are often shaped by their Nature; an Explorer might well gain Mega-Perception, while a Bravo might express his potential via Mega-Strength or a Quantum Bolt.

The archetypes listed here are a small sample of the many faces of humanity; feel free to create new Natures.

Analyst: You approach the universe as a riddle to be answered. You live by logic and deduction; any problem can be solved in a rational manner. Your goal is to uncover the truth, to understand everything. However, your intense interest in finding the answers to questions can be distracting, since you get caught up by minutiae and may lose sight of the larger issue.

Gain Willpower when a rational, scientific approach helps solve a situation.

Architect: You are driven to create something of lasting value for those who come after you, whether it be a new social order, a company, an art or some other legacy. Disorder and decay are your enemies; you hope to bring about order and progress through your efforts. If you become fixated on your goal, you may force your dream on others.

Gain Willpower when you accomplish a significant goal.

Bravo: There are winners and losers in life, and you are definitely a winner. You reinforce your self-worth by dominating situations, whether through physical brawls or political intrigues. You might terrorize or protect the weak, but such weakness is not something you tolerate in yourself. You don't know the meaning of fear, and failure is not an option. Then again, you're not sure what discretion means, either, and compromise isn't on your list of choices.

Gain Willpower whenever you make someone else back down.

Bureaucrat: Laws were created for a reason, and your primary concern is to follow them. No matter what the crisis, you follow the proper procedure. If people don't obey the System, chaos will run rampant. You take comfort in established processes, confident that they are the key to victory. Strict adherence to policy may blind you to better options.

Gain Willpower when a crisis is resolved by following correct procedures.

Caregiver: You always try to make a difference, helping those around you — and they depend on you for it. You're not blind to the flaws of others; if anything, that makes your desire to aid them stronger. You gain strength from knowing that you make a difference, that you ease the suffering in the world. Yet you have nowhere to turn for support.

Gain Willpower when you receive tangible proof that you have helped another.

Conniver: Why break your own back when you can talk someone else into breaking his for you? You always try to manipulate others before applying yourself. You advance your cause by coordinating your friends' efforts and sowing dissent among your enemies. You fear that others may be doing exactly the same thing to you, making it difficult for you to trust anyone.

Gain Willpower when you trick someone into doing what you want.

Critic: You find purpose in revealing weaknesses and faults, whether in artwork, an organization or a person's habits. You strive to perfect others by pointing out their shortcomings. You do this for their own good, whether they want your help or not. You can do your job too well, convincing someone that he isn't just flawed but worthless, perhaps driving away even those closest to you.

Gain Willpower when you point out a significant flaw that would have been harmful had it been overlooked.

Explorer: The prospect of finding new places, people and things — whether it's a new natural resource, an untapped power or a musical style — gives your life meaning. Discoveries are your passion, and you devote a great deal of time and effort to keeping up with current events. The routine and commonplace bores you, and learning of someone else's discovery fills you with envy. You constantly set your sights on the horizon, sometimes at the expense of the here and now.

Gain Willpower whenever you make a significant discovery.

Follower: Leaders need followers, and you await your orders. Taking charge isn't your style. It isn't in your nature to rebel. In fact, your strength comes from your ability to cooperate with a variety of personalities toward a common cause. Yet, while you might follow your commander into the sun, you tend to lack the self-esteem to question such a suicidal act.

Gain Willpower if you help the team succeed because you carry out your assigned duty.

Gallant: You are one of the noticeable ones, and others had better damn well recognize it! Your ego thrives on recognition and the admiration of others (though you'll settle for less desirable sorts of attention). You love being in the public eye, and nothing beats performing before an awestruck crowd. While you are certainly flamboyant and full of vivacity, others often see the potential in your overconfident approach to lead you to disastrous misjudgments.

Gain Willpower whenever your deeds are particularly impressive, awe-inspiring or likely to land you smack in the center of attention.

Hedonist: Life is too important to waste, so have as good a time as possible. You only go around once, after all. You don't mind a little hard work as long as a good time awaits you at the end of it. Pleasure is its own reward, and you pity those who take life too seriously to realize it. Even so, your pursuit of a good time can take you too far.

Gain Willpower whenever you have a truly good time (and bring others along for the ride).

Jester: The only sane defense against an insane universe is to laugh at it all. Sorrow and pain are your enemies, and humor is your weapon. You act the fool to take others' minds off gloom and despair. In your pursuit to spread smiles, you may cross the line, distracting and irritating those whom you mean to entertain.

Gain Willpower whenever you can lighten the mood or ease a tense situation.

Judge: You seek to solve the problems of others by acting as a mediator, arbitrator or even a friend. You pride yourself on your clear judgment and ability to find compromises. Conflict and dissent are abhorrent to you; you know there is always an option on which everyone can agree. Your greatest fear is that you may use poor judgment, and thinking this way makes you question even the most obvious of choices.

Gain Willpower any time you lead others to an amicable resolution.

Leader: You're meant to be in charge. You excel at organizing, and others look to you for direction. You trust your own judgment implicitly, and you have no qualms about taking over a project and shaping it the way you see fit. There are two ways to do a job: your way and the wrong way. While you may be a master of direction, ignoring others' suggestions could be your downfall.

Gain Willpower when others follow you without disputing your decisions.

Martyr: You're ready to put yourself at risk so that another person or a cause succeeds, even when the sacrifice isn't necessary. You drive yourself twice as hard as anyone else does, expecting no reward other than recognition of your efforts. Despite this suffering, you endure, clinging firmly to the belief that you make a difference. In your blind desire to throw yourself into the breach, you could sacrifice yourself for nothing.

Gain Willpower whenever you sacrifice yourself or something of yours to a higher goal.

Paragon: You have lofty and concrete ideals about what is right and noble in human nature, and you strive to embody those ideals. You consider your powers a great gift and a tremendous responsibility, and you feel dutybound to use them in the pursuit of righteousness and altruism. Though you aspire to be a role model, you are not a Gallant — public display is not as important as the knowledge of good deeds accomplished. Some might see you as self-righteous, but you are your own worst critic.

You are completely intolerant of human foibles (especially your own), and this lack of acceptance might well drive you over the edge one day.

Gain Willpower whenever you accomplish a significant task for the greater good.

Rebel: You're the ultimate free-thinker. Whether you champion a cause or simply feel contrary, you choose your own path. Others are welcome to join your march to a different drummer, but only if their beat matches yours. You defy authority in principle and deed, even if you have similar views.

Gain Willpower whenever you defy an established authority.

Survivor: You can endure nearly any circumstance. No matter what happens, you always persevere. Never say die and never give up — ever. You have no time for those who crumble at the first sign of adversity. In fact, to be safe, you avoid forming close ties with others. You'll pull through whatever the odds, even if it means sacrificing others.

Gain Willpower whenever you survive a difficult situation through your own cunning and perseverance.

Thrillseeker: You don't do things for the ends, but for the rush that the means provides. Risk gives your life meaning, and boredom is death. The stakes are never so high that they can't be made higher. As long as there's a thrill in it, you're willing to pay almost any price. Paybacks are a bitch, though, and you will get in over your head sooner or later.

Gain Willpower every time you put yourself in a life-threatening situation, then escape it.

Traditionalist: You believe the solutions for today's problems can be found by applying the methods of the past. Constant change destroys instead of creates. You wrap yourself in tradition, resisting innovations and breakthroughs. Not all change is bad, though; in holding too tightly to old ways, you can miss something better.

Gain Willpower when a tried-and-true method proves effective.

Visionary: You have a goal that only you can see, something to which you've dedicated your life. You may be a spiritualist, philosopher or inventor, but whatever you are, you search for something more. You create new possibilities by seeing beyond the bounds of conventional imagination. Though you are full of new ideas, your head is often among the stars.

Gain Willpower whenever you take a concrete step toward realizing your goal.

Allegiance

Ultimately, each nova stands alone. In the world of 2008, novas are among the prime movers and shakers; each is of potentially global significance. There are few "organization men" among their ranks; novas are courted as allies rather than recruited as minions.

Nonetheless, certain global organizations deal with novas more than the ruck and run of humanity, and novas have accordingly congregated to groups with the power and resources to play at something approximating the novas' own level. At the Storyteller's option, each nova character should select an allegiance for herself. This allegiance (supplemented by Background Traits like Backing and Allies) defines the organization or philosophy to which the nova adheres, if any. The Storyteller has a hand in this; for example, she is perfectly within her bounds to say, "This series is about a cadre of Team Tomorrow members, so all characters have allegiance to Utopia," or "The characters are all part of a nova performing act, so all characters are Individualists with no ties to anybody."

Many of these allegiances can suggest or even dictate Background expenditures. For example, rank in organizations such as Utopia requires the Backing Background; a member of Team Tomorrow will have high ratings in Backing, Allies, Resources and Influence (and his player will likely have to spend some bonus points to get the levels he needs). For double-agents or fugitives, the Cipher Background is absolutely essential.

Though many series will require all characters to have the same allegiance, it is entirely possible to run a series with mixed allegiances. An "all-Utopian" group could consist of one true Utopian, an Aberrant masquerading as a Utopian, an Individualist who's working with Utopia on a case-by-case basis, and a Teragen member masquerading as an Aberrant masquerading as a Utopian! Likewise, an Aberrant series could feature two Aberrants, two Individualists (friends of the Aberrants who are not convinced of the Utopia conspiracy, though they are standing by their pals for now) and a Teragen member (helping out her fellow novas against Utopia's duplicity in an effort to recruit the Aberrants to the Teragen cause). It is even possible to have Utopian and Aberrant members in the same series; after all, many Aberrants formerly belonged to Utopia, and two friends or lovers may maintain their relationship, each refusing to betray the other while trying to talk some sense into their "misguided" companion.

As a player, you do not have to broadcast your true allegiance publicly, or even to the other players. Indeed, all Proteus novas, and many Teragen, Aberrant and Directive novas, do not openly acknowledge their allegiance. In theory, a character can have many allegiances, open and secret. For example, some Utopians are actually moles for Project Proteus, making sure that Utopia remains focused on what it needs to be doing. A Directive agent could be a spy for the Teragen, or vice versa. Some novas might be triple or even quadruple agents, though these characters play a dangerous game indeed.

Here are the most common allegiances in the **Aberrant** world:

• **Aberrants:** The Aberrants are a very new faction, having appeared only in the last couple of months (as of May 2008); the name is an ironic adoption of a common anti-nova epithet. As of the game's beginning, there are only a few dozen Aberrants in the entire world; most work individually, though a few cells of three or more exist. Most Aberrants do not publicly identify themselves as such, since the group's founders, André Corbin and Sophia Rousseau, are being sought by Utopia and world authorities. Indeed, many Aberrants are still publicly affiliated with Project Utopia. These "closet Aberrants" attempt to find out the truth behind Utopia's agenda while avoiding the revelation of their true allegiance.

The Aberrants firmly believe that Project Utopia has been corrupted by a conspiracy; this conspiracy, they are certain, intends to enslave or destroy novas, and possibly the human race as well, through a variety of subversive operations. The Aberrants' primary goals, then, are to root out and expose the corruption in the organization and to recruit other novas to their banner. However, most Aberrants are aware of Utopia's many good works and would rather fix the problem than destroy Utopia outright. The Aberrants also realize that blatantly exposing Utopia's agenda would lead to worldwide panic. Accordingly, Aberrants are reluctant to go public with what they have learned, even if they thought it would be safe to do so (which they do not).

The Aberrants are aware of the existence of Project Proteus, though they have yet to uncover much of its true membership or agendas. The Aberrants are trying to convince as many Utopians and Individualists as possible that Utopia has been compromised, though their uncertainty as to the extent of Utopia's network forces them to do so furtively. Although the Aberrants realize that the Teragen also hates Utopia, they have not yet formed an alliance with it; most Aberrants consider the Teragen to be a dangerous band of radicals and terrorists, possibly even the root behind the corruption in Utopia. Most Aberrants are aware of a shadowy agency called the Directive, but they know little of its nature; the Aberrant stance is that the Directive could simply be a front for Project Proteus.

Suggested Backgrounds: Allies, Cipher, Contacts. Dormancy is useful to hide from pursuers.

• **Project Utopia:** Many novas are affiliated with this Aeon Society-founded international organization in a variety of capacities, ranging from the luminaries of Team Tomorrow to the support members who handle Utopia's less glamorous and more pragmatic concerns. Most novas experience Utopia's hospitality at least once in their lives, as they are invited to one of Utopia's Rashoud facilities and tutored in the rudiments of controlling their powers. Many novas elect to remain with Utopia following their initial eruption, and many more retain some ties to the group. After all, all Rashoud facilities are open to any nova so long as that nova is registered with the Project and not considered a threat.

Utopia's stated goal is to employ novas' vast power to better the world for nova and baseline alike. Less overtly, Utopia also takes great pains to cultivate a good public image for novas as a whole. The typical Utopian nova knows nothing of Project Proteus' existence and views the Aberrants' claims of a "shadow project" within Utopia as so much seditious propaganda. Most Utopians are highly disturbed by the recent "Slider scandal" and the rise of the Aberrants, viewing the Aberrants as traitors, murderers and dangerous subversives possibly allied with the Teragen. For its part, Utopia loathes the Teragen, seeing the movement as a band of selfish and destructive radicals. Not only is the Teragen the antithesis of everything Utopia stands for, but its actions could well turn the tide of public opinion against novas. Thus, Utopia does everything in its power to monitor Teragen sympathizers (and take them down when necessary). From what little Utopia knows of the Directive's existence, it considers the agency a hostile, reactionary cabal combining the worst aspects of J. Edgar Hoover and the Illuminati. Utopia takes a benevolent public stance toward unaffiliated novas. In practice, it makes an attempt to monitor and otherwise keep tabs on nova elements not directly tied to it; novas whose "selfish agendas" threaten the "cultivation of global harmony" are often approached and reasoned with, subtly or otherwise.

Suggested Backgrounds: Allies, Backing, Contacts, Influence, Mentor (experienced novas), Resources. Team Tomorrow Members *must* take Backing, Influence and Resources at 4 or greater, which may require an appropriate bonus-point expenditure.

• **Project Proteus:** Proteus is a true shadow organization. It exists so deep within the heart of Project Utopia that most Utopians are unaware of it. Few records of its presence exist, and those that do are highly encrypted and classified. Indeed, most Proteus "members" are unaware of their allegiance; Proteus tends to use mercenary elites, Utopians or other unaffiliated individuals, sending them on missions that advance the project's goals without ever letting the agents in question know for whom they're really working. Proteus is absolutely committed to secrecy, and it will do anything to maintain it, including terminating agents or entire branches.

Those Proteus novas who are aware of their affiliation believe that Proteus is a necessary adjunct to advance Utopia's less telegenic goals. They see Utopia as a good organization, necessary to continued harmony between humans and novas; their role, then, is that of the gardener, subtly pruning the Project where necessary, pulling up any weeds that surface and spraying destructive pests if need be. Most Proteus ops believe the Aberrants to be traitors, perhaps dupes of the Teragen, and they scoff at the Aberrants' claims of anti-nova sentiment permeating Utopia. After all, most Proteus agents are themselves novas.

Many Proteus novas hold "official" positions in Utopia, or even Team Tomorrow; some maintain covers as international celebrities or act as spies in government and corporate enterprises. No Proteus op ever admits to being a Proteus op except in absolute secrecy (and often not even then). As far as the world is concerned, Project Proteus does not exist, and Proteus' directors intend to do everything in their power to keep it that way.

Suggested Backgrounds: Cipher, Resources. "Official" Proteus ops have Allies and Backing. Other Backgrounds depend on the operative's cover identity.

• **The Teragen:** The Teragen movement is a philosophy particular to a few radical members of nova society. Though the movement was brought into the forefront by the shadowy nova, Divis Mal, the Teragen claims that Mal is not its leader, only its inspiration. The Teragen ascribes to the credo that novas are a separate species from the rest of humanity, and thus the laws, conventions, history and morality of *Homo sapiens* do not apply to them. The Teragen's stated goals are to "liberate" novas worldwide and help them realize their potential "by any means necessary."

Though the Teragen does not specifically call for separation from or aggression toward the rest of humanity, many of its members display a supremacist contempt toward baseline humans, and acts of revolutionary violence against "baseline fascism" are not unknown. Some members have also displayed a capricious callousness toward baseline "playthings," tarnishing the movement's image in the process. Since the Teragen claims not to be an organization as such, but merely a collection of like-minded individuals, radical acts by one sympathizer cannot be directly linked to other members; thus, for now, the Teragen as a whole has avoided massive retaliation. Nonetheless, the Teragen maintains a great deal of secrecy, and it is rumored to have hidden members and bases of operations worldwide.

The typical Teragen member hates Project Utopia with a passion and actively seeks the Project's destruction, believing the Project to have the worst of intentions for novas. The Teragen knows about the defection of the Aberrants, and has heard rumors of the existence of Project Proteus, but the group as a whole has not adopted a unified stance toward the Aberrants (not that the Teragen enacts "policy" anyway). Most Teragen feel that, with time, the Aberrants will come to them. The Teragen views the Directive with similar loathing, as a baseline agency attempting to suppress novas' rightful destiny. The Teragen takes a helpful, sometimes nurturing stance toward corporate, government and individualist novas, attempting to emancipate them from slavery to baseline concerns and help them realize their true place in the world to come.

Suggested Backgrounds: Allies (other Teragen), Cipher, Mentor, Node. The Teragen has no real structure or chain of command, so members do not need to take Backing. Likewise, many Teragen spurn human society and the Influence and Followers that come with it (though there are exceptions, such as Count Orzaiz).

• **The Directive:** The Directive is an international security, police and espionage agency founded by the United States, the UK, the Russian Confederation and Japan. Most members are baseline, but nova operatives fill out its ranks. The Directive's goals are to advance its member nations' interests and to act as a check against Utopia's growing power. Although the Directive has an "official" paper trail, its organizational structure and agenda are classified, and it takes pains to stay out of the public eye. Thus, most people do not know of it except as a name, and its activities and purpose are shrouded in rumor.

The typical Directive agent heartily distrusts Project Utopia and is very interested in the recent turmoil within the Project's ranks. The Directive also polices potentially dangerous international situations (terrorist factions, overly aggressive dictators, powerful novas), and it keeps a careful watch over China's large nova populace. The Directive shares Utopia's opinion that the Teragen is a very dangerous movement, though many Directive agents suspect that the Teragen and Utopia are secretly in cahoots, only staging an enmity for the cameras. A few Directive higher-ups have heard rumors of a "shadow cabal" within Utopia; certainly, such a group would explain many unusual occurrences over the past decade. The Directive knows that certain former members of Utopia have defected from the group, and agents are authorized to seek out and learn what they can about this situation, in hopes of finding out "the truth" about Utopia.

Suggested Backgrounds: Backing, Cipher, Contacts, Resources.

• **Corporate/Other:** Novas are certainly in demand, and there is no shortage of employers, sponsors and other backers all too willing to have a nova sign on the dotted line. In the United States, some large cities franchise one or more novas as PR reps and "public defenders"; residents hold these novas in the same reverence that they once held their 20th-century sports teams. Several corporations, including the DeVries Agency, the Hong Kong-based Novelty consulting firm, Exxon-Mobil, the N! network, ViaSoft, Third Millennium Motors and various Japanese technological firms, employ novas in various capacities. It is rumored that the global criminal cartels also retain one or more novas as "specialists."

Novas who work for a government or corporation by and large adopt their backers' views on global issues. Most novas view Utopia with equal parts fascination and suspicion. While many novas utilized Utopia's Rashoud facilities upon first erupting, many corporations hate Utopia's UN-granted authority to regulate potentially dangerous technology, viewing it as too powerful for its own good. Most government and corporate novas know little of the Teragen beyond gossip among novas and what they view in the media; only a few have even heard of the Aberrants, and none of them knows about Project Proteus. Novas working for a government or criminal cartel have likely heard of the Directive, but they know only spotty information about it; corporate novas may or may not know about the Directive.

Suggested Backgrounds: Allies, Backing, Influence, Resources.

• **Individualist:** Most novas have no defined allegiance to anything save their own goals and ends. A nova with Individualist "allegiance" is primarily motivated by self-interest, tempered with the agenda of whatever

Wheels Within Wheels

At heart, **Aberrant** is a game of mystery and conspiracy played at the highest levels of geopolitics. Part of the fun of the game is not knowing everything that's going on. Ideally, the secrets of the various novas and allegiances will reveal themselves over years of play and decades of game time, as the timeline ticks down toward the Aberrant War to come.

Accordingly, we're keeping our cards a bit close to our chest with regard to who the "real" good and bad guys are. The Aberrants *believe* that Utopia is corrupt... but then again, most Utopians believe that Aberrants harbor a sinister agenda and that its leaders are murderers. Utopians and Aberrants alike suspect the Directive of dissembling, and the Directive in turn trusts no one. *Nobody* trusts the Teragen, and almost no one's even heard of Proteus.

That having been said, the **Aberrant** timeframe will link up with the **Trinity** timeframe, and certain "official" events will lead to the gradual schism between baseline and nova, the rise of the psions, and the devastation of the Aberrant War. If you absotively, posilutely must do things "by the book," we'll have plenty of "official canon" support material for your (hopeful) enjoyment.

The thing about "official" and "canon," though, is that frankly, we don't put a lot of stock in 'em ourselves, and the needs of your series are more important than What Is Written on page XX, paragraph Yadda Yadda Yadda. Not only do we not require you to adhere to our vision of the 21st century, we encourage you to ignore it. Want Utopia to be a squeaky-clean, four-color New Deal for the world, with Team Tomorrow as the Justice League? Go for it. Want the Teragen to be blatant, snarling supervillains? Hey, it's your game. Want to ditch the entire concept of the Aberrant War and have the novas lead the human race to the stars? Make it so.

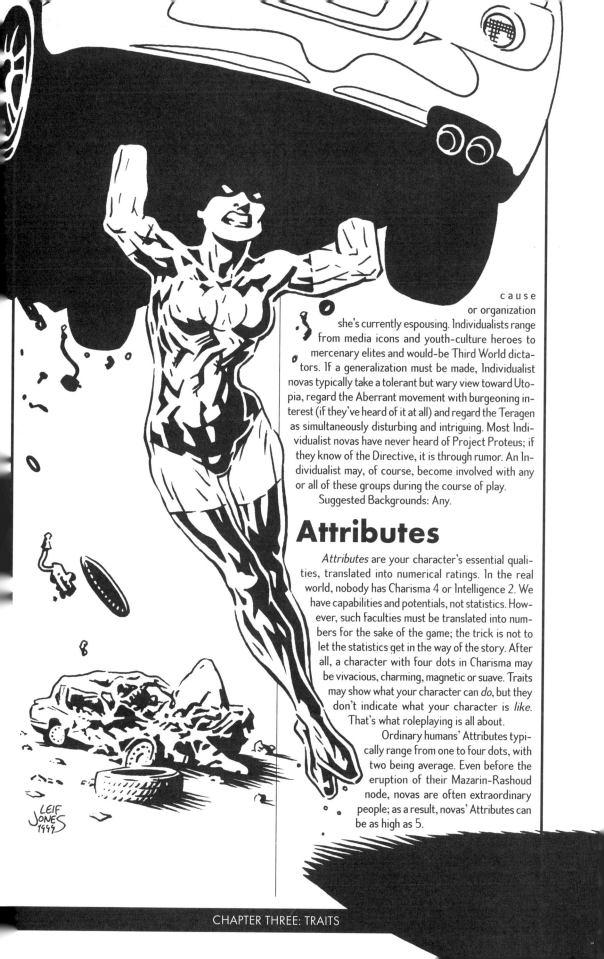

cause or organization she's currently espousing. Individualists range from media icons and youth-culture heroes to mercenary elites and would-be Third World dictators. If a generalization must be made, Individualist novas typically take a tolerant but wary view toward Utopia, regard the Aberrant movement with burgeoning interest (if they've heard of it at all) and regard the Teragen as simultaneously disturbing and intriguing. Most Individualist novas have never heard of Project Proteus; if they know of the Directive, it is through rumor. An Individualist may, of course, become involved with any or all of these groups during the course of play.

Suggested Backgrounds: Any.

Attributes

Attributes are your character's essential qualities, translated into numerical ratings. In the real world, nobody has Charisma 4 or Intelligence 2. We have capabilities and potentials, not statistics. However, such faculties must be translated into numbers for the sake of the game; the trick is not to let the statistics get in the way of the story. After all, a character with four dots in Charisma may be vivacious, charming, magnetic or suave. Traits may show what your character can *do*, but they don't indicate what your character is *like*. That's what roleplaying is all about.

Ordinary humans' Attributes typically range from one to four dots, with two being average. Even before the eruption of their Mazarin-Rashoud node, novas are often extraordinary people; as a result, novas' Attributes can be as high as 5.

Many novas have *Mega-Attributes*; a Mega-Attribute essentially increases the effectiveness of a normal Attribute by an exponential amount, allowing the character to transcend the limitations of normal humans. Even characters with Mega-Attributes, however, still retain their normal Attribute ratings, and these ratings indicate a character's capability within the range of the Mega-Attribute. For example, a character with a Strength of 1 who purchases the Mega-Strength Attribute at 1 can lift a ton or so of weight, but little more, whereas a character with a Mega-Strength of 1 and a normal Strength of 4 can push her lifting capacity to two, three or even more tons.

For more information on Mega-Attributes, see Chapter Four.

Qualities

You may select a *quality* for each of your character's Attributes rated 4 or higher. A quality reflects a Trait's aspect in which a person is remarkable, like Flexible (Dexterity), Suave (Charisma) or Discerning (Intelligence).

In game terms, a quality allows you to reroll any "10s" you roll for actions when that quality comes into play (like wriggling out of bindings for Flexible, impressing others for Suave or noting the relative worth of gems for Discerning). Any successes gained on the additional rolls are added to your total (including the original "10s"). And if you roll another "10" on a reroll, you keep rolling! Only one quality may be chosen per Attribute.

Physical Attributes

Physical Attributes indicate a character's raw strength, build, agility and sturdiness. Characters adept at physical combat or athletic activities have high Physical Attributes.

Strength

Strength rates physical power, including the capacity to lift objects and cause damage. This Attribute is used to resolve jumps, leaps and other actions that draw on raw physical power. Strength also determines the base number of damage dice rolled for successful physical attacks.

Of course, novas with Mega-Strength (p. 156) far exceed the capabilities of even the strongest normal human. Still, a character with a 4 or 5 Strength is very impressive by the standards of ordinary people.

Qualities: Athletic, Brutish, Rugged, Stout, Well-built, Wiry
- • Poor: Weakling (dead lift 15 kg).
- •• Average: That about says it all (dead lift 45 kg).
- ••• Good: Professional mover (dead lift 100 kg).
- •••• Exceptional: Linebacker (dead lift 165 kg).
- ••••• Superb: Olympic weightlifter (dead lift 240 kg).

Dexterity

Dexterity measures both agility and hand-eye coordination. It describes how fast a character runs, how precisely he aims at a target and everything else that relates to speed, grace and control. Dexterity also determines the base number of dice rolled to determine accuracy in combat, and it is combined with Wits to calculate Initiative.

Qualities: Coordinated, Delicate, Fast, Flexible, Nimble, Steady
- • Poor: Klutz.
- •• Average: You can dance without stepping on your partner's toes.
- ••• Good: You have a good deal of natural athletic potential.
- •••• Exceptional: You can juggle knives with flair.
- ••••• Superb: Olympic gymnast.

Stamina

Stamina indicates your character's health, tolerance for pain and how long she can maintain physical exertion. It encompasses endurance, physical will to live and sheer toughness. Stamina determines the character's base soak pool. Most novas develop reasonably high Stamina during eruption, as a side effect of channeling quantum energies.

Qualities: Determined, Enduring, Energetic, Resilient, Tenacious, Unflagging
- • Poor: You catch colds as a matter of course (1 bashing soak, 0 lethal soak).
- •• Average: You stay in moderately good health (2 bashing soak, 1 lethal soak).
- ••• Good: You seldom get sick, and you heal quickly (3 bashing soak, 1 lethal soak).
- •••• Exceptional: Marathon front-runner (4 bashing soak, 2 lethal soak).
- ••••• Superb: You can shrug off a strong man's punch (5 bashing soak, 2 lethal soak).

Mental Attributes

Mental Traits cover a character's perception, mental capacity, imagination and quick wits. Creative and intellectual individuals have high Mental Attributes.

Perception

Perception covers alertness and comprehension. It determines not only your character's attentiveness to the world around him, but how clearly he interprets it as well.

Qualities: Astute, Insightful, Intuitive, Nitpicky, Observant, Patient

- •   Poor: You misplace your keys routinely.
- • •   Average: You keep abreast of general goings-on.
- • • •   Good: You pick up on subtle subtext in books and conversations.
- • • • •   Exceptional: Your keen eye can pick out even the most minute of flaws.
- • • • • •   Superb: Sherlock Holmes was an amateur compared to you.

Intelligence

Intelligence measures raw mental processes — memory, retention, judgment, reasoning and imagination, as well as your character's ability to find connections between seemingly unrelated pieces of information or analyze complex ideas. This Attribute is not a measure of how fast your character thinks, but of how clearly he thinks.

Qualities: Bookworm, Bright, Clear-headed, Discerning, Pragmatic, Rational

- •   Poor: You're not the sharpest knife in the drawer (IQ 80).
- • •   Average: You remember family birthdays (IQ 100).
- • • •   Good: Your friends describe you as "bright" (IQ 130).
- • • • •   Exceptional: You're not just bright, you're downright brilliant (IQ 160).
- • • • • •   Superb: Genius (IQ 180+).

Wits

Wits ranks how quickly your character reacts to new situations and indicates general "grace under fire." This Attribute describes inherent common sense and how well your character thinks on the fly. Wits combines with Dexterity to determine base Initiative.

Qualities: Clever, Creative, Cunning, Ingenious, Level-headed, Shrewd

- •   Poor: Pull my finger.
- • •   Average: You know to quit while you're ahead.
- • • •   Good: You keep your cool in a firefight.
- • • • •   Exceptional: You always have the perfect comeback.
- • • • • •   Superb: You react almost before the other guy acts.

Social Attributes

Social Traits describe a character's influence, force of personality and looks. They often define interactions with others, from first impressions to leadership to dealing with people in general.

Appearance

Appearance is a combination of physical attractiveness and innate appeal. Call it animal magnetism or attractiveness, Appearance is your character's ability to make a good first impression or simply to generate an instinctive response in others.

Qualities: Alluring, Exotic, Imposing, Luminous, Pleasant, Sensual

- •   Poor: People suppress a cringe when they see you.
- • •   Average: Just that — another face in the crowd.
- • • •   Good: You turn heads when you enter a room.
- • • • •   Exceptional: You could be a model — or maybe you are.
- • • • • •   Superb: The "It Girl/ Guy" of your generation.

Manipulation

Manipulation measures your ability to influence others. This ability represents an aggressive persuasiveness, and it can be subtle or blatant. Manipulation covers everything from leading others to tricking them, from being sly to dominating. No one likes being fooled, though, so failing a Manipulation roll has risks.

Qualities: Authoritative, Cunning, Devious, Domineering, Persuasive, Witty

- •   Poor: You rarely get what you want.
- • •   Average: You fool some of the people some of the time.
- • • •   Good: You'd make a good lawyer.
- • • • •   Exceptional: Politicians envy your devious nature.
- • • • • •   Superb: Machiavelli had nothing on you.

Charisma

Charisma is used to charm others and to gain trust through natural appeal; your character's "force of personality," if you will. It reflects an air of confidence or social grace when dealing with people. Charisma defines how likable your character is to others and whether they actively seek her company.

Qualities: Charming, Cool, Eloquent, Genial, Polite, Suave

- •   Poor: People drift away when you approach.
- • •   Average: You're likable enough.
- • • •   Good: You're the life of the party.
- • • • •   Exceptional: Even your enemies respect you.
- • • • • •   Superb: You could lead a nation.

Abilities

Skill starts with raw potential (represented by an Attribute), combined with training or education (designated by an *Ability*). Abilities are grouped under the Attributes to which they relate most closely. When you perform an action, your dice pool is the combination of the appropriate base Attribute and the Ability most suited to the task (there may be exceptions to this process on occasion; see the "Cross-Matching Attributes and Abilities" sidebar in Chapter One). This combined rating is called the *skill total*.

Abilities are rated from • to • • • • •, and they are added to your character's Attributes. This combination can result in skill totals up to 10. Even one dot in an Ability implies at least basic proficiency. Although each Ability functions differently, all follow a similar scale of mastery.

x	Unskilled: No training in the Ability; rely on natural talent (default to related Attribute).
•	Novice: A basic grasp of the Ability; suitable for hobbies.
• •	Practiced: General familiarity with the Ability's applications; adequate professional training.
• • •	Competent: Detailed comprehension of the Ability's potential; skilled professional capacity.
• • • •	Expert: Profound understanding of virtually all of the Ability's aspects; peak talent in the field.
• • • • •	Master: Utter command of every possible way in which the Ability could be used; peerless mastery of the subject.

Specialties

Each Ability represents a fairly broad area of knowledge; it's unlikely that an individual would be equally skilled in all aspects of an entire category. To reflect this variety of specialization, Abilities have *specialties*, or areas of expertise. Specialties differ from qualities in that the former are areas of special training, while the latter are simply innate aspects of the individual.

Players buy specialties with bonus and/ or experience points. You may purchase a maximum of three specialties for each Ability. Refer to Chapter Two, p. 120, 124, for bonus point and experience costs. If you buy your character a specialty, simply write it after the Ability on your character sheet.

Once purchased, a specialty gives your character an extra die on all rolls related to that distinct qualification. A character with Drive 2 (Inclement Weather) adds two dice to his Dexterity for driving rolls, but since he's specialized in driving in bad conditions, he adds three dice to his Dexterity when making maneuvers in rain or snow.

Strength Abilities

Brawl: This skill covers styles of unarmed combat that rely more on power than on speed; they range from professional boxing to street fighting to wrestling. Brawl inflicts bashing damage, so while it isn't immediately fatal, it can inflict a fair amount of pain.

Specialties: Blind Fighting, Combinations, Dirty Maneuvers, Multiple Opponents, Fighting in Flight

Might: This Ability encompasses physical fitness and feats of focused muscle power. It rates lifting, climbing, jumping and throwing competence. While such tasks can be accomplished with brute force, Might helps your character use his physical power to maximum effect.

Specialties: Climb, Dead Lift, Leap, Throw

Dexterity Abilities

Athletics: A measure of fitness, this Ability concentrates on skills requiring balance, coordination and good reflexes. Athletics training can cover skill in various sports activities, knowing how to dodge and tumble or being able to maneuver in a microgravity environment.

Specialties: Acrobatics, Dodge, Gymnastics, Specific Sports, Tumbling

Drive: Most people are familiar with the basics of driving. This Ability gives you a detailed understanding of a vehicle's operation, including performing tricky maneuvers, driving at high speeds and engaging in pursuits. Drive is used to steer all forms of commercial land-based vehicles, from cars to motorcycles to trucks.

Specialties: Bootlegger's Reverse, Inclement Weather, Traffic

Firearms: This Ability covers weapon operation and basic maintenance, from personal sidearms to assault carbines to vehicle-mounted artillery. Weapons handle differently based on size, caliber and ammunition type. In the end, though, it still comes down to basic coordination and aim.

Specialties: Blind Fire, Cover Fire, Multiple Fire, Multiple Targets, Targeting

Legerdemain: This Ability describes skill with sleight of hand. Legerdemain is very useful for performing parlor magic, card tricks, filching small objects, switching items and even picking pockets. Legerdemain rolls are often made as resisted actions against a target's Awareness.

Specialties: Card Tricks, Palm Object, Parlor Magic, Pick Pockets, Switch Object

Martial Arts: This fighting Ability covers hand-to-hand styles such as aikido, capoeira, judo, karate, kung fu, tae kwon do, muay thai and more. Martial Arts styles inflict bashing damage. While it encourages speed over power, this Ability is as dangerous as any Brawl style.

Specialties: Blind Fighting, Combinations, Dirty Maneuvers, Multiple Opponents

Melee: A broad term for understanding the proper use of hand-to-hand armed combat and the proper care of weapons. Melee weapons range from knives to clubs to bottles.

Specialties: Ax, Chain, Club, Improvised Weapon, Knife, Nunchaku, Staff, Sword, Automobile (novas only)

Pilot: This Ability imparts skill in piloting airborne and submersible vehicles. Pilot covers not only basic control, but complicated maneuvers and combat techniques as well. Handling a craft in an atmosphere differs from maneuvering underwater, but all involve similar rudimentary piloting functions.

Specialties: Fighter, Frigate, Rotor, Submersible

Stealth: Stealth covers the capability to avoid notice, move quietly, trail someone and generally evade detection. Stealth rolls are usually made as resisted actions against another character's Awareness.

Specialties: Ambush, Camouflage, Hiding in Shadows, Sneak, Trail

Stamina Abilities

Endurance: This talent describes the capability to endure long-term exposure to severe conditions. This Ability differs from Resistance in that Endurance sustains your character's energy level over long periods of time. All novas start with at least three (free) dots in Endurance; see "Mega-Stamina" (p. 160).

Specialties: Fasting, Holding Breath, Long-Distance Exertion, Sleep Loss

Resistance: Resistance allows your character to temporarily combat the effects of physical pain or chemicals. This Ability can be used to restore dice lost due to injury and resist interrogation. All novas start with at least three (free) dots in Resistance; see "Mega-Stamina" (p. 160).

Specialties: Ignore Pain, Resist Disease, Resist Drugs, Resist Interrogation

Perception Abilities

Awareness: This Ability indicates how much your character notices about her surroundings. It's a measure of knowing what's physically nearby, covering input from all five senses. Awareness is useful for picking out a face in a crowd or for anticipating surprises that wait around a corner.

Specialties: Acute Hearing, Keeping Watch, Sharp Sight, Smell, Spot Ambush, Track

Investigation: Investigation is the skill of searching for relevant clues or information, whether at a crime scene, in a library or through speaking to witnesses. This Ability is vital to reconstruct (or uncover) events to gain insight into what really happened at a scene.

Specialties: Analysis, Concealed Objects, Deduction, Interviews, Quick Search, Research

Intelligence Abilities

Academics: Schooling reflects education in a given area of knowledge, such as history, law or philosophy. This Ability rates your character's degree of understanding of the topic, as well as her status in the field.

Specialties: Anthropology, Culture, Current Events, Geography, History, Law, Organization, Philosophy, Politics, Religion

Bureaucracy: This rating measures a person's understanding of general administration and the bureaucratic process. It enable your character to utilize the system beyond simple organizational skills to best achieve his own ends (and to prevent others from achieving theirs).

Specialties: Administration, Procedures, Regulations, Requisition, Rumors, UN

Computer: In the 21st century, most people have at least a rudimentary grasp of computers and the OpNet. However, this Ability allows much more than rudimentary expertise. A trained computer operator can access all sorts of data in the blink of an eye and even create complex programs. This Ability functions for OpNet and Internet protocols.

Specialties: Data Retrieval, Hacking, Programming, the OpNet

Engineering: Engineering rates your comprehension of electronic and mechanical devices. Your character not only understands how computers, vehicles, robots and other machines operate, but she can repair, modify and construct them. Certain novas with Mega-Intelligence and this Ability are beginning to change the very face of technology.

Specialties: Armaments, Computers, Construction, Electronics, Energy Sources, Mechanics, Telecommunications, Vehicles

Intrusion: Intrusion indicates knowledge of and ability to set up or avoid various security systems, and to set infiltration measures and countermeasures as well. Such understanding ranges from basic lock picking to advanced electronic systems.

Specialties: Countermeasures, Electronic Infiltration, Lock Picking, Security Procedures

Linguistics: An indication of the languages that your character knows. Linguistics also imparts a basic understanding of language systems. Due to the truly staggering number of languages that exist, specialization in Linguistics operates differently than do the specialties of other Abilities. Your character does not automatically understand all languages. Dots indicate an understanding of language "families" beyond native tongue. You must choose a language "family," and your character may comprehend tongues within that specific "family" (e.g., while Mandarin, Cantonese and Wu are different languages, they all belong to the Chinese language "family").

Your character knows an additional language family for each dot in this Ability (so at ● ● ● ● ●, he knows five language families in addition to his native tongue). Rolls are needed only to understand complex writing or speech, although a high Linguistics rating should reduce this necessity. The Specialties listed indicate most major language families.

Specialties: Arabic, Bengali, Cambodian, Chinese, English, French, German, Hebrew, Hindi, Italian, Korean, Japanese, Norwegian, Portuguese, Russian, Spanish, Swahili, Turkish

Medicine: This Ability details how well your character knows how the human body works, as well as how to repair it in case of injury. Medicine also includes an understanding of drugs and their use, along with the diagnosis and treatment of diseases and injuries.

Such knowledge can be used to harm as well as heal. Characters may use Medicine to take advantage of an opponent's injury, to apply harmful drugs (or helpful drugs in lethal doses) or to encourage a greater degree of illness in a subject due to improper treatment. Such attempts should be attended closely by the Storyteller.

Specialties: Emergency, First Aid, Novas, Pharmacy, Specialized Fields (Neurology, Oncology, etc.), Surgery

Science: Beyond an understanding of scientific theory, this Ability measures how well your character can put such knowledge to practical use. Science can be used to investigate advanced concepts or to cobble together a pipe bomb out of household chemicals.

Specialties: Astronomy, Biology, Botany, Chemistry, Geology, Mathematics, Physics, Quantum Theory, Zoology

Survival: This Ability is extremely useful to explorers and biologists. It enables your character to subsist in wilderness environments. He knows how to set traps, forage for food and water, build fires and separate dangerous flora and fauna from beneficial ones. With Project Utopia's recent environmental cleanups, this Ability is becoming in vogue once more....

Specialties: Fire-Building, Forage, Hunt, Navigation, Set Traps, Track

Wits Abilities

Arts: Arts rates level of talent in the visual or creative arts, from drawing to writing to sculpture. This Ability also imparts knowledge of the culture and society of a particular art form. Combined with high skill in one or more nova powers, Arts enables a nova to create artworks in media as diverse as light, flame or pure quantum energy.

Specialties: Composition, Design, Drawing, Painting, Poetry, Sculpture, Writing

Biz: Your character knows the ins and outs of business and finance, from marketing to licensing to balancing books. More commercial-oriented novas tend to have

at least rudimentary skill in this Ability; it's fun to figure out the royalties on licensed toys or T-shirts.

Specialties: Controller, Down Market, Merchandising, Positioning, Stocks & Bonds

Rapport: Rapport is used to sense and understand peoples' feelings. This Ability is not a nova power; it uses your character's own understanding of emotions and people to get an accurate reading of what others are feeling.

Specialties: Discern Motivation, Discern Truth, Emotional State, Intent

Appearance Abilities

Intimidation: This Ability enables you to coerce another into doing your will, whether through subtle menace or an outright threat. Whether you plan to follow through on your threat is not important as long as your subject truly believes that you will.

For the more vulgar forms of physical intimidation, use Strength instead of Appearance to calculate the skill total.

Specialties: Implied Threat, Overt Display, Silent Urging

Style: First impressions are important, and they are usually based on physical appearance. Style is more than simply presenting oneself to best effect. Beyond relating an awareness of proper fashions (clothing, hair, makeup, accessories) and how to accentuate appearance, Style can also be used to alter appearance using those same tools — even to the point of disguising oneself as someone else.

Specialties: Disguise, Fashion, Makeup, Seduction

Manipulation Abilities

Interrogation: Interrogation covers ways to draw information from a subject by manipulation, force, drugs or torture. Some techniques are more effective than others at breaking a subject's resolve, but they may leave him permanently disabled or dead.

Specialties: Drugs, Misdirection, Threats, Torture

Streetwise: Streetwise rates a character's knowledge of (and skill in interacting with) society's underbelly. This art involves knowing what is needed, who has it and the ways that it can be acquired. Streetwise helps your character fit into an unfamiliar city or country, giving her an understanding of attitudes and customs common in the underworld.

Specialties: Black Market, Customs, Fence, Information, Scrounge, Street Trade

Subterfuge: This Ability rates how well your character bends the truth and disguises her motives. Subterfuge also helps to sense when others are doing the same. Subterfuge can be used to separate gossip from truth and to discover if a person is lying.

Specialties: Con, Deception, Gossip, Lying, Seduction

Charisma Abilities

Command: Command is not only the ability to lead others, but also an indication of how willingly they follow your character. The better the ability to command, the more amenable people are to your character's decisions (even in extreme situations). Commands may be polite requests, written directives or strict orders.

Specialties: Crowd Control, Discipline, Field Command, Political Leadership, Tactics

Etiquette: This Ability measures understanding of the nuances and dynamics of polite society in a myriad of social circumstances. Etiquette combines grace and manners, and it is useful during diplomatic engagements, formal gatherings and in other encounters with "cultured society."

Specialties: Diplomacy, Negotiation, Social Graces, Sound Bites, Tact

Perform: Perform covers the gamut of live artistic expression, from public speaking to dancing to acting (including impersonating someone else). This Ability also imparts knowledge of the society surrounding a particular art form, as well as how well your character fits in it.

Specialties: Acting, Dance, Impersonation, Oration, Singing, Specific Instrument

Backgrounds

Backgrounds are not associated directly with your character's inherent capabilities, but they are key elements of who she is nonetheless. They help define her history and current circumstances.

Backgrounds tie closely to character concept. You must give each Background some sort of context beyond just a dot rating. After all, allies, contacts and mentors have their own lives, gear and resources don't just appear magically, and influence and status aren't handed out without reason.

Your Storyteller should have input into your choices. If your series begins before your character undergoes eruption, Mentor or Status may be inappropriate. Alternatively, if the characters form an elite squad, they may need a few dots in each of these Backgrounds. Ultimately, Backgrounds help the Storyteller ensure that the characters fit the series and complement one another.

You may occasionally need to roll for a task relating to a Background (say, to see if allies can come to your character's aid, or if he can afford a new piece of equipment). In such instances, the Storyteller chooses the Ability that he feels best suits the task (Command, Intimidation, Etiquette or Subterfuge may be appropriate for the first example, depending on how your character presents herself; Bureaucracy, Streetwise or Computer are good options for the second). Alternatively, the Storyteller may have you roll your character's Background rating (Allies or Resources, to continue the examples).

Allies

Almost everyone has at least one close friend. Allies are people with whom your character has intimate ties: friends, loved ones or simply someone with similar interests to whom she can turn for assistance and support. Allies represent truly dedicated individuals with whom your character has close bonds. Allies are not other members of the team; relationships with other players' characters are roleplayed.

Allies are people in their own right, with lives as involved as your character's. Friendship is a two-way street, and if your character takes but doesn't give, Allies are likely to desert her. Allies do what they can to help you, but they don't throw their lives away for nothing, nor are they on call to bail you out of trouble 24-7. They may also grow weary of repeated demands on their time and resources. Of course, allies can also call for assistance.

Each dot represents one ally (instead of signifying multiple allies, high ratings could represent a more powerful ally). An ally may be a fellow nova, detective, politician, soldier, philanthropist or old college pal. You should work with the Storyteller to detail the ally; as most readers of comics are well aware, a properly developed supporting cast makes for rich roleplaying.

x	None; you skulk about, having no one close to turn to.
•	One ally of moderate ability (equivalent to that of a starting character).
••	Two allies, or one significant one.
•••	Three allies, or fewer allies of correspondingly high power.
••••	Four allies, or fewer ones of great capability.
•••••	Five allies (popular, aren't you?), or fewer ones of immense power.

Attunement

Generally speaking, a nova's quantum powers affect only her own body. Novas with this Background have learned the trick of charging objects with their own quantum signatures, thereby permitting the objects to survive the rigors of the nova's powers so long as they remain in contact with the nova's body. Attunement is most commonly used to prevent a nova's clothing and small personal effects from being damaged or destroyed by her transformations. For example, a nova with Attunement 1 could "charge" her clothing, allowing it to remain undamaged even if she activates powers like Immolate, Growth, Density Decrease, Bodymorph or Shapeshifting. Attunement costs one quantum point per scene and confers absolutely no protection against other novas' quantum powers.

Charged objects may be organic or inorganic. Dots in Attunement govern the maximum amount of weight affected by Attunement:

- 2 kg (a set of clothes)
- •• 5 kg (a briefcase)
- ••• 10 kg (a household appliance)
- •••• 25 kg (a piece of light furniture)
- ••••• 100 kg (another person)

Backing

This Trait reflects standing in an organization (Utopia, Proteus, a government, a corporation or the Directive). This Background is less a measure of actual capability or achievement than it is of perceived influence or rank. At the Storyteller's discretion, you may take Backing multiple times for rank in different organizations. With this rank comes responsibility; if your character has high Backing, she is likely to be responsible for decisions involving great numbers of people and resources.

x None; you're a typical grunt.
• A low-ranking position of little authority, but a fair amount of (usually dull and unpleasant) responsibility.
•• A good post with most of the disagreeable duties pawned off on underlings.
••• Midlevel rank, usually with ill-defined authority and responsibility (such leeway can be both a blessing and a curse).
•••• A position of some direction and privilege. You have access to large resources and are trusted by the elite.
••••• You've reached the upper ranks; a leader in your own right. You hold significant power and respect.

Cipher

The world of **Aberrant** is a realm of secrets, covert conflicts and double-agents. Such being the case, many novas wish to maintain private lives away from the bustle of fame. The Cipher Background can represent a number of things — an aptitude for hiding secrets, lack of registration with governments or credit bureaus, possibly even one or more alternate identities. Cipher is particularly prized by the black ops of Project Proteus and the mask-wearing elite caste of novas, as both of these groups prefer to hide their true faces and names from public scrutiny.

For each dot you possess in Cipher, the Storyteller adds an additional level of difficulty to any investigations into your character. This Background may fluctuate if you don't maintain a certain level of secrecy. The Storyteller should determine if there's a risk that new information develops in the wake of your character's activities.

x Normal; just like everybody else, anybody can read your life story.
• A couple of your secrets are well hidden.
•• Your data trails are hard to follow.
••• You project the identity you wish to project.
•••• Even you have trouble remembering.
••••• Your secrets are completely safe.

Contacts

More casual than allies, contacts are people with whom your character has developed a mutually beneficial arrangement. Contacts use their talents, information or resources to help your character, but they always expect some favor in return. This favor could be a service, trade or even payment, but it generally matches the value of the contact's assistance. These associates don't risk themselves as far as a follower or even an ally will (although a well-cultivated contact could grow into one or the other over the course of the series).

Each dot represents major and minor contacts. Major contacts are individuals with whom your character interacts frequently. Major contacts know him personally and are from any walk of life, of any field of study, with access to a variety of information and resources, and they are willing to cut a deal. A contact could be a data-retrieval specialist at the local library, a fence specializing in vehicles or a Project Utopia field agent. Minor contacts specialize in fields of influence, like their major counterparts. They aren't as knowledgeable or resourceful, though. They may know of your character by nothing more than reputation or rumor, but they may be willing to work out an arrangement.

Tracking down a major contact doesn't usually require a die roll, but finding a minor contact does (typically Bureaucracy, Streetwise or Etiquette). Whether or not a contact feels inclined to help is another story, one that depends on the request. Of course, the more contacts your character has, the more people your character can go to if one doesn't come through.

x No useful contacts; you have to do your own legwork.
• One major contact (with whom you likely have a special arrangement) and a few minor ones.
•• Two major contacts in different areas and a smattering of minor contacts.
••• Three major contacts and a respectable number of minor ones.
•••• Four major contacts in different areas (although you may double up in a given field) and a large number of minor contacts.

• • • • • Five major contacts and a minor contact virtually anywhere you care to look.

Dormancy

Generally speaking, most novas are readily identifiable as such. Not only are their physiques too perfect, their bodies tailored to handle energies beyond human comprehension, but many "bleed" trace amounts of quantum energies into the environment. This effect is relatively harmless (except in the cases of novas with high amounts of Taint), but it makes the nova stand out. Even shapeshifters and novas with Mega-Appearance enhancements such as Copycat harbor large amounts of internal quantum energy; while their powers enable them to avoid casual detection, concentrated scans by novas looking for traces of quantum might reveal their true nature.

Novas with the Dormancy Background, though, are able to "power down" and avoid detection as novas. "Dorm'ing down" takes a turn of concentration, after which all quantum energies are completely internalized and shut down.

While dormant, the nova has no access to any of her nova characteristics, Mega-Attributes or quantum powers until she takes a turn of concentration to power up once more. Her appetite also reduces to something like a normal human level. Although she retains her basic nova characteristics (increased Endurance and Resistance, extended lifespan, etc.), she recovers quantum points at the reduced rate of one point per day.

However, each dot of Dormancy allows the player to roll one die in a resisted roll against any attempts to detect the dormant nova for what she is. Additionally, each dot of Dormancy allows a nova to suppress one dot of Taint, along with any accompanying aberrations, for as long as the character is dormant.

Novas with Dormancy ratings of 4 or 5 may choose to have a "human form" and "nova form," transforming between one and the other. At Dormancy 4, the nova form looks different, but it has certain basic features in common with the human form (fingerprints, retinas, blood type); at 5, the human and nova forms are completely different. However, novas who choose to switch forms have no access to any of their nova characteristics while in human form.

- • one die to resist detection attempts
- • • two dice to resist detection attempts
- • • • three dice to resist detection attempts
- • • • • four dice to resist detection attempts
- • • • • • five dice to resist detection attempts

Eufiber

The coming of novas has ushered in many technological advances, but few so universal as the bizarre substance known as eufiber. This organic polymer-esque substance was originally secreted from the epidermis of Costa Rican nova Aníbal Buendia; a synthetic version was later created from living colonies of the fiber. Eufiber and its derivatives have proved to have many industrial uses; OpNet cables and a considerable percentage of the world's clothing are made from a synthetic alloy derived from Buendia's creation. True, living eufiber, though, is even more prized by novas.

The Eufiber Background represents a colony of Buendia-secreted, living eufiber. The colony is most commonly "woven" into a garment of some sort. Eufiber shaped in this fashion can be worn by baselines, but it is most useful to novas, as its genetic and quantum pattern conforms to the nova's own. This property allows the colony to store a certain number of extra quantum points in its cell structure, giving the nova a quantum-point reserve; the nova can transfer a number of quantum points to the colony up to the Eufiber rating. The nova recovers the quantum points normally, while the eufiber colony stores them until the nova decides to use them.

While the eufiber is charged with quantum, the colony can use the stored quantum as an automatic defense for itself and its owner; this innate defense provides the nova with an amount of extra soak (versus bashing and lethal damage) equal to the number of quantum points currently stored in the colony.

As well, the colony adapts to the nova's own quantum powers, allowing it to remain intact and unharmed even while the nova uses body-altering powers like Bodymorph, Growth and Immolate. Perfect for the fashionable nova who doesn't want to run around naked every time he turns on the juice (though such an outfit provides absolutely no defense against other novas' quantum powers).

A eufiber outfit can adapt its shape, color and other parameters to the nova's whim, shifting at his mental command. Eufiber fashion shows are often wondrous and freakish affairs, as nova "supermodels" parade down runways attired in gravity-defying, shimmering, translucent, bioluminescent, scintillating or otherwise eye-catching constructs.

If a nova's eufiber colony is taken from him by another nova, that nova can attune the eufiber to herself by spending a quantum point. The colony is now attuned to the new nova's quantum signature. However, only one eufiber colony can be worn at a time.

- • one-point capacity
- • • two-point capacity
- • • • three-point capacity
- • • • • four-point capacity
- • • • • • five-point capacity

Followers

Your character has one or more assistants, steadfast companions in her journeys. These disciples are drawn to her for any number of reasons. Perhaps they're awestruck groupies or even worshippers; perhaps they're highly paid agents, managers and staff; perhaps they simply love your character.

Followers have some useful trade or skill (though not to the extent that allies or contacts do), and they are loyal to a fault. Such individuals can think for themselves, but they choose to stand by your character through thick and thin. Even so, poor treatment tests the patience of even the most devoted individual. A follower who is constantly sent to check for ambushes is bound to move on to a less abusive relationship (if he doesn't die first). Conversely, one treated with care and respect goes to tremendous lengths for your character.

Followers should not be novas, but they can be humans of any origin. They should be as flawed and as real as any character. Since player and Storyteller essentially share the duty of playing a follower, both must agree on the individual's history, personality and relationship with the nova. No follower should ever be the perfect assistant, nor should he constantly save the day; he's meant to add flavor to the series, not take center stage.

x	None; you haven't inspired anyone to rally to your banner.
•	One follower of average capability (equivalent to a typical extra).
••	Two followers or a notable one.
•••	Three followers or fewer disciples of significant ability.
••••	Four followers or fewer ones of high power.
•••••	Five followers or fewer ones of great ability.

Influence

If nothing else, novas are certainly persons of importance; people worldwide watch, look up to, emulate or (in the worst cases) fear them. The Influence Background reflects your character's pull and status in society. This status may derive from political office, running a business, being an entertainer or even being a religious figure. Whatever your character's specific credentials, people pay attention to his words and deeds.

Influence may be used to garner special favors from others, to promote a personal agenda in public or to simply get a good seat at the theater. Additionally, influence may be drawn on to network and to make important connections — or even to draw more people under your character's sway. Most novas eventually garner some degree of influence, if they don't start with it.

This Background doesn't cover standing or sway in a private organization; that's handled by Backing.

x	None; your 15 minutes of fame has yet to begin.
•	Moderately influential; you're a local celebrity.
••	Well-connected; you're a familiar face in the city, state or province.
•••	Influential; you are very important to one or more subcultures (fundamentalists, scientists, novox fans) and known to many others.
••••	Broad personal power; your words carry weight throughout the nation.
•••••	Vastly influential; you're a global media icon.

Mentor

A mentor is many things: a patron, teacher, defender and friend. Your character's relationship with her mentor is quite different from any relationship with an ally, contact or follower. While a mentor won't always respond to your character's requests for help, he always acts in her best interests (or what *he* considers best). A mentor-student relationship is a complex and personal association that entails responsibilities on both sides. It should be the subject of involved roleplaying.

A mentor may be a powerful nova, an organization as a whole (Project Utopia is happy to tutor any novas who pass the organization's background checks, though there is always a reciprocal price), or even someone seemingly unrelated to her circumstances who has taken a special interest in her development. Depending on his capabilities and means, a mentor may teach Abilities, make information or resources available, or even instruct in use of quantum powers. He may also serve as your character's advocate in dealing with a particular organization, or may simply show up in time to pull her out of a tight spot. It's advisable not to demand this sort of thing from a mentor too often, though.

The rating of this Background reflects a mentor's helpfulness. A minor patron is better than none (usually); a more significant mentor has a correspondingly higher rating. Even so, a low-ranking mentor can be a powerful influence in your character's growth.

| x | None; you haven't caught anyone's attention or you haven't found a patron worthy of *your* attention. |

x None; you haven't caught anyone's attention or you haven't found a patron worthy of *your* attention.

• Like an older sibling, your mentor is just a bit more worldly and wise than you are. He has a few connections.

• • A figure of some note, or a true power who has little time for you.

• • • A seasoned individual, your mentor is wise and moderately influential.

• • • • Canny and respected, your mentor has significant (perhaps even global) clout.

• • • • • Your mentor is potentially world-shaking, and he takes a great interest in your welfare. Beware, though: Such a mentor's enemies are now yours.

Node

It isn't much to look at. It's just a lump of grayish flesh about the size of a marble. It can grow bigger — some have been recorded which were the size of an apple or baseball — but it's still just a mass of tissue with a few blood vessels, nerve endings and tendrils extending from it. Yet it holds the key to the powers of the universe.

The Mazarin-Rashoud node is what gives novas their power. It provides them with the ability to channel quantum energies. But at the same time it can affect their psyches and their bodies in strange, often deadly, ways.

A character with this Background has a well-developed Mazarin-Rashoud node. Note the words "well-developed." All novas, even those without this Trait, have a Mazarin-Rashoud node. Most novas don't take the Node Background; they get by with the basic M-R node that all novas have. Node as a Background signifies that the nova's M-R is better developed, or channels quantum energies better, than the typical node. Thus, a nova with Node tends to be more powerful than others of his kind. He can use more quantum points per turn, can recover them quicker and possesses certain other powers. In general terms, he is more efficient at processing quantum energies than other novas. However, he is also more likely to suffer from Taint.

For example, a character with a fifth-instar Node (Node 4) gains two points of Taint. Aberrations associated with the Node Background are typically mental or psychological ones.

As the node grows, it presses upon other parts of the brain. In some cases it even causes the nova's forehead to bulge slightly. This pressure on the brain can result in mental problems for the nova. The larger the M-R node, the more likely that problems will occur, and the more extensive those problems are likely to be. By the time the node reaches the fourth instar, a problem of some sort is guaranteed. The human body and brain, even when augmented by quantum powers, are simply too fragile to handle the awesome energies coursing through them without being changed in some way.

Other effects of having a highly developed Node include:

Quantum Recovery

As mentioned under Quantum, a nova with Node recovers spent quantum points more quickly than one without, adding her Node rating to her normal rate of quantum-point recovery. Many novas think of the Node as a recharger that juices up their quantum batteries quickly.

Quantum Detection

As a receptacle for quantum energies, a Mazarin-Rashoud node also enables a nova to detect sources or conduits of quantum energies. Typically, these sources are other novas, though nuclear reactors, cyclotrons, generators or other large power sources might also be detected.

To detect a quantum source, the nova takes a full turn to concentrate, then the player rolls her Node rating as a dice pool. Range of the attempt is 10 meters per dot in Node. Difficulty is typically standard, though the Storyteller can increase it in the case of trace amounts of quantum energies. Success indicates the nova detects a source of quantum energy in the area. Succeeding on this roll does not let a nova pinpoint an invisible or hidden character, but it does enable her to detect a shapeshifted or "dormed down" nova for what it is.

The player of a nova with the Dormancy Background may roll his Background rating in a resisted roll against any attempt at quantum detection; successes on this roll cancel out the scanning nova's successes on a one-for-one basis.

Dots	Quantum Expenditure	Taint
x (1st instar)	Can spend 6 quantum points/turn.	—
• (2nd instar)	Can spend 8 quantum points/turn.	—
• • (3rd instar)	Can spend 10 quantum points/turn.	—
• • • (4th instar)	Can spend 12 quantum points/turn.	One
• • • • (5th instar)	Can spend 15 quantum points/turn.	Two
• • • • • (6th instar)	Can spend 20 quantum points/turn.	Three

Resources

Resources are a general indication of financial assets, but they are more than monetary wealth. Money can be gained and lost; this Background includes such things as property, clothing and basic equipment, as well as how easily your character can acquire more. While resources are not entirely liquid assets, possessions can be sold to gain money (though doing so may take some time depending on what is for sale).

Each Resource dot conveys a standard income beyond any gear or wealth your character gains during play. The source of this stipend must be detailed (contract work, employment, royalties, investments), since it may be increased, reduced or cut off entirely depending on events in the series. Wealth is listed in American dollars; the actual currency may differ depending on your character's origin.

As with influence, most novas have few problems acquiring resources — through one means or another.

x	None: You are homeless and broke.
•	Small savings: You have a tiny apartment and maybe an old used car. If you liquidated all your possessions, you'd have about $2,500.
••	Comfortable: You have a respectable flat and probably a reliable auto. If liquidated, your belongings would yield approximately $50,000.
•••	Affluent: You own a house, yacht or other sizable equity. If liquidated, these items would yield around $250,000.
••••	Wealthy: You own a significant amount of property (a mansion, apartment building, office tower or similar structure). You'd have at least $1,000,000 if you liquidated everything.
•••••	Amazingly rich: You have more money than you know what to do with. If you liquidated everything, you'd have at least $10,000,000.

Willpower, Quantum and Taint

The Willpower, Quantum and Taint Traits are at the core of your character's being, and they indicate who he is as much as his origin or Nature does.

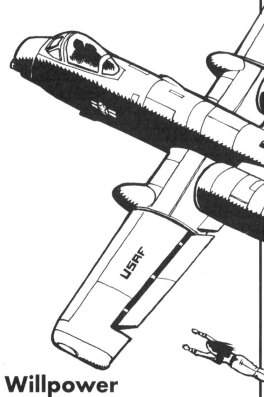

Willpower

The Willpower Trait measures drive and emotional stability. A high score reflects a confident, self-motivated individual, while a low score indicates someone with little confidence or perseverance.

Willpower has a permanent rating, also called the *score*, that reflect your character's total strength in the Trait (noted by the circles on the character sheet). Whenever a roll is called for, the dice pool is always based on permanent score. Willpower also has a current rating, called *points*, that indicate your character's present reserves. "Spending points" refers to removing points from the current rating (noted by the squares on the character sheet). Current rating can fluctuate greatly during a story.

•	Weak
••	Timid
•••	Hesitant
••••	Diffident
•••••	Certain
••••••	Confident
•••••••	Determined
••••••••	Secure
•••••••••	Iron-willed
••••••••••	Unshakable

Using Willpower

You spend Willpower when your character pushes himself beyond his normal limits in an attempt to do something extraordinary. You can spend only one Willpower point in a turn, unless otherwise stated.

• **Free success:** You can spend a Willpower point to earn an automatic success. This free success is separate from any that you roll, but it counts toward your success in an action. You must declare that you're spending Willpower in this fashion prior to rolling for the action. Only novas may use Willpower in this way.

• **Resist instinctual response:** Sometimes the Storyteller may have your character react to something out of instinct — whether fear of a monstrous aberrant, revulsion at the sight of a gruesome corpse or lust for a stunning individual. Your character can resist this urge with the expenditure of a Willpower point (although the urge may return depending on the circumstances, calling for further expenditures).

• **Resist Taint:** When a Taint-induced mental disorder causes your character to do something she would rather not do, you may spend a Willpower point to resist.

However, you must do so each time you make such an attempt.

• **Resist mental powers:** Your character can resist the effects of some mental powers with the expenditure of a Willpower point, or upon a successful Willpower roll. The specifics depend on the power being used; refer to Chapter Five: Powers for details.

• **Max quantum power:** A nova's player can spend a Willpower point to "max" a quantum power, enabling the nova to enhance the effects of the power. See p. 147 for details on this process.

Compulsion

Once all of your Willpower points are gone, your character is subject to a *compulsion*. His innermost Nature comes to the forefront of his personality, dictating his thoughts and actions. Compulsions are the weaknesses mentioned at the end of each Nature's description (see "Natures," p. 127). An Analyst becomes distracted even by the most mundane of puzzles. A Bravo acts without thinking, using brute force and bluster.

Acting at extremes can be very liberating, but it can also cause serious problems. While the likelihood of regaining Willpower increases (since your character behaves true to his Nature), operating under a compulsion can make your character ignore important information, disregard otherwise obvious warnings or be manipulated easily. When at least one Willpower point is regained, your character shakes off the compulsion, reasserting his self-will.

Recovering Willpower

Willpower points are regained whenever your character gets a chance to rest or restore his self-confidence. The Storyteller is always the final arbiter of when and how Willpower is regained. The following methods are entirely optional, and they should encourage roleplaying. The Willpower gained should serve as a reward for playing your character well in the story — it should not be the goal itself.

• For simplicity's sake, one point may be recovered every morning upon awakening — a fresh start each morning, as it were. If nothing else, this point guarantees some Willpower. (This rule should be ignored during downtime.)

• If your character performs an action that affirms her Nature, she may regain between one and three Willpower points. The exact amount is up to the Storyteller. He may deny your request if he feels the logic behind it is flimsy, or if it appears that your character performs certain actions solely to regain Willpower.

• You may receive a point (or more) if your character achieves some special success, like rescuing a friend or discovering a significant plot point, or if your character affirms his capabilities in some way.

• You get points equal to your character's Willpower score at the end of a series (not a single game session). The Storyteller may modify this return somewhat if significant story elements remain unresolved.

Quantum

Quantum energies flow throughout the universe and all things within it. These energies bind matter together and throw it apart, harmonize energy and disrupt it, and affect all living things every day of their existence. As mystic, even arcane, as this sounds, quantum energies in fact derive from scientific principles — albeit scientific principles of which humans have little understanding at present.

A nova's ability to control and manipulate quantum energies — and thus, in general, his "power" — is measured by his Quantum Trait. Quantum rates a character's ability to draw on and use the universe's quantum energies. This Trait is the primary distinction between novas and ordinary humans. A character with even a low Quantum is pretty powerful; one with a high Quantum — say, 4 or more — can wield powers previously unknown beyond the pages of outrageous fiction.

Every nova character starts the game with a Quantum rating of 1. Quantum can be increased with bonus and nova points. Though Quantum can theoretically reach as high as 10, no character may begin the series with more than a 5 Quantum, tainted or not. So far, only a few shadowy (and perhaps deeply twisted and warped) individuals have displayed abilities that might transcend the level of 5 Quantum.

Characters automatically acquire a point of Taint when their Quantum reaches 5. See p. 148 for further information on Taint.

A character's Quantum rating has several different effects and provides certain benefits, as follows:

Appearance

The more Quantum a nova has, whether tainted or not, the less human he looks. His Quantum may make him grotesque, or it may make him impossibly perfect and beautiful, but observers can tell he isn't a baseline. The exact effects of Quantum upon a character's appearance depend upon the character's powers, the player's desires and the Storyteller's whim.

Raw Power

Most powers' effects are based, at least in part, on a nova's Quantum rating. For example, a Quantum Bolt has a range equal to [15 meters x (dots + Quantum)] and inflicts [Quantum x 3] levels plus (power rating x 4) dice of bashing damage — or [Quantum x 2] levels plus (power rating x 4) dice of lethal damage.

Similarly, some powers have Quantum minima — they work only for novas who have Quantum ratings of a certain level or higher. A nova whose Quantum is not that high cannot purchase or use those powers. To the strong go the spoils.

Quantum Pool

Another important effect of Quantum is that it allows a nova to access the energy needed to fuel his powers. This energy is referred to as his *Quantum Pool*, and the points in that pool are *quantum points*. Each use of a power costs a certain number of quantum points from the quantum pool. For example, a Quantum Bolt costs two quantum points to fire.

A character's starting quantum pool is equal to 20 plus (Quantum x 2). Thus, a nova with Quantum 3 has a base Quantum Pool of 26 (20 + [3 x 2]). The Quantum Pool's capacity can be expanded, at the rate of two additional quantum points per nova point expended on the Quantum Pool. Capacity can also be improved with experience points, at the rate of three experience points per quantum point. Once purchased, the Quantum Pool dictates the maximum number of quantum points that a nova's body can contain under normal circumstances.

If a character loses all quantum points, she may not use any of her nova powers except for powers that don't require quantum points to use. She is depleted, spent and all too normal until she recovers quantum. She may sacrifice health levels for quantum points, as noted on p. 147.

Recharging Quantum Pool

All novas are natural collectors and receptacles of quantum energy. Accordingly, quantum points, once spent, gradually return to a character, in the same way that a tired person regains energy by resting for a while. If a nova is at ease but not completely relaxing (for example, going for a walk, doing some easy paperwork, watching television, talking with friends), he recovers quantum points at the rate of two per hour. If he is completely relaxed (sleeping, just sitting around doing nothing), he recovers quantum points at the rate of four per hour.

Novas can recover quantum points more quickly in several ways. First, if the nova has the Node Background, he adds his Node rating to the number of quantum points he recovers per hour when at ease or relaxing. For example, a nova with Node 2 would recover six quantum points per hour of relaxation. Second, some powers, such as Quantum Regeneration, allow a character to recover quantum points very quickly. Third, it is rumored that some drugs or foods allow a nova to boost himself back up to full Quantum Pool level much faster than normal.

Dying for Power

There are times when a nova's Quantum Pool just isn't full enough to get the effect she wants. In this case, a nova may trade health levels for a temporary boost to quantum points. The novas literally burns out her life force to ensure that she accomplishes some task or defeats some enemy. For each health level sacrificed, the character gains an additional two quantum points. Doing so allows a nova temporarily to increase her quantum pool above its normal maximum capacity. However, these points remain for only three turns, so the character should use them quickly or her sacrifice will be in vain. Health levels traded for quantum points are considered to be lethal damage (p. 253).

Look the Look

A nova's appearance depends, in part, on her Quantum Pool. When the Quantum Pool is full or close to it, the nova seems charged — vibrant, excited, vigorous. She may even crackle with energy, glow or otherwise display visible signs of her power. Conversely, a nova whose Quantum Pool is empty or low seems fatigued or drained. She may look completely healthy, but something about her suggests that she's running out of steam.

Maxing Powers and Special Maneuvers

Quantum powers are impressive enough. However, when a nova really puts her heart into channeling quantum energies, the effects can be truly awe-inspiring. By spending a point of Willpower, a nova can "max" a quantum power, enhancing its effects to far beyond normal levels. Only one power may be maxed at a time, and a nova may max a power only once per scene.

To max a power, the nova's player spends a point of Willpower and a variable number of quantum points, then spends a full turn in concentration. For each dot of Quantum the nova has, the player can roll one die, but he must pay one quantum point per die rolled. Each success on the roll may be "spent" to boost the nova's next use of quantum power, which happens on the following turn.

(Note: The max successes must be used on the next turn; they may not be "stored for later" or "built up" over several turns.)

Successes on this roll can be "spent" on the following options:

Damage/Successes: Each success spent adds one die (if an attack power) or success (if a mental power, power like Matter Creation).

Soak: Each success spent adds one to the character's soak versus bashing and lethal damage. Note that this option can be employed even if the character does not have any particular defensive powers (a last-ditch survival mechanism common to all novas), though the effects last for only one turn in any event.

Area: Each success spent doubles the area of an Area or Explosive power.

Range/Speed: Each success doubles the range or speed of a power.

Duration: Each success spent doubles the duration of a power.

Extras: A player may spend two successes to add the Area or Explosive Extra to an attack that does not have that Extra.

Each success enhances only one parameter, but multiple successes can be applied to different columns.

For example, the player of a nova with Quantum 5 aims a Quantum Bolt at her foe, spends a Willpower point, a full turn, and seven quantum points (five to activate her Quantum Trait, two to power the Quantum Bolt), then rolls her full Quantum Trait as a dice pool. She rolls four Quantum successes. She assigns two successes to the "Damage" column and two successes to the "Area/Extras" column. Her next Quantum Bolt inflicts +2 dice of damage; furthermore, even though the nova does not have the "Area" Extra, the shot will be an Area attack.

A maxed power (commonly known as a "special maneuver," "special" or "stunt") lasts for one turn or use, unless successes are used to increase its duration. For example, increased area, range or speed all last for one turn, decreasing to normal parameters on the following turn. Furthermore, activating and using a special maneuver is the only action the character can take that turn.

These special maneuvers are highly personal expressions of quantum power, and players are encouraged to design and name specific special maneuvers. For example, Core always does more damage (and over a greater area) when activating his Core Meltdown, while Jinshu Shan uses her Quantum to make herself virtually indestructible by shaping her Force Field into the Iron Chariot stance.

Example: *Lotus Infinite has Quantum 4 and Quantum Blast 3. Harried by a rival elite, she says "To hell with the contract!" and activates her devastating Infinity Justifier special maneuver. Lotus Infinite's player, Dana, spends a point of Willpower, two quantum points* (to activate Quantum Bolt) and four more points (to activate her maximum number of Quantum dice), for a total of six quantum points.

As Lotus Infinite spends a full turn in concentration, Dana rolls four dice, gaining three successes. She then spends two successes to turn her Quantum Blast into an Area effect and her third success into the "Damage" column to add a die of damage. Next turn, on her Initiative rating, the Infinity Justifier blossoms outward from Lotus Infinite in coruscating waves of pure quantum death.

Ultimately, maxing quantum power is a highly volatile and individual activity, and cannot be confined to a rigid set of rules. Particularly when many successes are scored on the Quantum roll, the effects can be whatever is cinematically appropriate, and can quite possibly affect the area for miles around the nova. Storytellers should keep this in mind, using power maxes to enhance the setting and provide spectacular scenes. Does the plot demand that the characters catch up to that space shuttle, blow that building to smithereens, or lift that mountain? If so, and if the power max roll is good enough, let 'em do it.

It should be noted, however, that botching a maxed power is deadly. Botching either the Quantum roll or the dice pool roll for the quantum power leads to the nova gaining one or more points of temporary Taint.

Taint

Quantum energies are powerful and, when channeled by the human mind via the M-R node, often unpredictable as well. Even when novas think they have those energies under full control, often they do not. The growth of an entire new gland — the M-R node — coupled with quantum energies seething through the body works changes on even the strongest nova. And the more powerful a nova gets, the more changed he becomes.

This effect on a nova is represented by a Trait known as Taint. All characters start the character-creation process with Taint ratings of zero. The more points of Taint a character accumulates, the stranger and more inhuman he becomes, until he becomes an unplayable god/monster and falls under the Storyteller's control.

As with Willpower, Taint ranges from zero to 10 and has a temporary and permanent track. Unlike Willpower, temporary Taint is not spent — it is gained as the character mishandles his power or tries to channel too much energy. Permanent Taint is a result of the nova's body and mind warping beyond human ken, the tragic side effect of channeling energies human beings were not designed to handle.

Characters begin the game with zero temporary Taint, but may have a number of permanent Taint points,

depending on the shortcuts they take during character creation.

Gaining Permanent Taint

Unfortunately for novas, there are many ways

for them to acquire Taint. They walk a razor's edge between power and insanity, might and destructive force. Ways in which to acquire permanent Taint include:

Too Much Quantum or Node

Quantum represents a basic measure of a nova's power, and the more power a nova has, the more tainted he becomes. When a nova's Quantum reaches 5, he acquires one point of Taint. Each point of Quantum gained thereafter adds another point of Taint. Power definitely has its price.

Similarly, a nova whose M-R node becomes too large (in game terms, whose Node rating is 3 or higher) acquires Taint. The exact amount of Taint, and some notes on the possible effects of that Taint, are discussed under the Node Background.

Buying Tainted Quantum or Powers

A player can voluntarily choose to give his beginning character some Taint by buying tainted powers. Doing so makes them cheaper (half normal cost), but imposes permanent Taint, and possibly the side effects of *aberrations*, on the character from the very start of the series. Each dot of tainted Quantum, Mega-Attribute or quantum power imposes one point of permanent Taint on the character.

Excessive Temporary Taint

If a nova gains 10 temporary Taint points, she immediately trades in those points for a point of permanent Taint. Her temporary Taint track is reset to zero, but she now has an extra point of permanent Taint, as well as any aberration that accompanies it.

Gaining Temporary Taint

A nova's body can be harmed by excessive channeling of quantum energies. Any of the following mishaps can net a character from one to three points of temporary Taint. Characters who gain three or more points of temporary Taint in one "sitting" might manifest one or more temporary aberrations lasting for about (15-Stamina/Mega-Stamina) days.

Remember that when temporary Taint reaches 10, all temporary Taint points are traded in for one point of permanent Taint.

Power Strain

Using vast amounts of quantum power sometimes backfires on a nova. Something goes wrong — her concentration slips, she is attacked at a crucial moment, or the energy warps out of her control — and the energy "feeds back" into her, creating Taint. This feedback is most likely to occur when a nova is exerting her will to draw on greater power or better manipulate the power she has.

In game terms, whenever a nova's player spends a point of Willpower to max a power in some way, then botches a roll associated with the use of that maxed power, the nova earns a point of temporary Taint. At the Storyteller's discretion, the nova might acquire more than one point of Taint, though three is the absolute maximum (and a nova should gain three points of Taint only from a truly spectacular failure).

Visually, what typically happens is that the power the nova is calling forth "explodes" inside her, or lashes back to hit her and not the target she was aiming at. Occasionally, the nova's body visibly warps, twists, mutates or otherwise alters itself. In some instances, particularly when mental powers such as Telepathy are being used, the Taint manifests itself psychically, in the form of madness and delusions.

Rapid Recovery

Quantum is a natural force of energy, meant to return to a nova *naturally*. That's why a nova's quantum points return at a set rate, based on how thoroughly the nova is resting and the strength of his Node. When a nova tries to enhance this rate of return, he runs the risk of acquiring Taint.

If a nova wishes to improve the rate at which her quantum points return, her player must make a Stamina + Node roll at a difficulty penalty of one for every quantum point she is trying to recover above her normal rate of recovery. If the roll is successful, the nova regains the quantum points without any problem. If it is failed, she acquires one point of temporary Taint. If the player botches the roll, the nova acquires two points of temporary Taint. Thus, a grievous failure when trying to boost the rate of recovery can leave a nova a warped, deranged wreck.

For Example: *Veldris Karim needs to recover the points in his Quantum Pool quickly before the next wave of Mite-crazed thugs attacks him. In his desperation he tries to boost his rate of recovery while he is at ease. The Storyteller calls for a Stamina + Node roll. Karim's Stamina is 4, he has no Node Background, and he wants to recover five quantum points instead of the usual two. Since this return equals three extra quantum points, the difficulty of his player's roll increases by three. The roll nets a result of 4, 6, 7 and 7 — failure. Karim not only fails to recover any quantum points, he acquires a point of temporary Taint as well.*

Mental Disorders

Some mental disorders, rather than being the result of Taint, actually impose temporary Taint upon a nova. According to recent (and Utopia-censored) psychological research, the mental instability affects the nova's quantum processes, gaining strength from them and making the nova more inhuman than ever. For further details on mental disorders, see the sidebar on p. 153.

Losing Temporary Taint

Temporary Taint can be forcibly "bled off," though this process is difficult. If the character undergoes an entire story or month of downtime either dorm'ed down or utilizing all quantum powers and Mega-Attributes at a maximum of half normal strength, and does not botch any power rolls in the process, the player may roll spend a Willpower point and roll the character's Willpower at the end of the story or downtime. The Willpower roll is made at +1 difficulty for each point of temporary Taint stored over the first. Success on the roll bleeds off one point of Taint; three or more successes bleed off two points of temporary Taint. Failure indicates that no Taint can be bled off during that time period; a botch *adds* another point of permanent Taint.

Permanent Taint, once acquired, is just that: permanent. No reliable means of reducing permanent Taint are known as of 2008. It is rumored in the nova underground that the Teragen has more effective means of bleeding off temporary, and perhaps even permanent, Taint, but the specifics of this are unknown.

Effects of Taint

The Taint Trait represents how inhuman a nova seems to be. Taint manifests as physical or psychic drawbacks, which are known as *aberrations*. A mental aberration can unbalance a nova's psyche, causing neuroses, psychoses or other mental disorders and derangements. Utopia's psychologists have begun referring to this effect as "Quantum Backlash Disorder," even though the effects can actually be classified as one of dozens of other mental disorders common to baseline humans.

With physical aberrations, a nova acquires an inhuman feature of some sort — an energy glow or discharge; thick metal plates in place of skin; possibly even horns or claws. The possibilities are, literally, endless. In some cases, an aberration even manifests as inhuman perfection — the nova is impossibly beautiful, athletic, muscular, you name it. This abnormality can be as disconcerting as extreme ugliness; superhuman beauty is as difficult for normal people to cope with as the disturbing mutations more often associated with Taint.

A nova suffers one detectable aberration when his permanent Taint score rises above 3. Thus, he acquires his first tangible manifestations of Taint when he "earns" his fourth permanent Taint point, and he earns one for each point thereafter. Though relatively few novas manifest overt aberrations as of 2008, recent research suggests that it might not take long for a powerful nova, or one who abuses her gifts, to become a twisted mockery of humanity.

Regardless of what form a nova's Taint takes, baseline humans can sense it. At first, this sensation manifests only as a slight sense of unease or eeriness; indeed, as of 2008, few novas inspire even this extreme a reaction. With time and additional Taint points, though, a nova may provoke disgust, revulsion or even hatred. The result, in game terms, is an increased difficulty to Social rolls when a nova tries to interact with a baseline human. The nova suffers a +1 difficulty on such rolls when his permanent Taint rating reaches 4; thereafter, every two full points of Taint inflict an additional +1 difficulty.

Needless to say, there may come a point at which powerful, and thus almost certainly tainted, novas stop trying to relate to normal humans in any sort of typical, healthy way.

Secondly, permanent Taint affects a nova's ability to use his Willpower in certain circumstances — specifically, when he is trying to resist succumbing to the effects of mental disorders. For each point of permanent Taint a nova has, the player must subtract one die from his Willpower dice pool when rolling to resist the effects of mental disorders (to a minimum of one die). Sooner or later a nova's mind simply cannot resist a descent (whether steep or slow) into insanity.

When a nova's permanent Taint reaches 10, he has become too inhuman to act as a player character. The Storyteller takes over the character; the player, if he wishes to continue playing, must create a new character.

Buying Tainted Powers

A nova may buy Quantum dots, Mega-Attributes or quantum powers as tainted, in order to save points on them. In effect he is taking the left-hand path to power, getting there quickly but sacrificing a part of his humanity in the process.

Quantum normally costs five nova points per dot. A dot of Quantum that is bought tainted costs only three nova points, but the character automatically gains one point of permanent Taint per Quantum dot bought in this fashion.

Similarly, the cost for a tainted Mega-Attribute dot or enhancement is two instead of three nova points, but at a price of one permanent Taint point per dot or enhancement purchased.

A nova may buy two dots in a Level 1 quantum power for one nova point, but doing so gives the nova one permanent Taint point per nova point spent. A tainted Level 2 or 3 power dot is only half of what the power normally costs (rounded up), but the character acquires one permanent Taint point per dot so bought. A power with a fixed cost, such as Body Modification, may be bought for half cost at the price of one permanent Taint point.

Differing levels of the same power may be bought with or without Taint; for example, a player may buy a tainted dot of Mega-Strength for two nova points, then pay full cost for the next dot in order not to accrue extra Taint. If there is some question about the cost of a power, consult the Storyteller.

When buying powers with experience points, the character can acquire a new Mega-Attribute/ enhancement/ quantum power or the next level of a power/ Mega-Attribute/ Quantum for half cost (rounded up) if he chooses to gain a point of permanent Taint in the process.

Possible Aberrations

The higher a nova's permanent Taint score, the more obviously inhuman she is. A list of suggested aberrations a Storyteller may inflict upon a nova follows, organized into low-, medium- and high-level aberrations (though even the low- and medium-level aberrations typically become more extreme at higher levels of Taint). Of course, players and Storytellers are always free to make up their own aberrations if none of the ones listed here is suitable. In that case, use the listed aberrations as guidelines for the possible effects and levels of power involved.

One important thing to remember when creating aberrations is that they should never be completely beneficial to a nova. Some of them may offer an advantage here or there, or provide some other benefit, but by and large, they should be disadvantageous. An aberration doesn't necessarily have to be disadvantageous in combat — an aberration that makes everyday life difficult for a nova is often as effective as (or more so than) one that inhibits his combat abilities.

Low-Level Aberrations

These aberrations are appropriate for novas with four to five points of permanent Taint.

• **Aberrant Eyes:** Something's strange about the nova's eyes. They may be a very weird color — glowing red, pure white, jet black — or they may display some sort of picture or pattern. In general, the more Taint a nova has, the more inhuman his eyes become. At lower levels they may simply be an unusual color or have an odd pattern — perhaps they appear to be covered with blood-red spiderwebs, have a matrix pattern overlaid on them, or are reflective or translucent (windows to the soul, indeed). At medium levels they may appear inhuman, looking instead like cat's eyes or something of the sort. At higher levels they may actually change physical form.

• **Anima Banner:** The nova's anima visibly manifests around her when she uses her powers, or even when she doesn't. This anima is a holographic, audial or telepathic manifestation of some object or symbol important to the character's subconscious; for example, a character who identified with a certain card in the Tarot might visibly manifest that symbol when she activates her quantum abilities. The anima has no tangible effect; it is merely a display of quantum energies.

• **Bulging Muscles:** The nova's muscles bulge inhumanly, making him appear like a bodybuilder on steroids. He isn't necessarily any stronger than he is normally, he just looks like a modern-day Hercules. Observers may wonder how he can keep his balance with such huge arms and chest and relatively tiny legs. This aberration may inhibit his ability to fit into cramped spaces.

• **Colored Skin:** The nova's skin turns an unusual, not necessarily unattractive, color — golden, bright cobalt blue, green, scarlet, silver or whatever else the Storyteller can think of. A particularly wicked Storyteller may even have the nova become splotched with different colors, or striped like a zebra or tiger. Whether the nova's hair or eyes also change color is up to the player Storyteller.

• **Feeding Requirement:** The nova develops a dependence on/addiction to some food, substance or form of energy, which she must ingest to fuel her powers. At low levels of Taint, this dependence should apply to some relatively ordinary food or substance, such as silver. At medium and higher levels, the demands become more extreme. The nova either requires enormous amounts of the substance, or her desire mutates. A high-Taint nova, for example, might need to consume blood, plutonium, or human flesh.

• **Glow:** This Taint is similar to Energy Emission. The nova is so filled with quantum energies that he can't completely hold them in. He intermittently emits them in a soft glow of some kind, or perhaps crackling sparks or some similar phenomenon. The color and nature of this effect usually depend on the type of powers the nova has manifested, as well as the Storyteller's fiendish imagination; it may or may not be attractive. In the dark, the difficulty to hit the nova with an attack is reduced by one.

• **Unearthly Beauty:** The nova is the paragon of handsomeness (or beauty, as the case may be). His hair is always perfect, his muscles show just the right amount of definition, his teeth are straight and white, his eyes a fascinating color, his build perfect, and it seems as if there's not an ounce of fat on him. In fact, he's just *too* perfect — it's eerie and disturbing. Even other "beautiful people" seem uneasy around him, sometimes expressing their unease through vicious jealousy, envy, barbed humor or the like.

Medium-Level Aberrations

These aberrations are appropriate for novas with six to seven points of permanent Taint.

• **Allergic Reaction:** The nova loses dice from dice pools, or possibly even takes damage, from exposure to a particular substance or phenomenon harmless to baselines. Examples include specific elements or substances, sunlight (or its absence) or certain types of energy fields. The Storyteller determines how much damage the nova takes (and what type of damage it is) based upon the amount, purity and/ or power of the substance.

• **Energy Emission:** The nova's ability to control the awesome energies coursing through his body has been compromised. He constantly gives off small "sparks" of energy, which may pose a danger to people and objects around him. The nature of the emissions depends upon

the nova's powers. For example, a nova with flame powers might emit tiny sparks of fire from his pores, or lava-like blood may drip down his body.

• **Hormonal Imbalance (Lust):** Members of the preferred sex, especially those who are in any way attractive, tend to inspire unabiding desire in the nova. More honorable novas will do their best to resist this unnatural attraction, but those of darker or more evil bent are perfectly capable of engaging in acts up to and including rape to get what they want.

• **Hormonal Imbalance (Rage):** The nova becomes prone to fits of blinding, destructive rage. When angered, she tends to attack without regard for her own defense, her surroundings or the situation; she simply lashes out at whatever has infuriated or annoyed her. Unless the player succeeds in a Willpower roll, the nova will use any and all power at her command in this sort of attack — usually with fatal results for the target. Once she is berserk, the nova's player must make a Willpower roll at difficulty +1 to "snap out of it"; at the Storyteller's option, the difficulty may be reduced if a friend talks to her soothingly, splashes water on her or uses a mental power to try to calm her down.

• **Mental Disorders:** This aberration is the most common form of mental Taint, and it is especially common in novas with mental powers or high-instar M-R nodes. The nova develops a mental disorder of some sort; the more tainted she becomes, the more the disorder affects her behavior (or she may develop additional, even stranger, psychoses).

• **Twisted Limbs:** The nova's arms and/ or legs are bent, twisted and warped. They may be unnaturally long, oddly slender (yet lacking nothing in strength), have joints which bend at disturbing angles or even an extra joint or two.

• **Vulnerability:** The nova's body becomes so changed that he takes extra damage from a particular type of attack (such as fire, electricity or Disintegration). The effect of any attack or power based on that type of attack is increased by three dice.

High-Level Aberrations

These aberrations are appropriate for novas with eight or more points of permanent Taint.

• **Contagious:** The nova's altered body exudes a virus that is harmful to baselines. This does not affect the character or other novas, but for baselines, the nova may well be a walking Typhoid Mary or Black Death.

• **Hardened Skin:** The nova's skin can no longer really be described as "skin." Instead, it's hardened into chitin, metal, horn, wood, scales, shell, sharklike "sandpaper skin" or something similar. It's obviously not normal to the touch or the eye. Unless the Storyteller decides otherwise, this Taint does not provide any sort of armor or protection. It may interfere with the nova's sense of touch or ability to manipulate fine objects. At the Storyteller's option, it may be covered with horns, spikes, barbs, ridges or similar features.

• **Megalomania:** The nova develops a "god complex." She truly believes herself to be the loftiest, mightiest, most power being in the world — of course, with a nova, this belief isn't so far-fetched. She requires absolute obedience (perhaps even worship) from her lessers. Megalomania is a particularly dangerous aberration, because the nova will wish to acquire more power as quickly as possible, which often means acquiring tainted quantum powers.

• **Oozing Skin:** The nova's skin is covered with slime, mucus or a similar loathsome substance. It may ooze out of his pores at a constant slow rate, or maybe it just somehow remains on him all the time — but regardless, it's disgusting to look at and worse to touch. At the Storyteller's option, the slime may be mildly poisonous or acidic.

• **Permanent Power:** One of the nova's powers becomes permanent, unable to be suppressed. This permanence has the advantage that the power costs no quantum points to use; however, the power might make it exceedingly difficult for a nova to interact with the rest of her environment. Examples of powers that might become permanent include Density Control, Immolate and Bodymorph.

• **Radioactive:** The nova cannot fully control her quantum emissions. She emits soft, or possibly even hard, radiation (see "Radiation," p. 257). The amount of radiation she emits increases as she spends additional quantum points.

• **Second Self:** One or more other bodies begins to sprout from the nova's body. Often the "extra" bodies are limited to just faces — a face on the side of the nova's head, in his chest, in his stomach or on his thigh. But in some cases more body parts, such as shoulders or limbs, emerge. This aberration seems to be more common among novas with powers such as Telepathy, though no one has offered a convincing explanation as to why.

• **Sheer Hideousness:** The nova is too horrifying for description. He is somehow warped, twisted, deformed or otherwise looks like he was broken and then put back together by someone who didn't know what a person should look like. He resembles something you'd see in your worst nightmare. His Appearance Attribute drops to zero, and he gains a permanent version of the Face of Terror Mega-Appearance enhancement (p. 172).

• **Sloughed Flesh:** The nova's skin and flesh no longer sit right on his bones. He looks as if he were made of wax and left too close to the fire — he seems slightly melted or askew, with skin and flesh bunched up where it should be thin, and paper-thin where it should rest thick on the skeleton.

• **Vestigial Limbs:** The nova has some extra, but functionally useless, limbs. These may be tiny withered arms, flightless wings (leathery or feathered) growing out of his back, a lifeless tail, or a set of tentacles below his arms or sprouting from his chest. The most any of these limbs can do is weakly hold on to very light objects, such as empty plastic cups.

Mental Disorders

• **Amnesia:** You forget a significant segment of your past due to physical trauma or mental scarring. This affliction can be so acute as to erase all memories or simply cause you to forget a few hours of time.

• **Delusions:** Your mind plays tricks on itself. You see and hear things that don't actually exist. Mild cases can be distracting, while potent delusions can cause a complete detachment from reality.

• **Multiple Personality Disorder:** Trauma can cause a single personality to splinter into distinct shards. Each personality possesses its own Nature and behaves differently from the others.

• **Obsessive/Compulsive Disorder:** You are unable to resist a certain urge. This urge may cause you to perform ludicrous tasks or to seek absolute perfection in every detail.

• **Polar/Bipolar Disorder:** Also known as depression, polar disorder causes lethargy, depression and an inability to function in normal society for months at a time. Manic-depressives suffer the same symptoms, but their bouts are interspersed with energetic bursts.

• **Schizophrenia:** This affliction causes a complete detachment from reality. Acute cases of paranoid schizophrenia are accompanied by severe delusions of persecution and elaborate paranoid theories.

CHAPTER FOUR: MEGA-ATTRIBUTES & ENHANCEMENTS

Mega-Attributes

All novas have the same nine standard Attributes — Strength, Dexterity, Stamina, Appearance, Manipulation, Charisma, Perception, Intelligence and Wits — that any other human has. However, novas' mastery of quantum energies enables their Attributes to go beyond those of mortal men into the realm of the superhuman. These enhanced Attributes are known as *Mega-Attributes*.

Buying Mega-Attributes

Like normal Attributes, Mega-Attributes are rated from 1 to 5. Each level of a Mega-Attribute increases the effectiveness of the base Attribute by an exponential amount. A nova must have a Quantum Trait equal to the level of Mega-Attribute the player wishes to buy, minus one.

Mega-Attributes supplement, not replace, normal Attributes, and a nova's normal Attribute level must match his Mega-Attribute level. For example, if a nova wants to buy Mega-Strength 3, he must have Strength 3 first; if his Strength is only 2, his Mega-Strength cannot exceed 2, either. Of course, the normal Attribute can exceed the Mega-Attribute if the player desires.

Tainted Mega-Attributes

With the Storyteller's permission, characters can buy tainted Mega-Attributes at a reduced cost per dot. However, doing so causes the character to acquire one point of Taint for each Mega-Attribute dot so purchased. If necessary, the Storyteller should choose an aberration appropriate to the Mega-Attribute. For example, a character with Tainted Mega-Strength might have Bulging Muscles or a Hunchback; one with Mega-Appearance might have Unearthly Beauty or Sheer Hideousness; one with a Mental Mega-Attribute might become megalomaniacal or otherwise mentally unstable.

Mega-Attribute Advantages

Possessing a Mega-Attribute gives a nova certain benefits. The first and foremost advantage to having Mega-Attributes is that they make Attribute rolls easier. The player of a nova with Mega-Perception uses her normal Perception Attribute when making any roll involving Perception. However, she may apply her Mega-Attribute dots to the roll in one of two ways:

1) She may apply an additional number of Mega-Attribute dice to the roll, up to a limit of her Mega-Attribute rating. These Mega-Attribute dice are rolled in addition to the character's normal dice pool. Like other dice, Mega-Attribute dice need to roll a 7 or higher to be considered a success. However, if one of these dice scores a 7 or higher, the character gains not one, but *two* additional successes; and if a Mega-Attribute die comes up "10," the character gains three additional successes.

2) She may subtract one from the difficulties of any rolls involving that Attribute, up to a limit of her Mega-Attribute rating. Thus, a character with Mega-Dexterity 4 attempting a Critical Athletics feat (+4 difficulty) may assign all of her Mega-dots to reducing the difficulty. Having done so, she rolls only her normal Athletics skill total, but makes the roll as though the task is of standard difficulty! This allocation cannot reduce any difficulty below standard difficulty (+0), but it makes it much easier for superhuman characters to accomplish even the most heroic feats.

The player may designate some of her Mega-Attribute dots as extra dice and others as difficulty reductions. She may also change the allocation of the dots from turn to turn and action to action. Moreover, assigned Mega-Attribute dots apply to all actions within the turn, including multiple actions. So, a player who assigns her Mega-Dexterity dots as dice gets those dice on all Dexterity actions for the turn, losing them only when her normal skill total drops below zero.

For Example: Toshiaki Iizumi, with Dexterity 4, Athletics 3 and Mega-Dexterity 3, is attempting to leap onto a speeding car. The Storyteller judges this to be a Critical Athletics feat (+4 to difficulty). However, Iizumi chooses to apply one of his Mega-Attribute dots to reducing the difficulty, making it Difficult (+3).

Iizumi's player, Linda, makes the roll, needing four successes. First, the player rolls Iizumi's Athletics skill total of 7. The dice come up 6, 9, 1, 1, 3, 5 and 6. Normally, this result would be a failure, as only one success was scored. However, Linda now rolls Iizumi's two remaining Mega-Dexterity dice. The dice come up 7 and 10! Iizumi gains five *extra* successes — two from the

"7" die and three from the "10" die — for six total successes. Not only can Iizumi land on the speeding car, he can land exactly where he wants and even do a jig on the roof.

Finally, each Mega-Attribute has certain special Traits, called *enhancements*, associated with it. When a nova buys a Mega-Attribute, he may select one of those enhancements for free. If he wants to have additional enhancements (or additional levels of the same enhancement), he can purchase them at the costs listed on p. 124. A nova may not buy enhancements for a Mega-Attribute he does not possess.

Mega-Attributes themselves cost no quantum points to use. However, most enhancements cost one or more quantum points whenever they are used. Unless stated otherwise, assume an enhancement costs one quantum point to activate.

Competing Mega-Attributes

Sometimes two novas with the same Mega-Attribute use their common Mega-Attribute to compete in a direct, head-to-head resisted roll (such as a grapple involving Mega-Strength or a puzzle contest requiring Mega-Intelligence). If they have the Mega-Attribute at differing levels (say, one has Mega-Strength 2 and the other has Mega-Strength 3), or if one character has a Mega-Attribute while another has an unenhanced Attribute, the character with the higher Mega-Attribute *always* wins. The only exception occurs if the weaker character expends a point of Willpower to push her limits for the duration of the contest. In this case, the characters roll their Mega-Attribute, and only Mega-Attribute, dice in a resisted roll. For example, two super-strong novas compete in an arm-wrestling contest. One nova has Mega-Strength 4, while his opponent has Mega-Strength 2. In most cases, the nova with the Mega-Strength 4 wins automatically. However, the weaker nova spends a point of Willpower, grits his teeth and twists for all he's worth. The contest now becomes a resisted roll, with the stronger nova rolling four dice versus the weaker nova's two dice. The stronger nova still has the edge, but the weaker nova at least has a chance.

Characters without a Mega-Attribute (including baseline humans) may also attempt to compete against a character with a Mega-Attribute; doing so is, however, phenomenally difficult. The character seeking to best the nova must have a natural Attribute of 5; any lower and the Mega-Attribute automatically dominates. If the character has a natural Attribute of 5, he may spend a point of Willpower *every turn* of the contest; by doing so, he gains one die to roll against the nova in a resisted roll. This die lasts for only one turn; subsequently, the unenhanced character must spend additional Willpower or get beaten automatically.

If competing characters have the same Mega-Attribute at the *same* level (both have Mega-Strength 3, for example), then Mega-Attributes and the bonuses they provide are *not* used. In effect, they cancel each other out. Instead, make any rolls using only the characters' normal Attribute (Strength, in this example). In short, don't think that just because you've got Mega-Strength 1, you can settle for a puny Strength of 1. If you do, sooner or later some other Mega-Strong nova will probably kick your ass around the block.

Note that these rules apply only in situations where one nova directly opposes another in a resisted roll. They do not apply in situations with a large number of variables, such as combat. Just because a nova has a higher Mega-Dexterity than her opponent does not mean she will hit the opponent every time; many other factors can come into play. Moreover, these rules are best used in direct Attribute-to-Attribute conflict, *sans* Abilities or other factors. A nova may well have Mega-Intelligence 5, for example, but if the supergenius has no training in Computer, he is unlikely to out-hack a character with lesser Intelligence but greater knowledge of the subject matter (e.g., the Computer Ability).

Exceptionally Normal

One of the benefits of Mega-Attributes is that they allow players to build characters who have minor abilities instead of the planet-busting quantum powers that many novas display. A character with several Mega-Attributes at a low level (typically level 1 or 2, rarely higher) is definitely superhuman, but not noticeably so — you might call him a "stealth nova."

When low Mega-Attributes combine with healthy levels in normal Attributes, a generous helping of Abilities and Backgrounds, and the latest technology and gear, you've got yourself a subtly powerful and highly intriguing character to play. Instead of thinking Superman, think Batman. Batman may not be able to toss buildings around or fly faster than a speeding bullet, but because of his unmatched intellect (Mega-Intelligence and Mega-Wits) and his ability to apply what power he does have exactly where and when it's needed, he's just as effective as the guy from Krypton.

Physical Mega-Attributes

Mega-Strength

Mega-Strength is perhaps the best known of the Mega-Attributes. It's certainly the least subtle. Novas with Mega-Strength usually have enormous muscles and a love of showing off what they can do with them. In nova circles it's commonplace to see them tossing cars around, smashing through buildings, picking up ships and crushing guns into paperweights.

In fact, many of the feats that novas with Mega-Strength perform defy the laws of science. For example, Mega-Strong novas have been observed picking up ships without having them break — even though the object's sheer weight should cause it to fall apart (not to mention the difficulty of getting a good grip on something that big). Experts on quantum powers speculate that a Mega-Strong nova unconsciously emits quantum energies to help keep the object together while he lifts it, but this hypothesis has not been proven conclusively.

Unlike other Mega-Attributes, *Mega-Strength provides no extra dice or reductions to difficulties*; when making Strength rolls, the character still rolls her base, unenhanced Strength, Brawl or Might skill total. Thus, a super-strong combatant still rolls her normal Strength + Brawl skill total to hit an opponent. However, each level of Mega-Strength provides a number of extra automatic successes that add to many Strength or Might rolls: for example, to inflict damage with a punch or smash through a vault door. Moreover, each dot of Mega-Strength provides an automatic minimum amount of weight the nova can lift: for example, a nova with Mega-Strength 1 can lift an object of 1000 kg (about one ton) without the necessity of a roll at all!

When Mega-Strength is used to lift something heavy, consult the table below to determine the nova's base lifting ability (such as 1000 kg for Mega-Strength 1). Then roll Might as normal (without adding the extra automatic successes). Each success on the roll increases the amount the nova can lift by 20%. Thus, a nova with Mega-Strength 1 and three successes on his roll could lift 1600 kg, or about 1.76 tons.

When hurling objects, characters with Mega-Strength may throw anything that weighs less than or equal to their base lifting capacity, using the normal rules for throwing (p. 236). However, when throwing an object of a mass is less than half their base lifting ability, Mega-Strong novas may multiply their normal throwing distance times their automatic successes.

Mega-Strength is particularly effective in personal combat. The following table indicates automatic damage successes applied to any close combat attack made by a character with Mega-Strength. When resisting, maintaining or breaking out of disarms, clinches and holds, use the rules for "Competing Mega-Attributes"; thus, most Mega-Strong combatants are deadly in grappling contests.

For each dot in Mega-Strength, a nova can carry up to 100 kilograms of weight without being encumbered. At higher levels, the Storyteller may wish to increase this capacity even further.

Mega-Strong novas almost always have Mega-Stamina as well.

• Stupendous: Olympic weightlifters look at you in awe. You deadlift 1000 kg (one ton) and gain [5] automatic successes to Strength/ Might rolls and close combat damage dice pools.

•• Amazing: When your moving truck breaks down, you just pick it up and carry it to your new home. You deadlift 10,000 kg (10 tons) and gain [10] automatic successes to Strength/ Might rolls and close combat damage dice pools.

••• Incredible: You can toss automobiles for blocks. You deadlift 25,000 kg (25 tons) and gain [15] automatic successes to Strength/ Might rolls and close combat damage dice pools.

•••• Spectacular: You can juggle tanks. You deadlift 50,000 kg (50 tons) and gain [20] automatic successes to Strength/ Might rolls and close combat damage dice pools.

••••• Godlike: Even other novas are impressed by your physical might. You deadlift 100,000 kg (100 tons) and gain [25] automatic successes to Strength/ Might rolls and close combat damage dice pools.

Mega-Strength Enhancements

Enhancements that characters with Mega-Strength may learn or purchase include:

Crush

Mega-Strength is, by itself, enough to cause deadly damage to many people — most normal humans can't survive blows from someone strong enough to pick up and throw cars. However, novas with this power have refined their ability to use Mega-Strength to kill. They are adept at grabbing and crushing people, delivering punches powerful and focused enough to go *through* a body, and so on.

System: Strength damage is normally bashing damage. A nova with this ability inflicts Brawl and Martial Arts damage (modified by his Mega-Strength, as usual) as *lethal* damage when he takes a full turn to focus his attack and spends a quantum point. The Crush attack is made the following turn, on the nova's Initiative. This enhancement lasts for one strike, but it can be reactivated as often as the nova likes, so long as she has the quantum points.

Shockwave

Who needs the San Andreas Fault? A Mega-strong nova with this ability can generate his own little earthquakes. All he does is stomp his foot or smash his fists against the ground, causing waves of force and pressure to radiate out away from him through the earth.

System: When a nova uses this enhancement, he may roll his Mega-Strength dice as a bashing damage dice pool to most targets within a radius equal to (Mega-Strength x 10 meters). Any target on the ground is affected; targets above the ground are not. Anyone affected falls to the ground unless he makes a Strength roll (at difficulty +3) to keep his feet. Targets may take extra damage if other objects (such as falling crockery or collapsing tunnels) fall on them. Additionally, the surface the nova is hitting also suffers damage as though the nova had made a normal Mega-Strength strike — so it isn't a very good idea for a character to use this maneuver when he is on things like aircraft, bridges or boats.

This enhancement stays active for a single attack, and the nova may make only one Shockwave attack per turn.

Lifter

A Mega-Strong nova with this enhancement is *really* strong — he makes even other Mega-Strong novas look puny. He's the guy to call when you need to move something like, say, a mountain.

System: The nova can double the amount of weight he can carry for each quantum point he spends. For example, a nova who spends four quantum points on Lifter can carry 16 times his normal weight limit (!). However, the character does not inflict any extra damage with punches or similar attacks. At the Storyteller's discretion, the character's ability to throw heavy objects may be increased in a similar fashion, but only to throw them for distance, not damage (for example, to throw a tank into orbit, but not to throw another character into a wall and hurt him).

This enhancement stays active for one scene or one "feat of strength," whichever comes first.

Quantum Leap

The character's leg muscles are prodigiously strong — so much so that she can leap enormous distances. Faster than the subway and twice as fun.

System: A character with this enhancement covers far more distance in a leap than the usual two meters per success on a Jumping roll. Instead, each success on a Jumping roll allows the nova to leap up to two kilometers horizontally, or half a kilometer vertically, times her number of dots in Mega-Strength (of course, she can choose to leap less far than this if she so desires). Thus, a nova with Mega-Strength 3 and Quantum Leap could cover six kilometers horizontally, or one and a half kilometers vertically, for each success.

Don't forget that such prodigious jumps are essentially an uncontrolled form of movement. Once she launches herself, a nova can't deviate from her line of "flight," do much to dodge attacks or avoid obstacles. Unless she has a power that allows her to see for many kilometers, she won't know where she's going to land until it comes into sight — and it won't necessarily be a pleasant landing spot.

The character may also use this enhancement to make a normal Dodge roll against area and explosive attacks, provided she spends the quantum point and takes a defensive action.

This enhancement stays active for one leap.

Thunderclap

When the nova claps his hands together, a tremendous burst of sound and air pressure cracks forth. The force of the effect is enough to hurt people, break windows and cause similar damage or harm in a nearby area.

System: When a nova uses this enhancement, he may roll his Mega-Strength dice as a bashing damage dice pool to most targets within a radius equal to (Mega-Strength x 10 meters). However, "hard" targets — such as most walls, vehicles or metal objects — and extremely "soft" targets — such as cloth — are not affected. Only living creatures and relatively brittle or fragile things, such as glass, take the damage.

This enhancement stays active for a single attack, and the nova may make only one Thunderclap attack per turn.

Mega-Dexterity

Mega-Dexterity is one of the more common Mega-Attributes. A Mega-dexterous nova is faster, more agile and stealthier than normal, and he often has a better re-action time. Mega-Dexterity is especially useful for novas whose powers are not quite so overt or "flashy" as most.

The Mega-Dexterity rating is added to the character's Initiative, run and sprint scores. Furthermore, when a nova with Mega-Dexterity is in combat and another character tries to use a delayed action to interrupt the nova's action, the interruption is not automatic. Instead, both characters must make Dexterity rolls; the one with the most successes goes first. If a nova with Mega-Dexterity and a character without it act at the same time, the Mega-Dexterous character is automatically considered to have the higher Initiative, and thus, he gets to go first. If both characters have Mega-Dexterity and the Enhanced Initiative enhancement (see "Mega-Wits"), the standard rule applies.

- • Stupendous: You can juggle knives in zero-g — with your feet. You may make Dodge rolls against bullets or other ranged attacks without seeking cover or hitting the ground.
- •• Amazing: Your reactions are so fast that even a martial-arts master cannot match them.
- ••• Incredible: Whenever you run by someone, they can barely see you — all they feel is the wind.
- •••• Spectacular: You can do your chores in just a few seconds. At this level or higher, you may pluck bullets out of the air by making a normal Block roll.
- ••••• Godlike: You can perform acts of manual dexterity so precise that even machines cannot duplicate them.

Mega-Dexterity Enhancements

Enhancements that characters with Mega-Dexterity may learn or purchase include:

Accuracy

Some Mega-Dexterous novas have an uncanny ability to aim attacks and judge how to place their blows for best effect. Certain novas claim that this enhancement is the ultimate in hand-eye coordination, while others speak of "mystic forces" guiding them. Whatever the reason, anyone who's seen them in combat can't help but admire their ability.

System: In addition to any other bonuses provided for having a Mega-Attribute, the character receives three more dice to roll when attempting to hit any target with any attack (whether close combat or ranged combat). The character must take a turn to aim the attack. This bonus applies only to firearms, martial arts, melee and quantum-power attacks; attacks involving Brawl do not get the bonus (since they depend on raw power and ferocity, not precise aim).

This enhancement stays active for a single attack (hit or miss).

Enhanced Movement

You're fast — *really* fast. You can run faster than the proverbial speeding locomotive at times. Your reaction time isn't any quicker than the normal Mega-Dexterous nova, but when you've got to cover the miles to get somewhere, you can cover them quicker than anyone else.

System: The character's pace when walking, running, sprinting or swimming is multiplied by (1 + Mega-Dexterity) for one turn (if the player spends one quantum point) or one scene (if the character spends three quantum points). Thus, a character with Mega-Dexterity 2 could spend a quantum point to triple her movement (1 + Mega-Dexterity 2) for one turn.

The effects of Enhanced Movement are cumulative with those of Hypermovement (p. 203). Apply the Enhanced Movement multiplier after determining the character's movement rate with Hypermovement.

Fast Tasks

When it's time to clean out the house, strip down and rebuild an engine or knit a sweater, your friends call you. You can do it much faster than they can — sometimes literally in the blink of an eye.

System: This ability allows a nova to perform tasks at extremely rapid speeds without sacrificing any care or workmanship. Depending upon the nature of the task, the nova can do it in less than half the time it would take a normal person; simple tasks may, as the preceding description indicates, take no more than a second or so. For example, a nova with Fast Tasks could paint a typical interior house wall in just a second or two; he could take apart and rebuild a reasonably complex machine (like an automobile engine) in something like half an hour. At the Storyteller's option, Fast Tasks may turn certain extended rolls (p. 109) into simple rolls.

The character must be able to perform the task in question; Fast Tasks does not grant any new or additional skills. For example, a nova who wants to repair engines at superspeeds must know the Engineering Ability. Furthermore, the player must make the standard rolls required to accomplish the work — Fast Tasks doesn't make the job any easier, it just gets it over with more quickly.

This enhancement stays active for one scene.

Flexibility

Dexterity isn't all speed and reaction time and things like that. Sometimes it reflects a character's ability to contort his body or reach into places ordinary characters cannot. That's certainly the case, at least in part, for novas who have this enhancement. In effect they can make their bodies sufficiently flexible or rubbery to stretch their arms for short distances or squeeze through narrow openings. They are often master contortionists and escape artists.

System: The character has the limited ability to contort and stretch his body. When he wants them to be, his flesh and bones become extremely flexible and malleable. This flexibility confers no protection from damage or harm, but it does allow the character to fit into places inaccessible to normal human bodies. The character may stretch his limbs up to two meters per dot of Mega-Dexterity. He can also contort and reshape his flexible form to fit through any opening big enough for his fist to pass through. The Storyteller is the final arbiter on which openings the character can squeeze through.

A player may select this enhancement multiple times. Each additional selection doubles the distance the character may stretch his limbs and body. The enhancement stays active for one scene.

Physical Prodigy

A nova with this ability possesses a certain "genius" for all physical activities, such as sports or running. Somehow he knows instinctively how to act, what to do and how to position himself for the best results in any given athletic endeavor. It's as if he had the greatest coaches in world history whispering in his ear and giving him tips.

Novas with this ability (and indeed, novas in general) have been banned from athletic competition with baselines, since they have an obvious unfair advantage. However, they can (and often do) compete with other novas on "supersports" pay-per-views.

System: In addition to any other dice received for Mega-Dexterity, the character receives three extra successes when making any roll involving Athletics, Performance (Dance) or similar skills. This bonus should not be applied to dodge dice pools, nor to skills such as Brawl, Firearms, Martial Arts, Melee or Stealth. If there is any doubt as to whether the bonus applies, the Storyteller must decide which Abilities are affected by Physical Prodigy. The effects last for a scene.

Catfooted

In a dangerous world, sometimes it's the unobtrusive person who survives the longest — and gets the most accomplished. A nova with this Mega-Dexterity ability is the stealthiest of the stealthy, able to walk on dead leaves without making a sound or run through sand without leaving footprints.

System: In addition to any other dice received for Mega-Dexterity, the character receives three extra successes when making any roll involving Stealth or similar skills. Furthermore, if the character makes a Dexterity roll, he can avoid leaving any tracks or similar marks showing where he walked. The difficulty of this roll increases by two if the character is running and three if he is sprinting. The effects last for a scene.

Rapid Strike

A nova with this enhancement can deliver a blur of rapid-fire punches or kicks to a single target. While the individual blows are not any more powerful than an ordinary strike, they strike so fast and furious that the cumulative effect is much more powerful.

System: For each dot he has in Mega-Dexterity, a nova using this enhancement adds one to his punch or kick damage dice pools; the effects last for one turn.

Mega-Stamina

A nova with Mega-Stamina is hardier, more durable and more resistant to injury than your average nova. Although not always as resilient as novas who actually buy defensive powers such as Force Field, novas with Mega-Stamina are still mighty tough. Furthermore, they tend to have a great deal of endurance; it's almost impossible to tire them out. Some of them display little need for sleep, staying up for days at a time.

Perhaps most importantly of all, a nova with Mega-Stamina feels very little pain. Regardless of the source — injury, disease, accident — a nova with Mega-Stamina can shrug off the pain and keep on going. Unconfirmed rumors speak of novas who were so resistant to pain that they didn't feel the effects of injury until their wounds killed them. In game terms, novas with Mega-Stamina suffer reduced dice pool penalties based on their health level, as indicated in the following table.

x — Normal nova metabolism: You're still pretty tough. You soak bashing and lethal damage as normal for your Stamina, but your healing rates are doubled. Base Resistance and Endurance ratings equal 3 each (before allocating any dots into Abilities). Lifespan 150+ years.

• Stupendous: You can go for weeks without sleep, and your healing rates are tripled. Base Resistance and Endurance ratings of 3 each. Lifespan 150+ years. Dice pool penalties due to injuries and pain are reduced by one. The character receives one extra soak against bashing damage and one extra soak against lethal damage.

•• Amazing: Torturers despair of breaking you. Your healing rates are four times faster than a baseline's. Base Resistance and Endurance ratings equal 3 apiece. Lifespan 150+ years. Dice pool penalties due to injuries and pain reduce by two. The character receives two extra soak against bashing damage and one extra soak against lethal damage, as well as one extra "Bruised" health level.

••• Incredible: Participating in a few triathlons in a row doesn't even phase you. Your healing rates are five times those of a normal human, and your base Resistance and Endurance ratings begin at 4 each. Lifespan 180+ years. Dice pool penalties due to injuries and pain reduce by three. The character receives three extra soak against bashing damage and two extra soak against lethal damage, as well as one extra "Bruised" health level.

•••• Spectacular: Bullets practically bounce off your chest, and your healing rates are six times that of a baseline. Base Resistance and Endurance ratings equal 4 each. Lifespan 200+ years. Dice pool penalties due to injuries and pain reduce by four. The character receives four extra soak against bashing damage and two extra soak against lethal damage, as well as two extra "Bruised" health levels.

••••• Godlike: Missiles practically bounce off your chest. Your healing rates are seven times better than any normal human's. Your base Resistance and Endurance ratings equal 5 each. Lifespan 250+ years. Dice pool penalties due to injuries and pain reduce by five. The character receives five extra soak against bashing damage and three extra soak against lethal damage, as well as three extra "Bruised" health levels.

Mega-Stamina Enhancements

Enhancements that characters with Mega-Stamina may learn or purchase include:

Adaptability

This enhancement allows the nova to survive nearly any adverse environmental condition. In effect, the nova uses ambient quantum energies to evolve and bolster her body's natural defenses, thus allowing her to survive in environments normally hostile to human life, such as the vacuum of outer space or underwater. Adaptability also allows the character to do without food, sleep or other necessities of life. Often, a nova with Adaptability spontaneously manifests gills, toughened skin or whatever feature is needed.

System: The character is able to sustain herself indefinitely on residual quantum energies, so long as she has at least one quantum point in her body. She does not need to eat, sleep or breathe, and can survive indefinitely in conditions as hostile as Death Valley, Antarctica, or outer space. She is automatically immune to most poisons, gases, diseases and drugs; against particularly virulent diseases or nova-derived poisons, she gains an extra six soak or Resistance dice. Moreover, the character's lifespan is increased by centuries, if not more.

Adaptability is normally an automatic enhancement and requires no quantum point expenditure. However, in particularly hostile environments (the vacuum of space, the bottom of the Mariana Trench, a conflagration), the character might need to spend a quantum point per scene, or even turn, of exposure. The Storyteller makes this decision.

Adaptability does *not* confer protection against weaponry or nova attacks such as flame blasts or the like, only against natural environmental conditions.

Durability

The nova is tough as nails. Although she's not necessarily capable of ignoring attacks outright, she instinctively channels deadly kinetic energy away from her body, rolls with otherwise lethal blows, or is otherwise capable of reducing an instant-kill attack to a "Gee, that stung" level of injury.

System: Whenever the character is hit with a kinetic attack inflicting lethal damage (bullet, knife, missile, etc.), she may spend a quantum point and roll her Mega-Stamina dice against a Standard difficulty. If she succeeds, the incoming damage is converted to bashing damage, which she may soak with her bashing soak score. The character may not convert energy attacks (fire, electricity, Quantum Bolts, etc.) in this manner, nor may she use this enhancement against bashing damage applied after she is Incapacitated.

Hardbody

This enhancement offers protection of a different sort from Resiliency. Although it doesn't help defend a character against ordinary damage, it allows him to soak certain forms of damage against which he ordinarily would have no protection at all.

System: A nova with Hardbody may use his lethal soak total to soak aggravated damage. This costs one quantum point, but the nova may activate the enhancement as an automatic feat. This enhancement stays in effect for one turn.

Regeneration

All novas heal more quickly than the human norm, but a nova with this enhancement heals even quicker than most novas. Sometimes her wounds literally close right before your eyes!

System: A nova with this enhancement may spend quantum points to instantly heal bashing and lethal damage, at the rate of one quantum point per health level healed. Doing so is an automatic action, but the nova may heal a maximum number of health levels per turn equal to her Mega-Stamina rating. Additionally, this enhancement allows a nova to regrow severed limbs or organs, but doing so takes a very long time (weeks or months, typically). Regeneration does not heal aggravated damage.

Resiliency

Toughened by the rigors of channeling quantum energies, the nova's frame is even more resistant to damage than are most Mega-Stamina novas' bodies.

System: The soak bonuses provided by the nova's Mega-Stamina rating are doubled. Thus, a nova with Mega-Stamina 3 and the Resiliency enhancement receives +6 soak against bashing, +4 against lethal damage, rather than the +3/+2 bonuses available to other novas with an equivalent level of Mega-Stamina.

This enhancement is "built in" and costs no quantum points to activate.

Mental Mega-Attributes

Mega-Perception

Scientists theorize that normal humans use only a fraction of their ability to observe things. Ask a normal person to describe what he just walked past, and he probably won't be able to tell you too many details about it, if any. That's not true of novas with Mega-Perception. They take it *all* in — every detail, every nuance, every little fact. They may not remember them very long (that's a function of Intelligence), but they don't overlook things. They make excellent sentinels, guards, detectives and trackers.

Novas with Mega-Perception almost always have a high Awareness skill. They often have high ratings in other "observational" skills, such as Investigation, but such is not always the case.

- **Stupendous:** You remember the license-plate numbers of all the cars you just walked past in the parking lot.
- • • **Amazing:** Even the tiniest details are like information beacons to you.
- • • • **Incredible:** You can tell what a person is thinking by the way the nerves in her face twitch.
- • • • • **Spectacular:** You can locate a single person in an auditorium by her body odor or perfume.
- • • • • • **Godlike:** You can hear wool growing on the backs of sheep.

Mega-Perception Enhancements

Enhancements that characters with Mega-Perception may learn or purchase include:

Analytic Taste/Touch

There are plenty of gourmets out there who can figure out what spices were used in a particular dish by tasting it. A nova with this power can go them one better: He can detect everything in the food. Give him a casserole, and he'll tell you every ingredient in it, as well as how much of each was used. Give him a pretzel, and he can tell you how many grains of salt there are on it. Give him poisoned food, and he will detect the poison as soon as he touches it with his tongue, then spit the food out immediately before the poison can affect him.

The character's sense of touch is also enhanced. Everyone knows what a dollar bill feels like — it's got a unique feeling like no other type of paper. Mix a dollar up with a bunch of pieces of newspaper and other papers, and someone can still find it by touch alone. But only a nova with Analytic Touch can tell you without looking whether it's a twenty or a c-note.

A character with this enhancement may use both functions.

System: With Analytic Taste, the character's sense of taste is so heightened that he can determine the composition and nature of food he eats, as described previously. This enhancement is most useful for detecting poison or other tampering, but it has other uses as well. If the Storyteller decides that a particular substance is present in only trace quantities, he may require a Perception or Awareness roll to allow the character to detect it. But even in such situations, the character receives a minimum of three extra dice when making any Perception roll based on taste. Furthermore, by flicking his tongue in and out of his mouth in the manner of a snake, the character can halve any penalties relating to darkness, as the character literally "tastes" vibrations in the air.

With Analytic Touch, the character's sense of touch is so heightened that he can differentiate many objects by touch alone. This ability can be extremely useful if the character cannot see. It also provides bonuses in situations where an acute sense of feel would be helpful — such as lockpicking or trying to figure out the combination to a safe by feeling the tumblers fall into place. The character receives a minimum of three extra dice when making any Perception roll based on touch. Furthermore, the character's skin is so sensitive that he can sense faint air currents, which adds two dice to Awareness skill totals when attempting to detect stealthy opponents like invisible novas.

This enhancement is always on and costs no quantum points to use.

Blindfighting

Most people are helpless when blind — particularly in combat — but not this character. Thanks to his enhanced senses, he can perceive where his foes are even when he cannot see them. Some Asian (or Asian-influenced) novas snidely refer to this enhancement as "Zen fighting."

System: The character is not subject to the difficulty penalty for fighting blind. In some situations, such as those with bad or glaring lighting, he might even be better off to shut his eyes and fight without using his sight. Similarly, if an opponent is using the power Invisibility to escape detection, a nova with Blindfighting can determine exactly where his invisible enemy is by making an Awareness roll (opponent resists with her Invisibility + Stealth dice pool).

This enhancement costs one quantum point and lasts for a scene.

Bloodhound

Like the animal for which it is named, this enhancement allows a nova to track a person by scent.

System: The character may make an Awareness roll to follow someone by scent alone. If the scent is particularly strong (for example, the person hasn't bathed in a week), reduce the difficulty by one. If the person being tracked passes through an area with a lot of other scents (like a crowded city street), walks through a stream or does anything else that might confuse or mask his scent, the nova must make another roll at an increased difficulty (+2 or more, usually).

If the nova is exposed to a particularly strong odor — such as having pepper thrown in her face — her Bloodhound ability is temporarily "blinded." Until she can get that scent out of her nose, which could take anywhere from a turn to an hour depending on the circumstances, she won't be able to follow any scents.

This enhancement is always on and costs no quantum points to use.

Electromagnetic Vision

By processing and amplifying waves in the middle end of the electromagnetic spectrum (infrared, visible light, ultraviolet), the character provides herself with a number of sensory abilities.

System: The character spends a quantum point to activate the power for (Perception + Mega-Perception) turns. While doing so, the character gains an additional three dice on any Awareness roll related to vision. Additionally, this enhancement provides a number of benefits:

• **Ultraviolet vision:** The character can see in the ultraviolet ("UV") spectrum, allowing her to see clearly and without penalty whenever UV illumination (such as from the sun, moon or stars) is present. Like a cat, she is able to see in conditions of very little light. The character can see as well in darkness as in daylight, provided that there is at least *some* light (even faint starlight is enough). If she is in total blackness (such as an unlit underground room), she cannot see.

• **Infrared vision:** The character is able to see in the infrared ("IR") spectrum. Not only can she see anything illuminated by an IR light, she can see the heat given off by living things and hot objects. Hot things appear "bright," cool things "dark."

• **Visible light attuner:** The character can magnify objects in her line of sight, as though she were a high-powered telescopic scope or electron microscope. Usually, novas use this ability to view tiny objects which would ordinarily be beyond the character's range of vision, but it can also help see objects at a distance. The character can also see distant objects as if they were close up. For each dot of Mega-Perception, the character can magnify distant or tiny images by a factor of 10 (x100 at Mega-Perception 2, x1000 at Mega-Perception 3, etc.). Use of this enhancement negates range penalties, as well as difficulty penalties suffered when striking at characters with the power of Sizemorph (Shrinking).

High-End Electromagnetic Scan

The character can transmit and receive waves from the gamma- and x-ray end of the electromagnetic spectrum. This allows him to "see" through solid objects, at a range equal to (Perception + Mega-Perception) x 20 meters.

System: By spending a quantum point, taking an action and making a Perception roll, the character may see through solid objects. The Storyteller may increase the difficulty to scan through particularly dense objects.

Extras: None

Hyperenhanced Hearing

A nova with this enhancement can hear and transmit sounds that are too high-pitched or low-pitched to be audible to the normal human ear, such as dog whistles, radio waves, or security devices that utilize ultrasonic sound.

System: The character spends a quantum point to activate the power for (Perception + Mega-Perception) turns. While doing so, the character gains an additional

three dice on any Awareness, Intrusion or other appropriate roll related to hearing. Additionally, this enhancement provides a number of benefits:

• **Infra/ultrasonic hearing:** Most characters cannot hear infrasonic or ultrasonic sound at all. A nova with this enhancement can, though the Storyteller may require an Awareness roll if the sound is extremely soft or distant — just like he would with any normal whisper or distant sound.

• **Sonar:** Like a bat, the nova can emit sonar waves which travel away from her, hit objects and "bounce" back to their source. This sense tells the character where things are, how big they are and other gross physical qualities. On the other hand, sonar does not reveal finer details or visual details, such as the number of fingers on a hand, color, fine texture or print. Sonar works in a 360-degree radius around the character and are sufficiently accurate to allow the character to launch attacks without any loss of dice or other penalties. Sonar can be detected with Radio Scan.

• **Radio scan:** The name of this technique is slightly misleading, since it actually allows the character to perceive all broadcast waves, including radio, television and cellular telephone transmissions. The character may also transmit along such wavelengths, though he can transmit voice only.

The character may voluntarily "shut off" the sense (to keep from being inundated with signals). He can also edit out specific frequencies so that he hears only a specific radio broadcast rather than all radio broadcasts, television, and other broadcasts.

Quantum Attunement

The character can sense the ebbs and flows of quantum energies in her vicinity. This gives her a hyperenhanced perception, allowing her to sense her surroundings on the molecular level, even if her other senses have been incapacitated. The character must still face in the general direction of what she wishes to perceive.

System: By spending one quantum point per turn, the character can attune herself to quantum energies in the area. Among other things, this allows the character to make an Awareness roll to sense her surroundings even if completely deprived of one or more senses. The character can also scan other novas by making a Medicine roll; this allows the character to sense the rough level of Quantum, Node and Taint Traits possessed by the other nova. With three or more successes, the character might be able to guess at the other nova's powers, though the Storyteller should describe this in narrative terms, as eddies and shifts in the local quantum flow (e.g., "Your foe clenches his fists, and quantum forces begin seething around his outstretched hands" as opposed to "He's going to throw a Quantum Bolt"; "When she stretches, nuclear forces scream and hiss around her frame," as opposed to "She's got Mega-Strength 4.").

Ultraperipheral Perception

Sometimes you'll hear someone described as "having eyes in the back of his head." A nova with this enhancement just about meets that description. He can sense all around himself more or less as readily as he can look straight ahead.

System: A character with Ultraperipheral Perception can perceive things in a 360-degree circle around himself without turning his head. This enhancement prevents a character from being surprised by people sneaking up on him from behind. Attackers do not gain flank or rear attack bonuses to hit him. It also allows him to keep track of everything surrounding him.

This effect costs a quantum point and lasts for a scene.

Mega-Intelligence

Intelligence, according to some, is the ultimate weapon. If that's the case, a nova with this Mega-Attribute is ready to fight in any war.

A character with Mega-Intelligence is intelligent beyond the dreams of even most geniuses. His ability to make deductive "leaps" from unrelated facts to a conclusion, to solve difficult problems and to analyze situations is nearly unparalleled. In some cases, novas with high Mega-Intelligence ratings have put powerful computers to shame. In fact, even one dot of Mega-Intelligence effectively indicates that the human IQ scale can no longer be applied to the Mega-intelligent nova.

Like Intelligence itself, Mega-Intelligence mainly represents the *quality* of a character's thinking processes — how clearly and precisely he can put facts together and draw conclusions from them. However, unlike Intelligence, to a certain extent it also measures the speed at which a character can analyze facts and perform calculations. Characters with high Intelligence solve problems quickly, but a nova with even Mega-Intelligence 1 makes them look like mental tortoises. When it comes to reacting fast under pressure, though, Wits and Mega-Wits still rule the day.

- • Stupendous: You do advanced calculus problems in your sleep.
- •• Amazing: Supergeniuses look on you with envy.
- ••• Incredible: An auditorium full of professors doesn't have as much brainpower as you.
- •••• Spectacular: Your memory for even the most trivial details never fails you.
- ••••• Godlike: You make supercomputers look slow and stupid.

Mega-Intelligence Enhancements

Enhancements that characters with Mega-Intelligence may learn or purchase include:

Analyze Weakness

Virtually everything — every object, every system, every procedure — has flaws, weaknesses and vulnerable points. In many instances these problems are so minor as to be unnoticeable to the average person. A nova with this ability, however, is not the "average person." By dint of her vast intellect and analytical prowess, she is able to detect where these weaknesses are, and she knows how to exploit them to her advantage.

System: A nova with this enhancement is able to detect weaknesses in objects, systems and procedures. Sometimes this flaw is physical (a place where a crack is likely to develop) and sometimes a less tangible weakness (a part of a security net where protection is lightest), but in either case, the nova can locate the problem.

To find and analyze a weakness, the nova must spend an action looking at and considering an object or system. Then she spends a quantum point and makes an Intelligence roll. The Storyteller can increase the difficulty of the roll if the nova is examining a particularly well-made or relatively flawless object or if the system or procedure being analyzed is so efficient that it generally lacks any vulnerabilities. If the roll fails, the object or procedure is without weaknesses or working at peak efficiency as far as the nova can tell. A nova can try to analyze the weaknesses in a particular object or system only once per scene; if she fails it will be a while before she can try again.

If the roll succeeds, there are several possible effects. If the nova is analyzing a physical object, such as body armor or a wall, the soak value of any armor provided by the object (both bashing and lethal) is reduced by one per success. This effect can be applied to anything that offers physical protection, such as another nova's Force Field, even though it is not literally a "physical object."

If a nova succeeds in analyzing the weaknesses in larger objects, such as buildings, vehicles or bridges, she knows where the cracks, weaknesses and/or stresses in the object are. This analysis allows her to place explosives where they will be the most effective, or to effect repairs as quickly and efficiently as possible. For each success the character achieves on his Intelligence roll, she receives an extra die (or sometimes more) for related Ability rolls to affect the object in some way. For example, if the nova's player achieves three successes on her Analyze Weakness roll when examining a spacecraft, she receives three extra dice for Engineering rolls to fix or modify the craft — or three extra dice for rolls to destroy the ship with a bomb, since she knows just where to put the bomb for maximum effect.

If the nova succeeds in analyzing a system or procedure — such as a security system or program, a plan of attack, a tactical situation or a bureaucratic system — she knows what aspects of it are not as good as they could be; what parts of it are flawed, weak or inefficient; and how the system or procedure could be improved. For each success the player achieves on her Intelligence roll, she receives one die (or sometimes more) for related Ability rolls to affect the object in some way. For example, if the nova's player achieves two successes when analyzing the guard patrols and other security measures protecting a mercenary base in Africa, she gains two extra dice for Intrusion rolls to sneak into that base. If she were trying to get information out of the federal court system, she would receive two extra dice for her Bureaucracy roll.

Eidetic Memory

Any nova with Mega-Intelligence has a well-developed memory. A nova with this enhancement, though, has a memory that's virtually foolproof. He can remember in precise detail just about anything that has happened to him. Anything he takes the time to study remains lodged in his mind. However, just because he can store a particular fact in his memory does not mean he can recall it instantly. Sometimes a character with Eidetic Memory has to stop and think for several seconds or minutes, slowly reading down a mental page or through a mental file until he retrieves the fact he wants.

System: A character with Eidetic Memory is assumed to have perfect, and nearly instantaneous, recollection of anything that has happened to him. For example, suppose that the characters have spent an hour working their way through the labyrinthine halls of some Teragen base. After the climactic encounter, the characters realize, to their dismay, that they cannot remember how to get out again. Fortunately, one of them has Eidetic Memory, and he can lead them back the way they came in without any problem.

Remembering studied information works a little differently. Theoretically, the character has perfect recall of anything he has studied, from the phone book to advanced quantum physics textbooks. However, the problem with this in game terms is that it can provide the character with many Abilities for free — a situation that isn't fair to the other characters. Therefore, the Storyteller needs to restrict this aspect of Eidetic Memory in a couple of ways. First, Eidetic Memory provides only *academic* knowledge. It doesn't teach a character how to do anything. The character might have memorized an entire book on plumbing, but since he's never actually put wrench to pipe in his life, he can't fix plumbing systems. He'd be qualified to advise a character who does have such skills, though.

Second, a character may not be able to recall a memorized fact quickly, as stated previously. Whenever the character wants to use his Eidetic Memory, the Storyteller should require an Intelligence roll. The Storyteller may increase the difficulty for particularly obscure facts. The Storyteller should also set a base time required for the nova to recall the fact; this base time can range from instantly, to one turn, to a minute or more. Each additional success achieved on the Intelligence roll cuts the recall time in half.

Characters with Eidetic Memory should be encouraged to spend experience points to buy Abilities related to facts they have memorized. Thus, this enhancement is an excellent justification for characters to buy all sorts of unusual and fun Abilities.

This enhancement is always in effect and costs no quantum points to activate.

Enhanced Memory

A nova with this enhancement lacks the long-term brainpower that a nova with Eidetic Memory has, but what he lacks in long-term memory he makes up for in short-term recall. He can study a subject and, for a brief period, remember everything he studied almost exactly. Although this information fades quickly after that period expires, it's there long enough for a character to make use of it — say, on a mission. Enhanced Memory is perfect for memorizing things like floor plans, guard patrol schedules and personal information about a target — just the sort of facts that come in handy on many missions.

System: The character chooses a particular subject or collection of data to memorize. The subject must not be too extensive — he can't choose the entire works of Shakespeare, for example. However, a complete mission briefing, or one or two textbooks, or the ability to speak a language enough to carry on a basic conversa-

tion, are all possible.

The player must spend a quantum point and make an Intelligence roll at +1 difficulty to memorize the chosen information successfully. Once memorized, the information remains in the character's short-term memory for a period equal to one day per dot of Mega-Intelligence. After that period has passed, the information begins to fade at the rate of about 25% per day until the character's recollection of it is virtually gone.

Characters may, if they wish, use their Enhanced Memory as a justification for buying a particular Ability, which reflects permanent recollection of a memorized subject.

Mathematical Savant

Calculator? Computer? Who needs them? A nova with this ability can run numbers in his head so fast that reaching for an electronic calculator is usually a waste of time.

System: A nova with the Mathematical Savant enhancement can perform complex mathematical equations in his head almost instantly. Multiplication and division, even involving four- to eight-digit numbers, takes only a second or two. More complex algebra, trigonometry or calculus problems may take up to a minute. Extremely complex mathematical operations, such as all the calculations necessary to launch a rocket to Jupiter, may take up to an hour.

Whenever the character is using a skill or Ability involving math, such as trying to decode an encrypted message, the Storyteller should allow the player to make an Intelligence roll. Each success bestows an additional die for any related Ability rolls.

This enhancement is always in effect, and it costs no quantum points to activate.

Linguistic Genius

Quelle heure et il?
¿Habla español, señor?
Bom dia!
Sprechen sie deutsch?

These phrases are all as good as his native language to a nova with this enhancement. A character with Linguistic Genius is, literally, a genius at linguistics and language interpretation. He can usually speak a lot of languages fluently, but more than that, he has an intuitive understanding of the structure and nature of language. Even if he has never heard a particular language before, if he listens to someone speaking it for a little while, he will be able to determine what the person is saying. He won't necessarily be able to speak the language himself, so he might not be able to respond or participate in a conversation, but he will know what's being said to him, and sometimes that's enough to solve any problems.

System: A character with this enhancement receives five automatic successes when the player makes Linguistics rolls. Furthermore, the number of language families with which he is familiar is quadrupled. Thus, a nova with Linguistics 5 and Linguistic Genius would be familiar with 20 language families.

Even better, the character has a limited ability to comprehend speech in languages with which he is not familiar. When he hears a language he does not know, the player may make an Intelligence roll. The Storyteller should add a difficulty modifier for especially complex languages, situations where the character has difficulty hearing the language being spoken or when the character is not able to listen to the language for very long.

This enhancement is always in effect and costs no quantum points to activate.

Mental Prodigy

This broad enhancement is actually several different enhancements grouped under a common heading. Each of them represents a nova who has an innate talent for, "feel for" or skill at a particular type of Intelligence-based (or -related) ability. The character must select a specific category of this enhancement.

When a character spends a quantum point to activate this enhancement, the effects and bonuses received last for a minimum of an hour, and possibly longer at the Storyteller's discretion.

Catergories include:

• **Engineering:** An Engineering Prodigy is a certifiable genius when it comes to working with electronic and mechanical devices. He has an innate understanding of how such devices work, how to repair or improve them and the synergies that result when particular technologies are combined. He can make intuitive leaps that leave ordinary engineers scratching their heads in puzzlement.

System: Whenever the character works with electronic or mechanical devices, the player may make an Intelligence roll. For each success he achieves, he may roll one extra die when making Engineering rolls or related rolls (it is the Storyteller's discretion as to what constitutes a "related" roll, based on the situation).

• **Financial:** Economics isn't such a "dismal science" to a nova with this ability. He has a natural understanding of economics and economic systems, high finance, market manipulation and money in general. Give him a few dollars to invest and he'll soon turn them into a fortune. Give him an economy to manage and it will soon be humming along efficiently and productively. Let him analyze the stock market for you, and you will be able to chart a productive investment strategy for years to come.

System: Whenever the character is involved with situations or problems concerning economics and finance, the player may make an Intelligence roll. For each success achieved, the player gains an additional die when making rolls related to such subjects.

• **Investigative:** Sherlock Holmes has nothing on a nova with this ability. The character is a deductive and investigative genius, able to read volumes of information from the smallest clues. Although he does not necessarily have any knowledge of forensic science, he has an intuitive ability to figure out what clues mean. This ability makes him a matchless detective — or a nearly uncatchable criminal.

System: Whenever the character is investigating a crime, interrogating someone, or trying to solve a mystery or puzzle, the player may make an Intelligence roll. For each success achieved, he may roll an additional die when making Investigation rolls, Interrogation rolls, Science rolls for specialties such as Criminology, Medicine rolls for the specialty Forensic Pathology or related rolls (it is the Storyteller's discretion as to what constitutes a "related" roll, based on the situation).

• **Medical:** Marcus Welby, eat your heart out — and if you do, this character might just be able to patch you back up. A nova with this enhancement is able to diagnose diseases, treat injuries and heal the sick as well as an experienced physician. If he actually has formal medical training (i.e., the Medicine Ability), he's even better.

System: Whenever the character is involved with situations or problems concerning medicine, healing injuries, fighting off illnesses and diagnosing diseases, the player may make an Intelligence roll. For each success achieved, he may roll an additional die when making Medicine rolls and any other rolls related to those tasks.

• **Scientific:** A Scientific Prodigy is to general science what an Engineering Prodigy is to working with technological devices. He has an intuitive understanding of scientific subjects in general, including the interrelationships of various scientific specialties and the best ways to perform experiments or analyze scientific data.

System: Whenever the character is involved with situations or problems concerning science or scientific subjects (but excluding subjects covered by Engineering Prodigy or Medical Prodigy, unless the Storyteller rules otherwise), the player may make an Intelligence roll. For each success achieved, he may roll an additional die when making Science rolls.

• **Tactical:** A nova with this enhancement is a genius when it comes to analyzing tactical and battlefield situations, evaluating resources and determining the best way to apply those resources to achieve victory in that situation. His ability to pull victory from the jaws of defeat, beat numerically superior enemies and concoct brilliant strategic and tactical plans is nothing less than phenomenal. And this ability often works just as well when applied to less dangerous, but no less violent, "battlefields" — such as the cutthroat corporate arena.

System: Whenever the character is involved with situations or problems concerning tactics, strategy or warfare (including such things as corporate economic warfare or political campaigns), the player may make an Intelligence roll. For each success achieved, he may roll an additional die when making rolls related to such subjects. The character also gains a permanent +3 to Initiative.

Speed Reading

A nova with this enhancement is able to process written and textual information far faster than the average reader. When he's studying something, sit back and watch the pages fly past.

System: The character is able to read text (whether in a book, on a computer screen or in any other medium) four times as fast as the average highly educated person without any loss of comprehension. Additionally, whenever he is using his Speed Reading ability, the player may make an Intelligence roll; each success adds one to the speed multiplier for his reading (one success means he is reading five times as fast, two successes mean six times as fast and so on).

This enhancement is permanent and costs no quantum points to use.

Taint Resistance

This nova is able to make amazingly efficient use of his brain cells, squeezing every last drop out of the old gray matter. As a result, the nova suffers less from mental aberrations brought on by expansion of the M-R node and tends to be more stable mentally.

System: When calculating permanent Taint from the Node Background, subtract the character's dots in Mega-Intelligence from the Node level. Thus, a nova with Node 3 and Mega-Intelligence 1 with Taint Resistance gets no Taint from the Node Background, and would get only one point of Taint if she increased her Node to 4.

Additionally, when the nova gains a mental aberration, subtract the nova's dots in Mega-Intelligence from the character's Taint to determine the severity of the aberration. This will not eliminate an aberration that is only mild, but will lessen the effect of higher Taint on mental aberrations, allowing the nova to function with less impairment as his brain reroutes around damaged areas.

This enhancement is permanent and costs no quantum points to use.

Mega-Wits

Mega-Wits is the flip side of Mega-Dexterity. Mega-Dexterity reflects how quickly some novas can move and react physically. Mega-Wits is how fast some novas can act and react *mentally*. As with Mega-Dexterity, each dot of Mega-Wits adds one to Initiative ratings.

Mega-Wits is one of the most disturbing Mega-Attributes for normal humans to deal with. Watching a nova pick up a truck or outrace bullets just seems sort of surreal after a while. But to see someone standing there calmly in the middle of a firefight or working a social situation like a grandmaster who can see 20 moves ahead is disconcerting. It's strange to see such level-headedness in the face of terrifying (to a normal human) danger or the application of superpowers in such "ordinary" situations.

•	Stupendous: Even when bullets are whizzing past your head, you remain calm and collected.
••	Amazing: Everyone around you hangs on your witty words.
•••	Incredible: Nothing surprises you — and even if something did, you'd never show it.
••••	Spectacular: Fooling you is about as easy as fitting an elephant through a doorway.
•••••	Godlike: Nothing on Earth can disturb your *savoir-faire*.

Mega-Wits Enhancements

Enhancements that characters with Mega-Wits may learn or purchase include:

Artistic Genius

A nova with this ability possesses an intuitive artistic sense and skill. He knows what "works" artistically, what doesn't, which colors complement each other and how to knock a chip off a sculpture here and there to turn a pedestrian piece into a masterwork. He may also be a skilled writer, able to express with a single sentence or paragraph what it takes others pages and pages to say. Novas who are Artistic Geniuses are often the darlings of the highbrow art scene.

System: Whenever the character is attempting to create or analyze art, literature, cinema or similar works or subjects, the player may make a Wits roll. For each success achieved, he receives one automatic success when making Arts rolls and related rolls.

This enhancement is always in effect, and it costs no quantum points to activate.

Enhanced Initiative

Reacting in combat isn't just a matter of physical reflexes — it's a matter of quick thinking and mental reaction time as well. Someone who is able to comprehend and analyze a combat situation quickly — such as a nova with this enhancement — has a definite advantage over combatants who react more slowly.

System: The player of a nova with Enhanced Initiative may add five points to his Initiative rating whenever he pays the standard one quantum point cost. This bonus lasts for only one turn; if the nova wants the bonus to continue, he must pay another quantum point next turn. A nova may purchase this enhancement more than once, thus gaining +10 Initiative, +15 Initiative and so on.

Additionally, if a nova with this enhancement delays his action and then acts at the same time as another character with a delayed action, the nova automatically goes first without having to roll. However, if the other character also has Enhanced Initiative or Mega-Dexterity, the two players must roll in the usual fashion to determine who acts first.

Lie Detector

No polygraph is needed when a nova with this enhancement is around. When she listens to a person talking and concentrates on what he is saying, she can instantly detect whether he is lying or not.

System: A nova with this Mega-Wits enhancement needs only concentrate on what someone is saying to determine (without a roll) if he is telling the truth or not. However, this ability does not reveal the truth *per se*, only that someone is telling a falsehood. Furthermore, it does not indicate that a character is lying if that character believes that what he is saying is the truth, even if it turns out to be wrong. If a "target" is particularly skilled at hiding the truth (for example, he has high Manipulation or Subterfuge Traits, or is a pathological liar), the Storyteller may require the nova to make a Wits roll to determine whether a lie is being told.

One quantum point activates this power for an entire scene.

Multitasking

Novas who wish for two heads and four hands so that they can get everything done appreciate this enhancement. It allows a nova to perform multiple actions with much more ease than the typical person. Indeed, some novas make taking multiple actions seem almost effortless.

System: The player of a nova with this enhancement may make a Wits roll at a difficulty penalty of one whenever he decides to perform multiple actions (see p. 110). If he succeeds, the multiple action penalty (the number of dice subtracted from his dice pool, in other words) is halved, rounding in favor of the character. Thus, a Multitasking nova who decides to perform three actions in a turn subtracts one die from the first task's dice pool, two dice from the second task's dice pool and two dice from the third task's dice pool (as opposed to the standard dice penalties).

This power costs one quantum point per turn of activation.

Natural Empath

Despite their inhumanity (or, as some would say, transcendence of humanity), some novas are very skilled at figuring out what people are feeling. They have an instinctive ability to gauge emotions and emotional states. More honorable novas use this power as a way to relate to (and offer comfort to) normal people; selfish novas use it as a tool to manipulate, harass or degrade humans.

System: Whenever his character is within 10 meters of a normal human, the player may make a Wits roll. If he succeeds, the nova has a general idea of the current emotional state of the person — happy, depressed, angry, lustful and so on. The more successes he achieves, the more accurate his assessment of the person's emotions. In the right circumstances, the nova might even be able to determine what is causing the person to feel that way, and what to do to change his emotional state (if necessary).

At distances greater than 10 meters, the nova can still try to determine what emotions a person is feeling, but it is harder. Out to 20 meters the difficulty increases by one; 30 meters, by two; 50 meters, by three. The power cannot work beyond 50 meters.

Regardless of the distance to the "target," the nova must be able to see him clearly. In some cases it may be necessary to observe him for several minutes in order to analyze his emotional state correctly.

Players of novas with Natural Empath gain three extra dice when making Rapport rolls. These dice come in addition to any bonuses received simply for having Mega-Wits.

This enhancement costs a quantum point to activate and lasts for an entire scene.

Quickness

Similar to both Enhanced Initiative and Multitasking, this enhancement allows a nova to take extra actions in combat. A nova with multiple levels of this ability becomes a whirlwind of carnage and destruction in combat, incapacitating his enemies before they can even react.

System: By spending a quantum point, the nova gains an extra physical action during the current combat turn. This action incurs no dice pool penalty — the nova may use his full dice pools with both of his actions. However, this action comes two places later than the character's Initiative rating for the turn.

A nova may purchase this enhancement multiple times, thus gaining the ability to act three, four or more times in a single combat turn with no dice pool penalties. However, each extra action costs an additional quantum point and incurs an additional -2 Initiative penalty. Actions taken must be physical actions; most quantum powers, even "physical" ones like Quantum Bolt, may not be activated multiple times, though super-strength punches or dodges may be. The effects of Quickness last only for the turn of activation.

Synergy

A nova with this enhancement works and plays well with others. He has an instinctive ability to figure out what other people he is working with are going to do and what he can do to assist them or complement their efforts. He becomes the oil that keeps the machine working at peak efficiency.

System: Whenever the nova performs a task with other players' characters in such a way that they combine successes to achieve a common goal, typically as an extended action (see p. 109), the nova's player may make a Wits roll. Everyone in the group receives an additional die for each success the nova's player achieves on his roll. This die applies to whatever rolls any given member of the group is making to advance the group's goal or complete their task. The die bonus applies to all rolls made for about an hour or until the job is finished, whichever comes sooner. The player may not make multiple Wits rolls to get multiple bonuses; only one Synergy bonus can apply to a given group during a given time period.

Social Mega-Attributes

Mega-Appearance

Mega-Attributes represent the extremes of nova nature (and thus, some would say, of human nature as well). Nowhere is this more apparent than Mega-Appearance. It shows, in the most obvious and up-front way possible, just how much better — and how much worse — novas can be than humans.

Typically, Mega-Appearance represents a nova who is extraordinarily handsome or beautiful. In this case the nova should have a standard Appearance score of 3 or higher, and 5 is not uncommon. Unlike the "Unearthly Beauty" aberration, the good looks deriving from Mega-Appearance generally are not especially unnerving to normal humans. They may inspire many emotions — love, lust, envy, worship, you name it — but they usually do not give rise to the feelings of unease, disquiet and even disgust that Unearthly Beauty does. Indeed, Mega-beautiful and -handsome novas are among the most popular of the "new humans," and they are frequently featured on television, in advertising campaigns and other media outlets.

Each dot of Mega-Appearance representing good looks grants an additional die on all Style rolls. The character's beauty or handsomeness is such that he is able to make even the worst clothes look good (not fashionable, maybe, but good). Similarly, the character usually makes a good first impression on looks alone.

In some rare instances Mega-Appearance can represent the opposite extreme, signifying a nova whose looks are Mega-ugly, even Mega-horrifying. In this case the nova's standard Appearance rating cannot be higher than 1 without special Storyteller permission (perhaps a half-beautiful, half terrifyingly ugly character could have a high Appearance and high "ugliness" Mega-Appearance, for example). Mega-ugly characters typically have high Taint ratings, and they often become as mentally twisted as their bodies are physically twisted — antisocial and cruel, and all too ready to destroy any beauty which confronts them. A Mega-ugly character is an exception to the rule that Mega-Attributes cannot transcend their normal human Attribute analogs; a character can have an Appearance of 1 and Mega-Appearance of any level so long as it is defined as Mega-ugliness.

Mega-ugly characters do not receive bonus Style dice. However, they receive a like amount of bonus dice to any Intimidation rolls.

- •   Stupendous: Miss or Mister America looks plain next to you. You receive one extra die for all Style rolls (in addition to your Mega-Attribute dice).
- • •   Amazing: A face that can launch at least a hundred ships, if not more. You receive two extra dice for all Style rolls.
- • • • Incredible: Okay, at least 500 ships. You receive three extra dice for all Style rolls.
- • • • • Spectacular: Helen of Troy, Adonis. You receive four extra dice for all Style rolls.
- • • • • • Godlike: Aphrodite, Freya. You receive five extra dice for all Style rolls.

Mega-Appearance Enhancements

Enhancements that characters with Mega-Appearance may purchase include:

Appearance Alteration

Don't like your looks? If you're a nova with this enhancement, you can do something about them.

Appearance Alteration allows a nova to make minor changes to his or her appearance. This can be done simply on a whim, or for fun. However, one of its main uses for novas who rely heavily on their good looks is to make sure they live up to a particular person's or culture's idea of what is "beautiful." Someone who is beautiful in, say, America may not meet the standards for beauty among certain Third World tribes; great beauty in China may be ugliness in Argentina. Even more importantly, individuals' ideas of what is beautiful differ wildly. One guy is a "leg man," another goes wild for women with red hair. Some women like men with "tight," muscular bodies, others look at the eyes or some other feature instead of the figure.

A nova with Appearance Alteration can satisfy all of these people. He can make minor changes or subtly remold his body to conform to the desires of those around him. "Minor changes" include: changing hair, eye or skin color; gaining or losing up to about 50 pounds; gaining or losing up to about four inches of height and increasing or decreasing any particular aspect of figure or appearance by no more than 20% or so.

System: The nova can make changes in his appearance within the aforementioned guidelines, either consciously or unconsciously. Any changes other than those listed require the Storyteller's permission. In no event can the character reshape his body to grow claws, wings or eyestalks, for example. Only outward physical appearance can change. Since this enhancement depends upon the perceptions and tastes of those observing the character, it cannot function as a disguise or to conceal the character's identity.

To change his appearance consciously, the nova need only pay the one quantum point and will the changes into effect. To change appearance to match what a particular person or group of people find desirable, the nova must pay the quantum point and be in that person or persons' presence for a minute or two. During that time the changes will slowly but surely take place. The nova can draw the changes out over a period of up to a day if he prefers, which is sometimes done to keep from frightening people who are not used to nova powers.

A nova cannot use Appearance Alteration to make himself resemble a specific other individual; that requires the Copycat enhancement. Nor can he use it to hide particularly grotesque aberrations unless the Storyteller specifically permits it. For example, some forms of Aberrant Eyes might be affected by Appearance Alteration; Vestigial Limbs could never be hidden this way.

The power lasts for one scene.

Awe-Inspiring

Many myths tell of gods and demons whose visages are too "awful" (awe-inspiring) for mortals to gaze upon directly. A nova with this enhancement has taken a page from that book, for his appearance, too, inspires awe.

A nova with the Awe-Inspiring enhancement has looks that, for whatever reason, give rise to awe, admiration and even worship. Normal humans often have trouble dealing with him in a straightforward manner. Weak-willed people feel more inclined to edge away nervously or be worshipful; even stronger-willed people feel intimidated, inadequate and cowed. It's not uncommon for an Awe-Inspiring nova to be surrounded by an entourage of fawning, adoring lackeys wherever he goes.

System: This effect works only when the people are in the nova's presence and looking at him; when they are away from him or not looking at him Awe-Inspiring cannot affect them. Of course, they may come to worship and revere him anyway, even if they are not near him, but that depends upon the individuals in question. Awe-Inspiring is not Domination; it's far weaker than that, and it shouldn't be played that way.

For each dot the player of a nova with Awe-Inspiring has in Mega-Appearance, he receives one automatic success when making Intimidation, Command and Interrogation rolls (in addition to the standard Mega-Attribute bonuses for Mega-Appearance). He should get similar bonuses to any roll related to persuading or inspiring people. This enhancement is one of many reasons why government officials are terrified of the idea of novas becoming heavily involved in politics or religion.

Awe-Inspiring is affected negatively by Taint. For each aberration the nova has, reduce the Awe-Inspiring automatic successes by one. If the nova's aberrations ever exceed his dots in Mega-Appearance, his Awe-Inspiring enhancement no longer has any effect on people. Similarly, a character with Awe-Inspiring generally should not be Mega-ugly; that does little to inspire worship in anyone.

This enhancement costs one quantum point to activate and lasts for a scene. Even when it isn't actively "on," the nova is still phenomenally captivating, and the Storyteller should keep this in mind (servers are deferential, groupies throw themselves at the nova, etc.).

Copycat

Being yourself gets kind of boring sometimes. Why not be a famous model or actor? Or the President?

Copycat will let a nova do just that, at least as far as outward appearance goes. After studying the subject to be imitated (either in person or from a good photograph), the nova can make himself look like that person — even a person of the opposite gender. However, these changes are purely cosmetic; no changes to internal organs occur.

System: Copycat allows a nova to shape himself into an exact duplicate of another person. Making the change does not require a roll. However, the nova must be in the presence of the person to be duplicated, or have a high-quality visual representation of him or her to work from. It takes about one minute to make the changes; the nova can cut this time in half by making an Appearance roll. Copycat costs one quantum point to activate, and the changes last for a scene.

Copycat does not allow the character to add to or remove anything from his physical form. He can't grow a tail, lose his Vestigial Limbs, create a sixth finger on his left hand, change his fingerprints or retina prints, or do anything similar.

Face of Terror

A nova with this enhancement can resemble something out of a horror movie. His appearance becomes so terrifying that few people can stand to spend any time with him. Instead, they run screaming in fear; if prevented from fleeing, they may gibber in terror, faint or suffer a heart attack.

System: Face of Terror allows a nova to assume a terrifying appearance. This ability is most common among novas who are Mega-ugly, but it is not restricted to them. Sometimes it is even more horrifying to see a form of great beauty slowly warp itself into something terrifyingly hideous.

To use this power, the nova simply spends a quantum point. If he is ordinarily ugly, the terrifying changes to his appearance may be slight, or even nonexistent — but something about his appearance becomes not just bad-looking, but very frightening. It's as if an aura of fear surrounds him. If the character is normally beautiful (or at least not ugly), the changes to his appearance will be much more extreme. They will take place over no more than a minute, and sometimes, it happens much more quickly than that.

In either case, the nova's appearance remains terrifying for a scene; this time limit can be extended by spending more quantum points. While this enhancement is in effect, the player receives three automatic successes when making Intimidation rolls or other rolls based on fear or disgust. This bonus includes any power or ability that allows the character to inspire those emotions in others.

To a certain extent, this power depends upon the psyche of the person(s) looking at the nova. Ugliness and horror, like beauty, are often in the eye of the beholder, so the nova's Face of Terror may look different when he confronts, say, a group of Asians instead of Americans.

First Impression

First impressions are just as important as everyone says. A character with a high Appearance rating is typically quite good at making them; one with Mega-Appearance even more so. However, a nova with this enhancement beats them both. Unless he deliberately tries to offend or annoy someone whom he is meeting, he always makes just the right impression. Depending upon what the person he meets is seeking, he may seem to be an enjoyable, likable person; someone who can get the job done; a potential mate; you name it. Whatever the other person is seeking, she will find it in the nova.

System: When meeting someone for the first time (or perhaps after a long time apart), the nova may spend one quantum point to activate this enhancement. If he does so, the other person automatically gains a good first impression of him. He may deliberately say or do something to negate this effect, but even an accidental *faux pas* or unthinkingly tactless remark will not be enough to shake the good impression he makes. That good impression will remain with the other person until the nova does something to ruin it (whether in the person's presence or not; bad reports about the nova in the media, for example, may ruin many uses of First Impression) or other people convince the target of First Impression that he has the nova all wrong. Of course, even a good first impression may not get the nova what he wants — making a good impression on the guards at the White House doesn't mean they'll let you in.

Furthermore, this effect also makes the nova seem like just what the other person is looking for. If the nova is on a job interview, First Impression will make him seem to be perfectly suited for the job. In a singles bar or nightclub, it will make him seem like the perfect date, potential spouse or one-night stand (depending upon what the other person is there for).

Mr. Nobody

In some ways, this paradoxical power is the opposite of Mega-Appearance, since it allows a nova to make himself look completely normal. The otherwise beautiful, handsome or ugly nova is able to convert his features into the unobtrusive ones of Joe or Jane Average. The bright side to this anonymity is that it becomes easy to pass for a normal human.

System: By spending a quantum point, the nova is able to mask his Mega-Appearance. For all intents and purposes he has an Appearance score of 2 — average. He looks just like the everyday man on the street. Although he cannot hide the fact that he radiates quantum energy (which other novas can often detect), to the average person he will seem like just another average person. Alternatively, the character can simply spend a quantum point to become completely unobtrusive ("I'm not the droid you're looking for.").

However, a character with this enhancement still may have difficulties passing for normal if he has acquired any aberrations. Mr. Nobody masks two point of Taint, plus one extra point per dot of the character's Mega-Appearance. Additional points of Taint still affect the nova's ability to interact with baselines without disturbing them. Furthermore, Mr. Nobody will not hide grotesque physical aberrations such as Vestigial Limbs or Sloughed Flesh; it will, however, cover up Unearthly Beauty.

The effects of this power last for a scene.

Seductive Looks

A nova with this enhancement has the ultimate in sex appeal. He looks just like the man (or woman) of the target's most lustful dreams. If the target is aroused by leggy women, for example, a female nova with this power would seem to the target to be a bit taller and leggier than she might really be — she'd be "just right" as far as the target is concerned.

System: By spending a quantum point, the nova makes himself seem extremely sexy and seductive to the target. (Note that the target need not be of the opposite gender as the nova.) The target perceives him as having

those attributes that the target finds most desirous or arousing, and the nova's appearance subtly changes to match that perception. The changes fade as soon as the target is no longer in the nova's presence; activating them again requires another quantum point.

While this enhancement is active, the nova receives three automatic successes on any roll to seduce or persuade the target. If there is any question, it is the Storyteller's discretion as to whether the bonus applies.

Players and Storytellers should remember that this enhancement is based entirely upon the nova's appearance. It does nothing to change his habits, attitude, or personality — as sexy as he looks, he may still turn the target off. However, Seductive Looks, and the bonuses it provides, can be used in conjunction with the Seductive enhancement for Mega-Charisma. Used together, the two enhancements make the nova both look *and* act like the target's ultimate sexual fantasy.

The effects of the power last for a scene.

Mega-Manipulation

A Mega-Manipulative nova has the world wrapped around his little finger. He is a master at influencing people in many different ways, from subtle methods (persuasion, personal charm, bribery) to more in-your-face tactics (intimidation, blackmail, devious trickery).

The fact that the nova is able to see through attempts to deceive or influence him is equally as important. Mega-Manipulative novas are so good at perceiving ways to affect others' opinions that they can tell when someone else is trying to do it to them. To simulate this effect, each level of Mega-Manipulation adds bonus dice (in addition to the standard bonus Mega-Attribute dice) to detect or resist being manipulated or tricked.

- Stupendous: Experienced con men regard your skills with reverence. You receive one extra die on any roll to detect or resist attempts to manipulate or trick you.

•• Amazing: Even lawyers can't twist facts and persuade others as well as you can. You receive two extra dice on any roll to detect or resist attempts to manipulate or trick you.

••• Incredible: People will follow you to the ends of the Earth if you ask them to. You receive three extra dice on any roll to detect or resist attempts to manipulate or trick you.

•••• Spectacular: Odysseus would admire your cunning. You receive four extra dice on any roll to detect or resist attempts to manipulate or trick you.

••••• Godlike: Loki and Anansi regard you as an equal. You receive five extra dice on any roll to detect or resist attempts to manipulate or trick you.

Mega-Manipulation Enhancements

Enhancements that characters with Mega-Manipulation may learn or purchase include:

Hypnotic Gaze

A nova with this enhancement possesses low-level hypnotic abilities. Although not as effective as the Hypnosis or Domination powers, it's still a useful ability when the character wants to persuade someone to do something.

System: The nova must be within three meters of the person to be hypnotized, and she must make eye contact with him. If they are separated or eye contact is blocked, the attempt to hypnotize the target automatically fails.

An attempt to hypnotize takes a little while — at least 10 seconds, and usually a minute or longer. The target must be willing to undertake (or at least not completely adverse to) what the nova is suggesting; Hypnotic Gaze cannot be used to make someone do something she is opposed to doing. However, the attempt to hypnotize the subject does not have to be obvious; it can, for example, be worked into normal conversation if the nova is clever. If necessary, the Storyteller can have the target make a Manipulation or Perception roll to figure out what the nova is trying to do.

Once the nova meets all these conditions, the player needs only spend a quantum point and make a Manipulation roll. If the roll succeeds, the target is hypnotized and will do as instructed. A posthypnotic suggestion can also be implanted to make the target do something (such as go to sleep or scream) when he experiences a certain outside stimulus. A posthypnotic suggestion lasts for one day per dot of Manipulation and Mega-Manipulation the nova has; thereafter it loses all effect.

Persuader

A nova with this enhancement is an expert at bringing people around to his point of view. He has an innate talent for knowing what people are thinking and subtly manipulating their opinions until they are thinking what he want them to think. He's a spin doctor supreme.

System: Whenever the nova wishes to persuade someone to change their opinion, perform a particular task, or the like, the player receives bonus successes. The exact number of successes depends upon what he is trying to persuade the target to do. If the request is something normal, relatively innocuous or harmless, the nova gets three automatic successes. Requests that involve changing strong opinions or expose the character to minor danger, embarrassment or trouble get two automatic successes. Requests which are dangerous or could get the target in extreme trouble get one automatic success (and the target normally has some kind of Willpower or other resisted roll).

The nova must spend a quantum point; the effects last for one request or series of related requests.

Trickster

Unlike P. T. Barnum, you can fool all of the people all of the time. Trickery, treachery, deceit and sneakiness are your stock in trade.

A nova with this enhancement possesses an intuitive talent for tricking and fooling people. She could trick Arabs into buying sand or Eskimos into buying refrigerators. Somehow she can sense a person's vulnerabilities and "soft" spots and use them against him. No one is safe from a Trickster's wiles.

System: Whenever the nova tries to trick, fool or deceive another character, the player receives three automatic successes on any roll necessary to the task. Usually, this roll involves Subterfuge, but other Abilities may be involved depending on the situation.

The nova spends a quantum point to activate the enhancement, and the effects last for the duration of the situation that the nova is seeking to turn to her advantage.

The Voice

Just talking to a nova with this enhancement can be dangerous. She is able to pitch her voice so that she uses infrasound and subharmonics, mixed in with her normal talk, to give nearly irresistible suggestions and commands to whomever her speech is directed at. Additionally, her voice is, in general, pleasant to listen to; her singing can be absolutely divine.

System: The nova exerts a subtle mental control effect through her voice. Only one person can be affected by this ability at a time. The subject must be within 20 meters of the nova, and must be able to hear the nova — deafness on the part of the subject, or other noises that drown out the nova's speech, prevent The Voice from being used successfully. The other major limitation on this ability is that any order given must be one that can be performed in one turn — "Drop the knife!" or "Untie me!", for example, but not "Play computer games until I tell you to stop" or "Torture your friend to death." Any orders or suggestions that would take longer than one turn to perform are automatically ignored by the target.

To use The Voice, the player makes a Manipulation roll. If he scores even one success, the attempt succeeds — but the target may stop himself from following the order or suggestion. The target makes a Wits roll to resist the command; each success he rolls counteracts one of the nova player's successes. If the net result is zero or less, the command fails. The target may also spend one or more points of Willpower to cancel successes at a 1:1 rate.

The player of a nova with The Voice may apply her Mega-Manipulation bonus dice to any Arts (Singing) or Perform (Singing) rolls she makes.

Mega-Charisma

Mega-Charisma represents the ultimate in personal charm and appeal. A nova with this Mega-Attribute exudes such self-confidence, poise and charm that she can win over just about anybody. Other people *want* to like and to please her, and they do.

Characters with Mega-Charisma are naturally at home in social situations. They carry themselves so well that they are the life of any party. They are *bon vivants par excellence;* even if they don't really feel like being at a party, they're able to mask their feelings and seem extremely amicable to one and all.

- •   Stupendous: Even your worst enemies find you likable.
- ••   Amazing: You could spill food and drink all over yourself and still seem elegant.
- •••   Incredible: Not even a tornado can ruffle your feathers; even in the most trying situations you are poised and charming.

- ••••   Spectacular: Bitter, lifelong enemies will make peace just to be able to spend time with you.
- •••••   Godlike: Even alien races find you fascinating and personable.

Mega-Charisma Enhancements

Enhancements that characters with Mega-Charisma may learn or purchase include:

Commanding Presence

A nova with this enhancement is a born leader. When he gives an order, people obey right away — even if it exposes them to harm. Even when they are away from him, people remember his words and try their best to fulfill his orders and live up to his example.

System: The nova's player receives three automatic successes on any roll that involves commanding people or giving orders. This bonus does not apply to attempts to persuade someone through reason or logic, appeal to people on a personal level, or the like; it works only when the character gives commands. The target of this enhancement may make whatever rolls he normally could to resist the order, or spend a Willpower point to refuse the order.

A nova with Commanding Presence does not necessarily have to be formally authorized to give orders to someone for this enhancement to work — he does not have to be the person's boss, commanding officer or parent. He can simply give orders and wait for them to be obeyed — that's what this power lets him do. However, if he is notably "beneath" the person — an ordinary citizen trying to order a high-ranking governmental official around, a corporal giving instructions to a major, or the like — the Storyteller may reduce the bonus for the power, at his discretion, or give the target a bonus on any rolls he makes to resist the order.

Dreadful Mien

When you really like someone, their anger or disappointment can come as a crushing blow. Some Mega-Charismatic novas use that phenomenon to their advantage. Their use their charm as a weapon — even in combat, enemies want to like them, and that, combined with the force of the nova's displeasure, makes it difficult for the enemy to attack.

System: The nova focuses his displeasure on one enemy, and the player makes a Charisma roll. Each success achieved subtracts one success from the victim's roll to hit the nova. If this cancellation results in no net successes for the attacker, he misses the nova, having flinched and pulled his attack aside rather than risk hurting such a likable fellow. A nova using this enhancement who takes any violent or threatening actions toward the target (as perceived by the target) while using it automatically negates its effects. The nova may attack the target's friends and compatriots; however, this allows the victim to make a Willpower roll to resist the successes scored by the nova. If the nova has previously attacked the victim during the scene, increase the difficulty for using Dreadful Mien by one per turn during which the nova attacked the victim.

Dreadful Mien does not work at range. If the target is more than three meters away from the nova, it is ineffective.

The enhancement costs one quantum point to activate, and the effects last for the duration of the confrontation.

Natural Agitator

When people like you, sometimes they will do things for you, or things that you ask them to do. That's doubly true for a nova with this power. Since everybody likes him so much, they hang on his every word. If he tells them to do something, they'll seriously consider it.

System: When he is speaking to a person, or even a crowd of people, the nova can use this enhancement to persuade them to do things. This enhancement's name derives from one of its obvious uses — sparking riots and agitation. The player makes a Charisma roll. If he succeeds, the person or crowd will do anything the nova says, so long as they would at least be inclined to perform the action in question. For example, people are inclined to buy food, so a nova could use Natural Agitator to convince them to buy all their food at a particular store or restaurant.

If the nova scores more than one success, he may be able to persuade the person or crowd to do things it wouldn't normally want to do — start a riot, for example. However, the targets get to make Willpower rolls to resist Natural Agitator; every success rolled cancels one of the nova's successes.

The effects of Natural Agitator usually linger for about an hour, or until someone else has the chance to talk some sense into the victim(s). More subtle, agreeable, effects may last longer; extreme effects may vanish almost as soon as the victims are out of the nova's presence.

For Natural Agitator to work, the nova must be physically present to talk to the victims. The enhancement does not work over radio, television or other broadcast media. The effects last for a single scene.

Seductive

This enhancement is the behavioral complement to *Seductive Looks*. A nova who possesses it is able to determine instinctively what behaviors a given individual finds sexy, desirable and attractive — then unconsciously adopt those behaviors.

System: The nova must be close to (i.e., within 10 meters of) his target, and the player must make a Charisma roll. If he succeeds, he has determined what sort of behavior the target finds sexy — coquettishness, self-confidence, sluttiness or vivacity. He automatically adopts that behavior as his own, thus making himself even more attractive than normal to the target.

While this enhancement is active, the player receives three automatic successes on any roll to seduce or persuade the target. If there is any question, it is the Storyteller's discretion as to whether the bonus applies.

Of course, this enhancement is based entirely upon behavior or body language; it does not alter looks at all. Altering looks in that fashion requires *Seductive Looks*. The two enhancements may be combined to create an almost irresistibly attractive package for any victim.

Soothe

The nova is a natural at soothing others' jangled nerves. Just being around him has a calming effect. He even makes it easier for normal humans to cope with novas.

System: When the player spends a quantum point and makes a Charisma roll, the character and everyone within 10 meters of him becomes calm. Stress drains away, leaving people happier and calmer. No one affected by Soothe (including the nova using it) can attack or take any other hostile action unless the person either makes a Wits roll and scores more successes than the nova achieved on his Soothe roll, or spends a point of Willpower to overcome Soothe's effects.

Additionally, Soothe can help to overcome the effects of Taint. For each success achieved on the Charisma roll, one point of Taint possessed by any novas within the radius of effect is temporarily negated as regards interaction with baselines within the affected area.

The power lasts for a scene. All effects of this enhancement disappear if an affected person wanders beyond the 10-meter radius.

CHAPTER FIVE: QUANTUM POWERS

More than any other Trait (except perhaps Taint), that which defines novas is their quantum powers — their superhuman abilities. Even more than Mega-Attributes, powers separate the superhumans from the humans in a way that's clear for all to see.

All novas have certain powers in common, most of which relate to their ability to resist and heal injuries and diseases. For further information on common nova powers, see p. 160. The powers discussed in this section are those which novas have to buy with nova points (during character creation) or experience points (after the game has begun).

The Nature of Quantum Powers

At their heart, all nova powers are exactly the same thing: manipulation of quantum energies. When you get right down to it, that's all a nova can do — control and work with quantum energies. There isn't a nova in the world who can actually, for example, ignite fire out of nothingness or fry a foe's synapses. The Mazarin-Rashoud node does not give any human the ability to manipulate the weather or disintegrate objects with a touch — what it does is allow a human to employ quantum energies in such a way as to do those things or mimic those effects.

However, just about everyone in 2008 has seen a nova (or footage of a nova) throwing blasts of fire, creating ice storms or manipulating magnetic fields. Their powers clearly seem to differ.

The solution to this paradox lies in the fact that humans — even those who have become novas — understand quantum energies imperfectly, at best. Although most novas are aware that quantum energies are at the root of their powers, they cannot always literally perceive those energies in their raw form. Their minds, for whatever reason, simply don't grasp their powers that way.

Instead, they often think of their powers in terms of phenomena they are used to: fire, ice, wind, superstrong muscles, magnetism or a thousand other forms of energy or matter that are familiar and comfortable. Thus, a given nova's powers may not actually *be* fire or lightning, but they *look and act* just like fire or lightning. For all intents and purposes they are the real thing, not "quantum energy." A power based on fire has all the chemical and physical properties of fire — it gives off heat, can set other objects on fire and consumes oxygen.

However, many novas' quantum powers are obviously not derived from "natural" forces. For example, a nova might Immolate herself with raw nuclear forces rather than fire, and even if she seems to wield "flame," it might burn eerie green, feel cold to the touch or in some other way betray its distinction from "real" fire.

Choosing Your Power's Effects

The upshot of this seeming variety in game terms, is that nova characters should choose some phenomenon or "special effect" for their powers. When you buy powers, customize them — or at least their names — to represent the type of phenomena they resemble. For example, if a nova has powers based on manipulating fire, when his player buys Quantum Bolt he can write "Fire Strike" on the character sheet to give the power a little bit of individuality. Each nova's powers are different, even though they are built using the same game effects and rules, and your character's powers should reflect his unique nature.

Adding an Extra (p. 230) can really help make a power distinctive. Many novas have Quantum Bolts, for example. But if a fire-manipulating nova wants to be able to toss fireballs around, he can create a "Fireball effect" by buying a Quantum Bolt and adding the Explosion Extra to it.

In some cases, a nova's manifestation of quantum energies might provide useful plot hooks for stories. For example, an Immolate power based on control of fire could be extinguished by dumping the nova in water or covering him up with sand. A nova whose Immolate is based on nuclear forces would probably be completely unaffected by such treatment. A nova with magnetic powers might not be able to work with computers or other magnetic storage media. In short, quantum powers always have an effect on the world around the nova, and *vice versa,* and the player and Storyteller should always keep that in mind.

A Nova's Origin

The primary factor that influences how a nova's powers manifest is the circumstances under which they first arise. Since the growth of a Mazarin-Rashoud node is commonly triggered by a traumatic or stressful situation (and the increased adrenaline levels that such situations cause), many novas' powers first appear in the midst of some crisis — a house fire, a car wreck, a riot or any of countless other emergencies. This trigger event often influences how their powers work and what they look like. For example, a fire-wielding nova might result from a house fire. A cryokinetic nova can result from exposure to the elements or avalanches. The possibilities are virtually endless.

Of course, this guideline is just that; not a rule. A nova whose powers first manifest while he's trapped in a house fire might end up with control over gravity fields — it's a function of the way his mind works as much as it is the traumatic situation. But the trauma often plays an important role, and it should not be ignored when creating a new character.

Creating and Altering Powers

We've tried to create a list of general quantum powers representative of what the novas of 2008 have been known to do. However, each nova is an individual, and no rigid guidelines can accurately capture every aspect of every nova's powers. These power descriptions are guidelines rather than absolutes. As such, feel free to twist them around to suit your concept and chronicle needs.

In general, when altering powers, try to balance one parameter against another. For example, maybe you want a Quantum Bolt that has an incredible range, but loses energy as it travels; if so, buy a normal Quantum Bolt, increase its maximum range, but dictate that the blast loses damage effect as it travels outward. If your character has a stronger or weaker version of a listed power — for example, claws that extend 30 feet and can slice diamond, or only the EMP technique of the Magnetic Mastery power — increase or decrease the power's level accordingly. And, of course, Storyteller permitting, you're free to create your own powers; simply compare your creation to the listed powers, decide if it's Level 1, 2 or 3, and run with it.

Power: General Rules

With a very few exceptions, all powers are rated from 1 to 5; this *power rating* adds to an appropriate Attribute when calculating the skill total of the power. Like any other Trait combination, the skill total is used to wield the power; thus, a nova with a Dexterity of 4 and a Quantum Bolt of 3 rolls seven dice to hit targets with her Quantum Bolt. The nova-point cost per dot in the power depends upon its level; so does the quantum-point cost per use of the power.

Powers activate automatically and instantaneously on the character's Initiative rating; for example, a character with a Quantum Bolt does not have to concentrate to fire. However, each activation of a power counts as an action for purposes of determining multiple actions. For the most part, powers are governed by the same rules that apply to other attacks. Hand-to-hand powers, such as Claws, can be blocked; ranged powers can be dodged. Mental powers (those noted as such in their description) may not be dodged or blocked, but they may typically be resisted; see the individual power description for specifics.

At the Storyteller's option, a character with a ranged power (such as Quantum Bolt) can use that power to block another character's use of that power — in effect, the defending nova is using his own power to shoot the other power out of the air. This "power block" is done using the normal rules for block, except that it works at range and the player uses the nova's dots in the power to determine success, rather than his Martial Arts or Brawl Ability.

Extra successes on an attack roll add to the damage dice pool of powers that inflict direct damage, such as Quantum Bolt or Disintegration, unless the text of the power indicates otherwise.

All novas are immune to all effects of their own powers; thus, a nova could shroud herself in her own Darkness, or stand at ground zero of her Explosive Bolt, with no ill effects. This immunity grants no immunity to similar or even identical effects generated by other novas, though.

Power Descriptions

Each power's description contains the basic information about that power, including:

Level: There are three "levels," or classifications of powers, in **Aberrant**. Most powers are Level 2. Minor abilities, ones that can be duplicated with technology or other means, are Level 1 powers. Level 3 powers are extremely powerful and flexible abilities, usually grouped around a particular theme or effect.

In game terms, a power's level indicates its cost in both nova points and experience points. Powers, like Abilities, are rated in terms of the number of dots the character has in the power. Each dot either provides a certain level of effect (such as three dice of damage per dot) or simply gives the player more dice to roll when wielding the power. A Level 1 power costs one nova point per dot. A Level 2 power costs three nova points per dot. A Level 3 power costs five nova points per dot. Powers can also be bought tainted for lower cost; see p. 120.

Unless the power description states otherwise, use of a power forces the character to spend a number of quantum points based on its level. A Level 1 power costs one quantum point to activate. A Level 2 power costs two quantum points, and a Level 3 power costs three quantum points. In the case of powers with multiple applications, such as Elemental Mastery, the quantum cost is levied for each technique activated. Of course, there's no requirement that a character use a power at full strength; he can save one quantum point by using it at half power.

If a power is bought with an Extra (p. 230), it is treated as one level higher. So, the Claws power (Level 1) bought with the Range Extra is purchased as a Level 2 power, and a Quantum Bolt bought with the Explosion Extra is purchased as a Level 3 power. A player cannot purchase an Extra for a Level 3 power.

Certain powers, such as Body Modification, are *miscellaneous* quantum powers. Rather than having a number of dots and a level, these powers simply have a fixed cost. Once this cost is paid, the nova has the listed power.

Quantum Minimum: This number sets the minimum Quantum Trait rating a nova must have in order to purchase this power. Many of the more powerful abilities aren't going to be available to beginning novas; they have to "grow into them" by earning experience points and increasing their Quantum Trait (which, while useful, also creates some problems).

Dice Pool: The dice rolled to determine whether the power is used successfully, as well as its effect. The nature of the roll, or sometimes multiple rolls, is detailed in the text. This dice pool typically combines the power rating plus an Attribute; if the nova has the appropriate Mega-Attribute, Mega-Attribute dice or difficulty reductions apply normally.

Some Level 3 powers have several different techniques, each with its own dice pool.

Range: The power's medium range in meters, if applicable.

"Touch" indicates the character must touch the target in order to affect it. The nova must make a roll (using the power's dice pool) to touch the victim. The victim can dodge, of course, but blocking the attack is ineffective since a block still allows the touch to occur.

For powers that work at a distance, the listed range is the power's normal effective range. The power's maximum range is twice the listed range. Attacks made at distances greater than the effective range are at +2 difficulty. Attacks at point-blank range (two meters or less) add two dice to the attacker's skill total.

Area: The area affected by the power, typically in a radius in meters, if applicable.

Using a power on an area has two effects. First, it presents the possibility of affecting multiple targets at the same time. Second, it gives the attack a +2 accuracy; however, extra successes on the attack roll do not increase the damage inflicted by the attack. The base difficulty for hitting an area is typically Standard, unless the attack is made at long range.

A character caught in an area of effect cannot block the effect, nor can he dodge it unless he is on the fringe of the area or has enough movement to get out of the area entirely.

Duration: The power's duration, if applicable.

"Instant" indicates that the power lasts only long enough for an attack to be launched — for example, the brief moment in which the flash of a Quantum Bolt is visible and blasts the target. The effects, of course, may last much longer; an injury does not go away just because the Quantum Bolt that caused it is no longer in existence.

An Instant power must be paid for each time it is used. Thus, each time a Quantum Bolt is fired, the nova using it must spend quantum points.

"Concentration" means the power lasts as long as the nova concentrates on it. While concentrating, the nova is at +2 difficulty on any other actions he takes. If the nova is Incapacitated or otherwise rendered unconscious, a Concentration power ceases immediately.

A Concentration power must be paid for when first activated; thereafter, it remains in effect without additional quantum-point cost for as long as the nova concentrates.

"Maintenance" indicates that the power, once activate remains in effect automatically for a period of time. Thereafter, the nova can automatically pay an additional number of quantum points to maintain the power. It does not require him to concentrate on maintaining it, however. Thus, once a Maintenance power is active, the nova does not lose any dice for any other actions taken while maintaining the power.

Unless specifically stated otherwise in the power description, assume a power used in combat or other stressful situations lasts for (Quantum + power rating) turns before needing to be maintained by spending additional quantum points; when used under more relaxed conditions, a power lasts for a scene. If a nova activates a power such as Flight during a routine mission, but subsequently enters combat or is otherwise involved in a dangerous situation, she must begin maintaining the power normally after (Quantum + power rating) turns have passed. If a Maintenance power has a variable effect (e.g., a Force Field, which can provide a varying degree of protection depending on the dice pool roll to activate it), the nova can choose to keep the same level of effect or can reroll the power upon spending additional quantum.

"Permanent" indicates that the power, once bought, is considered to be on or present at all times and does not cost quantum points to use or maintain.

Effect: An encapsulated description of what the power does.

In cases of powers that inflict damage, a distinction is made between damage adds (or automatic levels of damage) and damage dice, which a player rolls normally to determine damage. Damage adds are listed in [brackets], while damage dice are listed in (parentheses). When such an attack is soaked, damage adds are subtracted before damage dice.

Thus, a character with Quantum 3 buys the Quantum Bolt power at 2 and designates it as a bashing attack. A bashing Quantum Bolt inflicts [Quantum x 3] levels + (power rating x 4) dice of damage. The character's blast inflicts [3 x 3, or 9] automatic levels of bashing damage; plus the character may roll (2 x 4, or 8) dice to inflict extra damage.

Multiple Actions: Whether it is possible to use the power in a multiple action. "Yes" indicates that it is possible; "No" indicates that the power cannot be used as part of a multiple action.

Some powers (Cyberkinesis, Elemental Mastery, etc.) have many applications. If such a power is able to be used in a multiple action, the nova may use several aspects of the power simultaneously, so long as she pays the quantum-point cost for all uses. She must still subtract dice normally for multiple uses of the power in the same turn.

Description: A description of what the power does and the rules applicable to it.

Several powers (like Boost or Sizemorph [Grow]) are described as providing bonuses to Attributes. Sufficiently potent uses of these powers can raise Attributes above 5, thus effectively boosting the character into the Mega-Attribute range. If this situation occurs, the character gains the standard benefits of having that Mega-Attribute (as listed in its description and table), but he does not get to choose any enhancements. No Mega-Attribute can be raised above 5. However, Mega-Attributes gained through such temporary measures may be raised higher than the Quantum Trait limit (i.e., a character with Quantum 3 and the Boost power could raise his Mega-Strength as high as 5, even though his Quantum is only 3).

Extras: This heading comprises any unique Extras (see p. 230) available for purchase for the power, as well as its effects. Unique Extras should be bought like any other Extras, and they increase the power's level accordingly.

Mental Powers and Psi

In creating antagonists for your **Trinity** series or extending your **Aberrant** series into the **Trinity** timeline (as is not inconceivable for some of the longer lived **Aberrant** characters), it is important to keep the differences between a nova's and a psion's powers in mind. True, novas have manifested certain powers that mimic those of their psion counterparts through their control of quantum energies. However, even though a nova and a psion may both display telepathic abilities (for example), the two powers are not the same. Novas can control only quantum energies, while psions develop a mastery over *sub*quantum forces. A nova may never gain a Psi rating, just as a psion may never gain a Quantum score.

Nova "mental powers" are very individualistic, specific to the nova manifesting the powers; while an individual nova may improve her control through practice, the mental powers themselves are not codified and divided into "Aptitudes," as are those of the more disciplined psions. One nova's telepathic powers may manifest as a "brain-scan" in which the nova physically reads the patterns of the target's electrochemical impulses, while another's might manifest as a facsimile of the target's "soul" rising out of her body and imparting secrets. Though a nova's raw power might exceed that of a psion, the nova mentalist does not have a body of study and training to draw upon, as does the psion; nor can one nova mentalist necessarily tutor or "coach" another, even if the two mentalists have the same in-game power.

As mentioned, novas have no control over subquantum energies *per se*. Studies undertaken by Utopia, the Triton Foundation and other groups suggest that nova "mentalists" use quantum energies to alter brainwaves and brain patterns physically, while others simply hyperevolve their brains into brainwave-manipulating machines, in the same way that super-strong novas spontaneously develop muscles and mitochondria to levels exponentially outperforming their baseline counterparts.

Quantum Powers

Master Powers List

Level One Quantum Powers

Power	Quantum Minimum
Bioluminescence	1
Claws	1
Hypnosis	1
Intuition	1
Luck	1
Psychic Shield	1
Quantum Conversion	1
Sensory Shield	1

Level Two Quantum Powers

Power	Quantum Minimum
Absorption	1
Animal/Plant Mastery	1
Armor	1
Bodymorph	3
Boost	2
Density Control	3
Disorient	1
Disrupt	3
Domination	3
Empathic Manipulation	2
ESP	3
Flight	1
Force Field	2
Growth	1
Holo	1
Hypermovement	1
Immobilize	1
Immolate	2
Invisibility	1
Invulnerability	1
Mental Blast	3
Mirage	3
Poison	1
Premonition	1
Quantum Bolt	1
Quantum Leech	2
Quantum Regeneration	3
Quantum Vampire	3
Shroud	1
Sizemorph (Grow)	1
Sizemorph (Shrink)	1
Strobe	1
Stun Attack	1
Telekinesis	2
Telepathy	3
Teleport	2

Level Three Quantum Powers

Power	Quantum Minimum
Clone	5
Cyberkinesis	4
Disintegration	5
Elemental Anima	4
Elemental Mastery	5
Entropy Control	4
Gravity Control	4
Healing	4
Homunculus	4
Magnetic Mastery	4
Matter Chameleon	5
Matter Creation	5
Molecular Manipulation	5
Pretercognition	4
Quantum Construct	4
Quantum Imprint	4
Shapeshift	4
Temporal Manipulation	5
Warp	3
Weather Manipulation	4

Miscellaneous Quantum Powers

Power	Quantum Minimum
Body Modification	1

Absorption

Level: 2
Quantum Minimum: 1
Dice Pool: Stamina + Absorption
Range: Self
Area: N/A
Duration: Special
Effect: The nova converts damage or energy into Strength at the rate of one dot per success, to the limit of the damage done.

Multiple Actions: No

Description: This power allows the nova to absorb damage caused by attacks and convert it into Strength. The power works against either energy damage (like Quantum Bolts or fire) or kinetic damage (punches, knives or bullets); the character must define which phenomenon his Absorption works against when he buys it.

When the nova is hit with an attack of the type he can absorb, he may choose to absorb some or all of the effect. Doing so takes no time, may be applied before or after the character's normal soak, and the character may do it even if he has already acted for the turn; the character need not declare he will use Absorption until after an attack has hit and done damage to him. Each success rolled on a Stamina + Absorption roll subtracts one health level of damage from the attack; the character must pay one quantum point per health level absorbed. Every two health levels of damage are converted into one extra dot of Strength; above five dots of Strength they become dots of Mega-Strength. Dots in the power indicate the maximum dots of extra Strength (or Mega-Strength) the character can gain; the character may still use Absorption to reduce damage from attacks, though.

For Example: Jason Mercator has Absorption 4 that affects energy. He is hit with a Quantum Bolt that causes four health levels of damage to him. He decides to absorb the damage instead. He rolls Stamina + Absorption, scores six successes and spends four quantum points. He absorbs all four health levels of damage and suffers no injury. Furthermore, he now has two extra dots of Strength. He may gain two more dots of Strength before he maxes out.

*However, extra dots of Strength gained from Absorption don't last forever. They fade away at the rate of one point per (Quantum + power rating) turns. At the Storyteller's option, Absorbed dots may increase some-*thing other than Strength, such as Stamina or a Quantum Bolt (but never quantum points).

Characters cannot absorb more power than is available; the Storyteller should, if necessary, allow a certain number of dots of Strength to a power source to determine just how much power it can add to a character. For example, no matter how much Absorption a nova has, he should not be allowed to gain more than a single point of Strength from the power in, for example, a typical household appliance.

Extras: Extended Effect (dots of Strength gained from Absorption last for a scene); Energy Magnet (character with energy Absorption can absorb energy from sources at [Quantum x 10 meters] range as an attack; if absorbed from a nonsentient source [such as a fire or electrical socket], no roll other than the one to determine how much power is absorbed is required; if used on a sentient source, such as another nova, the player must roll Manipulation + Absorption to succeed with his attempt, then roll the normal Stamina + Absorption dice to determine how much energy is absorbed).

Animal/Plant Mastery

Level: 2
Quantum Minimum: 1
Dice Pool: Perception + Animal/Plant Mastery
Range: Variable
Area: Special
Duration: Special
Effect: Nova can communicate with and summon animals or plants.

Multiple Actions: No

Description: A nova with this power has the ability to communicate with animals or plants (she must choose only one when the player buys the power). This communication is telepathic, but if the creatures have the ability to make noises or communicate in other mundane fashions, she can understand those as well (though she may not be able to reply, and in any event such, "languages" are likely to be crude indeed).

Furthermore, the character can emit a telepathic call to summon a particular creature (or any creatures within range) to her side. This call has a range equal to two kilometers per dot in Animal/ Plant Mastery. Any creatures subject to the call will come to the character at their best speed; plants, of course, cannot move and will not be able to respond. Once in the character's presence, they will treat her in a friendly fashion and do their best to respond to her requests, though they are not obligated to take her orders.

Plants cannot physically uproot themselves; however, characters can attempt to animate foliage in the immediate vicinity. For example, trees might club at foes with their branches, while vines might wrap themselves around the character's enemies. The system for this power is treated as the Animation technique under the Molecular Manipulation power (p. 212), except that the character substitutes her Plant Mastery rating for the Molecular Manipulation rating.

Animals (or plants, depending on the power) will regard a character with Animal (or Plant) Mastery as their friend and boon companion until the character does something to prove otherwise. They will not harm her, and they will seek to prevent others from harming her as well. This power does not enable them to overcome their basic natures; the Storyteller should feel free to assign specific personalities to creatures based upon their natures. For example, lions and tigers might seem regal; poison ivy sarcastic and snide; antelopes nervous and edgy. However, whatever their natures, they will still try to help the character.

Extras: Nature Mastery (character can exercise both Animal Mastery and Plant Mastery).

Armor

Level: 2
Quantum Minimum: 1
Dice Pool: N/A
Range: Self
Area: N/A
Duration: Permanent
Effect: Character receives +3 soak against bashing and lethal damage per dot in Armor.
Multiple Actions: No
Description: This power represents a nova who is more resistant to damage than most. He may have thick, chitinous skin, a glowing force field of some kind (not to be confused with the power of the same name) or metal plates that cover his body. Usually the form of the protection is based on the nature of the character's powers. A character who can manipulate ice and cold might be covered with a suit of "ice armor," for example, while a shapeshifter might warp his skeleton into stegosaurlike plates. However, special effects are not required; it's possible for the character simply to be more durable than normal and still look the same as always. In any event, the power is permanent, costs no quantum points to maintain and can be turned on and off at will.

For each dot of Armor, the character may add three to soak bashing and lethal damage. At the Storyteller's option, the player may vary the ratio of the soak, assigning more to bashing and less to lethal or vice versa.

Extras: Superheavy Armor (nova can spend three quantum points to fortify his Armor for a scene; while so fortified, the nova's Armor provides four extra soak against bashing/lethal attacks, and the difficulty to hit him increases by one per dot of Armor; however, he loses three from Initiative [minimum 1], two from walking speed and five from running/sprinting speed, and loses one die from all Dexterity-based dice pools [minimum 1])

Bioluminescence

Level: 1
Quantum Minimum: 1
Dice Pool: Stamina + Bioluminescence
Range: Variable
Area: Special
Duration: 10 minutes per success
Effect: Character emits light.
Multiple Actions: No
Description: A nova with Bioluminescence can emit visible light. This light is not strong enough to blind other characters, but it definitely helps light the way through the dark places. To use it, the character spends one quantum point and rolls Stamina + Bioluminescence, allowing him to emit a soft glow for about 10 minutes per success. This light is bright enough to read by easily; it may make the character look either eerie or angelic (depending upon the character and his special effects).

For an additional quantum point, the character can project a beam of light like a flashlight. This beam has a range of 15 meters per success, and it lasts as long as his glow.

Extras: Increased Spectrum (normal Bioluminescence is only visible light; with this extra it emits infrared and ultraviolet light as well)

Body Modification

Level: N/A
Quantum Minimum: 1
Dice Pool: N/A
Range: Self
Area: N/A
Duration: Permanent
Effect: Modifies character's body in various ways.
Multiple Actions: N/A

Description: This power simulates a modification to the nova's body. This modification is permanent; it costs no quantum points to maintain or use, any more than the character's arms or legs do.

Listed here are some suggested modifications, along with the nova- or experience-point costs to buy them. Players may create others if they wish, but the Storyteller must approve all new modifications. See also the Claws power.

• **Adhesive Grip:** (two nova points/four experience points): The nova can physically or ionically bond with surfaces. This allows her to walk up walls or along ceilings at normal walking speed, and to cling to those surfaces with her normal Might rating.

• **Chromatophores:** (one nova point/ three experience points) The character's skin can change color, like a chameleon's or squid's. The player adds three dice to his Stealth skill totals, as long as the character is mostly naked or wearing attuned eufiber.

• **Extra Limbs:** (one nova point/ three experience points) The character has one or more extra limbs; he may define what they are and to what part of his body they are attached. These limbs are considered to be as useful as arms/ hands. The character subtracts one from multiple action penalties (so a character taking three multiple actions would act at -2, -3 and -4 penalties instead of the usual -3, -4 and -5). This bonus is applied before any reductions from the Multitasking enhancement (p. 169).

• **Extra Health Levels:** (one nova point/ three experience points) The character has extra health levels, perhaps because he has "duplicates" of some or all of his important organs. One nova point buys an extra "Bruised" health level or two extra "Maimed" health levels.

• **Gills:** (one nova point/ three experience points) The character has gills that allow him to breathe underwater.

• **Spines:** (two nova points/ six experience points) The character can extrude spikes from his body, or perhaps his body is naturally edged (for example, a nova made of living crystal). The spines change the nova's clinches, holds and tackles to lethal damage and inflict an amount of lethal damage equal to the attacker's damage dice pool (maximum 10 dice) on anyone contacting the nova with a Brawl or Martial Arts attack.

• **Tendril:** (one nova point/ three experience points) The character can extrude a tentacle, whip, flagellum or other similar "limb." This limb can be physical or made of energy; it can be used to grab, lash or constrict a target, or for the character to swing on. The tendril extends two meters per nova point/ three experience points spent. The tendril can inflict Strength +4 bashing damage (or Strength +2 lethal damage; player's choice); if the tendril is made of energy or some other unusual substance, it may, with the Storyteller's permission, do damage based on some other Attribute.

• **Webbed Hands/Feet:** (one nova point/ three experience points) The character's hands and/ or feet are webbed, allowing the character to swim at double running speed.

• **Wings/Patagia:** (three nova points/ six experience points) The nova grows a pair of leathery bat wings or feathered bird wings, or he simply stretches a flap of his own skin along his sides beneath his arms. This modification allows a character to control his falls safely or glide at his normal running pace. (This modification does not confer the same amount of control or speed as the Flight power.)

Extras: None.

Bodymorph

Level: 2
Quantum Minimum: 3
Dice Pool: Stamina + Bodymorph
Range: Self
Area: N/A
Duration: Maintenance
Effect: Allows character to take on aspects of one specific type of matter or energy.
Multiple Actions: Yes

Description: Bodymorph is a powerful ability possessed by only a few novas. It allows the nova to transform her body into a specific type of matter or energy. For example, she could transform her body to rock, to fire, to wind or to computer chips and circuitry. The player must choose what form that the character can assume when he buys the power. The Bodymorph power provides certain base abilities, depending on the form chosen; thereafter, Bodymorph dots essentially simulate enhancements or dots of other Level One and Two powers; when transforming, all Bodymorph powers activate simultaneously when the character pays the quantum cost to transform.

The character may transform herself automatically. However, the character's dots in Bodymorph define how effective the change is. It is up to the player to define where his character's Bodymorph dots are allocated, subject to Storyteller approval, but once they are defined, they cannot be changed. For example, when creating a character with a rock body, a player might buy Bodymorph 4 and assign one dot to Armor and three to Density Control (Increase). He cannot change that allocation later. Of course, if he buys another level of Bodymorph with experience points he can decide where that dot is allocated at that time.

If a nova wishes to use Bodymorph as a defense against an incoming attack (for example, to turn to flame to avoid being damaged by a flame blast), he may do so. This form of defense does not require an action, but it is easier if an action is available. If the character does not have a delayed action to use to do this, he must spend a point of Willpower instead. He then rolls Stamina + Bodymorph; even one success allows him to assume his alternative form in time to absorb some of the force of the attack, and each success reduces the damage the attack inflicts by one level.

Here are some guidelines for the general properties of most forms:

• **Stone/metal/hard solid:** The character automatically inflicts two extra dice of damage with Brawl and Martial Arts attacks, and all attacks directed at the character incur a difficulty penalty of one to hit him. Bodymorph dots often translate into levels of Density Control (Increase), Armor or Claws.

• **Liquid/amorphous:** The character automatically gains the ability to breathe and exist in water, may move through water at twice normal running speed, gains the Flexibility enhancement (p. 159), and may use the Asphyxiation combat maneuver (p. 246). Among other things, Bodymorph dots can translate into equivalent dots of Density Control (Decrease), Poison or Immolate (for characters who turn into acid). At least one Bodymorph dot *must* be assigned to Density Control (Decrease).

• **Gas:** While transformed, the character may automatically move through air at the character's normal running speed, gains +1 soak vs. physical damage (fists, bullets, etc.), gains the Flexibility enhancement (p. 159), and may use the Asphyxiation combat maneuver (p. 246). Among other things, Bodymorph dots can translate into equivalent dots of Density Control (Decrease), Poison, Flight or Storm (allows the character to become a whirling tornado, thus inflicting the equivalent of the Storm technique [p. 196] in her immediate vicinity). At least one Bodymorph dot *must* be assigned to Density Control (Decrease).

• **Energy:** While transformed, the character inflicts lethal damage with Brawl and Martial Arts attacks, and attacks directed at her incur a difficulty penalty of one to strike her. Bodymorph dots might be assigned to Immolate, Invulnerability (to the appropriate energy type), the EMP technique of Magnetic Mastery (p. 206), the Electromagnetic Vision enhancement (p. 162), Force Field, or Density Control (Decrease) dots.

These are general guidelines only; players can allow Bodymorph dots to represent a number of powers (or even invent their own) subject to the Storyteller's approval. Many of the techniques listed under Elemental Anima and Elemental Mastery are suitable as Bodymorph powers. However, all Bodymorph powers are available only while the character is transformed. Ultimately, the Storyteller must arbitrate the use of this power.

For Example: Houston Tornado 2 buys four dots of the Bodymorph (Air) power, defining this as the ability to turn into wind. She automatically may move through the air at running speed and use the Asphyxiation com-

bat maneuver (forcing air out of her foe's lungs); furthermore, she gains +1 soak versus physical attacks and may use the Flexibility enhancement. Now HT2 assigns her four dots to Density Decrease, Density Decrease, Density Decrease and Storm. Whenever HT2 is in wind form, she can make herself much harder to hurt (can activate up to three levels of Density Decrease) and can spin herself into a localized whirlwind (can activate the Storm technique as though she had one dot in Elemental Mastery). However, these powers work only while transformed, and the character must pay the Bodymorph quantum cost to activate them.

Extras: None

Claws

Level: 1
Quantum Minimum: 1
Dice Pool: N/A
Range: Self
Area: N/A
Duration: Maintenance
Effect: Converts character's close combat damage into lethal damage.
Multiple Actions: Yes
Description: This power allows the nova to grow claws, talons or similar natural weapons — maybe even a field of hissing quantum energy around the character's hands.

When used in close combat, Claws convert the bashing damage caused by the character's normal punches and strikes into lethal damage. Furthermore, the character may roll one extra damage die per dot he has in Claws. Thus, a Strike by a character with Claws 3 would do Strength +2 (for the maneuver) +3 (for the claws), or Strength +5, lethal damage.

Extras: Kinetic Discharge (the character actually stores up kinetic energy in her body, then channels it through anything she touches; this allows the character to add the extra damage to melee as well as hand-to-hand attacks or, by spending a quantum point per shot, to charge thrown objects and bullets with the extra damage)

Boost

Level: 2
Quantum Minimum: 2
Dice Pool: Quantum + Boost
Range: Touch
Area: N/A
Duration: Variable
Effect: Each success adds one dot to a specified Attribute; points fade at the rate of one per (Quantum + power rating) turns.
Multiple Actions: Yes
Description: Boost allows a nova to increase one of his Attributes temporarily. The Attribute affected by the power must be defined when the power is bought, and it cannot be changed thereafter. To use it, the nova must roll Quantum + Boost. Each success adds one dot to the Attribute. Above 5, the Attribute converts to Mega-Attribute 1, to a maximum of Mega-Attribute 5. The added dots fade at the rate of one per (Quantum + power rating) turns, and the power may be used only once per scene.

Extras: Extended Effect (dots of Attribute gained from Boost last for a scene); Extra Attribute (power affects one additional Attribute at the same time); Other Person (nova may boost either his or another character's Attributes; other person must be touched to be affected).

Clone

Level: 3
Quantum Minimum: 5
Dice Pool: Stamina + Clone
Range: Self

Area: N/A
Duration: One scene
Effect: Creates one duplicate of the character per success.
Multiple Actions: No
Description: This power allows a nova to create "clones" of himself from quantum energies and nearby molecules. To use it, he rolls Stamina + Clone. Each success equals one clone — assuming the character wants to pay for it. At this time, the character must spend one quantum point per clone created, up to the number of successes; he may, of course, spend fewer quantum points if he wishes fewer clones.

Clones are exact duplicates of the character — they have the same Attributes, Abilities, powers, clothes and equipment (except that clones do not have the Clone power themselves). However, they are separate persons in a game sense; if one is knocked unconscious or killed, the others are not affected. Clones do not have any sort of telepathic link; they communicate by talking just like ordinary groups of people.

Clones are not as powerful as the original character. Clones lose one die from all Traits (Attributes, quantum powers, etc.) for each clone created, to a minimum of 1. Thus, if a character created three clones, those clones would have -3 ratings in all Traits. Moreover, all clones have only half of their creator's Quantum Pool.

It takes only one turn for a nova to create clones, but the character can do nothing else that turn (not even walking). Once created, the duplicates remain for a scene or until they "recombine" with the original character (usually referred to as the "host" by the clones). To recombine, two or more duplicates need only touch and use an action; again, they can perform no other action during that turn. Recombining is automatic. Clones that do not recombine dissolve into nothingness at the end of the scene, as the energies forming them dissipate.
Extras: None

Cyberkinesis

Level: 3
Quantum Minimum: 4
Dice Pool: Variable
Range: (Quantum + power rating) x 10 meters or Special
Area: Special
Duration: Special
Effect: Controls computers and machines; the more successes achieved, the greater the control.
Multiple Actions: Yes
Description: Cyberkinesis is the ability to manipulate machines, particularly electronic machines and computers, encompassing a variety of related abilities. The

character does not have to possess any relevant Abilities (like Engineering) in order to use these abilities, but it is not uncommon for cyberkinetics to know such skills.

A cyberkinetic can send his consciousness through a computer network, allowing him to affect a distant computer, if he can locate the machine at all (typically a Hacking feat). Doing so costs one Willpower, requires total concentration (no other actions) and raises the difficulty of the skill roll as follows:

Computer Affected	Time to Accomplish	Difficulty
Same network	Three turns	+1
Same city	One minute	+2
Same continent	10 minutes	+3
Transcontinental	One hour	+4

As with Elemental Anima and Mastery, this power provides several techniques. A nova may learn and freely use one technique per dot in the power. She may attempt other techniques, but she must pay double quantum cost and roll against a difficulty penalty of one to activate these powers. Techniques include:

Alter Data
Dice Pool: Intelligence + Cyberkinesis
Area: N/A
Duration: Concentration
Upon a successful Intelligence + Cyberkinesis roll, the cyberkinetic can interface with a computer or similar piece of equipment to alter, read or remove existing data or insert or create new information. The character can read or alter approximately 100 megabytes x Quantum of information per minute. For each success achieved on the Intelligence + Cyberkinesis roll beyond the first, this time is cut in half. Any changes to or deletions of information are permanent; the data must be reentered into the computer by hand.

Control
Dice Pool: Manipulation + Cyberkinesis
Area: N/A
Duration: Concentration
The cyberkinetic can take control of any machine with electronic, mechanical or hydraulic parts. The number of successes achieved on a Manipulation + Cyberkinesis roll indicates the "Strength" of the cyberkinetic's control. If the machine (or its user or driver) tries to counteract the control, assign the machine a "Strength" to reflect its power and resolve the situation as a resisted action.

Fool
Dice Pool: Manipulation + Cyberkinesis
Area: N/A
Duration: Concentration
The cyberkinetic can insert false images in sensors, security systems or communications devices. The number of successes achieved on a Manipulation + Cyberkinesis roll indicates the "Manipulation" rating of

the cyberkinetic's control. The Storyteller should assign the device (or its user) a Perception rating; the more sophisticated and powerful the machine, the greater its Perception. A "Manipulation" versus Perception resisted action then determines whether the cyberkinetic's attempt to trick the machine succeeds.

Overload

Dice Pool: Wits + Cyberkinesis
Area: N/A
Duration: Instant

The cyberkinetic overloads the machine in some way — sends a pulse of electricity or electromagnetic energy through it, stresses it so that it jams or seizes up. If the nova's Wits + Cyberkinesis roll is successful, the machine will not work. The Storyteller may increase the difficulty of the roll for machines that are particularly advanced or difficult to affect for some reason.

Reprogram

Dice Pool: Intelligence + Cyberkinesis
Area: N/A
Duration: Concentration

A complement to Alter Data, Reprogram allows the cyberkinetic to change the instructions or programming used to run a computer or similar device. The difficulty of the Intelligence + Cyberkinesis roll should be determined by the Storyteller; the more sophisticated the computer and its software, the greater the difficulty. A standard desktop computer would incur no difficulty penalty, for example, while a highly defended military mainframe computer would incur a penalty of three. The changes or additions to a computer's software are permanent until otherwise altered.

Extras: None

Density Control

Level: 2
Quantum Minimum: 3
Dice Pool: Variable
Range: Self
Area: N/A
Duration: Maintenance
Effect: Increases or decreases the character's density, granting her armorlike protection or intangibility.
Multiple Actions: Yes
Description: This power allows the character to either increase her density or decrease it, but not both; the player must choose which ability the character has when the power is purchased.

A character who can increase her density becomes heavier but also tougher and stronger. To use this power, the character rolls Quantum, adding a number of automatic successes equal to her Density Control rating; each success doubles her weight and adds one dot of Strength (or one dot of Mega-Strength if Strength exceeds 5, to a maximum of Mega-Strength 5) and one extra soak against bashing and lethal damage. The extra Strength gained does not increase a character's jumping ability. In many characters an increase in density is accompanied by visible effects such as the character's body turning to rock or metal, but this effect is not required.

A character who can decrease her density can do so without a roll; however, the character must have, and use, an appropriate number of dots in the power to decrease density. Each level of Density Control adds one to the difficulties of hitting the character with all physical attacks except Area and Explosive attacks, so long as the character has the power activated.

Density Decrease	Effect
•	Reduced density; +1 die to dodge; character may ooze or seep through cracks and other tiny openings at the rate of one centimeter per turn.
••	Greatly reduced density; reduce by half the damage the character takes from any physical attack, correspondingly reduce the effec

tiveness of *the character's own attacks* by half; character may ooze through cracks at the rate of one meter per turn. +2 dice to dodge (character "flows" around attacks). Completely intangible to physical attacks; character is affected normally by energy attacks, gravity fields, psychic attacks and the like. While intangible, the character can walk through walls and ignore the effects of physical attacks. Attacks such as Strobe, which affects senses the character is still using, and any power which affects the character's mind (like Mirage or Mental Blast), still affect the character even though he is intangible. An intangible character needs to breathe, so cannot walk through the entire Earth; he can take damage from attacks such as gases unless he has the Adaptability enhancement. While intangible, the character cannot affect the tangible world in any way — he cannot fire a gun, pick up any object, punch someone or do anything of the sort. +3 dice to dodge.

•••• Completely intangible to physical attacks, takes half damage from energy attacks and suffers only half normal effects from energy fields. +3 dice to dodge; otherwise, effects are as at Density Control •••, above.

••••• Completely intangible to all forces except psychic attacks. Character may take an action to turn parts of her body solid, enabling her to attack with a solidified fist, foot, etc; attackers may target the solidified parts, but at normal targeting penalties. +3 dice to dodge; otherwise, effects are as at Density Control •••, above.

Extras: Full Control (character can both increase and decrease his density); Affects Others (character may change the density of persons or objects for a scene by touching them and rolling Manipulation + Density Control; an unwilling target may roll Resistance to resist; an object made superdense gains extra soak and weight, while an object made less dense loses soak or even becomes completely intangible)

Disintegration

Level: 3
Quantum Minimum: 5
Dice Pool: Dexterity + Disintegration
Range: (Quantum + power rating) x 10 meters
Area: N/A
Duration: Instant
Effect: Causes (Quantum + successes) levels of aggravated damage.
Multiple Actions: No
Description: This terrifying power allows the character literally to disintegrate (or in some similar way utterly destroy) a person or physical object. To use it, the character pays the quantum-point cost and rolls Dexterity + Disintegration. His successes, plus a number of automatic successes equal to his Quantum, equal the number of levels of aggravated damage the attack inflicts.
Extras: None

Disorient

Level: 2
Quantum Minimum: 1
Dice Pool: Manipulation + Disorient
Range: (Quantum + power rating) x 10 meters
Area: N/A
Duration: Maintenance
Effect: Allows character to confuse and weaken opponents.
Multiple Actions: Yes
Description: A nova with Disorient can cause another character to become confused, weakened, disori-

ented and unable to take action effectively. The effect can be physical (inducing nausea) or mental (creating hallucinations), depending on how the power is defined, but the end result is the same.

To use Disorient, the nova rolls Manipulation + Disorient; the target may oppose this with a Willpower roll. Each net success reduces all of the target's dice pools by one. If any dice pool is reduced to half or less, the target cannot use that power or ability at all unless she spends a point of Willpower; any dice pool reduced to zero cannot be used at all. The target may spend a point of Willpower to shake off the effects, but the attacking nova may use the power on the same target multiple times.

Disorient, as a Maintenance power, lasts for the normal (Quantum + power rating) turns. The nova may then spend extra quantum points to maintain the power automatically at the same level of successes. However, the opponent may make another Willpower roll, and she gains an automatic success on this roll. If the nova wishes to maintain the power for yet another period, the opponent's next Willpower roll gains two automatic successes, and so on.
Extras: None

Disrupt

Level: 2
Quantum Minimum: 3
Dice Pool: Intelligence + Disrupt
Range: (Quantum + power rating) x 10 meters
Area: N/A
Duration: Maintenance
Effect: Reduces the effectiveness of powers by one dot per success.
Multiple Actions: Yes
Description: This power represents a nova's great control over quantum energies. With it, he can disrupt another nova's control over any quantum power (but not Mega-Attributes or enhancements). To use it, he need only spend the quantum points and roll Intelligence + Disrupt. The target may resist with a Quantum + Node roll. Each net success the nova achieves over the number of successes achieved by his target reduces the power by one dot per success.

Disrupt can affect any power; the nova may, for example, disrupt his target's Quantum Bolt one turn, and his Force Field the next turn. However, without an Extra it cannot affect multiple powers at once. Moreover, it is difficult to use Disrupt multiple times in succession against the same target; each subsequent use of Disrupt against the same target incurs a +1 difficulty penalty.

Extras: Extra Power (Disrupt may affect any two powers at once)

Domination

Level: 2
Quantum Minimum: 3
Dice Pool: Manipulation + Domination
Range: (Quantum + power rating) x 10 meters
Area: N/A
Duration: Concentration
Effect: Take control of target's brainwaves; number of successes indicates degree of control.
Multiple Actions: Yes
Description: This mental power allows a nova to project his quantum consciousness into a sentient target's brainwaves. With sufficient successes, he can make his victim do anything, up to and including killing himself.

To use Domination, the nova must spend the necessary quantum points and roll Manipulation + Domination in a resisted action against the target's Willpower. If the nova scores more successes, he succeeds in achieving control. The degree of control depends upon how many successes the nova has left after subtracting the victim's Willpower successes, as follows:

After control has been achieved, a character affected by Domination may roll Willpower; if she succeeds, she may then spend one point of Willpower to decrease the attack's effectiveness — the Willpower point reduces the successes (and thus the command intensity) by one. For example, a character who is being Dominated is told to shoot a friend. She makes a Willpower roll at normal difficulty, succeeds, then spends a point of Willpower to reduce the effect to Major. The Storyteller rules that she summons up enough strength of will to turn the gun aside and shoot a wall instead of her comrade.

In order to use Domination, the nova must be able to communicate with his subject — Domination is not inherently "telepathic." If the target is too far away to hear a command or cannot understand a command for some reason, even Total Control may be useless.

Extras: Telepathic (Domination is telepathic — orders can be communicated automatically, without the need for speech); Parasitic Possession (nova spends three quantum and a Willpower point to discorporate and psychically possess victim; nova's body disappears, and nova becomes a being of quantum-charged brainwaves inhabiting victim's central nervous system; may substitute own personality for that of victim, up to the limit of the successes rolled; while in possession the nova gains the victim's physical Traits, Appearance and nova powers, as well as his own Mental Traits, Charisma, Manipulation, Willpower and mental powers, and may leave the host body via the expenditure of a further three quantum and one Willpower point; however, if nova-possessed victim dies while nova is possessing, the nova's consciousness dies as well; this power has a range of [Quantum + power rating] meters, and the nova must make eye contact with the victim; victim resists with Willpower per normal Domination rules)

Successes	Command Intensity
One	Minor/Quirky: Blink, eat a bug, wear a particular suit of clothes.
Two	Major/Noteworthy: Do the nova's chores; buy lunch for someone you hate.
Three	Complex/Antithetical: Worship a foreign god; follow a particular set of commands ("Fill out this form, mail it to Wilkes-Barre, PA from Boise, Idaho, and after doing so, take out a full-page newspaper ad which reads…"); attack (or refrain from attacking) whomever the nova indicates in combat.
Four	Total Control: Commit suicide; perform any task, no matter how difficult or vile.

Elemental Anima

Level: 3
Quantum Minimum: 4
Dice Pool: Variable
Range: Special
Area: Special
Duration: Variable
Effect: Character can control a particular substance or phenomenon.

Multiple Actions: Yes

Description: A nova with Elemental Anima can project her quantum consciousness into a particular element — fire, sound, ice, electricity or whatever the player can think of and the Storyteller will allow — investing it with "life." This power allows her to take control of it and shape it to her will. Note that the character cannot *create* the element (doing that requires the Elemental Mastery power) — she can only affect and manipulate elemental "matter" that already exists. The player must choose which element the nova can control when buying the power.

This control offers the nova a variety of techniques. The exact techniques differ from element to element,

based on the nature of those elements and the specific techniques the nova masters. The player may pick one of the listed techniques for each dot the nova has in the power; these techniques are ones the nova has "mastered" and may freely perform. The techniques chosen should be appropriate to the element that is being controlled — fire or water powers may provide movement abilities, for example, but it's unlikely that darkness would. The character may also try to perform other techniques, either ones listed here or entirely one-shot, off-the-cuff "stunts." However, such effects cost double the quantum points and suffer difficulty penalties of one; the nova has mastered only the techniques her dots allow her to. The Storyteller has the absolute right to allow or refuse a particular use of power, based on her interpretation of the element's inherent limits.

For Example: La Niña buys Elemental Anima at 3, defining the power as the ability to manipulate, focus and disperse air and wind. For her three mastered abilities, she chooses Enhance/ Diminish (can whip winds to a gale or calm them), Lethal Blast (knifelike "wind-serpents" that vaguely resemble hissing moray eels) and Movement (shapes winds into a cloaklike form, enabling her to sail aloft and glide through the air). She may use these abilities

at the standard difficulty. If Niña wished to focus air into a defensive screen (the Wall ability), she could try, but she'd have to pay double (six quantum points), and she'd suffer a difficulty penalty of one.

If the Storyteller or a player wishes to create additional techniques, the examples can serve as guidelines for levels of power and rules. As a basic rule of thumb, no technique gained through Elemental Anima should be as powerful as the same or similar ability bought on its own.

The duration of Elemental Anima techniques varies. Attacks are typically Instant; movement techniques usually have a duration of Maintenance; other durations are noted below. The range of a technique is typically the standard (Quantum + power rating) x 10 meters, but different ranges may be noted in the text, as is the area of any technique that covers one.

Alter Temperature

Dice Pool: N/A
Range: Variable
Area: (Quantum + power rating) x 10 meters
Duration: Maintenance

The character can increase or decrease the temperature of the air in an area around himself (which is appropriate for fire and ice powers primarily). The character can alter temperature by 10 degrees Celsius for each dot in the power. No roll is required, but quantum points must be paid.

Blast

Dice Pool: Dexterity + Elemental Anima
Range: (Quantum + power rating) x 10 meters
Area: N/A
Duration: Instant

The nova shapes, strengthens and redirects the element, turning it into a damaging blast that inflicts [Quantum x 2] levels + (power rating x 3) dice of bashing damage. If there is only a small amount of the element available, the Storyteller may reduce the range or damage.

Elemental Shield

Dice Pool: Wits + Elemental Anima
Range: Self
Area: N/A
Duration: Instant

The character can turn the element away from himself, thus protecting himself and anyone directly next to him from the brunt of its effects. Roll Wits + Elemental Anima; each success counts as four soak that apply only to attacks based on that element. This technique can be aborted to as a defensive action.

Enhance/Diminish

Dice Pool: Intelligence + Elemental Anima
Range: (Quantum + power rating) x 10 meters
Area: (Quantum + power rating) x 10 meter radius
Duration: Maintenance

The character can increase or decrease the effect of the element in an area — for example, brighten or dim light, or increase or decrease the damage caused by fire. The effect can be enhanced or diminished by 25% per success rolled. If the element is a damaging effect, each success increases or reduces the intensity of the element (or any element-based power) by two damage dice. The nova may not enhance her own or another character's powers with this effect, but she may attempt to reduce a rival elemental's powers. If another character's power is being reduced, a resisted action pitting the nova's Quantum + power rating against the target's Quantum + power rating is required; each net success reduces the target's power rating by one dot. If the power rating is reduced to zero, the target cannot use his power for a number of turns equal to the elemental's power rating.

No roll is required, but quantum points must be paid as usual.

Note: If the element controlled is air, and the nova reduces the effect to 0%, she creates a vacuum in the area. Characters without appropriate Life Support who are caught in a vacuum may suffocate; see "Suffocation and Drowning," p. 257.

Lethal Blast

Dice Pool: Dexterity + Elemental Anima
Range: (Quantum + power rating) x 10 meters
Area: N/A
Duration: Instant

The character can shape an existing quantity of the element into a deadly attack — sharp shards of stone, razor-sharp tendrils of water or air, a laser or the like. This attack inflicts [Quantum x 2] levels + (power rating x 2) dice of lethal damage.

Movement

Dice Pool: N/A
Range: Self
Area: N/A
Duration: Maintenance

The character directs the element in such a way that he can move quickly. The nature of the movement depends on the element: Novas who control wind have it pick them up and waft them where they wish to go; elementals who control earth and rock ride waves of earth or tunnel through the soil. The character can move at the rate of (power rating x 2) + 20 meters per action, or (40 x power rating) kilometers per hour out of combat.

Shaping

Dice Pool: Wits + Elemental Anima
Range: (Quantum + power rating) x 5 meters
Area: Special
Duration: Maintenance

The character may alter the shape of a quantity of the element. No more than (three cubic meters of the element x power rating) can be affected at once. The character can create geometric shapes or simple "sculptures" such as fire-people or ice statues. If the player makes an Arts (Sculpture) roll, the character can create extremely detailed and beautiful shapes. If the nova attempts to use this power offensively (for example, to sculpt a pit under a foe or trap an opponent in a burning ring of fire), the player must make an attack roll (Wits + Elemental Anima), which the target can dodge normally.

Wall

Dice Pool: N/A
Range: Special
Area: (Quantum + power rating) cubic meters
Duration: Maintenance (and see below)

The character raises a wall of the element in front of him. For each dot in the power, the nova gains two soak against appropriate attacks unless the attacker can somehow shoot around it. The wall moves as the character moves, but it immediately collapses if she intentionally leaves the ground (unless the character is creating a screen of hardened air molecules, for instance). The Storyteller may declare the wall useless against certain attacks; for example, a wall of wind would blow aside physical attacks and snuff fires, but it would have little effect on electricity.

Extras: None

Elemental Mastery

Level: 3
Quantum Minimum: 5
Dice Pool: Variable
Range: Variable
Area: Variable
Duration: Variable
Effect: The nova can create, alter and control various substances or phenomena.
Multiple Actions: Yes
Description: Elemental Mastery is similar to, but transcends, Elemental Anima. Whereas Elemental Anima allows a nova to manipulate an existing element, Elemental Mastery allows him actually to create that element or

phenomenon, thus greatly expanding the range of his elemental abilities.

Like Elemental Anima, Elemental Mastery provides a list of techniques, and characters may master one technique per dot in Elemental Mastery. Characters may attempt to use techniques they haven't mastered, but the players must pay double cost and roll against a difficulty penalty of one. The techniques chosen should be appropriate to the element being generated — fire or earth powers may provide Imprison, for example, but it's unlikely that light powers would.

Characters may choose from the techniques listed here or make up their own, with the Storyteller's permission and approval.

Blast

Dice Pool: Dexterity + Elemental Mastery
Range: (Quantum + power rating) x 10 meters
Area: N/A
Duration: Instant

The nova generates a blast or bolt of the element that inflicts [Quantum x 2] levels + (power rating x 3) dice of bashing damage.

Crush

Dice Pool: Dexterity + Elemental Mastery
Range: (Quantum + power rating) x 10 meters
Area: N/A
Duration: Instant

The nova is able to create a quantity of the element that picks up the target and slams him into a nearby sturdy object such as a building or tree, or simply crushes him. This attack could represent an intense burst of wind, a hand of stone which grows out of the ground and grabs the victim or phoenix-talons of fire. The character rolls Intelligence + power rating; each success allows the target to be moved up to 10 meters (if the nova so desires); the victim takes a number of bashing damage levels equal to twice the successes rolled, and her Initiative on the next turn is reduced by one per success.

Imprison

Dice Pool: Wits + Elemental Mastery
Range: (Quantum + power rating) x 10 meters
Area: N/A
Duration: Maintenance

The nova is able to confine a target within a quantity of the element. Examples include creating a fiery cage, suspending a victim in an invisible fist of air or causing someone to sink up to his neck into solid rock. The confining element has a Might equal to twice the number of successes rolled; the trapped character may break out of it just as he would from a clinch. Imprison inflicts no damage ordinarily, but if the nova spends an extra quantum point during the initial attack, it inflicts damage as would a clinch.

Lethal Blast

Dice Pool: Dexterity + Elemental Mastery
Range: (Quantum + power rating) x 10 meters
Area: N/A
Duration: Instant

The character can "throw" or project a lethal damage blast of the element — anything from a blast of freezing cold to a dehydrative attack that sucks the water out of the target's body. This attack inflicts [Quantum x 2] levels + (power rating x 2) dice of lethal damage.

Propel

Dice Pool: N/A
Range: Self
Area: N/A
Duration: Maintenance

By creating a "blast" of the element behind himself, the character can move at rapid speeds — (power rating x 2) + 20 meters per action, or (40 x power rating) kilometers per hour out of combat. Where and how the character can move depends on the element; Propel based on fire would be like Flight, whereas Propel based on water would work only in water and would be like Hyperswimming.

Shield

Dice Pool: N/A
Range: Self
Area: N/A
Duration: Maintenance

The character can create a Force Field-like protective barrier of the element around himself. This barrier provides two extra soak per dot versus bashing and lethal damage. For an extra quantum point, the Shield causes harm to anyone who touches it (it inflicts a number of dice of bashing damage equal to the character's power rating). The Shield slightly obscures others' view of the character, but it does not interfere with his vision at all.

Sphere

Dice Pool: Dexterity + Elemental Mastery
Range: (Quantum + power rating) x 10 meters
Area: (Quantum + power rating) x 3 meters
Duration: Instant

The character can project a large ball or sphere of the element, which injures anyone within its radius. The blast inflicts (power rating x 3) dice of bashing damage in the listed radius.

Storm

Dice Pool: Wits + Elemental Mastery
Range: (Quantum + power rating) x 10 meters
Area: (Quantum + power rating) x 5 meters
Duration: Concentration

The character can generate a stormlike area filled with the element. Examples include blizzards, firestorms, sandstorms, earthquakes, tornadoes, sonic fields and ice patches. Each turn, Storm typically inflicts two levels of bashing damage per dot in the power rating, reduces opponent's dice pools by two (from whipping winds, fiery gouts or poor footing) and halves movement and vision. Other effects are up to the Storyteller and should be based on common-sense views of the effects of the element. For example, anyone moving through a blizzard or earthquake might have to make an Athletics or Flight roll to keep from slipping and falling, and they would risk hypothermia; anyone in a firestorm would take lethal damage instead of bashing.

Extras: None

Empathic Manipulation

Level: 2
Quantum Minimum: 2
Dice Pool: Variable (Willpower resisted)
Range: (Quantum + power rating) x 20 meters
Area: N/A
Duration: Special
Effect: Controls and manipulates a target's emotions.

Multiple Actions: Yes

Description: Empathic Manipulation is, in essence, a highly specialized form of Domination or Telepathy. It allows a nova to detect and manipulate a single target's emotions. For example, the nova can make emotions stronger or weaker. Doing so does not necessarily prompt the target to do anything, but it does make it more likely that the target will take some kind of action. For example, if a nova detects that a target is angry at the government, he might heighten that emotion to a blinding rage. How the target deals with his range is beyond the nova's control. The target might begin a vitriolic letter-writing campaign, or he might pick up a submachine gun, walk into the nearest courthouse and begin firing.

To detect a target's emotions, the nova must roll Perception + Empathic Manipulation in an opposed roll against the target's Willpower. Even a single net success on the nova's part is enough for him to determine the target's emotional state and against whom or what that emotion is directed.

Manipulating those emotions requires a Manipulation + Empathic Manipulation roll, resisted by the target's Willpower. For each net success achieved, the nova can adjust the target's emotions up or down on the following table by one step. The Storyteller should use this table as a guideline for emotions not covered.

The emotional changes brought about by Empathic Manipulation last a scene or so (in the case of weaker emotions) or as long as the nova concentrates on them and pays quantum points per (Quantum + power rating) turns to maintain them (in the case of strong emotions). After that they abate normally. Lesser emotions take time to fade, but extreme emotions quickly "cool down" to lower levels. Circumstances may affect this, however.

Extras: None

Entropy Control

Level: 3
Quantum Minimum: 4
Dice Pool: Intelligence + Entropy Control
Range: Variable
Area: Variable
Duration: Special
Effect: Character can control and manipulate entropic forces.

Multiple Actions: Yes

Description: A character with this suite of abilities is a master of the forces of entropy that are always at work in the universe. His quantum consciousness is able to tap into, summon and manipulate entropy the same way other novas play with fire or ice.

Sadness/Happiness	Anger	Lust	Love	Hatred	Jealousy/Envy
Not sad/happy	Not angry	Not lustful	Apathetic	Not hateful	Not jealous/envious
Sad/happy	Angry	Interested	Like	Dislike	Jealous/envious
Depressed/elated	Enraged	Desirous	Love	Hatred	Greedy
Distraught/ecstatic	Berserk	Unabiding lust	Mad love	Blind hatred	Blind jealousy/envy

As with Elemental Anima and Mastery, this power provides several techniques. A nova may learn and freely use one technique per dot in the power; she may attempt other techniques, but she must pay double quantum points and roll at a difficulty penalty of one to use these alternative techniques. Techniques include:

Bioentropy Storm

Dice Pool: Dexterity + Entropy Control
Range: (Quantum + power rating) x 10 meters
Area: (Quantum + power rating) x 5 meters
Duration: Instant

The nova can create a field in which entropic effects pertaining to living creatures run riot. The victims age, suffer spontaneous injuries and experience other biological breakdowns. The nova rolls Dexterity + Entropy Control in an opposed contest against the victims' Stamina; each net success inflicts one health level of lethal damage. Victims cannot soak this damage unless they have the Hardbody Mega-Stamina enhancement.

Breakdown

Dice Pool: Intelligence + Entropy Control
Range: (Quantum + power rating) x 10 meters
Area: N/A
Duration: Special

The nova can cause any machine, device or similar object to stop functioning as some part of it breaks, wears out or loses power. This power's effects are permanent until someone repairs the device, provides it with more power or the like. To use Breakdown, the nova rolls Intelligence + Entropy Control in an opposed action against the device's "Stamina." The Storyteller should determine the device's Stamina rating for these purposes. The more complex or technologically advanced a machine is, the *lower* its Stamina — it's hard to use Breakdown on a simple object or one with few moving parts, but the more complicated a device becomes, the more opportunities there are for entropy to gain a foothold.

Entropic Shield

Dice Pool: Stamina + Entropy Control
Range: Self
Area: N/A
Duration: Maintenance

The character surrounds himself with a field of entropic energy. This field heightens the entropic reactions within any incoming attack (especially those based on physical objects, such as bullets), thus disrupting and weakening them. Each success achieved on a Stamina + Entropy Control roll grants the character an extra soak against bashing and lethal damage. However, this extra soak does not apply to attacks by living matter, such as fists or animals.

Probability Corruption

Dice Pool: Entropy Control
Range: (Quantum + power rating) x 5 meters
Area: N/A
Duration: Maintenance

This technique allows a nova to cause the forces of entropy to overwhelm a single target, making it more likely that he will fail disastrously. To use it, the nova rolls Entropy Control. Each success achieved results in a loss of one die (or one automatic success) for all rolls made by the target. Additionally, the target will botch a roll if he rolls no successes and any die comes up 1 *or 2.* These negative effects last as long as the nova pays quantum points to keep the entropic forces focused on the victim.

Extras: None

Successes	Clarity
One	Very hazy, as though sensing through fog; one sense (sight, hearing, etc.) only.
Two	Slightly blurry perception, one sense; or hazy perception, all normal senses.
Three	Perfect perception, one sense; slightly blurry perception, all normal senses; can use one nova sense, though it will be very hazy.
Four	Near-perfect perception with all normal senses; blurry perception with nova senses.
Five	Perfect perception with normal or nova senses.

Extras: Distant Scan (range is increased to [Perception + power rating] x 1000 km, but the process of scanning at this distance takes at least 15 minutes per 1000 km of distance, and the nova may take no other actions, or even perceive his immediate surroundings, while so scanning; furthermore, the Perception + ESP roll to target is at +1 difficulty per 2000 km)

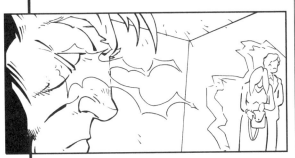

ESP

Level: 2
Quantum Minimum: 3
Dice Pool: Perception + ESP
Range: (Perception + power rating) x 20 meters
Area: N/A
Duration: Concentration
Effect: Allows character to sense his surroundings from a "focus point" at range.
Multiple Actions: No
Description: By attuning himself to quantum ebbs and flows, the nova may sense things at much greater ranges than he normally could. The sense that ESP affects must be chosen when the power is purchased and cannot be changed thereafter.

To use ESP, the nova need only spend the quantum points and concentrate. He then defines a "focus point" somewhere within the power's range. He can sense from that focus point as if he were standing right there. Thus, this power is perfect for "seeing through walls" or otherwise spying on people.

The nova must make a Perception + ESP roll (no range penalties) to target the power, and the clarity of the scan is based on the number of successes rolled:

Flight

Level: 2
Quantum Minimum: 1
Dice Pool: Dexterity + Flight
Range: Self
Area: N/A
Duration: Maintenance
Effect: Allows character to fly at the speed of (power rating x 4) + 40 meters per action.
Multiple Actions: Per normal movement rules.
Description: This power allows the character to fly through the air, outer space and similar three-dimensional areas. He can fly at a speed equal to (power rating x 4) + 40 meters per action in combat; out of combat his speed is (Quantum + Flight) x 50 kilometers per hour.

Normally, no roll is required to use Flight. If the character wants to perform aerobatic stunts or fly through narrow openings at high speeds without hurting himself, the Storyteller may require a Dexterity + Flight roll to determine whether the character succeeds. The character may also substitute Dexterity + Flight for a normal Dodge roll while in the air; depending on the character's movement, this may allow him to dodge explosions and area attacks, though particularly large-scale blasts might cost the character his entire action.

Extras: Underwater (character may use his Flight underwater and through other bodies of liquid)

Force Field

Level: 2
Quantum Minimum: 2
Dice Pool: Stamina + Force Field
Range: Self
Area: N/A
Duration: Maintenance
Effect: Quantum + (2/success) extra soak versus bashing and lethal damage.
Multiple Actions: Yes
Description: This power provides extra protection for a nova. Most novas are already pretty hardy, but one with this power may be virtually untouchable. Force Field provides a number of extra soak equal to the character's Quantum. The nova then rolls Stamina + Force Field. Each success adds another two soak. This soak protects versus bashing and lethal damage.

Force Field can be used to block or parry attacks, including attacks with quantum powers. The nova's Force Field rating is substituted for Brawl or Martial Arts.

Extras: Wall (allows character to project a "wall" of force at a range of three meters per dot in Force Field; the basic wall is two meters long by two meters high and can be made two meters taller or longer per dot in the power; the character can alter the dimensions with each use if he so chooses).

Gravity Control

Level: 3
Quantum Minimum: 4
Dice Pool: Variable
Range: Variable
Area: Variable
Duration: Variable
Effect: Character is able to manipulate gravity and gravitic fields.
Multiple Actions: Yes
Description: A nova with this power is a master of gravity. He is able to lift and move objects, fly by manipulating gravitic forces and otherwise control gravity.

As with Elemental Anima and Mastery, this power provides several techniques. A nova may learn and freely use one technique per dot in the power; she may attempt other techniques, but the player must pay double quantum cost and roll against a difficulty penalty of one to activate these powers. Techniques include:

Gravitic Blast

Dice Pool: Dexterity + Gravity Control
Range: (Quantum + power rating) x 10 meters
Area: N/A
Duration: Instant

By manipulating micropockets of intense gravity around a target, the nova can bash and tear it apart. The end result is similar to a Quantum Bolt. This attack does [Quantum x 2] levels + (power rating x 3) dice of bashing damage or [Quantum x 2] levels + (power rating x 2) dice or lethal damage (nova's choice).

Gravitational Field

Dice Pool: Wits + Gravity Control
Range: (Quantum + power rating) x 5 meters
Area: (Quantum + power rating) x 3 meters
Duration: Concentration

The nova can alter the gravity in a given area. For each success achieved on a Dexterity + Gravity Control roll, he can warp local gravity by up to .5 g (normal Earth gravity is 1 g). Weight of objects is increased or decreased by an equivalent amount; a 100 kg object in a 1.5 g field weighs 150 kg. Objects in a zero-g field weigh nothing, while objects in a negative-g field fall *upward* until out of the field. The nova can be selective if he wishes, increasing some objects' mass, decreasing others and leaving yet others alone. A creature or object that becomes too heavy cannot move (or be moved), and it may collapse under its own weight if it becomes heavy enough. If the nova tries to affect a living thing with a Gravitational Field, the target may resist with Willpower.

Weight vs. Mass

To determine an object's current weight, simply multiply its mass by the local gravitational field strength. A cargo bin that weighs just over 240 kg on Earth weighs only 91 kg in Mars' natural gravity (mass 240 kg x Martian gravity of .38 Earth-standard = 91 kg).

Gravity

Operating in nonstandard gravity is often difficult. People raised in a 1 g (normal Earth-gravity) environment are stronger and more durable in low gravity, but they are slowed down and weakened in high gravity. The effects of gravity changes are applied to characters in a straightforward fashion to reduce the need for formulas and complex mechanical systems.

Characters without Gravity Control operate with one extra dot in both Strength and Stamina in .6 g or lower, but they lose one dot from Dexterity; characters with Gravity Control gain the Strength and Stamina, but they do not lose the Dexterity. Characters without Gravity Control lose two dots from both Strength and Dexterity in 1.5 g or higher, since they're constantly resisting the increased pull of gravity. These adjustments affect not only dice pools, but jumping distances, Initiative, encumbrance and endurance as well.

A flying character caught in a G-field of 2 g or above must roll Strength + Flight against the gravity-wielder's skill total; if the flier scores fewer successes, he begins to fall (see "Falling," p. 256). Depending on the character's altitude, he might be able to make another Strength + Flight roll to pull out of his fall in time to avoid hitting the ground, but the player must spend more quantum points to reactivate his Flight.

Falling damage in altered gravity is multiplied by the strength of the G-field; thus, a character falling 20 meters in .5-G gravity would take damage as though she'd fallen 10 meters, while a character falling 20 meters in a 2-G field would take damage as though she'd fallen 40 meters. This also applies to falling or dropped objects; the damage they inflict is multiplied by the local G-field.

Gravitic Flight

Dice Pool: N/A
Range: Self
Area: N/A
Duration: Maintenance

The nova is able to manipulate gravity to pick himself up and fly crudely. His flying speed is equal to (power rating x 2) + 20 meters per action, or (40 x power rating) kilometers per hour out of combat.

Gravitic Shield

Dice Pool: N/A
Range: Self
Area: N/A
Duration: Maintenance

The character can project waves of gravity around herself. Doing so provides an excellent defense against incoming projectiles and deflects hand-to-hand physical attacks. Each turn, the character can subtract her dots in Gravity Control from the attack successes of any physical projectile attack (bullets, thrown objects, etc.); furthermore, the Gravitic Shield provides one soak per dot against any projectile attack that does connect. She may subtract half her dots in Gravity Control (round up) from the attack successes of any hand-to-hand physical attack. Gravitic Shield does not affect pure energy attacks, like flame attacks or electrical blasts.

Gravitokinesis

Dice Pool: Dexterity + Gravity Control
Range: (Quantum + power rating) x 10 meters
Area: N/A
Duration: Concentration

The nova may use his ability to manipulate gravity to pick up objects. He can then throw them or hit other characters with them. Doing so is performed in a fashion identical to use of the Telekinesis power (p. 224), except that the dice pool is Dexterity + Gravity Control and the nova must score two successes to gain one success on the Telekinesis lifting chart.

Extras: None

Healing

Level: 3
Quantum Minimum: 4
Dice Pool: N/A
Range: Touch
Area: N/A
Duration: Instant

Effect: Heals one health level of lethal or bashing damage per quantum point.

Multiple Actions: Yes

Description: This power enables a nova to heal herself or others. To use Healing, a nova must touch the per-

son to be healed and spend one quantum point per health level to be healed. The character may heal a number of bashing health levels up to twice her power rating, or a number of lethal health levels up to her power rating. This power may be employed only once per victim per scene.

Alternatively, if a character is suffering from poison or a disease, each quantum point adds one die to the afflicted character's Resistance roll. Once the roll succeeds, the poison or disease stops affecting the character. Any damage already taken can then be healed with a normal application of Healing.

Healing can even regenerate severed limbs or ruined organs, but to do so costs double quantum and a Willpower point.

Extras: None

Holo

Level: 2
Quantum Minimum: 1
Dice Pool: Manipulation + Holo
Range: (Quantum + power rating) x 10 meters
Area: (Quantum + power rating) x 5 meters
Duration: Concentration

Effect: Creates images; each success adds one to the difficulty of Perception rolls to determine the true nature of the image

Multiple Actions: No

Description: This power allows a nova to create images — illusions, if you will — with which to trick and befuddle other characters. The player must choose which sense the images affect when he buys the power. As its name suggests, Holo is usually used to create images which can be seen, but auditory images are also popular.

To use Holo, the nova rolls Manipulation + Holo to determine how precise and accurate his images are. Failure indicates that the nova fails to create an accurate image. Each success above the first increases the difficulty of Perception rolls to determine the true nature of the illusion by one. If an observer fails his Perception roll, he believes the images are real until he has reason to think otherwise (at which point he may roll Perception again). If he makes his Perception roll at any time, he instantly recognizes the images for what they are and can perceive what (if anything) they are hiding.

Images created by Holo cannot directly cause harm, even if they affect the sense of touch. However, they could trick a character into harming himself. For example, if Holo is used to make a cliff seem like a grassy meadow, anyone who fails his Perception roll could easily walk right off the cliff to his doom.

Extras: Extra Sense (power affects one additional sense at the same time).

Homunculus

Level: 3
Quantum Minimum: 4
Dice Pool: Stamina + Homunculus
Range: Self
Area: N/A
Duration: Special
Effect: Allows nova to separate parts of his body or create small creatures from his own body.
Multiple Actions: Special
Description: Similar in many ways to Clone, this power allows a nova to separate parts of his body yet retain control over them (for example, detaching his hands and letting them strangle someone on their own), to create small creatures from his own body, or even to break down his body into a swarm of tiny creatures. Use of the power does not cause the nova any damage.

To use Homunculus, the nova spends the required amount of quantum points and rolls Stamina + Homunculus. Success means that a body part can be detached or a creature can be created. The creatures in question cannot be perfect duplicates of the nova — that requires Clone — but they could be smaller, or warped and twisted, versions of him.

Detached body parts or creatures can move up to 10 meters per dot in Homunculus away from the charac-

ter. As long as the character has a line of sight to them, he can control what they do, just as if they were still a part of his body. If line of sight is lost, or if they somehow pass beyond the power's range, they will continue with whatever actions they were performing until their tasks are completed and then stop moving until line of sight and range are reestablished.

If a detached body part is attacked, it is considered to have the same Attributes and Traits as the character, but it acts separately from the character (i.e., if the character decides to dodge in a particular turn, his detached body parts do not have to dodge; they can attack, block, or do whatever else they want, just as if they were separate characters). If one is stunned or knocked unconscious, the other may continue to act. If the detached body part is killed, the character loses that part of his body permanently.

A "small creature" homunculus has no quantum powers, but it is otherwise considered to have half ratings in the character's normal Traits (i.e., if the character has a Strength of 4, the homunculus has a Strength of 2), half normal soak and a Bite/ Claw attack of Str +1 lethal damage. The player may shift points around if he likes (reducing Strength to add to Dexterity, for example). If killed, the main character takes one automatic health level of lethal damage.

At two dots and higher, the character can create more than one homunculus. At two dots he can create two homunculi; at three dots, four homunculi; at four dots, six homunculi; at five dots, 10 homunculi. These homunculi can all be the same, or can be different. It costs no additional quantum points to create multiple creatures.

Furthermore, if the character has Homunculus 4+, she can break down her entire body into a "homunculus swarm" of thousands of insect-sized creatures. The swarm moves at the character's normal speed and can flow over an opponent, automatically inflicting a number of levels of lethal damage per turn equal to the power rating (soak protects normally against this damage). The swarm can flow over multiple opponents; the character simply divides the levels of lethal damage between or among all appropriate targets. Thus, if the homunculus swarm could potentially inflict four levels of lethal damage per turn, the character could flow over three opponents, inflicting two levels per turn to one foe and one level per turn to the other two. A homunculus swarm takes a maximum of one health level of damage from most attacks, but fire, explosion and area attacks affect it normally.

It takes only one turn for a nova to create a single homunculus, but the character can do nothing else that turn (not even walking). Once created, the homunculus does not cost quantum points to maintain; it remains at no cost until it recombines with the original character. To recombine, two or more homunculi need only touch and use an action; again, this is the only action they can perform that turn. Recombining is automatic; it does not require a roll.

Extras: None

Hypermovement

Level: 2
Quantum Minimum: 1
Dice Pool: Dexterity + Hypermovement
Range: Self
Area: N/A
Duration: Maintenance
Effect: Increases character's running, flying or swimming speed.
Multiple Actions: N/A
Description: A nova with Hypermovement can run, swim or fly at super-fast speeds. At higher levels, Hypermovement allows a character to outpace bullet trains, jetfighters and other vehicles. The player must specify which mode of movement Hypermovement enhances (running, swimming or Flight, but not techniques from powers such as Elemental Mastery or Gravity Control) when he buys the power.

Hypermovement works by increasing the multiplier used to calculate the character's movement rate. Each dot adds six to the multiplier. For example, in combat all characters can sprint at a rate equal to (Dexterity x 3) + 20 meters per action. A character with Hyperrunning 1 moves at (Dexterity x 9) + 20 meters per action. If he increases the power to Hyperrunning 4, he moves at (Dexterity x 27) + 20 meters per action. A character with Hyperswimming treats his base swimming score as equal to his sprinting score, then adds the modifiers accordingly.

Out of combat, Hypermovement simply converts to a speed of 500 kilometers per hour times the dots in the power. Thus, a character with Hyperrunning 4 moves at 2000 kph — breaking the sound barrier, thus causing significant damage to structures he runs past because of

the sonic booms (consider this effect the equivalent of causing damage equal to the Mega-Strength enhancement Thunderclap along the character's backward trajectory, but substituting dots in Hypermovement for dots in Mega-Strength). Characters using Hypermovement have to be very careful about their effect on the world around them.

A character who moves at full tilt may take no other actions (except Hyperspeed or Aerial Slam) while so doing, but the difficulty to hit him increases by one per dot in the power; thus, anyone attacking a nova mentioned with Hyperrunning 4 has to roll against a difficulty penalty of at least four if the target is moving at full speed.

If a character has to maneuver suddenly while using Hypermovement, the Storyteller can have him make a Dexterity + Hypermovement roll to do so.

Extras: Extra Mode (power affects one additional mode of movement)

Hypnosis

Level: 1
Quantum Minimum: 1
Dice Pool: Intelligence + Hypnosis
Range: (Quantum + power rating) meters
Area: N/A
Duration: Special
Effect: Hypnotizes target; number of successes defines degree of control.
Multiple Actions: Yes
Description: Hypnosis is, in effect, a weaker version of Domination. While it allows characters to exert some control over the minds of others, it is harder to use, and it establishes a lower degree of control over the victim than Domination does.

A nova with Hypnosis can do anything a character with the enhancement Hypnotic Gaze (p. 174) can do (though all rolls made are Intelligence + Hypnosis, not Manipulation or Mega-Manipulation rolls). Additionally, he can establish more powerful mental control. To do so, he need only spend the required quantum points and roll Intelligence + Hypnosis in a resisted action against the target's Willpower. If the nova scores more successes, he succeeds in achieving control. The degree of control depends on how many successes the nova has left after subtracting the victim's Willpower successes, as follows:

Successes	Command Intensity
One	Very Minor: "You are getting sleepy...."
Two	Quirky: Wear a particular suit of clothes, pet an imaginary dog
Three	Minor: Eat a bug; go to a particular, easily accessible location
Four or more	Major/Noteworthy: Perform a relatively easy task for the nova

Obviously Domination is much more effective in most situations. However, when used cleverly, Hypnosis can be very effective. Hypnosis also has a longer duration than Domination. As long as the nova concentrates on the target, Hypnosis remains in effect. Once he stops concentrating, Hypnosis remains in effect, if appropriate, for a number of days equal to the character's dots in Hypnosis. This grace period usually lasts long enough for the nova to make his getaway, use an implanted post-hypnotic suggestion or take some similar action.

Extras: None

in an opposed test against the victim's Dexterity. Each net success, plus a number of automatic successes equal to the nova's Quantum, reduces the target's Dexterity by one (Mega-Dexterity dots are lost first). Attacks on a partially immobilized target gain bonuses to hit (see p. 249 for specifics). When the target's Dexterity reaches zero, he is completely immobilized.

To break out of Immobilize, the victim must exert his Strength or some other Attribute. In most cases Strength is the proper Attribute, but the Storyteller may choose another Attribute if he feels that is more appropriate — for example, if the Immobilize is defined as "locking up the victim's mind," Willpower or Wits would work better for breaking out. The Immobilize is considered to have an effective Strength, soak and number of "health levels" equal to the nova's Quantum + power rating. If this total ranges above 5, every two additional dots provide the Immobilize with effective levels of Mega-Strength — thus, a nova with Quantum 4 and Immobilize 5 creates Immobilize effects that bind targets as though they had Mega-Strength 2. When the victim does enough damage to the Immobilize to break free, it shatters or otherwise vanishes. A fully immobilized target can be automatically hit, but the Immobilize power's soak total protects the victim!

Extras: Supertough (the Immobilize effect's health levels are doubled); Intangible (Immobilize's soak and health levels do not protect victim)

Immobilize

Level: 2
Quantum Minimum: 1
Dice Pool: Dexterity + Immobilize
Range: (Quantum + power rating) x 10 meters
Area: N/A
Duration: One scene or until destroyed
Effect: This power renders a target immobile; each success subtracts one from the target's Dexterity. At zero Dexterity, the target is paralyzed.
Multiple Actions: Yes
Description: A nova with this power is able to paralyze or ensnare targets in some way, which ranges from creating blocks of ice around them, to secreting a paralytic poison, to imprisoning them within a quantum field.

To use Immobilize, the character spends the required quantum points and rolls Dexterity + Immobilize

Immolate

Level: 2
Quantum Minimum: 2
Dice Pool: N/A
Range: Self
Area: N/A
Duration: Maintenance
Effect: Character surrounds his body with a damaging effect; anyone who touches the nova takes (Quantum + power rating) x 2 dice of bashing damage or (Quantum + power rating) dice of lethal damage.
Multiple Actions: Yes

Description: This power, a variant of Quantum Bolt, allows a nova to surround himself with flame, electricity, raw quantum forces or some other dangerous substance. The player must choose when he buys the power precisely what surrounds the nova, and this decision cannot change thereafter.

When a nova Immolates, he damages anything he touches, or anything that touches him. His touch inflicts Quantum + (power rating x 3) dice of bashing damage, or Quantum + (power rating x 2) dice of lethal damage. The player must choose upon purchasing the Immolate power whether the effect is bashing or lethal, and this decision cannot be changed thereafter.

If the nova deliberately tries to touch someone, doing so counts as an attack. However, the nova can use a normal close combat attack (such as a punch) and *also* cause damage from Immolate without the use of Immolate counting as a separate action. Similarly, anyone who touches or grabs the character automatically takes the Immolate damage. This damage does not count as an action or attack by the nova.

Immolate can be extremely effective in combat, but it can also cause problems, since *anything* the nova touches takes damage. If he bumps into an innocent bystander, smashes through a wall or gas pump or simply walks down the street, he damages those people and objects — with potentially disastrous results.

Extras: Variable (Immolate may be either of two damaging substances; character may switch between them as an action); Aggravated (Immolate inflicts [power rating] levels of aggravated damage)

Intuition

Level: 1
Quantum Minimum: 1
Dice Pool: Perception + Intuition
Range: Self
Area: N/A
Duration: Permanent
Effect: Heightens character's awareness of dangers.
Multiple Actions: Yes

Description: Intuition is a lesser form of the Premonition power. Like Premonition, it warns a nova of potential threats and dangers. However, it is less sensitive, and it works somewhat differently.

As with Premonition, the player must make a Perception + Intuition roll to determine if there is danger. The differences are twofold. First, Intuition is permanent. The character does not have to spend quantum points or otherwise turn his Intuition on; it's constantly active and on the lookout for dangers. Second, the warning provided by Intuition is much less precise than the one given by Premonition. When the character makes his roll, the Storyteller simply tells him that he feels that "something is not right here." The more successes the character achieves on the roll, the more precise the Storyteller should be, but in no instance should he provide as much information as Premonition does.

Intuition alerts the character only to dangers to himself. It provides no warning if someone nearby is in danger.

Extras: None

Invisibility

Level: 2
Quantum Minimum: 1
Dice Pool: Wits + Invisibility
Range: Self
Area: N/A
Duration: Maintenance
Effect: Quantum + number of successes versus opponent's Perception to remain undetected
Multiple Actions: Yes

Description: Invisibility renders a nova undetectable to vision, and possibly other senses as well. Invisibility works against all variants of visual senses (Electromagnetic Vision, High-End Electromagnetic Scan, machines and security devices), but attempts to detect the invisible character with such enhanced vision gain an extra die unless the nova spends a Willpower point to fortify his invisible state.

To use Invisibility, the player needs only pay the quantum points and roll Wits + Invisibility. The number of successes achieved, plus a number of automatic successes equal to the character's Quantum rating, is compared to an Awareness roll for any persons directly attempting to detect the character. Players of characters who are not specifically trying to perceive the invisible character (such as the average person the invisible character passes on the street) are not allowed to roll Awareness at all. If the nova achieves the same or more successes, those trying to perceive him are completely unable to do so. Any attacks made based on that sense suffer Blind Fighting/ Fire penalties (assuming the attacker is making his attack in the proper direction or location at all).

If the onlookers achieve more successes, they perceive the character dimly — enough to launch attacks against the character at a difficulty penalty of only one.

Invisibility does not cloak a character against detection by other senses — he may still be heard, smelled, or registered on sonar, for example. However, the Enhanced Effect Extra, below, allows Invisibility to cloak the character against detection by additional senses. In the case of other senses, the Storyteller should determine any appropriate effects. For example, Invisibility to smell might require a character with Bloodhound (p. 162) to make his tracking rolls at increased difficulty.

Invisibility works only for the character's body; rendering one's clothes, effects or carried items invisible requires the Attunement Background (p. 139).

Extras: Enhanced Effect (Invisibility works versus one additional sense per success rolled)

Invulnerability

Level: 2
Quantum Minimum: 1
Dice Pool: N/A
Range: Self
Area: N/A
Duration: Permanent
Effect: Provides +6 soak per dot against a specific type of attack.
Multiple Actions: N/A

Description: Invulnerability is just what it says — it makes a character invulnerable, or nearly so, to a specific form of attack. Each dot in the power adds six soak when resisting damage from that kind of attack, even if the attack is aggravated. In the case of mental powers such as Domination, each level of Invulnerability provides six extra successes to any Willpower roll to resist the power's effects.

The character must choose the type of attack to which his Invulnerability applies. Typically this application is based on a given phenomenon (fire attacks) rather than a specific power (Quantum Bolt). Some possible examples include: any one attack form defined by an Elemental Anima or Elemental Mastery (fire, ice, earth or light); magnetic attacks or mental powers. Characters may not choose to be Invulnerable to "quantum powers," "physical attacks" or "energy attacks."

Extras: Broad Category (player can choose to be Invulnerable to "physical attacks" or "energy attacks," but not "quantum powers")

Luck

Level: 1
Quantum Minimum: 1
Dice Pool: Luck
Range: Self
Area: N/A
Duration: Permanent
Effect: Successes achieved on roll reduce damage and make tasks easier.
Multiple Actions: N/A

Description: A nova with this power is extraordinarily lucky. Somehow his quantum consciousness is able to tap into and manipulate fate, probabilities and perhaps even reality itself. Regardless of how it's done, Lady Luck smiles on the character and looks out for him.

Once per scene, a character may ask to roll his Luck. It is in the Storyteller's discretion whether the character may roll Luck; sometimes it's better for the game if the character depends on his own abilities. When the character rolls Luck, each success achieved influences the outcome of other events. Exactly what happens is up to the Storyteller, but here are some guidelines.

Combat: When the character is in combat, the player may divide the successes he gets for Luck in a given turn between his attack and his defense. Successes added to an attack grant one die per success to make the attack and determine its effects. Successes added to defense provide one success (not one die) to all dodge, parry or block rolls (or similar rolls to avoid other effects, such as Willpower rolls to counteract Domination).

Abilities: Each Luck success adds one success (not one die) to any use of Abilities out of combat. If a character makes two or more Ability checks during the same time frame (turn, minute, or whatever else the Storyteller decides is appropriate), he must divide his Luck successes among the different rolls.

Backgrounds: Luck affects rolls associated with Backgrounds just as it does with Abilities.

Remember, though, that Fate is a fickle bitch. If a character botches a Luck roll, he suddenly becomes *really* unlucky for a scene. An unlucky character botches if he rolls no successes and any die comes up 1 *or* 2.

Extras: None

Magnetic Mastery

Level: 3
Quantum Minimum: 4
Dice Pool: Variable
Range: Special
Area: Variable
Duration: Variable
Effect: Character is able to manipulate magnetism and magnetic fields.
Multiple Actions: Yes
Description: A nova with this power is a master of magnetism. She is able to lift and move metallic objects, project magnetic blasts and pulses and otherwise control and manipulate the forces of magnetism. If this power is active, a nova may Block any incoming metal attack, using Dexterity + Magnetic Mastery as the dice pool. The character may automatically make a Perception + Magnetic Mastery roll to accomplish minor feats like sensing magnetic north, gauging the strength of local magnetic fields, and the like.

As with Elemental Anima and Mastery, this power provides several techniques. A nova may learn and freely use one technique per dot in the power; she may attempt other techniques, but the player must pay double quantum points and roll against a difficulty penalty of one to use these powers. Techniques include:

EMP

Dice Pool: Wits + Magnetic Mastery
Range: (Quantum + power rating) x 10 meters
Area: N/A
Duration: Instant

The nova can emit an electromagnetic pulse that disrupts electronic equipment. To use it, the character pays the required quantum points and rolls Wits + Magnetic Mastery. The Storyteller opposes this power with a roll based on the target device's "Stamina." The Storyteller should determine the machine's Stamina based on how well shielded it is against such attacks. Most machines have a Stamina of 1 (at most); some military equipment, though, might have a Stamina of 5 or higher. For each net success the nova achieves, the machine is unable to function for one hour. At the Storyteller's option, minor technological devices may be permanently shorted out.

Magnetic Blast

Dice Pool: Dexterity + Magnetic Mastery
Range: (Quantum + power rating) x 10 meters
Area: N/A
Duration: Instant

The nova can project a damaging blast of magnetic force, similar to a Quantum Bolt. This attack inflicts [Quantum x 2] levels + (power rating x 3) dice of bashing damage.

Magnetic Field

Dice Pool: Wits + Magnetic Mastery
Range: (Quantum + power rating) x 5 meters
Area: (Quantum + power rating) x 3 meters
Duration: Concentration

The nova can create an intense magnetic field in a given area. This field interferes with electronic equipment. Each success achieved on a Wits + Magnetic Mastery roll imposes a difficulty penalty of one for any tasks attempted by or with electronic equipment. At the Storyteller's option, some shielded equipment may be able to resist this effect with a "Stamina" roll, as with the EMP power.

Magnetic Levitation

Dice Pool: N/A
Range: Self
Area: N/A
Duration: Maintenance

The nova is able to manipulate ambient magnetic fields to pick himself up and fly crudely. His flying speed is equal to (power rating x 2) + 20 meters per action, or (40 x power rating) kilometers per hour out of combat.

Magnetic Shield

Dice Pool: N/A
Range: Self
Area: N/A
Duration: Maintenance

The character can polarize metal weapons and projectiles away from herself. Each turn, the player can subtract her dots in Magnetic Mastery from the attack successes of any metal weapon used against her character. This defense also works against novas whose powers involve metal.

Magnetic Storm

Dice Pool: N/A
Range: Special
Area: (Quantum + power rating) x 5 meters
Duration: Concentration

This power allows the nova to telekinetically lift all in-range ferrous objects of 40 kgs or less, then whirl them around him in a sort of "magnetic tornado." He will not be hurt by the flying objects, but anyone within the area of effect acts at -2 to all dice pools and takes (power rating x 2) dice of bashing damage. The damage depends in part on the objects available. If there are few metallic objects in the vicinity, the Storyteller may reduce the damage done proportionally. If there are a lot of sharp objects (like knives or nails), the damage may be lethal.

Magnetize

Dice Pool: Perception + Magnetic Mastery
Range: (Quantum + power rating) x 10 meters
Area: N/A
Duration: Maintenance

The nova magnetically charges ferrous metal items within the vicinity, causing them to attract or repel one another. This could, for example, wrench a gun from a foe's hand or trap an armored guard against the metal bars of a prison cell. A magnetically charged ferrous object exerts an effective "Might" equal to the character's Quantum plus the successes scored on a Dexterity + Magnetic Mastery roll.

Magnetokinesis

Dice Pool: Dexterity + Magnetic Mastery
Range: (Quantum + power rating) x 10 meters
Area: N/A
Duration: Concentration

The nova may use his awesome magnetic powers to pick up metallic objects. Once he has them he can throw them or hit other characters with them. This feat mirrors the use of the Telekinesis power (p. 224), except that the dice pool is Dexterity + Magnetic Mastery, and only metal objects can be manipulated.

Extras: None

Matter Chameleon

Level: 3
Quantum Minimum: 5
Dice Pool: Stamina + Matter Chameleon
Range: Self
Area: N/A
Duration: Maintenance
Effect: Allows character to duplicate properties of specific types of matter.
Multiple Actions: No
Description: Matter Chameleon is similar to Bodymorph, but instead of allowing a character to assume only one form, it gives her the power to have her body take on the properties of any type of matter or energy she touches. If she touches rock, her body becomes as durable and strong as stone. If she touches tear gas, she becomes intangible and can blind people with her touch. If she touches water, she can flow through pipes and ignore many forms of attack. If she touches fire, she becomes a living flame.

To use Matter Chameleon, the nova must pay the required quantum and touch the form of matter or energy whose properties she wishes to assume (doing so does not cause her any damage, even if the substance would normally be damaging), and the player must roll Stamina + Matter Chameleon. Even one success is sufficient to allow her to assume the properties of that form; as long as she keeps paying quantum points, she will retain those properties.

Specific Traits granted by Matter Chameleon depend entirely on the material copied, often including extra Strength, soak, or damaging effects. The possibilities are nearly endless, and the Storyteller must ultimately adjudicate as she sees fit. Some general guidelines are: No substance may provide more damage or soak than the lower of a) the substance's normal properties; b) the nova's power rating x 3. No substance may provide more extra Strength levels than the nova's power rating. Exceptional levels of success may allow for modification of these guidelines.

For Example: Karen Roper has Strength 4 and Matter Chameleon 4. She sticks her hand into a junction box and scores four successes on a Stamina + Matter Chameleon roll, thus changing into living electricity. Although her Matter Chameleon rating is quite high, she can normally inflict no more than six dice of lethal damage — the amount of current available from the energy source. However, since Karen scored four successes on her roll, the Storyteller allows her to inflict eight dice of lethal damage by touch (after all, she's bigger than a junction box, thus might have more current running through her).

Next, Karen touches a flawless diamond, scoring a single success on the Stamina + Matter Chameleon roll. The Storyteller judges that a being made entirely from diamond would have at least 18 extra soak; however, because Karen has Matter Chameleon rating of only 4, she may gain a maximum of 12 extra soak by duplicating the diamond's structure. The Storyteller rules that Karen gains two extra dots of Strength (raising Karen's Strength to Mega-Strength 1) and the equivalent of four dots in the Claws power, as Karen's fingernails become diamond-hard.

If a nova wishes to use Matter Chameleon as a defense against an incoming attack (for example, to assume the properties of fire based on being hit by a blast of flame), she may do so. Doing so does not require an action, but it is easier if an action is available; if the character does not have a delayed action to use to do so, she must spend a point of Willpower instead. She then spends quantum points and rolls Stamina + Matter Chameleon; even one success allows her to assume that attack's properties, and each success reduces the damage the attack inflicts by one die or level.

For Example: Karen Roper is attacked by nerve gas. She rolls Stamina + Matter Chameleon, scoring three successes. The Storyteller rules that Karen completely ignores the effect of the gas and changes to gas herself. She gains properties similar to Bodymorph (gas); additionally, anyone enveloped by Karen will be affected as though doused with nerve gas (see the Appendix, p. 280, for details).

Matter Chameleon has a few other nice side effects, too. By spending a quantum point, the character can walk on water or other fluids at normal speed (this does not protect against the effects of fluids like acid or magma). By spending three quantum points and touching a solid such as a wall or floor, the character can attune her molecular composition to that substance, allowing her to "phase" through the solid at normal walking speed.

See Bodymorph (p. 185) for guidelines on the properties possessed by various substances.
Extras: None

Matter Creation

Level: 3
Quantum Minimum: 5
Dice Pool: Wits + Matter Creation
Range: (Quantum + power rating) meters
Area: N/A
Duration: Special
Effect: Creates matter of various sorts
Multiple Actions: Yes
Description: A nova with Matter Creation can literally create matter out of nothingness. He can create matter in its raw form — such as ordinary iron or wood — or he can create actual objects and devices — such as a sword, computer or chair.

When creating raw materials, the nova simply rolls Wits + Matter Creation. The amount of matter created depends on the number of successes rolled:

Successes	Amount of Matter
One	1 kg
Two	10 kg
Three	100 kg
Four	1,000 kg
Five	10,000 kg

Creating objects and working devices is a little more difficult. The number of successes required depends upon the nature of the object and the object's size.

Successes	Object Complexity
One	Simple Objects: A knife, a cup
Two	Complex Objects: Furniture, a book
Three	Simple Devices: A clock, a lamp
Four	Complex Devices: A desktop computer, an automobile
Five	Very Complex Devices: An airplane, a supercomputer, a missile

Difficulty	Object Size
+0	Small: Anything you could hold in one hand or arm
+1	Medium: Anything you would need two arms to hold
+2	Large: Anything you would need two or more people to hold
+3	Very Large: Anything you would need a forklift to hold

Additional Difficulties

+2	Radioactive
+3	Unknown substance; substance that

defies normal properties of physics (eufiber, for example)

There is an additional restriction on Matter Creation. The soak, health levels, and/ or dice of damage the object provides/ causes may not exceed the creator's Quantum + power rating total. Thus, a character with Quantum 5 and Matter Creation 3 can create objects that have eight health levels, provide eight soak and/ or inflict eight dice of damage (or less); he cannot create an object hard or durable enough to have nine health levels or provide nine soak.

At the Storyteller's option, creating complicated devices may require the character to have the skills necessary to build such a device from scratch. Those Abilities substitute for Wits in the roll. For example, to create a car, the character would have to roll Engineering + Matter Creation.

Once created, the substance or object remains in existence for one hour per dot in Matter Creation. A substance or object can be made permanent at the cost of a point of *permanent* Willpower.

Extras: None

Mental Blast

Level: 2
Quantum Minimum: 3
Dice Pool: Intelligence + Mental Blast
Range: (Quantum + power rating) x 10 meters
Area: N/A
Duration: Instant
Effect: Causes one level of bashing damage per success.
Multiple Actions: Yes
Description: This power allows a nova to project his "quantum consciousness" directly into another being's mind, causing psychic pain and injury. To use Mental Blast, the character pays the required quantum points and rolls Intelligence + Mental Blast in a resisted roll against the target's Willpower. Each net success achieved causes one health level of bashing damage; if bashing health levels go below zero, further Mental Blast damage is lethal.
Extras: None

Mirage

Level: 2
Quantum Minimum: 3
Dice Pool: Manipulation + Mirage
Range: (Quantum + power rating) x 20 meters
Area: N/A
Duration: Concentration
Effect: Creates illusions in target's mind.
Multiple Actions: No
Description: Unlike Holo, which creates an image that many different characters can see at once, Mirage allows a nova to project an image directly into a single target's mind. To use Mirage, the nova must spend the necessary quantum points and roll Manipulation + Mirage in a resisted action against the target's Willpower. If the nova scores more successes, he succeeds in implanting the illusion. The more net successes he has, the more complex and believable the illusion is.

Successes	Illusion Intensity
One	Simple Illusion: Change appearance or nature of existing objects or persons; create illusion that there are minor objects or people where none actually exist.
Two	Complex Illusion: Change appearance or nature of important existing objects or persons; create illusion that there are important objects or people where none actually exist; minor changes to overall environment.
Three or more	Very Complex Illusion: Illusion can completely change the target's environment or the people and objects around him.

Once the nova establishes the illusion, he must concentrate on it to maintain it. He will know how the target is reacting to it, and he can cause it to react accordingly. If the illusion does not react as the target expects (for example, someone who is the target's friend does not know who he is), the target may make a Perception roll, opposed by an Intelligence + Mirage roll, to break free from the illusion.

Unless the nova achieves three or more successes, a target cannot take damage from illusory attacks, though he might, for example, be tricked into running in front of a car as he reacts to an illusion. At three or more successes, the victim's mind will cause him to suffer injuries corresponding to those caused by illusory attacks — if shot with an illusory gun, he will take the same damage which he would take from a real gun — but regardless of the type of damage the attack would normally do, the damage is Stun Attack damage only (see Stun Attack, p. 223).

Extras: None

Molecular Manipulation

Level: 3
Quantum Minimum: 5
Dice Pool: Variable
Range: Variable
Area: Variable
Duration: Special
Effect: This power gives a character the ability to manipulate and control molecules.
Multiple Actions: Yes
Description: A nova with this power wields ultimate control over inorganic and unliving organic molecules. While he cannot change or affect living things in any way, his power is still quite impressive.

By spending a quantum point, a molecular manipulation can make a Perception + Molecular Manipulation roll to identify the chemical composition and properties of any substance within a range of [Quantum + power rating] x 20 meters.

As with Elemental Anima and Mastery, this power provides several techniques. A nova may learn and freely use one technique per dot in the power; she may attempt other techniques, but the player must pay double quantum cost and roll against a difficulty penalty of one to activate these powers. Techniques include:

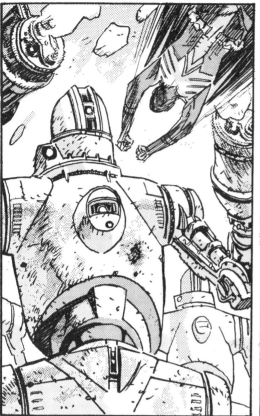

Animation

Dice Pool: Manipulation + Molecular Manipulation
Range: (Quantum + power rating) x 3 meters
Area: N/A
Duration: Concentration

The nova may "animate" inanimate objects, giving them a crude sort of quasi-life. Wheeled objects roll, furniture and other items with legs walk or run and other objects do their best to hop or otherwise motivate themselves. The character may animate one object of roughly human size for each success on the player's Intelligence + Molecular Manipulation roll. Thus, animating a couch, which is approximately twice the size of a normal human, would take two successes. Animated objects move at the character's walking pace, but this speed may increase to his running pace if he spends an additional quantum point.

Animated objects can attack targets. The Storyteller determines the objects' Strength, Stamina and health levels based on their size and the materials they are made of (the Material Strength chart on p. 257 provides some guidelines); an object's Dexterity is equal to the character's normal Wits Attribute. If the object has any special abilities (such as a gun, which could shoot others while animated), it may use them; the Storyteller should determine the exact effects and appropriate damage.

Destruction

Dice Pool: Dexterity + Molecular Manipulation
Range: (Quantum + power rating) x 10 meters
Area: N/A
Duration: Instant

The character unravels or destroys the molecular bonds holding an unliving object together, causing it to disintegrate. Doing so inflicts Quantum + Molecular Manipulation health levels of damage to the target object. Objects may soak; the Storyteller should determine how much damage they can soak based on the materials they are made of and how well they are constructed.

Molecular Alteration

Dice Pool: Intelligence + Molecular Manipulation
Range: (Quantum + power rating) x 5 meters
Area: N/A
Duration: Permanent

The character can convert the molecules of an unliving solid or liquid into molecules of another unliving solid or liquid, thus, for example, transforming a wooden chair into a steel chair. The nature of the changes a char-

Successes	Transmutation
One	Change Substance: The character may change the elements or substance of which an object is made, but he cannot change the object's shape or size. A wooden chair becomes a chair of solid gold; a steel knife becomes a knife of silk.
Two	Change Size: As Change Substance, plus the character can make the object larger or smaller by up to 20% per success over one (20% at the minimum two successes needed for this effect; 40% at three successes; and so forth).
Three	Change Shape: As Change Size, plus the object's shape can be changed. A wooden chair can be transformed into a lump of gold; a steel knife becomes a dress of silk.
Four	Change Complexity: As Change Size, plus the object's nature or complexity can be transformed — it can be made into working electrical circuits and moving parts. Thus, a tree can be changed into a working computer or a car.

Second Skin

Dice Pool: N/A
Range: Self
Area: N/A
Duration: Maintenance

By hardening air molecules in a film about himself, the nova can protect himself with a layer of armor. For each dot in Molecular Alteration, the nova gains +2 soak versus bashing and lethal damage.

Shape Alteration

Dice Pool: Wits + Molecular Manipulation
Range: Touch
Area: N/A
Duration: Special

The character can alter the shape of inanimate objects. He can alter the shape of 10 kilograms of any given substance per success rolled on an Intelligence + Molecular Manipulation roll. He need not affect an entire object to alter its shape, but he can alter only that part of the object which he is able to affect. He can cause a hole to open in the object (handy for getting through locked doors), make it grow crude arms or legs, or just change its appearance or ability to function. The changes remain until the nova reverses them or repairs are made.

A nova with this power can attempt to repair inorganic objects. The nova must have at least some knowledge of the subject to be fixed (generally speaking, at least one dot in Engineering). The nova then rolls Molecular Manipulation + Engineering (or other appropriate Ability); each success repairs one "health level" of damage suffered by the object.

Extras: None

acter can enact with Molecular Alteration depends upon the number of successes he achieves on an Intelligence + Molecular Manipulation roll.

The character may not create objects from thin air; that requires Matter Creation.

At the Storyteller's option, creating devices with Change Complexity may require the character to have the skills necessary to build such a device from scratch. Those Abilities substitute for Intelligence in the roll. For example, to create a car, the character would have to roll Engineering + Molecular Manipulation.

Once created, the substance or object remains in existence for one hour per dot in Molecular Manipulation. A substance or object can be made permanent at the cost of a point of *permanent* Willpower.

Poison

Level: 2
Quantum Minimum: 1
Dice Pool: Stamina + Poison
Range: Touch
Area: N/A
Duration: Instant
Effect: Character's touch can poison or infect another person.
Multiple Actions: Yes

Description: A nova with this ability can poison or drug someone with a touch or infect him with a disease. For purposes of this power, poisons, venoms, toxins, drugs and similar substances are considered to do Stun Attack (per the power of the same name), bashing or lethal damage; some poisons subtract from dice pools instead. The amount of damage the character's touch can inflict depends upon the type of damage and a Stamina + Poison roll; the character may add a number of successes equal to his Quantum. Each success gives him one level of Stun Attack damage; two successes are required to get a level of bashing damage, or to subtract one die from the victim's dice pools, and three successes are required for each level of lethal poison damage.

Diseases are handled differently. The number of successes achieved on the roll determine the virulence of the disease that can be inflicted. The victim may resist with a Resistance roll; net successes are compared to the table below:

Successes	Virulence Equivalent
One	Minor, nonfatal diseases: Colds, influenza
Two	Major, nonfatal diseases: Many types of fever, chicken pox
Three	Fatal diseases: HIV, leprosy
Four	Extremely fatal diseases: Ebola fever, Marburg fever, Lhasa fever

Conventional armor, including powers such as Force Field, usually offers little protection against poisons and diseases. A nova with the Adaptability enhancement may soak poison effects with his Stamina/Mega-Stamina soak; at the Storyteller's option, a Resistance roll may help to counteract a poison's effects (in whole or in part). Remember that most poisons and diseases do not work instantly — they have an "onset time" measured in hours, days, or weeks. Characters who expect to use this power to cause fatalities in combat are likely to be disappointed.

Extras: Projectile (can spit, exhale or otherwise expel a venom or virus at a range of 10 meters x power rating).

Premonition

Level: 2
Quantum Minimum: 1
Dice Pool: Perception + Premonition
Range: Variable
Area: Special
Duration: One scene
Effect: Allows character to detect danger or threats to himself.
Multiple Actions: Yes
Description: This sensory power warns the nova of impending dangers or threats. To use it, the character pays the quantum-point cost, which allows her to detect danger for one scene. Whenever she is confronted with any danger during that time — she is about to trip a trap, someone points a gun at her, etc. — the player may make a Perception + Premonition roll to detect it. The difficulty should be set by the Storyteller, depending on the severity of the danger (the greater the potential harm, the easier it is to detect) and how likely it is to affect the character (a direct threat is easier to detect than something that might adversely affect the character but isn't intended for her).

Premonition can detect threats specifically directed at the character (someone about to stab her with a knife) as well as threats directed at her general area (a terrorist's bomb that's about to destroy the building she's in). The danger must be within about (100 x Premonition) meters of him in most cases, though the Storyteller may, at her discretion, expand this range. Specific dangers (such as a sniper pointing a gun at the character from a thousand meters away) can usually be detected further away than general threats.

A successful Premonition roll does not tell the character exactly what the danger is, only that she is exposed to it and from roughly which direction or location it is coming. In most cases warning is enough to provide the character with the information she needs to avoid the danger. For example, suppose the character is about to walk through a door and her Premonition alerts her to a possible threat. If the Premonition indicates that the danger is coming from the door itself, the door is probably rigged for some kind of booby trap. If the danger comes from beyond the door, a more likely explanation is that someone — or something — is waiting on the other side of the door to attack or hurt the character.

Premonition does not detect danger to those near the character unless the character herself is somehow exposed to the threat.

Extras: Others (the character's Premonition can detect dangers to anyone within about [10 x Premonition] meters of the character)

For dramatic purposes, the Storyteller may, at his discretion, increase the timeframe. For example, if a nova with Pretercognition found an ancient Egyptian artifact, the Storyteller might let her "read" images associated with its creation, even though it is thousands of years old, because those visions contain a clue she needs to solve a mystery.

Storytellers should be very careful about allowing this power in their series. It can have an enormous impact on the characters' actions and on society, and it can make it virtually impossible to run scenarios that revolve around mysteries or puzzles. However, there's no guarantee that the visions received are absolutely accurate....

Extras: None

Pretercognition

Level: 3
Quantum Minimum: 4
Dice Pool: Perception + Pretercognition
Range: Self
Area: N/A
Duration: Instant
Effect: Allows character to foresee future (or view past) events; number of successes determines timeframe.
Multiple Actions: No
Description: Pretercognition allows a nova to foresee future events or grants glimpses of the past.

The timeframe within which the character can "view" events is based on the number of successes achieved on a Perception + Pretercognition roll.

Successes	Timeframe
One	Up to one hour per dot
Two	Up to one day per dot
Three	Up to one week per dot
Four	Up to one month per dot
Five	Up to one year per dot
Six	Up to 10 years per dot

Psychic Shield

Level: 1
Quantum Minimum: 1
Dice Pool: N/A
Range: Self
Area: N/A
Duration: Permanent
Effect: Provides two extra successes per dot on all attempts to resist mental powers.
Multiple Actions: N/A
Description: Psychic Shield is a potent defense against powers that directly affect a nova's mind (Domination, Hypnosis, Mental Blast, Mirage or Telepathy). Each dot grants two extra successes to any roll to resist mental powers. If the power causes damage, like Mental Blast, then Psychic Shield also provides two extra soak per dot. Psychic Shield is permanent, but a character may voluntarily shut it off if he wishes (he can reactivate it at any time, which does not require an action).

Psychic Shield does not work against emotion-controlling powers (Empathic Manipulation, many of the Mega-Social enhancements), only direct mind control.

Extras: Extra Mind (character may extend his Psychic Shield to protect one other person whom he is touching)

age, not [power rating x 4]; however, each such shot inflicts a bashing health level of damage on the nova due to the stress of channeling the excess energy, and any botch on the targeting roll inflicts a point of temporary Taint)

Quantum Bolt

Level: 2
Quantum Minimum: 1
Dice Pool: Dexterity + Quantum Bolt
Range: (Quantum + power rating) x 15 meters
Area: N/A
Duration: Instant
Effect: Inflicts [Quantum x 3] levels + (power rating x 4) dice of bashing damage or [Quantum x 2] levels + (power rating x 4) dice of lethal damage (player's choice).

Multiple Actions: Yes

Description: Quantum Bolt, in its myriad forms, is one of the most common offensive powers used by novas. It allows a nova to project a damaging blast of energy at a target. The damage may be either lethal or bashing (the player must choose what type of damage the power does when he buys it). The target takes [Quantum Trait x 3] levels + (power rating x 4) dice of bashing damage or [Quantum Trait x 2] levels + (power rating x 4) dice of lethal damage.

A nova might try to pull an unusual "stunt" with her Quantum Bolt, such as bouncing it off a surface to hit an opponent in the back. The Storyteller may, at his discretion, allow this effect if the nova achieves a sufficient number of successes on a Dexterity + Quantum Bolt roll.

A nova's Quantum Bolt must be defined as a specific type of energy or power, such as fire, ice, lightning, bioenergy or a laser, when the character is created. The energy type cannot be changed thereafter.

Quantum Bolt cannot normally use the standard Ranged Combat Maneuvers, such as Automatic Fire (p. 247). However, for each dot in the power above three, a nova may choose one such maneuver for her Quantum Bolt. She does not have to use the maneuver unless she wishes to, but it's available as a "power stunt" that she has trained herself to perform. Performing a maneuver costs one extra quantum point in addition to the points spent to fuel the power itself.

Extras: Extra Energy Type (power may manifest as one additional form of energy); Supercharge (character can spend three quantum points to have her Quantum Bolt inflict [power rating x 6] dice of appropriate dam-

Quantum Construct

Level: 3
Quantum Minimum: 4; must also have Force Field • or better
Dice Pool: Manipulation + Quantum Construct
Range: (Quantum + power rating) meters
Area: N/A
Duration: Maintenance
Effect: This power enables the character to create "creatures" or objects out of quantum force; the number of successes achieved indicates what beings can be summoned and how many.

Multiple Actions: No

Description: A nova with Quantum Construct is capable of generating raw quantum forces, then shaping them into animate creatures that act at the nova's whim. Many novas with this power use it to summon "demons" and other such creatures of legend. Regardless of the creatures' appearance, though, they are obviously made from quantum forces — a character with control over electromagnetic energies might summon constructs of living lightning, radiant energy or the like. Quantum Construct cannot create a duplicate of a specific person or the like.

To use Quantum Construct, a nova must spend the required quantum points and roll Manipulation + Quantum Construct. The number of successes indicate what type of creature can be summoned.

Characters may create more than one being in some circumstances. First, if they want a being smaller than those listed on the chart, they may "divide" the listed size up among multiple beings. For example, with two successes, a nova could create one human-sized being, two beings of half human size, four beings of one-quar-

Successes	Being(s) Summoned
One	One being no larger than a sheep (Strength and Stamina 1, Dexterity 3, four health levels)
Two	One being no larger than a human (All Physical Attributes 2, normal human health levels)
Three	One being no larger than twice human size (Strength and Stamina 4, Dexterity 2, eight health levels)
Four	One being no larger than four times human size (Mega-Strength 1/Strength 4, Stamina 4, Dexterity 2, +1 soak, 10 "Hurt" health levels)
Five	One being no larger than eight times human size (Mega-Strength 2/Strength 4, Stamina 4, Dexterity 2, +2 soak, 12 "Hurt" health levels)

Constructs are simply shaped matrices of quantum energy; they are directed by their creator, have no Mental, Social or Willpower Traits, and are immune to attacks dependent on those Traits (for example, Domination or Dreadful Mien). Furthermore, constructs feel no pain and suffer no wound penalties. Constructs can, however, be dispelled by powers such as Disrupt.

ter human size or a larger number of mouse- or insect-sized creatures. Second, if the character achieves more successes than needed to create the being he wants, he may use the extra successes to increase the numbers — each extra success doubles the number of constructs. For example, suppose a nova wants to summon a human-sized demon, and the player rolls four successes. The two additional successes double his numbers twice, allowing him to summon four demons.

Some constructs may have additional powers. A creation success can be converted into five nova points, which are used to provide Mega-Attributes or quantum powers to the summoned creatures. All such creatures have a Quantum Trait of 1 and 22 quantum points unless the nova spends creation successes to raise Quantum (one success per one additional Quantum dot).

The nova who summoned the constructs may (at any time and any range) "banish" them, dispersing them into the surrounding medium. No roll is required to do so.

Ultimately, the Storyteller is responsible for coming up with the game statistics and rules for created constructs, though he may let the player do the work and

simply review and approve what the player creates. The Storyteller should be careful not to let this power unbalance or ruin the game; just because a nova has the ability to summon an army of demonic soldiers doesn't mean he should be allowed to.

This power is extremely wrenching to the surroundings, and it is best used only once a scene. If a nova attempts to use it more than once per scene, each additional attempt costs double the quantum points and incurs a difficulty penalty of one.

Extras: None

Quantum Conversion

Level: 1
Quantum Minimum: 1
Dice Pool: Stamina + Quantum Conversion
Range: Touch
Area: N/A
Duration: Special
Effect: May convert up to one quantum point per dot into standard forms of energy.
Multiple Actions: Yes
Description: Quantum Conversion is sometimes considered one of the more unusual powers novas display, yet it is undoubtedly one of the more useful ones in a practical, everyday sense. It allows a nova to convert part of his personal quantum energies — his Quantum Pool — into standard forms of superquantum energies such as heat, fire or electricity. The player must choose what type of energy the nova can convert his quantum points into.

Quantum Conversion can convert up to one quantum point per dot into another form of energy. If converted into electricity, one quantum point would be enough to power a typical large television for about an hour. The Storyteller is the final arbiter of how much electricity is needed to power a given device, and for how long. He also determines the effects and uses of other forms of energy.

Quantum Conversion can also be used to cause damage to other people if the nova touches them while emitting the energy. Doing so causes one health level of bashing damage per quantum point converted (or one health level of lethal damage per two quantum points converted), but the person touched may soak this damage normally.

Extras: Extra Energy Type (power may convert quantum points into one additional type of energy; character chooses which type of energy to emit with any given use of the power)

Quantum Imprint

Level: 3
Quantum Minimum: 4
Dice Pool: Dexterity + Quantum Imprint
Range: Touch
Area: N/A
Duration: Maintenance
Effect: Copies the powers and abilities of character touched.

Multiple Actions: No

Description: Quantum Imprint allows a nova to copy the quantum signature of another nova. By touching another nova, he can duplicate some or all of that nova's powers in himself. The nova touched does not lose any of his powers or suffer any injury.

To use Quantum Imprint, the nova must make a Dexterity + Quantum Imprint roll to touch the victim. If the touch succeeds, the nova may copy one of the victim's Attributes, skills, abilities or powers for each dot he has in Quantum Imprint — but he may only copy them up to his number of dots in Quantum Imprint. For example, if a nova has Quantum Imprint 2 and wants to copy two of another nova's powers, he may do so, but he only gets two dots in each power, even if the other nova has five dots in them. He may also never gain more dots or use the power at a greater level of effect than the target nova — for example, if a nova with Quantum 5 and Quantum Imprint 5 steals a Quantum Bolt from a nova with Quantum 2 and Quantum Bolt 2, the Quantum Bolt can inflict no greater damage than permitted with Quantum 2 and Quantum Bolt 2. The nova must also pay one more quantum point to use a stolen power than he would have to pay if he had that power "naturally." Thus, the nova in the previous example would have to pay three quantum points to throw his copied Quantum Bolt.

Furthermore, when using his imprinted powers, the nova may only roll the base Attribute — he does not get to roll any dice for the power itself. For example, if a nova imprinted two dots' worth of Quantum Bolt, he would roll only his Dexterity, not Dexterity + Quantum Bolt, when determining the power's effects.

Extras: None

Quantum Leech

Level: 2
Quantum Minimum: 2
Dice Pool: N/A
Range: Touch
Area: N/A
Duration: Instant
Effect: A successful use transfers (Quantum + power rating) quantum points from the target nova to the nova using Quantum Leech.

Multiple Actions: Yes

Description: Many novas fear this power, for it takes from them the one thing they treasure most — quantum power, in the form of quantum points. To use this power, a nova pays *one* quantum point and touches the victim (standard contest of Dexterity if the touch is resisted). The player rolls Intelligence + Quantum Leech against the victim's Willpower. If the nova wins the contest, he transfers a number of quantum points equal to his (Quantum + power rating) from the victim to his (the nova's) own Quantum Pool. This transfer even allows the nova to exceed his natural Quantum Pool limit, up to twice his normal Quantum Pool; however, if the nova botches a roll to steal power exceeding his normal limits, he gains one or more points of temporary Taint. He retains those points until he uses them or becomes unconscious (including going to sleep). The nova from whom the points have been leached recovers them in the usual fashion at the normal rate.

Extras: Energy Siphon (may use Quantum Leech at a range of [Quantum + power rating] x 5 meters)

Quantum Regeneration

Level: 2
Quantum Minimum: 3
Dice Pool: N/A
Range: Self
Area: N/A
Duration: Special
Effect: Spend one Willpower to add (power rating x 2) to the amount of quantum points recovered per hour

Multiple Actions: Yes

Description: Most novas recover the spent quantum points at a steady, predictable rate — two points per hour while at ease, or four points per hour if completely relaxed. A nova with Quantum Regeneration can recover them far more quickly than that.

To use Quantum Regeneration, the character waits until he is about to start resting to recover quantum points. He spends one or more points of Willpower (not quantum points). For each point of Willpower spent, he may add twice his power rating to the amount of points he will recover in the next hour. For example, if a nova spent two points of Willpower and had Quantum Regeneration 4, he would recover 20 quantum points (4 + 8 + 8) in an hour of complete relaxation.

Extras: Double (doubles the effect of Willpower spent when using this power; each point of Willpower spent counts as two points).

Quantum Vampire

Level: 2
Quantum Minimum: 3
Dice Pool: Stamina + Quantum Vampire
Range: Touch
Area: N/A
Duration: Special
Effect: A successful use transfers a defined Attribute or power from the target nova to the nova using Quantum Vampire.

Multiple Actions: Yes

Description: Quantum Vampire is similar to Quantum Leech, but it allows a nova to steal powers or abilities other than quantum points from another person (nova or not). The player must define which single power, Attribute or Trait the nova can steal when he buys the power. Quantum Vampire cannot steal Mega-Attributes or quantum powers from a dormant nova, nor can it steal quantum powers that have been affected by the Disrupt power (p. 190).

To use this power, a nova pays the normal quantum-point cost and touches the victim. The player then rolls Stamina + Quantum Vampire against the victim's Willpower. If the nova wins the contest, he transfers a number of dots of the Trait equal to his number of successes from the victim to his (the nova's) own Trait. He retains those dots of power for one hour per dot in Quantum Vampire; the victim loses them for that period of time. No Trait can be reduced below zero.

If stealing an Attribute from a victim with a Mega-Attribute, the nova steals the Mega-Attribute dots first; however, the nova must transfer stolen dots to his normal Attribute (raising it to 5) before gaining the appropriate Mega-Attribute. If the energy vampire is in the Mega-Attribute range, points transferred from a similar Mega-Attribute raise the nova's own Mega-Attribute normally; however, if stealing normal Attribute dots to raise a Mega-Attribute, the nova must steal two Attribute dots to raise the Mega-Attribute by one dot.

For Example: Abyss, with Strength 3, no Mega-Strength and Quantum Vampire 4, attacks Core, who has Mega-Strength 3. Abyss hits Core and rolls three net successes. Core loses all three dots of his Mega-Strength, reducing him to his normal Strength rating of 5. Abyss gains three dots of Strength, pushing him to Mega-Strength 1 (Strength 4, then Strength 5, then Mega-Strength 1). If Abyss uses the power on Core again, he must score two net successes (reducing Core to Strength 3) to raise his Mega-Strength to 2.

If a nova uses Quantum Vampire to steal a power or ability he does not possess on his own (for example, he leaches Quantum Bolt, but he does not possess that power himself), the nova may roll only the base Attribute — he does not get to roll any dice for the power itself. For example, if a nova leached two dots' worth of Quantum Bolt, he would roll only his Dexterity, not Dexterity + Quantum Bolt (or Dexterity + Quantum Vampire, for that matter), when determining the power's effects. Furthermore, he must pay an additional quantum point when using any such power.

A nova may define this power as the ability to steal "life energy" (health levels) from his victim; if this option is chosen, the target may resist with Willpower or Resistance (whichever is greater). The target takes automatic bashing damage, while the nova gains "Bruised" health levels. If Quantum Vampire reduces the target below Incapacitated, the nova may begin inflicting lethal health levels of damage with the power, gaining life-force (extra health levels) normally. Damage inflicted by Quantum Vampire is treated as normal damage and may be healed normally; this does not affect the vampiric nova's stolen health levels.

Extras: Extended Duration (the nova keeps stolen powers for two hours per dot, and the victim loses them during that time); Multiple Traits (nova may steal dots from two Traits at once; successes rolled must be divided between the two Traits in whatever proportion the nova's player wishes)

Extras: None

Sensory Shield

Level: 1
Quantum Minimum: 1
Dice Pool: N/A
Range: Self
Area: N/A
Duration: Permanent
Effect: Each dot cancels two successes on Strobe attacks made against the character.
Multiple Actions: N/A
Description: Sensory Shield provides novas with protection against Strobe attacks and other phenomena that might interfere with their senses. It can represent eyes which are accustomed to extremely bright lights, armored skin which is so tough the character's nerves cannot be numbed and many other abilities.

Sensory Shield requires no rolls. Instead, each dot in the power counts as two successes to cancel out successes achieved on Strobe rolls and successes from attacks such as tear gas.

Extras: None.

Shapeshift

Level: 3
Quantum Minimum: 4
Dice Pool: Stamina + Shapeshift
Range: Self
Area: N/A
Duration: Maintenance
Effect: Allows character to alter her shape; the degree of alteration depends upon the successes achieved.

Multiple Actions: Yes

Description: Shapeshift is one of the most versatile nova powers. It allows a nova to use quantum energies to reshape her own body. With the proper degree of power and skill, she can turn herself into various animals, pieces of furniture or just about anything else she can think of.

Once a character has so much as a single dot in this power, she is able to alter her shape. However, she might not be able to make her transformation complete — it requires considerable precision to copy every detail of an object. An untrained nova might, for example, turn himself into a tiger but not manage to create the claws; or she could change shape into a bird but not create the wings properly, so she would not be able to fly. More experienced shapeshifters rarely have these problems.

The degree of change a character can work on her own body depends on the number of successes achieved on a Stamina + Shapeshift roll. If even one success is achieved, the character can alter her shape, but not her size or mass, and she cannot simulate any powers or Mega-Attribute enhancements. Successes beyond the first may be divided among the powers or enhancements that the character wishes to simulate. For example, if the character wants to assume the form of an eagle and rolls five successes, she could allocate one success each to Claws and Flight and two to Shrinking to simulate her eagle body. Some examples of powers and enhancements often used by shapeshifters include: Armor, Body Modification (each Body Modification costs one dot), Claws, Clinging, Flight, Growth, Shrinking and Life Support. When simulating a power that requires a roll, the character substitutes her Stamina + Shapeshift skill total for the power's normal dice pool. A nova may put no more dots into a duplicated power than she has in the Shapeshift power; for example, a nova with Shapeshift 3 who wishes to turn her skeleton into armored plates may not convert more than three Shapeshift successes into Armor dots.

A nova can use Shapeshift to disguise herself as someone else. Looking like a generic "other person" requires only one success. Imitating a specific person requires at least two successes. Doing so allows the character to simulate the Mega-Appearance enhancement Copycat.

Note that the Storyteller is perfectly within her rights to deny simulated powers she feels are unreasonable for the shape assumed. Generally speaking, Shapeshift may duplicate only physical powers; for example, a character who shapeshifts into a dragon might well gain Sizemorph (Grow), Claws and Armor powers, but he could not gain the ability to breathe fire (Quantum Bolt).

Extras: None

Shroud

Level: 2
Quantum Minimum: 1
Dice Pool: Dexterity + Shroud
Range: (Quantum + power rating) x 15 meters
Area: (Quantum + power rating) x 5 meter radius
Duration: Concentration
Effect: Creates a field that stifles senses; each success subtracts one from effective Perception Traits.

Multiple Actions: Yes

Description: The nova creates a field of opaque quantum energy, inky blackness, blinding mist or other such effect. This Shroud is difficult for other characters to see through. By spending a Willpower point on activation, the character can also hinder other forms of vision; for example, the Shroud could also affect Electromagnetic Vision.

To use Shroud, the character must roll to target the area he wants to affect with his Shroud field, using Dexterity + Shroud. Failure indicates the power misses outright. Each success achieved subtracts one from the effective Perception Traits of all beings immersed in the Shroud (or who are trying to perceive into the Shroud). Characters whose Perception Traits are reduced to zero cannot perceive into or through the area at all and are considered "blind" if fighting within it. See the Strobe power (p. 223) for more information on the effects of blindness.

Extras: Sensory Deprivation Field (Shroud affects one additional normal or nova sense per success on the power roll — for example, hearing, sonar or Quantum Attunement); Semisolid (Shroud halves movement of characters trapped within it and can be formed into a "wall" to soak one level of bashing or lethal damage per dot in the power rating)

then takes all four extra Bruised boxes and his normal Hurt box. If he then returns to normal size, those four extra boxes of Bruised damage are applied normally to reduce him to Crippled.

Extras: None

Sizemorph (Grow)

Level: 2
Quantum Minimum: 1
Dice Pool: N/A
Range: Self
Area: N/A
Duration: Maintenance
Effect: Double height and mass, +2 Strength, +1 Stamina and one extra "Bruised" health level per dot.

Multiple Actions: N/A

Description: By channeling quantum forces into his molecular structure, the character may increase his height. Each dot doubles the character's height, reach and mass. Each dot of Sizemorph (Grow) also increases the character's Strength by two and his Stamina by one and adds two to his Dexterity solely for purposes of determining how fast he can walk or run. If Strength or Stamina exceeds 5, the power then provides the appropriate Mega-Attribute, up to a maximum of 5. Additionally, each dot of Sizemorph (Grow) adds an extra "Bruised" health level to the character's damage track, making it much harder to incapacitate him.

However, all is not sunshine and roses. Every two dots of Sizemorph (Grow) grants opponents an extra die to attack or perceive the character. Furthermore, if the character suffers more than two boxes' worth of damage (bashing or lethal) while grown, those boxes may be absorbed (in whole or in part) by the extra "Bruised" health levels, but if the damage is not healed before he returns to normal size (and loses those extra levels), the boxes of damage are applied to the character's damage track normally — so a seemingly trivial wound suffered while using Sizemorph (Grow) may actually prove fatal when the character returns to his ordinary size.

For Example: Abelard Smith has Sizemorph (Grow) 4 and a normal Strength 3, Stamina 3, providing him with +8 Strength (which equates to Strength 5, Mega-Strength 5), +4 Stamina (which equates to Stamina 5, Mega-Stamina 2) and four extra "Bruised" health levels. While using Sizemorph (Grow), he takes six boxes of bashing damage. This damage reduces him to Bruised,

Sizemorph (Shrink)

Level: 2
Quantum Minimum: 1
Dice Pool: N/A
Range: Self
Area: N/A
Duration: Maintenance
Effect: Each level halves height and reduces mass to 1/8 normal, adds one to all Stealth attempts and increases difficulty to hit character by one.

Multiple Actions: Yes

Description: Sizemorph (Shrink) allows a nova to become smaller and lighter than normal — sometimes much smaller. Each dot of (Quantum + Sizemorph (Shrink)) reduces a nova's height by half and his mass to 1/8 of normal. Furthermore, each (Quantum + Sizemorph (Shrink)) level adds one die to all Stealth attempts and increases the difficulty to hit the character with attacks by one. Sizemorph (Shrink) also has less tangible benefits, such as allowing a character to fit inside small pipes, crawl under doors and be carried in a friend's pocket.

Each level of Sizemorph (Shrink) reduces the character's Strength and offensive powers by one dot (to a minimum of 1), though not against creatures who are likewise shrunk or just very small. Additionally, each level of Sizemorph (Shrink) halves the character's walking/ running and swimming movement rates while he is shrunk (but not other modes of movement, like Flight or the expansion of running provided by Hyperrunning). By greatly decreasing the character's mass, Sizemorph (Shrink) also makes it easier to throw the character, knock him around with attacks or bowl him over with gusts of wind.

Extras: Full Power (character's Strength and offensive capabilities do not decrease as he shrinks)

Strobe

Level: 2
Quantum Minimum: 1
Dice Pool: Wits + Strobe
Range: (Quantum + power rating) x 10 meters
Area: N/A
Duration: Instant
Effect: Each success disables one of the target's senses for one turn.
Multiple Actions: Yes

Description: This power allows a nova to project an energy field that disables one of an opponent's senses temporarily. It is usually used to blind a character's sight (typically through a flash of bright light or something similar), but it can also deafen a target (through extremely loud focused sound), deprive him of his sense of smell or numb his sense of touch.

The player must choose which sense his power affects when he buys it, which cannot be changed thereafter; exotic senses, such as ESP and Premonition, are also susceptible to this power. To use the power, he spends the required quantum points and rolls Wits + Strobe. Each success deprives the target of the use of that sense for one turn; five or more successes wipe out the sense for an entire scene. A blind character is subject to Blind Fighting/ Fire penalties; a numb character has a +3 difficulty on all tasks involving touch (including holding and wielding a weapon or gun). The Storyteller should adjudicate the effects of the loss of other senses on a case-by-case basis.

Extras: Sensory Deprivation Wave (power affects one normal or nova sense per success on the targeting roll)

Stun Attack

Level: 2
Quantum Minimum: 1
Dice Pool: Dexterity + Stun Attack
Range: (Quantum + power rating) x 15 meters
Area: N/A
Duration: Instant
Effect: (Quantum + successes) levels of damage only to daze or knock out target.
Multiple Actions: Yes

Description: This attack power is similar to Quantum Bolt, but it does not cause lasting harm to a target. All it can do is daze the target or knock him unconscious. For this reason it has no effect on unliving targets, such as buildings, vehicles or devices.

To use Stun Attack, the character spends the required quantum points and rolls Dexterity + Stun Attack. The successes achieved, plus the nova's Quantum, are compared to those rolled by the target with his Stamina. If the nova has the greater number of successes, the net successes are compared to the target's Stamina. If they equal the target's Stamina or exceed it by one, the target is Dazed; if they exceed the target's Stamina by two or more, the target is rendered Unconscious. See p. 249 for information on Dazed and Unconscious characters.

The target may spend Willpower to reduce the nova's successes. Each point of Willpower spent negates one success.

Extras: None

Telekinesis

Level: 2
Quantum Minimum: 2
Dice Pool: Dexterity + Telekinesis
Range: (Quantum + power rating) x 10 meters
Area: N/A
Duration: Maintenance
Effect: Character may lift and move physical objects without touching them; the more successes obtained, the greater the weight that can be lifted.

Multiple Actions: Yes

Description: Telekinesis is the ability to lift and move objects without touching them by applying quantum energies to them. This ability may manifest as a mental power, focused winds, energy "tentacles" or "talons," gravity manipulation or many other powers.

To use Telekinesis ("TK"), a nova must pay the required quantum points and roll Dexterity + Telekinesis, adding a number of automatic successes equal to Quantum. The number of successes indicates how much weight

Successes	Weight
One	50 kg
Two	100 kg
Three	200 kg
Four	500 kg
Five	1,000 kg
Six	2,000 kg
Seven	5,000 kg
Eight	10,000 kg
Nine	25,000 kg
Ten	50,000 kg

Each success beyond 10 doubles the weight that can be lifted.

the character can lift.

A character can move an object he has picked up a number of meters per action equal to 10 meters per dot

in Telekinesis.

Telekinesis has other uses as well. For example, a nova might use it to grab another character and keep him from moving. Doing so requires a resisted action pitting the nova's player's successes against the victim's successes on a Might roll. Ties go to the nova, and the victim remains trapped. TK can also be used to throw objects as if the nova's successes were successes on a Might roll (see p. 236). It is usually easier to throw objects at another character than to try to hold him telekinetically.

Telekinesis can be used to bash other characters with objects or telekinetically "punch" or crush them. In this case, the successes on a Dexterity + Telekinesis roll count as health levels of bashing damage, which may be soaked as normal. Additionally, TK can be used to guide and/or accelerate a thrown weapon, object or similar projectile; the character spends quantum points normally, throws the object, then may assign dots in her Telekinesis power rating to the object's attack or damage dice pool. Dots in the power rating may be split between attack and damage dice pools (e.g, a character with Telekinesis 4 can add two dice to her roll to hit and two dice to her damage effect).

Performing delicate tasks with Telekinesis can be difficult; it works better for cruder activities like lifting and moving. If a character tries to use a Dexterity Ability with TK, he first must be able to perform that Ability naturally — Telekinesis doesn't automatically teach a character how to pick locks or pilot aircraft. Assuming he has the required skills, every two successes on his Dexterity + Telekinesis roll count as one success for purposes of performing the skill.

Telekinesis has no action/ reaction; a character cannot be dragged by something which he is holding onto telekinetically (say, a vehicle). Nor can he use TK to pick himself up and fly.

Extras: None

Telepathy

Level: 2
Quantum Minimum: 3
Dice Pool: Perception + Telepathy
Range: Line of sight or Special

Area: N/A

Duration: Concentration

Effect: Allows character to read minds, scan for minds and alter memories.

Multiple Actions: No

Description: This versatile and efficient power grants a nova several related abilities which typically manifest as "mental powers." A telepathic nova is able to use his quantum consciousness to read the minds of others and perform similar tasks.

Specifically, Telepathy can do three things: read another person's mind and "talk" with him mentally, sense other minds and alter another person's memories. For each use, the player must pay the required quantum points and roll Perception + Telepathy; the more successes he gets, the greater the nova's degree of power.

Telepathy can be used to read and communicate with any mind within range, provided the nova can establish a line of sight to his target. A character whose mind is being read is automatically aware of that fact and of who is doing the reading. Each success achieved on the Perception + Telepathy roll allows the telepath to find and read one fact per action. Thus, with five successes a nova could find and "read" five facts per action. The Storyteller may, in his discretion, rule that some facts are so well-hidden that they require multiple successes to find and read. For example, intimate or very personal thoughts might require three successes each; criminal activities or information with which the character could be blackmailed require four successes each and the deepest, most hidden thoughts or facts require five successes each. Mental conversation takes place at the same rate as normal conversation, but Telepathy overcomes the language barrier — two characters who cannot speak to each other verbally because they don't know the same languages can communicate without difficulty using Telepathy.

Telepathy can also be used to scan for another person's mind or "mental signature." The telepath may find a specific mind within a variable distance, provided he scores at least one success on his roll. That one success tells him the person's general location and direction, but nothing more. The more successes, the more precisely the location can be determined. A telepath must have a specific mind to search for. If he can only describe the mind "generically" ("I'm looking for the mind of the nearest UN official"), the difficulty of the roll increases by one or more (Storyteller's discretion). Once he finds the victim's mind, the telepath may attempt mental communication/ reading normally.

Telepathic Scanning

Successes	Distance
One	two kilometers
Two	20 kilometers
Three	200 kilometers
Four	2000 kilometers
Five	20000 kilometers

Each success beyond five multiplies the scanning distance by a factor of 10.

Lastly, Telepathy can be used to alter existing memories or false memories. The number of successes needed to alter or implant a memory depends upon how important that memory is.

Successes	Memory
One	Trivial memories: What you did yesterday, your favorite food
Two	Minor memories: Your birthday or anniversary, crucial job facts
Three	Important memories: Vital personal facts, blackmail information, insider information
Four	Very important memories: Security codes, national security data

Extras: Surreptitious (victim will not be aware his mind is being read if nova does not wish him to be); Telepathic Channeling (the telepath may use other mental powers, such as Domination, Mental Blast or Mirage, through a telepathic link, regardless of distance between the telepath and target)

Teleport

Level: 2

Quantum Minimum: 2

Dice Pool: Perception + Teleport

Range: Self

Area: N/A

Duration: Instant

Effect: Allows character to move without passing through the intervening space.

Multiple Actions: No

Description: Teleport is an advanced form of movement in which a nova does not cross through the intervening space. Instead she simply "disappears" at Point A and "reappears" at her desired destination of Point B, bypassing completely any intervening barriers, such as walls or buildings.

To use Teleport, a nova spends the required quantum points, and the player rolls Perception + Teleport. In combat or other stressful situations, a nova may teleport up to 100 meters per success. Provided the nova has a full turn to concentrate, she may teleport a variable distance, as indicated on the chart. In either case, each point of Quantum she has counts as an additional automatic success. Using Teleport counts as a character's entire action for a turn.

If a character is unable to see her destination, or is not familiar with it due to previous visits there, she is "teleporting blind" and may miss her destination and end up somewhere else. The character must make a Perception + Teleport roll to "hit" her specified destination. The difficulty is one higher if she is teleporting more than two kilometers, two higher if she is teleporting more than 20 kilometers and three higher if she is teleporting more than 100 kilometers.

Teleport Distance

Successes	Distance
One	two kilometers
Two	20 kilometers
Three	200 kilometers
Four	2000 kilometers
Five	20000 kilometers

Each success beyond five multiplies the teleport distance by a factor of 10.

If the nova misses, the Storyteller should determine randomly where she went. Roll one die to determine the direction (1 = north, 2 = northeast, and so on; reroll 9s and 10s) and another die to determine how many units of measurement the character is "off" (if she is teleporting a distance in meters, it's one to 10 meters; if kilometers, one to 10 kilometers; if tens of kilometers, one to 10 times 10 kilometers). If she accidentally teleports into a solid object, she reappears in the nearest empty space but takes 1d10 health levels of lethal damage, reduced by one for each success achieved on a Stamina + Teleport roll.

Teleporting one's clothes, carried objects and the like requires the Attunement Background (p. 139).

Extras: Safe Blind Teleport (difficulty for teleporting blind is reduced by one, and the character takes bashing damage instead of lethal damage if she accidentally teleports into a solid object); Combat Teleport (teleport does not take an action; character may, for example, teleport to a foe's flank or rear, then make an attack normally; the character gains three extra dice to dodge if using Teleport while doing nothing except taking a defensive action; moreover, the character can dodge an area or explosive attack as though it were a normal attack)

Temporal Manipulation

Level: 3

Quantum Minimum: 5

Dice Pool: Variable

Range: Variable

Area: N/A

Duration: Variable

Effect: Character can manipulate time.

Multiple Actions: Yes

Description: This exceedingly rare power gives a nova control over that most basic, yet mysterious, of phenomena — time itself. He can alter or reverse time to achieve a number of effects, but he cannot actually travel through time. That has proved beyond the abilities of even the most powerful novas.

As with Elemental Anima and Mastery, this power provides several techniques. A nova may learn and freely use one technique per dot in the power; she may attempt other techniques, but the player must pay double quantum cost and roll against a difficulty penalty of one to activate these powers. Techniques include:

Internal Clock

Range: Self

Area: N/A

Duration: Permanent

This technique is known automatically by all time-manipulators and does not use up a dot in the power. A character with Temporal Manipulation possesses a highly accurate internal clock. He always knows exactly how much time has passed between two events, and he can mentally time events as if using an extremely precise stopwatch. This ability requires no roll and costs no quantum points; it functions automatically.

Age Alteration

Dice Pool: Manipulation + Temporal Manipulation
Range: (Quantum + power rating) x 5 meters
Area: N/A
Duration: Instant

This ability allows a nova to make another person age rapidly or regress back to his youth. For each success achieved on a Manipulation + Temporal Manipulation roll, the nova may add or subtract up to two years from the target's age; the target may resist with a Stamina roll. For reasons as yet unknown to science, this ability has no effect on the size or power of another nova's Mazarin-Rashoud node. It also does not affect the victim's mind or memories. A victim of Age Alteration will simply have to live with the effects ever after unless he can get another time-manipulator to reverse them.

Age Alteration can also be used on objects. Decreasing their age will repair minor damage (wear and tear) and make them look newer and shinier. Every two years added to an object inflicts one health level of damage on it, possibly causing it to crumble into ruin.

Accelerate Time

Dice Pool: Wits + Temporal Manipulation
Range: (Quantum + power rating) x 10 meters
Area: N/A
Duration: Maintenance

This ability allows a nova to put himself or another person inside a bubble of "fast time." Doing so makes the character move and act much more quickly than a person in a normal time frame. Each success on a Temporal Manipulation roll allows the character to take one additional action per turn. These actions are not multiple actions; they are extra actions. However, they may be used only to take additional physical actions (punching, running, or dodging, for example, but not using more Temporal Manipulation powers). The nova's power rating dictates the maximum number of extra actions that may be gained.

Dilate Time

Dice Pool: Wits + Temporal Manipulation
Range: (Quantum + power rating) x 10 meters
Area: N/A
Duration: Maintenance

Dilate Time is the reverse of Accelerate Time; it allows a nova to slow down another character by slowing the flow of time around him. Each success on an Intelligence + Temporal Manipulation roll reduces the victim's Initiative rating by one. If Initiative falls below 1, the victim is treated as having an Initiative rating of 1, but he may act only once every other turn.

Stop Time

Dice Pool: Intelligence + Temporal Manipulation
Range: (Quantum + power rating) meters
Area: N/A
Duration: Maintenance

This power is perhaps the most potent one in the Temporal Manipulator's arsenal. It allows him literally to stop time around a specific person or object. That person cannot move or use any powers or Abilities, he does not age and he cannot be affected by (and is unaware of) any outside force, phenomenon or attack while in suspension. Stop Time is very difficult to set up — the nova's player must achieve a success on an Intelligence + Temporal Manipulation roll at a difficulty penalty of two, and a living victim may make a Willpower roll to resist. Once established, the effect lasts as long as the character pays quantum points to maintain it.

Extras: None

Warp

Level: 3
Quantum Minimum: 3
Dice Pool: N/A
Range: (Quantum + power rating) meters
Area: N/A
Duration: Special

Effect: Allows character to create "gates" permitting her or other characters to move without passing through the intervening space.

Multiple Actions: No

Description: Warp is similar to Teleport in many ways — it involves the same method of moving without passing through intervening space. However, whereas Teleportation normally works on one person only (the nova who possesses it), Warp creates a "gate" that anyone can use.

It takes an entire turn to create a warp; the nova may take no other actions during this turn. Warps are typically three meters square; the nova may alter the shape by one meter (either dimension) per dot. Anything that cannot fit through the warp cannot use it. Warps are usually opened up at ground level, but a nova may create a warp anywhere within his range.

To use Warp, a nova simply spends the required quantum points. In combat or other stressful situations, a warp can teleport anyone who passes through it up to 100 meters per success; if the nova has a full turn to concentrate, Warp can teleport persons a variable distance, as shown on the accompanying table. In either case, each point of Quantum she has counts as an additional automatic success. Passing through a warp voluntarily counts as one of a character's actions for a turn.

Warp Distance

Successes	Distance
One	two kilometers
Two	20 kilometers
Three	200 kilometers
Four	2000 kilometers
Five	20000 kilometers

Each success beyond five multiplies the warp distance by a factor of 10.

A nova may use Warp as an attack by opening it up in front of a target. A moving target may dodge to avoid passing through it; this dodge takes no time. A nonmoving target may be "enveloped" by the warp if the nova's player succeeds with a Dexterity + Warp roll; the target resists that roll with an Athletics roll. Doing so is always a "combat" warp; a nova could not, for example, warp a foe into the vacuum of space unless she had a full turn to concentrate and the victim was helpless to dodge the warp.

Characters can see through the warp (unless conditions on one "side" of it prevent sight) and will know where they are going before they pass through it.

Extras: None

Weather Manipulation

Level: 3
Quantum Minimum: 4
Dice Pool: Variable
Range: Variable
Area: Variable
Duration: Variable
Effect: Character may alter and manipulate weather.
Multiple Actions: Yes
Description: Weather Manipulation provides the character with power over weather in its many aspects. As with Elemental Anima and Mastery, this power provides several techniques. A nova may learn and freely use one technique per dot in the power; she may attempt other techniques, but the player must pay double quantum cost and roll against a difficulty penalty of one to activate these powers. Techniques include:

Alter Temperature

Dice Pool: N/A
Range: (Quantum + power rating) x 2 kilometers
Area: (Quantum + power rating) x 5 kilometers
Duration: Maintenance

The character can increase or decrease the temperature of the air in an area around himself. The temperature can be altered by 10 degrees Celsius per dot in Weather Manipulation. No roll is required to do so, but quantum points must be paid.

Fog

Dice Pool: Intelligence + Weather Manipulation
Range: (Quantum + power rating) x 5 meters
Area: (Quantum + power rating) x 10 meters
Duration: Maintenance

The character is able to create a thick bank of fog over a wide area (or, if the player prefers, hard, driving rain which is so thick as to inhibit vision). The fog interferes with sight, making driving and other forms of movement hazardous. Each success achieved on an Intelligence + Weather Manipulation roll adds one to the difficulties of all visual Perception rolls made to see into or through the fog. The fog lasts as long as the character pays quantum points to maintain it, then dissipates at normal rates for the current environmental conditions.

Lightning Bolt

Dice Pool: Dexterity + Weather Manipulation
Range: (Quantum + power rating) x 10 meters
Area: N/A
Duration: Instant

The character may project bolts of lightning. These inflict [Quantum x 2] levels + (power rating x 2) dice of

lethal damage. Typically the bolts are projects from the character's hands, but the player may have them strike down from stormclouds, for dramatic purposes, if he wishes; however, this effect should not provide any bonuses to hit a target or other combat benefits.

Weather Alteration

Dice Pool: Intelligence + Weather Manipulation
Range: (Quantum + power rating) x 2 kilometers
Area: (Quantum + power rating) x 5 kilometers
Duration: Maintenance

This effect is the most basic of the Weather Manipulator's abilities. He can, as the power's name indicates, alter weather patterns over a large area. For each success achieved on an Intelligence + Weather Manipulation roll, he may adjust the current weather conditions up or down one step on the following table.

Weather Phenomena Table
Sweltering Heat
Clear/Sunny
Cloudy/Hazy
Drizzle
Rainstorm (or snow, if temperature makes it possible)
Strong Rain/Thunderstorm
Gale
Hurricane/Tornado/Typhoon/Blizzard

Thus, if the current weather is a rainstorm (and the player of a nova achieves two successes on his Intelligence + Weather Manipulation roll), a nova may increase it up to a gale or decrease it to cloudy/ hazy. If the nova changes the weather conditions to gale or higher, the effect is treated as the Storm technique of Elemental Mastery (p. 196).

Windriding

Dice Pool: N/A
Range: Self
Area: N/A
Duration: Maintenance

The character manipulates winds so that they carry him, similar to Flight. The character can move at the rate of (power rating x 2) + 20 meters per action, or (40 kilometers per hour x power rating) out of combat.

Players can create other Weather Manipulation techniques if they wish, but the Storyteller must review and approve all such techniques.

Extras: None

Extras

Extras are special advantages that can be added to existing powers. They make the power better in some way — more effective, able to work at greater ranges or effective against more targets. The choice of whether to take an Extra, either the ones listed with specific powers or the ones described here (which can apply to any appropriate power) is up to the player and requires the Storyteller's permission. Extras are never required.

Taking an Extra has two effects beyond the benefits of the Extra itself. First, it raises the power's level by one for purposes of the cost to purchase it with nova/experience points and power it with quantum points. For example, a Level 2 power with an Extra becomes a Level 3 power in terms of its cost to buy and use. Since there are no powers above Level 3, Level 3 powers *cannot* take Extras. A player can purchase up to two Extras for a Level One power.

A power with an Extra is considered a separate, distinct power. A character may not buy one power and several Extras and then "trade off" the Extras from turn to turn to get the most effective attack. An Extra, once purchased for a power, must always be used when that power is used.

Gaining Extras with Experience

A character may "upgrade" her power by purchasing an Extra later in the game, with the Storyteller's permission. The cost of doing so is equal to the total difference between the costs of all the dots without the Extra and the cost of all the dots with the Extra. A character may halve this cost by taking a point of Taint at the time the Extra is purchased.

For Example: Lotus Infinite has Quantum Bolt 3. After practicing a good bit with her Infinity Justifier special maneuver, she wishes to buy the Area Extra as a permanent feature of her power. The total experience-point cost to purchase Quantum Bolt 3 "from the ground up" is 30 points (5 + 10 + 15), while the similar cost to buy the power with an Extra is 44 points (9 + 14 + 21). The difference between the two costs (14 points) is what LI must pay to buy the Extra.

That's pretty expensive, so LI takes a point of Taint to purchase the Extra for half cost. After spending seven experience points, she may now use the Area Extra with every shot of her Quantum Bolt; however, she pays three, not two, quantum points to fire the attack.

Aggravated

This Extra, when applied to a power that causes bashing or lethal damage, makes that damage aggravated. The character inflicts a base amount of aggravated damage equal to Quantum, then adds attack successes from her skill roll to determine the total aggravated damage inflicted. For information on aggravated damage, see p. 253.

Area

This Extra allows a power to affect an area. It applies only to powers, such as Quantum Bolt, that do not already have an area of effect. The typical area is (Quantum + power rating) x 5 meter radius, but players should confer with their Storyteller to determine the area he wants a power to have.

For information on the effects of powers that affect an area, see p. 248.

Armor Piercing

A power with this Extra is able to pierce soak easily. For every attack success, the attack may ignore two levels of soak. Armor Piercing cannot be applied to powers that do not inflict damage.

Burning

This Extra is typically applied to an attack power, but it is appropriate for a few other types of powers as well. A Burning attack inflicts normal damage when it first hits, but it continues to "burn" the victim on subsequent turns. The victim of a Burning attack automatically takes half damage from the attack (which, of course, may be soaked as normal) for an additional number of turns equal to the attack's power rating.

Cloud

This Extra allows a nova to generate an attack in the form of a cloud of gas or energy. It fills an area equal to three meters radius per dot, which adds one die to attack rolls; extra successes on the attack roll do not increase the attack's damage or effect. However, the attack lingers in the area for one extra turn, during which it inflicts half damage on anyone who moves into it or remains inside it. The cloud will tend to fill up enclosed spaces and sink to the lowest part of the area it fills.

Explosion

Explosion is similar to Area, but it works differently — it covers a bigger area, but its effect decreases gradually over that distance. A power with Explosion inflicts full damage/ effect on the three-meter-diameter area at "ground zero" of the attack. However, for every three meters after the three meters at ground zero, one success (or health level of damage) is subtracted from the total applied. When the successes/ damage reaches zero, the Explosion has reached its maximum radius. Damage adds are lost before damage dice.

For Example: Derrick Tremaine uses a Quantum Bolt, Explosion against an enemy, Ral Karnazian. The center of the explosion is seven meters away from Karnazian. The first three meters radius covered by the explosion take the full damage — 18 health levels of damage. The three meters beyond that take 17 health levels of damage. The three meters beyond that, where Karnazian is, take 16 health levels. Karnazian may soak this damage normally.

Homing

A Homing attack can "lock on" to its target and follow it no matter where it tries to move or dodge. The attack suffers no penalties or modifiers for range (though it cannot move beyond its maximum range) and the attack ignores the target's first dodge success.

Impervious

Impervious is an Extra for defensive powers like Force Field. Impervious soak is not reduced by Armor Piercing, and it converts any aggravated damage into normal lethal damage, which can be soaked normally.

Increased Duration

A power with this Extra lasts longer than normal — it is doubled. Obviously, this Extra can be applied only to powers that have a duration defined by some unit of time.

Increased Range

This Extra, which applies only to powers with a defined range in meters, doubles the medium range of the power. The power can be used at long range all the way out to line of sight.

MIRV

A MIRV ranged attack power is able to split itself up among separate targets. The attacking character declares which targets he wishes to affect and makes one roll to hit them using the worst modifiers for any single target; die bonuses apply only if all targets would provide that bonus. If he succeeds, all targets are hit, though each target may dodge normally. He must then divide his damage dice among the various targets. If the power has a damage add, every target takes the base damage — only the additional damage dice must be split.

For Example: *Derrick Tremaine, with Quantum 2, has a bashing MIRV Fire Blast (Quantum Bolt 5). He wants to use it to hit five targets — one at point-blank range, three at medium range and one at maximum range (+2 difficulty). He must make one attack roll at +2 difficulty; he gets no bonuses for a point-blank attack, since not all targets are at point-blank range. He manages to achieve two successes, so he hits all five of his targets. Each target takes the damage add of six health levels of damage, and he splits his extra 20 damage dice evenly among the targets. Each target, then, takes [6] + 4d10 damage from the MIRV attack.*

Range

Powers with a range of Touch can work at a range of 10 meters per dot if they have this Extra. To attack, use the normal dice pool for the power; if there is none, use Dexterity + power rating to hit.

Reduced Quantum Cost

A power with this Extra costs only half as many quantum points to use and maintain (round in favor of the character). A Level One power with this Extra costs no quantum points to use.

Spray/Jet

This Extra allows the nova to use a power (typically a Quantum Bolt) as a "spray" or "jet" attack, like a living flamethrower. Each turn, the nova can choose to use a jet or spray. When using the power as a jet, the nova makes a normal attack roll; the range of a jet power is halved, but each turn the nova uses the power, she gains an additional die to accuracy, to a maximum of five extra dice.

When using the power as a spray, the nova emits a steady stream of energy, not unlike a fire hose, which is swept over an area. This energy spray functions like the Strafing maneuver (p. 248), adding 10 dice to a standard attack roll, with a difficulty penalty of one for each meter in area of effect covered beyond the first. Successes are divided up just as in strafing and applied to the damage effect.

Difficulties of dodge rolls against a jet or spray are increased by one.

CHAPTER SIX: DRAMA

Aberrant's focuses on roleplaying and character interaction. Still, we know you're just itching to blast some punk through a building, and such drama often involves an element of dice rolling. As Chapter One shows, the rules are designed to streamline this process as much as possible so that you can pay attention to the story. To assist you and the Storyteller further, this chapter covers more specific dice mechanics, including general dramatic systems, combat, damage and recovery.

Dramatic Systems

The only things limiting your actions are your imagination and your character's skill. During a game session, characters — both player and Storyteller personalities — attempt numerous diverse and complicated activities. The Storyteller is responsible for keeping all of this action organized while determining success or failure for all characters.

Dramatic systems simplify the Storyteller's job by supplying rules for a number of common activities. The appropriate Ability is bracketed after the system in question in each case. If a task requires a specialty, you may add a die to your character's dice pool for that test.

Storytellers should, and will undoubtedly have to, invent their own dramatic systems for new situations. The list of systems below is in no way exhaustive, but it provides a solid foundation on which to base events. Bear in mind that characters lacking a specific Ability may default to the Attribute on which the Ability is based, unless stated otherwise.

A number of these systems may be tried again if the first attempt is unsuccessful. Subsequent efforts may require additional difficulties, however, at the Storyteller's discretion (see "Second Chances," p. 111).

Physical Tasks

These systems cover tasks involving the three Physical Attributes (Strength, Dexterity and Stamina). Remember that players of characters with Mega-Attributes have extra dice to roll, and they act at reduced difficulties.

- **Climbing [Athletics]:** When your character climbs an inclined surface (rocky slope, cargo container or building), roll Athletics. For an average climb with available handholds and nominal complications, your character moves three meters per success. The Storyteller adjusts this distance based on the climb's difficulty (easier: four meters per success; more difficult: two meters per success). The number of handholds, smoothness of the surface and, to a lesser extent, weather can all affect rate of travel. A short, difficult climb may have the same difficulty as a long, easy climb. The extended action lasts until you've accumulated enough successes to reach the desired height. On a mild botch, your character may only slip or get stuck; on a more severe one, she may fall.

If your character has the Claws power, each level adds one die to all climbing attempts unless your character's "claws" are really discharged kinetic energy or the like. A character with the Clinging power may climb without a die roll.

- **Driving/Piloting [Drive, Pilot]:** A Drive or Pilot roll isn't needed to steer a vehicle under normal circumstances — assuming your character has the appropriate skill. However, bad weather, the vehicle's speed, obstacles and performing complex maneuvers can challenge even the most competent drivers. Specific difficulties based on these circumstances are up to the Storyteller, but they should increase as the conditions become more hazardous.

For example, driving in heavy rain increases the difficulty by one, but going fast while also trying to lose a tail jumps the penalty up three. Similarly, piloting a plane through artillery fire is +1, but adding a breakneck pace while avoiding pursuit bumps it to +3. A failed roll indicates trouble, requiring an additional roll to avoid crashing or losing control. Players of characters in control of a vehicle who have no dots in the appropriate Ability, must roll for almost every change in course or procedure. On a botch, the vehicle may spin out of control or worse.

- **Encumbrance [Might]:** The temptation to carry loads of equipment to satisfy every situation can be overwhelming. The Storyteller should make life difficult for players whose characters have extensive equipment and weaponry lists. Characters without Mega-Strength can carry 10 kilograms (22 pounds) per dot in their Might skill total without penalty; characters with Mega-Strength use the systems listed under that Mega-Attribute.

Should your character exceed this total, all actions involving physical skills incur an automatic difficulty penalty of one due to the added weight. Also, for every 10 kg over the allocation, your character's base movement drops by one meter (see "Movement," p. 106). If the total weight carried is double her Might allocation, your character can't move. This system is a guideline; the Storyteller should not call for an inventory check every time your character picks up a pen.

• **Feats of Endurance [Endurance]:** Endurance determines how well and for how long your character can run beyond her normal capacity, stay awake after a day of activity or hold her breath for an abnormally long time. Sustaining such acts depends on your character's Endurance skill total (see "Sources of Injury," p. 255), and it requires Endurance rolls after that point. The frequency of the rolls can range from every hour for trying to stay awake, each half-hour or so for maintaining physical activity or every few seconds to keep holding breath. Characters with Mega-Stamina find such feats exponentially easier, perhaps even automatic.

The Storyteller should add one to the difficulty (cumulative) to each subsequent roll after the first to reflect the increasing strain on your character's vitality. Botches should suit the feat attempted (e.g., stumbling, reflexively gasping for air, nodding off, lunging for the nearest available food).

• **Jumping [Might]:** In normal Earth gravity, each success on a Might roll launches your character half a meter vertically or two meters horizontally. On a botch, your character may trip over her own feet, leap right into a wall or do something similarly embarrassing. The Quantum Leap enhancement (p. 157) allows novas to cover truly amazing distances.

• **Lifting [Might]:** The chart below provides Might skill totals needed to deadlift various mass categories. The Storyteller determines any difficulties involved in lifting; generally, the number of dots by which your character is below the minimum Might rating required is the additional difficulty incurred to lift the object. However, if her Might skill total is at least one dot higher than the minimum needed, the Storyteller may allow your character to pick up the item without having to roll.

Might skill total	Mass (kg)	Example
•	15	Chair
••	45	
•••	100	Grown person
••••	165	
•••••	240	Empty cargo bin
••••••	300	
•••••• ••	360	Motorcycle
•••••• •••	420	
••••• •••••	480	Girder
••••• ••••••	550	

Characters can work together to lift an object, which requires a teamwork roll with the individual players rolling separately and combining any resulting successes.

Lifting is all or nothing — if you fail the roll, nothing happens. At the Storyteller's discretion, the difficulty may be reduced by one if all your character wants to do is drag something a short distance. On a botch, your character may strain something or drop the object on her own foot.

Characters with Mega-Strength use a different system for lifting. Each dot of Mega-Strength provides a base lifting ability:

•	1000 kg/1 ton (automobile)
••	10,000 kg/10 tons (truck)
•••	25,000 kg/25 tons (fighter plane)
••••	50,000 kg/50 tons (tank)
•••••	100,000 kg/100 tons (blue whale)

To lift more weight, the player rolls Might normally, and each success allows 20% more weight to be lifted. Thus, a character with Mega-Strength 2 may lift 20 tons on a Might roll of five successes.

• **Opening/Closing [Might]:** Opening a door with brute force calls for a Might roll. A standard interior door requires only one success to bash open or slam shut. A reinforced door or airlock generally takes five successes. A magnetically locked blast door might take 10 successes. These successes may be handled as an extended action. While teamwork is possible (and recommended), a door can still be forced open through a single individual's repeated hammering. Obviously, a door not held in some way can be opened without resorting to force. A botch causes a level of bashing damage to your character's shoulder.

Novas with Mega-Strength add their automatic damage successes to their players' Might rolls, should the Storyteller decide they even have to roll at all.

• **Pursuit [Athletics, Drive, Pilot]:** Catching someone who's trying desperately to avoid your character involves several different rolls, which can include Tracking or Investigation. Basic pursuit is an extended action. The target starts with a number of free extra successes based on his distance from pursuers. This system breaks down as follows: on foot, one for every two meters ahead of pursuers; in vehicles or flight, one for every 10 meters ahead of pursuers. Exceptionally long foot chases might involve Endurance tests.

If one participant has Hypermovement or Enhanced Movement and the other does not, or if one participant has Hypermovement at a higher level than the other, the faster character always escapes/ catches up unless the Storyteller dictates otherwise. In all other cases, the target and pursuers roll the appropriate Ability (depending on the type of pursuit) each turn, adding new successes to any successes rolled in previous turns. When the pur-

suer accumulates more total successes than the target, she catches up and may take further actions to stop the chase. As the target accumulates successes, he gains distance from his pursuers and may use that lead to lose his opponents. Each success that the quarry accumulates beyond the pursuer's total acts as a difficulty penalty of one to any Awareness rolls that pursuers have to make to remain on the target's tail. The Storyteller may call for the pursuer to make an Awareness roll at any time (although not more than once per turn). If the pursuer fails this roll, her target is considered to have slipped away (into the crowd, off the sensor screen). On a botch, the pursuer loses her quarry immediately. If the quarry botches, he stumbles or ends up at a dead end.

• **Resistance [Resistance]:** The Health track on your character sheet normally declares the number of dice you lose from dice pools as your character takes damage. You may roll Resistance once each turn; a successful roll restores a number of dice to your pool equal to your Resistance Ability rating (*not* skill total). The restored dice last for as many turns as successes you roll. This benefit requires the Resistance Ability; it cannot be performed as a default task.

• **Shadowing [Stealth]:** Shadowing someone requires that your character keeps tabs on the target without necessarily catching her — *and* while not being noticed by her! The target's player can roll Awareness whenever she has a chance to spot her tail (the Storyteller decides when such an opportunity arises); the pursuer opposes this roll with a Stealth roll. The target must get at least one more success than her shadow does to spot the tail; if so, she may act accordingly. This resisted action is handled individually for each person shadowing the target (if the target is being followed by three people, her player makes three separate Awareness rolls, one against each target's Stealth roll).

• **Sneaking [Stealth]:** Rather than fight through every situation, your character can use stealth and cunning. A sneaking character uses Stealth as a resisted action against Awareness rolls from anyone able to detect her passing. Unless observers receive more successes than the sneaking character does, she passes undetected. Noise, unsecured gear, lack of cover or large groups of observers can increase Stealth difficulty. Security devices, scanners or superior vantage points may add dice to Awareness rolls. On a botch, the character stumbles into one of the people she's avoiding, accidentally walks into the open, or performs some other obvious act.

Certain nova powers, particularly Invisibility, make sneaking much easier.

• **Swimming [Endurance]:** Assuming your character can swim at all (being able to do so requires one dot of Athletics and enables a maximum movement of the character's walking speed plus one meter per dot in Athletics), long-distance or long-duration swimming requires successful Endurance rolls. The first roll is necessary only after the first half-hour of sustained activity, and it requires only one success. A cumulative difficulty penalty of one applies for each subsequent half-hour. If a roll fails at any time, your character tires; she may float, but she is too exhausted to swim. Your character can rest by floating, but the current difficulty doesn't drop until she can get to solid ground and recuperate. On a botch, your character sinks and, if she doesn't have gills or appropriate Life Support powers, begins drowning (see p. 257).

• **Throwing [Might]:** Objects (grenades, knives) with a mass of one kilogram or less can be thrown a distance of the character's Might skill total x 5 in meters. For each additional kilogram of mass that an object has, this distance decreases by five meters (particularly heavy objects don't go very far). As long as the object's mass doesn't reduce throwing distance to zero, your character can pick up and throw it without having to make a Might roll. A character with 5 Might skill total can throw a 1 kg object 25 meters. He can throw a 2 kg object 20 meters and a 5 kg object five meters. If an object can be lifted, but its mass reduces throwing distance to zero, the object can be hurled aside at best — about one meter's distance. Obviously, if an object can't be lifted, it can't be thrown at all (refer instead to "Lifting," p. 234).

The Storyteller may reduce throwing distances for particularly unwieldy objects, or increase them for aerodynamic ones. On a botch, your character may drop the object or strike a companion with it.

Characters with Mega-Strength may throw objects of weights equal to their base lifting ability; to do so, they use the normal rules for throwing. However, when throwing objects whose mass is less than half their base lifting ability (e.g., a nova with Mega-Strength 2 attempting to hurl a 1000-kg automobile), they may multiply their normal throwing distance times their automatic damage successes!

Mental Feats

These systems cover tasks involving the three Mental Attributes (Perception, Intelligence and Wits). Mental tests provide you with information about things your character knows, but you don't, or they determine your character's skill at certain mental tasks. Still, depend on your creativity when solving problems — not on dice-rolling.

• **Awareness [Awareness]:** This feat involves picking a face out of a crowd, keeping an eye on someone and being aware of one's surroundings. Awareness covers anything that doesn't require specific training in observation, as Investigation does. Awareness is often used in resisted rolls against Abilities like Stealth.

• **Hacking [Computer]:** A person seeking to hack into a computer system makes an extended roll using the Computer Ability. The difficulty can be normal (for an ordinary PC) or up to +4 (for hacking into military mainframes). Likewise, successes needed can range from five or so up to 50 (or even more!).

Actively blocking a hacker is a resisted action; the adversary with the most successes wins. On a botch, you may trip a flag or even reveal your identity to the system you're trying to breach. Hacking requires the Computer Ability; your character cannot perform it as a default task. Note that characters with the Cyberkinesis power (p. 187) may substitute that power for these rules.

• **High Finance [Biz]:** The Biz Ability covers any attempt to amass wealth, from international banking to licensing oneself to a toy company. The character or sponsor typically invests an amount of money (usually equal to a Resource dot) and rolls Biz. Each additional Resource dot invested adds one die to the Biz roll. One success means the deal breaks even; the character/sponsor neither gains nor loses from the deal. More successes allow the character to gain one temporary unit of Resources for each success rolled; these units equal one month's worth of one Resource dot.

For Example: Harvey Wilder, with Resources 2 and a Biz skill total of 7, needs cash fast. In an all-or-nothing gamble, he invests his entire fortune (two Resource dots) in the stock market. His player now rolls eight dice (seven for his Biz skill, +1 for the additional Resource dot invested). The player scores three successes — two over the total to break even — so Harvey gains two units of Resources. The player may choose for Harvey to have an effective Resources of 4 for one month or Resources 3 for two months.

Five or more successes on the Biz roll allow the character to raise his Resources by one dot permanently. Failure means the character loses all invested Resource dots for one month, then regains them at one invested dot per month thereafter. A botch means all invested Resources are lost permanently.

• **Investigation [Investigation]:** Any search for clues, evidence or hidden contraband involves Investigation. The Storyteller may add a difficulty to investigations involving obscure clues or particularly well-concealed objects. One success reveals basic details; multiple successes provide detailed information and may even make deductions possible based on physical evidence. On a botch, he may miss or accidentally destroy obvious clues.

• **Intrusion [Intrusion]:** Intrusion covers breaking and entering, evading security devices, picking locks, bypassing keypad and retinal countermeasures — and preventing others from doing the same. When bypassing active security, your roll must succeed on the first attempt; failure activates any alarms present (opening manual locks may be attempted multiple times, though). Intrusion rolls are usually standard actions, but they may be difficult actions depending on a security system's complexity (the Storyteller decides the actual difficulty). On a botch, the clumsy break-in attempt goes horribly awry.

Setting up security measures is a standard action, but multiple successes achieved in the effort increase the system's quality (essentially adding to its difficulty to be breached).

• **Repair [Engineering]:** Before repairing a device that's on the fritz, your character must identify its problems (accomplished as a standard research roll). The Storyteller then sets the difficulty of the repair roll, if any. This difficulty depends on the problems' severity, whether the proper tools or any replacement parts are on hand and if adverse conditions exist. An inspired research roll may offset these factors somewhat. A simple tire change is a standard action, while rerouting power through a secondary system is more difficult. Basic repairs take at least a few turns to complete. More complex ones are extended actions that last 10 minutes per success needed. On a botch, your character may simply waste time and a new part, or may make the problem worse.

• **Research [Academics, Science, Engineering]:** A character performs research when searching computer databases for historical facts, when looking for obscure loopholes in anti-terrorism laws or when trying to learn a device's function or origin. In all cases, the number of successes achieved determines the amount of information discovered; one success gives you at least basic information, while extra successes provide more details. The Storyteller may apply difficulties for particularly obscure data. On a botch, your character may not find anything at all, or he may uncover completely erroneous information.

• **Tracking [Awareness, Survival]:** Unlike shadowing, tracking requires you to follow physical evidence to find a target. Discovering footprints, broken twigs, blood trails or other physical signs lead the tracker right to the subject. Following such a trail is a standard action; multiple successes provide extra information (subject's rate of speed, estimated weight, number of people followed). The quarry can cover her tracks with a successful Survival roll. Each success on a Survival roll modifies any tracking difficulties by one. Abnormal weather, poor tracking conditions (city streets, installation corridors) and a shortage of time also add to tracking difficulty. On a botch, your character not only loses the trail, but he runs the risk of destroying the physical signs of passage as well.

Social Graces

These systems cover tasks involving the three Social Attributes (Appearance, Manipulation and Charisma). Roleplaying usually supersedes any Social skill roll, for better or worse. Storytellers may ignore the Social systems when a player exhibits particularly good or excruciatingly bad roleplaying.

• **Carousing [Style, Streetwise]:** You influence others to relax and have fun. Applications of this roll might include showing a potential client a good time, loosening an informant's tongue or making instant drinking partners who come to your aid when a brawl starts. It's a standard action when dealing with an individual, though difficulties may be added for large or surly groups. On a botch, your character comes off as an obnoxious boor, if not worse.

• **Credibility [Subterfuge]:** Subterfuge is used when perpetrating a scam or trying to detect one (a scam can range from impersonating the authorities to using a forged passport). All parties involved, whether detecting the lie or perpetrating it, roll Subterfuge. The scam's "marks" must roll higher than the perpetrator to detect any deception. False credentials and other convincing props may add to the difficulty of uncovering the dupe, while teamwork may help reveal the scam. On a botch, the entire plan falls apart.

• **Disguise [Perform, Style]:** Disguise usually involves two Abilities, although only one may be called for at a time. Style is used to copy someone's appearance successfully. The Storyteller may apply difficulties depending on the resources at your character's disposal. A standard roll is suitable if ample visual references of the subject (and appropriate makeup, wig and wardrobe) are available. Going by a photo or having access to a limited wardrobe may be more difficult. Trying a disguise from memory or with little resources could be increase the difficulty by as much as three. A proper disguise takes at least 10 minutes to create (the Storyteller may add additional difficulty for such a rush job); an hour or more offers the best results.

To act like someone requires a Perform roll (the Oratory Specialty is useful only to imitate someone's voice, while Acting can be used to imitate someone's mannerisms). It is necessary to study a subject to create a believable disguise. A standard roll is adequate if the subject is in your character's presence for at least an hour (or suitable photos are on hand). Working from poor-quality photos or rushing things can result in +1 or +2 difficulty. Meeting the subject briefly (or simply faking it) may result in +3 or +4 difficulty.

Aside from these systems, the Storyteller should take into account the player's roleplaying. An adequate disguise roll may still succeed if the player does an impressive imitation, while even the most inspired disguise is ineffectual if the player acts no differently than usual. On a botch, the disguise may be simply transparent or patently ridiculous, but it is obviously not convincing.

• **Fast-Talk [Subterfuge]:** When there's no time for subtlety, baffle them with nonsense. A target can be overwhelmed with a rapid succession of almost-believable half-truths. Hopefully, the subject believes anything she hears just to get away from the babble — or becomes so annoyed that she ignores your character completely. Trying to Fast-Talk someone is a resisted action — your character's Subterfuge against the target's Willpower. Whoever scores more successes wins. On a tie, more babbling is needed. On a botch, your character goes too far, angering the target and rambling without effect.

• **Intimidation [Intimidation]:** Intimidation has two effects. Intimidation's passive effect doesn't involve a roll; it simply gives your character plenty of space — whether on a shuttle, tram or in a bar. The higher your Intimidation skill total, the wider the berth that others give him.

Intimidation's active application works through subtlety or outright threat. Subtlety is based on a *perceived* threat (losing one's job, going on report, pain and agony later in life). Roll Intimidation in a resisted action against the subject's Willpower; the target must get more successes or be cowed effectively.

The blatant form of intimidation involves direct physical threat. In this case, you may pair Intimidation with Strength in a resisted roll against the subject's Willpower. On a botch, your character looks patently ridiculous and doesn't impress anyone in attendance for the rest of the scene.

• **Interrogation [Interrogation]:** Anyone can ask questions. With the Interrogation Ability, you ask questions and have leverage. Interrogating someone peacefully involves asking strategic questions designed to reveal specific facts. This method is a resisted action between your character's Interrogation and the subject's Willpower. Rolls are made at key points during questioning, probably every few minutes or at the end of an interrogation session.

Violent interrogation involves torturing the victim's mind and/ or body until he reveals what he knows. Doing so is a resisted action between your character's Interrogation and the target's Resistance or Willpower (whichever is higher). Rolls are made every minute or turn, depending on the type of torture used. The subject loses a health level for each turn of physical torture, or one current Willpower point per turn of mental torture. Damage inflicted depends on the tools used — fire and electricity cause lethal damage; punches and kicks cause bashing damage. The combined effect of physical and mental torture has devastating results. A botched Interrogation roll can destroy the subject's body or mind.

Whatever the interrogation method used, if you roll more successes in the resisted action, the target divulges something for each extra success rolled. If your extra successes exceed the victim's Willpower score, she folds completely and reveals everything she knows. The extent and relevancy of shared information are up to the Storyteller (details are often skewed to reflect what the subject knows or by what she thinks her interrogator wants to hear).

• **Oration [Perform]:** From a general's rousing speeches to a politician's slick double-talk, the capacity to sway the masses emotionally creates and destroys empires. When your character speaks publicly, whether to a small board meeting or to an entire N! TV audience, roll Perform. The Storyteller may increase the difficulty for a huge, dispassionate or openly hostile audience. Oration is hit or miss — your character either succeeds or fails. On a botch, your character may damage her reputation or even be assaulted by the audience.

• **Performance [Perform]:** Perform can be used to impress an audience or to pay the bills. As with oration, the audience's mood can increase the difficulty, as can the performance's complexity. One success indicates an enjoyable if uninspired effort, while additional successes make the performance a truly memorable event to even the most surly crowd. On a botch, your character forgets lines or makes a gaffe.

• **Seduction [Streetwise, Etiquette, Style, Subterfuge]:** The particular situation and style of the seduction determine which Ability is used. In pleasant, cultured circumstances, roll Etiquette. In a seedy underbelly bar, Streetwise is appropriate. Style encompasses any attempt to physically attract an individual or even a group. Roll Subterfuge when your character makes a seduction attempt through exaggeration or fabrication. In all cases, the target rolls Willpower. As long as you get more successes, the target is definitely interested (the degree depends on the number of extra successes rolled). Otherwise, the subject hasn't bitten yet, but you may try again (although at an increased difficulty). On a botch, your character ends up with a drink in his face (at best).

Combat Systems

Combat in **Aberrant** attempts to capture the larger-than-life feats common to nova-level conflict without downplaying the grim reality of injury and death. What results is a system true to the dynamics, limitations and viciousness of real combat — particularly combat involving superheated plasma blasts and building-rattling punches — that leaves room for the spectacular elements that novas bring to it.

The Storyteller should be flexible when arbitrating combat situations; no rules can fully reflect the variety of situations encountered in warfare. If any part of these systems slows the game or causes bickering, don't use it. Combat systems are meant to add depth to the game, not create out-of-game conflict.

Types of Combat

There are three types of combat, each involving the same basic system with minor differences:

• **Close Combat:** This designation covers unarmed combat and melee. Unarmed combat can involve two Mega-strong bruisers wailing on each other or skilled martial artists facing off. Opponents must be within touching distance (one meter) to engage in unarmed combat, unless one or more combatants is superflexible, has the Tendril power, or is otherwise able to strike from a distance. Melee involves hand-held weapons, from broken bottles to katanas. Opponents must be within one or two meters of each other to engage in melee.

• **Ranged Combat:** This designation covers combat using projectile weapons or powers — guns, telekinesis and Quantum Bolts, for example. Normally, opponents must be within sight (and weapon range) of each other to engage in a firefight.

• **Armored Combat:** This term covers combat between vehicles using mounted weaponry — from tanks to fighter planes. Opponents must be within weapons range to engage in armored combat.

Combat Turns

In combat, many things happen at virtually the same time. Since this fact can make things a bit sticky in a game, combat is divided into a series of roughly three-second intervals called turns. Each combat turn has three stages — *Initiative*, *Attack* and *Resolution* — to make keeping track of things easier.

Stage One: Initiative

This stage organizes the turn, and it is the point at which you declare your character's action. Various actions are possible — anything from leaping behind a wall to shouting a warning. You must declare what your character does, in as much detail as the Storyteller requires.

Describing the Scene

Before each turn, the Storyteller should describe the scene from each character's perspective. Sometimes this description will be a wrap-up of the last turn, making what occurred clear to all players. This constant description is essential to avoid confusion.

This narration is the Storyteller's chance to organize and arrange events so that all goes smoothly when the players interact with the environment she has created. The Storyteller should make her descriptions as interesting as possible, leaving open many possibilities for characters' actions.

Each player rolls a die and adds it to her Initiative rating [Dexterity + Wits]; the character with the highest result acts first, with the remaining characters acting in decreasing order of result. If two characters get the same total, the one with the higher Initiative rating goes first. If Initiative ratings are also the same, roll again until the tie is resolved. (Note that novas with Mega-Dexterity or the Enhanced Initiative enhancement often transcend the normal Initiative order.)

Although you declare your character's action now (including stating that your character delays her action to see what someone else does), you wait until the *attack* stage to implement that action. At this time, you must also state if any multiple actions will be performed, or if Willpower points will be spent.

All of your character's actions are staged at her rank in the order of Initiative. There are only two exceptions to this rule. The first is if your character delays her action, in which case her maneuvers happen when she finally takes action. Your character may act at any time after her designated order in the Initiative, even to interrupt another, "slower" character's action. If two characters both delay their actions, and both finally act at the same time, the one with the higher Initiative score for the turn acts first.

The second breach of the Initiative order occurs in the case of a defensive action (see "Aborting Actions," p. 242, and "Defensive Maneuvers," p. 243), which your character may perform at any time as long as she has a maneuver left.

Stage Two: Attack

Attacks are the meat of the combat turn. An action's success or failure and potential impact on the target are determined at this stage. You use a certain Ability depending on the type of combat in which your character is engaged:

• **Close Combat:** Use Brawl, Martial Arts or Melee.

• **Ranged Combat:** Use Firearms or the quantum power skill total.

• **Armored Combat:** Use Firearms.

Remember, if your character doesn't have points in the necessary Ability, simply default to the Attribute on which it's based (Strength for Brawl; Dexterity for Melee, Martial Arts and Firearms).

In ranged combat, your weapon or power may modify your dice pool "accuracy" (due to rate of fire or a targeting scope, for example); check the weapon's vital statistics or power description for details. Attacks are usually standard actions, but a difficulty may apply depending on the circumstances of the attack. If you get no successes, the character fails her attack and inflicts no damage. If you botch, not only does the attack fail, but something nasty happens; the weapon jams or explodes, you hit an ally or your power backlashes into your body.

Stage Three: Resolution

During this stage, you determine the damage inflicted by your character's attack, and the Storyteller describes what occurs in the turn. Resolution is a mixture of game and story; it's more interesting for players to hear "Your Quantum Bolt knocks your foe through the air and into the side of the nearby building" than simply "Uh, he takes four health levels." Attacks and damage are merely ways of describing what happens in the story, and it's important to maintain the narrative of combat even as the dice roll.

Puny Human...

Some novas are truly impervious to injury. As an optional rule, the Storyteller can declare that, if a nova has natural defenses (not artificial armor) in the superhuman levels (six extra soak against bashing; three extra soak against lethal), and the nova's soak subtracts twice the amount of the attacker's damage effect, the attacker may not even roll his one die in hopes of attaining a single damage success. In this manner, novas with soak ratings of 12, 15 or even higher can wade through human-level attackers or small-arms fire without a care.

Normally, additional successes gained on a skill roll simply mean that you do exceptionally well. *In combat, each extra success you score on an attack roll equals an additional die you add automatically to your damage effect!* This addition creates fatal and cinematic combat. A maximum of five damage dice may be added in this fashion. Furthermore, area and explosive attacks may not add attack successes to damage, as there is little opportunity for finesse when delivering such an attack.

Damage Types

All weapons, powers and other attacks have specific damage ratings, indicating the number of dice that

you roll (or successes you apply) for the attack's damage (called the *damage effect*). Each success on the damage effect roll inflicts one health level of damage on the target. Most damage consists of one of two types:

• **Bashing:** Punches and other blunt trauma that are less likely to kill a victim instantly. Characters use their full Stamina ratings to resist bashing effects, and the damage heals fairly quickly. The maneuver and weapons charts (p. 250, 274-275) list bashing attacks with a "B," and damage is applied to the Health boxes on your character sheet with a "/."

• **Lethal:** Attacks meant to cause immediate and fatal injury to the target. Baseline human characters may not use Stamina to resist lethal effects, and the damage takes quite a while to heal. Most novas have a small degree of defense against lethal attacks, but even they tend to heal lethal attacks more slowly than they heal bashing attacks. The maneuver and weapons charts (p. 250, 274-275) list lethal attacks with an "L," and damage should be marked on the Health boxes on your character sheet with an "X."

A few particularly virulent nova powers deliver an even deadlier type of damage, which is referred to as *aggravated*. Aggravated attacks include things like disintegration attacks, molecular disruptions and other horribly destructive forces. Aggravated attacks are treated as lethal damage, but they take five times as long to heal, and they cannot be soaked except with certain special quantum powers. When necessary, use an asterisk (*) to denote aggravated damage.

Damage effect rolls cannot botch; a botched roll simply means the attack glances harmlessly off the target. Specifics on applying damage effects are described under "Health," p. 252.

Damage Adds versus Damage Dice

Novas and heavy weapons deliver a wallop far deadlier than the average human being can withstand. While most human-level attacks are made in terms of damage *dice* — thus inflicting a fair bit of damage or none at all, depending on the roll — particularly destructive attacks often do a certain minimum level of damage even on a glancing blow. Thus, many nova powers deliver a certain number of automatic damage successes, which are delivered in addition to the damage roll.

These automatic damage successes are known as damage adds and are always presented in brackets.

For Example: Overkilla nails some schmuck with his Quantum Bolt. His attack inflicts [10] + 12d10 bashing damage. The attack delivers 10 levels of bashing damage automatically, plus an additional number of health levels equal to the number of successes Overkilla's player rolls on his damage effect.

Pulling Your Punches

Novas don't have to hit at full force. A nova may subtract any amount she wishes, from damage adds and/or damage dice, before rolling damage. If this reduction takes the nova's damage effect below half of its normal value, the nova pays only half the normal quantum-point cost of the effect (round up).

For Example: Overkilla just got jumped by a skinny, 14-year-old and obviously stupid street kid. Overkilla fires back; however, not wanting to kill the li'l rugrat, Overkilla's player declares that he will pull all of his damage adds and use only eight of his damage dice in the attack. Since this is less than half of Overkilla's full-force blast, Overkilla has to pay only one quantum point to attack. If he hits, his attack will inflict a bashing dice pool of eight dice plus whatever successes he rolls on the attack — likely knocking the kid out, but not killing him.

Soak

All characters can resist a certain degree of physical punishment; doing so is called "soaking" damage. Your character's *soak* is based on her Stamina.

Baseline humans can soak one die of damage per point of Stamina, but they can apply this reduction only to bashing damage (reflecting the body's natural resilience to such attacks). Novas likewise subtract a base of one die per Stamina dot from bashing attacks.

Baselines cannot use Stamina to soak lethal damage, due to the brutal and invasive nature of such attacks. The human body can endure some abuse, but it's not capable of dealing with a bullet's traumatic impact or a laser's searing intensity. However, most novas have

Lethal Soak

The human body isn't designed to withstand the brutal physical trauma inflicted by gunshots and knife wounds. Most novas, however, automatically gain a certain amount of lethal soak as part of the eruption process. The transformation of the body into a Quantum-channeling dynamo makes it hardier and tougher, even with regard to novas who don't otherwise display any sort of special resiliency.

Novas, and only novas, have a certain automatic amount of lethal soak. A nova's natural lethal soak equals half her bashing soak, rounded down. The soak functions just like a natural bashing soak, except that it applies to lethal damage.

Additionally, novas with Mega-Stamina, Armor and/or Force Field gain extra lethal (and bashing) soak.

Stamina Rating	Base Lethal Soak
One	Zero
Two	One
Three	One
Four	Two
Five	Two

a small amount of lethal soak (p. 241). A side effect of eruption, lethal soak enables novas to withstand small amounts of lethal damage.

Soak rating is subtracted automatically from your attacker's total damage effect before it is rolled. Moreover, you subtract soak from automatic damage successes before you subtract damage dice. Even if your soak is higher than your attacker's damage effect, your opponent *still* rolls one die.

Armor, whether from Mega-Stamina, quantum powers or artificial sources, provides extra soak against bashing and/ or lethal effects (see "Armor"). Especially in the case of quantum powers, this extra can provide extremely impressive soak scores, enabling novas to laugh off weapon strikes, small-arms fire or even heavy artillery.

For Example: *Overkilla fires his Quantum Bolt at 2 Bigg Bettie, who has 15 soak versus bashing damage. Overkilla's attack inflicts [10 successes] + 12 dice of damage. Bettie's 15 soak completely cancels Overkilla's automatic successes and removes an additional five of his damage dice. Overkilla's player may now roll seven dice in an attempt to inflict damage on Bettie.*

Armor

Though most novas scorn artificial armor such as flak jackets and Kevlar vests, many baselines and a few novas wear this type of protection. Simply put, armor adds to your character's soak. The armor's rating combines with your base soak for purposes of reducing damage. Light armor offers a small amount of protection, but it doesn't hinder mobility. Heavy armor provides a lot of protection, but it can restrict flexibility. Some armor is designed to shield against bashing effects, some against lethal — and some protects against both.

Armor is not indestructible. If the damage applied from a single attack equals twice the armor's rating, the armor is destroyed.

Armor types, their ratings and other specifics are described in the Appendix (p. 277).

Personal Combat

These maneuvers give you a variety of choices in combat. Roleplaying combat is more entertaining if you can visualize your character's moves instead of simply rolling dice.

Maneuver Characteristics

Maneuvers with specific combat effects may modify your attack roll, difficulty or damage effect.

Ability: The Trait used for the action taken. If your character doesn't have a rating in the Ability, default to its base Attribute.

Accuracy: The dice added to the roll to hit an opponent. A "+3" adds three dice to the dice pool for that attack.

Difficulty: The added successes beyond the base one needed to accomplish the action. A "+2" difficulty means you need a total of three successes.

Damage: The modifier to the damage dice pool. A "+1" means you add one die when rolling the damage effect.

Combat Summary Chart

Stage One: Initiative

• Roll Initiative. Everyone declares actions. The character with the highest Initiative performs her action first. Actions can be delayed to any time later in the order of Initiative.

    • Declare any multiple actions, reducing dice pools accordingly.

Stage Two: Attack

• For unarmed close-combat attacks, roll Brawl or Martial Arts.

• For armed close-combat attacks, roll Melee.

• For ranged (with hand weapons) or armored combat (with vehicles), roll Firearms.

• For power use, roll the skill total listed with the appropriate power.

• A character can abort to a defensive action (block, dodge, parry) at any time before her action is performed as long as the player makes a successful Willpower roll (or a Willpower point is spent).

Stage Three: Resolution

• Determine total damage effect (weapon type or maneuver), adding any extra dice gained from successes on the attack roll.

• Subtract the target's soak (if applicable), then apply the remaining damage effect.

General Maneuvers

• **Aborting Actions:** You can abort your character's declared action to a defensive action as long as your character hasn't acted in the turn. Actions that can be aborted to include block, dodge and parry. A successful Willpower roll (or the expenditure of a Willpower point) is required for a character to abort an action and perform a defensive one instead. (See "Defensive Maneuvers," p. 243, for descriptions of block, dodge and parry.)

• **Ambush:** Ambushes involve surprising a target to get in a decisive first strike. The attacker rolls Stealth in a resisted action against the target's Awareness. If the attacker gets more successes, she can stage one free attack on the target and adds any extra successes from the resisted roll to her attack roll. On a tie, the attacker still attacks, although the target may perform a defensive maneuver. If the defender gets more successes, he spots the ambush, and both parties roll Initiative normally. Targets already involved in combat cannot be ambushed.

• **Blind Fighting/Fire:** Staging attacks while blind usually incurs a +2 difficulty penalty. The Ability specialties Blind Fighting and Blind Fire reduce that penalty. Specialties normally add a die to the rolls to which they apply. Blind Fighting and Blind Fire reduce the penalties imposed by fighting without seeing by one; all difficulty penalties for being in pitch darkness or for being flashed by bright light reduce to one. Novas with certain enhanced senses (pp. 162-164) may act without penalty even if they cannot visually perceive their targets.

• **Flank and Rear Attacks:** Characters attacking targets from the flank gain an additional die to accuracy, and they gain two additional dice to accuracy when attacking from behind.

• **Movement:** A character may move half of her running distance [Dexterity +12 meters, or half of whatever a nova's enhanced move is] and still take an action in a turn. Other maneuvers such as leaping or tumbling may be considered separate actions, depending on their complexity.

• **Multiple Actions:** If you declare multiple actions, subtract dice from the first dice pool equal to the total number of actions taken. Each subsequent action loses an additional die (cumulative). If a character performs *only* an abort action in a turn, use the appropriate block, dodge or parry system.

• **Targeting:** Aiming for a specific location incurs a difficulty, but it can bypass armor or cover or result in an increased damage effect. The Storyteller should consider special results beyond a simple increase in damage, depending on the attack and the target.

Target Size	Difficulty	DmgEffect
Medium (limb, briefcase)	+1	None
Small (hand, head, computer)	+2	+2
Precise (eye, groin, lock)	+3	+4

Defensive Maneuvers

It's a given that your character tries to avoid being hit in combat — that's why everyone makes attack rolls. Sometimes all your character wants to do is avoid attacks. You may announce a *defensive action* at any time before your character's opponent makes an attack roll, and as long as your character has an action left to perform. You can declare a defensive action on your character's turn in the Initiative or can even *abort* to a defensive maneuver. You must make a successful Willpower roll (or may simply spend one point of Willpower) to abort. If the Willpower roll fails, your character must carry out the action that you declared originally.

There are three basic types of defensive actions: block, dodge and parry. Some novas have access to a fourth defensive action: the power block. Using these three (or four) maneuvers, your character can defend against virtually any kind of attack. However, your character may not be able to avoid every single attack that's directed at her. She can't dodge when there's no room to maneuver, and she can't block or parry if she doesn't know an attack is coming.

Each defensive maneuver uses the same basic system: The defensive action is a resisted roll against the opponent's attack roll. Unless the attacker gets more total successes, he misses. If the attacker gets more successes, those that he achieves in excess of the defender's successes, if any, are used to hit (the attacker doesn't necessarily use *all* the successes he rolled). So even if the defender has fewer successes than the attacker does, the defender's maneuver can still reduce the effectiveness of the attack, even if the maneuver can't counteract it completely.

• **Block:** A Brawl or Martial Arts maneuver using your character's own body to deflect a hand-to-hand bashing attack. Lethal attacks cannot be blocked unless the defender has an appropriate quantum power or armor that provides special protection.

• **Dodge:** An Athletics or Martial Arts maneuver useful for avoiding attacks of all types. Your character bobs and weaves to avoid Melee or Brawl attacks (if there's no room to maneuver, she must block or parry instead). In firefights, your character moves at least one meter and ends up behind cover (if there's no room to maneuver and/ or no cover available, she can drop to the ground). If your character remains under cover or prone thereafter, cover rules apply against further Firearms attacks (see "Cover," p. 247).

Novas with at least one level of Mega-Dexterity may dodge ranged attacks without the necessity of seeking cover; they simply move out of the way, as with any other attack.

• **Parry:** A Melee maneuver using a weapon to block a Brawl, Martial Arts or Melee attack. If a character makes a Brawl or Martial Arts attack and the defender parries with a weapon that normally causes lethal damage effects, the attacker can actually be hurt by a successful parry. If the defender rolls more successes than the attacker does in the resisted action, the defender rolls the weapon's base damage plus the parry's extra successes against the attacker as automatic damage.

• **Power Block:** Many quantum powers can be used as part of defensive actions. Force Field is the most likely power for such a feat, but Gravity Control, Elemental Mastery and similar powers can also provide protection against certain attacks. Some attack powers can literally shoot an incoming projectile out of the sky.

To perform a power block, the player takes a defensive action as normal, then simply substitutes her Dexterity + power rating skill total for the normal block, parry or dodge roll. Each success on the power block roll subtracts one from the attack successes, as normal.

A power might be able to perform a power block against some maneuvers, but not against others. For example, Magnetic Mastery can certainly pull bullets off their trajectories, but it is useless against a flamethrower attack. The Storyteller must arbitrate power blocks on a case-by-case basis.

Block, dodge, parry and power block can be performed as part of a multiple action in your character's turn (punching then blocking, shooting then dodging, parrying then striking, blasting a tank shell out of the sky then blasting the tank to smithereens). Using a multiple action to act and defend is advantageous because your character can still accomplish something in a turn other than avoiding attacks.

For Example: *Jimmy the Body wants to punch two thugs, then be ready to dodge two attacks — a multiple action. Doing so is considered four separate actions using his 9 Martial Arts for the punches and his 10 Athletics for the dodges. The first punch is reduced by four dice (giving Jimmy five dice in his dice pool) because Jimmy performs four actions. The second punch is reduced by five dice (four actions plus an additional cumulative penalty), giving Jimmy four dice to strike. The first dodge is reduced by six dice (for a dice pool of four dice) as per the multiple-action rules. The final dodge is reduced by seven dice (leaving three dice).*

Rather than make defensive maneuvers a part of a multiple action, you may declare that your character spends an entire turn defending. The multiple-action rules are not used in this case. Instead, you have a full dice pool for the first defensive action, but you lose one die, cumulatively, for each subsequent defense action made in the same turn. It is difficult to avoid several incoming attacks.

For Example: *Jimmy the Body spends a whole turn dodging. With a 10 Athletics skill total, he can dodge up to 10 attacks! Jimmy's player rolls 10 dice against the first attack, nine dice against the second, eight dice against the third, seven dice against the fourth, six dice against the fifth, five dice against the sixth, etc. Jimmy can't do anything else that turn but dodge.*

Close Combat Maneuvers

This list comprises the most common maneuvers used in close combat; feel free to develop your own moves (with the Storyteller's approval). All hand-to-hand attacks inflict bashing damage unless stated otherwise. Damage inflicted by melee attacks depends on the weapon type (see the Melee Weapons Chart, p. 274).

Difficulty and damage for these maneuvers may be modified at the Storyteller's discretion, depending on the combat style the character uses. As always, drama and excitement take precedence over rules systems.

• **Clinch:** On a successful attack roll, the attacker goes into a clinch with the target. In the first turn, the attacker may roll Strength +2 damage effect. In each subsequent turn, combatants act on their orders in the Initiative. A combatant can inflict another Strength +2 damage effect automatically, or attempt to escape the clinch. Neither the attacker nor the defender may use any other standard combat maneuvers until one combatant breaks free; however, characters with body-altering powers such as Density Decrease, Shapeshift, Flexibility or Immolate may attempt to use them normally. To escape a clinch, make a resisted Brawl or Martial Arts roll against the opponent. If the escaping character rolls more successes, she breaks free; if not, the characters continue to grapple in the next turn.

> **Ability:** Brawl or Martial Arts
> **Difficulty:** Normal
> **Accuracy:** Normal
> **Damage:** Strength +2

• **Disarm:** To knock a weapon from an opponent's hand, the attacker rolls at +1 difficulty; if the attacker is unarmed, she rolls at +2 difficulty. If successful, the attacker rolls damage normally. If successes rolled exceed the opponent's Strength score, the opponent takes no damage but is disarmed. A botch usually means the attacker drops her own weapon or is struck by her target's weapon.

> **Ability:** Martial Arts or Melee
> **Difficulty:** Special
> **Accuracy:** Normal
> **Damage:** Special

• **Hold:** This attack inflicts no damage, as the intent is to immobilize rather than injure the subject. On a successful roll, the attacker holds the target until the subject's next action. At that time, both combatants roll resisted Brawl or Martial Arts actions; the subject remains immobilized (able to take no other action) until she rolls more successes than the attacker does.

> **Ability:** Brawl or Martial Arts
> **Difficulty:** Normal
> **Accuracy:** Normal
> **Damage:** None

• **Kick:** Kicks range from simple front kicks to aerial spins. The base attack is +1 difficulty and inflicts the attacker's Strength +3 in damage. These ratings may be modified further at the Storyteller's discretion, increasing in damage and/ or difficulty as the maneuver increases in complexity.

> **Ability:** Brawl or Martial Arts
> **Difficulty:** +1
> **Accuracy:** Normal
> **Damage:** Strength +3

- **Multiple Opponents:** A character who battles multiple opponents in close combat suffers attack and defense difficulties of +1, cumulative, for each opponent after the first (to a maximum of +4).

- **Strike:** The attacker lashes out with a fist. The base attack is a standard action and inflicts the character's Strength +2 in damage. The Storyteller may adjust the difficulty and/ or damage depending on the type of punch: hook, jab, haymaker, karate strike.
  Ability: Brawl or Martial Arts
  Difficulty: Normal
  Accuracy: Normal
  Damage: Strength +2

- **Sweep:** The attacker uses her own legs to knock the legs out from under her opponent. The target takes Strength +1 damage and must roll Athletics at +3 difficulty or suffer a knockdown (see "Maneuver Complications," p. 248).
  The attacker can also use a staff, chain or similar implement to perform a sweep. The effect is the same, although the target takes Strength + Weapon type damage.
  Ability: Martial Arts or Melee
  Difficulty: Normal
  Accuracy: Normal
  Damage: Special

- **Tackle:** The attacker rushes her opponent, tackling him to the ground. The attack roll is +1 difficulty and inflicts Strength +3 damage. Additionally, both combatants must roll Athletics at +2 difficulty or suffer a knockdown (see "Maneuver Complications," p. 248). Even if the target's Athletics roll succeeds, he is unbalanced, suffering +1 difficulty to his actions for the next turn.
  Ability: Brawl
  Difficulty: +1
  Accuracy: Normal
  Damage: Strength +3

- **Throw:** The attacker grabs her opponent at +1 difficulty to hit, then uses the target's own momentum to throw him. The target is launched a number of meters equal to the attacker's Strength (opponents with a lot of momentum may travel up to an extra two meters). The target suffers a knockdown (see "Maneuver Complications," p. 248) automatically, and he takes Strength +1 damage plus an additional die of damage for every two meters he was thrown (rounded down). Characters with Mega-Strength automatically throw a target two additional meters per automatic damage success. Landing on harmful objects or debris can increase the damage effect.

Ability: Brawl or Martial Arts
Difficulty: +1
Accuracy: Normal
Damage: Special

• **Weapon Strike:** A slashing blow, thrust or jab, depending on the weapon used.
Ability: Melee
Difficulty: Normal
Accuracy: Normal
Damage: Strength + Weapon type

Special Nova Maneuvers

• **Aerial Slam:** The nova flies full-tilt into a target. The nova inflicts a base Strength + 3 dice of bashing damage. Additionally, assuming the nova is moving at full speed, each dot of Flight adds an extra two dice of damage. The nova herself takes half damage from the slam (though her soak might well reduce this damage to zero), and she can reduce the total damage of her slam by any amount she chooses, so long as she announces this ahead of time and slows her pace accordingly. The victim of the slam must check for knockback (p. 249), while the attacker makes a Flight roll to keep herself oriented. If the defender suffers no knockback and the attacker fails her roll, the attacker also takes full damage from the slam (she just ran into the equivalent of a brick wall).

If the nova has Hypermovement (Flight), each dot of Hypermovement adds another +1 to damage dice pool.
Ability: Flight
Difficulty: +1
Accuracy: Normal
Damage: Special

• **Aerial Strike:** The nova whizzes by a target, bashing it with a limb or weapon as she passes. The move is treated as a Strike or Weapon attack, but the player adds her dots in Flight and/ or Hypermovement to the damage dice pool inflicted.
Ability: Flight
Difficulty: +1
Accuracy: Normal
Damage: Special

• **Asphyxiation Attack (Prereq: Appropriate Bodymorph power):** Some novas can transform into liquids, gases or other altered states, then use their altered form to smother foes dependent on an oxygen supply. A nova seeking to deliver an asphyxiation attack must have the Bodymorph power and must have it currently active. Furthermore, due to the nature of the asphyxiation attack, the nova may apply it at full effect even if partially intangible (i.e., is using Bodymorph to simulate Density Decrease • or ••).

To administer this attack, the nova must successfully enter a clinch with her victim, using her Strength + Bodymorph skill total rather than Strength + Brawl. On the following turn, the nova rolls Strength + Bodymorph against the victim's Endurance skill total. Success on the nova's part indicates the nova cuts off the character's oxygen supply; the victim immediately begins taking one automatic bashing health level of damage per turn the nova maintains the attack, and must also make a Willpower check to avoid panic (see "Suffocation and Drowning," p. 257, for details on this roll). Once the victim falls to Incapacitated from this attack, he will die in [Stamina + Mega-Stamina] turns if the nova maintains the attack.

Failure on the attack roll means the attack has no effect that turn, but the nova may attempt the attack again on the following turn, so long as the clinch is maintained. If the victim breaks the nova's clinch, he immediately ceases taking damage from the asphyxiation attack.

Obviously, this attack has no effect on novas who have no need to breathe.
Ability: Bodymorph
Difficulty: Normal
Accuracy: Normal
Damage: Special

• **Hyperspeed Slam:** The nova runs into someone at superspeed. This move is treated as a Tackle (Str +3 bashing damage). Assuming the nova is moving at full speed, each level of the Hypermovement power adds two dice to tackle damage, while the Enhanced Movement enhancement adds an additional two. The nova herself takes half damage from the slam (though her soak might well reduce this damage to zero), and she can reduce the total damage of her slam by any amount she chooses, so long as she announces it ahead of time and slows her pace accordingly. The victim of the slam must check for knockback (p. 249), while the attacker makes an Athletics roll to stay upright, just as with a normal Tackle maneuver. If the defender suffers no knockback and the attacker fails her roll, the attacker also takes full damage from the slam (she just ran into the equivalent of a brick wall).
Ability: Brawl
Difficulty: +1
Accuracy: Normal
Damage: Special

• **Hyperspeed Strike:** The nova races by a target, bashing it with a limb or weapon as she passes. The maneuver is treated as a Strike or Weapon attack, but the player adds two dice for Enhanced Movement and/ or one die per dot of Hypermovement.

Ability: Brawl or Martial Arts
Difficulty: +1
Accuracy: Normal
Damage: Special

• **Smackdown (Prereq: Mega-Strength •, Brawl or Martial Arts 2):** Sometimes you just gotta lay the Smackdown on some punk. A Smackdown attack represents any of the various insane, over-the-top custom combat maneuvers available to novas. Smackdown attacks are unique to the novas using them; a Smackdown can be a Giant Haymaker, Super Uppercut, Triple Spinning Crescent Death Kick, Thunder Fire Jackhammer Slam or whatever the player wishes it to be.

A Smackdown can be a Striking Smackdown or Grappling Smackdown; the two use different systems. A Striking Smackdown typically involves throwing a devastating punch, kick or other blow, while a Grappling Smackdown involves grabbing the victim, hoisting him up and slamming him with great force.

To use a Striking Smackdown, the player declares the action, spends a point of Willpower and takes a full turn to "wind up." During this turn, the nova may take no actions except to defend against a single attack. Next turn, on her Initiative rating, the nova launches the Smackdown attack at +2 difficulty. If it hits, the victim takes Strength + 6 dice of bashing damage and is automatically knocked down or back unless he rolls Athletics at +3 difficulty. If it misses, the Willpower point is wasted.

To use a Grappling Smackdown, the player declares the action, spends a point of Willpower and attempts a Hold maneuver. Following the successful completion of the maneuver, the nova must hold the victim relatively immobile for a full turn, taking no other action in the meantime, while hoisting the victim into position. If the victim escapes the hold, the Smackdown maneuver fails. The following turn, on her Initiative rating, the nova's player makes another Brawl roll to slam, suplex, power-bomb or otherwise wreck her victim, administering Strength + 6 dice of damage and automatically knocking the victim down. If this second roll fails, the victim partially slips from the hold, takes only half damage and may make an Athletics roll to avoid knockdown.

Ability: Brawl or Martial Arts
Difficulty: Special
Accuracy: Normal
Damage: Strength +6

Ranged Combat Maneuvers

Most physical conflicts involve ranged weapons at some point. The following maneuvers allow for a number of useful actions during a firefight, but don't feel limited by this list. If the need arises, try developing a new maneuver (at the Storyteller's discretion). Most ranged weapons inflict lethal damage. Refer to the Ranged Weapons Chart, p. 275, for specific information.

• **Aiming:** The attacker adds one die, up to her total Perception rating, to her accuracy on a single shot for each turn spent aiming. A scope adds two more dice to the attacker's pool in the first turn of aiming (in addition to those added for Perception). The attacker may do nothing but aim during this time. Additionally, it isn't possible to aim at a target that is moving faster than a walk.

Players of characters with Mega-Perception may add those dice to the roll, but only once they've added their normal Perception dice.

• **Automatic Fire:** The weapon unloads its entire ammunition clip in one attack against a single target. The attacker makes a single roll, adding 10 dice to her accuracy. However, the difficulty on the attack roll increases by two due to the weapon's recoil. Extra successes add to the damage effect, to a maximum of five extra dice.

This attack is permissible only if the weapon's clip is at least half-full. Also, full-auto is possible only with automatic weapons and certain quantum powers. When using this maneuver with quantum powers, a player must pay two additional quantum points for the automatic fire.

Ability: Firearms
Difficulty: +2
Accuracy: +10
Damage: Special

• **Cover:** Cover increases an attacker's difficulty to hit a target (and often the target's ability to fire back). The difficulties listed here are the extra number of successes that the attacker needs to hit a target under cover. A character who fires back from behind cover is also at something of a disadvantage to hit, as he exposes himself and ducks back under protection. Ranged attacks made by a defender who is under cover are at one lower difficulty than listed below. (If a listed difficulty is +1, then the defender suffers no penalty to make attacks from under that cover.) If your character hides behind a wall, attackers' ranged attack rolls have a +2 difficulty. Your character's attacks staged from behind that wall are at +1 difficulty.

Note that difficulties for combatants who are both under cover are cumulative. If one combatant is prone and one is behind a wall, attacks staged by the prone character are at +2 difficulty, while attacks staged by the character behind the wall are also at +2 difficulty.

Cover Type	Attacker Difficulty
Light (lying prone)	+1
Good (behind wall)	+2
Superior (only head exposed)	+3

• **Cover Fire:** This maneuver isn't meant to hit targets; it is used instead to force opponents to dive for cover (allowing attackers to advance, withdraw or perform some other strategic action). Cover fire is a resisted action between the attacker's skill total and each opponent's Willpower. Each opponent who gets fewer successes than the attacker does abandons any planned action and dives for cover automatically, losing any further actions that turn. If an opponent's successes tie the attacker's, the opponent perseveres, but he takes his next action at a base +1 difficulty. If an opponent gets more successes, he steels his nerve and endures the volley. If an opponent botches, he's struck by a shot and takes the attack's base damage.

• **Multiple Shots:** An attacker may take more than one shot in a turn by declaring a multiple action (the first shot's dice pool is reduced by the total number of shots fired, and each subsequent shot is reduced by an additional die, cumulative). The attacker can fire a number of shots up to the weapon's full rate of fire. If using this maneuver with quantum powers, a nova may make as many shots as he wishes, but he must pay the normal quantum-point cost for each attack.

Ability: Firearms
Difficulty: Normal
Accuracy: Special
Damage: Weapon type

• **Range:** The Ranged Weapons Chart (p. 275) lists each weapon's medium range; no modifiers apply when shooting at this range. Twice that listing is the weapon's maximum range. Attacks made up to maximum range are +2 difficulty. Attacks made at targets within two meters are considered *point blank*. Point-blank shots add two dice to the attacker's accuracy. Ranges for quantum powers are listed under each power's description.

• **Reloading:** Reloading takes one full turn and requires the character's concentration (like any other maneuver, reloading can be performed as part of a multiple action; no die roll is required to reload, but doing so counts as an action for reducing other die rolls in a turn).

• **Semiautomatic Burst:** The attacker gains two additional dice on a single attack roll, and he expends three shots from the weapon's clip. Only one burst may be fired each turn. All firearms may perform this maneuver, although at +1 difficulty on the attack due to recoil. If used with quantum powers, this maneuver costs an extra quantum point to evoke.

Ability: Firearms
Difficulty: Special
Accuracy: +2
Damage: Weapon type

• **Strafing:** Instead of aiming at one target, full-automatic weapons can be fired across an area. Strafing adds 10 dice to accuracy on a standard attack roll, and he empties the clip. A +1 difficulty (in addition to any other modifiers) is added for each meter in area of effect covered beyond the first.

The attacker divides any successes gained on the attack roll evenly among all targets in the covered area (successes assigned to hit an individual are added to that target's damage effect, as well). If only one target is within range or the area of effect, only half the successes affect him. The attacker then assigns any leftover successes as she desires. If fewer successes are rolled than there are targets, only one may be assigned per target until they are all allocated.

Dodge rolls against strafing are at +1 difficulty.
Ability: Firearms
Difficulty: Special
Accuracy: +10
Damage: Special

• **Two Weapons:** Firing two weapons gives the attacker a distinct advantage, but it has its share of complications. Doing so is considered performing a multiple action, complete with reduced dice pools for total shots taken and for any recoil. Additionally, the attacker suffers +1 difficulty for her off-hand (unless she's ambidextrous); if the attacker has Mega-Dexterity, she is automatically considered to be ambidextrous.

Pistols, carbines and other small arms incur no further penalties. However, wielding a sidearm and a heavy weapon requires a minimum 4 Might skill total; using two heavy weapons at once requires a minimum 6 Might skill total (default to Strength). Each point the attacker is under this minimum is an additional difficulty applied to each shot. The attacker can fire a number of shots up to each weapon's rate of fire.

Ability: Firearms
Difficulty: Special
Accuracy: Special
Damage: Weapon type

Maneuver Complications

The following are some of the common types of combat complications. The Storyteller should add any others as the situation warrants (see "Sources of Injury," p. 255, for further information).

• **Area and Explosion Attacks:** Area and explosion attacks add two dice to accuracy, and targets cannot block or parry them, even with nova powers. Targets may dodge, but they must have and use sufficient movement to get clear of the affected area. Area and explosive attacks do not add attack successes to damage dice pools.

- **Blinded:** Add two dice to attack rolls made against a blinded target. Furthermore, blind characters are at +2 difficulty on all actions.
- **Dazed:** If, in a single attack, the attacker rolls a number of damage successes greater than the target's Stamina, the victim is dazed. The target must spend her next available turn shaking off the attack's effects. Characters with Mega-Stamina may add double their Mega-Stamina dots to their Stamina to determine whether or not they're dazed. Also, see "Unconscious."
- **Immobilization:** Add two dice to attack rolls made on an immobilized (i.e., held by someone or something) but still struggling target. This penalty applies to characters whose Dexterity has been reduced by the Immobilize power. Attacks hit automatically if the target is completely immobilized (tied up or otherwise paralyzed).
- **Knockback:** Nova attacks pack a lot of punch. Sometimes, an attack hits with such force that a defender is blasted halfway across the battlefield, or even further. This phenomenon is known as knockback. Bashing attacks such as punches are the phenomena most likely to cause knockback, but lethal attacks of sufficient force may also inflict knockback.

Knockback is cinematic and very appropriate to the genre, but including it in a game inevitably involves boring, un-fun stuff like math and physics and whatnot. Accordingly, we present two systems to represent knockback:

The simple way: If an attack does a lot of damage, it may blast the target back a ways. Combatants who are big or heavy (for example, those with Density Increase or Growth) won't fly back far, if at all. Combatants who are light (like those with Shrinking) get knocked around real good. A combatant who is knocked back suffers some amount of bashing damage — whatever the Storyteller decides is appropriate — when she smashes into the ground, through a wall or whatever. That's it. Simple, up to the Storyteller and fun.

The complicated way: Some players aren't going to be happy with the simple system, and some Storytellers actually enjoy incorporating complicated formulas into their games. If you feel the need for a precise formula, try the following: Compare the attack's damage dice pool to the target's Might skill total. Each active dot of Density Control (Increase) adds three to the target's effective Might skill total, while each active dot of Shrinking subtracts three. (Note that even an attack that does not actually inflict damage on the target may still knock the target back.)

If the damage dice pool equals the defender's adjusted Might, the defender must check for knockdown.

If the damage dice pool is greater, the target flies back two meters per damage die above the Might skill total, plus two extra meters for each net success on the initial attack roll (that is, successes left after defensive actions such as dodges). The target takes one die of bashing damage for every two meters of knockback inflicted. If a knocked-back target smashes into something (a wall, another combatant, the side of a building), he effectively suffers a collision. The person or thing takes the same amount of damage that the knocked-back combatant suffers, and depending on the sturdiness of the substance, a collision may change the knockback damage dice to lethal damage. If the target hits with sufficient force, he might even blow right through the intervening material and continue on his trajectory. See "Material Strengths," p. 257, for specifics.

A knocked-back target may make an Athletics roll at +2 difficulty; success on this roll reduces knockback damage by half, as the target rolls with the blow. A target who collides with something may not make this roll.

Lethal attacks cause only half the normal knockback. Additionally, the Storyteller has the option to declare that certain attacks simply don't cause knockback. For example, a Quantum Blast that manifests as a laser beam or flame gout may do a lot of damage, but neither one is likely to cause much knockback.

Finally, if an attack is extremely potent (say, 20+ raw damage dice) and inflicts 10 or more dice of knockback damage, the Storyteller may decree that the knocked-back victim flies as far as is cinematically interesting. The target takes the normal amount of knockback damage, but he might be blasted back a kilometer or even more.

- **Knockdown:** Quite simply, the victim falls down. After suffering a knockdown, the subject makes an Athletics or Martial Arts roll. If successful, she gets back on her feet immediately, but her Initiative is reduced by two in the next turn. On a failed roll, the subject spends her next action climbing to her feet. On a botch, she lands particularly hard or at a severe angle; the Storyteller rolls a bashing damage effect equal to the botches rolled.

Maneuvers like Tackle, Throw and Sweep are intended to knock an opponent down. However, an especially powerful attack of any kind may send the target to the ground. Such instances are best left to the Storyteller's discretion, and they should occur only when appropriately cinematic or suitable to the story.

- **Unconscious:** If, in a single attack, the attacker rolls a number of damage successes greater than the target's Stamina plus two, the victim blacks out. Unconsciousness lasts from five turns to an entire scene (specific duration is at the Storyteller's discretion). Again, characters with Mega-Stamina add double their Mega-Stamina ratings to their Stamina.

Close Combat Maneuvers Table

Maneuver	Ability	Accuracy	Difficulty	Damage
Block	Brawl, Martial Arts	Special	Normal	0
Clinch	Brawl, Martial Arts	Normal	Normal	Strength + 2
Disarm	Martial Arts, Melee	Normal	Special	Special
Dodge	Athletics, Martial Arts	N/A	Special	0
Hold	Brawl, Martial Arts	Normal	Normal	0
Kick	Brawl, Martial Arts	Normal	+1	Strength +3
Parry	Melee	Special	Normal	0
Power Block	Dex+power rating	Special	Normal	0
Strike	Brawl, Martial Arts	Normal	Normal	Strength +2
Sweep	Martial Arts, Melee	Normal	Normal	Special
Tackle	Brawl	Normal	+1	Strength +3
Throw	Brawl, Martial Arts	Normal	+1	Special
Weapon Strike	Melee	Normal	Normal	Weapon

Special Nova Maneuvers

Maneuver	Ability	Accuracy	Difficulty	Damage
Aerial Slam	Flight	Normal	+1	Special
Aerial Strike	Flight	Normal	+1	Special
Asphyxiation	Bodymorph	Normal	Normal	Special
Hyperspeed Slam	Brawl	Normal	+1	Special
Hyperspeed Strike	Brawl, Martial Arts	Normal	+1	Special
Smackdown	Brawl, Martial Arts	Normal	Special	Strength +6

Ranged Combat Maneuvers Table

Maneuver	Ability	Accuracy	Difficulty	Damage
Automatic Fire	Firearms	+10	+2	Special
Multiple Shots	Firearms	Special	Normal	Weapon
Semiauto Burst	Firearms	+2	Special	Weapon
Spray	Firearms	+10	Special	Special
Strafing	Firearms	+10	Special	Special
Two Weapons	Firearms	Special	Special	Weapon

Armored Combat

Vehicle combat systems differ from those of personal combat in only two ways: damage effect and maneuvers. The weaponry involved in vehicle combat does a significantly higher amount of damage (though some novas' attacks equal or exceed those of vehicular weaponry), and the character directs a craft's maneuvers instead of performing them herself. Otherwise, Initiative, attacks and resolution are handled in the same way as in personal combat.

As of 2008, space travel is still in its infancy, although certain novas are theoretically spaceworthy. Should your chronicle require rules for space travel, consult **Aberrant**'s sister game, **Trinity**.

Damage and Armor Adds

As with nova powers, vehicle weapons are designed to deal significant amounts of damage to vehicles and other durable structures (buildings, orbital stations). A craft can also take more punishment than a person can. Essentially, people and vehicles fight on different scales. To reflect this, vehicle armament has *damage adds*, while vehicles themselves have *armor adds*. A damage add is listed in brackets next to a weapon's damage effect (e.g., 5d10 [10] L), while an armor add is bracketed after the vehicle's soak (e.g., 4 [10]). Armor adds are applied against both bashing and lethal damage.

The damage add is the number of damage successes inflicted automatically, just as with a nova's damage adds. If a person fires a weapon at a vehicle, the armor add is the number of dice subtracted from the weapon's damage effect.

When a vehicle weapon fires on another vehicle, the damage and armor adds are ignored. Instead, the weapon's base damage effect and the craft's base soak are rolled normally. This system reflects that artillery and armor are specifically designed to inflict and resist huge amounts of punishment, while still keeping dice pools to manageable totals.

The damage in vehicle combat is applied just like in personal combat. While the systems are identical, a damaged ship isn't the same as a damaged person. Refer to the Appendix, p. 278, for specifics on vehicle weapons and applying damage to vehicles.

Vehicular Slams

Vehicles that collide into pedestrians, flying novas or other vehicles inflict one die of lethal damage per 20 kph of speed. Base damage can be reduced for smaller vehicles (a motorcycle) or increased for large/ heavy vehicles (a tank).

Flying Objects

Novas (and aircraft) can perform a selection of maneuvers; dice actions usually come into play when the nova is either closing on or avoiding another flyer. The skill total for most such rolls is Pilot (for vehicles) or Dexterity + Flight (for novas). New maneuvers can be added with the Storyteller's permission.

• **Spin:** If traveling at no greater than one-half speed, the nova can rotate directly on her axis, thereby turning around or even spinning in a complete circle. Helicopters, ducted-fan craft and hovercraft may perform this maneuver as well. Conventional fixed-wing aircraft and aquatic craft cannot change direction without covering distance, and they must make a turn.

• **Turn:** Anything from a casual left to a severe swerve or U-turn. The Storyteller may assign difficulties depending on the sharpness of the turn.

• **Climb:** The nova (or pilot) heads up. Ascent can range from a slow climb to a sharp-angled ascent. The Storyteller may apply a +1 or +2 difficulty for a sharp climb, since such a maneuver involves high g-forces (characters with Gravity Control are assumed to compensate automatically for such things).

• **Dive:** The opposite of a climb; the character plummets downward. The Storyteller may apply a difficulty to the die roll for a hard dive due to g-force stresses, as with a sharp climb.

• **Loop:** The character makes a vertical loop, ending up in roughly the same position that he started in at the beginning of the move. Difficulty depends on the loop's tightness, usually between +1 and +3.

• **Roll:** The character flips upside down (and usually right-side up again). Repeated rolls are possible (a "corkscrew") with increasing difficulty, at the Storyteller's discretion.

Health

This section deals with your character's current physical or mental state, as well as various factors that can improve or worsen these conditions. Health can be affected by anything that injures the body or the mind, such as simple lack of sleep, mental assault or a bullet to the head. Depending on her condition, a nova's current health can greatly impede her ability to perform even the simplest of tasks.

Physical States

The coming of novas has contributed to considerable advances in medicine. The Human Genome Project has been completed, HIV and many forms of cancer have been wiped out and people are healthier and live longer, on the whole, than ever before. Which is good in theory, but a few Mega-Strength punches or Quantum Bolts can put a damper on anyone's good day.

The Health Chart

The Health chart on the character sheet helps you track your character's current physical condition. It also lists the penalty imposed on your dice pool for each level of injury that your character sustains. As your character suffers more injuries, her health declines until she becomes incapacitated — or dead.

Humans have eight health levels, ranging from Bruised to Dead. Some novas, particularly those with the Growth or Body Modification powers, have more. When an attacker rolls a success on a damage effect, your character takes one health level of damage. This damage is marked on your character sheet in the appropriate box, although the mark you make depends on the type of damage inflicted (see "Applying Damage").

The number to the left of the lowest marked box indicates your current dice penalty. As your character gets more and more battered, it's increasingly difficult for him to perform even the simplest of tasks. The dice penalty is subtracted from your dice pool for every action (except damage effect and soak) until the wound heals.

The penalty also indicates impaired movement, translating into the number of meters by which your movement is divided. Furthermore, at Wounded and below, your character can no longer sprint. A character with a 3 Dexterity who's at Maimed can walk only two meters a turn, or can run four meters. At Crippled, your character can only walk (or crawl) one meter per turn.

Health Level	Dice/Move Penalty	Description
Bruised	0	You're slightly battered, suffering no penalties.
Hurt	-1	Some scrapes and bumps; not seriously impaired.
Injured	-1	Minor injuries; noticeable damage.
Wounded	-2	You can walk and run, but you cannot sprint.
Maimed	-3	A bloody mess, you hobble about in pain.
Crippled	-4	You're severely injured, stumbling and wrecked.
Incapacitated		You lose consciousness from the pain and trauma. No actions are possible.
Dead		Simply that. Notify the next of kin.

• **Incapacitated:** The stage immediately before death, Incapacitated differs from unconsciousness in that your character collapses from the combined effects of physical trauma and pain. She falls to the ground and remains comatose until her Health recovers to Wounded. Successful medical treatment that restores at least one health level can bring her around before this. Any more damage suffered by an Incapacitated character kills her.

• **Dead:** When your character suffers a total of eight levels of lethal damage, she dies. Medicine being what it is in the 21st century, a trained professional has a brief amount of time to resuscitate her. Your character is beyond help after a number of turns equal to her total Endurance.

Applying Damage

Most damage in **Aberrant** consists of one of two types. Bashing damage includes all forms of temporary injury. Lethal damage covers permanent, killing wounds. All injuries are cumulative, whether lethal or bashing, and the combined injury determines your character's current health level. Specifics on each type of damage are provided.

When your character takes bashing damage, it's recorded as a slash ("/") in the appropriate Health chart box. Lethal damage is marked with an "X" for each level inflicted. Lethal damage always gets marked above bashing. So if you mark a level of bashing damage in the Bruised box, then take one lethal health level later, "move down" the bashing level to the Hurt box by marking that box with a "/." Bashing levels taken after lethal levels are simply drawn in on the next open box. Bashing damage isn't as severe as lethal, so it's always marked last and healed first.

HEALTH	
Bruised -0	◹
Hurt	☐
Injured	☐
Wounded	☐

For Example: Lotus Infinite has already taken a level of bashing damage from a Mitoid's glancing punch (Ms. Infinite's player marks her Health chart with a "/" in the Bruised box). A Teragen nova shoots LI with a flame blast, scoring three lethal health levels. LI's chart is marked with an "X" in the Bruised, Hurt and Injured health levels, and a "/" in the Wounded box (essentially moving the punch's damage down the chart). The combined damage puts LI at -2 dice to all rolls. Trying to escape, Lotus Infinite activates her Flight and hightails it.

HEALTH	
Bruised -0	☒
Hurt	☒
Injured	☒
Wounded	◹

Bashing Damage

Bashing damage, from a distracting headache to a punch in the nose, covers all forms of injury that aren't likely to kill instantly, or which fade relatively quickly. Most forms of hand-to-hand combat inflict bashing damage, as do mental "injuries" such as headaches, drunkenness or other mental distractions. Bashing damage generally impairs less than lethal damage does, and it heals faster.

Your character can die from bashing damage, though. A punch may not cause as much trauma as a bullet does, but enough punches can kill. After your character reaches Incapacitated on the Health chart, each new bashing injury, while soaked like a normal bashing effect, is marked with a second slash on the highest bashing level. This way, bashing levels turn progressively into lethal damage. Once your character's Health chart is filled to Incapacitated with lethal damage, the next level of damage taken, whether bashing or lethal, kills her.

For Example: Lotus Infinite, flying with three levels of lethal damage (X, X, X) and one of bashing (/), is swatted out of the sky by her nemesis Geryon. A squad of Mitoids catch up and batter LI (inflicting three more bashing health levels — /, /, /) until she blacks out. LI is at Incapacitated with four bashing damage levels left.

Lotus Infinite's merciless opponents then smash her prone body with punches and kicks. The first hit after LI falls to Incapacitated causes one level of bashing damage. So LI's Wounded level, previously bashing, has another slash drawn through it (for "X"), making it lethal. This process can be repeated three more times until LI's remaining health levels are changed from bashing to lethal. Regardless of whether it's bashing or lethal, the fourth level of damage will kill her.

If your character falls to Incapacitated due to bashing damage but then takes a level of lethal damage, she's dead.

Lethal Damage

Lethal damage is intended to cause immediate and grievous injury. Knives, pistols, claws and flame gouts all cause lethal wounds. Such wounds don't heal easily, and they usually require medical attention for any hope of recovery. Nature, too, provides numerous health hazards for humans and even novas. Electricity, vacuum exposure, hard radiation and fire all cause lethal wounds.

Lethal damage kills with ruthless efficiency. When your character's Health chart fills to Incapacitated with lethal damage, any further damage taken, whether bashing or lethal, kills her.

Aggravated Damage

A few particularly virulent nova attacks inflict aggravated damage. Aggravated damage represents disintegration, flesh-eating viruses, molecular disruption or some other form of complete tissue destruction. Aggravated damage may not be soaked except by novas with the Hardbody enhancement or other similar powers. To record aggravated damage, mark an asterisk ("*") in the Health box. Aggravated damage is marked over all other kinds of damage.

Against baselines, aggravated damage is *permanent*: the wounds never heal. Novas may heal aggravated damage, but they get no multiplier for their metabolisms; they heal aggravated damage no faster than a baseline human heals lethal damage. The Healing and Regeneration powers can heal aggravated damage, but each level healed costs triple the normal quantum-point cost.

Soak

As noted above, bashing damage isn't as immediately fatal as lethal damage is; bashing damage also heals more quickly (see "Recovery"). The human (and nova) body can take more punishment from bashing damage than it can from lethal effects. Use your character's full Stamina rating to soak bashing attacks. Baselines cannot use Stamina to soak lethal attacks; however, all novas may use half their Stamina, rounded down, to soak lethal attacks. See p. 241 for specifics.

Aggravated damage *cannot* be soaked unless the nova has the Hardbody enhancement or other similar protection.

Even with soak, most humans crunch real good when caught in the midst of nova-level combat. Many nova powers, though, protect against both bashing and lethal damage, and their benefits may add to your base soak against attacks.

Certain types of artificial armor protect against bashing and lethal attacks as well, though even if your character wears such protection (considered laughably wussy in many nova circles), most nova attacks worthy of the name shred conventional armor easily. See "Armor," p. 277, for specific ratings.

Recovery

Minor injuries simply require time to heal. Medical attention or quantum powers are required to recover from serious levels of bashing damage or from any form of lethal damage. If your character reaches Crippled, whether from bashing or lethal damage, she must get professional help. At that level, your character can barely walk.

The preceding charts list the time involved in healing damage. Bashing and lethal damage recover differently. Recovery Time lists how long it takes to heal that specific health level; the time is cumulative. A nova without Mega-Stamina who takes three levels of bashing damage takes 30 minutes to heal each one before he's

Healing Bashing Damage

Bashing damage up to the Wounded level can be cared for without medical skill; these wounds heal on their own, without treatment. Bashing damage beyond Wounded may have deeper consequences. Your character's vision or hearing may be altered due to a concussion, she may suffer excruciating pain from internal bruising or experience some other extreme discomfort. Receiving adequate medical attention negates these effects.

Health Level	Recovery Time
Bruised to Wounded	One hour
Maimed	Three hours
Crippled	Six hours
Incapacitated	12 hours

Once bashing levels reach Incapacitated, any further bashing wounds are X'd over previous bashing ones, making them lethal (see "Bashing Damage"). At that point, recovery is handled as lethal damage.

Healing Lethal Damage

Lethal damage of any sort can be deadly — that's why it's called lethal. Lethal wounds that go unattended may continue to bleed until your character passes out and dies from blood loss. Other dangers can also arise from infection, cellular damage or broken limbs.

Any lethal damage past Hurt requires medical treatment to prevent further harm. Untreated lethal wounds worsen by one level of lethal damage per day. When someone sustains lethal damage down to Incapacitated, he's one health level away from death. If he takes one more wound (whether bashing or lethal), he dies.

If the individual is at Maimed or higher, he may recover with rest over the times listed below. However, if your character is Crippled or Incapacitated, no recovery is possible unless he receives medical attention. Indeed, at Incapacitated the individual is comatose at worse and delirious at best, and he could still die.

Health Level	Recovery Time
Bruised	One day
Hurt	Three days
Injured	One week
Wounded	One month
Maimed	Two months
Crippled	Three months
Incapacitated	Five months

Note that these healing times are for baseline humans. *All novas heal at least twice as fast as the times listed on the charts*, and novas with high Mega-Stamina heal much faster. See "Mega-Stamina," p. 160, to calculate a nova's normal healing time.

fully fit. A nova without Mega-Stamina who suffers five lethal damage levels takes one month to recover from Maimed to Wounded. After that, he needs an additional two weeks, five days and 12 hours to recover from the rest. If the same character takes four levels of lethal damage and one of bashing, he needs 90 minutes to recover the bashing level before he starts recovering from the lethal wounds.

These recovery times assume the individual receives only basic care (first aid and bed rest). The times improve if the individual has access to modern health care. If he's treated by a physician with adequate skills (Medicine 2 rating) and medicine during his recovery time, the character heals each health level at one time category higher on the Health chart. If the patient forgoes special treatment at any point, he heals at normal rates.

If the individual receives care from advanced medical techniques (Medicine 4 rating), he recovers each health level at two categories higher on the Health chart. If this advanced treatment is not received at any point, normal healing rates apply.

No matter the quality of the treatment processes involved, each level of bashing damage still takes at least five minutes to heal, and lethal damage still takes a minimum of one hour per level to heal.

These recovery times don't take into account quantum powers. The systems described for the Regeneration enhancement or the Healing power take precedence over these systems.

For Example: Lotus Infinite is saved by fellow DeVries agents before the Mitoids finish her off. They take LI to a nearby clinic where a resident (Medicine 2) tends LI's injuries (she has currently taken lethal damage to Wounded and bashing damage to Incapacitated).

Thanks to the resident and the clinic's medical resources, LI heals everything one category more quickly. She is a nova and has one dot of Mega-Stamina, so she heals all damage three times as quickly as a baseline human. LI heals the Incapacitated bashing level in two hours, the Crippled bashing level in one hour and the Maimed bashing level in 20 minutes. LI then heals her Wounded lethal level in two days and eight hours, her Injured lethal level in a day and her Hurt lethal level in eight hours. Finally, her Bruised lethal level takes another eight hours to heal.

In short, LI recovers completely in four days, three hours and 20 minutes. If she had been a normal human and had not received medical care, it would have taken 41 days and 18 hours to heal fully.

Sources of Injury

Novas live in a hostile universe. The dangers inherent to such an environment are many, and they inflict the same kinds of harm that combat does.

Some sources of injury require that a damage effect be rolled, while others cause the subject to take damage automatically. If a system states that the Storyteller "rolls damage effect," the damage is treated like an attack, including applying the character's soak. If it says the character "takes a health level," she takes the damage automatically, regardless of any defenses.

Disease

Novas, though still human, are much more resistant to illnesses than their baseline counterparts. Still, a virulent enough disease — for example, a biological weapon — can affect novas. For game purposes, diseases are applied as bashing damage, although a soak roll isn't normally possible (Mega-Stamina may allow one, while appropriate Life Support enables the nova simply to ignore the disease). A fever or flu inflicts one or more bashing health levels, while rare diseases or genetically engineered viruses can be more devastating, even inflicting lethal damage.

The Storyteller should decide on the exact effects (including altered perception and delirium) of severe sicknesses. Permanent Attribute reductions may even occur. The Resistance Ability (of which all novas have at least three dots) can help combat infection and sickness; Storytellers should adjust appropriately.

Electrocution

The strength of the electrical flow determines the amount of lethal damage your character takes from electrocution. She suffers the damage effect noted below each turn until contact with the source is severed (not always an easy thing to accomplish, since electrocution tends to contract the victim's muscles, locking her in place as the electricity flows through her body).

Electrical damage is a lethal effect. Artificial armor doesn't protect against it (depending on the subject's defenses, the circumstance and the Storyteller's decision), though novas' natural soak against lethal damage does.

Damage Effect	Electrical Source
Two	Minor; wall socket
Four	Major; protective fence
Six	Severe; vehicle battery, junction box
Eight	Fatal; main feed line, subway rail

Falling

Even a nova can suffer great damage from falling significant distances. The Storyteller rolls one die of bashing damage for every three meters (rounded down) that your character falls before hitting something solid. However, on a controlled fall, roll Athletics; each success equals one meter that your character may fall before suffering injury. With two successes, your character could drop five meters before taking a die of bashing damage — however, if she falls eight meters, she takes two dice.

Falling damage may be soaked as normal, but the Storyteller always rolls at least one die. Each success is a bashing health level that your character takes. Landing on sharp objects can change the damage from bashing to lethal, at the Storyteller's discretion.

If your character plummets 30 meters or more, she reaches terminal velocity. The damage effect reaches a maximum of 10 dice at this point, and it is considered lethal damage. Additionally, all soak is halved against a terminal-velocity fall; only the toughest novas are designed for this sort of punishment.

Fire

A fire's size and fuel determine the amount of lethal damage your character endures. She suffers the damage effect each turn that she's in contact with the flames; she must leave the area and/ or put out any fire on her to stop taking damage. Fire damage is a lethal effect that may ignore artificial armor (depending on the armor type, the fire type and the Storyteller's discretion), though novas' lethal soak protects them against it.

Damage Effect	Type of Fire
Two	Lighter
Four	Campfire
Five	Bonfire
Six	Welding torch
Seven	Raging inferno
Fire type x 2	Chemical fire

If your character falls to Maimed, she is scarred temporarily by the flames (reduce Appearance by one until her wounds recover to Bruised). If she is reduced to Crippled or Incapacitated by the fire, the burns cover

ABERRANT

the majority of her body, resulting in permanent scarring (reduce Appearance by one if Crippled, by two if Incapacitated). These results may be corrected with advanced plastic surgery or the Regeneration enhancement.

Although a fair number of novas can walk unhurt through flames, the intense heat may still overwhelm them. A player whose character is trapped in the middle of a severe conflagration may have to make a Stamina roll or lose dice due to dizziness and overheating; novas with Mega-Stamina, particularly with the Life Support enhancement, typically ignore this effect.

Material Strengths

Combat in this genre inevitably involves someone being put through a building, water tower or other "immovable" object. To simulate this enjoyable pastime, we provide a chart listing protection ratings and health levels for various solids.

This chart, of course, applies to knockback. If someone or something goes flying into a solid, the substance immediately takes the knockback damage; if that damage exceeds the substance's soak, the solid breaks, while if it completely wipes out the health levels, the solid is completely destroyed and the knocked-back person/item continues on *through* the object.

Material	Health Levels (per cubic meter)	Soak
Glass	2	0
Ice	3	2
Wood	5	3
Stone and soft metals	8-10	5
Hard metals	10	6+

Radiation

Radiation covers the broad range of energy emissions that surround and penetrate everything. All things reflect and create a certain amount of radiation; life requires it, but too much radiation can kill. For the purposes of game play, radiation is divided into two simple categories: soft radiation and hard radiation. Damage from either type cannot be soaked normally, although Life Support, Absorption (energy), Invulnerability (radiation) or Mega-Stamina of 4 or greater will bestow protection against radiation.

Victims of large or extended doses of radiation may suffer cancer, hair loss, brittle bones, mental problems and other debilitating effects.

• **Soft Radiation:** This category includes all types of radiation that bombard humanity each and every day. High doses of soft radiation (x-rays, infrared) can cause sickness and even physical injury. A character suffers one bashing health level for each turn that she is exposed to high doses of soft radiation.

• **Hard Radiation:** This category includes all other types of radiation, including gamma rays, cosmic rays and microwaves. Even minimal doses of hard radiation can be lethal. A character suffers one lethal health level for each turn that she's exposed to hard radiation.

Suffocation and Drowning

A character without the Life Support enhancement can hold her breath one minute per point in her Endurance skill total. After this duration, you must roll Endurance each turn (at an increasing level of difficulty; see "Feats of Endurance," p. 234). When you fail a roll, your character suffers one bashing health level of damage. Your character automatically suffers a level of bashing damage every minute after your first failed Endurance roll, until she can breathe again. After reaching Incapacitated, your character dies if she is not resuscitated (Medicine 1 required to do so).

Temperature Extremes

Most human facilities are kept at a comfortable 20 degrees Celsius. Still, humanity can survive far warmer or colder temperatures. When exposed to dangerously high (35 degrees Celsius or higher) or low (-10 degrees Celsius or lower) temperatures, characters without appropriate Life Support suffer one lethal health level for every day in that environment — this damage cannot be soaked, nor can it be recovered until your character gets to a more hospitable climate.

This rate of damage increases if the temperature exceeds the survivable range (say, inside a freezer, where the temperature can drop as low as -20 degrees Celsius). A temperature far beyond human survivability (the heart of the sun, deep space) kills in moments.

Vacuum

Exposure to the vacuum of space involves many dangers. First of all, the temperature can range from over 1000 degrees Celsius when exposed to the sun, to -273 degrees Celsius in a planet's shadow — either way, death is instantaneous to anyone exposed without adequate protection. Space also transmits cosmic radiation unimpeded — even minor exposure can be lethal.

Assuming your character is trapped in a vacuum, but he is not exposed to outer space, survival chances increase dramatically. In that case, asphyxiation is the main threat (refer to "Suffocation and Drowning").

CHAPTER SEVEN: STORYTELLING

At its heart, **Aberrant** isn't a game about competition. There's only one goal for an **Aberrant** game — to tell a story about these beings of great power and have fun along the way. However, the difference between playing an **Aberrant** game and standard "storytelling" comes in the interaction. Here, the audience doesn't just sit passively and watch the story unfold — they wander through it as principal players, uncovering the plot and manipulating the setting. They meet people and do things that ultimately decide the story's outcome. And who defines where they are and what they see?

You do.

As the Storyteller, your role in all this is a pretty demanding one — to use a comic book-style metaphor, you're part artist, part writer and mostly editor. You design the overall plots and subplots, draw out the backgrounds, design the greater part of the book's cast and improvise dialogue as the stories unfold. Everything the players' characters see, hear and react to — yes, you're responsible for providing it all. You describe their surroundings, the people and things therein, and you generally adjudicate "what would happen next." By describing the world around them, you help to define the characters — who they are and what they're trying to accomplish. Daunting? Sure. But it's not as impossible as it sounds.

Being a good Storyteller requires a mixture of qualities, but you don't have to master them all — or even any. The primary objective of any game session is to entertain the players and have fun. That's all. However, the more you practice, the more involved your stories can get. Before long, you can be escorting your players on journeys that work on multiple levels, with symbolism and foreshadowing alluding to the greater picture. You'll be able to help your players *live* the story.

The Story

Developing a story requires some work. As a Storyteller, you have to not only devise the basic plot, but add hooks to keep the players interested and make provisions for whatever actions the characters might take as well. This responsibility is particularly important when you're trying to sustain the players' interests over the period of an entire series. Although there isn't a magical formula for "the ultimate story" that can be used time and time again, always keeping the players hungry for more, there are some basics that can ease your task quite a bit.

First and foremost, you need ample preparation. Preparing doesn't mean devising an impossibly convoluted plot and forcing the players to adhere precisely to your vision of the storyline, scene by scene. Rather, you should create a flexible outline of probable events and characters. Start the players with the first event on the outline — say, having them witness an upstanding member of Team Tomorrow brutally murder a spike dealer in an alleyway. How they react to that first scene — where they go from there — will start the story in motion. You don't need to script every line for every possible scene following, but you should have some idea of what will happen if they try to capture the "hero," or if they try to reason with him, or even if they ignore the whole thing.

Hand in hand with preparation is flexibility — this is a valuable trait for the Storyteller. At least once in every game session, a player will do something you won't expect. This is virtually a guarantee. If you can react quickly and logically to whatever twists the players throw at you, your story will run smoothly and maintain its strength. On the other hand, if you were absolutely, positively relying on them to turn the datadisc over to the Directive, the story will suffer if they decide to keep it for themselves. When snags come along, you can either work them into the framework of the story or try to find some other way of bringing things back on track. If you can't immediately think of a way to repair the story, don't panic — there's still opportunity to fix things over the course of the next few scenes. And besides, sometimes great inspiration can strike in the heart of desperation.

Motivating your players is also key. Never force them along the plotline — lead them along with tempting story hooks and strange riddles. If they take off enthusiastically in a direction you hadn't expected, you can let the story go along without directly intervening; either follow them along and improvise the outcomes to their actions, or wait until an appropriate point to reinsert the next plot point. For example, if the players decided to let the T2M hero off the hook after the spike dealer's murder, hit them a few days later with an OpNet headline about some new nova-powered presence in the drug trade. If they decided to go to the "hero's" superiors, maybe they find it even more difficult to get Project

Utopia to believe that one of their chosen is a common criminal than it would have been to confront the nova then and there. But above all, don't punish the players for deviating from the "script" — let them explore other avenues, and subtly try to nudge them back on track when you can.

One final piece of advice: Devise the agendas of the story's major players, particularly the antagonists, in as much detail as you see fit. Try to get a good feel for your antagonist's sinister plot, as well as any backup plans he might have made should interference arrive. If the players don't interfere, you can always hit them with the aftereffects of the antagonist's success. If they do, it's much easier to improvise his backup plans if you had some idea of what they are ahead of time.

Creating a Story

When you start to plan your story, any number of things can spark an idea. You might draw inspiration from a movie or book, or even from your environment. Ultimately, though, most stories are based on one of three things: a strong character, an event or a powerful atmosphere.

The character-based story is easy enough. Look at *Romeo and Juliet* or *Hamlet* for classic ideas of how one or two people can propel an entire story. With such a story, you generally center events on one or two characters — generally an antagonist or archvillain. Perhaps you have an image in your head of a powerful, elementally attuned Indian nova who's taken it into his head to purify the Ganges — by turning all the human cities along its length into wilderness. Or maybe the character in question is one of the characters' allies; perhaps their contact in the DeVries Agency is suddenly having personal troubles with the Medellín Cartel, but he doesn't dare move against them himself because his daughter is one of their enforcers. You can even focus a story on one of the players' characters if you feel that the character in question has been overshadowed by his teammates for a while. Naturally, you should be careful with this last one, so as not to be perceived as "playing favorites."

An event-based story is also pretty easy to define; look at the rash of disaster movies that were out a couple of years ago. Although each of these stories made an effort to have strong characters, a definite atmosphere and even an interesting plot, there was never really any question what the story's basic premise was. The situation was always the starting point for the story idea. If you prefer a less sensational (and rather more powerful) example, look at *The Seven Samurai* — although it had a fascinating set of characters and a strong atmosphere, the premise could be traced to the event "seven unemployed samurai are hired by peasants to protect a village." And look what came out of that.

Atmospheric stories can be tricky, but there's no lack of those, either. The most obvious example is, of course, the horror story. *Alien* was obviously more atmospheric than situation-based — the situation was original, yes, but the movie was devised to explore the atmosphere of horror in a new fashion. An atmosphere-based story can also be based on a moral or theme; if you want to illustrate the cutthroat violence of the criminal underworld, you can certainly pick characters and events to do so. And, of course, you can always use an atmospheric story to give the players what they want; if they've had a little too much politicking over the last few stories and are ready to have their hearts beat a little faster, there's nothing wrong with giving them a breakneck story that makes them fight for their lives and appreciate the adrenaline rush.

Story Elements

There are a few things that all good stories have in common. A well-told story typically has a single theme and a single mood. The setting is evocative, and a conflict lies at the heart of the story. The plot has a beginning, middle and end, with a climax and (usually) a resolution. And of course, the Storyteller has some sort of purpose in mind when he devised the story.

Theme

A story can't have it all; it's next to impossible to depict a scene of massacre early on in the evening and then expect the players to enjoy a more light-hearted scene later on. To keep events coherent and help devise ideas for the story, you should probably think about the story's theme. For instance, say you decide that your story's theme will be "the power of a nova is dehumanizing." Already this suggestion begs a few possible events and characters — a nova who has lost touch with humanity, a scene in which the Mega-Intelligent character suddenly realizes that he doesn't have a thing in common with his girlfriend any more.

Most of the story's events and characters should somehow be relevant to the story's theme. Even so, that doesn't mean you should paint the theme in mile-high, glowing letters for the players. They don't have to notice it at all. The theme is there to provide internal consistency, and it doesn't have to be blatant to be effective. Even if the players don't pick up on the connection between the emotionless Teragen "emancipator" and the difficulties they're experiencing with their home lives, they'll still subconsciously perceive the strength of the story as a whole. And they'll resent it a lot less than they would if you started preaching the theme from on high.

Aberrant's overall theme is that of power, both actual and perceived. A nova has enough raw power to shape the course of a country if unopposed; what's more, the public's perception of that power adds a new element. Where does the power pick up and the human leave off? Will the absolute power of the novas corrupt them absolutely? What will the people in control do in order to remain in control? Although this theme doesn't have to be the default theme of your stories, you should at least think about what kind of impact it has on your series.

Mood

If a theme is an intellectual hook into the story, a mood is an emotional hook. Once the players are able to respond to the story emotionally in much the same way that their characters would, the game experience becomes much more vivid.

Different moods lead to different kinds of stories. A dark, sinister story about Project Proteus is entirely different from a wild story about going on a musical world tour. Don't limit yourself to just one kind of mood; sure, you may find that you're talented at creating a mood of paranoia in your stories, but you shouldn't limit your series by maintaining that mood exclusively.

Start early. If you want to establish a mood of dread, begin with a nightmare that one of the characters is experiencing. If you want a mood of awe, begin by describing wondering masses far below, shading their eyes and pointing up to the characters flying by overhead. First impressions are as vital in storytelling as they are anywhere else. Once you've got them hooked, remember to reinforce the mood whenever you can; before long, they'll be helping you out by anxiously checking every corner

of their penthouse or firing off even more impressive displays of power, just because such actions seem appropriate.

If **Aberrant** has a common mood, it's probably that of awe. The novas are like unto gods. Everything they do is much larger than life. While the novas hollow out asteroids for their summer retreats and catch solar flares in their hands, humanity stares up at them slack-jawed. There's fear there as well — but the novas are so much more than humanity that they cannot help but inspire awe. Again, this shouldn't be the mood of every story you run (or even most stories), but it should be a consideration.

Setting

Theme and mood aren't necessarily tangible elements of a story, but the setting is. Working out a believable, vivid setting makes the rest of the story flow smoothly. If properly described, it'll probably even inspire your players to interact all the more enthusiastically with their surroundings.

The setting for a story may require several different "backdrops" — an **Aberrant** story could well have separate scenes set in India, on the Eiffel Tower, on a luxury cruise liner and finally on the moon's surface! It's

your duty to describe these settings as vividly as you can, so that the players don't start lagging and losing interest. Bear in mind that you don't want to use too much detail, either! Keep your descriptions brief, but make every word count. The players don't need to know all the different beers advertised in the bar's neon signs — but mentioning that the neon throws an unhealthy blue light over everything is a detail they'll remember.

Describe things accurately and completely. Take into account things like temperature, weather, open space (or the lack thereof), physical objects, sights, smells, sounds — all the details that make a place come alive. You can even use the setting to reinforce theme or mood — horror writers do this all the time. The world of **Aberrant** is a vibrant, colorful place. Help your players experience it.

Conflict

The core of every story is conflict — not *combat* (although that's certainly one aspect of it), but *conflict*. The characters should always face some level of opposition in pursuing their goals, or else there's really no point in bothering to tell a story at all. A Proteus op refusing an order to turn his powers on human soldiers, a Teragen member trying to convince another nova to come over to the Teragen's way of thinking and a Directive agent discovering that his brother is somehow entrenched in the cartel he's investigating are all examples of conflict. Each one has the potential to break out in a battle at some point, but the real conflict comes between the Proteus op and his superiors or between the Teragen member and his "recruit." In fact, these situations could even result in multiple conflicts; consider the Directive agent, who will be pitted not only against the cartel, but who will have to work against the Directive in order to somehow "go easy" on his brother — or against his conscience to bring his brother to justice in the first place.

The actual conflicts involved in a story vary widely, depending on the players' roles. For instance, a Team Tomorrow cell will probably have fewer clashes with public opinion than a group of Aberrants would. For the most part, of course, the conflict will usually boil down to nova vs. human or nova vs. nova. If the conflict is one of novas versus humans, it will usually pit novas against human society or an organization, something that is bigger than any one person. Struggles against other novas can involve anything from a *mano y mano* struggle with the local bruiser to a convoluted struggle against the peer pressure of nova society as a whole.

Of course, there are plenty of other potential sources of conflict — the characters might have to struggle against a hostile environment, against their own inner taint, or against the unknown. It all depends on what sort of story you want to tell.

Plot

Every story has a beginning, middle and end. A story is composed of a series of events that come together — the opening scene usually attracts the players' interest and sets the stage, the middle scenes expand and develop the conflict, and the final scene is a chance for a resolution. The plot, plain and simple, is the order in which these events occur.

A plot can be highly complicated and layered in mystery, but this complexity isn't necessary. It can also be pretty simplistic, but sometimes, simplicity isn't necessarily desirable, either. A good plot allows the characters some free will, yet retains an overall sense of progression. It's paced well, with simple plot advances balanced by the occasional twist or subplot, just to keep things interesting.

Think of a good plot as a roller coaster. Start out by setting things in motion. You can either have them climb the first hill slowly, learning to anticipate the first plot twist, or you can drop them without warning into the thick of things with the first scene. In either case, it's vital that you set the scene — make sure they understand where they are and what's going on.

Then you go into the scenes in the middle, the series of ups, downs, spirals and loops, that allow the characters to enjoy the ride as a whole but are still a buildup for the final stretch. Throw in subplots and plot twists here and there (just as a roller-coaster designer adds the occasional spiral or loop) to keep things interesting.

Finally, you hit the climax — the biggest spiral or the steepest drop. Now the players have the final conflict ahead of them.

Climax and Resolution

Every good story has a climax — the point where all the building tension hits the fan. The climax is the penultimate moment of the story — do or die time — the point where the characters succeed or fail, fight or compromise. It's the pivotal point of the story, so important that it can overshadow or color everything else that's happened along the way. The actual nature of the climax may have changed entirely from your plans, but you should still play it up — after all, this is what everything else has been leading up to.

A common thing to do is to continue play for one final scene after the climax, letting the players wind down. This allows them to look back over the story and wrap up any loose ends. Of course, they probably shouldn't take care of *all* the loose ends — those are the stuff that future stories are made of.

Telling the Story

There's more to telling a story than simply memorizing the plot. You can just set things in motion and tell the story by rote, but there are a few elements of style that you should be aware of. Part of becoming an expert Storyteller is finding your voice, but there are also a few guidelines that can make your job a lot easier.

• **Work with your players.** This one's very, very important. Don't design your series without their input — otherwise you might find yourself spending days on a plotline requiring the players to face down the Teragen, only to discover that your players want to roleplay Teragen members themselves. Encourage them to flesh out their characters' Background Traits, thus contributing supporting cast members and other details. ("So, Aaron, who *is* your old beat partner? How did you guys get along? Where's your apartment, and what does it look like?") Don't force them into roles. On a similar note, make sure that everyone understands the rules of the game, as well as any house rules you might enforce — the players deserve to know how level the playing field is.

Baselines

One of the advantages of **Aberrant**'s two-phase character creation process is the fact that Storytellers can have the players generate and play normal human characters, without any nova Traits at all. A Storyteller could have all the characters begin the chronicle as baseline humans, playing through one or even several stories before being given their nova points and erupting. Or, for a real challenge, try playing unenhanced, "inert" baselines in the **Aberrant** world — Utopia support staff, government agents, cartel operatives or other baselines whose duties force them to interact with novas, often far too close to ground zero.

• **Know the system — or be able to fake it convincingly.** You never, ever want your game to bog down in an argument over whether Timmy Typhon's magmablast should have slagged that support column or not. It's your responsibility to keep up with what your players' characters are able to do, and likewise for the major Storyteller characters in the series. If contention arises, don't be afraid to make an on-the-spot ruling and get on with the game — look up the exact rules later, if need be.

• **Maintain the mood.** Comic relief is all well and good, but if you decide to take the characters on a trip through Carroll's Wonderland, don't act surprised if the players have difficulty taking next week's session seriously. You shouldn't be tyrannical when enforcing the mood, but you do need to keep the players focused to some extent. Don't start punning in the middle of a manhunt for a virally contagious, high-Taint aberrant. Don't litter the street with children's corpses in the middle of a light-hearted story about greedy agents and overzealous fans. You owe it to your players and yourself to see a story through in more or less the same tone that it started — unless the change in tone is a major facet of the story. There's certainly nothing wrong with starting the game out in high spirits only to hit the players with something horrific or brutal — it happens all the time in stories. However, be careful about reversing the order. If even one game starts out in a grim, paranoid mood and suddenly lightens up, it'll be more difficult to get your players to take the next horror-themed story seriously.

• **Let your players accomplish things.** Remember, the characters are the stars of the show; nobody would pay to see the latest Indiana Jones movie if Marcus did all the trap-dodging and Nazi-outwitting. This rule is doubly important for **Aberrant**, where the novas are rapidly becoming the most important beings in the world. You don't have to give the players their every wish on a silver platter, but let them make progress. Their environment should be visibly changed by their very presence; they should be affecting lives. Even if their influence is purely local, it should be real. Make them feel like they're all stars now, and they'll be dying to come back for the next installment.

The Series

Creating a series can be a fair amount of work, but it's a lot less arduous than it might seem. After all, the comic-book industry was built on the concept of ongoing chronicles; limited series are nice, but the ongoing titles are what keep the fans coming back. An **Aberrant** series can continue for years — theoretically, one might even last until the **Aberrant** timeline ends and the **Trinity** timeline begins in AD 2120. You never know.

In order to make your series worthwhile, it should have a life of its own. A good series is more than just a string of scenes featuring the protagonists goofing around — it's a story with a plotline of its own. As it progresses, the players and characters alike share in the overarching themes and moods that link story to story. There's a sense of continuity, of belonging. One story influences the next; things change around the characters. The stories grow bigger and grander; the antagonists more fierce and awe-inspiring. The characters start planning for the future, and they work their changes on the world. By the time you're finally done with the series (if indeed you ever end it at all), you and the players alike should be well and rightly satisfied by what you've accomplished.

Gathering the Group

So what sort of group are your players interested in playing? Do they want to be heroes of a fairly classical mode, or are they more interested in playing around with what a self-centered demigod might be like? **Aberrant** offers hundreds of possibilities for a series' direction, but the roles the characters play in the world should help you narrow down the field.

It's important to realize that it's very unusual for novas to gather in numbers. To be frank, your average nova (although that's as oxymoronic a term as ever was) just doesn't *need* anybody else; he can get what he wants on his own. These are possibly the most important (and rarest — approximately one in one million) people in the world; as such, a gathering of like-minded novas will attract a tremendous amount of attention, as well as paranoia. Everyone from Joe Civilian to the Directive command will want to know what this group's going to be up to; after all, four to six like-minded novas is a force equal to a small country.

• **Utopians:** On the face, this is one of the most "black-and-white" series directions, and it can be played several ways. Naturally, there's the straightforward approach of playing true heroes in a tarnished world, backed by the benevolent Utopia in your efforts to make a better place. Another, more cynical (or realistic) approach is one of a more-or-less idealistic band of novas doing their best to live up to Utopia's ideals, even as they become involved in intrigues and gradually discover that perhaps Utopia itself — or at least certain elements within it — aren't quite so dedicated to the highest ideals. There's even the option of roleplaying a band of cynical, Proteus-affiliated novas who have *no* illusions about Utopia's less telegenic aspects and are willing to do the dirty work necessary to improve the world as a whole (and their bank accounts in the process). If you want to get really messy, you can even have a group consisting of all these types of characters — expect your series to take on a paranoid tone, as conflicts arise and the players start trying to figure out who's in the right. As series options go, the Utopian series is one with lots of latitude; the characters can be as well-known or covert as you like, and the game can take on any sort of theme, from "shining armor" to unapologetic grimness. You can easily switch from pitched battles with nova dissidents to ethical dilemmas over keeping too-nosy journalists quiet to careful intrigues at the heart of the project. Project Utopia is a big place, with a lot of room to play.

• **Aberrants:** A good choice for players who like the role of the underdog, an Aberrants series sets the characters against the doubly massive forces of Project Utopia and disapproving conventional authorities. This series is certainly one about heroism — presumably the characters' ideals compelled them to join Utopia, only to strike out on their own when the project's secret policies came to light. The characters will find themselves with powerful enemies on all sides, and few allies to be found. Perhaps they can get assistance from the Teragen — but would they want it? This isn't a series about glamour and fame, but every one of the characters' deeds is thrown into sharper relief because they struggle on without expecting a reward. An Aberrants series is good for players who like a great deal of say in how their organization is run — as of mid-2008, there are only a couple dozen Aberrants in the entire world, and so the characters will constitute a considerable percentage of the entire group!

• **Corporate/City Novas:** The characters may be a collection of novas in the employ of one very wealthy megacorporation, individually employed by various corporations, or even the founders and top brass of a corporation they've founded themselves. Naturally, a nova employee is of tremendous value, so the characters will command excellent salaries and significant benefits (encourage the appropriate Background Traits). Many of your stories will involve the players protecting their employers' interests, whether it's undertaking high-profile charity work for PR purposes, using their powers to speed up industrial processes, or playing security guard for important projects and personnel. There's ample opportunity for conflict with Utopia's scientific regulation policies; after all, the players will probably want to work in the corporation's (and even the world's) best interests by disseminating new technologies. This sort of series can continue on with the players remaining to offer their services to their employers and eventually earning enough of a position in the corporations to finally have a say in corporate policy — CEO sure sounds nice, doesn't it? Alternatively, the characters can have a falling-out with their benefactors (possibly over ethical issues, possibly as a side effect of personality conflicts), and either try to pursue new employment with their old corp's rivals or find some other use for their abilities. Either way, the corporation probably won't respond well to such ingratitude — and the corporation that can afford to hire a nova (or novas) can afford to make life very miserable for its enemies.

In the United States, certain large cities retain one or more novas as highly paid public servants and franchised PR reps, in the manner of a sports team. This job tends to be cushy (and thus not overly suitable for an adventuring troupe), but it still provides opportunity for stories. Franchised novas are expected to supplement the local police/ fire department in times of crisis (especially when the cameras are rolling) and represent the city in highly publicized "athletic" and power competitions with rival cities' novas. Competition among novas for these plum positions is high, and watch out for the sleazy agent who signs the novas to a "sweet" contract that includes some unforeseen fine print....

• **Government Agents:** The characters are all members of a specific government agency (likely the Direc-

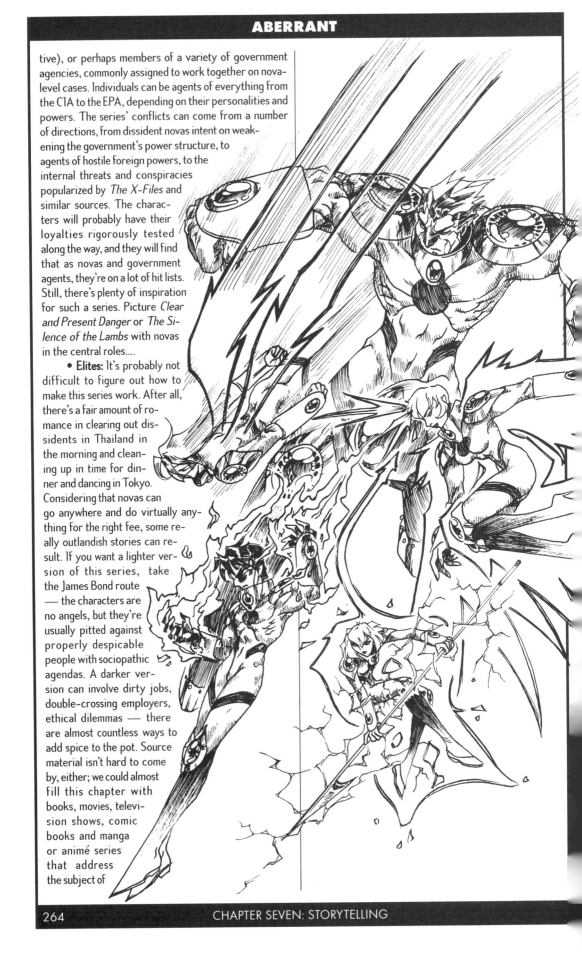

tive), or perhaps members of a variety of government agencies, commonly assigned to work together on nova-level cases. Individuals can be agents of everything from the CIA to the EPA, depending on their personalities and powers. The series' conflicts can come from a number of directions, from dissident novas intent on weakening the government's power structure, to agents of hostile foreign powers, to the internal threats and conspiracies popularized by *The X-Files* and similar sources. The characters will probably have their loyalties rigorously tested along the way, and they will find that as novas and government agents, they're on a lot of hit lists. Still, there's plenty of inspiration for such a series. Picture *Clear and Present Danger* or *The Silence of the Lambs* with novas in the central roles....

• **Elites:** It's probably not difficult to figure out how to make this series work. After all, there's a fair amount of romance in clearing out dissidents in Thailand in the morning and cleaning up in time for dinner and dancing in Tokyo. Considering that novas can go anywhere and do virtually anything for the right fee, some really outlandish stories can result. If you want a lighter version of this series, take the James Bond route — the characters are no angels, but they're usually pitted against properly despicable people with sociopathic agendas. A darker version can involve dirty jobs, double-crossing employers, ethical dilemmas — there are almost countless ways to add spice to the pot. Source material isn't hard to come by, either; we could almost fill this chapter with books, movies, television shows, comic books and manga or animé series that address the subject of guns for hire. To be sure, if you start borrowing plots, you'll have to adjust some factors — *Ronin* didn't account for people who could bounce bullets and melt steel — but inspiration is everywhere.

• **Slackers:** This sort of series may seem directionless at first, but it can also have a lot of potential. This can be the classic "road trip" series, with the characters finding themselves in a new location every week and almost invariably stumbling into trouble there pretty quickly. After all, if you can fly around the world in under an hour, what's to stop you from going and hanging out in Monaco whenever the itch strikes you? The only trouble with such a series is that there's no long-running source of conflict endemic to the ongoing story — if the characters don't have anything better to do than wander around and amuse themselves, they obviously aren't going to be pursuing some vital goal. Still, there's no shortage of recurring antagonists and possible hunters for even a motley crew of slacker novas; remember, novas are just so damn important that nobody in their right mind will pass up a chance to try and bring an unaligned nova over to their side.

• **Media Icons:** The most common version of this series is, of course, the music band. There's no denying that an all-nova act, whether a novox sideshow or a psychedelic retro band, would draw crowds that would make Elvis spin in his grave. However, that's far from the only option. Movie stars, performance artists, solo musicians — even XWF contenders and *real* supermodels are all possibilities. It's not even much of a stretch to have them all know one another — look how incestuous the lives of our own media icons are. This series focuses largely on fame and its price, and it is likely to bring its own strange look at heroism to the table; after all, when you're both a nova and a household name, you're *always* going to be a role model of some sort, whether you like it or not. Some conflict is likely going to arise from the demands of the public, agents and studios; more hazardous conflict is available in the role of criminal cartels and similar threats. After all, a media icon nova is worth *billions* — and you can bet that someone's going to want a piece of that pie. And don't forget all the people who want to plug *their* cause, whether it's cloning the snow leopard or "liberating" Egypt. Some of them just won't take no for an answer.

• **Teragen Members:** Sometimes it's relaxing to play the bad guys for the change. A series in which the players take the roles of various Teragen members, however, is going to be a particularly interesting kettle of fish. Divis Mal's "children" are more than just a hodge-podge of supremacist novas — they're philosophers, and some of their views hold a certain degree of logic. To be sure, the Teragen harbors a few mindless nihilists and heedless buffoons — blunt weapons are useful, after all

— but the important members, and thus the characters, should be something more. A Teragen series can be played as lightly as a "what city shall we wreck today?" beer-'n'-pretzels game, or it can delve into the ethics of strength and species, encouraging the players to roleplay through a series of interesting moral choices. As for conflict, this series won't disappoint — when your organization's leader is Public Enemy Number One on most governments' lists, there's no shortage of people lining up to take you down. DeVries bounty hunters, Directive agents, criminal cartels and Utopia's soldiers — there are plenty of antagonists to go around, and not person one outside the Teragen is going to stand up for you. Good luck.

• **Criminals:** No, not "supervillains." One of the major differences between the **Aberrant** setting and, say, the Marvel Universe is that in **Aberrant**, there are very few costumed supercriminals. After all, most novas can parlay their powers into all the wealth, fame and gratification they require through entirely legal channels. (Besides, when seeking to attract lovely young companions, a tuxedo is much more practical than a set of purple tights with a skull on the chest.) Why bother to knock over First National when you can make more money as a contracted "consultant," on the talk-show circuit, or even entirely through licensing fees?

However, antisocial types exist in every society — and eruption doesn't lessen sociopathic tendencies one little bit. In fact, it usually aggravates such problems, alienating the deviant even further from humanity as a whole. If your group's interested in such a series, it can be a cathartic experience (as long as you don't take it too far — most people have a limit to the amount of disgusting behavior they can "witness" or "perpetrate"). There's plenty of opportunity for the enterprising antisocial nova. Many criminal novas eventually drift into positions as enforcers and bosses of the criminal cartels, but certain elites also specialize in terrorist work and enforcement. Mental powers are perfect for blackmail, espionage or worse. A few nova criminals have even become quite popular among the young, bored and rebellious; black-market merchandise and convenient N! interviews can prove as lucrative for charismatic hoodlums as the initial acts that imparted their notoriety. Of course, a whole group of affiliated nova criminals can become Public Enemy Number One on most governments' hit lists. Worse, they'll be ruthlessly and mercilessly hunted down by Utopia — Utopia doesn't want too many antisocial novas to appear and prosper, lest a public backlash against all novas result. What's more, if rogue novas harm other novas in the course of their criminal activities, they can also be targeted by the Teragen. What's that — hunted by Utopia *and* the Teragen? Yep. Welcome to a very interesting life....

Realism

One of the most important things to think about when designing your series is the level of realism you plan to maintain. It's vital that you think about how "realistic" you want your game to be, and that you talk this over with the players. If you want a gritty, *Watchmen*-esque story where there are no real heroes or villains, and your players start generating four-color characters based on their favorite '70s *Legion of Super-Heroes* issues, you have a problem.

That's why it's important that everyone be on the same page. Talk it over with your players — how outrageous do they want things to get? Do they want an over-the-top game reminiscent of anime superheroics, or do they want a world without costumes and codenames? And will you be happy running what they'd like? It's important to find a happy medium, a style that you and the players will both enjoy — otherwise, why play the game?

The default realism level for **Aberrant** can be summed up as "mostly realistic" — there are some people who dress up in uniforms, adopt *noms du guerre* and try to save the world from itself. However, most novas use their powers to achieve fame and fortune through more "normal" channels (show business, industry, academia), and there isn't much of a tradition of supercriminals dressing up in tights and knocking over jewelry stores. (After all, if you can make ten million on the stock market in a couple of months, why risk arrest?)

More "four-color" games (named after the days when color comic books got their coloration from combinations of tiny dots in four colors) can actually have "villains" with codenames and agendas, as well as "heroes" who stop them. In this setup, Team Tomorrow becomes more like the Justice League and spends more time fighting supercriminals; similarly, you might want to introduce more archetypal antagonists, either by putting a more four-color spin on groups like the Teragen or by debuting actual teams of supercriminals. A really good source for four-color themes while still maintaining some plausibility is the *Astro City* comic — it's hard to find a better example of a classic superhero setting where the superheroes, villains and supporting cast actually act like real people.

Conversely, more "realistic" games might focus on a more gritty approach, one where superpowers are treated like the deadly weapons they are. You might want to halve the points given out in character creation, in order to have a less epic scale of conflict — in such a setting, novas don't have near the amount of influence they do in mainstream **Aberrant** games, and they can't change the world as readily. There are plenty of sources for such games, from *Watchmen* to the *Wild Cards* series of novels (although the latter gets bogged down in shock-value scenes and themes pretty quickly).

It's impossible to chart all the different degrees of realism an **Aberrant** series might take. The best thing for it is to think about what you'd like to do, then talk it over with your players. Odds are, you'll strike a level of realism that's not quite like anybody else's game — but that suits your group perfectly.

Common Bonds

It's worth asking: Why are the characters together? No, not just because that's the series' setup — *why* are they a group?

It's easy enough to just say, "Well, you were all recruited by the Directive and assigned to a single unit." However, this isn't necessarily what you want to do. If the characters are thrown together randomly, you'll miss out on a lot of potential group dynamics. Television has recently shown a heightened interest in the ensemble cast show — that's because if done well, an ensemble works much better than would a prima donna and a few costars orbiting his celestial glory.

Talk to your players beforehand; get a feel for what sort of characters they're planning to run, and extrapolate some interesting connections from there. We don't mean the soap-operatic clunkers like having everyone be estranged siblings, ex-lovers or shady characters from each other's pasts — instead, try to figure out relationships that could provide interesting drama even if the characters have never met before in their lives. If one person's playing a world-weary type whose eruption has given him a newfound vigor, try to arrange things so that he has an interesting first meeting with another player's youthful nova who's now having to learn responsibility. Sure, the older nova would be a terrible role model for the younger one — but that dynamic would be a lot of fun for the players to roleplay, as well as potentially very interesting to the entire group.

Consider the example of Team Tomorrow — they weren't all friends from the same college, or relatives, or anything of the sort. They didn't have much in common at all, save their powers, but the dynamics that formed were the core of everything interesting that happened later. Who would have thought that Slider would have befriended, of all people, the libertine Corbin? And yet, because she did, the group's history worked out in a fascinating fashion. If she'd warmed to the authoritative Caestus Pax, there might never have been an Aberrant movement at all.

This group dynamism is what you should work to achieve. Get the players interested in each other's characters. You don't have to require them to share all the details of their characters, but everyone should probably have some idea of the other sorts of personalities they'll be dealing with. Encourage those who have interesting potential links to sit down and work out what their characters might have in common.

After all, the alternative is winding up with a situation where your players create "moody loners" who do nothing but hang around, act taciturn and wait for the other characters to become fascinated with their mystique. Everyone takes the passive road, no bonds are formed and your series loses all its energy into a black hole of self-absorbed entropy.

It happens *all the time*. But you won't let it happen to you, right? Great.

Heroism

There's no way to tell a story about "superheroes" without actually touching on heroism. Even if your series is of the sort where the characters are in it for the money, fame and luxuries, you still can't ignore the basic premise that superhuman power can indeed create superhuman responsibility. **Aberrant** doesn't require that the characters wear white hats and dedicate their lives to stopping injustice; indeed, most novas do not. Ultimately, novas are individuals just like the rest of us; heroism comes from the person, not the powers. Nonetheless, in a world where the characters' every action can have grave or even world-shattering consequences, it's vital to have a strong idea of just how heroism is applicable to your series.

One Person

The most basic tenet to the whole concept of heroism is that one person can indeed make a difference. In **Aberrant**, this holds as true as anywhere else — in fact, more so, since a single nova is capable of doing almost anything he puts his mind to. Even the nova who decides to withdraw from the world and spend the rest of his days fishing for bass (which hardly makes for an interesting character, but it is a logical decision for a person to make) is probably going to have some impact on his environment, like it or not. Maybe he doesn't want to use his power, but what happens when the Teragen shows up on a membership drive? What if Utopia or Proteus operatives decide they don't like the thought of a nova with no obvious allegiances, and they begin investigating? Certainly the remaining criminal cartels aren't above threatening family and friends to compel cooperation. After all, every last nova in the world is that one nova who could tip the scales, who might be the difference between a project's success or failure. These people are *that important*.

Of course, the novas' relative importance doesn't mean that you should hand the player every goal he sets out after — changing the world shouldn't be like using a vending machine. (Deposit two quantum, make selection — ooh, you've taken over Bolivia!) After all, all the finest heroes — and virtually the same percentage of antiheroes — have to bust their asses to get what they want. Nothing's ever free — the one true law of the world. But with a little effort, a person can change things significantly. With a nova's powers behind him, he can change things almost completely. Naturally, the greater the forces that align against him, the more dramatic his success will eventually be — and even failure can work a lasting effect on the character's environment. After all, the Alamo fell — and that made all the difference.

Icons and Archetypes

It's only appropriate to follow up by noting the iconic level of an **Aberrant** game. It's no coincidence that a good portion of recent superhero literature directly compares superheroes to gods. In many ways, they are. Spider-Man really is the mortal turned demigod, the Everyman gifted with sudden power and responsibility. Batman is a Plutonian king of the underworld who constantly struggles to keep his damned subjects in line (and the same could be said of Spawn), while the shining young sun-god archetype is visible in characters from Captain Marvel to the Human Torch. The same should hold true of novas. Even an average, everyday person who receives power on this level has managed to ascend into the mythic. They stand for something — whether they like it or not.

Naturally, there are ways you can use this to your advantage. Plenty of writers are retelling various myths with modern superbeings in the place of demigods and legendary heroes — why ignore such a fine source of ideas? Consider the underworld ruler who abdicates his throne for a while and sets up a mortal in his place. Would one of the players find it interesting to take over a corporate nova's position for a while? Then there's the trickster who steals the sun for the benefit of mankind. Is there a character in your series who'd be appropriate to liberate some strange new science from Project Utopia? What about a solar-system-wide version of Jason and the Argonauts? Take a look at your players' characters. Consider what roles they'd play in such epic stories. Think big.

Antiheroes

Not everyone has what it takes. Some people have the courage and determination to become heroes — and simply don't care enough. The antihero hasn't always been a popular staple of superhero fiction, but with the advent of *The Dark Knight Returns* and *Watchmen*, suddenly the "grim warrior who doesn't give a damn about anything but destroying his enemies" started cropping up in a lot more comics. Although industry critics are still divided on whether this was a good thing or not, ultimately it all boils down to one thing: Like any other archetype, the antihero is a strong character only when he is a *character*, not a cardboard stand-up. Batman hasn't lasted as long as he has just by treating readers to tales of one guy beating up crooks, after all. The myriad of complications in his life — his aversion to guns, being haunted by the ghosts of his parents, the struggle between his desire for justice and his obvious sexual attraction to certain criminals, the gradual loss of touch with "Bruce Wayne" — is what keeps *Batman* comics still selling today.

The real problem with antihero characters is that their admittedly lax approach toward ethics can wind up working against the series. It can get a lot harder to make a story properly dramatic when the characters (and sometimes, the players) are jaded toward death and suffering in all but the most extreme circumstances. After all, when the characters have strolled into the Nakato gambling den and effortlessly snuffed out every last tattooed, missing-a-pinky hatchetman in the building, how exactly are you going to get them emotionally involved in the death of a bystander?

If the players want to play antiheroes (and at least one of them will certainly want to), you shouldn't discourage them to do so out of hand. However, you'll definitely have a lot of work on your hands with such a series. You'll need to develop a revolving stable of antagonists and not get too attached to any one. You should also make certain to focus on the characters' personality traits, hangups and weaknesses, perhaps even more so than usual. Such a series is an intense endeavor, and it *should* be — otherwise, it's just a bunch of shallow kill-em-where-they-stand scenes, and you can get *that* from Hollywood.

Sample Story Hooks

There are hundreds of possible story hooks for an **Aberrant** series, and the characters' backgrounds and personalities should lend themselves to dozens more. From stories that take place before the characters' eruptions (as a sort of prologue) to the final conflict between the characters and their worst rivals, the possibilities are virtually endless. The following ideas are only the tip of the iceberg, but if you've never run an **Aberrant** game before, they might offer a good starting point.

• **Disaster Relief:** Whether flooding in the American Midwest, a hurricane in the tropics or earthquakes battering Japan, the world offers plenty of opportunities for novas to help their fellow man. Most powers can be useful in these situations — telekinesis to rescue people caught in floodwaters, superhuman strength to support a bridge for a few minutes more, and even plasma generation to burn firebreaks with incredible speed. Give the characters a personal reason to involve themselves,

be it conscience, excellent PR, family members in trouble, patriotism, loyalty to the Utopian ideal or what have you. To throw in a couple of monkeywrenches, what if a new nova spontaneously erupts in the confusion — how do the players contain him as well as the disaster, and where will they guide him afterwards? What if a Teragen member arrives and heaps scorn on the characters' efforts, trying to coerce them into "not being such suckers"? The characters will certainly earn new admirers for their help — are there possible romantic interests, political contacts or rivals to be gained? This story seed can be a good introduction for new players, allowing them to test their powers in creative fashions and find ways to make even the most destructive powers do some good.

• **Publicity Stunts:** The world may all but worship novas, but nobody is immune to bad publicity. No matter what sort of series you're running, the characters can easily run afoul of the media. And when you're a nova, it's virtually impossible to hide. So what do you do when the global media starts wondering if you're on the take, or criticizing your employers' policies? What about the vocal anti-nova groups? What if some teenager kills himself in a half-baked attempt to emulate his role model, and someone suggests that the nova himself is to blame? Remember, in **Aberrant**, critics of nova behavior are actually in the minority — thus far — so this sort of story can actually serve as a sharp relief to the hero-worship to which even Teragen characters might have grown accustomed. Do the characters' accusers have an ulterior motive, or is this a sign of things to come?

• **Young Novas in Love:** Although romantic interests are usually relegated to the status of subplot, there's no reason that *amour* can't be the focus of an entire story. The romance in question doesn't even have to focus on one of the players' characters, although it tends to be a little more immediate when the players are more directly involved. What if one of the characters is being stalked by an obsessive nova, someone who's convinced that they'd make the perfect genetic match? How about a genuine story of love (or at least genuine attraction) from the opposite sides — say, between a Utopian and a Teragen member? The chemistry between lovers from opposite sides of the fence is pretty damned potent. Love triangles and the usual amount of soap-opera clichés can add to the tension, but one of the most distinct problems is that even if all goes well, the couple can't expect much privacy — an individual nova doesn't quite get the media attention that the President of the United States does, but they get a lot more than the occasional mention in *People*. Can a relationship last in the bright lights of global attention?

• **Mob War:** Only four crime syndicates have survived Utopia's purges to prosper in the underground of the world of **Aberrant**. And to many of these syndicates' higher-ups, that's three syndicates too many. Although

the international crime market is pretty neatly divided up at this point, there are still plenty of areas — such as the United States — where the territorial lines are constantly shifting. What happens when the characters are caught between two (or more) warring underworld factions, some of which may have brought along nova enforcers? What if the characters themselves and their resources or contacts are part of the "stakes" in the war? How can the characters act to preserve their interests without bringing down the wrath of the syndicates on their loved ones' heads?

• **Exploration:** To novas, there may well not be a final frontier. If the characters are capable of exploring the solar system without benefit of a ship, wouldn't someone pay them quite a bit of money to see what's *really* on Mars? Even if the characters need a space shuttle or the like, the heightened survivability of novas (to say nothing of complementary powers) are a valuable asset in exploration. The deep seas would be a similarly appropriate venue for exploration, possibly even more so (easier for novas to survive, and rather more convenient). Of course, who's to say that other novas haven't beaten them to the punch? A resource war could result from a particularly rich find, or Utopia might try to keep the characters from disclosing any unusual scientific discoveries. The sky's the limit — well, not really, but you get the idea.

Antagonists and Supporting Cast

You're only as good as what you know — or in this case, *who* you know. No hero ever amounted to anything without proper enemies. Similarly, it's damn rare to find an interesting story with only one character. Just as every comic-book character who's managed to last more than a couple of years has his or her own vibrant supporting cast, your series should be stocked with intriguing people who seem *real.* It's no coincidence that the world is more familiar with Lois Lane than it is with the latest faddish bad girl or muscleboy.

When designing Storyteller characters, the first thing you should probably consider is the character's motive. You probably know what they're going to be doing in the series when you create them — but you also need to know *why.* If you know that the scientist is driven by intense jealousy of nova powers, you can better judge how he'll react to the players' characters when they show up at his lab. Figuring out whether the hitman is in it for the money, family loyalty or desperation can help you refine his tactics, to say nothing of his personality. Treat your important characters as if they're actors who just asked what their motivations are in this scene — they'll be much more vivid for the trouble.

It can't be stressed too highly that motivation is *very* important for antagonists. Even the most avaricious criminal has some idea of what he's actually going to do with all that money he's trying to steal. Similarly, the thuggish XWF fighter who "just likes to beat people up" has to have some reason for that, whether it's cold sadism or some sort of revenge against perceived tormentors. If your antagonists don't have believable goals, hopes and dreams, they're not really going to be that effective. Many of the best antagonists are people who aren't "evil" — they simply have goals that are at odds with those of the characters. And even if you do bring in a sadistic monster with only one redeeming value to his name, you have the option of making him a recurring threat in the series. Nothing gets the players into the game better than some bastard that they love to hate and can't wait to catch.

After motivation, your next step is probably to make sure that the character is distinctive. Doing so is pretty easy. A detailed physical description is a great place to start. Be certain to stress details that give away the character's personality; pretty red-haired reporters are a dime a dozen, but if you give the local journalist a habit of showing up in rumpled skirts and jackets, you've established something about her personality — maybe she's too busy to keep up with her ironing, or maybe she's just a slob. Either way, it's a hook.

Mannerisms are also important. Does the Utopian agent constantly polish his glasses during debriefings? Does the Interpol detective munch on slightly withered carrot sticks that he keeps in his jacket pocket? Is the up-and-coming starlet desperately trying to tone down her strong Southern accent? It helps if you can come up with at least one slightly distinctive feature for each cast member; this keeps the stain of generica out of your series and gives you a headstart on creating a supporting cast with a collective personality all its own.

Advanced Storytelling

Some techniques require a little more work on the Storyteller's part, and they don't offer much help in streamlining stories or advancing the plots. These techniques are tricky to use, but they can really enhance the story in which they're used.

It should be stressed that advanced storytelling techniques aren't for the benefit of the players' characters; they don't appear to give the characters access to information they wouldn't otherwise have. They're tools to entertain the players and bring them more fully into the world of **Aberrant** — tools to make the story more vivid and meaningful. They obviously aren't for every-

one, and there's no reason you should use them if you don't feel comfortable with them. But if you're looking for something to make the story touch the players a little more deeply, give one or two of these a try.

Flashbacks

You've seen them in comics, movies, novels, television shows and even video games. The flashback has become such a staple of our storytelling vocabulary that it's only *technically* an advanced technique. You know the basics: Something triggers a memory in one or more of the characters, and the scene shifts to a scene from the past that is relevant to the present. In many cases, you can just describe the scene and how it plays out, but to make things really interesting, you can let the players roleplay through the flashback.

The characters in the flashback are only rarely the players' main characters. It's important that the players not use any information gained in the flashback that their characters wouldn't have access to; the flashback is to flesh out the story and make it more vivid, not to give the characters an edge. For instance, a flashback might recreate the *Galatea* explosion, with the players taking the roles of various people on board the *Galatea*. Although the characters won't be any the wiser (for there's no way they'd know just what went on aboard the space station prior to its explosion), the players will be more fully immersed in the storyline of the series — and that's what's important.

Symbolism

Sometimes a cigar *isn't* just a cigar. That's symbolism for you. This technique allows you to splice in layers of meaning to your story that wouldn't otherwise be evident. Symbols can recur throughout the series, or only appear once or twice where appropriate. They needn't even be all that evident. However, the power of symbolism is such that even if the players don't realize what the tattered newspaper littering the street stands for, they may subconsciously pick up on the themes that it represents.

One example of symbolism might involve the players tracking a rogue nova through several scenes, many of which are marked by the presence of broken shards of mirrored glass. The glass represents the fragile self-esteem of their prey, and the players will almost certainly subconsciously associate the brittle, jagged substance with their target. Although definite examples of symbolism in comics are hard to come by (as they're rarely labeled as such), comics today are certainly littered with symbols. Read through a few titles and pay particular attention to the use of light and shadow, background elements and color. There's almost always a pattern, and it's a trick worth picking up.

Dream Sequences

Admittedly, although a dream sequence can be a particularly vivid storytelling device, you have to be careful how you use it. Even the best-laid, most masterfully crafted story is going to cause resentment in its audience if it ends with "...and then he woke up and realized it was all just a dream." But if you avoid this trap, you can wring a lot of drama out of a well-played dream sequence.

Such a scene can be shared by all the characters, or specific to only one. The players take the roles of their characters, or sometimes outlandish parodies of themselves. Even if only one character is doing the actual dreaming, the other players can still participate (either playing their characters in the dreamer's dreamscape, or other "supporting cast" in the dream).

Although the dream sequence can be brought on as a key element of the plot — the comic books are thick with villains who've hooked their captive nemeses up to "dream machines" — it is usually less of an obstacle that must be overcome and more of a means of providing the players with insight. Of course, you can always up the emotional stakes in such a scene — having the characters dream about losing their powers, or losing control of their powers, is a common enough theme. However, to make this even more effective, you can combine the characters' insecurities with some relevant plot twist. For instance, maybe C.G. Crescendo, the media icon, has a horrible dream about losing his movie-star girlfriend to a faceless stalker while he's powerless and invisible, unable to prevent the murder. Once you begin the game, you can introduce an antagonist that has even a tiny resemblance to the dream stalker, or have his girlfriend mention that some fan has gotten hold of her home phone number — and then watch Crescendo sweat.

Of course, the dream proper doesn't even have to belong to one of the characters. The characters might all be "guest stars" in a Storyteller character's dreams, playing some role that stresses their relationship to the unknown dreamer. For example, maybe a right-wing evangelist has a horrible nightmare in which the characters appear as devilish versions of themselves. This technique can really unsettle the players, although you should probably use it only when you're sure they'll enjoy the insights they gain and not try to have their characters abuse the information they wouldn't logically have access to. Of course, there's more than one way to make such a revelation.

Meanwhile...

Not every scene in the story has to involve the characters. Comic books, movies, novels and all manner of stories abound with scenes in which the protagonists aren't involved. For instance, we might see the scene, 20 years before, where the science lab noticed there was something strangely wrong with the test-tube babies they were growing. Similarly, the scene might shift to the antagonist's Alpine bungalow, where he carefully explains his plot to his henchmen (and, likely executing one of them for incompetence along the way).

Although such scenes can be essential for helping the audience understand the whole story, they're rather trickier to implement in a roleplaying game. After all, if you show the players the scene where the villain hides the bomb under the ballpark's press box, roleplaying the search for the bomb is meaningless. Never use such a scene to give the players information that you want them to figure out for themselves.

Naturally, you probably also want your players to handle any information gained honorably — don't show them the cartel hit that killed Borgia's fiancé if you think they might abuse that information in trying to negotiate with her. But if they're ready for it, go ahead and use this technique. Even though the characters might not be fully informed by the end of the story, the players may well be "fat and happy" for having seen the *entirety* of the story itself.

Parallel Stories

Something like a flashback and something like the "Meanwhile..." trick, parallel stories are another interesting way for the players to step out of their usual roles for a while. In a parallel story, nobody plays the same characters; only the theme remains the same. Usually the parallel story's protagonists are created by the Storyteller, in order to best showcase other elements of the main story. For instance, if the usual gang of characters is busying themselves in a prolonged struggle with the Heaven Thunder Triad, perhaps the parallel story might depict Hong Kong natives undergoing their own struggle with a different cell. As the two stories progress, the players learn more about the interconnected, almost incestuous nature of the tong.

Naturally, the lure of the parallel story is the vast amount of uncharted territory that it can explore. The players can see things they wouldn't otherwise see with their normal characters, and there are bound to be surprises aplenty. To be sure, this isn't a technique to overuse, but if you're willing to put in the work to craft the occasional parallel story, you can make your story all the richer.

Foreshadowing

It's a common trick, and a good one. Foreshadowing is the art of carefully placing certain elements in the story early on that allude to what's to come. This isn't the same thing as revealing a surprise — rather, it's a trick to build suspense. When a playwright places a gun in Act One, Scene One, the audience automatically knows that gun is going to get used at some point during the story. However, they don't know *when*, or on *whom* — and thus anticipation and suspense are created. The audience is at the playwright's — or in this case, the Storyteller's — mercy. They aren't going to find out the specifics until it's the right time, no matter how much they speculate on the outcome. The timing is what's key here, not the surprise itself.

The main thing to remember when using foreshadowing is to be subtle. Don't overuse the gimmick, or your stories will become predictable; similarly, don't make the clues too obvious, or there won't be any suspense. If your players pick up on the hints, that's great; if they don't, they'll be surprised by the plot twist rather than the timing. You win either way.

Repetition

By repetition we don't mean always using the word "sultry" to describe each and every one of the female characters your players encounter. Rather, repetition is a subtle way of enforcing a story's continuity. Again, subtlety is a key element; it doesn't have to be anything more outrageous than a recurring series of green neon signs (not even necessarily advertising the same thing) or multiple background radios tuned to the same oldies channel. This element can be powerful, and it's a favorite of many filmmakers today. Maybe those neon signs get your players subconsciously thinking about money. Maybe the oldies songs makes the veteran nova in the group feel old.

Once your players pick up on the repeated elements, the fun increases. They're very likely to get paranoid about the whole thing. Why exactly do their contacts and hired thug nemeses alike have empty Pompeii Pizza boxes somewhere nearby? Is there something about the local franchise they should know? Maybe there's a greater conspiracy at work here!

Well, probably not. But it's certainly worth it to get them thinking.

When It All Goes to Hell

It happens even to the best games: Sometimes the players go berserk, the die rolls get so improbable they'd get your group thrown out of Vegas and you find your game spinning rapidly out of control. What do you do then?

The first thing to remember, of course, is that it's not just your game — the game belongs to you and all the players, and you're all there to have a good time. It's unfair to force all the players to adhere to your vision of **Aberrant** if they have a different one; if your players are psyched to play a rollicking, high-spirited, white-knight T2M series, it's in poor form to force them to play Aberrants on the run from the sinister Project Utopia and its Proteus pitbulls.

That said, you shouldn't let the majority always bully you into doing their will. Most good stories requires that *something* goes against the characters, and not all players appreciate high adversity. If the players were in charge, none of their characters would ever get captured, die or even be slightly embarrassed. (Well, it isn't true of all groups, but if you know that your players are the kind to put their characters in losing situations for the benefit of the story, you probably don't need this advice anyway.)

Ultimately, you have to balance the requirements of a good story with the desires of the players. If the players really want to kill Divis Mal and take over the Teragen, maybe they'd have a good time in the process — but any story after something that dramatic and improbable would have to be insanely great, or else it's a letdown. Worse, sometimes through a mixture of luck and skill, the players kill the villain in Act One (or achieve a success or failure that's similarly anticlimactic). At this point, you have one of two options — proceed on and improvise, allowing them that victory (which is difficult, but it sometimes leads to even better stories), or cheat. What do you do?

The first thing to keep in mind is that players are a creative lot, and you can't always anticipate their actions. When you work up the plot for a story, think about the different directions each scene could go. Do the players interrogate the cartel hoodlum, or do they waste him without asking questions? How do you get them to the next scene in either case? Will the next scene have to change — for instance, will they wind up going to the ski resort instead of the luxury liner? If you do some preparation ahead of time and plan at least a little for your players' creativity, you won't be caught as flat-footed when they do something completely unexpected.

Cheating is unfair by nature, but it's not as unforgivable in roleplaying games as it is in competition. The difference is that you shouldn't cheat to make your players lose — you should cheat only if it would greatly improve the story. Allow them the majority of their victories, but if something happens that would greatly alter the focus of the story (they obliterate the Sons of Astaroth with one lucky shot to the fusion generator before discovering that one of the Sons is a traitor who can guide them to the series' climatic showdown), it's probably okay to fudge things just a little. Even then, don't take their efforts completely away from them; let them cut a more modest swath of destruction, maybe destroying one or two of the Sons out of hand and severely wounding the traitor.

Bear in mind that it's also okay to cheat *for* the players — something that rarely happens in competitive games, but which is also fine here. A fluky die roll has just killed a character through no fault of his own, without even the opportunity for a dramatic death scene? Roll some extra dice behind the screen, put on a grave expression and break the bad news of the character's severe injury and poor luck. Just don't tell them what the dice had dictated; it's really none of their business, anyway. Who's in charge of keeping the story running smoothly and entertainingly, anyway, you or the dice?

Of course, the most equitable way to cheat — and one of our favorites — is to balance everything out. So you fudged a die roll to keep the player's romantic interest alive? The next time things go easy for her in a tight situation, have them get a little more tense. Fudged a Heaven Thunder enforcer's dodge roll to keep him alive until the final showdown? That's fine; have him do poorly on another roll when the showdown occurs. What goes around comes around.

The best storytelling is a mixture of preparation and improvisation, the exact proportions of which are best left to the Storyteller to define. Even if your first few stories stick in places and don't go completely smoothly, don't give up; storytelling is a skill that only improves with practice. Before long, you'll be stirring up subplots and launching the players into orbit at the drop of a hat. Besides, it's not like putting in your hours of practice isn't any fun, right?

APPENDIX

Weapons

Many novas possess more firepower than an entire platoon of heavily armed soldiers. The following lists of weaponry are presented for those novas who choose to outfit themselves with standard weapons in addition to their quantum powers. The Storyteller can also outfit antagonists with weapons from this list, giving human opponents at least a small chance against the superenhanced novas.

The charts list weapons as generic types rather than specific models or name brands. The charts also list the damage each weapon inflicts and whether that damage is bashing (B) or lethal (L).

Melee Weapons

Melee covers all manner of close-combat weaponry. This category also covers items that may not be intended for combat, yet get thrown in the mix by desperate attackers.

• **Automobile:** When two heavyweight novas duke it out on a city street, the most convenient, effective melee weapon is the car. The overall size of a common vehicle makes it a highly accurate weapon, able to hit multiple targets in one swipe. It may also be thrown and (if it's large enough) employed as an area attack. Occasionally, trucks and buses come into play, with appropriately adjusted damage modifiers.

• **Ax:** Most modern-day axes chop firewood. In combat, the reinforced-steel blade, attached to a one-meter-long handle, makes an effective offensive weapon.

• **Chain:** Whether an improvised weapon or one designed for a martial artist, the chain is a painful weapon when used against baselines.

• **Club:** Just about any blunt object can be considered a club. Chairs, lumber and glass bottles all fall into this category. Larger objects make excellent clubs as well. Urban novas occasionally wield lampposts, while trees are effective in the wild.

• **Knife:** Any edged weapon less than 50 cm long is considered a knife.

• **Sword:** Not very popular as a modern form of defense, the sword remains in use by enthusiasts, martial artists and certain unorthodox novas.

Melee Weapons Chart

Weapon Type	Damage	Str Min	Str Max	Conceal	Mass	Cost
Automobile	Str + 6/10d10 B	Mega •	Mega • • •	N	1 mton	• •
Ax	Str + 4d10 L	• •	• • • • •	N	3 kg	•
Chain	Str + 5d10 B	•	Mega •	P	2.5 kg	•
Club	Str + 4d10 B	•	• • • • •	T	1 kg	•
Lamppost	Str + 6/10d10 B	Mega •	Mega • •	N	100 kg	• •
Knife	Str + 2d10 L	•	• • • • •	J	0.5 kg	•
Staff	Str + 6d10 B	• •	• • • • •	N	3 kg	•
Sword	Str + 5d10 L	• • •	Mega •	T	3 kg	• •
Tree	Str + 6/10d10 B	Mega •	Mega • • •	N	0.5 mtons	•
Truck	Str + 7/12d10 B	Mega • •	Mega • • • •	N	10 mtons	• • • •

Damage: Indicates the damage dice pool for the weapon. Nonstandard weapons (e.g., automobiles) have two damage codes: the lower level should be applied to normal swings; the higher level is applied when the nova swings at full force wrecking the vehicle in the process.

Str Min: Indicates the minimum Strength required to use the weapon in question. Characters who do not possess the indicated level of Strength simply cannot use the weapon effectively.

Str Max: Indicates the maximum Strength at which the weapon can effectively be used. Characters with higher levels of Strength than indicated will break the weapon on its first use, though they can "pull" their blows to the Str Max (reducing damage dice pools accordingly) in order not to break the weapon.

Concealment: P = Can be carried in a pocket; J = Can be hidden in a jacket; T = Can be hidden under a trenchcoat; N = Cannot be hidden on a person at all.

Mass: Indicates the mass of the weapon in kilograms or metric tons.

Cost: Represents the value of the weapon in Resource dots.

Ranged Weapons

Ranged weapons include firearms, archaic ranged weapons and new weaponry developed since the advent of novas. As with melee weapons, ranged weapons are listed in terms of generic categories rather than brand names.

- **Revolver:** The first modern handgun, these firearms have become outdated by the modern clip-loaded pistol. They're still readily available on the streets of most modern cities.
- **Pistol:** Modern pistols have overcome early jamming problems and nearly replaced their predecessor, the revolver. A standard among law-enforcement officials.
- **Rifle:** Highly accurate, even at long range, the rifle remains the hunter's number-one choice. Military and law-enforcement units use rifles to take down dangerous opponents at long range.
- **Flechette Rifle:** The flechette rifle is a highly experimental magnetically charged weapon combining the automatic fire of machine guns with the spray effect of shotguns. This lightweight weapon, available only to the military or on the black market, fires a deadly spray of depleted uranium fragments at ultra-high speed.
- **Taser:** The taser fires two small darts that conduct a massive jolt of electricity. The weapon is used throughout the world to subdue opponents without causing permanent damage.
- **Machine gun:** Capable of firing multiple rounds in seconds, these weapons vary from handheld semiautomatic submachine guns (SMGs) to high-caliber vehicular-mounted military variety.
- **Shotguns:** Deadly at short range, shotguns release a spray of lethal pellets that lose potency with distance. Multiple versions exist, including pump action and twin-gauge.
- **Thrown object:** Mega-strong novas often uproot and throw large objects at their foes. The variety of potential thrown objects is too vast for categorization. Most objects inflict Str damage (which, in the case of novas with Mega-Strength, is considerable), though some objects might inflict less (brittle objects) or more (aerodynamic or particularly dense objects). See "Throwing," p. 236, for information on range. Most objects inflict bashing damage, though sharp or edged objects inflict lethal.

Note that most thrown objects inflict about the same amount of damage; after all, a Mega-Strong nova can throw a mailbox or a car, but the mailbox will impact with much greater velocity. The primary advantage of large thrown objects (like automobiles) is that they can be treated as area attacks.

Ranged Weapons Chart

Type	Acc	Damage	Range	Mnv	RoF	Clip	Conc	Mass	Cost
Revolver, Lt.	0	4d10 L	50	Ms Tw	2	6	P	0.5	•
Revolver, Hvy.	0	5d10 L	50	Ms Tw	2	6	J	0.5	••
Pistol, Lt.	0	4d10 L	50	Af Ms Tw	4	17 + 1	P	0.5	•
Pistol, Hvy.	0	5d10 L	50	Af Ms Tw	3	7 + 1	J	0.5	••
Rifle	+2	8d10 L	200	n/a	1	5 + 1	N	3	••
Flechette Rifle	+1	6d10 L	35	Ms St	5	40	J	1	••••
Taser	0	6d10 B	20	Tw	1	20	J	1.5	••
SMG, Small	0	6d10 L	50	Af Ms Sa St Tw	40	40	J	2.5	••
SMG, Large	0	7d10 L	50	Af Ms Sa St Tw	45	50	N	3	•••
Shotgun	+5	6d10 L	30	Ms	2	8 +1	T	3	••
Thrown Object	0	(Str/MegaStr, +/- 1-3)	Spec.	n/a	1	n/a	n/a	Spec.	n/a

Acc: Accuracy indicates the number of dice added to the shooter's dice pool.

Damage: Indicates the damage dice pool for the weapon.

Range: This gives the practical shot range in meters.

Mnv: Maneuvers lists the special attacks available to the weapon. Effects of these maneuvers are listed in the Combat section. Af = Automatic Fire, Ms = Multiple Shots, Sa = Semiautomatic burst, St = Strafing, Tw = Two Weapons. Aiming, Cover, Cover Fire and Reloading apply to all weapons.

RoF: This represents the number of shots that can be made in one turn of combat.

Clip: The number of shots a gun can hold.

Conc: Concealability of the weapon. P = Can be carried in a pocket; J = Can be hidden in a jacket; T = Can be hidden under a trenchcoat; N = Cannot be hidden on a person at all.

Mass: The weapon's mass in kilograms.

Cost: Represents the value of the weapon in Resource dots.

Heavy Weapons

Most ordinary, personal weaponry has little chance of harming a fully powered nova. The military, on the other hand, has had decades of practice developing munitions capable of killing large groups of people or heavily armored opponents. The following list of weapons should be available only to military personnel, government agencies or well-connected criminals.

Like many nova powers, these weapons often have damage adds. Damage in brackets [ ] represents the number of automatic health levels of damage inflicted by the attack before a character applies soak.

• **30mm cannon:** A vehicle-mounted, belt-fed machine gun, the 30mm cannon uses armor-penetrating ammunition to punch through tank armor.

• **105mm gun:** The 105mm gun represents typical tank armament.

• **Antitank Missile:** The antitank missile can be a portable, shoulder-launched tank-killer or a vehicle-mounted guided missile. The portable versions tend to be both less accurate and less powerful.

• **Artillery:** The classic support weapon of the modern military, artillery pieces, such as the howitzer, can level buildings, collapse bridges and even knock novas off of their feet.

• **Flamethrower:** A backpack-mounted tank carries three canisters of napalm and a rifle-like nozzle focuses the spray of flame. Flamethrowers are highly effective against both armored and unarmored persons, as armor tends to conduct the intense heat. The napalm continues to burn for several turns (halving its damage dice pool every turn), and it is hard to extinguish.

• **Grenade Launcher:** Available only to the military and law enforcement, grenade launchers are capable of firing a variety of explosives or gas grenades. The damage this weapon inflicts varies with the ammunition used (see the Grenade Chart).

• **Mortar:** A portable, indirect-fire weapon, the mortar is a common field artillery piece used by most armies today. While the most common shells are fragmentation or armor-piercing, the mortar can also fire gas or smoke grenades.

• **Portable Laser:** Condensed power packs have made two-man laser units possible for the military. In the field, one soldier carries a two-way radio while the other carries the actual laser. Both soldiers carry a cumbersome, rechargeable power packs. Designed under the auspice of an antitank weapon, portable lasers have already seen use against novas.

• **Surface-to-Air Missile:** The surface-to-air missile (SAM) is designed to destroy enemy aircraft using "fire-and-forget" tracking technology. The missiles can lock onto their targets with radar or the target's own heat signature. As with the antitank missile, SAMs can be portable or vehicle-mounted, with the same variance in power, range and accuracy.

Heavy Weapons Chart

Type	Acc	Damage	Range	RoF	Capacity	Mass	Cost
30mm cannon	0	8d10 L [5]	800	21	100	50	••••
105mm gun	+2	15d10 L [10]	1200	1	1	Special	•••••
Antitank, portable	0	10d10 L [8]	200	1	1	10	•••
Antitank, vehicle	+4	12d10 L [10]	2500	1	8	120	••••
Artillery	-2	20d10 L [15]	10 miles	1	1	3 mtons	•••••
Flamethrower	+4	10d10 L/turn	10	1	30	100	•••
Grenade Launcher	-2	Varies	400	1	1	12	•••
Mortar	-2	10d10 L [8]	1300	1	1	100	•••
Portable Laser	+2	13d10 L [12]	1000	1	10	100	•••••
SAM, portable	+2	12d10 L [12]	4 km	1	1	50	••••
SAM, vehicle	+4	15d10 L [15]	40 km	1	4	3 mtons	••••••

Acc: Accuracy indicates the number of dice added to the shooter's dice pool.

Damage: Indicates the damage dice pool for the weapon. The rating in brackets indicates the number of automatic damage successes the weapon receives against human-sized targets. This bracketed rating also reduces the armor rating on armored vehicles or supertough novas.

Range: This gives the practical shot range in meters.

RoF: This represents the number of shots that can be made in one turn of combat.

Capacity: The number of shots a gun can hold.

Mass: The weapon's mass in kilograms.

Cost: Represents the value of the weapon in Resource dots.

Grenades

Grenades are the most portable explosives, and they are used for both antipersonnel and antitank attacks. Advanced grenades are designed to carry tear gas, flash powder, concussive explosives or even deadly hot white phosphorus. The grenades listed here can be hurled, set by hand or fired from a grenade launcher.

Grenade Chart

Type	Damage	Special
Fragmentation	8d10 L	Full damage to all targets within three meters, half damage to six meters from ground zero.
Shaped charge	10d10 L [8]	No blast effect.
Tear Gas	4d10 B	See tear gas (p. 280).
Concussive	6d10 B	Full damage to all targets within three meters, half damage between three meters and six meters from ground zero.
Flash	2d10 B	Blinds target (as Strobe ● ●).
White Phosphorus	8d10 L	Continuous damage, halved every turn after the first.
Chaff	0	Disrupts electronic sensors (as Cyberkinesis ●).

Armor

While novas tend to be tougher than normal humans, there is no guarantee they will develop exceptional physical defenses. Armor provides protection from physical harm when either baselines or novas come into conflict with one another. Armor tends to be bulky and therefore obvious to casual bystanders, as well as a hindrance to movement. Most heavy armor is available only to military or law-enforcement personnel. As with weaponry, developments in anti-nova defenses have led to enhanced armor for dealing with aberrant threats.

Armor ratings are split between protection from bashing and lethal attacks. Armor may also be limited to a certain part of the body, as noted.

• **Reinforced Clothing:** Although it provides only minimal protection, every attempt is made to make this armor resemble normal clothing.

• **Armored T-shirt:** Made from light, flexible material, an armored T-shirt can easily be hidden under a jacket or normal clothing.

• **Kevlar Vest:** Standard police issue, the Kevlar vest reduces the penetrating power of bullets and other projectiles. Although an expert could spot it, the vest can be hidden under a coat.

• **Flak Jacket:** Military-issue protection designed to prevent explosives from harming the wearer.

• **Full Riot Gear:** This suit covers the body completely from head to toe, including a handheld shield and helmet.

• **Bomb Squad Armor:** This armor is specifically designed for bomb-disposal units and is the highest protection available to civilian organizations.

• **Advanced Body Armor:** An enhanced version of full riot gear, Body Armor is an environmentally sealed, electrically insulated, steel-reinforced body suit. The armor provides enough oxygen for 30 minutes when sealed.

Armor Chart

Class	Bashing	Lethal	Protection	Penalty	Conceal	Cost	Destruction
Reinforced Clothing	0	2	Full body	0	*	●●	8
Armored T-shirt	2	1	Torso	0	J	●●	8
Kevlar Vest	2	3	Torso	1	T	●●●	10
Flak Jacket	4	4	Torso, arms	1	N	●●●	12
Full Riot Gear	5	5	Full Body	2	N	●●●●	12
Bomb Squad Armor	6	5	Full Body	2	N	●●●●	13
Advanced Body Armor	6	6	Full Body	2	N	●●●●●	15

Bashing: The armor's soak versus bashing attacks.
Lethal: The armor's soak versus lethal attacks.
Protection: The coverage provided by the armor.
Penalty: Each die of penalty subtracts one die from any Dexterity-based dice pool due to bulkiness.
Concealment: P = Can be carried in a pocket; J = Can be hidden in a jacket; T = Can be hidden under a trenchcoat; N = Cannot be hidden on a person at all.
Cost: Represents the value of the weapon in Resource dots.
Destruction: If an attack inflicts this many damage successes or greater, the armor is destroyed.
* Reinforced clothing passes for normal attire except under meticulous examination.

Vehicles

In terms of design, speed and power, the modern car has not changed much over the last decade. When speaking of efficiency, however, the automobile has changed dramatically. Hypercombustion engines have drastically reduced pollution and decreased the depletion of natural resources. Electrical and solar-powered cars have become more popular, but they remain a small percentage of civilian transportation.

Vehicles, because of their size and metal construction, provide a certain amount of protection to those in or behind them. Damage should be soaked by the vehicle before hitting any passengers.

• **Cars:** The standard mode of transportation for most industrial and postindustrial countries, the car comes in a multitude of shapes and sizes. The sports car stands out as the top performance model available for speed and maneuverability.

• **Motorcycles:** Capable of tight maneuvering, motorcycles can often go places inaccessible to automobiles. Motorcycles are a popular choice among novas with no movement advantages.

• **Trucks:** Trucks form the backbone of cargo transportation in any modern country. Each carries bulky loads on a heavy-duty suspension pulled by a powerful engine.

• **Prop Planes:** Prop planes vary in size from light personal aircraft to heavy commercial versions.

• **Jet Aircraft:** Available only to corporations, the wealthy or the government, jets are the standard means of long-distance travel. Commercial versions are designed for either cargo or passengers. Military planes carry a variety of armaments for various combat functions.

• **Military Jet Aircraft:** The backbone of modern armed forces, military jets fill a variety of roles, including close ground support, long-range bombing, reconnaissance and intercontinental nuclear deterrence. For simplicity, military jets are divided between bombers (long-range, ground-attack vehicles) and fighters (high-speed interceptors).

• **Helicopters:** An increasingly common sight in urban environments, helicopters can access any location with their vertical takeoff and landing capabilities. Most hospitals, police departments and news crews have access to helicopters.

• **Military Helicopters:** Military helicopters sport high-caliber machine guns and antitank missiles. Close

Vehicle Chart

Vehicle	Safe Speed	Max Speed	Maneuver	Passengers	Armor	Cost
Compact car	100	180	5	3	2	••
Midsize car	150	250	6	4	3	••
Large car	150	280	5	5	4	•••
Sports car	200	420	6	2	2	••••
Motorcycle	180	280	8	2	0	•
Small truck	125	200	5	2	3	•••
Large truck	100	200	4	2	4	••••
Small prop plane	220	340	5	4	2	•••
Large prop plane	540	760	3	40	5	••••
Jet aircraft	700	900	4	20	6	•••••
Fighter	700	Mach 3	7	2	3 [7]	•••••
Bomber	600	Mach 2	5	5	3 [10]	••••••
Helicopter	300	500	7	20	3	••••
Military helicopter	360	600	9	2-8	3 [8]	•••••
Personnel carrier	60	90	3	16	5 [10]	•••••
Urban assault vehicle	80	120	4	5	5 [10]	•••••
Main battle tank	60	90	2	4	6 [12]	•••••

Safe Speed: Indicates the safest possible speed (in kilometers per hour) at which to perform maneuvers in the vehicle.

Max Speed: The highest possible speed (in kilometers per hour) for the vehicle. Maneuvers are extremely difficult, if not impossible, at this speed.

Maneuver: The maximum dice pool allowable by the vehicle type. Penalties (i.e., damage penalties) should be applied to the character's dice pool before limiting the pool by the maneuver rating.

Passengers: The normal seating capacity of the vehicle.

Armor: The protection afforded to passengers of the vehicle. Damage should be soaked by the vehicle before hitting any passengers. The rating in brackets indicates the minimum number of damage successes required to penetrate the vehicle's armor. This rating is reduced by the damage add indicated for heavy weapons or nova attacks.

Cost: Represents the value of the weapon in Resource dots.

support and personnel deployment are their main roles on the battlefield.

- **Personnel Carrier:** An armored car or treaded vehicle capable of sustaining a lot of damage. Both military and law-enforcement versions exist.
- **Urban Assault Vehicle:** Changes in local law-enforcement priorities and increases in terrorism have led to the need for higher firepower in urban environments. As an alternative to martial law and its accompanying bad PR, many large-city police forces have acquired this minitank for dealing with particularly dangerous threats.
- **Main Battle Tank:** Every government capable of sustaining a modern army owns various versions of the tank. A treaded vehicle, the tank can take its heavy armament into almost any terrain or situation. Heavy armor protects its small crew and payload.

Vehicle Damage

Every vehicle has eight structural levels, much like your character has health levels. As a vehicle takes damage, its structural integrity is reduced until it is destroyed (and may blow up in the process). A vehicle's performance is reduced as it takes damage.

The chart below lists structural levels, along with vehicles' relative status at each level. The dice penalty listed is subtracted from your character's Driving/Piloting and Firearms rolls, reflecting the increasing degree of difficulty involved in holding the vehicle on course and getting its systems to respond. These modifiers apply until repairs are made. Vehicle damage is noted with a "X," as with lethal damage.

Structural Level		Dice Penalty Description
Scraped	0	Slight scoring and dents; nothing significant.
Dented	-1	Minor structural damage; not seriously impaired.
Battered	-1	Serious structural damage; top speed is limited to cruising speed.
Smashed	-2	Significant damage; cruising speed is halved.
Breached	-3	Structurally unsound, the vehicle is a death trap.
Wrecked	-4	Only basic systems function; speed is minimal.
Broken down		The craft is one step from being scrap metal. It cannot perform any maneuvers and has no power.
Demolished		The vehicle is destroyed completely (the Storyteller may have it disintegrate, explode or simply fall apart).

Repairing Vehicle Damage

A craft must be repaired before it returns to prime working condition. Fixing a vehicle's structural damage takes time, tools and appropriate parts. Minimal damage may be repaired using existing parts, but damage beyond Battered requires replacement materials. Vehicles

Optional Rule: Vehicles as "Extras"

Vehicle combat can take some time to resolve when all craft have eight structural levels. If the Storyteller wants to make vehicle combat fast paced, craft that are insignificant to the plot should be assigned only four structural levels [Dented -1, Breached -3, Broken down and Demolished]. Such vehicles are used to create cinematic effect, are piloted by nameless goons, and are under the direction of the powerful forces whom the characters are after.

The Storyteller may also wish to take things a step further, giving small craft four structural levels when battling significantly larger vehicles (e.g., a motorcycle against a tank, or a fighter plane against a battleship).

at Breached or lower must be taken to an appropriate maintenance facility to have access to necessary repair equipment.

Recovering each structural level requires a successful Engineering roll. The repair times listed below are cumulative. A Dented vehicle takes four hours to fix, while a Smashed vehicle takes almost a day to repair.

Structural Level	Repair Time
Scraped	One hour
Dented	Three hours
Battered	Six hours
Smashed	12 hours
Breached	One day
Wrecked	Three days
Broken down	One week
Demolished	It's scrap, remember?

If repairs are made using superior skill (4 Engineering rating) and equipment, repair time is moved one category higher on the repair chart (to a minimum of one hour).

Poisons and Drugs

Nova physiology has opened new doors for scientists. Not only have old ideas of human maximum potential been disproved, but a new species of humanity has emerged. Nova biology produces new hormones never before seen inside the human body or anywhere else on Earth for that matter. The medical uses for such chemicals seem limitless when applied to normal human systems.

On the darker side, a new black market has also emerged to exploit these new drugs. Drug cartels, still making a tidy profit trafficking in narcotics, realize the vast potential of nova drugs and their derivatives. Through bribery or coercion, organized crime syndicates have hired biologists to explore the most profitable abuses of nova-created chemicals.

For their part, certain novas have created a new

market demand for drugs powerful enough to overcome their high metabolism rates and enhanced tolerances. Combinations of cocaine and synthetic nova steroids have been the vanguards of this blossoming industry, but a true narcotic for novas has yet to be perfected.

The military, never to be left out, has used the studies to create virulent new poisons. Rumors persist of top-secret military research investigating nerve gases and poisons capable of subduing novas. Also, leaks in the intelligence community have pointed to genetic research to replicate nova physiology in baselines. The truth of these rumors, as well as their success or failure, remains a mystery.

Note that all novas are very resistant to most drugs. When ingesting normal, non nova-specific drugs, the player of a nova may (in fact, must) make a standard Resistance roll; even one success enables the nova to ignore the effects of the drug. Nova-specific drugs (soma, adrenocilin, moxinoquantamine) have been designed to overcome the nova metabolism, though a nova's player may make a single Resistance roll at +2 difficulty to purge these drugs from the nova's system.

Tear Gas

Description: Tear gas is commonly used by military and law-enforcement agents when killing the opponent is not the main goal. A grenade is launched into the target area, where the cloud of noxious fumes drives the victims out of hiding.

Vector: Contact or inhaled

Effect: Severe eye irritation, coughing and gagging incapacitate the victim. All dice pools are reduced by three dice for 10 minutes after exposure.

Protection: A gas mask, similar breathing apparatus or other forms of self-contained breathing (i.e., the Adaptability enhancement) prevents the effects of the gas.

Antidote: None

Nerve Gas

Description: Military-grade poison gases, the various types of nerve gas are designed to kill their victims quickly. Nerve gas typically targets the nervous system or the brain directly, rendering the target immobile before killing. Even low doses of nerve gas can be lethal.

Vector: Contact or inhaled

Effect: At low concentrations, nerve gas causes one lethal health level per minute, with no soak possible. At higher dosages, the rate increases to one health level per turn, again with no soak possible. Nerve gas typically disorients the victim, reducing all dice pools by three dice.

Protection: Nerve gas can pass through the skin but is most effective when inhaled. Gas masks prevent some forms of nerve gas, but more powerful types require a full environment suit. Novas with Mega-Stamina •• or higher are unaffected by most forms of nerve gas.

Antidote: Antidotes are notoriously ineffective against nerve gas, as it affects the victim so quickly. They are made strictly to help victims of accidental exposure.

Amphetamines and Cocaine

Description: Highly addictive drugs used recreationally on all levels of society. Cocaine and amphetamines used to be the most profitable controlled substances on the market until the advent of nova-derived drugs. Recently, a highly potent synthetic amphetamine called "spike" has been making the rounds among club kids and the junkie set.

Vector: Inhaled or swallowed

Effect: These drugs make the user excited and hyperactive. In this state, the user usually feels superior, even invincible. The drugs provide no game mechanic bonus, but after the effect wears off (one to three hours) the user will be sluggish and tired. Reduce the character's Stamina by two for purposes of endurance.

Users of spike gain +2 to Initiative and become either euphoric or jittery and paranoid. Each time spike is taken, roll Stamina; on a botch, the user immediately suffers a heart attack.

Long-term effects include heart problems, high blood pressure, paranoia and loss of judgment. These drugs are also highly addictive.

Antidote: Though not an "antidote" per se, depressants counteract amphetamines' effects; mixing drugs in this fashion, though, is highly dangerous.

Depressants

Description: Common depressants include alcohol and barbiturates. Medical depressants are often prescribed for individuals suffering from hypertension or who have difficulty sleeping.

Vector: Swallowed or injected

Effects: Depressants suppress pain and thought functions, putting the user in a listless, lethargic state. Subtract two from all dice pools while under the influence of these drugs.

Antidote: As depressants counteract amphetamines' effects, so amphetamines and other stimulants counteract depressants' effects; again, mixing the two types of drugs is dangerous and just plain stupid.

Hallucinogens

Description: Viewed by some as gateways to other forms of consciousness, hallucinogens affect the mind's ability to maintain contact with reality. Powerful doses can even cause full-environment hallucinations.

Vector: Contact or inhaled

Effect: Lower all dice pools by one to three dice, depending on the strength of the dosage. Powerful hallucinogens can produce an effect similar to Mirage ••. The effects can last from one to six hours.

Novas under the influence of powerful hallucinogens have been known to "accidentally" activate their powers, unconsciously tapping their M-R nodes.

Mite

Description: Extracted from nova steroids and developed from nova mitochondria, mite is a controlled substance in the United States and many other nations. Nonetheless, use of the drug to increase muscle mass in athletes has become popular. The First World's current obsession with physique and muscle toning has skyrocketed the price of black-market mite.

Vector: Injected

Effect: Mite has the same effect on novas that steroids have on humans (increased body mass over time, heart problem, sterility). Baselines who ingest mite, however, are overcome with elation and orgasmic pleasure. Combined with a rigorous workout, mite can dramatically increase muscle tissue to dangerous levels. Overdoses of mite are common, as the drug is still new to the market and highly addictive.

After taking mite, a normal human's Strength and Might are increased by one temporarily. Over several months of continuous use, the effects become permanent. Should the user continue to take mite, the effects increase in a mathematical progression until the baseline's Strength/ Might skill rating reaches 10. At this point, the baseline's muscle mass has reached grotesque levels (-1 to Appearance, minimum 1). Continued use of the drug at this point pushes the human to Mega-Strength 1 (and a further -1 to Appearance), but each week of use thereafter, the user must make a Stamina roll at +1 difficulty. If she fails, she suffers immediate and total cardiac arrest.

Gangbangers have discovered this drug to be an effective weapon against rivals and police. Addicted thugs, called "mitoids," lose control under stress, often displaying tremendous feats of strength and violence. A mitoid who has reached Mega-Strength 1 often goes berserk when angered; while berserk, he feels no pain and thus suffers no wound penalties, but mindlessly attacks his chosen target (or even his friends!) until subdued or killed.

Antidote: No known antidote exists, but the effects (good and bad) wear off gradually if the user stops taking the drug.

Adrenocilin

Description: Exclusive to Project Utopia's Rashoud facilities, adrenocilin is a drug given to newly erupted novas to help them control their powers. It also acts as an effective pain deadener for the debilitating headaches and other trauma common to new quantum-channelers.

Vector: Ingested

Effect: Adrenocilin adds one die to any quantum power skill total. As a side effect, it lowers wound penalties by one. Effects last for four hours.

While adrenocilin is obtainable at any Rashoud facility, it is somewhat addictive (Willpower roll to avoid addiction if used more than three times a month). A nova addicted to adrenocilin must have the drug in her body at all times; otherwise, all uses of quantum powers are at +2 difficulty. While on adrenocilin, a nova is also somewhat lethargic and passive (Willpower rolls at +1 difficulty). Other side effects may exist as well.

In baselines, adrenocilin is a deadly poison (each dose inflicts 10 - Stamina levels of lethal damage).

Antidote: Moxinoquantamine

Moxinoquantamine (Mox)

Description: Often given to newly erupted novas, moxinoquantamine is a regulator drug that interferes with signals from the M-R node. It is thus used when training novas who have little control over their quantum powers or novas who wish to exercise and train already existing powers.

Vector: Ingested

Effect: Moxinoquantamine makes it more difficult for novas to use quantum powers. All uses of quantum powers, including Mega-Attributes and enhancements, are at +2 difficulty. Additionally, any roll of "1" or "2" is treated as a botch; however, botched power rolls while on mox do not inflict temporary Taint. The effects last approximately six hours per dose.

In baselines, mox is a deadly poison (each dose inflicts 10 - Stamina levels of lethal damage).

Antidote: Adrenocilin

Soma

Description: The normal adrenal gland creates adrenochrome, one of the most powerful chemicals in the human body. Chemicals extracted from a nova's M-R node are many times more potent. A baseline ingesting M-R hormones, whose street name is soma, experiences the most potent high possible — if he survives.

Soma can be produced only through direct extraction from a living nova's M-R node. The process always kills the "donor." Obviously, the drug is extraordinarily rare, and most people believe it to be nothing more than an urban legend.

Vector: Swallowed

Effect: Soma kills a baseline user outright unless he makes a Stamina roll at +1 difficulty. The effects of the drug overwhelm the human system in a manner similar to a transplant rejection. In this case, soma rejects the frail human body, destroying it in the process.

Should the user survive, she gains some semblance of nova powers. Enhanced speed and strength (Mega-Strength •, the Quickness enhancement) are common to baseline users. The effects for baselines are temporary (four hours) but highly addictive.

Ingested by a nova, soma adds one dot to all Mega-Attributes, enhancements and quantum powers. The effects last for four hours.

When cut with cocaine, soma creates the only known narcotic capable of consistently overcoming a nova's enhanced metabolism (treat as amphetamines/cocaine, above). Again, rumors among the nova community suggest that a few repulsive epicures indulge, and even traffic, in the drug.

Antidote: None

Red 7

Description: Military research laboratories have managed to splice M-R node hormones with human adrenaline to produce a potent combat-enhancing drug. Safer and less powerful than soma, Red 7 increases the recipient's physical abilities but has detrimental side effects.

Vector: Injected

Effect: The recipient adds two to all Physical Attributes (maximum 5) for the one hour the drug lasts, but he becomes prone to aggressive behavior. There is an escalating chance the drug will kill the user, beginning at about five percent and increasing by five percent with every dose.

Antidote: None, although effects wear off with time.

Henchmen

The players might come into conflict with a wide variety of underlings used by corporations, law enforcement, criminal groups or other organizations. Henchmen are generic villain fodder who complicate the characters' lives. They need not be described in great detail, as the heroes should handle them with ease. Henchmen serve to fill out the forces of the antagonist and whittle down the players' quantum points before facing the real challenge.

Organized Crime

Most organized crime cartels have been eliminated, but the four primary survivors have consolidated power to become very strong indeed. Criminal cartels vary in character and organization across the world. From the Medellín Cartel in South America to the Heaven Thunder Triad in China, cartels' strength comes from their control of numerous activities. Each group controls its territory's gambling, prostitution, racketeering and money-laundering — in short, anything that will make money. Depending on the city or country, several different groups divide up activities, or all activities fall under the purview of one central organization.

While few altruistic "superheroes" have dedicated their lives to ridding the world of organized crime, T2M finds destruction of international syndicates to be good PR. Accordingly, syndicates all over the world interact with novas, quite often for less-than-legal reasons.

Most groups contain a number of grunts who perform the organization's legwork. These soldiers answer to the equivalent of a captain, who then answers to head

of the organization. The captain controls the soldiers and handles the day-to-day affairs of the boss in his designated area. The crime boss possesses the political and economic clout to maintain the entire organization while seeming to remain perfectly legitimate. Of course, names and even organization will vary from group to group and country to country.

Soldier

Physical Attributes 3, all other Attributes 2, Biz 1, Brawl 2, Drive 1, Firearms 2, Intimidation 2, Might 1, Resistance 2, Streetwise 1, Willpower 4; automatic pistol or SMG

Captain

Physical Attributes 4, all other Attributes 2, Awareness 2, Biz 1, Brawl/ Martial Arts 3, Command 3, Drive 3, Endurance 1, Firearms 3, Interrogation 1, Intimidation 3, Might 3, Resistance 3, Stealth 1, Streetwise 3, Willpower 6; automatic pistol, SMG or assault rifle

Crime Boss

Charisma, Manipulation and Wits 4, all other Attributes 3, Awareness 3, Biz 4, Brawl/ Martial Arts 3, Command 4, Drive 2, Endurance 1, Firearms 3, Interrogation 2, Intimidation 3, Might 1, Resistance 2, Streetwise 4, Style 1, Subterfuge 3, Willpower 7; automatic pistol (possibly with heavy weapons if given sufficient time to prepare)

Gangs

Gangs are largely disorganized bands of criminals who cling together for security and camaraderie. Most gangs, however, deal in drug trafficking, and they usually answer to organized crime cartels. It is their numbers and influence on the local community that make gangs a threat. Gangs feed off the local population like parasites, through larceny, drug dealing and extortion.

Gang Member

Physical Attributes 3, all other Attributes 2, Brawl 2, Drive 1, Firearms 2, Intimidation 1, Melee 1, Might 1, Resistance 2, Streetwise 2, Survival 1, Willpower 4; automatic pistol or SMG

Gang Leader

Physical Attributes 4, all other Attributes 2, Awareness 2, Biz 1, Brawl/ Martial Arts 3, Drive 3, Command 2, Firearms 3, Intimidation 3, Melee 2, Might 3, Resistance 3, Stealth 1, Streetwise 3, Survival 2, Willpower 6; automatic pistol, SMG or assault rifle; possibly with Mite or Red 7

Police

State and local police represent a significant portion of the United States of America's law-enforcement capabilities. Overall, they have limited ability to deal with nova-level threats, and they usually defer to those more capable. Individual city or state governments, however, vary their stance on nova intervention regardless of the dangers. While some cities franchise glitzy nova "public defenders," others seek to avoid the publicity and expense of these rent-a-cops. In this case, the local police are forced to handle even renegade novas with normal tactics. Police forces across the globe face similar difficulties.

Characters who run afoul of the law will inevitably have to deal with the police. The average police officer has little chance of apprehending even the least powerful nova. When taken as a whole, however, an entire city's police forces can become a hazardous opponent. Larger cities have special Crisis Response teams, helicopters and urban assault vehicles, and they are thus somewhat more effective against novas.

Police Officer

Physical Attributes 3, all other Attributes 2, Awareness 1, Brawl/ Martial Arts 2, Bureaucracy 1, Drive 2, Firearms 2, Interrogation 2, Investigation 1 (or 3 if plainclothes detective), Medicine 1, Might 1, Resistance 2, Stealth 1, Streetwise 2, Willpower 5; automatic pistol, police car, night stick, armored T-shirt (possibly flak jacket if expecting serious trouble)

SWAT Officer

Physical Attributes, Perception and Wits 3; all other Attributes 2, Awareness 2, Brawl/ Martial Arts 3, Drive 3, Endurance 3, Firearms 4, Melee (taser) 2, Might 2, Resistance 3, Stealth 1, Streetwise 2, Willpower 6; automatic pistol, SMG or assault rifle, flak jacket or full riot gear

Crisis Response Specialist

Physical Attributes 4 (plus bonuses for Red 7), Perception/Wits 3, other Attributes 2, Awareness 3, Bureaucracy 2, Endurance 3, Firearms 4, Martial Arts 4, Melee (taser) 3, Might 3, Resistance 3, Stealth 3, Streetwise 2, Willpower 7; automatic pistol, assault rifle, grenade launcher, bomb squad or (rarely) advanced body armor, Red 7

Government/Directive Agents

In the postindustrial, nova-altered world of 2008, espionage and subtlety are more important geopolitical commodities than massive standing armies. Many nations have devoted significant resources toward investigating novas and their threat to national security. The most important is the multinational Directive, but national agencies also deal with novas. Within the United States, the Central Intelligence Agency and National Security Agency keep detailed files on all known novas, tracking their movements and associations whenever possible. The Federal Bureau of Investigation works in concert with local law enforcement, dealing with nova-level threats as carefully as possible.

The players may come into conflict with the government in any number of ways. Breaking the law or posing some other threat to public safety is sure to draw attention. The players might also find themselves being watched as part of the Directive or CIA's ongoing nova investigations. Government intelligence agencies receive

millions of dollars in financing for a wide variety of activities handled under the umbrella of "national security." Any one of these programs might easily conflict with characters' values or lives.

Government agencies usually have access to powerful weaponry. If conflict with novas is a possibility, agents are likely to be heavily armed. The Directive in particular is developing both energy- and toxin-based weapons to deal with aberrant threats.

Special Agent

All Attributes 3 (or higher in the case of elite agents), Awareness 2, Brawl/ Martial Arts 3, Bureaucracy 1, Drive 3, Endurance 1, Firearms 3, Interrogation 2, Intrusion 3, Investigation 3+, Medicine 1, Might 1, Resistance 3, Stealth 3, Streetwise 2, Style 2, Subterfuge 3, Willpower 7+; automatic pistol, armored T-shirt, electronic communication and surveillance gear

"Mitoids"

"Mitoids" are 'roid freaks, 2008-style. Only now the lunatic not only feels no pain in his drug-induced frenzy, but he lifts cars and tosses them at innocent bystanders. "Mite" is the common street name for a strength-enhancing drug developed from nova mitochondria. Baselines who use mite on a regular basis develop abnormal strength levels, bordering on superhuman. Unfortunately, continual use of mite induces paranoia and even psychosis. Victims of a mite overdose have been documented twisting metal lampposts and tearing up concrete. A few street gangs, tongs and other criminal groups use mite to gain an edge over their rivals or the police.

Strength 5, Dexterity 3, Stamina 4, all other Attributes 1 or 2, Athletics 2, Brawl 3, Endurance 2, Might 5, Resistance 3, Willpower 4; chain or other improvised weapon Mega-Strength ● (no enhancements); punch damage [5] + 7D (B); chain damage [5] + 10D (B); no wound penalties

Nova Threats

Novas are as varied as any other human being. Their motivations, characteristics and powers make nova antagonists new and dangerous threats. Conflict between novas occurs for any reason, from differences in political ideology to ego-driven conflicts of interest. The antagonists below represent the smallest sample of possible threats posed by other novas.

El Cuchillo

Cuchillo's superspeed and agility are renowned in Southern California and Mexico. An independent nova of limited imagination, El Cuchillo seeks only personal gain at the expense of others' reputations. He works with media agencies to arrange "mask duels" between himself and local nova favorites. For a not-so-modest fee, Cuchillo will duel a local favorite in a public bout. In exchange for exclusive footage, and therefore higher ratings, the local media give El Cuchillo fuel for his ego, intelligence on his opponent, a large sum of cash and a quick trip out of town.

Cuchillo's true identity remains unknown, as he prefers a mask. He claims never to have lost a duel, and he refuses to remove his mask until he is defeated. Whether he will stick to his bargain is unknown. What is known is that he takes full advantage of the media's hospitality, often leaving them with thousands of dollars in room-service fees and other bills.

Nature: Gallant
Allegiance: Independent
Attributes: Strength 5, Dexterity 5, Stamina 4, Perception 3, Intelligence 2, Wits 4, Charisma 4, Manipulation 4, Appearance 2 (?)
Abilities: Arts (Performance) 2, Athletics 5, Awareness 2, Drive 1, Endurance 5, Intimidation 3, Legerdemain 3, Linguistics 1, Martial Arts 4, Might 3, Resistance 4, Stealth 3, Style 3
Backgrounds: Attunement 1, Cipher 4, Influence 2, Resources 3
Quantum 3, Quantum Pool 30, Willpower 6, Taint 2
Powers: Mega-Dexterity ••• (Rapid Strike, Fast Tasks, Enhanced Movement), Mega-Stamina • (Regeneration), Mega-Wits •• (Quickness x2), Hypermovement •

Hugo the Bouncer

Hugo "the Bouncer" Pinnela works for Luciano Camparelli of the Camparelli-Zukhov megasyndicate. Hugo was a simple bouncer in one of Camparelli's establishments until a near-fatal beating erupted his M-R node. Hugo now possesses brutal strength, armored skin and a preternatural danger sense. With such enhancements, Hugo immediately moved up in stature in the syndicate, eventually finding himself in an enviable position as the higher-ups' bodyguard.

Hugo has shown himself to be every bit as smart as he is strong. Whether his intellect grew with his physique is unclear, but he continues to surprise his boss at every turn. It has been whispered in back rooms that Hugo has too much influence over the boss and should be removed. No one dares execute this plan, however, as Hugo would no doubt see it coming and deal with it.

Nature: Conniver
Allegiance: Camparelli-Zukhov megasyndicate
Attributes: Strength 4, Dexterity 3, Stamina 4, Perception 5, Intelligence 5, Wits 3, Charisma 2, Manipulation 5, Appearance 3
Abilities: Academics 3, Athletics 1, Awareness 5, Biz 4, Brawl 5, Computer 3, Endurance 4, Intimidation 4, Might 4, Rapport 4, Resistance 4, Streetwise 4, Style 2, Subterfuge 4
Backgrounds: Allies 2, Backers 4, Followers 2, Node 2, Resources 4
Quantum 3, Quantum Pool 26, Willpower 8, Taint 2

Powers: Mega-Strength ••• (Crush, Thunderclap), Mega-Stamina ••• (Resiliency), Armor ••, Danger Sense •••, Mega-Perception • (Nightvision)

Marissa Dunlop

A seasoned combat veteran before she erupted, Marissa has taken her experience and abilities to the private sector. As a nova for hire,

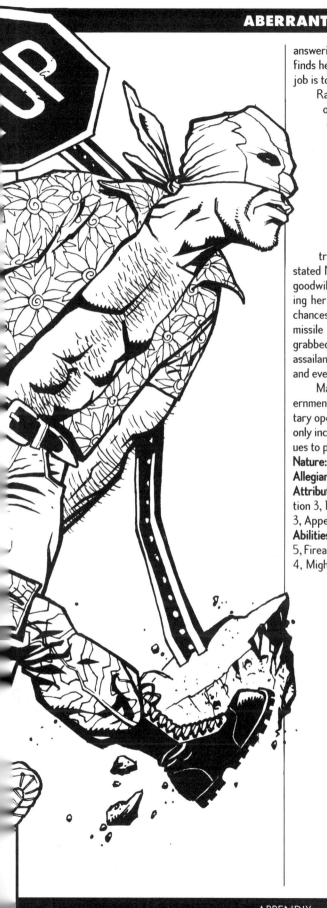

answering only to her Swiss bank accounts, she often finds herself working for the wrong side of the law. No job is too dirty for her, and no fee is too large.

Raised by her mercenary father, Marissa grew up on battlefield after battlefield, where the horrors of war and the blatant facts of life in a combat zone scarred her psyche. When her father finally died fighting for the "good guys," who could barely cover his expenses, she had had enough. Thereafter, she opened her services to the highest bidder. More often than not, she ended up working for criminal cartels, corrupt governments and the CIA.

Marissa was captured as part of a CIA betrayal — they turned her over to the newly instated Nicaraguan government in the name of political goodwill. Never one to go quietly, Marissa started shooting her way out. The Nicaraguan regulars, taking no chances with such a dangerous woman, fired an antitank missile at her. A moment before impact, she mentally grabbed the projectile out of the air and hurled it at her assailants. In the confusion, she escaped into the jungle and eventually out of the country.

Marissa now has a bone to pick with the US government, and she gladly works for anti-American military operations worldwide. Her telekinetic powers have only increased the value of her services and she continues to pay the bills with money from the highest bidder.

Nature: Survivor

Allegiance: Independent

Attributes: Strength 4, Dexterity 4, Stamina 3, Perception 3, Intelligence 2, Wits 4, Charisma 2, Manipulation 3, Appearance 4

Abilities: Athletics 3, Awareness 4, Drive 2, Endurance 5, Firearms 4, Intimidation 4, Linguistics 2, Martial Arts 4, Might 3, Pilot 2, Politics 2, Resistance 5, Stealth 3, Style 1, Subterfuge 2, Survival 3

Backgrounds: Cipher 3, Contacts 2, Dormancy 2, Eufiber 1, Node 3, Resources 3

Quantum 3, Quantum Pool 30, Willpower 7, Taint 3 (Glow)

Powers: Mega-Dexterity • (Rapid Strike), Force Field ••••, Telekinesis ••••, Flight ••

CREDITS

Original Concept and Design: Robert Hatch, with Andrew Bates, Ken Cliffe, Greg Fountain, Sheri M. Johnson, Chris McDonough, Ethan Skemp, Mike Tinney, Richard Thomas, Stephan Wieck, Fred Yelk

Additional Design: Justin R. Achilli, Steven S. Long, Mark Moore

Authors: Justin R. Achilli, Andrew Bates, Robert Hatch, Sheri M. Johnson, Steven S. Long, Mark Moore, Ethan Skemp, Fred Yelk

Additional Material: Brooks Miller, Dave Van Domelen

Storyteller Game System: Mark Rein·Hagen

Revised Storyteller System: Andrew Bates

Developer: Robert Hatch

Editor: Carl Bowen

Art Direction: Richard Thomas

Artists: Guy Davis, Glenn Fabry, Thomas Fleming, Langdon Foss, Michael Gaydos, Jeff Holt, Mike Huddleston, Mark Jackson, Phil Jimenez, Leif Jones, Matt Millburger, Christopher Moeller, William O'Connor, Paolo Parente, Steve Prescott, Jeff "Send Me More Powers" Rebner, Steve Rude, Alex Sheikman, Uko Smith, Larry Snelly, Richard Thomas, Melissa Uran

Cover Art: Tom Fleming

Layout: Ron Thompson

Limited Edition Design: Richard Thomas

Playtesters: Bryan Armor, Bruce Baugh, R. Sean Borgstrom, Deird'Re M. Brooks, James V. Coleman, Bryant Durrell, Brian Goodson, Jess Heinig, Chris Hemphill, Brooks Miller, Clayton Oliver, Charlsie Patterson, Mikki Rautalahti, Eric Thompson, Dave Van Domelen, Will Van Meter, Dave Weinstein, Dave Wendt, Alex Williams

WHITE WOLF PUBLISHING

735 PARK NORTH BLVD.
SUITE 128
CLARKSTON, GA 30021
USA

ABERRANT CHARACTER SHEET

Birth Name: _____   Eruption: _____
Nova Name: _____   Nature: _____
Series: _____   Allegiance: _____

ATTRIBUTES AND ABILITIES

PHYSICAL

STRENGTH ●○○○○
Brawl _____ ○○○○○ ☐
Might _____ ○○○○○ ☐
_____ ○○○○○ ☐

DEXTERITY ●○○○○
Athletics _____ ○○○○○ ☐
Drive _____ ○○○○○ ☐
Firearms _____ ○○○○○ ☐
Legerdemain _____ ○○○○○ ☐
MartialArts _____ ○○○○○ ☐
Melee _____ ○○○○○ ☐
Pilot _____ ○○○○○ ☐
Stealth _____ ○○○○○ ☐
_____ ○○○○○ ☐
_____ ○○○○○ ☐

STAMINA ●●○○○
Endurance _____ ●●●○○ ☐
Resistance _____ ●●●○○ ☐
_____ ○○○○○ ☐
_____ ○○○○○ ☐

MENTAL

PERCEPTION ●○○○○
Awareness _____ ○○○○○ ☐
Investigation _____ ○○○○○ ☐
_____ ○○○○○ ☐

INTELLIGENCE ●○○○○
Academics _____ ○○○○○ ☐
Bureaucracy _____ ○○○○○ ☐
Computer _____ ○○○○○ ☐
Engineering _____ ○○○○○ ☐
Intrusion _____ ○○○○○ ☐
Linguistics _____ ○○○○○ ☐
Medicine _____ ○○○○○ ☐
Science _____ ○○○○○ ☐
Survival _____ ○○○○○ ☐
_____ ○○○○○ ☐

WITS ●○○○○
Arts _____ ○○○○○ ☐
Biz _____ ○○○○○ ☐
Rapport _____ ○○○○○ ☐
_____ ○○○○○ ☐

SOCIAL

APPEARANCE ●○○○○
Intimidation _____ ○○○○○ ☐
Style _____ ○○○○○ ☐
_____ ○○○○○ ☐

MANIPULATION ●○○○○
Interrogation _____ ○○○○○ ☐
Streetwise _____ ○○○○○ ☐
Subterfuge _____ ○○○○○ ☐
_____ ○○○○○ ☐
_____ ○○○○○ ☐
_____ ○○○○○ ☐

CHARISMA ●○○○○
Command _____ ○○○○○ ☐
Etiquette _____ ○○○○○ ☐
Perform _____ ○○○○○ ☐
_____ ○○○○○ ☐
_____ ○○○○○ ☐
_____ ○○○○○ ☐
_____ ○○○○○ ☐

ADVANTAGES

BACKGROUNDS
_____ ○○○○○
_____ ○○○○○
_____ ○○○○○
_____ ○○○○○
_____ ○○○○○

WILLPOWER
○○○○○○○○○○
☐☐☐☐☐☐☐☐☐☐

TAINT
○○○○○○○○○○
☐☐☐☐☐☐☐☐☐☐

ABERRATIONS
_____
_____
_____
_____

QUANTUM
○○○○○○○○○○

MEGA-ATTRIBUTES
_____ ○○○○○
_____ ○○○○○
_____ ○○○○○
_____ ○○○○○
_____ ○○○○○
_____ ○○○○○
_____ ○○○○○
_____ ○○○○○
_____ ○○○○○
_____ ○○○○○
_____ ○○○○○
_____ ○○○○○

QUANTUM POWERS
_____ ○○○○○
_____ ○○○○○
_____ ○○○○○
_____ ○○○○○
_____ ○○○○○
_____ ○○○○○
_____ ○○○○○
_____ ○○○○○
_____ ○○○○○
_____ ○○○○○

QUANTUM POOL

○○○○○○○○○○○○○○○○○○○○○○○○○○○○○○○○○○○○○○
☐☐☐☐☐☐☐☐☐☐☐☐☐☐☐☐☐☐☐☐☐☐☐☐☐☐☐☐☐☐☐☐☐☐☐☐☐☐

COMBAT

ATTACK

	ACC	DMG	ROF	FT
_____	☐		☐	☐
_____	☐		☐	☐
_____	☐		☐	☐
_____	☐		☐	☐
_____	☐		☐	☐

ARMOR

	RTG		BULK	FT
	B	L		
_____	☐	☐	☐	☐
_____	☐	☐	☐	☐
_____	☐	☐	☐	☐
_____	☐	☐	☐	☐
_____	☐	☐	☐	☐

INITIATIVE

MOVEMENT

Walk	Run	Sprint	_____

SOAK

Bashing	Lethal

DESCRIPTION

HEALTH

Bruised	-0	☐
_____		☐
_____		☐
_____		☐
_____		☐
_____		☐
_____		☐
_____		☐
_____		☐
_____		☐
_____		☐
_____		☐
_____		☐
_____		☐
_____		☐
_____		☐
_____		☐
Incapacitated		☐
Dead		☐

(Write in health levels as needed)

EXPERIENCE

Quantum Powers: Level One powers costs one nova point (or one nova point/two dots tainted) per dot purchased. Level Two powers cost three nova points (or two points tainted) per dot purchased. Level Three powers cost five nova points (or three points tainted) per dot purchased.

Power	Level	Dice Pool	Range	Area	Duration	Multiple Actions	Effect
Absorption	2	Stamina + Absorption	Self	N/A	Special	No	Convert damage/energy into Strength
Animal/Plant Mastery	2	Perception + Animal/Plant Mastery	Variable	Special	Special	No	Communicate/summon animals
Armor	2	N/A	Self	N/A	Permanent	No	+3 soak/dot vs. B/L
Bioluminescence	Misc.	Stamina + Bioluminescence	Variable	Special	10 minutes per success	N/A	Character emits light
Body Modification	2	N/A	Self	N/A	Permanent	N/A	Modifies character's body in various ways
Bodymorph	2	Stamina + Bodymorph	Self	N/A	Variable	Yes	Take aspects of one specific type of matter/energy
Boost	1	Quantum + Boost	Self	N/A	Maintenance	Yes	Adds 1 dot per success to specific Attribute
Claws	1	N/A	Touch	N/A	Variable	Yes	Close combat damage is lethal damage
Clone	3	Stamina + Clone	Self	Special	1 scene	Yes	Creates 1 duplicate of character per success
Cyberkinesis	3	(Variable) + Cyberkinesis	(Q+PR)x10 meters or Special	Special	Special	No	Control computers and machines
Density Control	3	Variable	Self	N/A	Maintenance	Yes	Increase or decrease character's density
Disintegration	3	Dexterity + Disintegration	(Q+PR)x10 meters	N/A	Instant	No	Causes (Q+successes) levels of aggravated damage
Disorient	2	Manipulation + Disorient	(Q+PR)x10 meters	N/A	Maintenance	Yes	Allows character to confuse and weaken opponents
Disrupt	2	Intelligence + Disrupt	(Q+PR)x10 meters	N/A	Maintenance	Yes	Reduces effectiveness of powers
Domination	2	Manipulation + Domination	Self	N/A	Concentration	Yes	Take control of target's brainwaves
Elemental Anima	2	(Variable) + Elemental Anima	Special	Special	Variable	Yes	Control particular substance or phenomenon
Elemental Mastery	3	(Variable) + Elemental Mastery	Variable	Variable	Variable	Yes	Create, alter and control various substances or phenomena
Empathic Manipulation	3	Variable (Willpower resisted)	(Q+PR)x20meters	N/A	Special	Yes	Control and manipulate target's emotions
Enhancement	Misc.	N/A	Self	N/A	Permanent	N/A	Player buys an enhancement
Entropy Control	3	(Variable) + Entropy Control	Variable	Variable	Special	No	Control and manipulate entropic forces
ESP	2	Perception + ESP	(P+PR)x20meters	N/A	Concentration	No	Sense surroundings
Flight	2	Dexterity + Flight	Self	N/A	Maintenance	Per normal rules	Fly at speed of (PRx4)+40meters per action
Force Field	2	Stamina + Force Field	Self	N/A	Maintenance	Yes	Quantum + (2 per success) extra soak vs. B/L damage
Gravity Control	3	(Variable) + Gravity Control	Variable	N/A	Maintenance	Yes	Manipulate gravity and gravitic fields
Healing	2	N/A	Touch	N/A	Instant	Yes	Heals 1 health level of B/L damage per quantum point
Holo	2	Manipulation + Holo	Self	N/A	Concentration	No	Creates images
Homunculus	3	Stamina + Homunculus	Self	N/A	Special	Special	Separate parts of body or create small creatures from body
Hypermovement	2	Dexterity + Hypermovement	Self	N/A	Maintenance	Yes	Increase running, flying or swimming speed
Hypnosis	1	Intelligence + Hypnosis	(Q+PR) meters	N/A	Special	Yes	Hypnotizes target
Immobilize	2	Dexterity + Immobilize	(Q+PR)x10 meters	N/A	I scene or until destroyed	Yes	Renders target immobile
Immolate	2	N/A	Self	N/A	Maintenance	Yes	(Q+PR)x2 B damage/(Q+PR) L damage
Intuition	2	Perception + Intuition	Self	N/A	Permanent	Yes	Heightened awareness of danger
Invisibility	2	Wits + Invisibility	Self	N/A	Concentration	Yes	Quantum + number of success vs. opponent's Perception
Invulnerability	1	N/A	Self	N/A	Permanent	N/A	+6 soak per dot vs. specific type of attack
Luck	2	Luck	Special	N/A	Variable	N/A	Successes on roll reduce damage/make tasks easier
Magnetic Mastery	3	(Variable) + Magnetic Mastery	(Q+PR) meters	N/A	Maintenance	No	Manipulate magnetism and magnetic fields
Matter Chameleon	3	Stamina + Matter Chameleon	Self	N/A	Maintenance	Yes	Duplicate properties of specific types of matter
Matter Creation	3	Wits + Matter Creation	Special	Variable	Special	Yes	Creates matter of various sorts
Mental Blast	3	Intelligence + Mental Blast	(Q+PR)x20 meters	N/A	Instant	No	1 level B damage per success
Mirage	2	Manipulation + Mirage	Variable	N/A	Concentration	No	Creates illusion in target's mind
Molecular Manipulation	3	(Variable) + Molecular Manipulation	Touch	Special	Special	No	Manipulate and control molecules
Poison	2	Stamina + Poison	Self	N/A	Instant	Yes	Poison or infect another person
Precognition	2	Perception + Precognition	Self	N/A	Instant	Yes	Detect danger or threats
Premonition	3	Perception + Premonition	Variable	Special	Special	No	Foresee future or view past events
Psychic Link	1	N/A	(Q+Psychic Link+Node)x1000 km	N/A	Permanent	N/A	Establish mental link between 2 or more characters
Psychic Shield	2	Perception + Psychic Link	Special	N/A	Special	N/A	+2 successes per dot on all attempts to resist mental powers
Quantum Bolt	2	Dexterity + Quantum Bolt	(Q+PR)x15 meters	N/A	Instant	Yes	[Qx3]+(PRx4) B damage; [Qx2]+(PRx4) of L damage
Quantum Construct	3	Manipulation + Quantum Construct	(Q+PR) meters	N/A	Maintenance	No	Create "creatures" or objects from quantum force
Quantum Conversion	1	Stamina + Quantum Conversion	Touch	N/A	Special	Yes	1 Q point per dot into standard forms of energy
Quantum Imprint	2	Dexterity + Quantum Imprint	Touch	N/A	Maintenance	No	Copy powers and abilities of charcter touched
Quantum Leech	2	N/A	Touch	N/A	Instant	Yes	(Q+PR) quantum points transferred from target to character
Quantum Regeneration	2	N/A	Self	N/A	Special	No	Spend 1 Willpower to add (PRx2) to quantum points recovered per hour
Quantum Vampire	2	Stamina + Quantum Vampire	Touch	N/A	Special	No	Transfer defined Attribute or power from target to character
Sensory Shield	1	N/A	Self	N/A	Permanent	N/A	Cancel 2 successes per dot on Blind attacks vs. character
Shapeshift	3	Stamina + Shapeshift	Self	N/A	Maintenance	Yes	Alter charcter's shape
Shroud	2	Dexterity + Shroud	Self	N/A	Concentration	Yes	Creates field to limit vision
Sizemorph (Grow)	2	N/A	Self	N/A	Maintenance	N/A	Double height and mass; +2 Strength, +1 Stamina, +1 "Bruised" per dot
Sizemorph (Shrink)	2	N/A	Self	N/A	Maintenance	N/A	Reduce height and mass to 1/8 normal; +1 to all Stealth attempts, +1 difficulty to hit character
Strobe	2	Dexterity + Strobe	Self	(Q+PR)x5 meter radius	Instant	Yes	Disable 1 of target's senses for 1 turn per success
Stun Attack	2	Dexterity + Stun Attack	(Q+PR)x10 meters	N/A	Instant	Yes	(Q+successes) levels of damage to daze or knock out target
Telekinesis	2	Dexterity + Telekinesis	(Q+PR)x15 meters	N/A	Maintenance	Yes	Lift and move physical objects without touching
Telepathy	2	Perception + Telepathy	(Q+PR)x10 meters	N/A	Concentration	No	Read minds, scan for minds and alter memories
Teleport	2	Perception + Teleport	Line of sight or Special	N/A	Instant	No	Move without passing through intervening space
Temporal Manipulation	3	(Variable) + Temporal Manipulation	Variable	N/A	Variable	Yes	Manipulate time
Warp	3	N/A	(Q+PR) meters	N/A	Special	No	Create "gates" to pass through intervening space
Weather Manipulation	3	(Variable) + Weather Manipulation	Variable	Variable	Variable	Yes	Alter and manipulate weather

Mega-Attributes:
Mega-Attributes cost three nova points per dot to purchase (two if tainted) and grant one free enhancement. Additional enhancements cost three nova points to purchase (two if tainted).

Physical	Enhancements

Physical

Mega-Strength
- Crush
- Shockwave
- Lifter
- Quantum Leap
- Thunderclap

Mega-Dexterity
- Accuracy
- Enhanced Movement
- Fast Tasks
- Flexibility
- Physical Prodigy
- Catfooted
- Rapid Strike

Mega-Stamina
- Adaptability
- Durability
- Hardbody
- Regeneration
- Resiliency

Mental

Mega-Perception
- Analytic Taste/Touch
- Blindfighting
- Bloodhound
- Electromagnetic Vision
  - Ultraviolet vision
  - Infrared vision
  - Visible light attuner
- High-End Electromagnetic Scan
- Hyperenhanced Hearing
  - Infra/ultrasonic hearing
  - Sonar
  - Radio scan
- Quantum Attunement
- Ultraperipheral Perception

Mega-Intelligence
- Analyze Weakness
- Eidetic Memory
- Enhanced Memory
- Mathematical Prodigy
- Linguistic Genius
- Mental Prodigy
  - Engineering
  - Financial
  - Investigative
  - Medical
  - Scientific
  - Tactical
- Speed Reading
- Taint Resistance

Mega-Wits
- Artistic Genius
- Enhanced Initiative
- Lie Detector
- Multitasking
- Natural Empath
- Quickness
- Synergy

Social

Mega-Appearance
- Appearance Alteration
- Awe-Inspiring
- Copycat
- Face of Terror
- First Impression
- Mr. Nobody
- Seductive Looks

Mega-Manipulation
- Hypnotic Gaze
- Persuader
- Trickster
- The Voice

Mega-Charisma
- Commanding Presence
- Dreadful Mien
- Natural Agitator
- Seductive
- Soothe

Index

UPCOMING RELEASES FOR ABERRANT

Aberrant Storytellers Screen
What Lies in Wait for the New Gods?
The Aberrant world is full of mysteries and hidden secrets. Some things only the Storyteller should know. Have the mysteries of the Aberrant setting at your fingertips.
The Secrets Revealed
The Aberrant Storytellers Screen is the first supplement for Aberrant. It presents all the charts and tables necessary to run Aberrant, as well as additional setting information and a ready-to-run story in a 72-page book.
August 1999

Aberrant: Year One
To Bask in the Light...
The Aberrant world is a vast and often terrifying place. Who knows what secrets lurk in the Nova Age of 2008? From the mazy alleys of Hong Kong to the eerily sterile paradise of Addis Ababa, this sourcebook provides all manner of exotic locales for characters to control... or die exploring.
Or Lurk in the Shadows
This sourcebook details the Aberrant world as it stands in the year 2008. A host of cities from around the globe, as well as various dangerous technological items, give Aberrant characters all the hotspots and heat they can handle.
September 1999

Exposé: Aberrants
The Center Cannot Hold
Fugitives... murderers... or unsung heroes? The controversial Aberrants faction is outgunned, outnumbered and has the weight of the world against it. Aberrants wouldn't have it any other way.
The Price of Liberty
Exposé: Aberrants details the nascent Aberrants organization and its fight against Aeon's Project Utopia. At only $4.95, this book's a steal for Aberrant players and Storytellers alike.
November 1999

Aberrant: Project Utopia
Guiding Humanity to a Better Tomorrow...
It is more powerful than nations. It controls more novas than any other entity in the world. It is Project Utopia, stalwart guardian of Earth. Utopia has ended wars, cured diseases and saved entire populations from starvation. So why are some novas so hell-bent to take it down?
Along a Path of Blood
This sourcebook details Project Utopia and the novas who serve it. An entire organization — including subsidiaries Team Tomorrow and Project Proteus — is covered in minute detail in this 144-page tome.
December 1999

EXTRA! EXTRA!

1925 - 2008 - 2120
EVERY AGE HAS ITS HEROES.

HUNT'ER
THE RECKONING

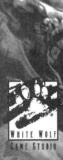

Taking back the night,
one monster at a time.